Irish Americans

A Versified Company

compiled, edited, and annotated

by

Richard Demeter

Cranford Press • *Pasadena, California*

Irish Americans

A Versified Company

Published by
Cranford Press
500 Cliff Drive, Pasadena, California 91107
Tel: 626-351-9263 • Fax: 626-568-0152

First Edition

Library of Congress Catalog Card Number: 99-096230

Printed in the United States of America

ISBN 0-9648253-4-1

Copyright Acknowledgments

For permission to use the copyrighted material included in this volume, the editor is indebted to the authors, their representatives, and the publishers named below, whose courtesy is gratefully acknowledged. All rights to these poems are reserved by the holders of the copyright.

Basic Books for: "Jacqueline" by Will Inman, "In Arlington Cemetery" by Stanley Koehler, and "For John Kennedy of Harvard" by Edward Pols from *Of Poetry and Power: Poems Occasioned by the Presidency and by the Death of John F. Kennedy* edited by Erwin A. Glikes and Paul Schwaber. Copyright © 1964 by Basic Books, a member of Perseus Books, L.L.C. Reprinted by permission of Basic Books, a member of Perseus Books, L.L.C.

Barbara M. Beecher for: "Escort for a President," "Jefferson Davis Inaugural," and excerpts from "And I Will Be Heard" and "The Chautauqua" from *The Collected Poems 1924-1974* by John Beecher. Copyright © 1974. Reprinted by permission of Barbara M. Beecher, widow of John Beecher.

James Benét for: "Jesse James" from *Golden Fleece* by William Rose Benét. Copyright 1933, 1935 by Dodd, Mead & Company. Copyright renewed. Reprinted by permission of James Benét.

Bloodaxe Books for: "De Valera at Ninety-Two" from *A Time for Voices: Selected Poems 1960-1990* by Brendan Kennelly, Bloodaxe Books, 1990. Reprinted by permission of Bloodaxe Books.

Brandt & Brandt Literary Agents, Inc. for: "Jesse James" and "Dolly Madison"

In Memoriam

A Remembrance

by Richard Demeter

As with the finger of a stealthy thief,
undoing Death unties the phantom barque
from 'mid the coils of its earthly moorings.
An unshod pilgrim borne on by the ghostly barge,
the sleepless soul ascends the Holy Mount
to bear the sole-scourging, unscrupulous pebbles,
to face the soul-searching, penultimate scruple.
There in the sacred grove of the Celtic "oak house"
a Druidess — Brigit-like — proclaims her decree:
"The soul that once through Tara's halls did reign
so like an ancient king shall reign no more.
A stringless harp, it 'hangs as mute on Tara's walls.'"
A holy monk from Cavan come stands steady to reply:
"To mourn unduly would unseemly seem, though, aye,
we'll miss his many kindnesses, his passion to do good,
his Celtic hospitality, his story-telling grace.
No more St. Patrick's Day we'll keep without
his integrity and faith."
From Inishturk to Doonloughan to Lettermullan way,
from Donegal to Kerry Head to Inishvickillane,
the ghostly barge skirts 'round the Em'rald Isle,
until from Finan's Bay it rounds the Skellig Rock.
Two haloed crosses, hooded monks atop the eastern ledge,
with arms outstretched call welcome to the sin-purged soul.

Holy Mount: Croagh Patrick, a 2,500-foot-high peak on the south shore of Clew Bay in County Mayo, Ireland, where St. Patrick is believed to have spent 40 days and nights in fasting and prayer. The route to the summit is strewn with sharp-edged stones. **sacred grove of the Celtic "oak house":** a site in Kildare ("Church of the Oak"), so named from a pagan sanctuary in which stood a tree sacred to the Druids, members of a pre-Christian religious order among the Celts in Ireland. **Druidess:** a female Druid. (See the previous entry.) **Brigit:** originally the Celtic goddess of healing, fertility, and poetry. The perpetual fire in her sanctuary in Kildare was tended by vestal virgins whose high priestess was regarded as an incarnation of the goddess and successively bore the name Brigit. One theory posits that in the sixth century A.D. the last of the high priestesses of this cult became a Christian and transformed the pagan sanctuary into a Christian shrine.

This Christian Brigit later founded a community of nuns, whose chapel in Kildare was built from a tree which the Druids held sacred. **"The soul that once . . .":** a variation on "The harp that once through Tara's halls," the first line of a song of the same name by the Irish poet Thomas Moore (1779-1852). **Tara:** the Hill of Tara (in County Meath), the site of the ancient palace of the High Kings of Ireland (who ruled at least the northern half of the country). The site seems to have been abandoned sometime after Christianity came to Ireland. **Cavan:** a town and county in north-central Ireland. This area was part of the ancient kingdom of Breffni, whose Celtic rulers — the O'Reillys — managed to retain power until the county was divided among English and Scottish settlers in the 1600s. **Inishturk, Doonloughan, Lettermullan:** islands or peninsulas along the Connemara coast of western Ireland. **Donegal:** Donegal Point on the west coast of County Clare. **Kerry Head:** a coastal site north of Tralee in County Kerry. **Inishvickillane:** one of the Blasket Islands off the west coast of the Dingle Peninsula. **Em'rald Isle:** Ireland. **Finan's Bay:** St. Finan's Bay at the far western end of the Iveragh Peninsula in County Kerry. **Skellig Rock:** Great Skellig (Skellig Michael), a rocky island off the west coast of County Kerry. Between the sixth and the twelfth centuries, the island was the site of a monastic community.

Contents

Introduction

The idea for this anthology of verse arose while I did research in preparation for writing the two volumes of *Irish America: The Historical Travel Guide*. In that pursuit I occasionally came across poems about historical figures of Irish birth or ancestry who had played a significant role in American history and whom I mentioned in the pages of *Irish America*. In a sense, this anthology is a literary companion to the two earlier volumes.

The first such verse which serendipitously fell to my gaze were poems about John Barry and Hercules Mulligan, both natives of Ireland. The former is the well known "Father of the American Navy," while the latter is a little known spy who served General Washington during the Revolutionary War. Readers of Volume 1 of *Irish America* will find numerous references to Barry as well as the location of nine memorials in his honor, the most prominent a statue of him outside Independence Hall in Philadelphia.

Some other early discoveries were verses in honor of three famous Civil War personalities. One of the men, Fr. William Corby, was chaplain of the Eighty-Eighth New York Infantry, one of the many Celtic units in the Irish Brigade during the Civil War. (A statue of the Catholic priest stands on the battlefield at Gettysburg, where he gave general absolution to the men of the brigade.) Two other "versified" figures were generals James Shields and Patrick Cleburne, who, though sharing a common love for their Irish homeland, fought on opposing sides of the American conflict.

Irish Americans: A Versified Company contains 267 poems and songs grouped into ninety-nine sections. Each section is named for a particular figure, event, or subject from Irish-American history and is placed in chronological sequence. Biographical or historical information about the subject of the poems in each group appears at the beginning of each section, and many of the poems are annotated. The number of poems in each section ranges from one in many cases to seventeen in honor of Ulysses S. Grant.

The verse in this anthology represents the work of 156 poets identified by name and another twenty-eight known only anonymously. Among the former group are some of the most well known poets in American literature — Thomas Bailey Aldrich, Richard Armour, John Beecher, Stephen Vincent Benét, Ambrose Bierce, Paul Laurence Dunbar, Robert Frost, Allen Ginsberg, Bret Harte, Robinson Jeffers, Joyce Kilmer, Sidney Lanier, Vachel Lindsay, James Russell Lowell, Robert Lowell, Herman Melville, John Boyle O'Reilly, Thomas Buchanan Read, James Whitcomb Riley, Carl Sandburg, and Walt Whitman. That so many prestigious wordsmiths wrote about figures of Irish-American history reflects the influence which the latter had on the nation and its historical consciousness.

The majority of the poems in this anthology are narrative, recounting in verse and meter some historical event or biographical tale. In "The Man of Machias" A. M. Sullivan retells the stirring account of Jeremiah O'Brien, under whose lead a band of hardy colonials captured two British sloops off the coast of Maine in 1775. A century later, John Jerome Rooney versified the bravery of Captain Henry J. Reilly, killed soon after he and his men had blasted their way into Peking in 1900. His actions helped end the siege of the legation district during the Boxer uprising:

> Then "Forward," called Reilly—and forward they swept
>   To the walls where the foe had rallied his horde.
> Like a boy, to a ladder the Captain has leapt,
>   You can see, far in front, the gleam of his sword.
> Then up thro' the smoke, like a wraith, he has gone—
> And Reilly went on—bold Reilly went on!

More in the biographical vein is "The Ballad of Billy the Kid," a poem about the notorious outlaw Henry McCarty by Henry Herbert Knibbs.

While many of the poems in this anthology were written to commemorate the lives of individuals long dead, some were penned for a particular occasion. In 1893 the state of Illinois placed a statue of James Shields in Statuary Hall in the nation's capitol building. For the occasion Charles J. Beattie composed the poem "The Shields Statue," which summarized the famous military leader's career. Almost twenty-five years later, Denis McCarthy wrote "John Boyle O'Reilly" for the dedication in 1917 of a memorial to the exile/journalist on the grounds of the latter's home in Hull, Massachusetts.

Despite the common narrative character of much of the verse in this volume, the tone employed in the poems runs the gamut of human expression. Some are boastful (e.g., "The Irish Name" and "The Fighting Irish"), others are deferential (e.g., "Woodrow Wilson" by Robinson Jeffers), and many are proudly patriotic (especially those about the Irish-American heroes of the War of 1812). While numerous poems laud their subjects in heroic terms (e.g., "Jackson at New Orleans" and "Kearny at Seven Pines"), a few belittle them (e.g., "James Buchanan" by Martha Keller). The tone of many other poems falls somewhere in between — critical (of Henry Ford, for example, in "And I Will Be Heard"), satirical (as in "Mourning Becomes Eugene O'Neill"), and ironic (as when "Doxolgy" praises the godlike William Randolph Hearst). The reader encounters a lighter tone in the humorous "Slide, Kelly, Slide," but tragedy pervades "In Memoriam" and "Kennedy *Ucciso*" — the former about the death of the five Sullivan brothers in World War II and the latter about the assassinated president.

Two of the poets in this volume deserve special mention because their poetry helped raise the nation's consciousness of Irish-American history. The first — Joseph Clarke — worked as a journalist in New York after emigrating from Ireland and later became president of the American Irish Historical Society in that city. In his poetry he celebrated the Revolutionary War heroes John Barry and John Sullivan, fellow Irish-born newspaperman John Boyle O'Reilly, and the Rough Rider William "Buckey" O'Neill. His verse also acknowledged the military prowess of the Irish and their offspring ("The Kinship of the Celts," "The Ballad of the Sixty-Ninth," and "The Fighting Race") and the achievements of the Irish in California ("Ireland at the Fair").

Clarke's fellow popularizer, A. M. (Aloysius Michael) Sullivan, combined a career in the advertising and public relations fields with a passion for writing poetry. Mention has already been made of his poems about Jeremiah O'Brien and the Sullivan brothers, but other works highlighted the lives of Irishmen John O'Neil, Dick Dowling, and John Goff as well as Irish Americans Tim Murphy and John F. Kennedy. Sullivan was a director of the American Irish Historical Society and once described a poem as "a group of words walking on tiptoe to the rhythm of the senses." His surviving daughter, Catherine Rose Sullivan, kindly granted permission to reprint the works of his which are included in this volume. What A. M. Sullivan said about Dick Dowling and his Confederate band at Sabine Pass, Texas, can be said of the poet himself: He "Will live forever . . . / Inviting the ghosts of the Irish bards / Who sing by the sandless hourglass."

Catalogue of Poems

1. The Irish in America

The American Irish

by Robert P. Troy

They surged like ocean billows deep
    On Freedom's golden shore,
They pledged allegiance at her shrine
    And kept it evermore;
They gave their hearts, their arms, their blood,
    That Liberty might live;
They gave the best that God bestows,
    And all that man may give.

They came in legions o'er the sea,
    Defying storm and gale,
Lest tyrant's might should crush the flag
    And heroes' arms should fail.
The heritage of centuries
    Equipped them for the fight,
Unsheathed their swords and nerved their hearts
    To battle for the right.

They found their Celtic brothers here,
    Who pioneered the land
In happier days when rural peace
    Inspired the patriot band.
Their magic touch established town
    And school and mart and mill;
They founded here a continent
    Which breathes their spirit still.

They swelled the ranks that swept the foe
    From every battlefield,
From Lexington to Yorktown's works,
    Where England's banners yield;
And when the foeman crept away
    To Albion's plighted shore,
The blood of Erin in our soil
    Took root forevermore.

And from that root its petals rare
    Have purged like gentle flowers,

Whose spreading breath has scented all
    This loyal land of ours.
And centuries now swing along
    In Time's eternal space,
Exalting our Americans
    As mankind's noblest race,

While all the world its tribute pays
    This nation pure and free,
Extolling every blood that flowed
    To mould its destiny,
The Irish in America
    Are numbered with the rest,
As braver than the bravest
    And better than the best.

Lexington: the first major battle of the American Revolution, fought at Lexington, Massachusetts, on April 19, 1775. **Yorktown:** the last major engagement of the Revolutionary War, during which the British surrendered at Yorktown, Virginia, on October 19, 1781. **Albion:** a literary name for England or Great Britain. **Erin:** a literary name for Ireland.

The Irish Name

by John Jerome Rooney (1866-1934)

Who fears to claim the Irish name?
    Who will forswear his blood?
Who holds in shame the deeds and fame
    Of Emmet, Grattan, Flood?
Their hearts held true through death and rue,
    Through death and sore disgrace,
Then who'll forget the boundless debt
    We owe our Irish race?

Ere Learning's sun had found the road
    Above the Eastern hill,
Her lamp of art and wisdom glowed
    By Irish lake and rill;
To Scotia's crags it flashed a ray,
    And Albion spoke reply;
From tower and shrine it beamed benign,
    A beacon in the sky!

Where'er the rights of man were pressed
    Beneath the heel of wrong—
Where'er, from utmost East to West,
    The helpless sought the strong—
There—there the son of Erin found
    His soul's appointed place—
When Freedom calls, oh, what appals
    The dauntless Irish race.

Within the mighty woods of Maine
    You hear their cheery word;
Upon the boundless Texan plain
    They drive their thundering herd;
They smite the veins of golden ore,
    They gird the earth with plans—
But first and most (their proudest boast),
    They're true Americans!

Then, who would shame the Irish name
    By one ignoble deed?
He—he alone we will not own
    Who would belie his seed!
We claim our line—your blood and mine—
    From out a sacred sod.
Then, hand in hand, we'll take our stand—
    True to ourselves and God!

Emmet: Robert Emmet (1778–1803), an Irish patriot arrested and executed for his involvement in an uprising against British rule in 1803. In his speech to the jury he asked that no man write his epitaph until "my country takes her place among the nations of the earth." **Grattan:** Henry Grattan (1746–1820), a Protestant lawyer and the leader of the anti-British party in the Irish parliament. **Flood:** Henry Flood (1732–1791), a Protestant member of the Irish parliament who led the opposition to British rule prior to Henry Grattan. **Scotia:** a literary name for Scotland. **Albion:** a literary name for England or Great Britain. **Erin:** a literary name for Ireland.

2. James Wolfe

Although James Wolfe was born in England in 1727, his ancestors had lived in Ireland since the fifteenth century. His most famous Irish ancestor (Captain George Woulfe) led the unsuccessful resistance to Ireton's siege of Limerick in 1651. The young James Wolfe advanced so rapidly in the military that at the age of eighteen he was a major and a deputy quartermaster under his father during the latter's campaign against Scottish rebels. The young soldier spent the following decade in either garrison duty or active service in the Netherlands, Scotland, Ireland, and England. In 1752 he visited Belfast, Londonderry, and Dublin and probably his ancestral seat in Limerick. By 1758, however, he was in America, a brigadier general in command of a division under General Amherst at the siege of Louisbourg, Nova Scotia.

In June 1759 Wolfe was en route to Quebec for the final act in the epochal struggle against the French for control of Canada. Arriving at the head of a large fleet and a force of 8,000 men, Wolfe, now a major general, erected batteries at Point Lévis and on the island of Orleans. After an unsuccessful attack on the French position at Montmorency, he landed his troops above the city and — by scaling a precipice — gained the heights behind the town. There, on the Plains of Abraham, on September 13, the British surprised the French under the Marquis de Montcalm. Toward the beginning of the ensuing battle, Wolfe sustained two severe wounds, one in the wrist and the other in the groin. He continued to lead his men, however, until struck again, this time in the chest. Informed that the enemy was retreating, Wolfe ordered that a regiment be sent to cut off the retreat. He then murmured his last words: "Now God be praised, I will die in peace." The French surrendered five days later.

Brave Wolfe

author unknown

Cheer up, my young men all,
    Let nothing fright you;
Though oft objections rise,
    Let it delight you.

Let not your fancy move
    Whene'er it comes to trial;
Nor let your courage fail
    At the first denial.

I sat down by my love,
    Thinking that I woo'd her;
I sat down by my love,
    But sure not to delude her.

But when I got to speak,
    My tongue it doth so quiver,
I dare not speak my mind,
    Whenever I am with her.

Love, here's a ring of gold,
  'T is long that I have kept it,
My dear, now for my sake,
  I pray you to accept it.

When you the posy read,
  Pray think upon the giver,
My dear, remind me,
  Or I'm undone forever.

Then Wolfe he took his leave,
  Of his most lovely jewel;
Although it seemed to be
  To him, an act most cruel.

Although it's for a space
  I'm forced to leave my love,
My dear, where'er I rove,
  I'll ne'er forget my dove.

So then this valiant youth
  Embarked on the ocean,
To free America
  From faction's dire commotion.

He landed at Quebec,
  Being all brave and hearty;
The city to attack,
  With his most gallant party.

Then Wolfe drew up his men,
  In rank and file so pretty,
On Abraham's lofty heights,
  Before this noble city.

A distance from the town
  The noble French did meet them,
In double numbers there,
  Resolved for to beat them.

A Parley:
Wolfe and Montcolm together

Montcalm and this brave youth,
  Together they are walking;
So well they do agree,
  Like brothers they are talking.

Then each one to his post,
  As they do now retire;
Oh, then their numerous hosts
  Began their dreadful fire.

Then instant from his horse,
  Fell this most noble hero,
May we lament his loss
  In words of deepest sorrow.

The French are seen to break,
  Their columns all are flying;
Then Wolfe he seems to wake,
  Though in the act of dying.

And lifting up his head
  (The drums and trumpets rattle),
And to his army said,
  "I pray how goes the battle?"

His aide-de-camp replied,
  "Brave general, 't is our favor,
Quebec and all her pride,
  'T is nothing now can save her.

She falls into our hands,
  With all her wealth and treasure."
"O then," brave Wolfe replied,
  "I quit the world with pleasure."

ring of gold: an allusion to Wolfe's betrothal, at age thirty-two, on the eve of his departure for Canada. **Abraham's lofty heights:** the Plains of Abraham, a high plain adjoining the city of Quebec.

Brave Wolfe

author unknown

Come all you young men all, let this delight you.
Cheer up, you young men all, let nothing fright you.
Never let your courage fall when you're brought to trial,
Nor let your fancy move at the first denial.

I went to see my love only to woo her,
I went to gain her love, not to undo her;
Whene'er I spake a word my tongue did quiver,
I could not speak my mind while I was with her.

Love, here's a diamond ring, long time I've kept it,
'This for your sake alone, if you'll accept it.
When you the posy read, think on the giver,
Madam, remember me, or I'm undone forever.

Brave Wolfe then took his leave of his dear jewel,
Most sorely did she grieve, saying, "Don't be cruel."
Said he, "'tis for a space I must leave you,
Yet love, where'er I go, I'll not forget you."

So then this gallant youth did cross the ocean,
To free America from her commotion.
He landed at Quebec with all his party,
The city to attack both brave and hearty.

Brave Wolfe drew up his men in form most pretty,
On the Plains of Abraham, before the city;
There just before the town the French did meet them,
With double numbers they resolved to beat them.

When drawn up in a line, for death prepared,
While in each other[']s face their armies stared;
So pleasantly brave Wolfe and Montcalm talked,
So martially between their armies walked.

Each man then took his post at their retire,
So then these numerous hosts began to fire;
The cannon on each side did roar like thunder,
And youths in all their pride were torn asunder.

The drums did loudly beat, colours were flying,
The purple gore did stream and men lay dying;
When shot off his horse fell this brave hero,
And we lament his loss in weeds of sorrow.

The French began to break their ranks and flying,
Brave Wolfe then seemed to wake as he lay dying,
He lifted up his head while guns did rattle,
And to his army said, "How goes the battle?"

His aide-de-camp replied, "'Tis in our favor,
Quebec with all her pride, we soon shall have her;
She'll fall into our hands with all her treasure."
"Oh, then," replied brave Wolfe, "I die with pleasure."

Plains of Abraham: a high plain adjoining the city of Quebec. **weeds:** mourning garments.

The Death of Wolfe

author unknown

Thy merits, Wolfe, transcend all human praise,
The breathing marble or the muses' lays.
Art is but vain—the force of language weak,
To paint thy virtues, or thy actions speak.
Had I Duché's or Godfrey's magic skill,
Each line to raise, and animate at will—
To rouse each passion dormant in the soul,
Point out its object, or its rage control—
Then, Wolfe, some faint resemblance should we find
Of those great virtues that adorned thy mind.
Like Britain's genius shouldst thou then appear,
Hurling destruction on the Gallic rear—
While France, astonished, trembled at thy sight,
And placed her safety in ignoble flight.
Thy last great scene should melt each Briton's heart,
And rage and grief alternately impart.
        With foes surrounded, midst the shades of death,
These were the words that closed the warrior's breath—
"My eyesight fails!—but does the foe retreat?
If they retire, I'm happy in my fate!"
A generous chief, to whom the hero spoke,
Cried, "Sir, they fly!—their ranks entirely broke:

Whilst thy bold troops o'er slaughtered heaps advance,
And deal due vengeance on the sons of France."
The pleasing truth recalls his parting soul,
And from his lips these dying accents stole:—
"I'm satisfied!" he said, then wing'd his way,
Guarded by angels to celestial day.
    An awful band!—Britannia's mighty dead,
Receives to glory his immortal shade.
Marlborough and Talbot hail the warlike chief—
Halket and Howe, late objects of our grief,
With joyful song conduct their welcome guest
To the bright mansions of eternal rest—
For those prepared who merit just applause
By bravely dying in their country's cause.

Duché's or Godfrey's magic skill: Reverend Jacob Duché, at one time chaplain to the Continental Congress, was known for his emotional sermons; Thomas Godfrey (1736–1763) was a poet, whose play *Prince of Paradise* was the first by an American colonist to be produced professionally. **Gallic:** French. **Marlborough:** John Churchill (1650–1722), First Duke of Marlborough, the British general whose military victories were among the most glorious in European history. **Talbot:** Charles Talbot (1660–1718), the leader of the movement to replace King James II with William of Orange, the husband of James's daughter Mary.

3. The Irish Donation

This short poem relates an incident which occurred in Massachusetts Bay Colony during the winter of 1630–31. The provisions in the colony having become so scare that the people were forced to eat mussels and acorns, William Pierce was sent to Ireland to seek additional supplies. When the gentleman failed to return by the beginning of February, the colonists feared that he had been lost at sea or taken by pirates. Thus a day of fasting and prayer to God for relief was appointed for February 6. The day before, however, Pierce arrived at Nantasket, Massachusetts, aboard the *Lion*, laden with provisions. The ship sailed on to Boston, where the governor distributed the provisions to the people "proportionate to their necessities." To acknowledge God's mercy to them, the colonists appointed February 22 as a day of thanksgiving.

The Irish Donation
by Rev. Michael Earls, S.J.

God save old Ireland, say we all,
    God heal her woes, we pray;
What fitter time to bless her call
    Than here Thanksgiving day,
Than here where far-off echoes fall
    Of Massachusetts bay?

Oh, dreadful is the famine
    And the burning drought of fears,
When yesterdays walk ghostlike
    And fill tomorrow's fears.

Tomorrow's fears were plentiful,
    They clouded land and sea,
That year in Massachusetts bay
    And the starving colony.

For starving was the harvest,
    When autumn reaped a blight;
And winter looked to springtime
    With a blacker look than night.

Yet in the night are God's good stars,
    And across the sea a star;—
Distress will find the latchstring out
    On Irish hearts afar.

Afar the Irish hearts and hands
    Brought quick a valiant store,
And welcomed well good William Pierce,
    And filled his ship ashore.

The good ship *Lion* westward sailed
    To Nantasket of the bay,
And a colony blessed Ireland
    That first Thanksgiving day.

Then God save Ireland, say we all,
    God heal her woes, we pray:
What fitter time to bless her call
    Than here Thanksgiving day,
Than here where far-off echoes fall
    Of Massachusetts bay?

4. George Berkeley

George Berkeley was a native of County Kilkenny, Ireland, where he was born in 1685. After attending Kilkenny College, he began a lengthy career as a teacher of Hebrew, logic, classics, and theology at Trinity College, Dublin. While there, he wrote works on his philosophy of immaterialism, including an essay on the psychology of perception published in 1709, the year of his ordination as a priest in the Church of Ireland.

Following his appointment as dean of the cathedral in Londonderry in 1724, Berkeley proposed the creation of a university in Bermuda to educate pastors for colonial parishes and train missionaries to the Native Americans. Prospects for the project seemed promising when Parliament pledged £20,000. Berkeley resigned his deanery and sailed for Bermuda in September 1728, but his ship lost its direction and landed instead in Newport, Rhode Island, the following January. For the next two years he resided on his ninety-acre farm "Whitehall."

After realizing that his educational proposal would never receive the financial support he had expected from England, Berkeley returned to Ireland and bequeathed Whitehall to Yale College. The income from his farm was subsequently a source of scholarship funds for Yale students. Though he had resisted requests to become the first bishop in the British colonies, he did accept appointment as bishop of Cloyne in County Cork.

Bishop Berkeley

Stanza #9 from "Power" by Robert Lowell (1917-1977)

The Bishop's nihilism is clerical,
no one was much imperiled by his life,
except he visited Newport and was Irish,
and he was not Rimbaud or Attila,
unhinged, amused to crack the world on his skull.
He lived with quality, and thought the world
is only the perception we perceive. . . .
In Mexico, I met this private earthquake,
when the soil trembled in the soles of my feet;
it was only my high blood of the decline,
my river system saying: I am weak,
I am Whitman, I am Berkeley . . . all men,
bathing my feet in a tub of lukewarm water;
one foot scalds the water, one foot chills the water.

Rimbaud: Arthur Rimbaud (1854–1891), a French poet. **Attila:** a fifth-century king of the Huns. **Whitman:** Walt Whitman (1819–1892), an American poet.

5. The Friendly Sons of St. Patrick

Both during and soon after the colonial period several fraternal and charitable organizations bearing the name of St. Patrick were established in America. The Friendly Brothers of St. Patrick, for example, composed largely of Irish-born officers serving in the British forces in North America, appeared in New York City in 1768. Three years later a similarly-named organization was formed in Charleston, South Carolina, while the Friendly Sons of St. Patrick was established in Philadelphia that same year. A New York branch of the Friendly Sons was organized in 1784, with Daniel McCormick, a native of Ireland and a director of the Bank of New York, as its first president.

One of the founders and the first secretary and treasurer of the Friendly Sons of St. Patrick in Philadelphia was William Mitchell. He served from the founding of the society in March 1771 until his death in the late summer of 1775.

To William Mitchell

by Thomas Augustine Daly (1871-1948)

When first you trimmed your goose-quill pen
    And spread your minute-book before you,
Ah, William Mitchell, surely then
    Two watchful spirits hovered o'er you!
St. Patrick, first of all, who blessed
    The thankless pains that you are taking;
And pagan Clio, to attest
    Much golden history in the making.

As well becomes a Friendly Son,
    Whose faith no sundering seas can smother,
You may, indeed, have sensed the one—
    The saintly presence—not the other.
You'd scarcely think that History's Muse,
    Whose records must outlast the ages,
Could rate as news, the rules, the dues
    The roll of names upon your pages.

Yet Clio watched you ply your pen,
    And her quick glance across your shoulder
Marked names that would be deathless when
    The world and they were five years older;
But you, good William, man of trade,

Whose days were full of goods and chattels,
How little must you have paid
    To dreams of fame and far-off battles.

A solid merchant, quite content
    To live at peace among his neighbors,
I fancy with what joy you went,
    That peaceful spring, about your labors.
You prospered, for the times were good
    And war was but an ugly rumor;
Then came your Celtic brotherhood
    To put you in still finer humor.

Your minutes of the Friendly Sons,
    (We treasure still that faded, gray book,
Where year by year the record runs
    Like your own ledger, or your daybook)
Gave little news in any form
    How wagged the world outside, no tiding
Of rumblings of the gathering storm,
    Of marching men, or courtiers riding.

Although with all his dogs at heel
    Grim Mars was arming in his cavern,
Your words dealt most with some good meal
    At Burns's [*sic*] or the City Tavern,
And named the special committee
    (Good trenchermen and practised "pickers")
Whose duty it would be "to see
    The food bespoke, and chuse the liquors."

Thus four full years your records ran
    With scarcely any warlike inkling;
But ah! good William, modest man,
    Full well we know your eye was twinkling,
And while you wrote of trivial things,
    You and your fellows but dissembled;
And soon the vaunted pride of Kings
    Before the Irish onset trembled.

But ah! for you, good man and true,
    Fate spared no part in all the fighting;
Before the rallying bugles blew,
    Death closed the record YOU were writing.

Here, too, these halting lines should end.
    Their work is done, so why continue?
The only mission they intend
    Is centered round about and IN you.

Not mine the task with florid pen
    To glorify your valiant brothers,
And tell of their great deeds again,
    So oft and better told by others.
My pleasure, William Mitchell, lies
    In one slight service I can do you:
Bid your pathetic figure rise
    That we may pay our tribute to you.

We brush the grave-dust from your brow,
    And as our true blood-brother boast you!
If we could "chuse the liquors" now
    Right gladly, William, we would toast you:
Least-known of all that gallant tribe,
    You found no laurels for your winning;
But, blessings on you! faithful scribe,
    Who saw our glorious beginning!

St. Patrick: the fifth-century Briton whose missionary work in Ireland led to its conversion to Christianity. **Clio:** in classical mythology the muse of history. **Mars:** the Roman god of war. **Burns's [*sic*]:** Byrne's, from James Byrne, a tavern-keeper in Philadelphia. It was either at his tavern (the Golden Fleece) or at his home on March 17, 1769, that the first recorded celebration of St. Patrick's Day in Philadelphia was held. He was one of the earliest members of the Society of the Friendly Sons of St. Patrick. **City Tavern:** after 1775 the finest public house in America; located on Second Street and Bank Alley in Philadelphia.

The Friendly Sons of St. Patrick

by Clare Gerald Fenerty (d. 1952)

O! God of our fathers, behold us tonight,
Sons of St. Patrick, as one in our cause,
Children of those who through tyranny's night
Championed for Irishmen, Irishmen's laws!
What do we hear? 'Tis the roll of the drum,
As Washington, Moylan—a brave ghostly band
From Lexington, Yorktown and Gettysburg come—
Sons of the Saint of the little green land.

Fearless in battle, for justice our lance
Unbroken remains, as we answer the call
Of duty, in Erin, Columbia, France,
Eternal our war-cry: "To conquer or fall!"
Valiant in peace, let our labor and art
Garner their harvest as gifts to a shrine,
Fraught with the zeal of a patriot's heart,
Flaming with faith in your country and mine.

For kingdoms have fallen and yet we are young,
Serene in the glory that streams from our past,
Singing the songs that our fathers have sung,
Upholding the truths that they kept to the last;
Our heritage holy—bequest from the God
Who ennobled our land with peace, freedom and mirth,
And sent us, as sentinels, sons of the Sod
Whose offspring have hallowed the nations of earth.

As long as the grass grows in famed Innisfall,
As long as our dawn-tinted emblem unfurled
Entwines with the battle-scarred green of the Gael,
Or chivalry lives in a recreant world,
So long are we true to the mother that bore us—
Columbia, foremost in Liberty's van—
True as the fathers who loved her before us,
Fighting for God and the birthright of man.

Here Loyalty lingers, daughter of God,
Here Virtue and Knowledge and Fortitude meet,
Authority, child of the chastening rod,
And Friendship and Tolerance render them sweet;
May heaven's own breezes to Ireland coast
On invisible waves through the lightning and gale
Bear our message of hope—our perennial toast:
"The Sons of St. Patrick—the Knights of the Grail!"

Moylan: Stephen Moylan (1737–1811), the Irish-born quartermaster general of the Continental Army, the commander of the Fourth Pennsylvania Light Dragoons, and the first president of the Friendly Sons of St. Patrick in Philadelphia. **Lexington:** the first major battle of the American Revolution, fought at Lexington, Massachusetts, on April 19, 1775. **Yorktown:** the last major engagement of the Revolutionary War, during which the British surrendered at Yorktown, Virginia, on October 19, 1781. **Gettysburg:** the most famous battle of the Civil War, when Union troops repulsed a Confederate thrust into the North in July 1863. **Erin:** a literary name for Ireland. **Columbia:** the United States, usually personified as a female figure. **Innisfall:** also *Inisfail,* a Gaelic word meaning "Isle of Destiny" (Ireland). **Knights of the Grail:** King Arthur's knights, one of whom, Sir Galahad, sought the Holy Grail, the cup reputedly used by Christ at the Last Supper.

6. Jeremiah O'Brien

In 1770 Jeremiah O'Brien and his Dublin-born father were among a group of settlers who were granted land in Machias, Maine, on condition "that they build a suitable meeting house for the public worship of God and settle a learned Protestant minister and make provision for his comfortable and honorable support."

Five years later, in June 1775, the H.M.S *Margaretta* arrived off Machiasport, Maine, with two sloops to take on lumber for the British barracks in Boston. Tempers flared when Midshipman James Moore of the 100-ton British ship refused to heed Jeremiah O'Brien's warning to abandon his mission. Moore raised the ante by ordering the colonials to remove the Liberty Pole which they had erected in town only a month before. When O'Brien's brother John challenged the order, Moore repeated his demand that "That liberty pole must come down or it will be my painful duty to fire upon the town."

In response, a heavily armed band of forty colonials — including Jeremiah and his five younger brothers — leaped aboard the sloop *Unity* and seized it. After provisioning the captured vessel with twenty shotguns, a small cannon, hay forks, and axes, the colonials gave chase to the *Margaretta.* When O'Brien ordered Moore to surrender, the British commander opened fire, killing two of the American crew. The Irishman then maneuvered his ship next to the *Margaretta* and lashed the two together, thereby making it easier to subdue the British crew. After outfitting the *Unity* with the *Margaretta's* guns, O'Brien rechristened her *Machias Liberty,* the first American armed cruiser of the Revolutionary War. This engagement — the first naval encounter of the Revolution — prompted the Continental Congress to create an American navy.

The Man of Machias

by A. M. Sullivan (1896–1980)

Farmer and woodsman and sailor was he,
    Jeremiah O'Brien,
And he met the British upon the sea
And he sailed the captured "Unity"

And he won a Yankee victory
With a lumber sloop and forty-three.
        Praise Jeremiah O'Brien.

Seventeen-seventy-five's the year
        That Jeremiah O'Brien
Told how Concord's guns rang clear
With defiance for all the world to hear
And the woodsmen gathered from far and near
And listened to him who had no fear,
        Jeremiah O'Brien.

"The British navy is waxing strong,"
        Said Jeremiah O'Brien,
"On Machias oak but not for long.
None of our trees shall stand for wrong
But one shall stand for freedom among
Men of Machias, old and young,"
        Said Jeremiah O'Brien.

"We'll search the wood for the tallest tree,"
        Said Jeremiah O'Brien,
"And plant it deep for Liberty
In Machias Common for all to see
Macias men who will bend no knee
To tax or tyrants or Tories," said he,
        Jeremiah O'Brien.

Axe and scythe and muskets four
        Had Jeremiah O'Brien,
Three rounds of powder and nothing more
When they left Machias' rocky shore,
But they were ready to wage a war
For Freedom's sake and the angry roar
        Of Jeremiah O'Brien.

Ichabod Jones was the Tory foe
        Of Jeremiah O'Brien.
His lumber sloops went to and fro,
To Boston town with a craft in tow
And many a tree the men laid low
In Machias' woods till one said, "NO,"
        Jeremiah O'Brien.

Ichabod Jones denied the food
       For Jeremiah O'Brien
And a hundred others who cut the wood
When the British spilled New England's blood[,]
And Ichabod said, "The rebel brood
Will get no bread till they eschewed
       Jeremiah O'Brien."

A sloop rode high in the morning swell
       When Jeremiah O'Brien
Summoned his brothers with the tavern bell.
"The 'Unity[,]' lads, could serve us well,
What else is there to ask or tell."
The meeting was over and silence fell
       On Jeremiah O'Brien.

The 'Unity[,]' lads, is a pretty sloop,"
       Mused Jeremiah O'Brien
As his brothers five and the council group
Slacked the hawser and slipped the loop
While Ichabod drowsed on the tavern stoop
And woke in a rage to play the dupe
       For Jeremiah O'Brien.

"Let Ichabod and his Tories gloat,"
       Cried Jeremiah O'Brien,
"Our river is never a British moat
Though the sword of choice is at our throat,
If it's kneel or starve, then starve I vote,
Never for bread shall I turn my coat,"
       Said Jeremiah O'Brien.

The "Margaretta" was a comely craft
       To Jeremiah O'Brien,
Twenty-foot beam and ten-foot draft
But her guns were aimed at the Liberty shaft
In Machias town, and the Rebels laughed
When a townsman said, "We'll scuttle the raft."
       'Twas Jeremiah O'Brien.

Captain Moore showed buttons and braid
       To Jeremiah O'Brien
And he vowed that Machias would be amply paid

With ball and powder for the stand it made
But no man fled from the shining blade
And least of all stood unafraid
        Jeremiah O'Brien.

Ichabod Jones was a coward in haste
        From Jeremiah O'Brien,
But an arrogant sailor whenever he paced
By the side of Captain Moore and faced
His surly neighbors and bade them taste
A beggar's bread and be disgraced
        To Jeremiah O'Brien.

Five proud brothers, they stood beside
        Jeremiah O'Brien
And there were others who risked their hide,
Some of them lived and some of them died,
One was a blackamoor, Machias' pride,
Richard Earle went far and wide
        With Jeremiah O'Brien.

Benjamin Foster was the fighting friend
        Of Jeremiah O'Brien.
He captured the "Polly" on the river bend
From Ichabod Jones, and that was the end
Of Ichabod's fleet with none to lend
A keel to the king as the townsmen send
        For Jeremiah O'Brien.

The men elected a Captain bold,
        Jeremiah O'Brien,
Who grieved when Foster's craft was shoaled
On Machias' river where the tide ran cold,
But hope ran high as the "Unity" rolled.
"It's now or never," the men were told
        By Jeremiah O'Brien.

The "Unity" filled her cheeks with air
        As Jeremiah O'Brien,
The terrier[,] took the lion's dare
And sprung at the foeman waiting there
Baring his teeth in his chosen lair
And woodsmen stood with breastbones bare
        By Jeremiah O'Brien.

"Strike your colors," a young man said.
      'Twas Jeremiah O'Brien.
But the schooner answered with ball and lead
And John McNeill at the bow fell dead
And Coolbroth mortally wounded bled
On the deck as the flying "Unity" sped
      With Jeremiah O'Brien.

"Make fast and board," a young man cried.
      'Twas Jeremiah O'Brien.
The "Unity" bumped the schooner's side
And bounded from her bristling hide,
And once again, she was not denied,
As the rigging fouled and the ropes were tied
      By Jeremiah O'Brien.

Woodsmen, farmers and sailors all
      With Jeremiah O'Brien
Bounded over the smoking wall
Armed with axe and fork and maul
And they met the sword and the musket ball
And charged the foemen at the call
      Of Jeremiah O'Brien.

Commander Moore with pride and poise
      Faced Jeremiah O'Brien.
He laughed at the men who fought like boys
Armed for war with awkward toys
But above the curses and musket noise
His warriors brought a thousand joys
      To Jeremiah O'Brien.

A dozen musket balls were aimed
      At Jeremiah O'Brien,
And four beside him were struck and maimed
And four men died and none were shamed
By breath of powder, and none were tamed
By gun or sabre, heroes acclaimed
      With Jeremiah O'Brien.

"Drown the rabble," cried dapper Moore
      Toward Jeremiah O'Brien.
His shining buttons were a musket lure
And a woodman's eye was sharp and sure

And Death gave Pride the ancient cure
And a brave foe fell for his royal boor
    Near Jeremiah O'Brien.

"Strike your colors," they heard the shout
    Of Jeremiah O'Brien
And fifty Britons left no doubt
Who were the victors in the bout,
They dropped their weapons in the rout
And never a Briton turned to flout
    Jeremiah O'Brien.

Into the halyards leaped a man,
    Jeremiah O'Brien,
Swift as a spider the sailor ran
For all on Machias' shore to scan
And the woodsmen cheered as heroes can
When the flag came down according to plan
    Of Jeremiah O'Brien.

And there was joy in Machias town
    When Jeremiah O'Brien
Hauled the British ensign down
And tilted askew the British crown
And there was many a Tory frown
For neighbors who shared the bright renown
    Of Jeremiah O'Brien.

Concord's guns: an allusion to the battle of Concord, Massachusetts, on April 19, 1775, when local militia met and fired upon advancing British troops. **his brothers five:** Gideon, John, William, Dennis, and Joseph O'Brien. **Richard Earle:** an African American who was employed by Jeremiah O'Brien in his saw mill. **Benjamin Foster:** captured the *Polly* with a group of picked men but later reported that she had run aground. **John McNeill:** killed when musketry fire from the *Margaretta* tore through the timbers of the *Unity*. **Coolbroth:** James Coolbroth, mortally wounded during the engagement between the *Margaretta* and the *Unity*. He died a few hours later.

The Prize of the *Margaretta*

by Will Carleton (1845–1912)

I

Four young men, of a Monday morn,
Heard that the flag of peace was torn;

Heard that "rebels" with sword and gun,
Had fought the British at Lexington,

While they were far from that bloody plain,
Safe on the green-clad shores of Maine.
With eyes that glittered, and hearts that burned,
They talked of the glory their friends had earned,

And asked each other, "What can we do,
So our hands may prove that our hearts are true?"

II

Silent the *Margaretta* lay,
Out on the bosom of the bay;

On her masts rich bunting gleamed:
Bravely the flag of England streamed.

The young men gazed at the tempting prize—
They wistfully glanced in each other's eyes;

Said one, "We can lower that cloth of dread
And hoist the pine-tree flag instead.

"We are only boys to the old man and sage;
We have not yet come to manhood's age;

"But we can show them that, when there's need,
Man may follow and boys may lead."

Tightly each other's hand they pressed,
Loudly they cried, "We shall do our best;

"The pine-tree flag, ere day is passed,

Shall float from the *Margaretta's* mast."

III

They ran to a sloop that lay nearby;
They roused their neighbors, with hue and cry;

They doffed their hats, gave three loud cheers,
And called for a crew of volunteers.

Their bold, brave spirit spread far and wide,
And men came running from every side.

Curious armed were the dauntless ones,
With axes, pitchforks, scythes, and guns;

They shouted, "Ere yet this day be passed,
The pine-tree grows from the schooner's mast!"

IV

With sails all set, trim as could be,
The *Margaretta* stood out to sea.

With every man and boy in place,
The gallant Yankee sloop gave chase.

Rippled and foamed the sunlit seas;
Freshened and sung the soft May breeze;

And came from the sloop's low deck, "Hurray!
We're gaining on her! We'll win the day!"

A sound of thunder, echoing wide,
Came from the *Margaretta's* side;

A deadly crash, and a loud death-yell,
And one of the brave pursuers fell.

They aimed a gun at the schooner then,
And sent the compliment back again;

He who at the helm of the schooner stood,

Covered the deck with his rich life-blood.

V

Each burning to pay a bloody debt,
The crews of the hostile vessels met;

The Western nation now to be,
Made her first fight upon the sea.

And not till forty men were slain,
Did the pine-tree flag a victory gain;

But at last the hearts of the Britons quailed,
And grandly the patriot arm prevailed.

One of the youths, the deed to crown,
Grasped the colors and pulled them down;

And raised, 'mid cries of wild delight,
The pine-tree flag of blue and white.

And the truth was shown, for the world to read,
That men may follow and boys may lead.

Lexington: the first major battle of the American Revolution, fought at Lexington, Massachusetts, on April 19, 1775. **pine-tree flag:** possibly a banner like the Bunker Hill flag, one with a blue background and a white field adorned with a red cross and a pine tree. **Western nation now to be:** the future United States.

7. Richard Montgomery

Richard Montgomery was born in County Donegal in 1737, the son of an Anglo-Irish father who was a member of the Irish parliament. After enlisting in the British army, the younger Montgomery served under James Wolfe at the capture of Quebec in 1759. Although he sailed home after the French and Indian War, he returned to America in 1772 and married into the family of Robert Livingston.

As part of the American offensive against the British during the Revolutionary War, the Continental Congress placed Montgomery, America's first Irish general, at the head of an expeditionary force into Canada. Montgomery headed north via Lake Champlain, captured Montreal in November 1775, and reached Quebec with his army on December 1, thereby bringing the attack force to 2,000 men. Although he subsequently erected batteries on the high ground commanding the St. John and the St. Louis gates, the ensuing American bombardment produced few results. Deciding to storm the town by night, Montgomery and his men set out at 2 a.m. on December 31, crossed the Plains of Abraham, and descended into what is now Champlain Street. By 4 a.m., however, a blinding northeast snowstorm was raging as Montgomery descended the cliff and advanced along a ledge flanked by the crags of Cape Diamond. Although the Americans' objective — the Près-de-Ville barricade — was defended by only fifty Canadian seamen and militiamen, the defenders peppered Montgomery's advancing column with cannon and musket fire. Montgomery, two of his aides, and ten of his men were killed in the first discharge, a surprising turn of events that caused the remaining 700 Americans to turn and flee. Montgomery's body was first buried in Quebec, but in 1818 his remains were reinterred in St. Paul's Chapel in New York City.

Montgomery at Quebec

by Clinton Scollard (1860–1932)

Round Quebec's embattled walls
 Moodily the patriots lay;
Dread disease within its thralls
 Drew them closer day by day;
Till from suffering man to man,
Mutinous, a murmur ran.

Footsore, they had wandered far,
 They had fasted, they had bled;
They had slept beneath the star
 With no pillow for the head;

Was it but to freeze to stone
In this cruel icy zone?

Yet their leader held his heart,
    Naught discouraged, naught dismayed:
Quelled with unobtrusive art
    Those that muttered; unafraid
Waited, watchful, for the hour
When his golden chance should flower.

'T was the death-tide of the year;
    Night had passed its murky noon;
Through the bitter atmosphere
    Pierced nor ray of star nor moon;
But upon the bleak earth beat
Blinding arrows of the sleet.

While the trumpets of the storm
    Pealed the bastioned heights around,
Did the dauntless heroes form,
    Did the low, sharp order sound.
"Be the watchword Liberty!"
Cried the brave Montgomery.

Here, where he had won applause,
    When Wolfe faced the Gallic foe,
For a nobler, grander cause
    Would he strike the fearless blow,—
Smite at Wrong upon the throne,
At Injustice giant grown.

"Men, you will not fear to tread
    Where your general dares to lead!
On, my valiant boys!" he said,
    And his foot was first to speed;
Swiftly up the beetling steep,
Lion-hearted, did he leap.

Flashed a sudden blinding glare;
    Roared a fearsome battle-peal;
Rang the gloomy vasts of air;
    Seemed the earth to rock and reel;
While adown that fiery breath
Rode the hurtling bolts of death.

    Woe for him, the valorous one,
        Now a silent clod of clay!
    Nevermore for him the sun
        Would make glad the paths of day;
    Yet 't were better thus to die
    Than to cringe to tyranny!—

    Better thus the life to yield,
        Striking for the right and God,
    Upon Freedom's gory field,
        Than to kiss Oppression's rod!
    Honor, then, for all time be
    To the brave Montgomery!

Wolfe: James Wolfe (1727–1759), the British general who defeated the French on the Plains of Abraham in Quebec in 1759. **Gallic foe:** the French troops under the Marquis de Montcalm.

A Song of the Brave General Montgomery

author unknown

    Come soldiers all in chorus join
    To pay the tribute at the shrine
        Of brave Montgomery,
    Which to the memory is due
    Of him who fought and died that you
        Might live and yet be free.

    With cheerful and undaunted mind,
    Domestic happiness resigned,
        He was a chosen band,
    Through deserts wild, with fixed intent,
    Canada for to conquer went,
        Or perish sword in hand.

    Six weeks before St. John's they lay,
    While cannon on them constant play,
        On cold and marshy ground;
    When Prescott forced at length to yield,
    Aloud proclaimed it in the field,
        Virtue a friend had found.

To Montreal he winged his way,
Which seemed impatient to obey
        And opened wide its gates,
Convinced no force could e'er repel
Troops who had just behaved so well,
        Under so hard a fate.

With scarce one third part of his force
Then to Quebec he bent his course,
        That grave of heroes slain;
The pride of France, the great Montcalm,
And Wolfe, the strength of Britain's arm,
        Both fell on Abraham's plain.

Having no less of fame required,
There too Montgomery expired
        With Cheeseman by his side.
Carleton, 'tis said, his corpse conveyed
To earth in all the grand parade
        Of military pride.

St. John's: St. Jean-sur-Richelieu, a town southeast of Montreal along the Richelieu River north of Lake Champlain. **Prescott:** General Richard Prescott, who surrendered the British garrison at St. John's (St. Jean-sur-Richelieu) on November 2, 1775. **Montcalm:** Marquis de Montcalm (1712–1759), the French general whose troops were defeated by the British on the Plains of Abraham in Quebec in 1759. Montcalm died on the battlefield. **Wolfe:** James Wolfe (1727–1759), the British general who defeated the French on the Plains of Abraham in Quebec in 1759. **Cheeseman:** Captain Jacob Cheeseman, one of Montgomery's aides. **Carleton:** General Guy Carleton (1724–1808), governor of Canada from 1768 to 1778 and again from 1786 to 1796. Born in County Tyrone, Ireland, in 1724, Carleton was descended from an originally English family that had resided in Ireland since the beginning of the seventeenth century. His father and mother were from counties Down and Donegal, respectively.

Montgomery's Return

by Arthur Guiterman (1871–1943)

How black the barge of trailing pall
        And nodding sable plume
That Hudson bears by mountain wall
        And fields of golden bloom
A cloud upon the azure flow,

           A shadow in the sun,
To drumhead roll and church-bell toll
           And boom of minute gun!
By night the ruddy beacons flame
           On crested Kaaterskill.
Great heart that beat for Love and Fame
           Why liest thou so still?

How blithe and brave he left his hall
           Beside the Hudson's wave!
He heard his struggling country's call,
           His uttermost he gave.
He bade his bonny bride farewell;
           In wastes of nor'land snow
He battled, conquered, failed, and fell—
           Full twoscore years ago
They've wrapped him in a noble sheath,
           The flag without a fleck;
They've borne him from the grave beneath
           The walls of old Quebec.

The land he left in doubtful strife
           Has triumphed, free and blest;
And him that died to give it life
           His people bear to rest.
The bride he kissed a blooming lass
           Is wrinkled, old, and gray;
She hears the drums; she sees him pass;
           She droops and swoons away.

          *   *   *   *   *   *   *   *

Loud boomed the bell of high St. Paul's
           From out the hollow dome;
And thus below those ivied walls
           Montgomery came home.

barge of trailing pall: Montgomery's funeral barge, which passed the general's home near Rhinebeck, New York, as it made its way down the Hudson River. Rhinebeck is located on the eastern side of the Hudson, about fifteen miles north of Poughkeepsie. **Kaaterskill:** Kaaterskill Clove, a gorge on the edge of what is now Catskill State Park, between Palenville and Haines Falls, New York. **bonny bride:** Janet Livingston.

8. John Barry

John Barry was born near Wexford, Ireland, in 1745 but left his native land for America at the age of fourteen. Until 1776 he was employed in various capacities in the Philadelphia merchant marine, serving as captain at age twenty-one and eventually becoming an influential shipmaster and shipowner.

Following the start of hostilities with Britain, Barry achieved fame as a naval commander for the aborning nation. In January 1776 he was placed in command of the *Lexington*, the first regular cruiser to put to sea under the authority of the Continental Congress. On April 17 the *Lexington* became the first vessel so commissioned to capture a British warship in actual battle. Barry's was also the first vessel flying the new striped American flag to capture an armed British ship.

The Irishman's reputation was further enhanced when he refused a bribe from the British. During the war General Howe offered Barry up to 20,000 guineas and command of the best British frigate if he would abandon the American cause. Barry replied that he had devoted himself to the cause of his adopted land and that neither wealth nor the promise of command over the whole British fleet would tempt him from continuing to serve her.

The episode that forms the basis of the "Ballad of Saucy Jack Barry" — the last poem in this section — occurred on February 26, 1778, while the British occupied Philadelphia and a British fleet commanded the Delaware River. At first intimidated by the superior British fleet, Barry held his ship the *Effingham* and two smaller vessels in the upper waters of the Delaware at Burlington, New Jersey. After about a month of inaction, however, Barry petitioned the Continental Congress for permission to attack the *Alert*, a British warship anchored in the lower Delaware which was convoying two transports (the *Kitty* and the *Mermaid*) filled with food and forage for the British in Philadelphia.

In the last year of the war, Barry was appointed commander of the frigate *Alliance*. During a subsequent engagement with two British vessels, he was wounded in the shoulder and was forced below to tend to his injury. After his ship's colors had been shot away, one of his men asked him if he would surrender. "No," the captain replied. "If the ship can't be fought without me, I will be brought on deck." A reenergized crew and a favorable wind allowed the *Alliance* to pound the enemy with a broadside, soon forcing the two British vessels to surrender.

In 1794 President Washington named Barry the senior captain of the United States navy, an appointment which led to Barry's honorific as "Father of the American Navy."

John Barry — A Poem
by Joseph I. C. Clarke (1846–1925)

The Continental Captains

Bold captains of the stormy seas,
    Whose hearts rose stalwart on the blast,
When first our star-flag took the breeze,
    And all the lift with gloom o'ercast,
Ye fearless souls, we hail ye all.
    From rock-bound Maine to Delaware,
Who cried "ay, ay," to Freedom's call
    And flashed the biting cutlass bare.

Ye recked not whether tempests slept,
    Or lashed the waters with their gales,
Ye cared not that the foemen swept
    The oceans with a swarm of sails.
Five hundred ships, ten thousand guns
    And thirty thousand fighting men
'Gainst scant a thousand Freedom's sons
    And ships that counted barely ten.

The cannon chorus of the foe
    Mighty roar in thunder loud and long.
You rammed your guns and let them go—
    The sounding staves in Freedom's song.
Ye climbed the hillocks of the deep
    When foam and fume in spindrift flew,
Our ocean outposts still to keep,
    No matter whence the wild winds blew.

Ye fought at sight or sped at need,
    Nimble of heel or yard to yard;
Like tigers ye could strike or bleed,
    Else haul your sheets and stand at guard.
Their tow'ring fleets might crowd the waves,
    Their 74's your stout ribs rake;
Ye trembled not at ocean graves
    While glory glimmered in your wake.

Honored be all who took the stand
    That under God we must be free.

Hard pressed, our true men held the land,
    While ye kept open paths at sea.
For ye Fame's silver trumpet tones
    To earth's last hour the tale will carry
Hopkins, Whipple, O'Brien, Jones,
    Beside the glowing name of Barry.

John Barry

Blithe and bold and bred to the sea
That beats and frets on Ireland's shore,
He turned his face from a land unfree,
And westward over the ocean bore,
Better to battle with winds and waves
Than cringe for crusts among fellow-slaves.
Here, too, deep planted he had found
Oppression's tree before our gate.
This tree whose flower is a people's hate,
With bitter fruitage of revolt,
And which, to keep the forest sound,
You must uproot with ax and bolt.

On many seas and in many climes,
Trusty and tireless, stern or bland,
He manful rose to his ship's command,
A captain at twenty-one;
And so for a decade his race was run.
But when on his ear rang out the chimes
That told of our young republic born,
"Count ye on me," he smiling cried,
"Give me a ship, and I'll sail at morn."

True as he spoke, he sailed amain
And romped back, bringing a British prize,
With heart of cheer and brave man's blow,
With quick resort of a fertile brain,
And a passionate stream of love,
Ever on land and sea he strove
To keep the star flag in the skies.
And the foeman learned his name to know.
"A frigate and clear ten thousand pounds
If you'll fight for us," they tempting cried,
His answer through the years resounds:
"Not for your fleet and your wealth beside."

The Ballad of Barry's Prayer

John Barry, ho! they're speeding you to France.
The west wind hums: the sunny waters dance
Around your lofty frigate, the *Alliance*,
    With her long guns, forty-four,
    Off the Massachusetts shore,
And her ensign at the peak in defiance.

The ragged Continentals call for gold,
Their powder running short, too, we are told;
So crowd your studding sails, and never tarry.
    Good King Louis there beyond
    Will with ships and gold respond.
And who will bear the message but John Barry?

The king has sent a royal fleet, and, more,
In cash a hundred thousand louis d'or,
And Barry sails to fight whate'er he matches;
    Takes a British brig or two,
    And mans them from his crew,
Then sails on with the Britons under hatches.

One hazy morn in May the breezes fail;
No puff to raise the corner of a sail.
And Barry spies two warships on his quarter,
    "What ships," he shouts, "are ye"? [*sic*]
    "Why, *Atalanta*, *Trepassy*:
John Bull will cut John Barry's cruising shorter."

John Barry stamps; no wind his ships to wear;
He scarce can bring a brace of guns to bear.
The British ships steal up with sweeps and pound him:
    Their balls and grape come fast,
    Shiv'ring rigging, spar and mast.
And Barry falls, his brave men gath'ring round him.

His flag's shot down: his guns make no reply.
They carry Captain Barry down to die.
The first lieutenant asks: "Shall we surrender?"
    "No, never;" answers Barry;
    "Their hides I still can harry.
On deck with me; I'll fight her and defend her."

The first lieutenant, shamefaced, springs away,
And Barry, in his bandage, turns to pray:
"O mighty Lord, who rules the storm and thunder;
    Here I beg as on my knees
    For a capful of a breeze.
A capful, and I'll rip their ribs asunder."

His prayer is heard. A light breeze swings her head,
Her broadsides pile the British ships with dead,
And rend their sides with splitting crash and rattle,
    Till the union jacks are low'red,
    And our prize crews jump aboard,
With grateful hearts to Barry's God of battle.

So Barry anchors safe off Boston town,
The Continentals drink to his renown,
And bravely on to Yorktown, runs the story,
    For the king's help that he sought
    And the great news that he brought
High heartened us and paved our way to glory.

Father of the Navy

O brave John Barry, whom Washington,
Our godlike leader, dearly loved,
Who a hundred times his valor proved
In a dash, a cruise, or a fight,
Never a conflict fair to shun
With a boarding crew or cannon shocks,
His ships in flames or on the rocks,
Or the foeman's ensign flutt'ring down,
True and ready by day or night.

 Then with the war for Freedom won,
And our nation, the United States,
Shaping a Navy to guard our gates,
Well may we see you, in true man's pride,
Take from the hands of Washington
Your Captain's charter, stamped, Number One.
You fought from the first till Freedom came,
And still you carried a freeman's sword,
And led once more through the perilous fight,
Wherever the red-hot cannon roared.

You trimmed your ships and handled your guns,
And called to your men, "Fight on, my sons."
So, first of our captains by your right,
Long as the star-flag lights our land
And Justice rules with even might,
John Barry, Father of our Navy, stand.

The Guns of Peace

The turreted leviathans of steel
Now sentinel a hundred million souls.
They bear our flag and watch our weal
On ev'ry mile of sea between the poles.
And in our breast a world-pride they evoke;
But ever shall the greater tale be told
Of men like Barry in their ships of oak,
Who held the sea for us in days of old.
They won their fight; they won an honored peace—
The heritage that we are guarding still;
Untempted to the swinging of the sword,
In patient might beneath God's kindly will.
We'll hold that peace, and only flash the word,
Our ton-weight bolts of thunder to release,
Should Freedom's foes rise reckless, armed to kill.
And victory shall light our way once more,
And Barry's soul be with us as of yore.

Their 74's: ships carrying seventy-four guns. **Hopkins:** Stephen Hopkins (1707–1785), a governor of Rhode Island and a signer of the Declaration of Independence. **Whipple:** William Whipple (1730–1785), a signer of the Declaration of Independence, who helped negotiate the surrender of the British after the battle of Saratoga in 1777. **O'Brien:** Jeremiah O'Brien (1744–1818), whose capture of a British ship off the coast of Machias, Maine, in 1775 was the first American naval victory of the Revolution. **Jones:** John Paul Jones (1747–1792), the American naval hero famous for an apocryphal boast attributed to him ("I have not yet begun to fight"), allegedly made while his ship the *Bonhomme Richard* captured the British ship *Serapis* in 1779. **John Bull:** England. **union jacks:** British national flags. **turreted leviathans of steel:** the new ships of the American navy.

Ballad of Saucy Jack Barry

by John Jerome Rooney (1866–1934)

They have taken the old rebel city of Penn;
Lord Howe, he has filled it with red-coated men.
"What terror," said he, "has the winter for me,
Since I hold the town and my ships hold the sea?"

But it never is safe, in making a boast,
To reckon too easy, not counting your host;
Or is it quite prudent to count on your boat
When saucy Jack Barry is up and afloat?

There were banquets for Captains and plenty for all;
The horses had forage, too much for the stall;
Double rations were served—in truth 'twas a feast,
And prospects were cheery for man and for beast.

But bins have a bottom and larders grow thin
When plenty comes out and nothing goes in;
But his Lordship smiled blandly such trifles away—
"The 'Alert' and two transports are down in the Bay!"

But it never is safe, in making a boast,
To reckon too easy, not counting your host;
Or is it quite prudent to count on your boat
When saucy Jack Barry is up and afloat?

The Delaware waters come down with a sweep
Past Burlington town, snow-clad and asleep,
And there lay our "Effingham," silent and stark,
A ghost of the sea, looming up thro' the dark.

Then, sudden, four boats sweep out from her side,
With oars swift and muffled swing down in the tide;
The moon has gone black, the wind whistles high,
And the scud of the thunder-storm darkens the sky.

Down the river they went, like the flight of a bird;
The twenty and seven said never a word—
They are after the fox of the ocean again,
And they'll make not a stir as they enter his den.

It was three o' the clock when, faintly ahead,
The lights of the city flashed yellow and red—
Then, sudden, a gleam, a cannon's dull roar,
A challenge and halt from the river and shore.

But, surely, no need then to speak to them twice—
Four nautical heels were shown in a trice;
Down thro' the night, like a hound, they're away
To the lair of their quarry in Delaware Bay.

The sun had come up when they rounded Port Penn.
And O what a sight there for gods and for men!
A schooner (ten guns pointed out from her side,
With the flag of the Briton) swung free in the tide.

With a leap like a tiger the boats swung around,
Then straight for the Briton, with bound upon bound.
"Grapple tight!" cried the Captain, and guiding his band,
Up the side went Jack Barry, with cutlass in hand!

He is over the rails in the flash of an eye,—
"Strike, strike yonder flag or, by heaven, you die!"
But never a hand or a foot there did turn;
They were frozen with terror from stem unto stern.

With a yell the bold Britons their weapons let go,
Then, like mice in a pantry, they scurried below.
"Boys, batter [batten?] the hatches," called Jack to his men;
"We have got the red fox, at last, in his den."

The "Kitty" and "Mermaid" awoke, with a start,
With the guns of their gallant trained straight at their heart.
Their "Alert" was caught napping (drowsy lovers, beware!)
And saucy Jack Barry had captured the fair.

"Ho, run her in shore to yonder good pier;
We'll see how the foxes are burrowing here.
Now loosen the hatches! Come foe or come friend!
You'll find Yankee sailors will take either end!"

Then up came a Major; forsooth, he was glum;
Two Captains, lieutenants, a man with a drum;
Ten soldiers paced out, then a hundred marines,
Like a troop in a play, strode out from the scenes!

O the twenty and seven who came down thro' the night
Were as proud as the Caesars to see such a sight;
Three cheers, and three more boomed up, like the seas,
As the flag of the Stars broke out on the breeze!

O it is never safe, in making a boast,
To reckon too easy, not counting your host;
Nor is it quite prudent to count on your boat
When saucy Jack Barry is up and afloat!

old rebel city of Penn: Philadelphia. **Lord Howe**: Richard Howe (1726–1799), British naval commander in the early years of the American Revolution. His less-than-vigorous pursuit of George III's war policies may have contributed to the ultimate American victory. **Burlington:** a town in New Jersey along the Delaware River between Trenton and Philadelphia.

9. Timothy Murphy

Born in 1751 to Irish immigrant parents living in New Jersey, Timothy Murphy grew to manhood on the frontier of Pennsylvania's Wyoming Valley. Although unable to read and write, he was a legendary marksman during the Revolutionary War and earned the nicknamed "Sure-shot Tim." In July 1777 he joined Colonel Daniel Morgan's elite Rifle Corps. During the fighting at Saratoga, New York, the following October, Morgan ordered Murphy and a few other sharpshooters to kill the British brigadier general Simon Fraser. After setting his rifle in the fork of a tree, Murphy took aim at his target. Although two bullets missed their mark (hitting Fraser's horse instead), the third struck the general, who was removed from the field and died the next morning. Murphy is also said to have been responsible for mortally shooting Sir Francis Clerke, General John Burgoyne's aide-de-camp.

The following excerpts are from *Tim Murphy, Morgan Rifleman*, a sequence of fifteen long poetic ballads recounting Murphy's exploits during the Revolutionary War, his skill with the double-barreled Golcher rifle, and his elopement with the daughter of a wealthy farmer. Murphy was said to have killed more than 100 Indians, Tories, and regulars with his rifle and yet never suffered a bullet wound.

From *Tim Murphy, Morgan Rifleman*
by A. M. Sullivan (1896–1980)

Toward Boston Town

Tim Murphy was a laughing man
Of jet black hair and bright blue eyes;
Faster than redskin foe he ran
When life and freedom were the prize,
Half ruffian, half Samaritan,
Of giant deeds and David's size;
He made Schoharie's challenge heard
By Johnson, Brant and George the Third.

With risk and gamble at his side
Through seven years of wit and war,
Hate never pinked his lucky hide
Though foemen kept the bitter score
Where redskins and the redcoats died,
A hundred silent men or more.
Seven years he played the game
And no black bullet bore his name.

Tim Murphy, born at Minnisink
Along the craggy Jersey shore,
Watched the deer come down to drink
And saw the moonlight lay its floor
Across the river, saw the wink
Of fire flies like jewels pour
Upon the rapids in a snare
Of splendor on the Delaware.

Along the Susquehanna's bank
The lad Tim Murphy learned the craft
Of woodsmen where the panther drank.
Black bear he slew, and trout he gaffed,
And from no adversary shrank
And in face of danger laughed.
He knew all tricks the red men knew
And past their kin he learned a few.

North toward Shamokin strangers came
With compass, chains and measured poles,
And Tim went with them shooting game,
Or clearing brush, and climbing knolls,
Building shelters, and fanning flame,
And by the campfire warmed the souls

Of lonely men who heard big talk
About Cuchullin of Dundalk.

Tim sang the songs his father taught him,
The keens of Carlow and Kellistown;
He sang of Finn and the men who fought him,
And Maeve the queen with a rakish crown
Who chased a bull but never caught him,
Who lost ten champions of renown.
One night Tim paused and his searching eye
Fixed on a branch, and they wondered why,

But not for long, as he seized his gun
And seemed to fire at a star.
Before the echoing steps had run
Like clumsy ghosts gone off to war
They heard sounds like a rolling tun
Upon the earth, then heard no more;
But in the dawn surveyors found
The panther stretched upon the ground.

And when the call to battle came
For men who had the fighting mood,
Fact and legend vaunt the fame
Of Murphy from Shamokin's wood,
The lad from Sunbury with the aim
That made its mark in foemen's blood
And Murphy's rifle drank its fill
Of vengeance after Bunker Hill.

Golcher of Easton forged the gun
That Indian and Tory hated,
And Boston redcoats learned to shun
The woodsmen, telling how with bated
Breath a rifleman had won
A battle with a barge that grated
On tidal flats, and half a score
Of dead and dying reached the shore.

When echoes of the Concord battle
Rumbled toward the Blue Ridge hills
The farmers left their fields and cattle
And millers left their grinding mills.
"Take your choice. Free men or chattel?"

Asked Colonel Thompson at the drills
Of the riflemen and he showed the way
From the Delaware to Boston Bay.

Murphy came from a rebel region
Where Thompson, Kelly and the Brady brothers—
Hugh, John and Sam—rose in high dudgeon
Against the despot's brutal tethers,
Marching men whose names were legion,
Men whose glory never withers—
William Butler, Boyd and Parr
Who led Penn's riflemen to war.

The long squirrel rifles scared the British,
Cowed the Minute Men as well,
The folk in Cambridge Town were skittish
When raucous woodsmen charged pell-mell
Toward Charlestown, waving gun and fetish
Of coonskin tails with hoot and yell,
And Boston said it was a sin
To show such lack of discipline.

The men from Pennsylvania stood
In proud review for Washington
And they were brash and young and crude,
But each caressed a smooth-bore gun
And each man wore his weapon proud,
As Murphy, back against the sun,
Hit targets on young maple trees
And cut the saplings to their knees.

Though redcoats sat on Bunker Hill
They wore a tarnished crown of fear.
For day by day the hidden quill
Of Thompson's rifles bristling near
Darted through the ports to kill
The men in braid who dared to jeer
The woodsman with the six-foot barrel
Who strutted past in strange apparel.

In Boston Bay a man-of-war
Growled and spat at Prospect Hill,
But someone answered from the shore—
A David with ten Davids' skill—

As bullets from a rifle's bore
Began to speak, began to spill
The blood of redcoats on the bay,
Trapped on a barge, half-mile away.

Wonder and terror swept the craft;
No musket ball could answer back,
And they who tumbled on the raft
Never heard the rifle's crack;
And some ran fore and some ran aft
Prisoned in the tidal slack.
(Tim Murphy resting on his arm
Felt his rifle growing warm.)

It was the proud brig *Somerset*
That splashed the turf in the rising sun,
But on the barge a rivulet
Ran warm and red as the day begun,
And death and a host of foemen met
Without a battle lost or won.
(Tim Murphy crouching in the swamp
Felt his buttocks growing damp.)

All morning long the batteries bellowed
Their malice over Prospect crest,
But on the barge the dead were pillowed
With crimson badges on each breast
(With empty horn Tim Murphy wallowed
Out of the mire of his nest),
And the King's Own counted ten men lost
When David answered Goliath's boast.

. . . .

Samaritan: the Good Samaritan, the New Testament character who rescued a man who had been robbed and beaten and left by the wayside. **Of giant deeds and David's size:** diminutive in size (as the Hebrew David was to Goliath) but capable of heroic deeds. **Schohaire's challenge:** defiance of the British and their allies by the inhabitants of the Schohaire Valley in eastern New York. **Johnson:** John Johnson (1742–1830), a loyalist who directed Indian and Tory raids along the frontiers of New York and Pennsylvania. **Brant:** Joseph Brant or Theyendanega (c. 1742–1807), the Mohawk chief who supported the British during the Revolution. Between 1778 and 1780 he led raids against settlers on the New York frontiers. **George the Third:** the British king during the American Revolution. **redcoats:** British soldiers, so called from the red jackets of their uniforms. **Shamokin:** See Sunbury below. **Cuchullin:** in Celtic mythology a mortal endowed with superhuman powers which he exercised to protect the people of Ulster. **keens:** wailing laments for the dead. **Carlow and Kellistown:** Carlow and Kells, towns in Ireland. **Finn:** Fionn mac Cumal, in Celtic mythology a mortal possessed of superhuman powers. **Maeve:** also Mebh, in Celtic mythology the warrior queen of Connaught. Jealous that none of her bulls equalled any of her husband's, Maeve asked the chief of Cualigne to loan her his prize brown bull, reputedly the best in all Ireland. But when Maeve's messenger boasted that if the chief of Cualigne refused her request she and her troops would seize the bull, the chief expelled the messenger. After a series of wars with Cuchullin, the hero of Ulster, Maeve did succeed in capturing the brown bull. **lad from Sunbury:** Timothy Murphy. **Golcher of Easton:** a rifle manufacturer in Easton, Pennsylvania. **Concord battle:** one of the first major engagements of the Revolutionary War, April 19, 1775, in Concord, Massachusetts. **Colonel Thompson:** William Thompson (1736–1781), a native of Ireland and the commander of a battalion of riflemen raised in Pennsylvania during the Revolution. After leading an invasion force of 2,000 men into Canada, he was captured at Three Rivers. **Brady brothers:** Hugh, John, and Samuel were the grandsons of Irish immigrant Hugh Brady and the sons of Captain John Brady. Samuel served in the Revolution as first lieutenant of Captain Doyle's Company of Lancaster Men and also belonged to units commanded by General Edward Hand and General Anthony Wayne. The younger John Brady was wounded at the battle of Brandywine in 1777. The reference to the brother Hugh seems out of place, since he was only seven years old at the time of the battle of Concord (1775) mentioned in the poem. (Hugh's illustrious military career spanned the later period 1792 to the 1830s.) The poet may have confused him with a fourth Brady brother — James, who died from an Indian scalping in 1778. **William Butler:** a native of Ireland who led a significant raid against the Indians of upper New York state during the Revolution. He was almost killed during the mutiny of the Pennsylvania Line regiments in 1781. **Boyd:** Thomas Boyd, a sergeant in William Thompson's Pennsylvania rifle battalion and a leader in General John Sullivan's campaign against the Iroquois. He was captured by Indians and tortured to death in 1779. (One of his eyes was put out; his nose, tongue, head, and genitals were cut off; and he was skinned alive.) **Parr:** Major James Parr, according to the poem a native of Ulster, Ireland. He was in command of Daniel Morgan's riflemen at the battle of Newtown, New York, in August 1779. **Penn's riflemen:** Pennsylvania riflemen, from the name of William Penn, the founder of Pennsylvania. **Minute Men:** American militia. **Cambridge Town:** Cambridge, Massachusetts. **Charlestown:** now a section of Boston but formerly a separate town, the site of the battle of Bunker Hill, June 17, 1775.

The Death of Simon Fraser

. . . .

When Morgan chose his Partizans
Tim Murphy's name was written first,
And next he wrote Dave Elerson's
With a host of riflemen accurst
By redcoats with their thwarted guns,

Who met the scouts and learned the worst
And died in the siege of Boston Town
When distant rifles cut them down.

. . . .

Johnny Burgoyne, he feared no danger
As he journeyed out of the wilderness,
Flanked by the savage and the ranger.
But Johnny loathed the buckskin dress,
At Bemis Heights he caught a stranger
With a coonskin cap and flowing tress
And he asked, "Are you the fiend of Gorgon?"
And the answer came, "A scout of Morgan."

Tim Murphy with a catlike tread
Was a shadow in the British line;
He overheard the password said
And caught the pious countersign—
The sentry called "Our Daily Bread,"
The officer bawled "The Holy Wine"—
And Murphy sniffed the chilly musk
Waiting the first star of the dusk.

The password brought him into camp
And he wandered through the sleepy aisles
Where soldiers shivered in the damp
Or built their stores in clumsy piles.
Murphy paused at a tapered lamp
Where a British captain copied files,
Tim drew his hunting blade and went
Swift and silent toward the tent.
"That you, Samson? Bring some rum
And make a toddy. I'm getting chill."
"Chill you'll be in Kingdom Come,"
Said Tim, his blade poised for the kill.
The man of Sandhurst rose up numb.
"Walk," said Murphy, "and keep still.
You're going to visit friends, and stay
With country cousins for the day."

No pistol near, no sword in hand,
The startled captain looked about
In silence at the soft command.
He murmured, "You a Morgan scout?"

"Yes," said Murphy, "I understand
You are my prisoner; any doubt?"
He pressed the steel against his spine,
Said, "March, I'll give the countersign."

On Bemis Heights the British lost
Three hundred slain and half their hope.
"Get word to Clinton at any cost,"
Said Johnny Burgoyne on the russet slope
Glistening in the October frost,
"By heaven or hell or the hangmen's rope
Tomorrow at dawn we shall attack.
Go on we must, for we can't go back."

Burgoyne attacked, and back he reeled
(Gates to the right and Morgan left
And Arnold all over the bloody field).
The British line was bruised and cleft
With the battle issues almost sealed
As redcoats ran like knaves bereft
When Simon Fraser dashed from the wood
And with his Scot's burr stemmed the flood.

Fraser's steel-gray gelding rode
Through the hail of death, and Fraser said
The words shame-pointed to a goad
That turned his men to the field they fled
Where a deadly scythe of bullets mowed.
"Never were British foemen led
By a better soldier or braver man
Than Simon Fraser," said Colonel Dan.

"But Fraser dies today, I swear,
For the redcoats' chances live with him;
Sir Francis Clark [*sic*], who's standing there
With epaulets and fancy trim,
He rides as if to make a dare.
Then both shall die. You take them, Tim."
And Murphy, as Dan Morgan spoke,
Sprang to the first bough of an oak.

Fraser, three hundred yards away,
Banters a moment with Francis Clark [*sic*],

As if it were a hunting day
With fowling guns and the beagle's bark.
Tim Murphy watches the prancing gray
Until he pauses, then fails the mark;
His bullet with an erring course
Cuts the check rein of the horse.

With the second flash of Murphy's gun,
Fraser sees Sir Francis tumble—
Burgoyne's young aide-de-camp is done.
Fraser hears in the cannon's rumble,
"Take cover, General." "I shan't run,
Nor shall my men though heavens crumble,"
Cries Simon Fraser unafraid,
And Murphy watches the glinting blade.

Fraser boasts, "I'll take my chances,"
Scorns the enemy before him,
"Forward, men." He never glances
As the fading eyes of youth implore him.
"You're a target," moans Sir Francis,
But Fraser's stubborn ears ignore him,
And Murphy, taking careful aim,
Says, "Fraser, this ball knows your name."

There came a gun flash from the oak—
Fraser reeled and Fraser fell;
The redcoats paused, the redcoats broke,
Tim's bullet ended Fraser's spell
Of magic in the words he spoke.
There's little more of the tale to tell,
Save Morgan's men went on to harry
Johnny Burgoyne, the cornered quarry."

. . . .

Morgan: Daniel Morgan (1736–1802), the leader of a company of Virginia riflemen during the Revolutionary War. He played a crucial role in the American victory at Saratoga. **redcoats:** British soldiers, so called from the red jackets of their uniforms. **Johnny Burgoyne:** the British army officer (1722–1792) whose plan to invade the American colonies from Canada ended in his surrender at Saratoga in 1777. **Bemis Heights:** the southern end of the battlefield at Saratoga. **Gorgon:** any of three sister monsters of Greek mythology. Each had snakes for hair, and their eyes turned anyone who looked at them into stone. **Kingdom Come:** heaven; the hereafter. **Sandhurst:** the Royal Military Academy for potential British army officers. **Gates:** General Horatio Gates (1728–1806), who commanded the 9,000 American troops at Saratoga. **Arnold:** Benedict Arnold (1741–1801), an American officer who lost his leg during the battle of Saratoga. **Simon Fraser:** a British brigadier general who was killed at the battle of Saratoga. **Francis Clark [*sic*]:** Francis Clerke (1748–1777), aide-de-camp to the British general John Burgoyne at Saratoga.

Saratgoa

by Joseph I. C. Clarke (1846–1925)

"Give me six thousand fighting men,"
   Said General John Burgoyne,
"Or better, Your Majesty, make it ten,
   Our line of battle to join,
And I will scatter the rebel host
   Like straw in a stormy wind,
As down the Hudson stream we'll post,
   With treason dead behind,
While Howe comes marching from the coast,
   With Washington groping blind.

"From Canada by stream and lake
   To the river by Albany town,
Small trouble or none their forts to take,
   And their bumpkin troops strike down.
Then southward Howe and I will forge,
   And pay them in leaden coin,
Till the crows upon all traitors gorge
   Who would our honor purloin,—
Sure as Your Majesty's name is George,
   And mine is John Burgoyne."

So redcoats, Hessians, Kanucks and scouts,—
   Horse, foot and artillery,—
Came down and captured our lake redoubts,
   Tho' we fought them knee to knee,
Till grim upon the Hudson's banks,
   They came up against our line.
On Bemis Heights we'd formed our ranks
   To check their bold design,
And the fight was fierce their line to pierce,
   With bayonet charges nine.

In vain we charged, for counter-charge,

Led by a lion of war,
Would push us back to the river's mirage,
    And sinking seemed our star.
'Twas Fraser, gallant, tigerish Scot,
    Whose valor and skill inspired
Their dogged files with a courage hot,
    That if but a gun retired,
He'd send it back with shout and shot,
    And full in our faces fired.

'Twas then brave Morgan lowered his glass,
    And pointing where Fraser stood,
Cried, "Woodsmen say when a man must pass,
    'He's the log that jams the flood.'
Six thousand men of the new-born states,—
    American, Irish, Dutch—are we.
One man holds back the flood of the fates
    That sweeps us on to be free;
Let Heaven open for him its gates."
    And Tim Murphy climbed a tree.

John Burgoyne: the British army officer (1722–1792) whose plan to invade the American colonies from Canada ended in his surrender at Saratoga in 1777. **Your Majesty:** George III, the British king during the American Revolution. **Hudson stream:** the Hudson River. **Howe:** William Howe (1729–1814), a British general during the American Revolution. **redcoats:** British soldiers, so called from the red jackets of their uniforms. **Hessians:** a generic name for German mercenaries, although they were not only from Hesse but also from other small German principalities (Ansbach, Anhalt-Zerbst, Brunswick, and Waldeck). **Kanucks:** Canadians, especially French Canadians. **Bemis Heights:** the southern end of the battlefield at Saratoga. **Fraser:** Simon Fraser, the British brigadier general who was killed at the battle of Saratoga in 1777 by the Irish-American sharpshooter Timothy Murphy. **Morgan:** Daniel Morgan (1736–1802), the leader of a company of Virginia riflemen during the Revolutionary War. He played crucial roles in the American victories at Saratoga (1777) and Cowpens (1781).

10. The Brady Riflemen

The frontier exploits of the "Brady riflemen" are the topic of the following poem by Martha Keller. The Brady brothers John, James, and Samuel were the grandsons of Irish emigrant Hugh Brady and the son of Captain John Brady. The latter forebear saw action in the French and Indian War and the Pontiac War of the 1760s. In 1776 he built a half-fortified residence, later known as Brady's Fort, near Muncie, Pennsylvania. He was wounded at Germantown the following year and was killed by Indians in 1779.

The younger John Brady was wounded at the battle of Brandywine in 1777, and his brother James died from an Indian scalping the next year. The third son, Samuel, served in the Revolution as first lieutenant of Captain Doyle's Company of Lancaster Men. After the battle of Monmouth he was promoted to a captaincy. The deaths of his father and his brother at the hands of Indians so incensed him that he spent the rest of his life avenging their memories. When he finally killed Chief Bald Eagle, Captain Brady allegedly placed the Indian's body in a canoe, stuck a piece of 'johnnycake' between the dead man's lips as a gesture of derision, and let the craft drift downstream. At the place where it grounded Bald Eagle was buried.

Brady's Bend

by Martha Keller

This is the story of
The brawny Brady riflemen,
John,
    James,
And the celebrated Samuel—
Who fought Bald Eagle with
The Pennsylvania rifle when
Chief Bald Eagle was
The tomahawk of hell.

Old John Brady was
At Valley Forge and Germantown,
Some
    say,
At the battle of Brandywine.
He brought a many of
The tomahawking vermin down,
Before they fixed him with
The Indian sign.

Young Jim Brady was
A-harvesting a field in ear,
Long
    gun
Left a-leaning on a stubble stack,
When Chief Bald Eagle like
A weasel come a-eeling near,
And dropped Jim Brady with
A bullet in his back.

Left him lying like
A chicken when its head is chop-
    ped,
Scalped
    him
With a whooping-coughing
    caterwaul.
But sure and as soon as
The shooting and the shouting

    stopped,
The dead man dying there
Begun to crawl.

Crawled to the river bank
A-hunting for a boat he had
Hid
        there,
Half rotting in the river mud.
For help was afar away,
And forty mile to float he had,
Young Jim Brady with
His head all over blood.

Down the Susquehanna he
Slipped across the river sand,
Wet
        rock
A-shining like a scalping knife.
Sunset, sunrise
Burned upon the river and
Reddened, like his forehead with
The blood of life.

"Tell my brother how
Bald Eagle took my hair away.
Tell
        Sam
To remember, like I told him, to
Trail Bald Eagle like
A beagle over there away,
And lift the scalping lock
The Indians do."

Up the Alleghany where
The Great Chief made his stand,
Sam
        went
A-harrying and hunting him.
Till back by the river bend,
That's named now for Brady's
        band,
He scalped Bald Eagle like
He promised Jim.

He killed Bald Eagle by
The river Alleghany—a
Great
        Chief—
Did the Samuel, aforesaid,
Who scalped more Indians in
The State of Pennsylvania
Than any other white man
Alive or dead.

This is the story of
The brawny Brady riflemen,
John,
        James,
And the celebrated Samuel—
Who fought Bald Eagle with
The Pennsylvania rifle when
Chief Bald Eagle was
The tomahawk of hell.

Susquehanna: a river flowing south from central New York through eastern Pennsylvania and northeast Maryland into Chesapeake Bay. **Alleghany:** also Allegheny, a river flowing northwest from Pennsylvania into southwestern New York and then south through western Pennsylvania.

11. John Sullivan

The son of an Irish schoolmaster, John Sullivan was born in New Hampshire and studied law in Portsmouth. As relations with England worsened in the early 1770s, he was chosen to attend both the first and the second continental congresses. Following his appointment as brigadier general in the newly formed Continental Army, he served in the siege of Boston until the British evacuation in March 1776. He subsequently accompanied the American army in its retreat across New Jersey and took a prominent role in the battles of Trenton and Princeton.

After spending the winter of 1777–78 at Valley Forge, Sullivan was ordered to take command in Rhode Island. His siege of Newport failed, however, after the French withdrew their army and fleet to Boston. In the summer of 1779 the American general led an expedition against the Iroquois in New York and western Pennsylvania in retaliation for the atrocities committed by the Indians in the Wyoming Valley and the Cherry Valley massacres the year before. During that campaign the Americans destroyed forty Indian villages and 160,000 bushels of corn. After receiving reinforcements, Sullivan completely routed the Iroquois and their Loyalist allies at Newtown (now Elmira), New York, in August of that year. That victory is described in the following poem, read at the dedication of the Newtown Battlefield Monument on August 29, 1912.

After the war Sullivan held a variety of political posts. In New Hampshire he was a member of the state constitutional convention (1782), speaker of the Assembly (1785), governor (three times between 1786 and 1789), and chair of the state convention called to ratify the Federal Constitution (1788). With the creation of the new national government, he was appointed U.S. district judge for New Hampshire.

Sullivan

by Joseph I. C. Clarke (1846–1925)

> A spirit walked the smiling hills of morn,
> And over the waving forests at her feet
> The wild harps of the summer winds played sweet;
> And the rivers sang, now loud, now low,
> While the valleys echoed to their flow.
> The lakes flashed silver laughter back
> To the flaming sun on his mounting track,
> For joy that another day was born.
>
> The spirit gazed from her calm, clear eyes,
> And she saw the morning mists arise

To melt like a pray'r in the August skies.
The wild sharp scent of the mountain pine
Like the breath of Freedom her bosom filled,
As dewdrops clinging to branch and vine
Shed diamond spray by the night distilled.
And higher she rose in the fields of air
Till the broad expanse touched the ocean's rim,
Then northward turned her glance to where
The mountains lifted their foreheads dim;
West with the prairies spread beyond,
Then southward glanced where, bole and frond,
Arose the wide-plumed palm.
And it all breathed joy in its morning hymn,
And her lips replied in a golden psalm:—

"Lord of the worlds, the stars, the suns,
Within whose web existence runs,
And all stands open to thy ken,
If thou hast given this world to men,
Let it, O Father, ever be
A world of the true, a world of the free,
Where hearts may love and souls aspire,
And Faith pile high its altar fire,
Knowing no other God than thee."
Bathed in the glory that upon her shone,
The spirit still prayed bravely on:

"And, Lord, this virgin land implores
That kingdoms perish from its shores.
Already combating in Freedom's name,
My sons advance in blood and flame.
Strengthen their arms, make bold their feet;
Be with them, Lord and Master,
Through onset or retreat,
Through victory and disaster,
Till they reach the shining goal—
My land, America, one and whole;
Equal the rule from sea to sea,
The men, the land, the waters free."

Hark! to the spirit rise the calls
Of the forest and the waterfalls:
"O mighty spirit, what dost thou see
From the Susquehanna to the Genesee?"

"I see through a tangled, wooded glen
The glint of weapons shine,
And a long array of stalwart men
Marching in warlike line.
They stretch 'twixt the hills from crest to crest,
Their sweat is thick upon brow and breast,
Their muskets trailing low.
They peer through the forest round about
For pitfalls of the foe.
Their horses tug at the traces stout
Of cannon rumbling slow.
And swarms of boats and rustic floats
Up the babbling river come,
And I catch the thrilling of bugle notes
And the rolling of the drum.
On through the thickets a way they trace;
They pause at the river's bars.
They follow a man of the Fighting Race,
And he follows a flag of stars."

          *   *   *   *   *   *   *   *   *

Thus Sullivan, with battle-flag outflung,
Marched grimly by the banks of the Chemung;
Vengeance his mission, a mandate to destroy:
Death to the slinking murderers who crept
By night upon our settlers as they slept,
And slew them—woman, girl and boy—
By the blazing of their log-built homes,
Carved from the age-old wilderness
Where the Susquehanna foams.
Savage and Tory in a pact of shame:
Plunder and scalps for the Indian braves,
A dance of murder, a path of flame,
And the pride of trampling white men's graves.
For the Briton a grip on the mighty West,
An empire! if Freedom should win the rest.

But Washington clear in his ample view
(While he faced the English beside the sea)
Four thousand men from his scant force drew,
This their winter warrant to be:
To pierce the wilderness through and through;
To hunt out the recreant Tory crew;

To burn and waste where the Indians hived
Till they knew that no murder-treaty thrived
Where the flag stars shone and the eagle flew.
For leader he singled a true-souled man,
Brave of the brave—John Sullivan.

There be those who strive for the hero's meed,
And storm the hilltops of endeavor
With the onrush of one blazing deed,
And win to live forever.
And there be those of a hundred flights,
As bold of hand and high of spirit,
Who charge with eager feet the heights
Of victory and merit,
Only to find high fortune fail,
And foes and forces new assail.
Yet, beaten down, such grace inherit,
That at the foot, still constant, true,
They bare their sabres to ascend anew.

John Sullivan was of these last.
No thrice-crowned child of battle-rapture he,
But when he threw his law books by
And life and fortune for his country cast
That she should rise up free,
His sword shone dazzling in the front of war,
And over many a field
He saw the Briton and the Hessian yield
Or 'fore his onset turn and fly.

But of the great emprises nigh his grasp
Saw hazard snatch them ere he might enclasp.
All the more hero let him stand,
Whose splendid best went out to save our land.
His the long story of the Irish race,
Unconquerable though beaten oft,
And crushed and starved beneath the heavy chain,
Yet sent us battling sons of brawn and brain,
Who led and bled to hold our flag aloft;
And, having fought till victory won release,
Still led and ruled along the paths of peace.

Oft at his stern-browed Leader's feet,
He learned to hearken to the true-man's call:

That men upon the battledores of fate
Have but their Souls, their lives.
Hither and thither thrown; advance, retreat;
Smiting or falling, laden, ay, with gyves,
They must be single-minded to be great,
The cause they follow is their all.

The column writhes along its hard-won trail
In swelter of the noonday heat,
When a forest scout comes hurrying down
On noiseless, moccasined feet.
"At the river's bend an Indian town,
A score of rough-hewn huts tricked out
With barbarous colors, blue and brown,
But none make answer to our shout."
And Sullivan's face went death-like pale,
On his brow a deepened frown.
"Burn it to ashes; let the flames outspread
Till their fields are bare," he hoarsely said.
'Twas quickly done,
And the smoke still hung o'er the blasted vale,
When Sullivan gloomily rode ahead
In the blood-red setting of the sun.

War, the great curse of man,
If oft the only cure
Of man-wrought and intolerable ill,
And rightly waged to make the right endure,
And bring the world to God's great plan,
Sees horrors that we shrink from thinking o'er,
Things worse than killing or the lust to kill,
Until its very name we must abhor,
Cursing not warriors, but the cause of war.

Night, and the burning embers mock the stars;
Morn, and the ashes all are gray;
The soldiers toiling on the forest way;
The boatmen polling at the river's bars.
Sudden the rifles' stinging crack,
Shot after shot on the hot, dense air.
The scouts once more come hurrying back
Through the forest's dark defiles.
"The game we're hunting's at bay up there.

They've built them a breastwork of brush and logs.
From river to creek on a rising ground—
A thousand of Indians and Tory dogs."
And Sullivan shortens his rein and smiles

The riflemen, gaunt, lank pioneers,
Are rushed to the front, a sparse, fierce line.
"Amuse them, lads, till the trap is sprung."
A hill is found for the cannoneers
To sweep the curve of the Chemung,
And Poor and Clinton are marched to the right
Behind the woodland screen
To strike the foe in the flank.
The rifles ring by the river bank
In stealthy, deadly frontier fight.
The aides are moving to and fro,
While Sullivan hastily gathers his might
To strike the frontal blow.

Behind the heavy barricade,
Four hundred Tory picaroons
Have here the chance they boastful prayed
Till now unheard,
And with them, hapless dupes of fate,
A thousand Iroquois crouch and wait
Theyandenaga's word,
On white men's throats to pay the red man's debt
In scores of lives.
They fondle their crown muskets, and they whet
Their scalping knives.
A cannon booms; another and another rolls,
Till the valley quakes with the thundrous [*sic*] roar—
Thunder the red man never heard before.
The crashing round-shot and the rattling grape
Tumble the breastwork till its timbers gape,
Taking their toll of souls.

Tory and Indian rise and flee pell-mell,
As Poor comes charging on the frantic rout—
A chase and a race for a hiding place
Till the scattering mob on-stumbling blind,
A grave or a shelter in the forest find.

Sullivan views the quick-swept field with scorn;

The buglers call in the outflung men;
The torch is laid to the Indian's corn.
The column takes the rough trail again,
Through the virgin forest it hews a path,
And the breath of the young Republic's wrath
Goes up in a cloud of smoke by day,
And pillars of fire by night,
Like Israel in the wilderness of old,
Filling the wild things with affright,
While the red men far through the forest flee.
So, Sullivan out of the savage wold
Comes on the valley of the Genesee
In its glory of tasseled gold,
Swaying in beauty, mile after mile outrolled.

Leader and men stand fast and gaze,
In pity and amaze,
For this their goal where vengeance might expire—
The red man's homeland doomed to flame and spoil,
Silent of man but eloquent of toil.
Pity still whispers, bidding Duty fail,
But Duty sounds its loud insistent call,
And swift the bannerets of ruthless fire,
Have down the smiling valley waved.
Fields, houses, granaries and orchards, all
Are blotted out beneath the smoky pall.
Deep from the forest rises one long wail.
Vengeance is sated and the West is saved.

* * * * * * * * *

The hovering spirit through the clouds of dawn,
That o'er the valley of destruction loom,
Drops tears of pity in a gentle rain
For her forest children, homeless now or slain.
And when the sun wheels wondrous up from sea,
Gilding the mountains, lighting stream and lawn,
She prays the comfort of the boundless skies
That hold the miracle of the morning beam,
And feels a chrism immortal touch her eyes.
Higher she floats in rapture of a dream
That draws the curtains of all time to be.

Before a leaguered city far to South

She catches glint of Lord Cornwallis' sword
Surrendered to our Washington,
And loud thereafter from the cannon's mouth
Salvos of victory for freedom won,
And songs of peace that silence war's alarms,
A people's joyance from the heart outpoured.

She sees the forests shrinking from the hills,
The tall trees toppling to the woodman's axe,
Valleys and plains a-blossoming in farms.
A hum of industry the tense air fills.
The rutted trails give place to shining tracks,
Whereon strange engines lined-out wagons draw,
And towns and cities turreted and spired
Spring as by magic over all the land,
Elmira rising there below
Where Sullivan drove out the foe;
And in the cities, order; on the border, law.

Then sadly through a cloud of rifle smoke
She sees her people torn apart in strife,
And reunited rise to grander life,
Never in God's great mercy to invoke
The battle-gods but on a foreign foe.

Hears free democracy its gospel give;
The right to prosper and a way to live,
Where all estates make common cause,
And stand alike before the equal laws,
Nor poor nor rich a vantage know.
And sees in time still hidden to our ken—
Times of wide welfare and of vision clear—
Columbia, god-like with extended hands,
Speeding goodwill to nations and to men,
Ranged with her strong archangels forty-seven,
To bring her grace and strength at need from Heaven,
O'er all the world-peace that the ages sought for,
That Sullivan and his soldiers fought for,
The peace America wept for here.

Susquehanna: a river flowing south from central New York through eastern Pennsylvania and northeast Maryland into Chesapeake Bay. **Genesee:** a river flowing north from northern Pennsylvania into Lake Ontario. **Fighting Race:** the Irish, used here in a positive sense. **Chemung:** a river that flows past Elmira, New York, to the Susquehanna River at Athens, Pennsylvania. **Tory:** a supporter of the British cause during the American Revolution. **Poor:** Enoch Poor (1736–1780), who accompanied General John Sullivan on his expedition against the Iroquois in 1779 and who was commended for his "intrepidity" in the battle of Newtown. **Clinton:** James Clinton (1733–1812), an American general who accompanied General Richard Montgomery to Quebec in 1775 and helped General John Sullivan defeat the Indians and their Tory allies at the battle of Newtown in 1779. Clinton was the grandson of an emigrant from County Longford, Ireland. **picaroons:** rogues, brigands, or pirates. **Theyandenaga:** Joseph Brant (c. 1742–1807), the Mohawk chief who supported the British during the Revolution. Between 1778 and 1780 he led raids against settlers on the New York frontiers. **pillars of fire:** an allusion to the pillar of fire that preceded the Israelites on their journey through the desert. **leaguered city far to South:** Yorktown, Virginia. **Lord Cornwallis:** Charles Cornwallis (1738–1805), the commander of the British forces in the southern colonies during the last years of the American Revolution. His surrender in October 1781 to a superior force of French and American troops at Yorktown virtually ended the war. **Columbia:** the United States of America, usually personified as a female figure. **archangels forty-seven:** probably the forty-seven states in the Union at the time this poem was completed (August 22, 1912).

12. The Irish Brigade in the Service of France

By the middle of the eighteenth century the various armies of Europe contained as many as 250,000 soldiers and officers of Irish birth or descent. This situation was the climax of a development that had begun in 1607, when the English defeated Irish rebels under the command of the earls of Tyrconnell and Tyrone. These Irish nobles — and about 100 of their followers — fled to the Continent, where many of them became mercenaries in the armies of the European monarchs. By 1688 France alone had 6,000 such Irish troops in its service.

This "Flight of the Earls" swelled to a flood after 1690, when James II and his Irish Catholic supporters were defeated by William III at the battle of the Boyne. As a result, approximately 7,000 Irish Jacobites went into immediate exile in France. These "Wild Geese" and their descendants formed the Irish Brigade which served the French monarchs throughout the eighteenth century. It has been estimated that between 1691 and 1792, when the brigade was disbanded, more than 500,000 Irishmen died in the service of France. Among the more than a dozen regiments in the brigade were those of Charlemont, Clanricarde, Clare, Dillon, Mountcashel, O'Brien, and Walsh.

The Dillon Regiment was under the immediate command of Count Arthur Dillon (1670–1733), a member of an originally Irish family which had settled in France at the end of the seventeenth century. During the American Revolution, Dillon's regiment took part in an attack on British-held Savannah in 1779. (More than half of the regiment's 194 men were killed in the assault.) In the summer of 1781 the regiment was among the 6,000 French and Irish soldiers who marched from Newport, Rhode Island, to Yorktown, Virginia. These troops played a decisive role in assuring the American victory against the British at Yorktown that October. (The second poem in this section — "The Kinship of the Celt" by Joseph Clarke — was composed to commemorate that victory.) After returning to France, Dillon was placed in command of a division of the French army. Although he led his troops under the tricolor of the French Republic, he was suspected of being a royalist and was guillotined in 1794.

Dillon's Brigade

by Mary Sinton Leitch (1876–1954)

Savannah is fallen, the gallant, the brave!
Though the pride of her spirit no foe can enslave,
Yet with crimson the bayonet's staining the streets,
And tyranny triumphs as freedom retreats,
Over-borne and defenceless to save.
Outside of the town, stricken thus by the blight
Of the war, are bold Irishmen spoiling for fight.
In the service of France is their regiment led
By the dashing Count Dillon, each man of it bred
To consider all danger delight.

Yet the bravest might blench should their leader demand
That those walls shall be stormed. Can the stoutest withstand
The blasts from the ramparts the British have taken,
Or march toward those cannon, their valor unshaken
By the fire that shatters the land?

He does not demand it: too heavy the loss
That must follow. He cries, "Who has the mettle to cross
Yonder terrain and strike? Let who will, volunteer!
One hundred gold guineas to that grenadier
Who first plants a fascine in the fosse!"

Swiftly there runs through the ranks of the men
As flame in dry grasses a whisper, and then
They are silent. "What now! Is your valor but shoddy
And sham? Do you hold it less dear than your body,"

Count Dillon exclaims, and again
He exhorts them, "Who goes? Are the Irish afraid
That the sound of a gun turns them pale like a maid!
Remember the hundred gold guineas! Advance
And win them in honor of Erin and France!"
None moved in the Irish brigade.

But at last a man spoke: "You have taught us to flout
The enemy's fire and yet, sir, when out
In the field a man lies in the slime and the mud,
Who can figure in guineas the cost of his blood?
Not for gain would we storm the redoubt."

Count Dillon stands humbled. "Forgive me," he cries,
"That I bargained for something no gold ever buys;
That I thought your wild courage a thing I could tame.
On, on to the ramparts in Ireland's name!
God be with you—and death be the prize!"

Every man volunteered. Why they did, who shall say?—
Why they flung their young lives with abandon away.
For joy in the battle? Desire for glory?
For God or Saint Patrick?—Each man has his story
That is lost and forgotten today.

They charged, and yet vain the assault they made.
Only Death could stand up to that fierce cannonade.
Let the years pay them tribute—the few who returned,
And the many, the blinded, the broken and burned,
Who fell. For the sake of the gold that they spurned,
A toast to Count Dillon's brigade!

fascine: a bundle of sticks bound together, used as reinforcement in the construction of earthworks; probably used here to represent the brigade's flagstaff. **fosse:** a moat or ditch. **Erin:** a literary name for Ireland.

The Kinship of the Celt

by Joseph I. C. Clarke (1846–1925)

"It's the flag of France! the flag of France, I see!
      Life to it! Health to it! fold on fold,
With the silken glint on its colors three.
      Yet if it was white with lilies of gold—
The flag of a king—but the banner of France.
      With the flag of stars our love 'twould share,
And, my soul, I'm for either with sword or lance.
      It's a people we love not the flag they bear.
      Let the seas divide: let the green earth hide,
      And the long years come and go,
      When love has once dwelt in the heart of the Celt.
      It is there while the waters flow."

"And why do you Irish love France? It seems right
      When we sons of Plymouth read how they came,
And they shouldered their guns in the Yorktown fight,
      To feel grateful, and honor that nation's name.
To see plain Ben Franklin sit down with their king,
      And Rochambeau join Lafayette on guard,
'Longside of George Washington, and,—by jing!
      Paul Jones on the deck of *Bonhomme Richard*!
      Oh, it stirs us yet; no, we don't forget
      The days between storm and shine,
      With the ships of the French, and their men in the trench
      And their rush on the fighting line."

"The love of old Ireland for France? It has been
      In the first low lilt of our cradle croon;
Has twined with our longing for 'Wearing the Green';
      Has been wet with the tears of our 'Shule Aroon.'
No new love can bid it to wither and fall;
      Its roots have sunk in the deep past, and are strong
As the long, long mem'ry that marks out the Gael
      For loving old love and rememb'ring old wrong.
      Where the strong hands clasp, in the true man's grasp
      And the stout soul finds its mate,
      Let the great doors swing and the great bells ring
      For the love that laughs at fate.

"To France for a hundred sad years we turned

As our only friend and our hope-lit star.
And never our banished ones' prayers she spurned
But mustered for Ireland her lords of war.
Oh, the French on the sea, and the pikes on the plain,
The battle-joy strong in the eyes and breast;
And if in our Ireland their valor was vain,
God prospered their arms in the land of the West.
Man strikes and prays, but God's dim ways
Direct the red bolt that's hurled,
And the staggering blow of Rochambeau
Broke chains all round the world.

"They flung wide their hall to our priests and our youth,
When our schools were razed and our faith was banned;
They sent us the swords of De Tesse and St. Ruth,
And Humbert and Hoche to strike for our land.
And we, poor in all but our lives and our blades,
Sent Sarsfield and Dillon, O'Brien, O'Neill
And the passionate stream of the Irish brigades,
The sire of MacMahon went there with his steel.
With the years as they go, may its glory grow,
Fair France of the generous hand!
As for freedom it stood with its gold and its blood,
Still free and superb may it stand.

"From the loins of the grand old Celtic race,
Our fathers and theirs came stalwart and twin,
Wherever we've met on the round world's face,
Our souls knew their souls for clansman and kin,
And by us, who on many a blood-red field,
Poured out of our best by the best of France,
The compact of kinship again shall be sealed,
Whenever for freedom her colors advance.
May health and grace greet the Celtic race—
The Gaul and Gael—on sea and shore!
And the green banner ride the wide heavens beside
The starry flag and the tricolor!"

colors three: the blue, white, and red of the French tricolor, the national flag adopted during the French Revolution. **white with lilies of gold:** a description of the Bourbon flag used in France prior to the French Revolution. **Celt:** used here to refer to the Irish. **sons of Plymouth:** the descendants of the Pilgrims who settled in Plymouth, Massachusetts, in 1620 but used here to refer to Americans in general. **Ben Franklin:** the American representative in Paris during the American

Revolution. **their king:** Louis XVI. **Rochambeau:** Jean Baptiste Donatien de Vimeur, Count de Rochambeau (1725–1807), the commander of the French military forces sent to aid the American colonies during the Revolution. **Lafayette:** Marquis de Lafayette (1757–1834), the French nobleman who fought on behalf of the Americans during the Revolutionary War. **Paul Jones:** John Paul Jones (1747–1792), the American naval hero famous for an apocryphal boast attributed to him ("I have not yet begun to fight"), allegedly made while his ship the *Bonhomme Richard* captured the British ship *Serapis* in 1779. **Wearing the Green:** the custom of wearing a shamrock to indicate one's Irish identity or support for the cause of Irish independence; an allusion to the song "The Wearin' o' the Green." **Shule Aroon:** the English phonetic spelling of the Gaelic *Siuil a run*, a phrase commonly translated as "Come, (my) love." The phrase is the title of an old Gaelic song dating from the end of the seventeenth century, when many Irish patriots fled Ireland and enlisted in the French army. The verses refer to a lover's enlistment in the Irish Brigade, an all-Irish contingent in the armies of the French kings. One verse of the song reads: "Now my love has gone to France / To try his fortune to advance, / If he e'er come back, 'tis but a chance. . . . " **Gael:** used here to refer to the Irish. **De Tesse:** René de Frouay, Comte de Tessé. As marshal of France he led an expedition against Gibraltar in 1705 and participated in the victorious defense of Toulon against Imperial troops in 1707. He also served as ambassador to Rome and Spain. **St. Ruth:** Charles Chalmont Marquis de St. Ruth (d. 1691), the French nobleman and soldier who raised an army of 15,000 men in Ireland to support the cause of James II. **Humbert:** Jean Joseph Amable Humbert (1755–1823), the French general who landed an invasion force of 1,000 at Killala, Ireland, in 1799 as part of an unsuccessful Irish insurrection against English rule. In 1815 he lent his support to Andrew Jackson at the battle of New Orleans, the city in which he was buried. **Hoche:** Lazare Hoche (1768–1797), the general chosen to lead an aborted French invasion of Ireland in 1796 with forty-three ships and 14,450 men. **Sarsfield:** Patrick Sarsfield (d. 1693), the leader of the Irish Catholic resistance (1689–1691) to England's King William III. Sarsfield had earlier served in the army of Louis XIV and accompanied James II to France when the latter monarch was deposed in favor of William. After the Williamite victory in Ireland, Sarsfield and about 7,000 Irishmen went into exile in France. **Dillon:** Arthur Dillon (1670–1733), one of the Irish Jacobites who went into exile in France after James II failed to regain his throne from William III. One of the "Wild Geese" exiles, Dillon subsequently served as a general in the French army. **O'Brien:** possibly Charles O'Brien (d. 1706), Fifth Viscount Clare. After leaving Ireland for France in 1692, he was appointed captain of the *gardes du corps*. In 1696 he became colonel of the Clare regiment in the Irish Brigade in the service of France. **O'Neill:** possibly Gordon O'Neill (d. 1704), one of the "Wild Geese" who left Ireland for France following the collapse of the Jacobite cause. After recovering from wounds suffered at the battle of Aughrim in Ireland in 1691, he retired to France, where he was made colonel of the Irish infantry of Charlemont. **sire of MacMahon:** the Irish ancestor of Patrice MacMahon (1808–1893), the second president (1873–1879) of the French Third Republic. **The Gaul and the Gael:** by metonymy used here to refer to the French and the Irish respectively. **green banner:** probably the regimental banner of the Irish Brigade. **starry flag:** the American flag.

13. James Caldwell

Born in Virginia of Scotch-Irish and Huguenot descent, James Caldwell was graduated from the College of New Jersey (now Princeton) in 1759. Within two years he was ordained and installed as pastor of the First Presbyterian Church in Elizabethtown, New Jersey. Because of his service as chaplain of Drayton's New Jersey Brigade during the war against Britain, Loyalists called him the "high priest of the Revolution" and offered rewards for his capture.

In a battle near Union, New Jersey, in early June 1780, Caldwell's wife, Hannah, was killed by a random bullet, and the parsonage there was burned by the enemy. From then on, Caldwell always preached with pistols close at hand. At the battle of Springfield two weeks later, when the American soldiers ran out of wadding for their rifles, Caldwell broke open the church doors and began to distribute to the troops copies of the Watts hymnbook. "Now put Watts into them, boys!" he cried.

In 1781 Caldwell met his death during an unfortunate incident with a Patriot guard, an Irishman named James Morgan. After the parson had picked up a package from an acquaintance, Morgan ordered the minister to stop, apparently with the intention of questioning him about the item. When Caldwell failed to obey the command quickly enough, the sentry shot him through the heart. At Morgan's trial another soldier testified that he had heard the Irishman express his intention to "pop" Caldwell off whenever he had the chance, while still another soldier claimed that Morgan had been bribed to kill the parson.

Caldwell of Springfield

by Bret Harte (1839–1902)

Here's the spot. Look around you. Above on the height
Lay the Hessians encamped. By that church on the right
Stood the gaunt Jersey farmers. And here ran a wall,—
You may dig anywhere and you'll turn up a ball.
Nothing more. Grasses spring, waters run, flowers blow,
Pretty much as they did ninety-three years ago.

Nothing more, did I say? Stay one moment: you've heard
Of Caldwell, the parson, who once preached the Word
Down at Springfield? What, No? Come—that's bad; why he had
All the Jerseys aflame. And they gave him the name
Of the "rebel high-priest." He stuck in their gorge,
For he loved the Lord God,—and he hated King George!

He had cause, you might say! When the Hessians that day
Marched up with Knyphausen they stopped on their way
At the "Farms," where his wife, with a child in her arms,
Sat alone in the house. How it happened none knew
But God—and that one of the hireling crew
Who fired the shot! Enough!—there she lay,
And Caldwell, the chaplain, her husband, away!

Did he preach—did he pray? Think of him as you stand
By the old church to-day;—think of him and his band
Of militant ploughboys! See the smoke and the heat
Of that reckless advance,—of that straggling retreat!
Keep the ghost of that wife, foully slain, in your view,—
And what could you, what should you, what would you do?

Why, just what he did! They were left in the lurch
For the want of more wadding. He ran to the church,
Broke the door, stripped the pews, and dashed out in the road
With his arms full of hymn-books and threw down his load
At their feet! Then above all the shouting and shots,
Rang his voice,—"Put Watts into 'em,—Boys, give 'em Watts!"
And they did. That is all. Grasses spring, flowers blow
Pretty much as they did ninety-three years ago.
You may dig anywhere and you'll turn up a ball,—
But not always a hero like this, and that's all.

Hessians: a generic name for German mercenaries, although they were not only from Hesse but also from other small German principalities (Ansbach, Anhalt-Zerbst, Brunswick, and Waldeck). **Knyphausen:** Wilhelm, Baron von Knyphausen (1716–1800), the senior German military figure in America who fought with the British during the Revolution. **Farms:** Connecticut Farms, near Union, New Jersey, where Caldwell and his wife and family lived in the parsonage.

Parson Caldwell at Springfield

by Charles D. Platt

See the Red-coats in the distance!
    Here they come! To arms! To arms!
Get your powder-horn and musket!
    Call the neighbors from their farms!

Fire the roaring eighteen-pounder
    Signal gun from Prospect Hill!

Light the blazing black tar-barrel!
    Fight we must and fight we will!

Jump the stone wall by the roadside!
    Hide behind it! Prime your gun!
Now we're ready! See them gather!
    Farmers coming on the run!

Who's that riding in on horseback?
    Parson Caldwell, boys; Hooray!
Red-coats call him "Fighting Chaplain;"
    How they hate him! well they may!

When he preaches to us Sundays,
    Gathered in the Old Red Store,
Down he lays his cavalry pistols,
    Sets his sentinels at the door.

Boys, remember how the British,
    Passing through Connecticut Farms,
Shot the parson's wife! That murder
    Stirs us more than wild alarms.

Hah! The fight's begun! They're firing!
    See the flash of British steel!
Hear the crack of Jersey muskets!
    Doomed to make the Red-coats wheel!

Who's that riding on the gallop,
    Stopping by the meetin'-house door?
In he goes—comes out with arms full,
    Piled with hymn-books by the score.

Parson Caldwell!—Will he sing now,
    While the bullets round him hum?
Will he hold another meetin',
    Set the hymns to fife and drum?

Hear him shouting, "Give 'em Watts, boys!
    Put Watts into 'em, my men!"
Ah! I see they're out of wadding;
    That's the tune! We'll all join in!

Then the worn old hymn-books fluttered,

> And their pages wildly flew,
> Hither, thither, torn and dirty,
> On an errand strange and new.
>
> Making Short Partic'lar meter
> Parson Caldwell pitched the tunes;
> Jersey farmers joined the chorus,
> Put to flight those red dragoons.

Red-coats: British soldiers, so called from the red jackets of their uniforms.

14. Stephen Moylan

The son of a highly successful merchant and his wife, Stephen Moylan was born in 1737 in Cork, Ireland. Because educational opportunities for Catholics were limited in Ireland, Moylan pursued his education in Paris and later spent several years in Lisbon associated with his father's shipping business. In 1771, three years after coming to Philadelphia, he was elected president of the Friendly Sons of St. Patrick even though that charitable society was composed almost entirely of Protestants.

With the outbreak of the Revolution, Moylan joined the Continental Army at Cambridge, Massachusetts. Because of his commercial experience, he was at first assigned to the commissariat department. He quickly became General Washington's secretary and then quartermaster general of the army, with the rank of colonel. After only four months, however, he resigned from the latter position, apparently because of his failure to reorganize the army. In the field he was easily recognized by his unusual uniform: red waistcoat, bright green coat, bearskin hat, and buckskin breeches.

Moylan subsequently raised and led a cavalry unit known as the Fourth Pennsylvania Light Dragoons under the overall command of Casimir Pulaski. When Moylan and his Polish superior quarreled, the Irishman was court-martialed for insubordination but was later acquitted. Toward the end of the war, Moylan and his dragoons assisted Lafayette in forcing Cornwallis's surrender at Yorktown, Virginia.

Moylan's Dragoons

by Thomas D'Arcy McGee (1825–1868)

> Furl up the banner of the brave
> And bear it gently home,

Through stormy scenes no more to wave;
    For now the calm has come.
Through showering grape and drifting death,
    It floated ever true;
And by the signs upon our path,
    Men knew what troop went through.

Our flag first flew o'er Boston free,
    When Graves' fleet groped out.
On Stony Point, reconquered, we
    Unfurled it with a shout;
At Trenton, Monmouth, Germantown,
    Our sabers were not slack;
Like lightning, next, to Charlestown
    We scourged the British back.

And here at Yorktown now they yield,
    And our career is o'er.
No more thou'lt flutter o'er the field,
    Flag of the brave!—no more.
The Redcoats yield them to "the Line";
    Both sides have changed their tunes,
To peace the Congress doth incline;
    And so do we Dragoons.

Furl up the banner of the brave,
    And bear it gently home;
No more o'er Moylan's march to wave.
    Lodge it in Moylan's home.
There Butler, Hand, and Wayne, perchance,
    May tell of battles brave,
And the old flag on its splintered lance
    Above their heads shall wave.

Hurrah, then, for the Schuylkill side,
    Its pleasant woody dells!
Old Ulster well may warm with pride
    When each his story tells.
Comrades, farewell; may heaven bestow
    On you its richest boons!
So let us drink before we go,
    To Moylan's brave Dragoons!

Graves: Admiral Samuel Graves (1713–1787), the commander of the British fleet in American waters. On May 27, 1775, he sent forty marines on a small schooner under the command of his son, Lieutenant Thomas Graves, to defend Noodle Island in Boston Harbor against possible attack by colonials. **Stony Point:** the last major northern battle of the Revolution, when General Anthony Wayne's troops captured a 600-man British garrison on the Hudson River in June 1779. **Trenton, Monmouth, Germantown:** Revolutionary War battles fought, respectively, in December 1776, June 1778, and October 1777. **Charlestown:** Charleston, South Carolina. **Yorktown:** the last major engagement of the Revolutionary War, during which the British surrendered at Yorktown, Virginia, on October 19, 1781. **Redcoats:** British soldiers, so called from the red jackets of their uniforms. **the Line:** the regiments of the Pennsylvania Line. **Butler:** William Butler, an Irish native who led an expedition against the Indians of upper New York state during the Revolution. He was almost killed during the mutiny of the Pennsylvania Line regiments in 1781. **Hand:** Edward Hand (1744–1802), an Irish-born physician and a highly regarded officer during the Revolutionary War. He ended his military career as General Washington's adjutant general. **Wayne:** Anthony Wayne (1745–1796), a Revolutionary War general and the commander of the regiments of the Pennsylvania Line. **Schuylkill:** a river flowing southeast from eastern Pennsylvania to the Delaware River at Philadelphia. **Ulster:** Ulster County, Pennsylvania.

15. Anthony Wayne

The first ancestor of Anthony Wayne's to come to America was his grandfather, an Englishman who had settled in County Wicklow, Ireland, after fighting for King William at the battle of the Boyne. In 1722 the elder Wayne immigrated to Pennsylvania, and two years later he was followed to America by his Irish-born son Isaac.

The latter's son Anthony was born in Paoli, Pennsylvania, in 1745. The famous general was a member of various Pennsylvania legislative bodies (the provincial convention, the state assembly, and the convention called to ratify the U.S. Constitution) and served at the battles of Brandywine, Germantown, Monmouth, Stony Point, and Yorktown. To prove his sentimental attachment to the land of his father's birth, he always celebrated St. Patrick's Day and in later years became a member of the Friendly Sons of St. Patrick.

On January 1, 1781, while encamped at Morristown, New Jersey, the eleven regiments of Wayne's Pennsylvania Line mutinied. After seizing the guns and ammunition in the camp, approximately half of the line's 2,500 men headed off to Philadelphia to present their grievances to the Continental Congress. That a considerable number of Irish soldiers were involved in the mutiny can be surmised from the fact that Wayne selected two officers of Irish descent to accompany him to Princeton, New Jersey, where he hoped to negotiate with the leaders of the rebellion.

One of Wayne's most daring exploits was his capture of Stony Point, a British-held garrison along the Hudson River. In the dead of night on July 15, 1779, Wayne led a force of 1,200 men across the swamp dividing the fort from the mainland, reached the outworks before being discovered, and successfully stormed the fort. When Washington had asked him whether he could storm the garrison, Wayne boasted, "I'll storm hell, sir, if you'll make the plans!" Wayne's superior offered sounder advice: "Better try Stony Point first, General."

Mad Anthony Wayne

by one of Wayne's aides-de-camp

His sword-blade gleams, and his eye-light beams,
And never glanced either in vain;
Like the ocean tides, at our head he rides,
The fearless Mad Anthony Wayne!
Bang! bang! the rifles go,
Down falls the startled foe;
Bang! bang! the rifles go,
Down falls the startled foe;

And many a redcoat here tonight,
The Continentals scorning,
Shall never meet the blaze of the broad sunlight,
That shines on the morrow morning.
And many a redcoat here tonight,
The Continentals scorning,
Shall never meet the blaze of the broad sunlight,
That shines on the morrow morning.

Was e'er a chief of his speech so brief,
Who utters his wishes so plain?
Ere he speaks a word, the orders are heard
From the eyes of Mad Anthony Wayne!
Aim! Fire! exclaim his eyes,
Bang! Bang! each gun replies.
Aim! Fire! exclaim his eyes,
Bang! Bang! each gun replies.

It is best to fall at our country's call,
If we must leave this lifetime of pain;
And who would shrink from the perilous brink

When led by Mad Anthony Wayne?
Ran! Tan! the bugles sound,
Our forces fill the ground.
Ran! Tan! the bugles sound,
Our forces fill the ground.

Let them form their ranks in firm phalanx,
It will melt at our rifle-ball rain,
Every shot must tell on a redcoat well,
Or we anger Mad Anthony Wayne.
Tramp! Tramp! away they go,
Now retreats the beaten foe.
Tramp! Tramp! away they go,
Now retreats the beaten foe.

Mad Anthony Wayne: Wayne received his nickname from the following incident. After the general had ordered the arrest of his trusted spy — the Irishman "Jemmy the Rover" — for disorderly conduct, the bold subordinate asked whether Wayne was "Mad" or "in Fun." When told that he would receive twenty-nine lashes for any future misconduct, Jemmy replied, "Then Anthony is mad! Farewell to you! Clear the coast for the Commodore 'Mad Anthony's' friend."

Wayne at Stony Point

by Clinton Scollard (1860–1932)

'T was the heart of the murky night, and the lowest ebb of the tide,
Silence lay on the land, and sleep on the waters wide,
Save for the sentry's tramp, or the note of a lone night bird,
Or the slough of the haunted pines as the south wind softly stirred.
Gloom above and around, and the brooding spirit of rest;
Only a single star over Dunderberg's lofty crest.

Through the drench of ooze and slime at the margin of the river fen
File upon file slips by. See! are they ghosts or men?
Fast do they forward press, on by a track unbarred;
Now is the causeway won, now have they throttled the guard;
Now have they parted line to storm with a rush on the height,
Some by a path to the left, some by a path to the right.

Hark,—the peal of a gun! and the drummer's rude alarms!
Ringing down from the height there soundeth the cry, *To arms!*
Thundering down from the height there cometh the cannon's blare;
Flash upon blinding flash lightens the livid air;

Look! do the stormers quail? Nay, for their feet are set
Now at the bastion's base, now on the parapet.

Urging the vanguard on prone doth the leader fall,
Smitten, sudden and sore by a foeman's musket-ball;
Waver the charging lines; swiftly they spring to his side,—
Madcap Anthony Wayne, the patriot army's pride!
Forward, my braves! he cries, and the heroes hearten again;
Bear me into the fort, I'll die at the head of my men!

Die!—did he die that night, felled in his lusty prime?
Answer many a field in the stormy aftertime!
Still did his prowess shine, still did his courage soar,
From the Hudson's rocky steep to the James's level shore;
But never on Fame's fair scroll did he blazon a deed more bright
Than his charge on Stony Point in the heart of the murky night.

Dunderberg's lofty crest: Thunder Mountain, north of Stony Point. **James's level shore:** an allusion to Wayne's skirmish with British troops at Green Spring Farm along the James River near Jamestown, Virginia, on July 6, 1781. **Stony Point:** a British-held garrison along the Hudson River, which Wayne and a force of 1,200 men captured in the dead of night on July 15, 1779.

Anthony Wayne

by Arthur Guiterman (1871–1943)

Down the Ohio the flatboats go,
One by one and three in a row.
    "Wayne, Anthony Wayne!"
Faring still on the ancient quest,
Hundreds of flatboats drifting west.
    "Wayne, Anthony Wayne!"
The eddy swirls from the curving shores
And the steersmen chant as they shift their oars,
    "Wayne, Anthony Wayne!
Free is the river from source to mouth,
Free are the streams of the North and the South,
    Praise to Anthony Wayne!"

Wayne, Wayne, Anthony Wayne!
Who bore the brunt on Monmouth Plain,
Who marched by night with his picked command
And stormed Stony Point with spear in hand,

Who kept the steel of the bayonet bright,
Whose word in war was always, "Fight!"
     Wayne, Anthony Wayne!

Westward rode pirogue and raft,
     Freighted well with household gear,
Till the red man's hate and the red man's craft
     Stayed the march of the pioneer.

Shawnees lurked at the river shoals,
     Hurons claimed the woods for theirs.
Round the hamlet's reeking coals
     Yelled the braves of the Delawares.

Whelming all and sparing none,
     Dark Miamis mocked the slain.
"Give me a man!" cried Washington.
     "I am the man!" said Wayne.

Wayne, Wayne, Anthony Wayne,
Fiery heart and cool, clear brain,
Deep in the wilds of the Northwest region
Marched at the head of his hard-drilled legion,
Pressing where two had filed before,
Bringing the choice of peace or war.

Iroquois, Ottawa, Chippeway,
Back of the fallen timbers lay;
Wyandot, Shawnee, Delaware
Poured their shot from the sheltered lair.
Over the root-laced parapet
The legion stormed with the bayonet,
Hunting the warriors out and out;
Hard on the flank of the savage rout,
Leaping the trunks in their reckless course,
Thundered the mad Kentucky Horse,
Lunging, plunging, bridles ringing,
Pistols flashing, sabers swinging,
Till the woods were clear as a new-washed fleece
And the vanquished sachems sued for peace.

Down the Ohio the flatboats go,
One by one and three in a row.
     "Wayne, Anthony Wayne!"

With light canoes and blunt bateaux
Down the Ohio a flatboat goes.
    "Wayne, Anthony Wayne!"

Up in the bow in a rough-made chair
Granddad sits with his silver hair;
Safe in the waist is the placid cow,
The coop of fowls, the scythe and plow,
And the towhead children, five and more;
While staunch in the stern at the steering oar,
Brave and tall, is the man who goes
To a land new-cleared of ruthless foes,
With his strong-souled wife in her homespun dress
Who will make a home in the wilderness,
For they come of the same undaunted strain
    As Wayne, Anthony Wayne!

Monmouth Plain: the battle of Monmouth, New Jersey, in 1778, when Wayne and his division of 1,000 men exacted a heavy toll of British casualties. **Stony Point:** a British-held garrison along the Hudson River which Wayne and a force of 1,200 men captured in the dead of night on July 15, 1779. **Shawnees, Hurons, Delawares, Miamis, Iroquois, Ottawa, Chippeway, Wyandot:** various Native American tribes. **fallen timbers:** an allusion to the battle of Fallen Timbers in 1794, when Wayne and a professional army defeated an Indian force near present-day Toledo, Ohio. Wayne's victory temporarily checked Indian resistance in the region and led to the Treaty of Greenville, by which the Native Americans ceded much of the Ohio territory to the United States.

16. Hercules Mulligan

Hercules Mulligan was born in Coleraine, County Antrim, Ireland, in 1740 and came to America with his parents at the age of six. He probably worked for the haberdashery firm of Kortright and Company in New York City before opening a clothing and tailoring business of his own in the same city. As relations between the British and their American cousins continued to deteriorate, Mulligan was extremely active in the anti-British agitation in New York City. In July 1776 he led the mob that destroyed the famous bronze statue of King George III on Bowling Green.

Mulligan's most famous role during the revolutionary struggle, however, was as a "confidential agent" (spy) for General George Washington. In 1779 Mulligan informed the American commander-in-chief that the British intended to send 300 infantry to intercept Washington as he led his men through Connecticut on their way to Newport, Rhode Island. Mulligan later helped frustrate another attempt to seize Washington when he overheard a British officer in his shop boast that Washington would be a captive "before another day." Mulligan immediately dispatched an African American with a warning to the American general. In addition, sometime before April 1781 Mulligan warned Washington that he and the governors of New Jersey and New York were the targets of an assassination plot. Following Washington's return to New York City in 1783, the former American commander had breakfast with Mulligan at Fraunces Tavern, an event celebrated in the following poem.

Breakfast with Hercules Mulligan
by Shaemus O'Sheel (1886–1954)

The last red file of grenadiers halts at the grey sea-wall,
They have crowded into the last long boat that scarcely holds them all,
And the sullen oarsmen pull for the ships that shall sail and never
    return,
And the Union Jack of Britain droops, dejected, at the stern.
And now as the night's grey fleece is shown by the golden shears of the
    sun,
Slowly, astride his dappled grey,
Down to the Battery, down to the Bay,
Riding, comes Washington.

His aides-de-camp
Hold back the throng
As he reins his dappled grey,
And notes how the white sails take the breeze

And the black ships slink from the Bay.
Now sped by the sun's bright arrows
They have vanished beyond the Narrows,
And they'll come not back through the Narrows
This side of Judgment Day.

And the people's shout is mighty,
And all eyes turn as one
To the dappled grey and its rider,
The silent Washington.
But Washington broods apart;
His thoughts go back through the years
That heard no clamorous cheers
To ease disaster's smart.
The pageant unrolls before him
Of the days that tried and tore him,
When only faith upbore him,
And only the valiant heart.
What wonder that he can scarcely see
The radiant face of victory
As the last ship slinks away to the sea
And the last link falls
Of the chain that galls
The newborn daughter of Liberty?

The last tall mast has faded away;
Washington turns on the dappled grey,
And bows to a silent rider near him,
Speaking loudly that all may hear him,
"Hercules Mulligan, if I may,
I will break my fast with you this day!"

Over the Bowling Green they ride,
Washington, Mulligan, side by side;
Thus the Chieftain, in all men's view
Proves Hercules Mulligan staunch and true.

For Washington knows the Irish breed;
They sprung to arms in the hour of need,
Sullivan, first to strike on land,
O'Brien, first to strike at sea,
Knox and Moylan and Wayne and Hand,
Barry, Magaw and Shee.
They proved their mettle on many a field,

> First to charge and last to yield,
> In the cause of Liberty.
>
> Washington smiles and bows to his host;
> "Hercules Mulligan, here's a toast:
> If the land we have seen this day set free
> Ever shall be in danger
> From foe within or stranger,
> May Heaven grant, to save us then,
> The hearts and the hands of Irishmen."
> And the shout rings 'round the board, "Amen"!

Union Jack: the British national flag. **Battery:** the southern tip of Manhattan Island, overlooking New York Bay. **the Narrows:** a strait in New York Bay between Staten Island and Long Island. **Judgment Day:** the day at the end of world when the living and the dead will be judged by God. **Sullivan:** John Sullivan (1740–1795), the leader of a band of colonials who seized gunpowder and weapons from the British at Fort William and Mary in New Castle, New Hampshire, in 1774. **O'Brien:** Jeremiah O'Brien (1744–1818), whose capture of a British ship off the coast of Machias, Maine, in 1775 was the first American naval victory of the Revolution. **Knox:** Henry Knox (1750–1806), the Irish-American general whose troops dragged fifty-nine cannon from Fort Ticonderoga, New York, to Boston, between November 1775 and January 1776. **Moylan:** Stephen Moylan (1737–1811), the Irish-born quartermaster general of the Continental Army, the commander of the Fourth Pennsylvania Light Dragoons, and the first president of the Friendly Sons of St. Patrick in Philadelphia. **Wayne:** Anthony Wayne (1745–1796), a Revolutionary War general and the commander of the regiments of the Pennsylvania Line. **Hand:** Edward Hand (1744–1802), an Irish-born physician and a highly regarded officer during the Revolutionary War. He ended his military career as Washington's adjutant general. **Barry:** John Barry (1745–1803), the Irish-born "Father of the American Navy." Early in 1776 he was placed in command of the first regular cruiser to put to sea under the authority of the Continental Congress. **Magaw:** Robert Magaw (d. 1789), the Irish-born officer in the Continental Army who unsuccessfully defended Fort Washington (in New York) against British and German troops in November 1776. **Shee:** John Shee, the Irish-born colonel of the Third Pennsylvania Regiment. He personally subscribed £1,000 to supply provisions for American troops during the Revolution.

17. Hermann Blennerhassett

Although born in England, Hermann Blennerhassett was the son of an Irish gentleman who claimed to be a direct descendant of King Edward III. After attending Trinity College in Dublin, the younger Blennerhassett was admitted to the Irish bar in 1790. He was described as a cultured man with a talent for music and an interest in science. According to his contemporaries, he was blessed with all sorts of sense except common sense.

Two years after their arrival in the United States, Blennerhassett and his wife settled on an island in the Ohio River, near what is now Parkersburg, West Virginia. There he built a two-story mansion flanked by two wings — one with his library and his laboratory, the other with offices, the servants' hall, and the kitchen. The interior was decorated with frescoes, mirrors, carpets, and furniture imported from Europe, while the 1,000-acre estate boasted gardens, stables, slaves' quarters, orchards, and farmlands.

Blennerhassett fatally jeopardized his life as a country squire, however, by his involvement with Aaron Burr. While the latter maintained that he never entertained "any design to separate the Western from the Eastern States," the popular conception was otherwise. Whatever the case, Blennerhassett came under a cloud of suspicion by allowing his island to be used by armed recruits, supervising the construction of a supply boat and fifteen barges, and contributing funds for the purchase of land which Burr intended to colonize. In response the local militia took possession of the Anglo-Irishman's island and looted his mansion in December 1806. The fugitive Blennerhassett hastened to join Burr at the mouth of the Cumberland River but was arrested in Mississippi Territory.

The subsequent trial in Richmond, Virginia, centered on the nature of Burr's scheme. One witness testified that Blennerhassett had told him that the object of the scheme was an invasion of Mexico, which Burr would subsequently rule as king. The prosecuting attorney argued that Burr's plan involved secession of the western states, a Mexican invasion, and creation of a western empire centered around New Orleans. In the end, Chief Justice John Marshall acquitted Burr and Blennerhassett of charges of treason against the United States but ruled that the pair be tried for conspiracy against Spain. (Although the two men were indicted on that charge, the case never went to trial.)

Blennerhassett's Island

by Thomas Buchanan Read (1822–1872)

Once came an exile, longing to be free,
Born in the greenest island of the sea;

He sought out this, the fairest blooming isle
That ever gemmed a river; and its smile,
Of summer green and freedom, on his heart
Fell, like the light of Paradise. Apart
It lay, remote and wild; and in his breast
He fancied this an island of the blest;
And here he deemed the world might never mar
The tranquil air with its molesting jar.
Long has his soul, among the strife of men,
Gone out and fought, and fighting, failed; and then
Withdrew into itself; as when some fount
Finds space within, and will no longer mount,
Content to hear its own secluded waves
Make lonely music in the new-found caves.
And here he brought his household; here his wife,
As happy as her children, round his life
Sang as she were an echo, or a part
Of the deep pleasure springing in his heart—
A silken string which with the heavier cord
Made music, such as well-strung harps afford.
She was the embodied spirit of the man,
His second self, but on a fairer plan.
And here they came, and here they built their home,
And set the rose and taught the vines to roam,
Until the place became an isle of bowers,
Where odors, mist-like, swam above the flowers.
It was a place where one might lie and dream,
And see the naiads, from the river-stream,
Stealing among the umbrous [*sic*], drooping limbs;
Where Zephyr, 'mid the willows, tuned her hymns
Round rippling shores. Here would the first birds throng,
In early spring-time, and their latest song
Was given in autumn; when all else had fled,
They half forgot to go; such beauty here was spread.
It was, in sooth, a fair enchanted isle,
Round which the unbroken forest, many a mile,
Reached the horizon like a boundless sea:—
A sea whose waves, at last, were forced to flee
On either hand, before the westward host,
To meet no more upon its ancient coast.
But all things fair, save truth, are frail and doomed;
And brightest beauty is the first consumed
By envious Time; as if he crowned the brow
With loveliest flowers, before he gave the blow

Which laid the victim on the hungry shrine. . .—
Such was the dreamer's fate, and such, bright isle, was thine.
There came the stranger, heralded by fame,
Whose eloquent soul was like a tongue of flame,
Which brightened and despoiled whate'er it touched.
A violet, by an iron gauntlet clutched,
Were not more doomed than whosoe'er he won
To list his plans, with glowing words o'errun:
And Blennerhassett hearkened as he planned.
          Far in the South there was a glorious land
Crowned with perpetual flowers, and where repute
Pictured the gold more plenteous than the fruit—
The Persia of the West. There would he steer
His conquering course; and o'er the bright land rear
His far-usurping banner, till his home
Should rest beneath a wide, imperial dome,
Where License, round his thronèd feet, should whirl
Her dizzy mazes like an Oriental girl.
His followers would be lords; their ladies each
Wear wreaths of gems beyond the old world's reach;
And emperors, gazing to that land of bloom,
With impotent fire of envy should consume.
Such was the gorgeous vision which he drew,
As one in some enchanter's misty room,
His senses poisoned by the strange perfume,
Beholds with fierce desire the picture fair,
And grasps at nothing in the painted air,—
Gave acquiescence, in a fatal hour,
And wealth, and hope, and peace were in the tempter's power.
The isle became a rendezvous; and then
Came in the noisy rule of lawless men.
Domestic calm, affrighted, fled afar,
And Riot revelled 'neath the midnight star;
Continuous music rustled through the trees,
Where banners danced responsive on the breeze;
Or in the festoons, above the astonished bowers,
With flaming colors shamed the modest flowers.
There clanged the mimic combat of the sword,
Like daily glasses round the festive board;
Here lounged the chiefs, there marched the plumèd file,
And martial splendor over-ran the isle.
Already, the shrewd leader of the sport
The shadowy sceptre grasped, and swayed his court.
In dreams, or waking, revelling or alone,

Before him swam the visionary throne;
Until a voice, as if the insulted woods
Had risen to claim their ancient solitudes,
Broke on his spirit, like a trumpet rude,
Shattering his dream to nothing where he stood!
The revellers vanished, and the banners fell
Like the red leaves beneath November's spell.
Full of great hopes, sustained by mighty will,
Urged by ambition, confident of skill,
As fearless to perform as to devise,
A-flush, but now he saw the glittering prize
Flame, like a cloud in day's descending track;
But, lo, the sun went down and left it black!
He heard the shout, and "treason!" was the cry;
And that harsh word, with its unpitying blight,
Swept o'er the island like an arctic night.
Cold grew the hearthstone, withered fell the flowers,
And desolation walked among the bowers.
     This was the mansion. Through the ruined hall
The loud winds sweep, with gusty rise and fall,
Or glide, like phantoms, through the open doors;
And winter drifts his snow along the floors,
Blown through the yawning rafters, where the stars
And moon look in as through dull prison bars.
On yonder gable, through the nightly dark,
The owl replies unto the dreary bark
Of lonely fox, beside the grass-grown sill;
And here on summer eves, the whip-poor-will
Exalts her voice, and to the traveller's ear
Proclaims how Ruin rules with full contentment here.

exile: Hermann Blennerhassett. **naiads:** in Greek mythology the nymphs who presided over rivers and springs. **umbrous [*sic*]:** umbrose, an obsolete word meaning "shady." **Zephyr:** the west wind. **stranger:** Aaron Burr. **glorious land:** Mexico. **shrewd leader of the sport:** Aaron Burr.

18. Dolly Madison

Dorothea (Dolly) Payne, the wife of President James Madison, was born in 1768 in North Carolina, the maternal granddaughter of William Coles, a native of Enniscorthy, Ireland. While living in Philadelphia, the blue-eyed Dolly married John Todd Jr., a lawyer and, like Dolly, a Quaker. The marriage ended after only three years, though, when Todd died of yellow fever in 1793. Eleven months later the widowed Dolly became the wife of James Madison, at the time a noted congressman. Although Madison was twenty years older than Dolly, the marriage was a happy one.

Mrs. Madison became a major figure on the social scene in the nation's capital when her husband became President Jefferson's secretary of state. For the widower Jefferson she served as the unofficial first lady and made a name for herself as a gracious and charming hostess. She continued this role during her husband's two terms as president. When the Executive Mansion was torched by the British during the War of 1812, Mrs. Madison saved many state papers and a portrait of George Washington.

From 1817 until her husband's death in 1836, Mrs. Madison lived at "Montpelier," the couple's estate in Virginia. During that time Dolly cared for Madison's aged mother, served as his secretary, and carried on her tradition of hospitality as best she could. Although Mrs. Madison later benefited financially from the posthumous sale to Congress of her husband's famous notes on the Constitutional Convention, continued financial problems eventually caused her to sell Montpelier.

Dolly Madison
1772–1849

by Rosemary Carr Benét (1900–1962)

Dolly Madison
(Dorothea Payne),
Married, was widowed
And married again.

Passing by other
More dashing names
To set her cap
For "the great little" James.

She loved fine clothes,
Though she was a Quaker.
She wore linen masks
So the sun wouldn't bake her.

Her eyes were large,
Her manners urban,
And she posed for her portrait
Wearing a turban.

She brushed her satins,
Tended her beauty,
Smoothed her laces,
Minded her duty.

But, though fine and grand
On her at-home day,
She could still take snuff
With Henry Clay.

When the British began
To cut more capers
And burned the White House,
She didn't have vapors.

The roofs fell in
And the cut-glass burst—
But she saved George Washing-
     ton's
Portrait first.

She didn't talk much.
She eschewed all tears.
She went to a ball
At fourscore years.

But her very last words
Set us staring—for—
"There's nothing in this life
Worth caring for."

Said by a lady
Who loved her life
And, more than most,
Was a perfect wife,

Make us wonder a little,
Though with no stigma,
If Dolly could have been
An enigma.

Henry Clay: a U.S. congressman and senator (1777–1852).

19. Stephen Decatur

Stephen Decatur, whose maternal grandparents were Irish, first achieved fame in the annals of the American navy during two incidents in the Tripolitan War. Earlier in that conflict the frigate *Philadelphia* had run aground off Tripoli and had been captured by pirates. For more than three months the vessel lay at anchor under the guns of the viceroy's castle. On the night of February 15, 1804, however, Lieutenant Decatur and eighty other officers and men entered the harbor, boarded the *Philadelphia*, drove the pirate crew overboard, torched the frigate, and escaped with the loss of only one man. When Lord Nelson heard of this triumph, he called it "the most bold and daring act of the age."

In an engagement the following August, Decatur and twenty-three men captured two pirate craft off Tripoli. Armed with a cutlass, the dashing Decatur fought in hand-to-hand combat with a pike-wielding pirate. The American killed his assailant with a pistol just as the pirate was aiming a blow with a knife. During the scuffle Decatur was saved from the blow of another Tripolitan by the heroism of a devoted sailor — the Reuben James of the second poem below. Although James dies in the poetic rendition below, another version of the story says that he survived. It is said that when Decatur thanked his rescuer and promised him any favor he might ask, James replied that his only wish was to be promoted to the rank of gunner's mate.

Decatur earned additional glory for himself in a spectacular engagement at the beginning of the War of 1812. While cruising off Madeira, Captain Decatur's forty-four-gun frigate the *United States* captured the *Macedonian*, a British vessel of thirty-eight guns. During the ninety-minute battle on October 25, 1812, the Americans suffered only thirteen casualties, while the enemy sustained losses of thirty-six killed and sixty-eight wounded. (An incident recounted in one of the poems below — "Jack Creamer" by James Jeffrey Roche — reveals the unbounded confidence that the crew of the *United States* had in its captain.)

After the War of 1812 Decatur led a squadron to Algiers, offering the Dey the choice of war or peace on American terms. He then proceeded to Tunis and Tripoli to exact payment for injuries sustained during the recent war with Britain. Upon his return to the United States, he was feted as one of the nation's greatest heroes. It was to a toast in his honor in 1816 that he replied with his famous tribute: "Our country! In her intercourse with foreign nations may she always be in the right; but our country, right or wrong." Decatur's illustrious career came to an untimely end when he was killed in a duel with a fellow naval officer in 1820.

How We Burned the *Philadelphia*
by Barrett Eastman (1869–1910)

By the beard of the Prophet the Bashaw swore
*   He would scourge us from the seas;*
Yankees should trouble his soul no more —
By the Prophet's beard the Bashaw swore,
*   Then lighted his hookah and took his ease,*
And troubled his soul no more.

The moon was dim in the western sky,
    And a mist fell soft on the sea,
As we slipped away from the *Siren* brig
    And headed for Tripoli.

Behind us the hulk of the *Siren* lay,
    Before us the empty night;
And when again we looked behind
    The *Siren* was gone from our sight.

Nothing behind us, and nothing before,
    Only the silence and rain,
As the jaws of the sea took hold of our bows
    And cast us up again.

Through the rain and the silence we stole along,
    Cautious and stealthy and slow,
For we knew that the waters were full of those
    Who might challenge the *Mastico.*

But nothing we saw till we saw the ghost
    Of the ship we had come to see,
Her ghostly lights and her ghostly frame
    Rolling uneasily.

And as we looked, the mist drew up
    And the moon threw off her veil,
And we saw the ship in the pale moonlight,
    Ghostly and drear and pale.

Then spoke Decatur low and said:
    "To the bulwarks' shadow all!
But the six who wear the Tripoli dress
    Shall answer the sentinel's call."

"What ship is that?" cried the sentinel.
    "No ship," was the answer free;
"But only a Malta ketch in distress
    Waiting to moor in your lee.

"We have lost our anchor and wait for day
    To sail into Tripoli town,
And the sea rolls fierce and high to-night,
    So cast a cable down."

Then close to the frigate's side we came,
    Made fast to her unforbid—
Six of us bold in the heathen dress,
    The rest of us lying hid.

But one who saw us hiding there
    "*Americano!*" cried.
Then straight we rose and made a rush
    Pellmell up the frigate's side.

Less than a hundred men were we,
    And the heathen were twenty score;
But a Yankee sailor in those old days
    Liked odds of one to four.

And first we cleaned the quarter deck,
      And then from stern to stem
We charged into our enemies
      And quickly slaughtered them.

All around was the dreadful sound
      Of corpses striking the sea,
And the awful shrieks of dying men
      In their last agony.

The heathen fought like devils all,
      But one by one they fell,
Swept from the deck by our cutlasses
      To the water, and so to hell.

Some we found in the black of the hold,
      Some to the fo'c's'le fled,
But all in vain; we sought them out
      And left them lying dead;

Till at last no soul but Christian souls
      Upon that ship was found;
The twenty score were dead, and we,
      The hundred, safe and sound.

And, stumbling o'er the tangled dead,
      The deck a crimson tide,
We fired the ship from keel to shrouds
      And tumbled over the side.

Then out to sea we sailed once more
      With the world as light as day,
And the flames revealed a hundred sail
      Of the heathen there in the bay.

All suddenly the red light paled,
      And the rain rang out on the sea;
Then—a dazzling flash, a deafening roar,
      Between us and Tripoli!

Then, nothing behind us, and nothing before,
      Only the silence and rain;
And the jaws of the sea took hold of our brows
      And cast us up again.

By the beard of the Prophet the Bashaw swore
He would scourge us from the seas;
Yankees should trouble his soul no more —
By the Prophet's beard the Bashaw swore,
Then lighted his hookah and took his ease,
And troubled his soul no more.

Prophet: Mohammed (570–632), the Arab founder of Islam. **Bashaw:** a corruption of *Pasha*, a Turkish viceroy or provincial governor. **hookah:** a water-pipe used by Turks to smoke tobacco. *Mastico:* the captured ketch with which Decatur and his men boarded the *Philadelphia*.

Reuben James

James Jeffrey Roche (1847–1908)

Three ships of war had Preble when he left the Naples shore,
And the knightly king of Naples lent him seven galleys more,
And never since the *Argo* floated in the middle sea
Such noble men and valiant have sailed in company
As the men who went with Preble to the siege of Tripoli.

Stewart, Bainbridge, Hull, Decatur—how their names ring out like
    gold!—
Lawrence, Porter, Trippe, Macdonough, and a score as true and bold;
Every star that lights their banner tells the glory that they won;
But one common sailor's glory is the splendor of the sun.

Reuben James was first to follow when Decatur laid aboard
Of the lofty Turkish galley and in battle broke his sword.
Then the pirate captain smote him, till his blood was running fast,
And they grappled and they struggled, and they fell beside the mast.

Close behind him Reuben battled with a dozen, undismayed,
Till a bullet broke his sword-arm, and he dropped the useless blade.
Then a swinging Turkish sabre clove his left and brought him low,
Like a gallant bark, dismasted, at the mercy of the foe.

Little mercy knows the corsair: high his blade was raised to slay,
When a richer prize allured him, where Decatur struggling lay.
"Help!" the Turkish leader shouted, and his trusty comrade sprung,
And his scimitar like lightning o'er the Yankee captain swung.

Reuben James, disabled, armless, saw the sabre flashed on high,

Saw Decatur shrink before it, heard the pirate taunting cry,
Saw, in half the time I tell it, how a sailor brave and true
Still might show a bloody pirate what a dying man can do.

Quick he struggled, stumbling, sliding in the blood around his feet,
As the Turk a moment waited to make vengeance doubly sweet.
Swift the sabre fell, but swifter bent the sailor's head below,
And upon his 'fenceless forehead Reuben James received the blow!

So was saved our brave Decatur; so the common sailor died;
So the love that moves the lowly lifts the great to fame and pride.
Yet we grudge him not his honors, for whom love like this had birth—
For God never ranks His sailors by the Register of earth!

Preble: Captain Edward Preble (1761–1807), the commander of the American squadron in the Mediterranean. *Argo:* in classical mythology the vessel in which Jason and his companions sailed in search of the Golden Fleece. **middle sea:** the Mediterranean Sea. **Stewart:** Charles Stewart (1778–1869), the captain of the *Constitution* during its successful encounter with the British vessels *Cyane* and *Levant* on February 20, 1815. **Bainbridge:** William Bainbridge (1774–1833), an American naval officer who held commands in the Tripolitan War and the War of 1812. During the latter conflict he captured the British frigate *Java* while commanding the *Constitution.* **Hull:** Isaac Hull (1773–1843), the U.S. naval officer who, as captain of the *Constitution,* defeated the British frigate *Guerrière* during the War of 1812. **Decatur:** Stephen Decatur (1779–1820), the American naval hero who stopped the attacks of Barbary pirates on U.S. shipping and during the War of 1812 captured the British frigate *Macedonian.* **Lawrence:** James Lawrence (1781–1813), the U.S. naval officer whose command "Don't give up the ship!" became the motto of the U.S. navy. During the War of 1812 he was mortally wounded when his ship the *Chesapeake* was disabled and captured by the British vessel the *Shannon.* **Porter:** David Porter (1812–1891), the U.S. naval officer who assisted David Farragut and Ulysses S. Grant in the capture of New Orleans and Vicksburg, respectively, during the Civil War. Porter was later the superintendent of the U.S. Naval Academy. **Trippe:** John Trippe (1785–1810), an American naval officer in the Tripolitan War. In one encounter with the North African pirates, he was wounded eleven times by a single adversary before killing the man with his own sabre. **Macdonough:** Thomas Macdonough (1783–1825), the American naval hero best known for his victory against a British fleet at Plattsburgh Bay on September 11, 1814.

The *United States* and the *Macedonian*

author unknown

How glows each patriot bosom that boasts a Yankee heart,
To emulate such glorious deeds and nobly take a part;
When sailors with their thund'ring guns,

Prove to the English, French and Danes
That Neptune's chosen fav'rite sons
        Are brave Yankee boys.

The twenty-fifth of October, that glorious happy day,
When we beyond all precedent, from Britons bore the sway,—
    'Twas in the ship *United States*,
    Four and forty guns the rates,
    That she should rule, decreed the Fates,
        And brave Yankee boys.

Decatur and his hardy tars were cruising on the deep,
When off the Western Islands they to and fro did sweep,
    The *Macedonian* they espied,
    "Huzza! bravo!" Decatur cried,
    "We'll humble Britain's boasted pride,
        My brave Yankee boys."

The decks were cleared, the hammocks stowed, the boatswain pipes all
    hands,
The tampions out, the guns well sponged, the Captain now commands;
    The boys who for their country fight,
    Their words, "Free trade and Sailor's Rights!"
    Three times they cheered with all their might,
        Those brave Yankee boys.

Now chain-shot, grape, and langrage pierce through her oaken sides,
And many a gallant sailor's blood runs purpling in the tides;
    While death flew nimbly o'er their decks,
    Some lost their legs, and some their necks,
    And Glory's wreath our ship be-decks,
        For brave Yankee boys.

My boys, the proud St. George's Cross, the stripes above it wave,
And busy are our gen'rous tars, the conquered foe to save,
    Our Captain cries "Give me your hand,"
    Then of the ship who took command
        But brave Yankee boys?

Our enemy lost her mizzen, her main and fore-topmost,
For ev'ry shot with death was winged, which slew her men so fact,
    That they lost five to one in killed,
    And ten to one their blood was spilled,

So Fate decreed and Heaven had willed,
        For brave Yankee boys.

Then homeward steered the captive ship, now safe in port she lies,
The old and young with rapture viewed our sailors' noble prize;
        Through seas of wine their health we'll drink,
        And wish them sweet-hearts, friends and chink,
        Who 'fore they'd strike, will nobly sink
            Our brave Yankee boys.

Neptune: the Roman god of the sea. **Western Islands:** Madeira, a group of eight islands off the northwest coast of Portugal. **tampions:** plugs placed in the muzzle of a cannon to keep it free from dirt and moisture when not in use. **St. George's Cross:** a white flag emblazoned with a red cross, long the national banner of England. It was flown from the foremast of English ships. **stripes:** the American flag ("Stars and Stripes"). **chink:** probably coins, from the sound made when they strike one another.

Jack Creamer

by James Jeffrey Roche (1847–1908)

The boarding nettings are triced for fight;
Pike and cutlass are shining bright;
The boatswain's whistle pipes loud and shrill;
Gunner and topman work with a will;
Rough old sailor and reefer trim
Jest as they stand by the cannon grim;
There's a fighting glint in Decatur's eye,
And brave Old Glory floats out on high.

But many a heart beats fast below
The laughing lips as they near the foe;
For the pluckiest knows, though no man quails,
That the breath of death is filling the sails.
Only one little face is wan;
Only one childish mouth is drawn;
One little heart is sad and sore
To the watchful eye of the Commodore.

Little Jack Creamer, ten years old,
In no purser's book or watch enrolled,
Must mope or skulk while his shipmates fight,—
No wonder his little face is white!
"Why, Jack, old man, so blue and sad?

Afraid of the music?" The face of the lad
With mingled shame and anger burns.
Quick to the Commodore he turns:

"I'm not a coward, but I think if you—
Excuse me, Capt'n, I mean if you knew
(I s'pose it's because I'm young and small)
I'm not on the books! I'm no one at all!
And as soon as this fighting work is done,
And we get our prize-money, everyone
Has his share of the plunder—*I* get none."

"And you're sure we shall take her?" "Sure?
"Why sir, She's only a blessed Britisher!
We'll take her easy enough, I bet;
But glory's all that I'm going to get!"
"Glory! I doubt if I get more,
If I get so much," said the Commodore;
"But faith goes far in the race for fame,
And down on the books shall go your name."

Bravely the little seaman stood
To his post while the scuppers ran with blood,
While grizzled veterans looked and smiled
And gathered new courage from the child;
Till the enemy, crippled in pride and might,
Struck his crimson flag and gave up the fight.
Then little Jack Creamer stood once more
Face to face with the Commodore.

"You have got your duty," he said, "my lad,
And money to make your sweetheart glad.
Now, who may she be?" "My mother, sir;
I want you to send the half to her."
"And the rest?" Jack blushed and hung his head;
I'll buy some schoolin' with that," he said.

Decatur laughed; then in graver mood:
"The first is the better, but both are good.
Your mother shall never know want while I
Have a ship to sail, or a flag to fly;
And schooling you'll have till all in blue,
But little the lubbers can teach to you."

Old Glory: the American flag.

Decatur's Toast
by Arthur Guiterman (1871–1943)

Up rose, triumphant, from his seat
    The Bayard of the Sea—
The lion of our laureled fleet,
    The scourge of Barbary;
His glass abrim with bubbling light,
    He pledged that brilliant throng—
"Our Country!—be she ever right;
    Our Country!—right or wrong!"

Then round about the oaken board
    The goblets leaped and rang,
And fervent fingers pressed the sword
    As up the heroes sprang;
No mawkish qualms or doubts had they
    That echoed deep and strong,
"Our Country!—ever right, we pray;
    Our Country!—right or wrong!

Too well the stifling mists they knew
    That dimmed the Stars we bore—
The plots of banded traitors, who,
    Amid the stress of war,
Made weightier their nation's woes,
    Till rose the patriot song:
"When face to face with foreign foes,
    Our Country!—right or wrong!"

Stanch lovers of our free domain,
    We strive for truth and right
With honest force of heart and brain
    As God may give is light.
But doubts must yield and ties must break
    When darkening perils throng;
And when the sullen guns awake,
    "Our Country!—right or wrong!?

Bayard: Pierre du Terrail (c. 1473–1524), Chevalier de Bayard. This French soldier's courage, loyalty, piety, and feats of arms earned him the name *le chevalier sans peur et sans reproche* ("the knight without fear and without reproach").

On the Death of Decatur

by William Crafts (1787–1826)

Sweet-scented flowers on beauty's grave
We strew—but, for the honored brave,
The fallen conqueror of the wave—
     Let ocean's flags adorn the bier,
     And be the Pall of Glory there!

Britannia!—noble-hearted foe—
Hast thou no funeral flowers of woe
To grace his sepulchre—who ne'er again
Shall meet thy warriors on the purple main.
His pride to conquer—and his joy to save—
In triumph generous, as in battle brave—
Heroic—ardent—when a captive—great!
Feeling, as valiant—thou deplorest his fate.
And these thy sons who met him in the fray,
Shall weep with manly tears the hero passed away.

And thou, my country! young, but ripe in grief!
Who shall console thee for the fallen chief?
Thou envied land, whom frequent foes assail,
Too often called to bleed or to prevail;
Doomed to deplore the gallant sons that save,
And follow from the triumph—to the grave!

Thou starry streamer! symbol of the brave,
Shining by day and night, on land and wave;
Sometimes obscured in battle, ne'er in shame,
The guide—the boast—the arbitress of Fame!
Still wave in grateful admiration near,
And beam for ever on Decatur's bier;
And ye, blest stars of Heaven! responsive shed
Your pensive lustre on his lowly bed.

Britannia: Great Britain. **Thou starry streamer!:** the American flag.

20. Oliver Hazard Perry

The son of Christopher Perry and his Irish wife (Sarah Wallace Alexander), Oliver Hazard Perry joined the navy in 1799 at the age of fourteen. He first saw action in the West Indies during the naval war with France and then in the Mediterranean during the war with Tripoli. When the United States declared war against Britain in 1812, he was assigned the task of creating an American fleet to challenge British control of Lake Erie. From his headquarters at Erie, Pennsylvania, he supervised the building, equipping, and manning of nine vessels, the largest of which were the *Lawrence* and the *Niagara*. In the *Lawrence* Perry sailed up the lake to Put-in-Bay, Ohio, and reconnoitered the British fleet of six vessels at the Detroit River.

The fateful battle was finally joined on September 10, 1813. Early in the conflict the *Lawrence* was virtually destroyed by the *Detroit*, with a loss of eighty-three of her 103 men. Perry quickly transferred to the *Niagara*, which subsequently broke through the British line after a fifteen-minute barrage forced the limeys to surrender. Perry lost twenty-seven killed to the enemy's forty-one, although each side had about ninety-five wounded. The victorious American sent his famous message to General William Henry Harrison: "We have met the enemy, and they are ours. Two ships, two brigs, one schooner, and one sloop." (His dispatch to the secretary of the navy — similar to Nelson's report after the battle of the Nile — is less well known: "It has pleased the Almighty to give to the arms of the United States a signal victory over their enemies on this lake.") Perry's achievement won control of Lake Erie for the Americans and made possible Harrison's invasion of Canada. Harrison's victory at the battle of the Thames effectively ended the War of 1812 in the Northwest.

While in command of a squadron in the West Indies in the summer of 1819, Perry was attacked by yellow fever and died after a brief illness. His body was brought to the United States in 1826 and was buried at Newport, Rhode Island.

Perry's Victory
author unknown

Ye tars of Columbia, give ear to my story,
Who fought with brave Perry where cannons did roar;
Your valor has gained you immortal glory,
A fame that shall last until time is no more.
Columbian tars are the true sons of Mars,
They rake for and aft as they fight on the deep;
On the bed of Lake Erie, commanded by Perry,

They caus'd many Britons to take their last sleep.

'Twas just at sunrise, and a glorious day,
Our squadron at anchor snug in Put-in-Bay;
When we saw the bold Britons, and cleared for about,
Instead of Put-in-Bay, by the Lord we put out.
Up went Union Jack, never up there before,
"Don't give up the ship," was the motto it bore;
And soon as that motto our gallant lads saw,
They thought of their Lawrence, and shouted, "Huzza!"

O then, 'twould have raised your hat three inches higher,
To see how we dash'd in among them like fire;
The *Lawrence* went first, and the rest as they could,
And a long time the brunt of the battle she stood.
'Twas peppering work—fire, fury, and smoke—
And groans, that from wounded lads spite of them broke;
The water grew red round our ship as she lay,
Tho' 'twas never before so till that bloody day.

They fell all around me, like spars in a gale;
The shot made a sieve of each rag of a sail;
And out of our crew scarce a dozen remained,—
But these gallant tars still the battle maintained.
'Twas then our Commander—God bless his young heart!—
Thought it best from his well-peppered ship to depart,
And bring up the rest, who were tugging behind,
For why? They were sadly in want of a wind.

Then to Yarnall [*sic*] he gave the command of the ship,
And set out like a lark on his desperate trip,
In a small open yawl, right through the whole fleet,
Who with many a broadside our cock-boat did greet.
I steer'd her—and damme [*sic*] if every inch
Of these timbers of mine at each crack didn't flinch;
But our tight little Commodore, cool and serene,
To still ne'er a muscle by any was seen.

Whole volleys of muskets were level'd at him,
But the devil a one ever graz'd e'en a limb,
Tho' he stood up erect in the stern of the boat,
Till the crew pulled him down by the skirts of his coat.
At length, thro' Heaven's mercy, we reach'd t'other ship,
And the wind springing up, we gave her the whip,

And ran down the line, boys, thro' thick and thro' thin,
And bother'd their ears with a horrible din.

Then starboard and larboard, and this way and that,
We bang'd 'em, and rak'd 'em, and laid their masts flat;
Till one after t'other they hauled down their flag,
And an end put for that time to Johnny Bull's brag.
The *Detroit*, and *Queen Charlotte*, and *Lady Prevost*,
Not able to fight or run, gave up the ghost;
And not one of them all from our grapplings got free,
Tho' we'd fifty-four guns, and they'd just sixty-three.

Now give us a bumper to Elliot [*sic*], and those
Who came up in good time to belabor our foes;
To our fresh-water sailors we'll toss off one more,
And a dozen at least to our young Commodore.
And tho' Britons may talk of their ruling the ocean,
And that sort of thing—by the Lord, I've a notion—
I'll bet all I'm worth,—Who takes it? Who takes?
Tho' they're lords of the seas, we'll be lords of the Lakes.

Columbia: the United States of America, usually personified as a female figure. **Mars:** the Roman god of war. **Union Jack:** Perry's battle flag, inscribed with the motto "Don't give up the ship!" **Lawrence:** James Lawrence (1781–1813), the U.S. naval officer whose command "Don't give up the ship!" became the motto of the U.S. navy. During the War of 1812 he was mortally wounded when his ship the *Chesapeake* was disabled and captured by the British vessel the *Shannon*. **Yarnall** [*sic*]: Lieutenant John J. Yarnell, the battery officer who was left in command of the *Lawrence* when Perry took command of the *Niagara*. During the battle Yarnell's nose was perforated by a splinter. **Johnny Bull:** England. **Elliot** [*sic*]: Jesse Duncan Elliott (1782–1845), the ranking officer under Perry during the battle of Lake Erie. Elliott's failure to bring the *Niagara* into close action to help Perry as the latter's flagship was being shot to pieces by the British led to a continuing controversy. As a result of the recriminations, Elliott challenged Perry to a duel. Elliott's paternal ancestors hailed from County Donegal, Ireland.

Perry's Victory
author unknown

Ye tars of Columbia, give ear to my story,
    Who fought with brave Perry where cannons did roar;
Your valor has gained you immortal glory,
    A fame that shall last until time is no more.
Columbian tars are the true sons of Mars,

They rake for and aft as they fight on the deep;
On the bed of Lake Erie, commanded by Perry,
     They caus'd many Britons to take their last sleep.

The tenth of September, let us all remember,
     So long as the globe on her axis rolls round;
Our tars and marines, on Lake Erie were seen,
     To make the proud flag of Great Britain come down.
The van of our fleet, the Britain to meet,
     Commanded by Perry, the *Lawrence* bore down;
Her guns they did roar, with such terrific power,
     That savages trembled at the dreadful sound.

The *Lawrence* sustain'd a most dreadful fire,
     She fought three to one, for two glasses or more;
While Perry undaunted did firmly stand by her,
     The proud foe on her heavy broad sides did pour.
Her masts being shatter'd, her rigging all tatter'd,
     Her booms and her yards being all shot away;
And few left on deck to manage the wreck,
     Our hero on board her no longer could stay.

In this situation, the pride of our nation,
     Sure heaven had guarded unhurt all the while;
While many a hero, maintaining his station,
     Fell close by his side, and was thrown on the pile.
But mark you and wonder, when elements thunder,
     When death and destruction are stalking all round;
His flag he did carry on board the *Niagara*,
     Such valor on record was never yet found.

There is one gallant act of our noble commander,
     While writing my song, I must notice
While launch'd in the smack, that carried the s[tandard?]
     A ball whistled through her, just close to his side.
Says Perry, "the rascals intend for to drown us,
     But push on, my brave boys, you need never fear!"
And with his own coat, he plugg'd up the boat,
     And through fire and sulphur away he did steer.

The fam'd *Niagara*, now proud of her Perry,
     Display'd all her banners in gallant array;
And twenty-five guns on her deck she did carry,
     Which soon put an end to this bloody affray,

The rear of our fleet was brought up complete,
    The signal was given to break through the line;
While starboard and larboard, and from every quarter,
    The lamps of Columbia did gloriously shine.

The bold British Lion, roar'd out his last thunder,
    When Perry attacked him close in the rear;
Columbia's eagle soon made him crouch under,
    And roar out for quarter, as soon you shall hear,
Oh, had you been there, I vow and declare,
    Such a sight as you never had seen before;
Red bloody flags that no longer could wag,
    Shall lay at the feet of our brave Commodore.

Brave Elliot, whose valor must now be recorded,
    On board the *Niagara* so well play'd his part;
A gallant assistance to Perry afforded,
    We'll place him the second on Lake Erie's chart.
In the midst of the battle, when guns they did rattle,
    The *Lawrence* a wreck, and the men most all slain,
Away he did steer and brought up the rear,
    And by this manoeuvre the victory was gain'd.

Oh! had you but seen those noble commanders,
    Embracing each other when the conflict was o'er;
And viewing all those invincible standards,
    That never had yielded to any before.
Says Perry, "Brave Elliot, come, give me your hand, sir,
    This day you have gained an immortal renown;
So long as Columbia, Lake Erie commands, sir,
    Let brave Captain Elliot with laurels be crown'd."

Great Britain may boast of her conquering heroes,
    Her Rodneys, her Nelsons, and all the whole crew;
But none in their glory have told such a story,
    Nor boasted such feats as Columbians do.
The whole British fleet was captured complete,
    Not one single vessel from us got away;
And prisoners some hundreds, Columbians wondered,
    To see them all anchor'd and moor'd in our bay.

May heaven still smile on the shades of our heroes,
    Who fought in that conflict their country to save,
And check the proud spirit of those murdering bravos,

> Who wish to divide us, and make us all slaves.
> Columbians sing, and make the woods ring,
> We'll toast these brave heroes by sea and by land;
> While Britons drink cherry, Columbians, Perry,
> We'll toast him about with full glass in hand.

Columbia: the United States of America, usually personified as a female figure. **Mars:** the Roman god of war. **two glasses:** two hour glasses (i.e., two hours). **smack:** a fishing vessel. **Elliot [sic]:** Jesse Duncan Elliott (1782–1845), the ranking officer under Perry during the battle of Lake Erie. Elliott's failure to bring the *Niagara* into close action to help Perry as the latter's flagship was being shot to pieces by the British led to a continuing controversy. As a result of the recriminations, Elliott challenged Perry to a duel. Elliott's paternal ancestors hailed from County Donegal, Ireland. **Rodneys . . . Nelsons:** references to British admirals on a par with George Rodney (1718–1792) and Horatio Nelson (1758–1805). During his naval career Rodney took part in the capture of Louisbourg, Nova Scotia; captured the islands of Martinique, St. Lucia, Grenada, and St. Eustatius; defeated the Spanish off Cape Finisterre and Cape St. Vincent; and defeated the French off Dominica. Nelson was celebrated for his victory over a Franco-Spanish squadron off Cape Trafalgar, Spain, in 1805. The British suffered 449 dead to the enemies' 4,400 fatalities. **Columbians:** Americans. (See "Columbia" above.)

Perry's Victory
author unknown

We sailed to and fro in Erie's broad lake,
To find British bullies or get into their wake,
When we hoisted our canvas with true Yankee speed,
And the brave Captain Perry our squadron did lead.

We sailed through the lake, boys, in search of the foe,
In the cause of Columbia our brav'ry to show,
To be equal in combat was all our delight,
As we wished the proud Britons to know we could fight.

And whether like Yeo, boys, they'd taken affright,
We could see not, nor find them by day or by night;
So cruising we went in a glorious cause,
In defence of our rights, our freedom, and laws.

At length to our liking, six sails hove in view,
Huzzah! says brave Perry, huzzah! says his crew,
And then for the chase, boys, with our brave little crew,
We fell in with the bullies and gave them "burgoo."

Though the force was unequal, determined to fight,
We brought them to action before it was night:
We let loose our thunder, our bullets did fly,
"Now give them your shot, boys," our commander did cry.

We gave them a broadside, our cannon to try,
"Well done," says brave Perry, "for quarter they'll cry,
Shot well home, my brave boys, they shortly shall see,
That quite brave as they are, still braver are we."

Then we drew up our squadron, each man full of fight,
And put the proud Britons in a terrible plight,
The brave Perry's movements will prove fully as bold,
As the fam'd Admiral Nelson's prowess of old.

The conflict was sharp, boys, each man to his gun,
For our country, her glory, the vict'ry was won,
So six sail (the whole fleet) was our fortune to take,
Here's a health to brave Perry, who governs the Lake.

Columbia: the United States of America. **Yeo:** Sir James Lucas Yeo (1782–1818), the British commodore whom Captain Isaac Chauncey defeated on Lake Ontario in May 1813. **burgoo:** a picnic at which a highly seasoned stew of the same name is served. **Admiral Nelson:** Horatio Nelson (1758–1805), the British admiral celebrated for his victory over a Franco-Spanish squadron off Cape Trafalgar, Spain, on October 21, 1805. The British suffered 449 dead to the enemies' 4,400 fatalities.

The Battle of Lake Erie

by Philip Freneau (1752–1832)

["]To clear the lake of Perry's fleet
And make his flag his winding sheet
This is my object—I repeat—"
    Said Barclay, flush'd with native pride,
To some who serve the british crown;—
But they, who dwell beyond the moon,
Heard this bold menace with a frown,
    Nor the rash sentence ratified.

Ambition so bewitch'd his mind,
And royal smiles had so combined
With skill, to act the part assign'd
    He for no contest cared, a straw;

The ocean was too narrow fare
To be the seat of naval war;
He wanted lakes, and room to spare,
    And all to yield to Britain's law.

And thus he made a sad mistake;
Forsooth he must possess the lake;
As merely made for England's sake
    To play her pranks and rule the coast;
Where she might govern, uncontrol'd,
An unmolested empire hold,
And keep a fleet to fish up gold,
    To pay the troops of George Provost [*sic*].

The ships approach'd, of either side,
And Erie, on his bosom wide
Beheld two hostile navies ride,
    Each for the combat well prepared;
The lake was smooth, the sky was clear,
The martial drum had banish'd fear,
And death and danger hover near,
    Though both were held in disregard.

From lofty heights their colors flew,
And Britain's standard all in view,
With frantic valor fired the crew
    That mann'd the guns of *Queen Charlotte*.
"And we must Perry's squadron take,
And England shall command the lake;—
And you must fight for Britain's sake,
    (Said Barclay) sailors, will you not?"

Assent they gave with heart and hand;
For never yet a braver band
To fight a ship, forsook the land,
    Than Barclay had on board that day;—
The guns were loosed the game to win,
Their muzzles gaped a dismal grin,
And out they pulled their tompion pin,
    The bloody game of war to play.

But Perry soon, with flowing sail,
Advanced, determined to prevail,

When from his bull-dogs flew the hail
   Directed full at *Queen Charlotte*.
His wadded guns were aim'd so true,
And such a weight of ball they threw,
As, Barclay said, he never knew
   To come, before, so scalding hot!

But still, to animate his men
From gun to gun the warrior ran
And blazed away and blazed again—
   Till Perry's ship was half a wreck;
They tore away both tack and sheet,—
Their victory might have been complete,
Had Perry not, to shun defeat
   In lucky moment left his deck.

Repairing to another post,
From another ship he fought their host
And soon regain'd the fortune lost,
   And down, his flag the briton tore;
With loss of arm and loss of blood
Indignant, on his decks he stood
To witness Erie's crimson flood
   For miles around him, stain'd with gore!

Thus, for dominion of the lake
These captains did each other rake,
And many a widow did they make;—
   Whose is the fault, or who to blame?—
The briton challenged with his sword,
The yankee took him at his word,
With spirit laid him close on board—
   They're ours—he said—and closed the game.

Barclay: Robert Barclay (1774–1811), the commander of the British squadron which was defeated by Commodore Perry at the battle of Lake Erie on September 10, 1813. **George Provost [*sic*]:** George Prevost, the British commander-in-chief during the 1812–1814 campaign.

The Victory of Perry
by Alice Cary (1820–1871)

Lift up the years! lift up the years,
   Whose shadows round us spread;
Let us tribute pay to the brave to-day
   Who are half a century dead.

Oh, not with tears—no, not with tears
   The grateful nation comes,
But with flags out-thrown, and bugles blown,
   And martial roll of drums!

Beat up! beat up! till memory glows
   And sets our hearts aflame!
Ah! they did well in the fight who fell,
   And we leave them to their fame;

Their fame, that larger, grander grows
   As time runs in to the past;
For the Erie-waves chant o'er their graves,
   And shall, while the world shall last.

O beautiful cities of the Lake,
   As ye sit by your peaceful shore,
Make glad and sing till the echoes ring,
   For our brave young Commodore!

He knew your stormy oaks to take
   And their ribs into ships contrive
And to set them so fine in battle line,
   With their timbers yet alive.

We see our squadron lie in the Bay,
   Where it lay so long ago,
And hear the cry from the mast-head high,
   Three times, and three, "Sail Ho!"

Through half a century to-day
   We hear the signal of fight—
"Get under way! Get under way—
   The enemy is in sight!"

Our hearts leap up, our pulses thrill,
    At the boatswains' pipes of joy;
So loudly play o'er the dash o' the spray,
    "All hands, up anchor—ahoy!"

Now all is still, aye, deadly still;
    The enemy's guns in view;
"To the royal fore," cries the Commodore
    And up run the lilies and blue!

And hark to the cry, the great glad cry,—
    All a-tremble the squadron stands,—
From lip to lip, "Don't give up the ship!"
    And then "To quarters, all hands!"

An hour, an awful hour drags by—
    There's a shot from the enemy's gun!
"More sail! More sail! Let the canister hail!"
    Cries Perry, and forward, as one,

Caledonia, Lawrence, and *Scorpion,* all
    Bear down and stand fast, till the flood
Away from their track sends the scared billows back
    With their faces bedabbled in blood.

The *Queen* and her allies their broadsides let fall—
    Oh, the *Lawrence* is riddled with storm!
Where is Perry? afloat! he is safe in his boat,
    And his battle-flag up in his arms!

The bullets they hiss and the Englishmen shout—
    Oh, the *Lawrence* is sinking, a wreck!
But with flag yet a-swing like a great bloody wing
    Perry treads the *Niagara's* deck!

With a wave of his hand he has wheeled her about—
    Oh, the nation is holding its breath!
Headforemost he goes in the midst of his foes
    And breaks them and rakes them to death!

And lo, the enemy, after the fray,
    On the deck that his dead have lined,
With his sword-hilt before to our Commodore,
    And his war-dogs in leash behind!

And well, the nation does well to-day,
   Setting her bugles to blow,
And her drums to beat for the glorious fleet
   That humbled her haughty foe.

Ah, well to come with autumn flowers,
   A tribute for the brave
Who died to make our Erie Lake
   Echo through every wave—

"We've met the enemy and they're ours!"
   And who died, that we might stand
A country free, and mistress at sea
   As well as on the land.

On the Death of Commodore Oliver H. Perry
by John G. C. Brainard (1796–1828)

By strangers honor'd, and by strangers mourn'd.

How sad the note of that funereal drum,
   That's muffled by indifference to the dead!
And how reluctantly the echoes come,
   On air that sighs not o'er that stranger's bed,
   Who sleeps with death alone. O'er his young head
His native breezes never more shall sigh;
   On his lone grave the careless step shall tread,
And pestilential vapors soon shall dry
Each shrub that buds around—each flow'r that blushes nigh.

Let Genius, poising on her full-fledg'd wing,
   Fill the charm'd air with thy deservèd praise!
Of war, and blood, and carnage let her sing,
   Of victory and glory!—let her gaze
   On the dark smoke that shrouds the cannon's blaze,
On the red foam that crests the bloody billow;
   Then mourns the sad close of thy shorten'd days—
Place on thy country's brow the weeping willow,
And plant the laurels thick around thy last cold pillow.

No sparks of Grecian fire to me belong:
   Alike the uncouth poet and the lay;

Unskill'd to turn the mighty tide of song,
    He floats along the current as he may,
    The humble tribute of a tear to pay.
Another hand may choose another theme,
    May sing Nelson's last and brightest day,
Of Wolfe's unequall'd and unrivall'd fame,
The waves of Trafalgar—the fields of Abraham:

But if the wild winds of thy western lake
    Might teach a harp that fain would mourn the brave,
And sweep those strings the minstrel may not wake,
    Or give an echo from some secret cave
    That opens on romantic Erie's wave,
The feeble cord would not be swept in vain;
    And though the sound might never reach thy grave,
Yet there are spirits here that to the strain
Would send a still small voice responsive back again.

Nelson: Horatio Nelson (1758–1805), the British admiral who defeated a Franco-Spanish squadron off Cape Trafalgar, Spain, on October 21, 1805. The British suffered 449 dead to the enemies' 4,400 fatalities. **Wolfe:** James Wolfe (1727–1759), the British general who defeated the French in Quebec in 1759. **Trafalgar:** Cape Trafalgar, Spain. (See "Nelson" above.) **fields of Abraham:** also Plains of Abraham, a high plain adjoining the city of Quebec, Canada, where the British defeated the French in 1759.

21. John O'Neil

John O'Neil, who was born in Ireland in 1769, came to America at the age of eighteen. After serving under General Henry Lee in crushing the Whiskey Rebellion in western Pennsylvania, he enlisted in the American navy against the French. He operated a nail manufactory in Havre de Grace, Maryland, until that enterprise was destroyed when the British burned the town in May 1813.

In anticipation of the British attack, about 250 American militiamen gathered to defend the battery near the present lighthouse in Havre de Grace. When between fifteen and twenty British barges made their approach to Point Comfort, they were met with gunfire from the American position. The enemy replied with grapeshot and rockets that set fire to the town. As British landing forces advanced to seize the battery, all the militiamen but two — John O'Neil and Philip Albert — abandoned their posts. When Albert was wounded, O'Neil manned the largest gun alone, until its recoil injured his thigh. The Irishman was soon captured and spirited aboard the British frigate *Maidstone*. But when the American brigadier general Henry Miller threatened to execute two British subjects in retaliation, O'Neil was released on parole. For his valor, he was named lighthouse keeper in Havre de Grace.

The Ballad of John O'Neil of Havre de Grace
by A. M. Sullivan (1896–1980)

Fighters ashore were few in deed
When the War of 1812 began:
New England sulked for her waning trade
Caught in the British and French blockade
And William Hull in the Malden raid
Quit without the loss of a man.

But Isaac Hull absolved the name
When he conquered the frigate, *Guerriere*
With Dacres as skipper his foe and friend
With the *Constitution* to defend
And the right of sea search at an end
And the foe his pleasant prisoner.

John Randolph warned "The gates are open,
Machias south to the Chesapeake
And our fences down as fools go forth

To fight the foemen in the north
Without a man of tested worth
To share his valor with the meek."

And while the warning word was scorned
The British probed the pulsing heart
Of Yankee land and the swinging door
To Washington and Baltimore
And sent four vipered men-of-war
Hissing with many a poisoned dart.

George Cockburn wore a rakish crown
From Old Point Comfort to Craney's Isle
Where the Susquehanna meets the Bay.
Sir George, the knight[,] was blithe and gay
Or rude and ruthless as pleased the day
Strutting the bridge with despot's guile.

[']Twas May the second when John O'Neil
Of Havre de Grace woke in alarm
And from his pinking window spied
The British Lion in his pride.
Fifteen barges scraped their hide
Upon the beach and spilled a swarm

Of eighteen hundred men in red
As Cockburn's chanticleering gun
Swiveled toward redoubts on the hill.
The foemen tossed their bombs until
The shore militia lost its will
To meet invaders, and chose to run,

That is, all ran, excepting two
John O'Neil, and Albert his aide,
(Bowled over as the cowards scampered
Out of redoubt and over the rampart
Allowing the foe to climb unhampered
Amid the howitzer's loud tirade.)

Cockburn sprayed the mound with grape
As two men propped the cannon's wheel
And one man rammed the cannon's throat
And turned it toward the beast afloat

Spitting flame across the moat
And the glinting of British steel.

The gun rolled back, and Albert fell
And now O'Neil stood up alone,
Charged his cannon, and fired again
With anger bursting in the den
Of the lordly lion; alack, and then
The gun rolled back. O'Neil was prone.

He who dodged the Cockburn rockets
Was hors' de combat when the wheel
Of the 9-inch cannon crushed his leg
But he was not the man to beg
For mercy by a powder keg
But hobbled from the yeoman's steel,

Holding his musket and crying, "Shame,
Come back, faint-hearted and save our town[."]
But sons of the men who fought and won
At the summons of George Washington,
Ran in terror. There were none
But the cripples left to tilt the Crown
Symboled by Cockburn's cap and braid.
He gloried in a fiery name
As he put the torch to the Capital
While timid soldiers spurned the call
To meet invaders, stand or fall
With honor in a bloody game.

Too young to fight in Seventy-six
But never too old to face the foe
When Cockburn sailed the Chesapeake
And ravaged the inlet, marsh and creek,
O'Neil was a warrior who would speak
With tongue of flame, and blow for blow.

Albert escaped. O'Neil was taken
Limping alone in the empty street,
By a sworded centaur who climbed the marge
From the silted waters beside the barge
Seeking the Yankee foe at large,
But there was only one to greet,

And he was O'Neil, the Irishman,
Who took command at the Battery
When Cockburn charged. John won the praise
Of the horseman staring in sheer amaze
And as a captive, spent three days
On the *Maidstone* with due charity.

When John O'Neil wrote to a friend
Of "my defeat" where the Bay began
At Craney's Isle by a larger foe,
He said that Cockburn didn't know
His prisoner came long years ago
From an Ulster town on the river Bann,

Or he might have swung from a *Maidstone* yard
Instead of feeling Sir George's hand
On his shoulder with a generous word
Or living to sheathe an honored sword
Or manning the lighthouse as reward,
Had he said, "I was born in Ireland."

William Hull: the American general (1773–1843) who was court-martialed for surrendering Detroit to the British without firing a shot. Hull had earlier crossed into Canada with the intention of attacking Fort Malden. When his delay allowed the British to reinforce the fort, he returned to Detroit, which he surrendered on August 15, 1812. **Isaac Hull:** the American naval officer (1773–1843) who, as captain of the *Constitution*, defeated the British frigate *Guerrière* during the War of 1812. **Dacres:** James Dacres, captain of the British frigate *Guerrière* during its encounter with the *Constitution*. **John Randolph:** a Virginia statesman (1773–1833) and an outspoken champion of states' rights and an opponent of the War of 1812. **Machias:** a town on the coast of Maine. **George Cockburn:** the British rear admiral (1772–1853) whose fleet helped British military forces capture Washington, D.C., in August 1814. **Old Point Comfort:** a site on a small peninsula on the north side of the entrance to Hampton Roads, Virginia. **Craney's Isle:** actually Craney Island, a small island in the Elizabeth River just west of Norfolk, Virginia. **Susquehanna:** a river flowing south from central New York through eastern Pennsylvania and northeast Maryland into Chesapeake Bay. **chanticleering:** an unusual adjectival form of the word "chanticleer" (rooster), used here in its original French meaning ("singing out clearly"). **hors' de combat:** a French idiom meaning "disabled or out of action." **Ulster town on the river Bann:** perhaps Coleraine, a town in northern Ireland. Sullivan places O'Neil's birthplace in Ulster because that province in northern Ireland was the traditional stronghold of the O'Neills.

22. Robert Ross

Toward the end of the War of 1812, Major General Robert Ross, whose maternal great-grandfather was from County Cork, Ireland, led a British infantry brigade against the coast of the United States. The force, about 4,500 men by the time it arrived in Chesapeake Bay, was launched in retaliation for the burning of York (now Toronto) by American soldiers. On August 24, 1814, Ross's troops marched on Washington, D.C., by way of Bladensburg, Maryland, where they found an American force of about 6,500 men. After three hours of fighting, the Americans broke ranks and fled, but not before killing 250 British.

Emboldened by the American retreat, Ross and his men proceeded to Washington. During the night of September 24–25, they torched the Capitol and its library, the treasury building, and the executive mansion. Ross later said that he regretted burning the library and would not have set the presidential mansion on fire if the first lady (Dolly Madison) had not fled the building. ("I make war neither against letters nor ladies," he said.)

After returning unopposed to his ships, the British general set his sights on Baltimore. With a reduced force of less than 4,000 men, Ross marched a dozen miles to the city, where 6,000 militia had taken their stand. He was killed when a bullet passed through his right arm into his breast. Although the militia were routed, the British gave up the attack when their naval forces were unable to provide cover. Ross's body was transported to Halifax, Nova Scotia, and was buried in that city.

The Battle of Baltimore

author unknown

Old Ross, Cockburn, and Cochrane too,
    And many a bloody villain more,
Swore with their bloody savage crew,
    That they would plunder Baltimore.
But General Winder being afraid
    That his militia would not stand,
He sent away to crave the aid
    Of a few true Virginians.
        Then up we rose with hearts elate.
        To help our suffering sister state.

When first our orders we received,
    For to prepare without delay,
Our wives and sweethearts for to leave,

And to the army march away
Although it grieved our hearts full sore,
    To leave our sweet Virginia shore,
We kiss'd our sweethearts o'er and o'er
    And marched like true Virginians.
            Adieu awhile, sweet girls, adieu,
            With honor we'll return to you.

With rapid marches on we went,
    To leave our sweet Virginia shore,
No halt was made, no time was spent,
    Till we arrived at Baltimore.
The Baltimoreans did us greet,
    The ladies clapt their lily-white hands,
Exclaiming as we passed the street,
    "Welcome, ye brave Virginians.
    May Heaven all your foes confound,
    And send you home with laurels crown'd."

We had not been in quarters long,
    Before we heard the dread alarms,
The cannon roar'd, the bells did ring,
    The drum did beat to arms.
Then up we rose to face our foes,
    Determined to meet them on the strand,
And drive them back from fair Freedom's shore,
    Or die like brave Virginians.
            In Heaven above we place our trust,
            Well knowing that our cause is just.

Then Ross he landed at North Point,
    With seven thousand men or more,
And swore by that time next night,
    That he would be in Baltimore.
But Striker [*sic*] met him on the strand,
    Attended by a chosen band,
Where he received a fatal shot
    From a brave Pennsylvanian—
            Whom Heaven directed to the field,
            To make this haughty Briton yield.

Then Cockburn he drew up his fleet,
    To bombard Fort McHenry,
A thinking that our men, of course,

Would take affright and run away.
The fort was commanded by a patriotic band,
     As ever graced fair Freedom's land,
And he who did the fort command
     Was a true blue Virginian.
               Long may we have brave Armstead's [*sic*] name
               Recorded on the book of fame.

A day and a night they tried their might,
     But found their bombs did not prevail,
And seeing their army put to flight,
     They weigh'd their anchor and made sail,
Resolving to return again,
     To execute their former plan;
But if they do, they'll find us still
     That we are brave Virginians.
               And they shall know before they've done
               That they are not in Washington.

But now their shipping's out of sight,
     And each man takes a parting glass,
Drinks to his true love and heart's delight,
     His only joy and bosom friend,
For I might as well drink a health,
     For I hate to see good liquor stand,
That America may always boast
     That we are brave Virginians.

Cockburn: George Cockburn (1772–1853), the British rear admiral whose fleet helped the British military capture Washington, D.C., in August 1814. **Cochrane:** Alexander Cochrane (1758–1832), the British admiral who directed the unsuccessful British attempts to capture Baltimore and New Orleans during the War of 1812. **General Winder:** William Winder (1775–1824), the American adjutant general whose undisciplined militia retreated in the face of the British invasion of Washington, D.C., in August 1814. **seven thousand men:** actually more like 4,000. **Striker [*sic*]:** Brigadier General John Stricker, who led a force of 3,185 Americans to check the landing of the British near Baltimore. In the ensuing engagement the Americans lost 163 killed or wounded; the invaders suffered more than 300 casualties. **Where he received a fatal shot / From a brave Pennsylvanian:** General Ross was killed by either David Wells or Henry McComas. **Fort McHenry:** the fortification in Baltimore Harbor, named for James McHenry, a native of County Antrim, Ireland, and President Washington's secretary of war when construction was begun in 1798. **Armstead [*sic*]:** Major George Armistead, the commander of Fort McHenry during its bombardment by the British on September 12, 1813.

23. Thomas Macdonough

Thomas Macdonough was born in Delaware in 1783, the grandson of an emigrant who had left Ireland about fifty years earlier. The future naval hero served under Stephen Decatur against the pirates of Tripoli, but in 1810 he was seized by a British press gang and was forced aboard a frigate. The enterprising sailor escaped by disguising himself in the clothes of a British tar. At the time, he promised himself: "If I live through this I'll make England remember the day she impressed an American sailor!"

Soon after war broke out between Britain and the United States in 1812, Macdonough took command of the American fleet on Lake Champlain in upstate New York. By the spring of 1814 he had put together a fleet of thirteen ships (including the *Saratoga* and the *Eagle*), with eighty-six guns and 882 men. To counter the Americans, the British spent the summer building additional ships of their own, until they commanded a squadron of sixteen sail, ninety-two guns, and 937 men. When the fateful engagement finally occurred on September 11 off Plattsburgh, New York, the battle at first raged indecisively until Macdonough positioned his ships so that they could fire both broadsides into the British. (Tradition maintains that a rooster aboard Macdonough's flagship crowed during most of the battle. The cock's alleged good luck popularized the use of the bird's image on local weather vanes.) By the time the British surrendered they had lost eighty-four killed and 110 wounded, while the American loss amounted to fifty-two killed and fifty-eight wounded. Macdonough's victory frustrated Britain's attempt to control the Great Lakes and forced the enemy's army to retreat into Canada. As a result, Great Britain could press no claim upon American territory at the peace negotiations ending the war.

The Battle of Lake Champlain
by Philip Freneau (1752–1832)

Parading near Saint Peter's flood
Full fourteen thousand soldiers stood;
Allied with natives of the wood,
With frigates, sloops, and galleys near;
Which southward, now, began to steer;
    Their object was, Ticonderogue.

Assembled at Missisqui bay
A feast they held, to hail the day,
When all should bend to British sway
    From Plattsburgh to Ticonderogue.

And who could tell, if reaching there
They might not other laurels share
And England's flag in triumph bear
    To the capitol, at Albany!

Sir George advanced, with fire and sword,
The frigates were with vengeance stored,
The strength of Mars was felt on board,—
When Downie gave the dreadful word,
    Huzza! for death or victory!

Sir George beheld the prize at stake,
And, with his veterans, made the attack,
Macomb's brave legions drove him back;
And England's fleet approached, to meet
    A desperate combat on the lake.

From Isle La Motte to Saranac
With sulphurous clouds the heavens were black;
We saw advance the *Confiance*,
Shall blood and carnage mark her track,
    To gain dominion on the lake.

Then on our ships she poured her flame,
And many a tar did kill or maim,
Who suffered for their country's fame,
    Her soil to save, her rights to guard.

Macdonough, now, began his play,
And soon his seamen heard him say,
"No *Saratoga* yields, this day,
    To all the force that Britain sends.

"Disperse, my lads, and man the waist,
Be firm, and to your stations haste,
And England from Champlain is chased,
    If you behave as you see me."

The fire began with awful roar;
At first flash the artillery tore,
From his proud stand, their commodore,
    A presage of the victory.

The skies were hid in flame and smoke,

Such thunders from the cannon spoke,
The contest such an aspect took
    As if all nature went to wreck!

Amidst his decks, with slaughter strewed,
Unmoved, the brave Macdonough stood,
Or waded through a scene of blood,
    At every step that round him streamed:

He stood amidst Columbia's sons,
He stood amidst dismounted guns,
He fought amidst heart-rending groans,
    The tattered sail, the tottering mast.

Then, round about, his ship he wore,
And charged his guns with vengeance sore,
And more than Etna shook the shore—
    The foe confessed the contest vain.

In vain they fought, in vain they sailed,
That day; for Britain's fortune failed,
And their best efforts naught availed
    To hold dominion on Champlain.

So, down their colors to the deck
The vanquished struck—their ships a wreck—
What dismal tidings for Quebec,
    What news for England and her prince!

For, in this fleet, from England won,
A favorite project is undone;
Her sorrows only are begun—
And she may want, and very soon,
    Her armies for her own defence.

Saint Peter's flood: possibly St. Peter Lake, an expansion of the St. Lawrence River, extending thirty miles from Sorrel to Trois Riviéres, Quebec. **Ticonderogue:** Fort Ticonderoga on Lake Champlain. **Missisqui bay:** a body of water between Quebec and Vermont at the extreme northern end of Lake Champlain. **Sir George:** George Downie, the commander of the British fleet during the battle of Lake Champlain. He was killed during the action. **Mars:** the Roman god of war. **Macomb:** General Alexander Macomb (1782–1841), the commander of the American land forces at the battle of Lake Champlain on September 11, 1814. His army of about 1,500 regulars and some detachments of militia sent 15,000 British redcoats back into Canada. **Isle La Motte:** an island at the northern end of Lake Champlain, fifteen miles north of Plattsburgh, New York. **Saranac:** the Saranac River, which flows into Lake Champlain near Plattsburgh, New York. **Columbia:** the United States of America, usually personified as a female figure. **Etna:** Mount Etna, an active volcano in Sicily.

The Battle of Plattsburg[h] Bay
by Clinton Scollard (1860–1932)

Plattsburg[h] Bay! Plattsburg[h] Bay!
Blue and gold in the dawning ray,
Crimson under the high noonday
With the reek of the fray!

It was Thomas Macdonough, as gallant a sailor
    As ever went scurrying over the main;
And he cried from his deck, *If they think I'm a quailer,*
    And deem they can capture this Lake of Champlain,
    We'll show them they're not fighting France, sir, nor Spain!

So from Cumberland Head to the little Crab Island
    He scattered his squadron in trim battle-line;
And when he saw Downie come rounding the highland,
    He knelt him, beseeching for guidance divine,
    Imploring that Heaven would crown his design.

Then thundered the *Eagle* her lusty defiance;
    The stout *Saratoga* aroused with a roar;
Soon gunboat and galley in hearty alliance
    Their resonant volley of compliments pour;
    And ever Macdonough's the man to the fore!

And lo, when the fight toward its fiercest was swirling,
    A game-cock, released by a splintering ball,
Flew high in the ratlines, the smoke round him curling,
    And over the din gave his trumpeting call,
    An omen of ultimate triumph to all!

Then a valianter light touched the powder-grimed faces;
    Then faster the shot seemed to plunge from the gun;
And we shattered their yards and we sundered their braces,
    And the fume of our cannon—it shrouded the sun;
    Cried Macdonough—*Once more, and the battle is won!*

Now, the flag of the haughty *Confiance* is trailing;
    The *Linnet* in woe staggers in toward the shore;
The *Finch* is a wreck from her keel to her railing;
    The galleys flee fast to the strain of the oar;
    Macdonough! 't is he is the man to the fore!

Oh, our main decks were grim and our gun decks were gory,
    And many a brave brow was pallid with pain;
And while some won to death, yet we all won to glory
    Who fought with Macdonough that day on Champlain,
    And humbled her pride who is queen of the main!

Cumberland Head: Cumberland Bay, an inlet on the western shore of Lake Champlain just northeast of Plattsburgh, New York, where the battle of Lake Champlain was fought. **Downie:** George Downie, the commander of the British fleet during the battle of Lake Champlain. He was killed during the action. *Confiance, Linnet, Finch:* British ships. **queen of the main:** Britain.

The Blue Hen's Chickens
by Arthur Guiterman (1871–1943)

Sou'-sou'east of the Woods of Penn
Lies the Nest of the Old Blue Hen—
The garden spot beyond compare
Known as the State of Delaware.
Dutchman, Yankee, Finn, and Swede
Filled the land with a stalwart breed,
Cleared the forest, sowed the maize,
Back in the old Colonial days;
Then, in "the times that tried men's souls,"
Put their names on the muster-rolls
And marched away with courage stout
To drive King George's Redcoats out.

North with the Delaware Regiment
Captain Jonathan Caldwell went,
Taking along to amuse his men,
Sundry chicks of an Old Blue Hen.—
Yes, they had their minor crimes;
Men "fought cocks" in those wicked times,
And the best-plucked birds from the Gulf to Maine
Were the fighting cocks of the Old Blue strain;
And like those birds, the books declare,

Were the men who marched from the Delaware;
For fight they could, and fight like the dickens,—
So the Army called them "The Blue Hen Chickens!

* * * * * * * * *

Once again was the land at grips
With mad King George's troops and ships:
Macdonough sailed on Lake Champlain—
A fighting cock of the Old Blue strain.
His fleet, new-built of lakeside pine
And oak, he ranged in battle line
Where Plattsburg[h]'s headland rears its crag;
The *Saratoga* bore his flag.
The foe came down; the fight was hot;
Port and starboard crashed the shot;
Heavy broadsides, stroke on stroke,
Battered the Flagship's walls of oak,—

When,—a bolt from a British sloop
Broke the bars of the chicken coop!
Forth upon the blood-stained deck
Strutted a Bird with arching neck.
Up he flew to the splintering spars
Under the Flag of Fifteen Stars
And crowed and crowed and crowed again,
For he was a Cock of the Old Blue Hen!
And the grimy sailors down below
Laughed and cheered to hear him crow,
And kept the rapid guns aflame
Till down the British ensign came!

* * * * * * * * *

Bravely flung to the autumn breeze
Floats the Flag on the lakes and seas
From bending masts and dipping spars,
And two score–eight are its Clustered Stars.
Two score–eight, in their silver sheen,
Cluster the tars that were once Thirteen;
And there's Peace in the East, Peace in the West,
From the Golden Gate to the Blue Hen's Nest
There is Peace. And the Peace that ye hold so dear
Was won by men who laughed at Fear;
So may we have, in time of need,
More fighting Cocks of the Blue Hen's breed!

Woods of Penn: Pennsylvania. **Nest of the Old Blue Hen:** Delaware, whose best fighting men were known from Revolutionary days as "The Blue Hen's Chickens." **"the times that tried men's souls":** the Revolutionary War period. The words are a close parallel to a line from Thomas Paine's pamphlet *Common Sense*. **King George's Redcoats:** British soldiers of King George III. **Captain Jonathan Caldwell:** the officer whose company in the First Delaware Regiment took with them certain game chickens — of a brood of blue hens from Kent County — known for their fighting qualities. **A fighting cock of the Old Blue strain:** Macdonough, who, like the fighting men known as the "The Blue Hen's Chickens," hailed from Delaware. **Flag of Fifteen Stars:** the American flag, which at the time of the battle had fifteen stars. **two score–eight are its Clustered Stars:** the American flag, which between 1912 and 1959 had forty-eight stars. **Golden Gate:** a strait between San Francisco and the Pacific Ocean.

Sea and Land Victories

author unknown

With half the Western world at stake,
See Perry on the midland lake,
    The unequal combat dare;
Unawed by vastly stronger pow'rs,
He met the foe and made him ours,
    And closed the savage war.

Macdonough, too, on Lake Champlain,
In ships outnumbered, guns, and men,
    Saw dangers thick increase;
His trust in God and virtue's cause
He conquer'd in the lion's jaws,
    And led the way to peace.

To sing each valiant hero's name
Whose deeds have swelled the files of fame,
    Requires immortal powers;
Columbia's warriors never yield
To equal force by sea or field,
    Her eagle never cowers.

Long as Niagara's cataract roars
Or Erie laves our Northern shores,
    Great Brown, thy fame shall rise;
Outnumber'd by a veteran host
Of conquering heroes, Britain's boast—
    Conquest was there thy prize.

At Plattsburg[h], see the Spartan band,
Where gallant Macomb held command,
  The unequal host oppose;
Provost [*sic*] confounded, vanquished flies,
Convinced that numbers won't suffice
  Where Freeman are the foes.

Our songs to noblest strains we'll raise
While we attempt thy matchless praise,
  Carolina's godlike son;
While Mississippi rolls his flood,
Or Freemen hearts move patriots' blood,
  The palm shall be thine own.

At Orleans—lo! a savage band,
In countless numbers gain the strand,
  "Beauty and spoil" the word—
There Jackson with his fearless few,
The invincibles by thousands slew,
  And dire destruction poured.

O Britain! when the tale is told
Of Jackson's deeds by fame enrolled,
  Should grief and madness rise,
Remember God, the avenger, reigns,
Who witnesses Havre's smoking plains,
  And Hampton's female cries.

Perry: Oliver H. Perry (1785–1819), the American naval officer whose victory over a British fleet on Lake Erie in 1813 made possible a successful invasion of Canada that effectively ended the War of 1812 in the Northwest. **midland lake:** Lake Erie. **Columbia:** the United States of America, usually personified as a female figure. **Niagara's cataract:** the falls of the Niagara River, between western New York and Ontario, Canada. **Erie:** Lake Erie. **Great Brown:** Jacob Brown (1775–1828), the American brigadier general who in July 1814 led his army across the Niagara River and around the end of Lake Ontario in a campaign that ended in the British surrender of Fort Erie. The next month Brown successfully repulsed the enemy's attempts to retake the fort. **Plattsburg[h]:** the scene of the battle of Lake Champlain on September 11, 1814. **Spartan band:** an allusion to the 300 Spartans who gave their lives in defense of Thermopylae against the Persian invasion of Greece in 480 B.C. **Macomb:** General Alexander Macomb (1782–1841), the commander of the American land forces at the battle of Lake Champlain on September 11, 1814. His army of about 1,500 regulars and some detachments of militia sent 15,000 British redcoats back into Canada. **Provost [*sic*]:** George Prevost, the British commander-in-chief during the 1812–1814 campaign. His indecisiveness caused him to order retreats at Sackett's Harbor (on Lake Ontario) and at Plattsburgh (on Lake Champlain). **Carolina's godlike son:** Andrew Jackson. **Orleans:** the battle of New Orleans, an American victory against the British on January 8, 1815. **Jackson:** Andrew Jackson (1767–1845), the victor of the battle of New Orleans. **Havre's smoking plains:** an illusion to the British attack on Havre de Grace, Maryland, in May 1813. **Hampton's female cries:** an allusion to the British attack on Hampton, Virginia, during the War of 1812.

24. Charles Stewart

The son of a native of Belfast, Ireland, Charles Stewart (1778–1869) was born in Philadelphia and joined the merchant marine at the age of thirteen. By the turn of the century he was an officer in the U.S. navy and saw action against the pirates of Tripoli. Assigned as captain of the *Constitution* in 1813, he broke through the British blockade of Boston harbor and put out to sea. On February 20, 1815, the *Constitution* forced the surrender of the British vessels *Cyane* and *Levant* near Madeira, losing only four killed and ten wounded while the enemy suffered seventy-seven casualties.

After the surrender the two British captains blamed each other for their defeat and insisted that the outcome would have been different if they had executed different tactics. "Gentlemen," interrupted Stewart, "there is no use getting warm about it; it would have been all the same whatever you might have done. If you doubt that, I will put you all on board again and you can try it over."

During his subsequent naval career, Stewart commanded the Mediterranean fleet and the Pacific squadron and commanded the Philadelphia navy yard. Stewart's daughter, Delia, married the Irishman Charles Henry Parnell and was the mother of Charles Stewart Parnell, the champion of Irish home rule at the end of the nineteenth century.

The *Constitution*'s Last Fight
by James Jeffrey Roche (1847–1908)

A Yankee ship and a Yankee crew—
　　Constitution, where ye bound for?
Wherever, my lad, there's fight to be had
　　Acrost the Western ocean.

Our captain was married in Boston town
    And sailed next day to sea;
For all must go when the State says so;
    Blow high, blow low, sailed we.

"Now, what shall I bring for a bridal gift
    When my home-bound pennant flies?
The rarest that be on land or sea
    It shall be my lady's prize."

"There's never a prize on sea or land
    Could bring such joy to me
As my true love sound and homeward bound
    With a king's ship under his lee.

The Western ocean is wide and deep,
    And wild its tempests blow,
But bravely rides "Old Ironsides,"
    A-cruising to and fro.

We cruised to the east and we cruised to north,
    And southing far went we,
And at last off Cape de Verd we raised
    Two frigates sailing free.

Oh, God made man, and man made ships,
    But God makes very few
Like him who sailed our ship that day,
    And fought her, one to two.

He gained the weather-gage of both,
    He held them both a-lee;
And gun for gun, till set of sun,
    He spoke them fair and free;

Till the night-fog fell on spar and sail,
    And ship, and sea, and shore,
And our only aim was the bursting flame
    And the hidden cannon's roar.

Then a long rift in the mist showed up
    The stout *Cyane*, close-hauled
To swing in our wake and our quarter rake,

And a boasting Briton bawled:

"Starboard and larboard, we've got him fast
    Where his heels won't take him through;
Let him luff or wear, he'll find us there,—
    Ho, Yankee, which will you do?"

We did not luff and we did not wear,
    But braced our topsails back,
Till the sternway drew us fair and true
    Broadsides athwart her track.

Athwart her track and across her bows
    We raked her fore and aft,
And out of the fight and into the night
    Drifted the beaten craft.

The slow *Levant* came up too late;
    No need had we to stir;
Her decks we swept with fire, and kept
    The flies from troubling her.

We raked her again, and her flag came down,—
    The haughtiest flag that floats,—
And the lime-juice dogs lay there like logs,
    With never a bark in their throats.

With never a bark and never a bite,
    But only an oath to break,
As we squared away for Praya [sic] Bay
    With our prizes in our wake.

Parole they gave and parole they broke,
    What matters the cowardly cheat,
If the captain's bride was satisfied
    With the one prize laid at her feet?

A Yankee ship and a Yankee crew—
    Constitution, where ye bound for?
Wherever the British prizes be,
Though it's one to two, or one to three,—
"Old Ironsides" means victory,
    Across the Western ocean.

our captain: Charles Stewart. **"Old Ironsides":** the nickname given the *Constitution* after its encounter with the British ship *Guerrière* on August 19, 1812. Though the British ship was reduced to a wreck, the *Constitution* sustained so little damage to her hull that she was ever afterwards known as "Old Ironsides." **Cape de Verd:** also Cape Verde, a group of islands in the Atlantic, west of Senegal in West Africa. **lime-juice dogs:** British sailors, so called from the fact that lime juice was included in their rations as a way to protect them from scurvy. **Praya [*sic*] Bay:** Praia Bay, on Santo Tiago, one of the Cape Verde Islands, off the west coast of Africa. **With the one prize laid at her feet:** Stewart succeeded in getting only one of his prizes, the *Cyane*, to America; the other, the *Levant*, sought refuge in the neutral harbor of Port Praia.

The Old Admiral

by Edmund Clarence Stedman (1833-1908)

Gone at last,
    That brave old hero of the Past!
His spirit has a second birth,
    An unknown, grander life;—
All of him that was earth
    Lies mute and cold,
    Like a wrinkled sheath and old
Thrown off for ever from the shimmering blade
That has good entrance made
    Upon some distant, glorious strife.

From another generation,
    A simpler age, to our *Old Ironsides* came;
The morn and noontide of the nation
    Alike he knew, nor yet outlived his fame,—
    Oh, not outlived his fame!
The dauntless men whose service guards our shore
    Lengthen still their glory-roll
    With his name to lead the scroll,
As a flag-ship at her fore
    Carries the Union, with its azure and the stars,
Symbol of times that are no more
    And the old heroic wars.

He was the one
Whom Death had spared alone
    Of all the captains of that lusty age,
Who sought the foeman where he lay.

On sea or sheltering bay,
      Nor till the prize was theirs repressed their rage.
They are gone,—all gone;
      They rest with glory and the undying Powers;
      Only their name and fame and what they saved are ours!

It was fifty years ago,
      Upon the Gallic Sea,
      He bore the banner of the free,
And fought the fight whereof our children know.
      The deathful, desperate fight!—
      Under the fair moon's light
The frigate squared and yawed to left and right,
      Every broadside swept to death a score!
Roundly played her guns and well, till their fiery ensigns fell,
      Neither foe replying more.

All in silence, when the night-breeze cleared the air,
      Old Ironsides rested there,
Locked in between the twain, and drenched with blood,
      Then homeward, like an eagle with her prey!
      Oh, it was a gallant fray,
      That fight in Biscay Bay!
Fearless the Captain stood, in his youthful hardihood;
      He was the boldest of them all,
      Our brave old Admiral!

And still our heroes bleed,
Taught by that golden deed.
      Whether of iron or of oak
The ships we marshall at our country's need,
      Still speak their cannon now as then they spoke;
Still floats our unstruck banner from the mast
As in the story Past.

Lay him on the ground:
      Let him rest where the ancient river rolls;
Let him sleep beneath the shadow and the sound
      Of the bell, whose proclamation, as it tolls,
Is of Freedom and the gift our father's [sic] gave,
      Lay him gently down:
      The clamor of the town
Will not break the slumbers deep, the beautiful ripe sleep
      Of this lion of the wave,

Will not trouble the old Admiral in his grave.

Earth to earth his dust is laid.
Methinks his stately shade
    On the shadow of a great ship leaves the shore;
Over cloudless western seas
Seeks the far Hesperides,
    The islands of the blest,
Where no turbulent billows roar,—
    Where is rest.
His ghost upon the shadowy quarter stands
Nearing the deathless lands.
    There all his martial mates, renewed and strong,
    Await his coming long.
    I see the happy Heroes rise
    With gratulation in their eyes:
"Welcome, old comrade," Lawrence cries;
"Ah, Stewart, tell us of the war!
Who win the glory and the scars?
    How floats the skyey flag—how many stars?
Still speak they of Decatur's name,
Of Bainbridge's and Perry's fame?
Of me, who earliest came?
    Make ready, all:
    Room for the Admiral!
Come, Stewart, tell us of the wars!"

Gallic Sea: probably Biscay Bay. (See next entry.) **Biscay Bay:** a bay in the Atlantic Ocean between western France and northern Spain. **Hesperides:** also Islands of the Blessed, in classical mythology islands at the farthest end of the Atlantic Ocean to which the souls of heroes were believed to be transported after death. **Lawrence:** James Lawrence (1781–1813), the U.S. naval officer whose command "Don't give up the ship!" became the motto of the U.S. navy. During the War of 1812 he was mortally wounded when his ship the *Chesapeake* was disabled and captured by the British vessel the *Shannon*. **Decatur:** Stephen Decatur (1779–1820), the American naval hero who stopped the attacks of Barbary pirates on U.S. shipping and during the War of 1812 captured the British frigate *Macedonian*. **Bainbridge:** William Bainbridge (1774–1833), an American naval officer who held commands in the Tripolitan War and the War of 1812. During the latter conflict, as captain of the *Constitution,* he captured the British frigate *Java*. **Perry:** Oliver H. Perry (1785–1819), the American naval officer whose victory over a British fleet on Lake Erie in 1813 made possible a successful invasion of Canada that effectively ended the War of 1812 in the Northwest.

25. Andrew Jackson

Andrew Jackson was of Scotch-Irish descent, his ancestors having emigrated from Scotland to northern Ireland sometime after 1690. His parents were weavers from Carrickfergus, County Antrim, and had emigrated from Ireland about 1765. Though born along the border of North and South Carolina, Jackson came to maturity in Tennessee, where he quickly gained political prominence: congressman at twenty-nine, U.S. senator at thirty, and justice of the state supreme court at thirty-one. During a speech to the Charitable Irish Society in Boston, he proudly alluded to his Irish blood: "It is with great pleasure that I see so many of the countrymen of my father assembled on this occasion. I have always been proud of my ancestry and of being descended from that noble race, and rejoice that I am so nearly allied to a country which has so much to recommend it to the good wishes of the world. Would to God, sir, that Ireland on the other side of the great water enjoyed the comfort, contentment, happiness and liberty that they enjoy here." Jackson's reputation as a soldier and an Indian fighter earned him the support of the western settlers, whose growing political clout led to his election as president in 1828.

Jackson's name is forever linked to his victory over the British on January 8, 1815, at the battle of New Orleans. At the end of the previous December, Jackson had retreated with his 2,000 men to Chalmette Plantation after an inconclusive battle against an equal number of British troops farther south along the Mississippi. Shortly after the Americans had thrown up defensive earthworks on the plantation, the British attacked, this time with almost 9,000 men under the command of General Edward Pakenham, a native of Westmeath, Ireland, of Anglo-Irish descent. The American force, in the meantime, had grown to almost 5,500, swelled by the addition of civilians from town, Jean Lafitte's pirates, and a force of free African Americans. When Pakenham was shot in the spine during the battle, Major General John Keane, an Anglo-Irishman from County Waterford, assumed command. His efforts to turn the tide were in vain, however, and the British ultimately suffered 2,000 casualties to the Americans' thirteen.

Andrew Jackson

by Stephen Vincent Benét (1898–1943)

> The East and the South have ruled us long
> And they mean to keep on ruling,
> But the wild boy West is growing strong
> And tired of their constant schooling.
> He carries a rifle, long and brown,
> And his rough, free ways they fear.

But here comes
Old Hickory,
The pride of the frontier.

He's none of your old New England stock,
Or your gentry-proud Virginians,
But a regular Western fighting-cock
With Tennessee opinions.
When the gathered West, at New Orleans,
Mowed down the grenadier,
Who led the fight?
Old Hickory!
The pride of the frontier.

He was born and raised like a young raccoon
In the midst of death and dangers.
And his hair may be white as the hunter's moon
But his eyes are the forest-ranger's.
"This country's bigger than East or South.
Old ways must disappear.
Let the people rule!"
Says Hickory
"As they rule on the frontier!"

They follow behind him, the lusty crew
Of the States with the Injun trophies.
They'll sweep him into the White House, too,
And cock their boots on the sofys.
The rich and the staid may ring their hands
But how the people cheer!
To see him there,
Old Hickory,
The pride of the frontier.

Old Hickory: the nickname given to Jackson, probably because of his strong and
wiry build.

Old Hickory

by Clinton Scollard (1860–1932)

A Ballad for Andrew Jackson's Day

This is the day when we honor "Old Hickory,"

Honor him, aye, for the name that he bore!
Fierce as a fighter, and yet above trickery,
Virile and valiant and leal to the core!

Forth from Jamaica came faring the foemen,
    Sixty stout sail of them, ships of the line,
Who were to combat them? Patriot yeomen,
    Men of the forest as stanch as the pine!

Threading the bayou-ways, on pressed the barges,
    Ensigns a-flutter like birds on the wing;
Sounded the cheers as they landed their charges,
    While the bands echoed with "God Save the King!"

Haply they thought they were out for a holiday,
    They who filed forward so proud into view;
Sooth, but they found it was far from a jolly day
    Ere the morn's frolic of fighting was through!

For there was one who had thrilled with his bravery,
    For there was one who had filled with his fire
All of his men, and they struck at enslavery
    With the old Concord and Lexington ire.

Pakenham might rage, and the cannon might crack again,
    Vain was his valor, our praise to it be!
Thrice they made onset, and thrice they quailed back again,
    Thrice they reeled backward, then slunk to the sea!

Never since then has the land of our motherhood
    Known the encroach of hostility's tread;
Now we clasp hands with past foes in fair brotherhood
    Over the gulf of a century dead.

This is the day when we honor "Old Hickory,"
    Honor him, aye, for the name that he bore!
Fierce as a fighter, and yet above trickery,
    Virile and valiant and leal to the core!

Old Hickory: the nickname given to Jackson, probably because of his strong and
wiry build. **leal:** loyal and true. **Forth from Jamaica came faring the foemen:** the
British fleet en route to New Orleans. **Concord and Lexington:** towns in Massachusetts where the first two major battles of the Revolutionary War took place on
April 19, 1775. **Pakenham:** Major General Sir Edward Pakenham (1778–1815), in
command of the British troops during the battle of New Orleans in January 1815.

The Battle of New Orleans*
author unknown

'Twas on the eighth of January, just at the dawn of day.
    We spied those British officers all dressed in bat'l array;
Old Jackson then gave orders, "Each man to keep his post,
    And form a line from right to left, and let no time be lost."

With rockets and with bombshells, like comets we let fly;
    Like lions they advanced us, the fate of war to try.
Large streems of firey vengence upon them we let pour
    While many a brave Commander lay withering in his gore.

Thrice they marched up to the charge, and thrice they gave the ground;
    We fought them full three hours, then bugle horns did sound.
Great heaps of human pyramids lay strewn before our eyes;
    We blew the horns and rang the bells to drown their dying cries.

Come all you British noblemen, and listen unto me;
    Our Frontiersman has proved to you America is free.
But tell your Royal Master when you return back home
    That out of thirty thousand men but few of you returned.

*This song retains its original spelling.
Frontiersman: Andrew Jackson. **Royal Master:** the British monarch.

The Battle of New Orleans
by Thomas Dunn English (1819–1902)

Here, in my rude log cabin,
    Few poorer men there be
Among the mountain ranges
    Of Eastern Tennessee.
My limbs are weak and shrunken,
    White hairs upon my brow,
My dog—lie still old fellow!—
    My sole companion now.
Yet I, when young and lusty,
    Have gone through stirring
    scenes,
For I went down with Carroll
    To fight at New Orleans.

You say you'd like to hear me
    The stirring story tell,
Of those who stood the battle
    And those who fighting fell.
Short work to count our losses—
    We stood and dropped the foe
As easily as by firelight
    Men shoot the buck or doe.
And while they fell by hundreds
    Upon the bloody plain,
Of us, fourteen were wounded
    And only eight were slain.

The eighth of January,
    Before the break of day,
Our raw and hasty levies
    Were brought into array.
No cotton-bales before us—
    Some fool that falsehood told;
Before us was an earthwork
    Built from the swampy mould
And there we stood in silence,
    And waited with a frown,
To greet with bloody welcome
    The bull-dogs of the Crown.

The heavy fog of morning
    Still hid the plain from sight,
When came a thread of scarlet
    Marked faintly in the white.
We fired a single cannon,
    And as its thunder rolled,
The mist before us lifted
    In many a heavy fold—
The mist before us lifted
    And in their bravery fine
Came rushing to their ruin
    The fearless British line.

Then from our waiting cannon
    Leaped forth the deadly flame,
To meet the advancing columns
    That swift and steady came.
The thirty-twos of Crowley [*sic*]
    And Bluchi's [*sic*] twenty-four
To Spotts's eighteen-pounders
    Responded with their roar,
Sending the grape-shot deadly
    That marked its pathway plain,
And paved the road it travelled
    With corpses of the slain.

Our rifles firmly grasping,
    And heedless of the din,
We stood in silence waiting
    For orders to begin.
Our fingers on the triggers,

Our hearts, with anger stirred,
Grew still more fierce and eager
    As Jackson's voice was heard:
"Stand steady! Waste no powder!
    Wait till your shots will tell!
To-day the work you finish—
    See that you do it well!"

Their columns drawing nearer,
    We felt our patience tire,
When came the voice of Carroll,
    Distinct and measured, "Fire!"
Oh! then you should have marked
    us
    Our volleys on them pour—
Have heard our joyous rifles
    Ring sharply through the roar,
And seen their foremost columns
    Melt hastily away
As snow in mountain gorges
    Before the floods of May.

They soon re-formed their columns,
    And, mid the fatal rain
We never ceased to hurtle,
    Came to their work again.
The Forty-fourth is with them,
    That first its laurels won
With stout old Abercrombie [*sic*]
    Beneath an eastern sun.
It rushes to the battle,
    And, though within the rear
Its leader is a laggard,
    It shows no signs of fear.

It did not need its colonel,
    For soon there came instead
An eagle-eyed commander,
    And on its march he led.
'T was Pakenham in person,
    The leader of the field;
I knew it by the cheering
    That loudly round him pealed;
And by his quick, sharp movement

We felt his heart was stirred,
    As when at Salamanca
        He led the fighting Third.

I raised my rifle quickly,
        I sighted at his breast,
God save the gallant leader
        And take him to his rest!
I did not draw the trigger,
        I could not for my life,
So calm he sat his charger
        Amid the deadly strife,
That in my fiercest moment
        A prayer arose from me—
God save that gallant leader,
        Our foeman though he be!

Sir Edward's charger staggers;
        He leaps at once to ground.
And ere the beast falls bleeding
        Another horse is found.
His right arm falls—'t is wounded;
        He waves on high his left;
In vain he leads the movement,
        The ranks in twain are cleft.
The men in scarlet waver
        Before the men in brown,
And fly in utter panic—
        The soldiers of the Crown!

I thought the work was over,
        But nearer shouts were heard,
And came, with Gibbs to head it,
        The gallant Ninety-third.
Then Pakenham, exulting,
        With proud and joyous glance,
Cried, "Children of the tartan—
        Bold Highlanders—advance!
Advance to scale the breastworks,
        And drive them from their hold,
And show the stainless courage
        That marked your sires of old!"

His voice as yet was ringing,

When, quick as light, there
    came
The roaring of a cannon,
        And earth seemed all aflame.
Who causes thus the thunder
        The doom of men to speak?
It is the Baratarian,
        The fearless Dominique.
Down through the marshalled
    Scotsmen
        The step of death is heard,
And by the fierce tornado
        Falls half the Ninety-third.

The smoke passed slowly upward
        And, as it soared on high,
I saw the brave commander
        In dying anguish lie.
They bear him from the battle
        Who never fled the foe;
Unmoved by death around them
        His bearers softly go.
In vain their care, so gentle,
        Fades earth and all its scenes;
The man of Salamanca
        Lies dead at New Orleans.

But where were his lieutenants?
        Had they in terror fled?
No! Keane was sorely wounded
        And Gibbs as good as dead.
Brave Wilkinson commanding,
        A major of brigade,
The shattered force to rally
        A final effort made.
He led it up our ramparts,
        Small glory did he gain—
Our captives some; some slaugh-
    tered,
        And he himself was slain.

The stormers had retreated,
        The bloody work was o'er;
The feet of the invaders

Were soon to leave our shore.
We rested on our rifles
    And talked about the fight,
When came a sudden murmur
    Like fire from left to right;
We turned and saw our chieftain,
    And then, good friend of mine,
You should have heard the cheer-
        ing
    That rang along the line.

For well our men remembered
    How little, when they came,
Had they but native courage,
    And trust in Jackson's name;
How through the day he labored,
    How kept the vigils still,
Till discipline controlled us—

A stronger power than will;
And how he hurled us at them
    Within the evening hour,
That red night in December
    And made us feel out power.

In answer to our shouting
    Fire lit his eye of gray;
Erect, but thin and pallid,
    He passed upon his bay,
Weak from the baffled fever,
    And shrunken in each limb,
The swamps of Alabama
    Had done their work on him;
But spite of that and fasting,
    And hours of sleepless care,
The soul of Andrew Jackson
    Shone forth in glory there.

Carroll: William Carroll (1788–1844), the major general of the Tennessee militia which gave Andrew Jackson invaluable help at the battle of New Orleans. After the War of 1812 Carroll served twelve years as governor of Tennessee. His parents were natives of Ireland. **Crowley [*sic*]:** Lieutenant Charles Crawley, a naval officer who helped man the *one* 32-pounder in Jackson's Battery Number 4. **Bluchi [*sic*]:** Renato Beluche, one of two of Jean Lafitte's pirates who each manned a 24-pounder in Jackson's Battery Number 3. **Spotts:** Lieutenant Samuel Spotts, who with the Frenchman Chauveau commanded *one* eighteen-pound culverine and a six-pounder in Battery Number 7. **Abercrombie [*sic*]:** Robert Abercromby (1740–1827), the British lieutenant of the Forty-Fourth Regiment during the French and Indian War. He was present at the battle of Niagara and the capture of Montreal. **Pakenham:** Major General Sir Edward Pakenham (1778–1815), in command of the British troops during the battle of New Orleans in January 1815. **Salamanca:** the scene of an 1812 battle in Spain in which Sir Edward Pakenham led the Third Division. **Gibbs:** Samuel Gibbs, a British officer and the second in command to General Pakenham during the battle of New Orleans. He was killed while trying to rally his troops. **Baratarian . . . Dominique:** Dominique You (c. 1772–1830), one of the freebooter Jean Lafitte's lieutenants, so called after Barataria Bay, the infamous pirate's headquarters in an inlet of the Gulf of Mexico on the coast of Louisiana. Many of Lafitte's band fought with Jackson at New Orleans, where they distinguished themselves as artillerists. **man of Salamanca:** Sir Edward Pakenham, who had brilliantly led the Third Division at the battle of Salamanca, Spain, in 1812. **Keane:** John Keane (1781–1844), the Anglo-Irish officer in command of the Third Brigade during the battle of New Orleans. He assumed command of all the British troops after Pakenham was killed. **our chieftain:** Andrew Jackson.

Jackson at New Orleans
by Wallace Rice (1859–1939)

Hear through the morning drums and trumpets sounding,
Rumbling of cannon, tramp of mighty armies;
Then the mist sunders, all the plain disclosing
  Scarlet for England.

Batteries roll on, halt, and flashing lightnings
Search out our earthworks, silent and portentous.
Fierce on our right with crimson banners tossing
  Their lines spring forward.

Lanyards in hand, Americans and seamen,
Gunners from warships, Lafitte's privateersmen,
Roar out our thunders till the grape and shrapnel
  Shriek through their columns.

Shattered in fragments, thus their right is riven;
But on our left a deadlier bolt is speeding;
Wellesley's Peninsulars, never yet defeated,
  Charge in their valor.

Closing their files, our cannon fire disdaining,
Dauntless they come with vict'ry on their standards;
Then slowly rise the rifles of our marksmen,
  Tennessee hunters.

Cradles of flame and scythes of whistling bullets
Lay them in windrows, war's infernal harvest.
High through the onslaught Tennessee is shouting,
  Joying in battle.

Pakenham falls there, Keane and his Highlanders
Close from the centre, hopeless in their courage;
Backward they stagger, dying and disabled,
  Gloriously routed.

Stilled are our rifles as our cheers grow louder:
War clouds sweep back in January breezes,
Showing the dreadful proof of the great triumph
  God hath vouchsafed us.

That gallant war-host, England's best and bravest,
Met by raw levies, scores against its hundreds,
Lies at our feet, a thing for woman's weeping,
    Reddening the meadows.

Freed are our States from European tyrants:
Lift then your voices for the little army
Led by our battle-loving Andrew Jackson,
    Blest of Jehovah.

Lafitte: Jean Lafitte (c. 1780–c. 1825), a French-born adventurer, many of whose band fought with Andrew Jackson at New Orleans. Lafitte refused an offer of $30,000 from the British to help them attack New Orleans. **Wellesley's Peninsulars:** British troops that had served under Sir Arthur Wellesley in Spain and Portugal (the "Peninsula") during the war against the French (1809–1813). After Wellesley defeated Napoleon, these forces were sent to fight against the Americans, although Wellesley did not accompany them. **windrows:** rows of hay left to dry before being raked into heaps. **Pakenham:** Major General Sir Edward Pakenham (1778–1815), in command of the British troops during the battle of New Orleans in January 1815. **Keane:** John Keane (1781–1844), the Anglo-Irish officer in command of the Third Brigade during the battle of New Orleans. He assumed command of all the British troops after Pakenham was killed. Keane, who was wounded in the neck while leading his Highlanders in support of General Gibbs, later served as lieutenant governor of Jamaica.

The Victory at New Orleans

by Wallace Rice (1859–1939)

There's a blare of bugles blowing
    And a hum of rumbling drums,
Red upon the green plain flowing,
    See! the British army comes.
There are regiments in scarlet,
Renegade and negro varlet,
            Rolling on;
There are regiments half savage
That had aided Ross to ravage
            Washington.

Broad their banners forth are streaming
    In the January sun,
Bright their bayonets are gleaming
    Over every deadly gun;
Bold marine and bolder seaman

Who had fought like any demon
           On the main;
Thousands more black with the pillage
Gleamed in many a hapless village
           Back in Spain.

Here are Wellesley's trusted henchmen,
      Fiendish old Peninsulars,
Stained with blood of slaughtered Frenchmen
      Through the long and bitter wars;
Rank and file as ripe with evil,
Rape, and rapine as the devil
           And his dam;
At their head that hero-Briton
On whose brow success was written,
           Pakenham.

There are sixty war-ships heaving
      On the Mississippi sound,
Near ten thousand warriors weaving
      Through that tufted, swampy ground;
There are breastworks just before them—
One bold charge and they'll be o'er them,
           High or low;
Then an hour of British shooting,
And a wreck of British looting,
           Death, and woe.

But the frontiersmen with Jackson
      See there's powder in the pan,
They have never turned their backs on
      Savage beast or savage man;
Craven Spain at Pensecola [*sic*]
And the Creeks of Tallapoosa
           Know their glance,
Know the coonskin cap, and rifle,
And the bullet-clouds that stifle
           All advance.

For the fourth time now the Briton
      Since his coming in the night
Is to see his bravest smitten
      By the lightnings of our night:
When our gunboats meet their barges;

On the night our army charges
          Into flame;
When their cannon are dismounted:
Thrice they've learned we can be counted
          On for aim.

Yet they come in long ranks steady
       To take up the battle brunt,
With their courage tried and ready,
       Gallant officers in front;
Near the river Rennie's soldiers
With their muskets on their shoulders
          Hold their path;
'Gainst our right he leads his raiders.
Welcome now the bold invaders
          With our wrath!

On our first redoubt they're dashing,
       Rank on rank they rush a-swarm:
Down their files our cannon crashing
       Hurl an extirpating storm;
Thunder-stricken and astounded
They are hurled back crushed and wounded
          By our lead;
Patterson in wide swaths mows them
Humphrey's grape in huge gusts blows them
          Rennie's dead.

Steadily, not one a coward,
       Gibbs's men charge with a will;
Steadily our shrapnel's showered—
       They are coming closer still;
There Lafitte's bold men are aiming:
All our batteries are flaming
          For their fall;
But our hail of grape despising,
On they come, their broad front rising
          At the call.

Every rifleman with longing
       Gazes on the lines in red
As they come in columns thronging;
       But the word has not been said:
At two hundred yards, or nearer,

Sounds the signal for each hearer,
>> *Tennessee!*
Hurled to hell in quick disorder,
Britons leave a crimson border
>> As they flee.

Pakenham rides up to rally—
>> He is wounded in the arm;
Gibbs shall never from that sally
>> Ride again to war's alarm;
Quick to aid Keane's men are coming—
Hear our rifles' ceaseless humming!—
>> Keane is slain.
Spreads the panic's fitful pallor—
Pakenham in all his valour
>> Low is lain.

There's no blare of bugles blowing ,
>> Not a hum of rumbling drum.
Bitter is their overthrowing,
>> Thousands lie for ever dumb;
With backwoodsmen, to defend us
We have won the odds tremendous,
>> One to three.
Woe to him who dares to trifle
With the 'coonskin cap and rifle—
>> *Tennessee!*

Talluschatches, Talladega,
>> These our general's victories,
Bowyer's Fort, and Tohopeka:
>> Now New Orleans is his.
Silence! then a noise of cheering—
Louder—Louder—he is nearing—
>> Jackson comes!
Hear the song of triumph growing,
Hear the blare of bugles blowing,

Hear the drums!

Ross: Robert Ross (1766–1814), the British commander whose troops captured Washington, D.C., in August 1814 and set fire to various government buildings, including the Capitol and the executive mansion. **Peninsulars:** British troops that had served under Sir Arthur Wellesley in Spain and Portugal (the "Peninsula") during the war against the French (1809–1813). After Wellesley defeated Napoleon, these forces were sent to fight against the Americans, although Wellesley did not accompany them. **Pakenham:** Major General Sir Edward Pakenham (1778–1815), in command of the British troops during the battle of New Orleans in January 1815. **Pensecola [*sic*]:** Pensacola, a Spanish city in Florida which by 1814 was notorious for its lawlessness. Although conditions improved after British troops were stationed in the city in the summer of that year, General Andrew Jackson attacked Pensacola in November 1814, as a result of which the British withdrew. Jackson returned to Pensacola in 1818, when he set up a military government to stop raids by Florida Indians against the Georgia border. He was criticized for again invading Spanish territory. **Tallapoosa:** a river in Alabama, along which hundreds of Creek Indians gathered prior to the battle of Horseshoe Bend on March 27, 1814. **Rennie:** Colonel Robert Rennie, a British officer killed while leading his troops out of a captured American redoubt. **Patterson:** Daniel Todd Patterson (1786–1839), an American officer whose batteries on the river bank poured a murderous fire on the British army as it advanced across Chalmette Plantation toward Andrew Jackson's breastwork. The batteries were lost to the British, though, when the Kentuckians retreated, leaving their positions undefended. **Humphrey:** Captain Enoch Humphrey, an American officer who commanded the battery closest to the river. **Gibbs:** Samuel Gibbs, a British officer and the second in command to General Pakenham during the battle of New Orleans. He was killed while trying to rally his troops. **Lafitte:** Jean Lafitte (c. 1780–c. 1825), a French-born adventurer, many of whose band fought with Andrew Jackson at New Orleans. Lafitte refused an offer of $30,000 from the British to help them attack New Orleans. **Keane:** John Keane (1781–1844), the Anglo-Irish officer in command of the Third Brigade during the battle of New Orleans. He assumed command of all the British troops after Pakenham was killed. Keane was wounded in the neck while leading his Highlanders in support of General Gibbs. **Talluschatches, Talladega:** Creek Indian villages in Alabama that were destroyed in 1813 by an army of 5,000 militia led by General Andrew Jackson. **Bowyer's Fort:** an earthen fortification thirty miles below Mobile, Alabama, whose garrison of 130 Americans fought off a British force of five ships, 130 marines, and 600 Indians in September 1814. **Tohopeka:** the site in Alabama where the battle of Horseshoe Bend took place on March 27, 1814. A force of 3,000 men under General Andrew Jackson killed more than 800 Creek warriors and imprisoned 500 women and children. By the terms of a treaty which the Creeks accepted the following August, the Indians ceded 23 million acres of land, comprising part of southern Georgia and more than half of Alabama.

Old, Old, Old, Old Andrew Jackson
by Vachel Lindsay (1879–1931)

. . . .

I think of you, Andrew Jackson,
Two o'clock in the morning,
In the White House, alone,
You stand there, Old Hickory,

Lean as a bone.
It is now
The fifth of March,
1833,
And you wonder
With an aching heart,
Have you set your people free?

. . . .

Then he thinks of the time when the world was young
And Rachel was young,
When he threaded the black woods without guard,
        without guide,
And shot without trial all who slandered and lied;
He thinks of gigantic scoundrels he hung
In West Tennessee, when the Nation was young,
In Florida, when the Nation was young.
Then he thinks he will soon
Hang those
Nullifiers,
And make them a "terror to traitors—
And especially . . .
John C. Calhoun!
Then, he thinks on,
To Heaven,
Where heavenly Rachel is gone.
And the boy frontiersmen sense the mystery
Of the far-off eyes and the destiny
Of this man who could never change his mind,
Who put strange fight into humankind.

. . . .

Only the rich want his name to grow dim,
To have the American people forget
How they brought great white horses for him.
Do you think that I want some fool,
Statistical,
To picture that second inaugural
Who has read all the diaries of that day
And all that the Adamses have to say?
And the speeches of Calhoun, of Webster and Clay?
I must ask a boy who has faded away.
I must ask my own heart when it was so young
To speak of Jackson with a proud tongue,

As my father and my grandfathers taught me
To speak of Jackson with a proud tongue.
When I take the road and beg again,
In the first log cabin I will talk of Jackson.
There, the second inaugural night,
With a cane he drove the last revelers out,
For there were swine in the glamour and rout.
There were gourds on the floor,
Empty hard cider kegs,
Broken-up tables,
And broken chair legs.
But, far on the edge of the Maryland hills,
Bonfires burned high, the revelers danced,
Steeds and riders snorted and pranced;
Thebes had gone down,
Sparta gone down,
Babylon fallen,
Rome fallen,
London Tower fallen,
The Bastille fallen!
Gone were the blasphemous breeds—
Mankind was made new.
The only crown was Democracy's crown,
The only town left was Democracy's town,
And Jackson was king of it, too.

. . . .

Let us think of Democracy's proudest son,
The wilderness, brought to Washington,
The frontier, brought to its place of power,
To its proudest hour!—

Rachel: Rachel Donelson Robards, Andrew Jackson's wife. Jackson married Rachel in 1791, after she was told that her first husband had obtained a divorce. Almost two and a half years later, however, the new couple's marital bliss was disturbed when they learned that the divorce had not been granted until September 1793, fully two years after Jackson's marriage to Rachel. Although the two were remarried in Nashville, they became the object of vilification during the 1828 presidential campaign: Jackson was called a "paramour husband" while his wife was branded a "convicted adulteress." **shot without trial all who slandered and lied:** In response to a reported slur against his wife, Jackson in 1805 killed Charles Dickinson in a duel. Dickinson's bullet smashed two of Jackson's ribs and lodged in his opponent's chest. **gigantic scoundrels he hung:** During the campaign against the Creek Indians in Florida, Jackson hanged two British traders, creating a serious international crisis. **Adamses:** John Adams and his son John Quincy Adams, both of whom regarded Andrew Jackson as a barbarian and his election to the presidency as a victory for "mobocracy." **Nullifiers:** proponents of the theory that states could refuse to obey — or nullify — federal laws which they regarded as unconstitutional. **John C. Calhoun:** Andrew Jackson's vice president, although the two were political enemies, particularly on the nullification issue. **Webster:** Daniel Webster (1782–1852), a Massachusetts senator and orator. **Clay:** Henry Clay (1777–1852), a Kentucky congressman and senator who introduced and secured passage of censure motions against President Jackson in 1834. **Thebes, Sparta:** Greek city-states. **London Tower:** a complex of medieval buildings in London where enemies of the Crown were imprisoned. **Bastille:** the fortress in Paris captured by revolutionaries on July 14, 1789. The fortress was regarded as a symbol of royal absolutism.

Jackson

by Jason R. Orton

Man of the honest heart and iron will!
Cold is thy form and dim thine eagle eye;
Earth bids thee a good-night, and tower and hill
Wave their black flags upon the solemn sky.
The booming guns and pealing anthems, high,
Hallow thy exit to the realms of light.
The cot, the palace, heave alike and sigh,
And, sorrowing, tell thy deeds and honors bright—
A mighty nation weeps at bidding thee good-night!
Thou wast a star of glory to thy friends;
Thou wast a scourge of terror to thy foes;
As the soft sunshine with the torrent blends,
Blended thy mighty purpose and repose.
For thou wast all alive to human woes,
The loving husband and the gentle sire;
And as the sods upon thy mortal close,
Fame lights her altar with unwonted fire,
And gives thee to our hearts, thy paeans to the lyre.
Men of the age! thy voice of humble prayer,
Which called down blessings on thine enemy—
Thy battle cry, which terrified the air,
And woke of old the land of chivalry
Are mute; and yet their echoes will not die;
For thou hast left thine impress on the world.
They name shall light the nations, as they try
The issues of the future, and is hurled
Man's last defiance forth, and his last flag unfurled.

The Statue of Old Andrew Jackson
by Vachel Lindsay (1879–1931)

Andrew Jackson was eight feet tall.
His arm was a hickory limb and a maul.
His sword was so long he dragged it on the ground.
Every friend was an equal. Every foe was a hound.

Andrew Jackson was a Democrat,
Defying kings in his old cocked hat.
His vast steed rocked like a hobby-horse.
But he sat straight up. He held his course.

He licked the British at Noo Orleans;
Beat them out of their elegant jeans.
He piled the cotton-bales twenty feet high,
And he snorted "freedom," and it flashed from his eye.

And the American Eagle swooped through the air,
And cheered when he heard the Jackson swear:—
"By the Eternal. let them come.
Sound Yankee Doodle. Let the Bullets hum."

And his wild men, straight from the woods, fought on
Till the British fops were dead and gone.

And now old Andrew Jackson fights
To set the sad big world to rights.
He joins the British and the French.
He cheers up the Italian trench.
He's making Democrats of these,
And freedom's sons of Japanese.
His hobby horse will gallop on
Till all the infernal Huns are gone.

Yes,
Yes,
Yes!
By the Eternal!
Old Andrew Jackson!

Andrew Jackson was eight feet tall: probably an allusion to the bronze statue of Andrew Jackson in Lafayette Park in Washington, D.C. The work was cast in 1853 by Clark Mills from cannon captured by the former president in the War of 1812. An identical statue by Mills stands in Jackson Square in New Orleans. The inscription on that pedestal — "The Union Must and Shall be Preserved" — was a toast which Jackson made during the nullification controversy with extreme states' rights supporters in the 1830s. Another copy of the Mills statue is in Nashville, Tennessee. **set the sad big world to rights:** This poem was written in August 1918, toward the end of World War I, which Woodrow Wilson said was fought "to make the world safe for Democracy." **Huns:** a derogatory term for German soldiers during both world wars.

Andrew Jackson

by Martha Keller (b. 1902)

He was a man as hot as whiskey.
He was a man whose word was good.
He was a man whose hate was risky—
          Andrew Jackson—hickory wood!

He was in love with love and glory:
His hopes were prospered, but at a price—
The bandying of the ugly story
          He'd had to marry his Rachel twice.

Hot he was and a hasty suitor,
But if he sinned he was poor at sin.
She was plain as a spoon of pewter,
          Plain and good as a safety pin.

Andrew Jackson, man of honor,
Held her name like he held his head.
He stopped a bullet for slurs upon her.
          All his life he carried lead.

All his life wherever he went he
Wore the scar of a pistol shot—
Along with others he had in plenty.
          Hickory wood is hard to rot.

Hard to rot and a fiery fuel—
When faith and freedom both burned dim,
He stood his guns as he fought a duel,
          And heartened others to stand with him.

With any man who was good at sighting,
No ally but the thief Lafitte,
And no campaigns but Indian fighting,
        He brought the British to black defeat.

The odds against him were more than double.
His gunmounts sank like a heart that fails,
Sank in mud and the frosty stubble—
        So he set his cannon on cotton bales.

And over the cane and the silver sedges—
The redcoats' coats were as red as flame—
In a hundred rows like a hundred hedges,
        The bayonets of the British came.

The smoke of his cannon rolled and scattered
Like bursting flowers, like cotton blooms.
Like teeth from a comb the red ranks shattered,
        While water lifted in yellow plumes.

White and red on the silver carpet,
Scarlet tunics by crossbelts crossed,
They fell and died—and a flood of scarlet
        Covered over the field of frost.

He was a man whose hand was steady.
He was a man whose aim was good.
He was a man whose guns were ready—
        Andrew Jackson—hickory wood!

He'd had to marry his Rachel twice: In 1791 Jackson married Rachel Donelson Robards after the bride-to-be was told that her first husband had obtained a divorce. Almost two and a half years later, however, the couple learned that the divorce had not been granted until September 1793, fully two years after Jackson's marriage to Rachel. Although the two were remarried in Nashville, they became the object of vilification during the 1828 presidential campaign: Jackson was called a "paramour husband" while his wife was branded a "convicted adulteress." **redcoats:** British soldiers, so called from the red jackets of their uniforms.

26. David Crockett

The frontiersman David Crockett was of Norman-French and Irish ancestry. His great-great-great-great-grandfather was Antoine de Crocketagne, a French Protestant of the late seventeenth century. When Louis XIV expelled the Protestants from France, de Crocketagne fled with his family to Bantry Bay on the west coast of Ireland. There his third son married Sarah Stewart, presumably of Scotch-Irish ancestry, and soon joined the Irish migration to America. By 1775 descendants of this couple — now calling themselves Crocketts — had settled in Tennessee, where the famous "Davy" was born in 1786.

Later known as the "King of the Wild Frontier," Crockett was legendary for his "tall tales." In one such "whopper" he told of how, when caught in a hollow tree by a mother bear, he held on to the animal's tail and jabbed her with his knife until she pulled him out. Another story related how he had fought hand to claw with a vicious black bear until he stabbed it to death. According to his own count, he killed 105 bears during a nine-month period.

Crockett later went into politics when someone jokingly suggested to him that he run for Congress. After his election to the House of Representatives in 1826, the young Tennessean caught the attention of official Washington with his frontier dress and speech. Following his election to a third term in Congress, Crockett was mentioned by the French observer de Tocqueville in his classic description of American democracy. After repeating the usual slanders against the Tennessean — that he owned no property, lived most of the time in the woods, was uneducated and almost totally illiterate — the French aristocrat cited Crockett's career as a reason for opposing universal suffrage. When he lost his seat in 1835, Crockett moved to Texas, where he was killed the next year while defending the Alamo from a Mexican army.

The Alamo, or the Death of Crockett
(Air — "The Star-Spangled Banner")
by Robert Taylor Conrad (1810–1858)

To the memory of Crockett fill up to the brim!
　　The hunter, the hero, the bold yankee yeoman!
Let the flowing oblation be poured forth to him
　　Who ne'er turned his back on his friend or his foeman
　　　　And grateful shall be
　　　　His fame to the free;
Fill! fill! to the brave who for Liberty bled—
May his name and his fame to the last—GO AHEAD!

When the Mexicans leaguered thy walls, Alamo!
   'Twas Crockett looked down on the war-storm's commotion,
And smiled, as by thousands the foe spread below,
   And rolled o'er the plain, like the waves of the ocean.
      The Texans stood there—
      Their flag fanned the air,
      And their shout bade the foe try what freemen will dare.
What recked they, tho' thousands the prairies o'erspread?
The world of their leader was still—GO AHEAD!

They came! Like the sea-cliff that laughs at the flood,
   Stood that dread band of heroes the onslaught repelling;
Again! And again! yet undaunted they stood;
   While Crockett's deep voice o'er the wild din was swelling.
      "Go ahead!" was his cry,
      "Let us conquer or die;
      "And shame to the wretch and the dastard who'd fly!"
And still, mid the battle-cloud, lurid and red,
Rang the hero's dread cry—*Go ahead!* GO AHEAD!

He fought—but no valour that horde could withstand;
   He fell—but behold where the wan victor found him!
With a smile on his lip, and his rifle in hand,
   He lay, with his foemen heaped redly around him;
      His heart poured its tide
      In the cause of its pride,
      A freeman he lived, and a freeman he died;
For liberty struggled, for liberty bled—
May his name and his fame to the last—GO AHEAD!

Then fill up to Crockett—fill up to the brim!
   The hunter, the hero, the bold yankee yeoman!
Let the flowing oblation be poured forth to him,
   Who ne'er turned his back on his friend or his foeman!
      And grateful shall be
      His fame to the free,
      For a bolder or better they never shall see.
Fill! fill! to the brave who for Liberty bled—
May his name and his fame to the last—GO AHEAD!

recked: heeded or cared about.

27. Sam Houston

Sam Houston, a descendant of Irish-born emigrants from northern Ireland, was born in Virginia in 1793. Both his grandfather and great-grandfather had immigrated to Philadelphia in 1735, and his father, Major Samuel Houston, had been a member of Daniel Morgan's rifle corps during the Revolutionary War.

The younger Houston moved to Tennessee in 1807 with his widowed mother and his eight brothers. A few years after the family had opened a store in Maryville, the wild Sam ran away to Cherokee territory, explaining that he preferred "measuring deer tracks to [measuring] tape." For three years he lived with the Indians, learning their language, hunting with them, and developing an appreciation for their way of life. The Indians called him "The Raven" and assigned him the eagle as his totem or guardian. His experiences with the tribe caused him to believe that the American settlers were to blame for much of the conflict between the two races on the frontier.

Houston went on to enjoy a varied political career. Besides serving as a congressman and the governor of Tennessee, he was the Texan commander at the battle of San Jacinto, the president of the Texas Republic, and the first governor of Texas. Because of his determined opposition to secession, however, he was removed from the governorship of Texas and was henceforth regarded as a traitor. Prior to his dismissal he made an eloquent plea for American nationhood: "Men who never endured the privation, the toil, the peril that I have for my country call me a traitor because I am willing to yield obedience to the Constitution and the constituted authorities. Let them suffer what I have for this Union, and they will feel it entwining so closely around their hearts that it will be like snapping the cords of life to give it up. . . ."

Sam Houston

by Stephen Vincent Benét

Whenever Sam Houston felt ill at ease
He'd go and live with the Cherokees,
For he liked their ways and he liked their dress
And the free, proud life of the wilderness.

This buckskin hero from Tennessee
Had a life as checkered as lives can be.
There was speech and duel and love and ire,
And all of it lived like a prairie fire.

He was up and down, he was hissed and cheered,
But there was never anything Houston feared.
His dreams were huge and his costumes showy
And his private honor bright as a bowie.

He's the pride and boast of the Lone Star State
For he fought her battles and made her great,
And, on either side of the wide Atlantic,
You won't find anyone more romantic.

bowie: a heavy sheath knife having a long, single-edged blade. **Lone Star State:** Texas. **battles:** especially San Jacinto, the battle fought in Texas in April 1836 during which the Texans avenged the massacre at the Alamo and effectively achieved independence from Mexico. Approximately 100 Irish-born — or one-eighth of the Texan army — participated in the battle.

28. The Alamo

The Alamo was destined to become the focal point of the Texan Revolution when, in February 1836, the Mexican dictator General Santa Anna led 5,000 troops north across the Rio Grande in an attempt to crush the Texans' struggle for independence. Of the 187 men who gave their lives during the subsequent siege of the Alamo, thirty-four were either Irish natives or men of Irish ancestry or bearing traditional Irish surnames.

Each of those thirty-four defenders is mentioned in *The Alamo*, a 275-page epic poem written by Michael Lind (b. 1962) and published in 1997. The names of the thirty-four are listed below, each with a reference to its first appearance in *The Alamo* (book.stanza.line) and some with a descriptive verse from the epic.

• The known Irish natives were twelve: Samuel Burns (10.37.6), who "fought like one of his native Eire's old kerns"; Stephen Dennison (11.29.3), "who had come from Ireland, / dreaming of acres and a hefty purse, / was trapped beside a soldier from a worse / nation than Mexico, an Englishman / named James R. Dimkins"; Andrew Duvalt (11.3.6), "Missouri Irishman"; Robert Evans (8.44.7); Joseph Hawkins (10.39.1); William Daniel Jackson (11.10.1), who "fell, but not before / his pistol's single shot blew out a skull, / speckling him with his opponent's gore"; James McGee (11.4.1), "propped up, old bandages now freshly stained"; Robert McKinney (10.50.2); James Nowlan (11.7.5), ". . . Blue steel began to flay / James Nowlan, as the mattress where he lay / gorged like a leech"; Jackson Rusk (12.24.4), "Irish-bred, / a colonist whose waiting land-grant spred

/ no heirs would ever claim"; Burke Trammel (10.26.3), "a son of Ireland" who "knocked a pair / of stormers from the edge, fought for a gun / with yet a third"; and William Ward (12.22.5).

• Another five were from the Irish colonies in eastern Texas and for that reason were most likely Irish-born: Samuel Blair (11.15.1), whose "contortions showed the route / of what had killed him"; James Brown (12.27.2); James Hannon (or Hannum) (12.21.4), whose corpse was "still warm"; Edward McCafferty (or McAfferty) (10.34.6), who "down fell bandaged"; and William Parks (10.65.7).

• Five others had Irish-American ancestry: Peter James Bailey, Daniel William Cloud and William Fauntleroy (10.58.4), "Together they had ridden here; each one / alone on that cold morning would confront a separate death, hot, whistling, sharp, or blunt"; David Crockett (4.37.7) and William Travis (1.15.5). (Crockett was of French and Irish ancestry, while Travis's grandmother was Jemima McNamara.)

• Another twelve casualties were men with Irish surnames: John Blair (11.4.3), "heartlessly cut open" where he lay; John Cane (or Cain) (10.70.3), "always keen / to pull a prank"; William Carey (7.14.3); Robert Cochran (11.10.6); John Garvin (11.10.4), who "flailed, a maddened, streaming bull / beneath a crowded stadium's howling hull"; Patrick Henry Herndon (10.50.3); James Kenny (10.71.2); William Malone (5.10.2), "who shivered with relief / while guzzling"; Albert Martin (7.29.6), on whom "three hundred muskets were trained / . . . as he made his way / beneath the second flag of truce that day"; James (or Jesse) McCoy (11.34.5), who "waited to unfurl / his full six feet, guns flaming"; John Purdy Reynolds (10.59.1), who "seized / a frightened Mexican private's bayonet / and shoved him back"; and Isaac Ryan (10.71.2).

The Irishmen who died at the Alamo are honored each St. Patrick's Day with a memorial wreath placed in front of the Alamo by members of the Harp and Shamrock Society of Texas.

The Men of the Alamo

James Jeffrey Roche (1847–1908)

To Houston at Gonzales town, ride, Ranger, for your life,
Nor stop to say good-bye to-day to home, or child, or wife;
But pass the word from ranch to ranch, to every Texan sword,
That fifty thousand Mexicans have crossed the Nueces ford,
With Castrillon and perjured Cos, Sesmá and Almonté,
And Santa Anna ravenous for vengeance and for prey!
They smite the land with fire and sword; the grass shall never grow
Where northward sweeps that locust herd on San Antonio!

Nor who will bar the foeman's path, to gain a breathing space,
Till Houston and his scattered men shall meet him face to face?
Who holds his life as less than naught when home and honor call,
And counts the guerdon full and fair for liberty to fall?
Oh, who but Barrett Travis, the bravest of them all!
With seven score of riflemen to play the rancher's game,
And feed a counter-fire to halt the sweeping prairie flame;
For Bowie of the broken blade is there to cheer them on,
With Evans of Conception, who conquered Castrillon,
And o'er their heads the Lone Star flag defiant floats on high,
And no man thinks of yielding, and no man fears to die.

But ere the siege is held a week a cry is heard without,
A clash of arms, a rifle peal, the Ranger's ringing shout,
And two-and-thirty beardless boys have bravely hewed their way
To die with Travis if they must, to conquer if they may.
Was ever valor held so cheap in Glory's mart before
In all the days of chivalry, in all the deeds of war?
But once again the foemen gaze in wonderment and fear
To see a stranger break their lines and hear the Texans cheer.
God! how they cheered to welcome him, those spent and starving men!
For Davy Crockett by their side was worth an army then.
The wounded ones forgot their wounds; the dying drew a breath
To hail the king of border men, then turned to laugh at death.
For all knew Davy Crockett, blithe and generous as bold,
And strong and rugged as the quartz that hides its heart of gold.
His simple creed for word or deed true as the bullet sped,
And rung the target straight: "Be sure you're right, then go ahead!"

And were they right who fought in the fight for Texas by his side?
They questioned not; they faltered not; they only fought and died.
Who hath an enemy like these, God's mercy slay him straight!—
A thousand Mexicans lay dead outside the convent gate,
And half a thousand more must die before the fortress falls,
And still the tide of war beats high around the leaguered walls.
At last the bloody breach is won; the weakened lines give way;
The wolves are swarming in the court; the lions stand at bay.
The leader meets them at the breach, and wins the soldier's prize;
A foeman's bosom sheathes his sword when gallant Travis dies.
Now let the victor feast at will until his crest be red—
We may not know what raptures fill the vulture with the dead.
Let Santa Anna's valiant sword right bravely hew and hack
The senseless corse; its hands are cold; they will not strike him back.

> Let Bowie die, but 'ware the hand that wields his deadly knife;
> Four went to slay, and one comes back, so dear he sells his life.
> And last of all let Crockett fall, too proud to sue for grace,
> So grand in death the butcher dared not look upon his face.
>
> But far on San Jacinto's field the Texan toils are set,
> And Alamo's dread memory the Texan steel shall whet.
> And Fame shall tell their deeds who fell till all the years be run.
> "Thermopylae left one alive—the Alamo left none."

Houston: Sam Houston (1793–1863), who, as military commander-in-chief of the provisional rebel government in Texas, ordered that the Alamo be destroyed since he thought it could not be defended by volunteers. He later was commander-in-chief and president of the Texas Republic and first governor of Texas. **Gonzales:** a town in southeast Texas. In 1836 thirty-two citizens from Gonzales answered the call of Colonel William Travis at the Alamo for reinforcements. **Nueces:** a 315-mile-long river in southeastern Texas. **Castrillon, Cos, Sesmá and Almonté:** Mexican generals under the command of Santa Anna. **Santa Anna:** Antonio Lopez de Santa Anna (1795?–1876), a Mexican general, revolutionary, and president. **San Antonio:** the town in Texas in which the Alamo was located. **guerdon:** a reward. **Barrett Travis:** William Barrett Travis (1809–1836), a leader in the movement for Texas independence and a defender of the Alamo during its final days in March 1836. **Bowie:** James Bowie (1796–1836), an American adventurer and slave trader and a defender of the Alamo in its final days. **Evans:** Robert Evans, the Irishman who tried to ignite a room full of gunpowder at the Alamo (to fulfill an agreement which the defenders had made before the assault). Within a foot of the powder, however, he was killed by a Mexican officer. **Lone Star flag:** the red, white, and blue banner of the Texas Republic and now the Texas state flag. The defenders of the Alamo most likely did not fly this banner. One theory claims that the flag flown at the Alamo was the Mexican tricolor emblazoned with the date 1824, an allusion to the liberal Mexican constitution of that year. Although it is true that the Texas rebels originally fought in defense of that constitution, by 1836 their loyalty to Mexico had given way to a desire for independence from that country. The flag most likely flown during the siege of the Alamo was the azure blue banner of the New Orleans Greys. **Davy Crockett:** David Crockett (1786–1836), the colorful frontiersman who served three terms in Congress before moving to Texas, where he was killed while defending the Alamo from a Mexican army. **A thousand Mexicans lay dead:** actually closer to 500. **convent gate:** the gate of the Alamo, a former Franciscan mission. **corse:** corpse. **deadly knife:** a bowie knife, a heavy sheath knife having a long, single-edged blade. The knife was designed by James Bowie's brother. **San Jacinto:** the battle fought in Texas in April 1836 during which the Texans avenged the massacre at the Alamo and effectively achieved independence from Mexico. Approximately 100 Irish-born — or one-eighth of the Texan army — participated in the battle. **Thermopylae:** a pass in eastern Greece where a force of 6,000–7,000 Greeks under King Leonidas of Sparta initially held off a Persian invasion force of perhaps 180,000 in 480 B.C. Most of the Greeks fled, however, when the Persians gained access to the pass. In the end, only 300 Spartans and 800 Thespians under Leonidas fought to the death to defend Thermopylae. The sole survivor mentioned by Roche may be Ephialtes, the Greek traitor who informed the Persians of a path around the pass. **Alamo left none:** Actually at least fourteen people in the Alamo survived the siege: one member of the garrison, three Americans (Susannah Dickinson, her daughter, and Travis's slave), and ten Mexican women and their children.

The Defence of the Alamo

by Joaquin Miller (1841–1913)

Santa Ana [*sic*] came storming, as a storm might come;
 There was rumble of cannon; there was rattle of blade;
There was cavalry, infantry, bugle and drum—
 Full seven thousand in pomp and parade,
The chivalry, flower of Mexico;
And a gaunt two hundred in the Alamo!

And thirty lay sick, and some were shot through;
 For the siege had been bitter, and bloody, and long.
"Surrender, or die!"—"Men, what will *you* do?"
 And Travis, great Travis, drew sword, quick and strong;
Drew a line at his feet. . . . "Will you come? Will you go?
I die with my wounded, in the Alamo."

Then Bowie gasped, "Lead me over that line!"
 Then Crockett, one hand to the sick, one hand to his gun,
Crossed with him; then never a word or a sign
 Till all, sick or well, all, all save but one,
One man. Then a woman stepped, praying, and slow
Across, to die at her post in the Alamo.

Then that one coward fled, in the night, in that night
 When all men silently prayed and thought
Of home; of to-morrow; of God and the right;
 Till dawn; and with dawn came Travis's cannon-shot,
In answer to insolent Mexico,
From the old bell-tower of the Alamo.

Then came Santa Ana [*sic*]; a crescent of flame!
 Then the red escalade; then the fight hand to hand;
Such an unequal fight as never had name
 Since the Persian hordes butchered that doomed Spartan band.
All day—all day and all night; and the morning? so slow

Through the battle smoke mantling the Alamo.
Now silence! Such silence! Two thousand lay dead
   In a crescent outside! And within? Not a breath
Save the gasp of a woman, with gory gashed head,
   All alone, all alone there, waiting for death;
And she but a nurse. Yet when shall we know
Another like this of the Alamo?

Shout "Victory, victory, victory ho!"
   I say 'tis not always to the hosts that win!
I say that the victory, high or low,
   Is given to the hero who grapples with sin
Or legion or single; just asking to know
When duty fronts death in his Alamo.

Santa Ana [*sic*]: Antonio Lopez de Santa Anna (1795?–1876), a Mexican general, revolutionary, and president. **Travis:** William Barrett Travis (1809–1836), a leader in the movement for Texas independence and a defender of the Alamo during its final days in March 1836. **Bowie:** James Bowie (1796–1836), an American adventurer and slave trader and a defender of the Alamo in its final days. **Crockett:** David Crockett (1786–1836), the colorful frontiersman who served three terms in Congress before moving to Texas, where he was killed while defending the Alamo from a Mexican army. **save but one:** Louis Moses Rose, a Frenchman and a friend of Bowie's. Rose escaped from the Alamo by climbing over one of its walls. **a woman stepped . . . to die at her post in the Alamo:** There is no evidence that any of the women at the Alamo were killed during the siege. **one coward:** Louis Moses Rose, who escaped from the Alamo by climbing over one of its walls. **escalade:** the scaling of the Alamo walls by the Mexican troops. **Persian hordes:** the 180,000 Persian troops assembled by King Xerxes in his attempt to invade Greece in 481– 480 B.C. **Spartan band:** a group of 300 Spartans who gave their lives in defense of Thermopylae against the Persian invasion of Greece in 480 B.C. **Save the gasp of a woman:** Susannah Dickinson, the wife of Almerion Dickinson, a lieutenant belonging to the garrison. Actually at least fourteen people in the Alamo survived the siege: one member of the garrison, three Americans (Susannah Dickinson, her daughter, and Travis's slave), and ten Mexican women and children.

Hymn of the Alamo

Reuben M. Potter (1802–1890)

"Rise, man the wall, our clarion's blast
   Now sounds its final réveille;
This dawning morn must be the last
   Our faded band shall ever see.
To life, but not to hope, farewell!

> Yon trumpet's clang, and cannon's peal,
>   And storming shout, and clash of steel,
> Is ours, but not our country's knell!
> Welcome the Spartan's death—
>   'Tis no despairing strife—
> We fall!—we die!—but our expiring breath
>   Is Freedom's breath of life!"

> "Here, on this new Thermopylae,
>   Our monument shall tower on high,
> And 'Alamo' hereafter be
>   In bloodier fields the battle cry."
> Thus Travis from the rampart cried;
>   And when his warriors saw the foe
>   Like whelming billows move below,
> At once each dauntless heart replied,
> "Welcome the Spartan's death—
>   'Tis no despairing strife—
> We fall!—we die!—but our expiring breath
>   Is Freedom's breath of life!"

> They come—like autumn leaves they fall,
>   Yet, hordes on hordes, they onward rush;
> With gory tramp they mount the wall
>   Till numbers the defenders crush—
> Till falls their flag when none remain!
>   Well may the ruffians quake to tell
>   How Travis and his hundred fell
> Amid a thousand foemen slain!
> They died the Spartan's death,
>   But not in hopeless strife—
> Like brothers died, and their expiring breath
>   Was Freedom's breath of life!

Spartan's death: an allusion to the 300 Spartans who died while defending Thermopylae against the Persian invasion of Greece in 480 B.C. **Thermopylae:** a pass in eastern Greece where a force of 6,000–7,000 Greeks under King Leonidas of Sparta initially held off a Persian invasion force of perhaps 180,000 in 480 B.C. Most of the Greeks fled, however, when the Persians gained access to the pass. In the end, only 300 Spartans and 800 Thespians under Leonidas fought to the death to defend Thermopylae. **Barrett Travis:** William Barrett Travis (1809–1836), a leader in the movement for Texas independence and a defender of the Alamo during its final days in March 1836. **a thousand foemen slain:** actually closer to 500.

No Quarter, No Quarter
by Martha Keller (b. 1902)

"Blow it up! Blow it up!" said Houston, Sam Houston.
"They have six thousand men—it's a sin and a snare.
         Get out of Bexar and do not delay or
You'll die like a dog—you'll be massacred there.
When they sound the no quarter, they'll close for the slaughter—
When they play the degüello, *the wail of despair.*
         Colonel Travis,
                 Davie Crockett,
                         Jim Bowie,
                                 Major Evans,
                                         Major Bonham,
         It can never be held with as few men as these.
         Bee-hunting hunter,
                         and gambler,
                                 and pirate,
         You never can hold it, so fire it, so fire it . . . .
         Or you'll nevermore roam on the Texas prairies."

With the greasers as thick as the fleas on a dog is,
Or bugs on a blanket—they paid him no heed.
For the boys in the buckskin said, "Surely our luck's in.
And if it is not, we will see how they bleed."

"If the Alamo go," said Travis, Bill Travis,
"All Texas is stuck like a pig in a pen.
By the god-damn *degüello* the so-and-sos wail, though
We're less than two hundred we still will be men."

Then some say the pirate, some Bonham, some Bonham,
Rode out to get help, and got through, and got through.
Rode out to get Fannin more men and more cannon.
But Fannin was bogged and his cannon were, too.

Some say it was Bonham, and some the old pirate,
That rode back to Bexar, alone, all alone.
Though he knowed good and well he'd be going to hell—he'd
Gotten no help so he'd brought back his own.

But thirty rode in from Gonzales, Gonzales.
Thirty more men put their necks in the knot.

So they opened the whiskey. And though it were risky,
Laid bets with the gambler, and swilled while they shot.

Crockett, he played on the fiddle, the fiddle,
Till thy yelled like coyotes and fired to the tune.
And banged all the bungs out, and hollered their lungs out,
And sang, for they knowed that the end would be soon.

The hunter-of-bees killed eleven, eleven.
But the twelfth shot he shot come a little too late.
"Tell Kate," he says, "Kate, she's in old Nacogdoches.
Tell Kate I am dead. Who will tell my poor Kate?"

Evans, he died with a ball in his bosom,
Saying, "Sam, he were right. But we done what we could.
If you'll give me a hand up, I think I can stand up.
And I'll blow up the fort." But he died where he stood.

Bowie, Jim Bowie, was flat with the fever,
Weaker'n water, too seedy to stand.
But living or dying, from where he was lying,
He fought till he died, with his knife in his hand.

Crockett, Dave Crockett, got five of their gunners,
As pretty sharpshooting as ever were done.
But they got him, they got him, the Mexicans shot him.
And he lay in his blood by his sweet-shooting gun.

Travis, Bill Travis, what happened to Travis?
As broad as the Brazos, as high and as wide—
The Mexicans filled him with lead till they killed him.
When they played the *degüello*, Bill Travis, he died.

"Blow it up! Blow it up!" said Houston, Sam Houston.
"They have six thousand men—it's a sin and a snare.
Get out of Bexar and do not delay or
You'll die like a dog—you'll be massacred there.
When they sound the no quarter, they'll close for the slaughter—
When they play the degüello, *the wail of despair.*
Colonel Travis,
Davie Crockett,
Jim Bowie,
Major Evans,

> *Major Bonham,*
> *It can never be held with as few men as these.*
> *Bee-hunting hunter,*
> *and gambler,*
> *and pirate,*
> *You never can hold it, so fire it, so fire it . . . .*
> *Or you'll nevermore roam on the Texas prairies."*

Houston: Sam Houston (1793–1863), who, as military commander-in-chief of the provisional rebel government in Texas, ordered that the Alamo be destroyed since he thought it could not be defended by volunteers. He later was commander-in-chief and president of the Texas Republic and first governor of Texas. **Bexar:** the town of San Antonio de Bexar, Texas, where the Alamo was located. **degüello:** a Spanish bugle call signaling that no quarter will be given. The word is derived from the Spanish verb *degollar* ("to slit the throat"). **Colonel Travis:** William Barrett Travis (1809–1836), a leader in the movement for Texas independence and a defender of the Alamo during its final days in March 1836. **Davie Crockett:** the colorful frontiersman (1786–1836) who served three terms in Congress before moving to Texas, where he was killed while defending the Alamo from a Mexican army. **Bowie:** James Bowie (1796–1836), an American adventurer and slave trader and a defender of the Alamo in its final days. **Major Evans:** Robert Evans, an Irish native, who tried to ignite a room full of gunpowder at the Alamo (to fulfill an agreement which the defenders had made before the assault). Within a foot of the powder, however, he was killed by a Mexican officer. **Major Bonham:** James Bonham of South Carolina, one of those who died while defending the Alamo. **Bee-hunter, gambler, pirate:** three fictitious characters from *Col. Crockett's Exploits and Adventures in Texas*, written in 1836 by Richard Penn Smith but published as Crockett's autobiography. The bee-hunter's name was Edward or Ned, and the gambler bore the assumed name Thimblerig; the pirate, however, was nameless. The three purportedly accompanied Crockett to the Alamo and were killed in the final Mexican assault. **greasers:** swaggering young toughs, used here to refer to Mexicans. **Fannin:** James Fannin (1804?–1836), a leader in the movement for Texas independence. He and most of his soldiers were massacred at Goliad, Texas, while they were prisoners of Mexican troops. Forty-seven of the killed were Irish natives or men with Irish surnames. **Gonzales:** a town in southeast Texas. In 1836, thirty-two (not thirty) citizens from Gonzales answered the call of Colonel William Travis at the Alamo for reinforcements. **Brazos:** one of the principal streams of Texas.

Lament for the Alamo

by Arthur Guiterman (1871–1943)

Davy Crockett in his woodman dress,
    His shirt of the hide of a yearling doe
And his coonskin cap and his rifle, Bess—
    Dead he lies in the Alamo.

Ned the Bee-hunter with the coal-black curls,
    Straight as a spear shaft, lithe as a bow,
With a song for the world and a laugh for the girls—
    Dead he lies in the Alamo.

Colonel Bowie of the twelve-inch blade,
    Gentle of speech and sure of blow,
Prone on the heap that his sword arm made—
    Dead he lies in the Alamo.

Stout were their hearts the red week long
    That they strove with the hordes of Mexico,
But their powder failed and the odds were strong—
    Dead they lie in the Alamo.

Back to back in the slaughter pen,
    Steel to the steel of a ruthless foe,
Travis fell with his nine-score men—
    Dead they lie in the Alamo.

Gone from the wood and the waterside,
    Gone from the haunts of the buffalo,
They ride no more where they loved to ride—
    Dead they lie in the Alamo.

Texans, plainsmen, pioneers,
    Pay the debt that your rifles owe:
Pay your debt of blood and tears
    For those who died in the Alamo!

Davy Crockett: the colorful frontiersman (1786–1836) who served three terms in Congress before moving to Texas, where he was killed while defending the Alamo from a Mexican army. **Bess:** sometimes Betsey or Old Betsy, Davy Crockett's nickname for his rifle. **Ned the Bee-hunter:** a fictitious character from *Col. Crockett's Exploits and Adventures in Texas*, written in 1836 by Richard Penn Smith but published as Crockett's autobiography. The bee-hunter's name was Edward or Ned and purportedly accompanied Crockett to the Alamo. **Colonel Bowie:** James Bowie (1796–1836), an American adventurer, a popularizer of the Bowie knife (designed by his brother), and originally the co-commander (with William Travis) of the Alamo in its final days.

29. Thomas Fitzpatrick

Thomas Fitzpatrick was born in County Cavan, Ireland, about 1799 and came to America as a teenager. During the 1820s and 1830s he became forever identified with the Rocky Mountains, first as an explorer and then as a trapper. In 1836 while exploring the desert regions of the Rockies, the Irishman was pursued by a party of Blackfeet until he and his stead were forced to jump from a forty-foot precipice into the Yellowstone River. Hardly had he emerged on the opposite bank when the savages were again at his heels. In his haste to pull off the cover on his rifle, he accidentally discharged the weapon, whose contents shattered his left wrist. Undaunted, he reloaded and fired, killing two of his pursuers before shaking them off his trail. From then on, he was known as "Broken Hand."

Beginning in the 1840s, Fitzpatrick's name became associated with the nation's westward migration. In 1841 he led the first emigrant train to reach Oregon and California through northern Montana. Two years later he served as guide for Charles Fremont's second and longest expedition. The thirteen-month trek took the young Fremont from Kansas Landing to Idaho, across the Sierra Nevada to Sutter's Fort, south through the San Joaquin Valley, and back across the Sierras into Utah and then home to Missouri. After hardly a breathing space, Fitzpatrick was again heading west, this time on two successive expeditions with Colonel Philip Kearny.

In 1848 Fitzgerald was appointed Indian agent to the Arapahoes, Cheyennes, and Sioux in the Upper Platte. During the next five years he helped negotiate treaties with various Plains tribes north of the Platte. In 1865 Chief Little Raven of the Arapahoes described Fitzpatrick as "the one fair agent" they had ever had.

Broken Hand, Chief of the Mountain Men
by Ann Woodbury Hafen (1893–1970)

Trapper, Guide, Indian Agent

On frosted nights,
When the Great Bear turns in his starry bed,
The trapper creeps from his furry roll
To feed the midnight fire.
At an hour when the moon back-tracks the dawn,
Where then and now hold breathless rendezvous,
The Mountain Men come back.
I built a camp beside a mountain stream.
And when the night was silent as spent fire
A hand reached from the past to feed the coals.

Pine cones that leaped to flaming ghosts, revealed
A horny hand spread out to catch the warmth—
A grease-smeared hand, three fingers stubbed.
"Why, you — you're Broken Hand, the trapper-chief!"
Scarred fingers fed the cones
But not a word the Mountain Man replied. . . .

Trapper

You, buckskin-clan adventurer, son of a frontier breed,
What dull safe lands did you escape to be
A captive of the mountain peak and pine?
Trails your restless moccasins wore down
Lured from deep-rutted ways the covered caravans.
I think I see you in the campfire gleam—
Young sun-bronzed weathered face
That glows as an autumn leaf.
Long wind-tossed hair . . . .
Keen eyes like winter stars
That glisten crystals of the new-laid snow.
No book reveals the winding of your ways.
But a smoke-etched suit records—
As parchment traced by ancient hands—
The dangers and the doings of your days:
Grease smears of skinning knife,
Dark stains of trickled blood,
Fringe snagged by thorn of brush
Or ripped by grizzly claw.
Knife-cut
Where a challenger at Summer Rendezvous
Hot with bad liquor
Slashed but missed his mark.
Your coat's gay porcupine adornment
Sings the art of some bright Indian maid.
Does it speak too her love for you,
Adopted by her mountain tribe?
Your days, an endless search for beaver sign:
The fresh-gnawed aspen, brushwood dam,
Mound castle moated in a tiny lake,
Moist glassy slides in clay of river banks,
Stirred water paddle-slapped by wary wisdom.
Up virgin streams that swallow human scent
You lug steel cunning traps,
And manwise trick to death with castor bait

Sleek masters of the lodge.
Spring trapping done, what then?
Like pirate to his chest
You dig from secret cache
Pelt treasures to fur-hat the world!
With stacks of hairy banknotes
Off to Rendezvous where trappers holiday
And barter furs. Three beaver pelts
You wrested from an icy stream at dawn
Will buy vermilion paint and beads
To win a Cheyenne maid.
That grizzly skin that cost your partner's life
Will stake you at the gambler's monte game.
What care you if in one gay day
Go dearly-bought blood earnings of a year!
Then back again to autumn hunt
And Winter Rendezvous. Content.
Still captive to the solitude.
A campfire . . . pipe . . . a wonder tale . . .
A bed of buffalo robes . . . a sighing wind . . .
A canopy that drips the gold of stars!

Guide

Guardian of the west-bound caravan!
Director of the mighty sweep and stream
Of nation builders surging to their dream.
From water-front, across the gullied plain,
Up table land, on through the mountain gates,
Explorer, soldier, missionary band,
Home-seekers, visioning a sunset land,
     Follow your footsteps.
Master of frontier arts and mountain craft,
Sign-talker with palavering Indian bands
Builder of bullboats, tamper of quicksands,
Reader of landmarks, corraller of the train.
You turn a buffalo herd in wild stampede
Or lead the way through rivers high in flood.
You choose a camp with water, grass, and wood.
You husband the supplies; you ration food.
You bolster courage, reconstruct disaster—
     Guide of the western trail!

Indian Agent

Not with a forkéd tongue
Not with an evil heart
Not with aloofness nor disdain
For sacred medicine and solemn rite
Nor smirking with a maudlin sentiment
Do you come from the great White Father.
Ambassador of peace
Promoter of understanding
You mediate between
The feathered warrior and the rash dragoon,
The Indian village and the covered caravan.
To red men groping through a maze
Of ways disaster-fraught,
You point a path
To bloodless peace!

Great Bear: the constellation of Ursa Major, the most prominent northern constellation, containing the seven stars that form the Big Dipper. **Rendezvous:** a gathering of trappers and traders, during which time they exchanged goods and amused themselves with horse racing, wrestling, gambling, and shooting contests,

30. James K. Polk

James K. Polk, the eleventh president of the United States, was born in North Carolina in 1795, the son of a farmer and surveyor of Scotch-Irish descent. Polk's great-great-great-grandfather was Robert Pollock (pronounced "Poke" or "Polk"), who had left County Donegal, Ireland, for Maryland late in the seventeenth century. At age eleven James K. Polk moved with his family to Tennessee but returned to attend the University of North Carolina. There the young student excelled in mathematics and the classics and delivered the Latin oration for his graduating class. He was later so renowned for his oratory that he was dubbed the "Napoleon of the Stump."

Polk began his political career as a protégé of Andrew Jackson. In 1824 the young lawyer was elected to the first of seven terms in the House of Representatives, over whose proceedings he presided as Speaker for four years. After completing one term as governor of Tennessee, he was selected in 1844 as the dark horse presidential candidate on the Democratic ticket. He ran on a platform that emphasized the nation's "manifest destiny" to advance across the continent to the Pacific.

Despite his relative obscurity to many Americans, Polk is generally regarded by historians as one of the country's most effective presidents. During his single term he successfully pursued policies which rivaled the Louisiana Purchase for increasing the territorial size of the nation. Through annexation he extended American sovereignty to Texas, for example, while his bluster toward the British resulted in the acquisition of the Oregon Territory. In turn, the annexation of Texas led to a war with Mexico which resulted in the sale of California and the vast reaches of "New Mexico" to the Northern Colossus.

1845   (written 24 May 1963)
by Jackson Mac Low (b. 1922)

. . . .

The main things about James Knox Polk were
that first he had Texas & then a war with Mexico on his hands
that he was no ox but a man with a conscience who made war anyway
that "we" got all of Texas, Utah, Nevada, & California
        & most of Arizona and New Mexico   because
                of conscience-stricken Mr. Polk's war
that   Mr. Polk's war
                    extended "us" to the   waters of the
                                    Pacific   (Ocean)
(how "pacific" can an ocean be   if   "we"
 got
 "our"
window on it thru a war?)
                                    (Answer: just as
        "pacific"
                    as any other ocean)
                    ("window"   hell:
                        "our"
                            teeth
snapped up a whole damn coast *that* time
            & everything up   *to* it)
                    that   *that* war
                                    was
                                    why
                Thoreau refused to pay his tax
            & stayed in jail a night
            & wrote *Civil Disobedience*
            &   eventually
                was read by a little Indian lawyer   (*Indian* Indian)

     who invented another way to fight
     & thought it wasn't violent
     &
       used it
          so shrewdly that
   he &   circumstances made
   the British Empire lose a whole sub-continent.

In the palm of his hand
    a man who ate no fish or meat
  held   for a time
     an
   empire on which the sun never set
       his eye
    controlled that vast melange of
       hungry peoples
  he
       didnt
       fight
 not
     that is
      as
 other people fought
   he thought
  he made no threats
    thought
  he   used no violence
    thought
  he   used only
     Satyagraha
   the force of truth
to pull away the British Empire's props.

Thus we've come by word of mouth
    from James Knox Polk
    America's
    first "dark horse" president
to the eye of Mohandas Gandhi:
  that   ox-goad
    small enough to be
  hidden in the palm of a hand.
         (to here at 1:10 am Sat 25 May 1963)

Thoreau: Henry David Thoreau (1817–1862), an opponent of the Mexican War and the author of *The Necessity of Civil Disobedience*. **little Indian lawyer:** Mohandas Gandhi (1869–1948), the Hindu religious leader and nationalist who led India to independence from Britain through a campaign of nonviolent civil disobedience. (See "Satyagraha.") **Satyagraha:** "Devotion to truth," a slogan used to describe Mohandas Gandhi's technique of redressing wrongs (e.g., by the British in India) by resisting the adversary and fighting him without violence.

31. James Shields

A native of County Tyrone, Ireland, James Shields enjoyed a number of distinctions. He challenged Abraham Lincoln to a duel, served in three of the nation's military conflicts (the Black Hawk War, the Mexican War, and the Civil War), and was the only American to represent three states in the U.S. Senate (Illinois, Minnesota, and Missouri).

Shields served with extraordinary distinction in the conflict with Mexico. At the battle of Cerro Gordo in 1847, his right lung was pierced by a cannon grapeshot an inch and a third in diameter, although luckily the missile exited before hitting his spine. On the field at Churubusco he led the charge of New York Irish and South Carolina volunteers. Later at the battle of Chapultepec he fought on foot, with sword in hand, after his horse had been shot out from under him. Although he subsequently suffered a fractured arm during the assault on Mexico City, the men under his command were the first to plant the Stars and Stripes over the city.

An example of Shields' romantic daring was evident in an episode which occurred on the eve of the capture of Mexico City. That night an English boy entered the general's tent and informed him that his — the boy's — sister was being held captive in the city by a Mexican desperado. With Shields in the lead, he and his men stealthily followed the boy back into Mexico City, rescued the woman, and had almost returned to camp when the Mexicans opened fire on them, although without effect. The next morning when General Winfield Scott reprimanded Shields for his unauthorized expedition, the Englishwoman pleaded her rescuer's case. Scott was unyielding, however, and threatened the Irishman: "Shields, I shall court martial you; I shall have you dishonorably discharged, and disgrace you." Shields nobly replied: "General Scott, you can court martial me, you may have me dishonorably discharged, but no one, except myself, can disgrace me."

During the Civil War, Shields offered his services to Lincoln's war effort. As brigadier general of volunteers, he campaigned in the Shenandoah Valley, where he won recognition for his part in the battle of Winchester.

Incident of the Siege of Mexico
by Katherine Brownlee Sherwood (1841–1914)

"Halt!" 'Twas the picket's ringing cry,
    And halt 'mong the cactus spears,
A little, trembling, wild-eyed lad
    Lay smitten by his fears.
"Who comes there?" Not a soul replied,
    And now the sturdy guard
Puts down his gun and drags the boy,
    Half naked, from the sward.
All this was thirty years ago,
    As many of you know;
It happened when the boys in blue
    Laid siege to Mexico.

"What do you here, you skulking spy?"
    The rough-voiced soldier said,
"To-morrow, boy, prepare to die,
    A bullet through your head!"
The lad sprung up in terror then
    And clasped the soldier's knees,
And moaned and moaned between his sobs
    Such broken cries as these:
"Oh, soldier, by your English speech,
    And English face, I know
You will not harm a Union lad
    Who flees from Mexico."

The soldier's face grew grave and sad,
    He thought him of his home,
And how just such a lad as this
    Would joy to see him come.
Love lent a pathos to his speech,
    A radiance to his face.
Till, grown more bold, the stranger boy
    Made known his piteous case:
"Oh, sir, unto the General
    One moment let me go,
To plead for her who cries for help
    In cruel Mexico."

No braver man than General Shields

E'er wore the Union blue;
He curbed his soldier spirit
    Till he heard the story through;
Then kissed the forehead of the lad
    And said, "Godspeed us all;
This night my men shall pass the squares
    Of Santa Anna's Hall."
The soldier's blood was hot and high,
    He chafed that he might go
To rescue her who blessed our flag
    In bonds of Mexico.

The camp was in commotion,
    'Twas a cry for volunteers,
Men fit for any danger,
    Men void of any fears.
"'Tis not for fame or conquest,
    To storm redoubt or line;
To save a woman's honor
    Let hearts and swords combine!
A woman of the Union,
    Who says a Spaniard 'No,'
We'll dare a thousand deaths to wrest
    From alien Mexico!"

By twos and tens they gather—
    Four hundred men and true—
New York and Illinois they came,
    And South Carolina, too;
By twos and tens they gather
    To follow General Shields,
The man who never falters,
    The man who never yields.
By twos and tens they scale the heights,
    They pass the sleeping foe,
And one fair woman clasps our flag
    In haughty Mexico.

What ho! the alarm! the foe awakes!
    The muskets flash and roar,
The streets are filled with angry men,
    A cloud behind, before!
"Unsheath your swords and follow me!"
    The General led the blow;

And no man spared his sword for her
    They bore from Mexico.

'Tis morning in the plaza,
    And General Scott is there.
His conquering hosts around him,
    And cheers rend all the air.
Above the stately palaces
    The Stars and Stripes are run,
And music joins her clamor
    With the booming of the gun.
But not a braver deed was done,
    The conquering siege will show,
Than General Shields for woman wrought,
    Defying Mexico.

Shout, little refugee, and toss
    Your cap for General Shields,
The man who never falters,
    The man who never yields;
Break forth in merry laughter
    With the sister by your side;
She shall be no ruffian's mistress,
    She shall be a soldier's bride!
Cheers for the brave four hundred,
    With their faces to the foe,
And three times three for General Shields
    Who fought at Mexico.

Santa Anna: Antonio Lopez de Santa Anna (1795?–1876), a Mexican general, revolutionary, and president. **General Scott:** Winfield Scott (1786–1866), the general-in-chief of the U.S. army from 1841 until his retirement in 1861. During the Mexican War he enjoyed victories at Vera Cruz, Cerro Gordo, Contreras, Churubusco, and Chapultepec.

The Sword of Cerro Gordo

by Charles J. Beattie

Sound the loud bugle!—roll the drum!
    Your standard flag unfurl to-day,
From every state the people come,
    Their debt of gratitude to pay
To him who in the battle van

Gave heart and soul and sword to man—
            The Sword of Cerro Gordo!

From the glad north—the sunny south,
    The east—the west—from shore to shore,
And from the cannon's iron mouth
    Let salutations loudly roar—
For him whose sword in siege and field
Was freedom's bulwark—honor's shield—
            The Sword of Cerro Gordo!

For Shields, the statesman, pure and true,
    For Shields, the hero of two wars,
Who led the gallant boys in blue
    To victory 'neath the stripes and stars,
Whose sword flashed in the hottest fight
For home and country—truth and right—
            The Sword of Cerro Gordo!

That peerless sword in fight was seen—
    To flash upon a foreign strand
By mountain ford and forest green;
    And here in freedom's holy land
At Winchester it gain'd the day—
And vanquished Stonewall in the fray—
            The Sword of Cerro Gordo!

Son of fair Erin—let the place
    That gave him birth, be honor'd here.
Sons of his land—a hero race—
    Remember him with sigh and tear;
Though sheath'd that sword—the bronze unveil
To glad the Saxon and the Gael—
            The Sword of Cerro Gordo!

Raise high for him the sculptur'd stone,
    Three states the august statesman claim,
Missouri calls him all her own,
    Fair Minnesota loves his name,
In Illinois he is adored,
Columbia glories in his sword,
            The Sword of Cerro Gordo!

Cerro Gordo: the pass in Mexico at which an American force of 8,500 men overcame 12,000 Mexican troops in 1847. The Americans lost sixty-three killed and took 3,000 prisoners. **stripes and stars:** the American flag ("Stars and Stripes"). **foreign strand:** Mexico. **freedom's holy land:** the United States. **Winchester:** Shields actually defeated "Stonewall" Jackson at Kernstown (not Winchester), Virginia, on March 23, 1862, in what was the only time a Union general bested the Confederate commander. In the long run, though, Shields failed to destroy Jackson's force in the Shenandoah Valley and was defeated at Port Royal the following June. **Stonewall:** Thomas "Stonewall" Jackson (1824–1863), a Confederate general who was accidentally killed by his own men soon after his victory against the right wing of the Union line at the battle of Chancellorsville. **Erin:** a literary name for Ireland. **Saxon:** used here to refer to the English and their American descendants. **Gael:** used here to refer to the Irish. **Columbia:** the United States of America, usually personified as a female figure.

The Shields Statue

by Charles J. Beattie

Unveil the statue! Let the bronze reveal
The gallant soldier, true through woe and weal;
Son of the island green, beyond the wave—
Adopted by Columbia, free and brave;
To her he gave his heart, his love, his life,
In peace his counsel, and his sword in strife.

When the wild war drum with its dread alarms
Wakes the dread echoes with the call to arms,
We heard the trumpet and the bugle shrill,
Call to the camp, the muster and the drill—
When on our Southern border massed the foe,
And fierce invaders storm'd from Mexico.

When fell marauders shed our soldiers' blood,
And stained our soil by Rio Grande's flood,
We saw the patriot host to battle throng,
For our lov'd land—our country right or wrong—
When soldiers mustered or for Aztec fields,
First in the line was seen the gallant Shields.

When the fierce storm of iron hail and rain
At Vera Cruz swept over hill and plain,
When Hell's red fires were hurled from fort and crag,
He braved their furies and upheld our flag;

In the wild cyclone's mass of wounds and death,
He won the soldier's crown—the hero's wreath.

In the advance on Cerro Gordo's height,
He seemed the master-spirit of the fight;
When the grim batteries from the ramparts frowned,
He climbed the hill with all death's engines round,
Leading the storm 'gainst embattl'd walls,
With Spartan courage captured its high halls.

Hero of heroes! in his bright career,
He sought the post of danger, void of fear;
Foremost in fight—he led the crimson way—
Into the hottest of the bloody fray,
And proud as Mars amid the battle wreck,
Was hailed proud victor at Chapultepec.

Again war's sanguine sounds spread on the gale,
Fraternal strife convulsed the hill and vale,
Wild civil war with all its untold woes—
The North and South embattl'd—bitter foes;
Troop mustered past by field and ford,
Again the country claimed his trusty sword.

Again the hero led in war's red brunt—
The patriot men who mustered at the front
In battle grand array, who nobly stood
Like living bulwarks 'gainst the crimson flood;
On Winchester's proud heights he led the free
And crown'd our flag with glorious victory.

Yet war was not his choice—his destined path—
He loved not bloodshed—and he sought not wrath,
His sphere was law—a Senator profound,
'Gainst slavery and injustice ever found,
Who represented 'mong our greatest—best—
Three sovereign states that gild the mighty West.

Hail, soldier of two wars! Hail, statesman true!
To-day we raise the cenotaph to you;
Though in our hearts your company ever bright,
Outlasts the chaos of the field and fight—
And ever green be watered by our tears,
Through all the cycles of the coming years.

Columbia: the United States of America, usually personified as a female figure. **Rio Grande:** the river forming the boundary between Texas and Mexico. **Aztec:** pertaining to the ethnic group that ruled much of central and southern Mexico prior to the Spanish conquest in 1521. **Vera Cruz:** a port on the east coast of Mexico, from which the American general Winfield Scott led an expeditionary force toward Mexico City. **Cerro Gordo:** the pass in Mexico at which an American force of 8,500 men overcame 12,000 Mexican troops in 1847. The Americans lost sixty-three killed and took 3,000 prisoners. **Mars:** the Roman god of war. **Chepultepec:** the fortress defending Mexico City, where 7,200 American soldiers outfought 16,000 Mexicans in September 1847. The U.S. troops had to fight their way up steep slopes and smash through city walls with picks. **Winchester:** Shields actually defeated "Stonewall" Jackson at Kernstown (not Winchester), Virginia, on March 23, 1862, in what was the only time a Union general bested the Confederate commander. In the long run, though, Shields failed to destroy Jackson's force in the Shenandoah Valley and was defeated at Port Royal the following June. **cenotaph:** a sepulchral monument erected in memory of a deceased person whose body is buried elsewhere.

In Memoriam: General James Shields
by T. O'D. O'Callaghan

A month since thine ashes were laid, Shields,
    To rest in thy Western grave,—
A month in death's trappings arrayed, Shields,
    Lying stark by Missouri's wild wave,
And not one Irish poet or bard, Shields,
    Though rhymers a legion there be,—
O'er thy heroic clay, battle-scarred, Shields,
    Has chanted a requiem for thee!

Old Ireland is mother of sons, Shields,
    Right famous in historic lore,—
Of soldiers who stood by their guns, Shields,
    On battle-fields crimson with gore,—
The O'Neills—Shaun, the valiant, and Owen, Shields,
    Fought bravely for freedom of yore;—
'Mongst the hills of thy native Tyrone, Shields,
    Their memory is green evermore.

And Sarsfield was clever and brave, Shields,—
    Defender of Limerick's wall;—
At Landon [*sic*] he found a red grave, Shields,
    And Ireland long mourned his fall;
Tom Meagher was brilliant and bold, Shields;—

Gallant soldier of Freedom proved he,
Where battle's mad billows high rolled, Shields,
    Like the waves of a storm-lashed sea!

Phil Kearney [*sic*] was found in the front, Shields,
    When freedom stood struggling for life;
In many a fierce battle's brunt, Shields,
    His sword-flash illumined the strife!
Kilpatrick rode fearless and free, Shields,
    On many a dead-cumbered plain;—
When Sheridan gave greeting to Lee, Shields,
    Dark treason fled, routed amain!

Soldier-heroes besides those we've named, Shields,
    Have sprung from the old Gaelic sod,—
Before whom pale cowards slunk, shamed, Shields,
    In the presence of man and of God;
But 'mongst all her soldiers of fame, Shields,
    In ancient and modern day,
Thy country shall treasure *thy* name, Shields,
    In story and record and lay.

And Freedom will never forget, Shields,
    Her gallant and chivalrous knight,
Who on many a battle-field met, Shields,
    The foes who dared question her right;
Those wounds on thy cold clay attest, Shields,
    How freely thy blood had been shed,
Neath the star-spangled flag of the West, Shields,
    In Heaven's own glory outspread!

On Mexico's tower-capped hills, Shields,
    Old Echo is whispering thy name;
By Mexico's rivers and rills, Shields,
    The peasants remember thy name;
Though years nigh two score have flown by, Shields.
    Over Mexican valleys and bowers,
Since you planted the starry flag, high, Shields,
    On her Capitol's turrets and towers.

CONTRERAS, in letters of gold, Shields,
    Is blazoned on history's scroll;
CHERUBUSCO'S proud story'll be told, Shields,
    While men deeds of valor extol;

CHEPULTEPEC'S record shall stand, Shields,
  While the "Star Spangled Banner" floats free;
CERRO GORDO towers solemn and grand, Shields,
  Monumental forever of thee!

The memory of Winchester's day, Shields,
  Is linked with thy name evermore,—
Where Jackson's grim host in dismay, Shields,
  Fled, vanquished, thy onset before;
Till the last flickering moment of time, Shields,
  Expires in the red flame of Doom,
The light of that story sublime, Shields,
  Shall shine 'mid thy sepulchre's gloom!

No "Soldier of fortune" wert thou, Shields,
  Save fortune (uncertain) of war;
And nought of war's fortune, I trow, Shields,
  Was thine, save the red battle-scar!
Ah! meagre and mean the reward, Shields,
  Dead soldier of Freedom, they gave;
But Honor shall evermore guard, Shields,
  The ashes which hallow thy grave.

On this, Freedom's memorial day, Shields,
  While her cannon triumphantly boom,
This tribute I tearfully lay, Shields,
  With reverent heart, on thy tomb.
May Heaven grant peace to thy soul, Shields,
  High o'er the fierce storms of War!
While Missouri may oceanward roll, Shields,
  Undimmed be the light of thy star.

Western grave: at Carrolton, Missouri, where Shields died on June 4, 1879. **Missouri's wild wave:** the Missouri River. **Shaun O'Neill:** probably Shane O'Neill (c. 1530–1567), the Irish patriot whom Elizabeth I recognized as chieftain of Tyrone in order to prevent him from becoming a tool of Spanish intrigues against her. **Owen O'Neill:** Owen Roe O'Neill (1590–1649), an Irish rebel commander during a major Catholic revolt (1641–1642) against English rule in Ireland. **Sarsfield:** Patrick Sarsfield (d. 1693), a leader in the Irish Catholic resistance (1689–1691) to England's King William III. Sarsfield had earlier served in the army of Louis XIV and had accompanied James II to France when that monarch was deposed in favor of William. After the Williamite victory in Ireland, Sarsfield and about 7,000 Irishmen went into exile in France. **Landon [*sic*]:** Landen, the battlefield in Flanders where the French defeated William III of England in 1693. The Irish exile Patrick Sarsfield was killed during the engagement and was buried on the battlefield.

Tom Meagher: Thomas Meagher (1823–1867), the Irish native who formed the Irish Brigade in the Union army during the Civil War. **Phil Kearney** [*sic*]: Phil Kearny (1814–1862), a veteran of the Mexican War and the commander of the First New Jersey Brigade in the Civil War. He was killed after unwittingly crossing the Confederate lines just before the second battle of Bull Run. **Kilpatrick:** Hugh Judson Kilpatrick (1836–1881), a Union brigadier general, whose cavalry assaulted the Confederate right flank at Gettysburg. **Sheridan:** Philip Sheridan (1831–1888), generally regarded as the third most important Civil War Union general (after Ulysses S. Grant and William T. Sherman). **Gaelic sod:** Ireland. **Echo:** in classical mythology the mountain nymph who pined away for love of Narcissus until only her voice remained. **Contreras-Churubusco:** a double battle during the Mexican War in which Santa Anna lost about 8,000 men and General Winfield Scott lost 200 killed and 900 wounded. The victory left the Americans only five miles from Mexico City. **Chepultepec:** the fortress defending Mexico City, where 7,200 American soldiers outfought 16,000 Mexicans in September 1847. The U.S. troops had to fight their way up steep slopes and smash through city walls with picks. **Cerro Gordo:** a pass in Mexico at which an American force of 8,500 men overcame 12,000 Mexican troops in 1847. The Americans lost sixty-three killed and took 3,000 prisoners. **Winchester:** Shields actually defeated "Stonewall" Jackson at Kernstown (not Winchester), Virginia, on March 23, 1862, in what was the only time a Union general bested the Confederate commander. In the long run, though, Shields failed to destroy Jackson's force in the Shenandoah Valley and was defeated at Port Royal the following June. **Freedom's memorial day:** July 4, 1879.

32. Matthew C. Perry

Matthew C. Perry, who was born in Rhode Island in 1794, was the son of an Irish woman whom his father had met in Ireland and who accompanied him home to America. Prior to his success in opening Japan to American trade, the younger Perry enjoyed a varied career in the U.S. navy. In 1820 he served as executive officer of a naval vessel that escorted the first group of African Americans to be settled in Liberia, and he later commanded a squadron that helped suppress the slave trade and protect the African-American colonies on the west coast of Africa. During the Mexican War he commanded the naval forces that helped General Winfield Scott force the surrender of Vera Cruz, Mexico.

In 1852 Perry was chosen to lead a historic diplomatic mission to Japan. He was commissioned to negotiate with that isolated nation a treaty that would ensure the protection of American sailors and property in Japan and bring about the opening of Japanese ports to American trade. After anchoring in Yedo Harbor in July 1853, Perry proceeded to insist that he be greeted by a Japanese emissary equal to his own rank. Perry's bluster finally won for him an elaborate welcome by representatives of the emperor. Although a full-scale commercial treaty was not negotiated until 1858, Perry and his men gave the Japanese their first introduction to Americans and western technology. The American commander was especially complimentary about Japanese resourcefulness: "Their curiosity to learn the results of the material progress of other people, and their readiness in adapting them to their own uses, would soon . . . raise them to a level with the most favored countries."

Despite his reputation for gruffness and strict discipline, "Old Bruin" was at the forefront of reform efforts within the navy. Early in his career he stressed the importance of proper hygiene among his men in order to prevent diseases, and he proposed a naval apprenticeship system that was finally adopted by Congress. He later led the way to creation of the U.S. Naval Lyceum for the further education of naval officers, and he helped prepare the first curriculum for the Naval Academy at Annapolis.

To Commodore Matthew Calbraith Perry
by Arthur Guiterman (1871–1943)

When Commodore Perry with banners unfurled
Unbottled Japan on a wondering world,
How little he dreamed what a demon of war
Emerged from that bottle so harmless before—
A demon remorseless to rave and kill,
Obeying no law but its arrogant will.
Oh, Commodore Perry, come quickly and pen
That spirit of wrath in its bottle again!

33. Edgar Allan Poe

Edgar Allan Poe traced his Irish ancestry to his grandfather, David Poe, who had emigrated from Londonderry, northern Ireland, and settled about 1748 in Pennsylvania, where he married Elizabeth Cairnes, also of an Irish family.

From 1832 to 1835, a period which some biographers call his "dark and mysterious years," Poe lived in Baltimore, where he wrote "MS in a Bottle," "Berenice" (his first sensational horror story), and his only play, *Politan*. At the time, he was living with his grandmother, his aunt, his brother, and two cousins, one of whom — Virginia Clemm— he later married, although she was only thirteen years old.

While living in Philadelphia from 1842 to 1844, Poe wrote "The Gold-Bug," "The Black Cat," "The Tell-Tale Heart," "The Murders in the Rue Morgue," "The Fall of the House of Usher," and the first draft of "The Raven." Poe, his dying wife, and his mother-in-law were in such an impoverished condition that his wife's mother sold most of their furnishings to pay the rent and to cover her daughter's medical expenses. When Poe moved from Philadelphia, he reputedly left with only his books and two cats.

In 1844 Poe lived in the area of what is now West Eighty-Fourth Street in New York City, at the home and farm of Patrick Brennan. It was there that he completed "The Raven." When Poe first met Brennan and his wife and their six children, he described the pair as "a hospitable agriculturalist and his consort." Poe later described their farm as "a perfect paradise," where he hoped that his consumptive wife would soon regain her health. As the poet revised his earlier drafts of "The Raven," he incorporated into it the statue of the goddess Athena — the "pallid bust of Pallas" — which stood above one of the doors in the Brennan home. Poe described his experience with the Brennans as "playing hermit in earnest, nor have I seen a living soul out of my family."

From *A Fable for Critics*
by James Russell Lowell (1819–1891)

"There comes Poe, with his raven, like Barnaby Rudge,
Three fifths of him genius and two fifths sheer fudge,
Who talks like a book of iambs and pentameters,
In a way to make people of common sense damn metres,
Who has written some things quite the best of their kind,
But the heart somehow seems all squeezed out by the mind,
Who— . . . ."

Barnaby Rudge: a feebleminded young man in the novel of the same name by Charles Dickens. The work is built around the anti-Catholic riots and destruction of Newgate Prison in London in 1780. **iambs and pentameters:** metrical feet used in poetry.

Poe's Cottage at Fordham
by John Henry Boner (1845–1903)

Here lived the soul enchanted
By melody of song;
Here dwelt the spirit haunted

By a demoniac throng;
Here sang the lips elated;
Here grief and death were sated;
Here loved and here unmated
    Was he, so frail so strong.

Here wintry winds and cheerless
    The dying firelight blew,
While he whose song was peerless
    Dreamed the drear midnight through,
And from dull embers chilling
Crept shadows darkly filling
The silent place, and thrilling
    His fancy as they grew. . . .

Proud, mad, but not defiant,
    He touched at heaven and hell.
Fate found a rare soul pliant
    And rung her changes well.
Alternately his lyre,
Stranded with strings of fire,
Led earth's most happy choir,
    Or flashed with Israfel.

No singer of old story
    Luting accustomed lays,
No harper for new glory,
    No mendicant for praise,
He struck high chords and splendid,
Wherein were fiercely blended
Tones that unfinished ended
    With his unfinished days.

Here through this lowly portal,
    Made sacred by his name,
Unheralded immortal
    The mortal went and came.
And fate that then denied him,
And envy that decried him,
And malice that belied him,
    Have cenotaphed his name.

Here loved and here unmated: It was in this cottage that Poe and Virginia Clemm
spent the last years of their married life, and it was here that she died. **Israfel:**

according to the Koran an angel "whose heartstrings are a lute, and who has the sweetest voice of all God's creatures." **cenotaphed his name:** A cenotaph is a monument to the memory of someone who is buried elsewhere.

Edgar Allan Poe

by Timothy Thomas Fortune (1856–1928)

I know not why, but it is true—it may,
In some way, be because he was a child
Of the fierce sun where I first wept and smiled—
I love the dark-browed Poe. His feverish day
Was spent in dreams inspired, that him beguiled,
When not along his path shone forth one ray
Of light, of hope, to guide him on the way,
That to earth's cares he might be reconciled.
Not one of all Columbia's tuneful choir
Has pitched his notes to such a matchless key
As Poe—the wizard of the Orphic lyre!
Not one has dreamed, has sung, such songs as he,
    Who, like an echo came, an echo went,
    Singing, back to his mother element.

where I first wept and smiled: the South. Fortune spent his early life in Florida. **Columbia:** the United States of America, usually personified as a female figure. **Orphic lyre:** the lyre of Orpheus, a poet of Greek myth who tried to free his dead wife, Eurydice, from the underworld by charming the god Hades with his music.

To Edgar A. Poe

by Sarah H. Whitman (1803–1878)

When first I looked into thy glorious eyes,
And saw, with their unearthly beauty pained,
Heaven deepening within heaven, like the skies
Of autumn nights without a shadow stained,
I stood as one whom some strange dream enthralls;
For, far away in some lost life divine,
Some land which every glorious dream recalls,
A spirit looked on me with eyes like thine.
Even now, though Death has veiled their starry light,
And closed their lids in his relentless night,—
As some strange dream, remembered in a dream,
Again I see, in sleep, their tender beam;

Unfading hopes their cloudless azure fill,
Heaven deepening within heaven, serene and still.

At the Grave of Poe
by Clinton Scollard (1860–1932)

Spring's glow and glamour over Baltimore
     Above the green God's acre where he lies,
The sunlight, amber as some fabled ore,
     And the ethereal blue of vernal skies,
     He who so long since solved the great surmise,
And haply now tunes an immortal lyre
     (He who could tune a mortal lyre so well)
     With the rapt Israfel,
And the celestial choir.

As white as snow the marble of his tomb
     Against the climbing ivy on the wall;
No cypress bough, with its unhallowed gloom,
     Here flings its sombre shade funereal;
     Even the church-tower, turreted and tall,
Speaks not of dolor, and the slender spines
     Of arbor-vitae tell of life, not death,
     The life that quickeneth
His immemorial lines.

Yet he was phantom-haunted; eldritch things
     Peopled the silent chambers of his brain;
Forevermore the winnow of dark wings
     Beat round about him, as when autumn rain
     Is hurtled by wild gusts against the pane.
Weird wraiths companioned him, but none the less,
     Amid the forms of ghoul and ghost and gnome,
     Figures were wont to roam
Of light and loveliness.

His was the master's magic; every chord
     He touched gave forth a throb of melody;
No music welled whereof he was not lord,
     Whether he sang some city by the sea,
     Or some strange palace built in Faëry;
He wove the spell of immaterial chimes

Into his fabric; e'en the midnight bird
And unforgotten word
Breathed through his charmèd rhymes.

He walked with shadows, and yet who shall say
We are not all as shadows, we who fare
Toward one dim bourn along life's fateful way,
Sharing the griefs and joys once his to share
Who passed erewhile to that fair Otherwhere
Beyond the poignancy of bliss or woe!
There hangs the immitigable pathos of dead years,
High hopes bedewed with tears,
About the grave of Poe.

the green God's acre where he lies: Poe is buried in Westminster Burying Ground in Baltimore, Maryland. **Israfel:** according to the Koran an angel "whose heartstrings are a lute, and who has the sweetest voice of all God's creatures." **arbor-vitae:** any of several evergreen trees of the cypress family. **eldritch:** eerie, weird, spooky. **Faëry:** the imaginary land of the fairies.

A Poet's Grave

by Thomas Bailey Aldrich (1836–1907)

In this pleasant beechen shade,
Where the crocus blossoms red,
Lieth one who, being dead,
Is neither matron, man, nor maid.

But once he wore the form of God,
And walked the earth with meaner things:
Death snapt him. See! above him springs
The very grass whereon he trod!

Let the world swing to and fro,
The slant rain fall, the wind blow strong:
Time cannot do him any wrong
While he is wrapped and cradled so!

Ah, much he suffered in his day:
He knelt with Virtue, kissed with Sin—
Wild Passion's child, and Sorrow's twin,
A meteor that had lost its way!

He walked with goblins, ghouls, and things
Unsightly,—terrors and despairs;
And ever in the starry airs
A dismal raven flapped its wings!

He died. Six people bore his pall;
And three were sorry, three were not:
They buried him, and then forgot
His very grave—the lot of all!

But strains of music here and there,
Weird children whom melody owns,
Are blown across the fragrant zones
Forever in the midnight air!

pleasant beechen shade: Westminster Burying Ground in Baltimore, Maryland, where Poe is buried.

Haunting Poe's Baltimore

by Allen Ginsberg (1926–1997)

I

Poe in Dust

Baltimore bones groan maliciously under sidewalk
Poe hides his hideous skeleton under church yard
Equinoctial worms peep thru his mummy ear
The slug rides his skull, black hair twisted in roots of threadbare grass
Blind mole at heart, caterpillars shudder in his ribcage,
Intestines wound with garter snakes
midst dry dust, snake eye & gut sifting thru his pelvis
Slimed moss green on his phosphor'd toenails, sole toeing black tomb
     stone—
O prophet Poe well writ! your catacomb cranium chambered
eyeless, secret hid to moonlight ev'n under corpse-rich ground
where tread priest, passerby, and poet
staring white-eyed thru barred spiked gates
at viaducts heavy-bound and manacled upon the city's heart.

II

Hearing "Lenore" Read Aloud
at 203 Amity Street

The light still gleams from the brazen fire-tongs
The spinet is now silent to the ears of silent throngs
For the Spirit of the Poet, who sang well of brides and ghouls
Still remains to haunt what children will obey his vision's rules.

They who weep and burn in houses scattered thick on Jersey's shore
Their eyes have seen his ghostly image, though the Prophet walks no
      more
Raven bright & cat of Night; and his wines of Death still run
In their veins who haunt his brains, hidden from the human sun.

Reading words aloud from books, til a century has passed
In his house his heirs carouse, til his woes are theirs at last:
So I saw a pale youth trembling, speaking rhymes Poe spoke before,
Till Poe's light rose on the living, and His fire gleamed on the floor—

The sitting room lost its cold gloom, I saw these generations burn
With the Beauty he abandoned; in new bodies they return:
To inspire future children 'spite his *Raven*'s "Nevermore"
I have writ this antient riddle in Poe's house in Baltimore.

church yard: Westminster Burying Ground in Baltimore, Maryland, where Poe is buried. **"Lenore":** a poem by Poe lamenting the death of a beautiful young woman, a theme which he regarded as the "most poetic topic in the world." **"Nevermore":** the refrain uttered by the mysterious bird in Poe's poem "The Raven."

To the Least American, if not the Greatest, of all American Poets

by William Griffith (1876–1936)

They say that Edgar Allan Poe was buried in Baltimore,
And only the other day
A signal tomb was lifted for sightseers to find,
As though he were *resting* there.
Surely Poe is not resting in Maryland soil,
Nor is he resting in any mortal thought of him. . . .
Being a strange and illusory presence,
Such as prevails in the rareness of poetry,
He is restless everywhere,
Searching, moving, having a passion to explore
Regions that reach beyond the attic or the cellar door.

Walt Whitman at the Reburial of Poe
by Nicholas Christopher (b. 1951)

*". . . of the poets invited only Walt Whitman
        attended."*   —Julian Symons

They got him in the end, of course.
In a polling booth, dead-drunk.
Vagrant, ballot-stuffer . . .
Four Baltimore coppers to carry that meager frame.
Our first detective of the broken heart,
he picked through its rubble
with his frenzied calculations,
his delirium of over-clarity,
until he found too many clues . . .
Once I dreamt of a man on a schooner,
compact and handsome, alone on the Sound,
thrilling to a violent storm,
threaded to this world by the silver
of a dying spider:
that man was Edgar.
He loved the moon, and the night-torch,
the notion of blood sea-temperatured,
of the cold rush impelling him . . .
In life, in poetry, my antithesis—
detached from the true life,
of rivers and birds and swaying trees,
of soil red with tubers and pregnant clay,
detached from the wondrous release of sex,
his spleen beating heavier than his heart—
two or three men (at least)
packed in among a dozen demons.
He never much cared for my work.
I admired only a fraction of his.
But I happened to be in Washington
last night . . . and I'm old now, half-wise,
too old not to have a sixth sense—
for the genuine article, anyway . . .
I marvel at all he accomplished
in such a hatcheted life,
electrifying his losses.
celebrating the deer park, the potter's field,
as I celebrated forest and plain . . .

But then to finish here,
another half-forgotten city,
wearing another man's rags—
a scene he might have written:
streets snaking around him,
steaming and sulphurous,
rain dirty as it left the sky—
one last maze before the foothills of hell . . .
And that polling booth . . .
the drinking pals who dumped him there,
frightened perhaps by that dying wolf's voice;
it strikes me now, the eulogies concluded
(I wouldn't give one and I wouldn't say why),
how appropriate he should go that way,
how perversely American in the end—
a man who had consumed himself with exotica,
green as the Republic itself,
poet of our bloodied ankles and ashen
bones, our cankers and lurid dreams:
I wonder who he voted for.
I wonder if he won.

In a polling booth, dead-drunk: En route from Richmond, Virginia, to Philadelphia to accept $100 for completing an editing job, Poe stopped in Baltimore. There he broke his temperance pledge and was found senseless in the gutter near a polling place on Lombard Street on October 3, 1849. He died in a hospital four days later of "congestion of the brain." **coppers:** a slang term for police officers. **Sound:** probably Long Island Sound, the body of water between Connecticut and Long Island, New York. **my work:** Walt Whitman's. Christopher uses Whitman as the narrator of this poem.

The Bad Habit
(For Poe)

by Charles Henri Ford (b. 1913)

Drug of the incomprehensible
engenders the freak of desire.
The bleeding statue, the violin's hair,
the river of fire:

the blood grows, the hair flows, the river groans,
from the veins, from the skin, by the home of the child
pulled and repelled by Bloody Bones;

renewal of the swoon

mastered, the raw egg of fear,
doped with mystery, the hooded heart:
perpetually haunted, hopeless addict,
herding unheard of cattle!

hopeless addict: by the time of his death, Poe was addicted to both alcohol and opium.

Mysteries

by Terence Winch (b. 1945)

All last night I kept speaking in this
archaic language, because I had been reading
Poe & thinking about him. I read "The Murders
in the Rue Morgue" which is supposedly the first
detective story. Who dun it? I wondered.
It turns out an orangutan was the murderer.
It looks to me like the detective story genre got off
to a pretty ridiculous start. I used to visit
Poe's house in the Bronx. I used to think,
God, Poe must have been a midget. Everything
was so small. Poe died in Baltimore and I can see why.
In Baltimore, all the people are very big and sincere.
During dinner last night, I told Doug and Susan
about "Murders in the Rue Morgue." I said I hadn't
finished it yet, but it looked like the murderer
was going to turn out to be an orangutan, unless
the plot took a surprising new twist. Then Doug
suggested that he and I collaborate
on a series of detective stories in which
the murderer is *always* an orangutan.

"Murders in the Rue Morgue": a mystery by Edgar Allan Poe, published in 1841 and regarded as the first detective story.

Streets of Baltimore

author unknown

Woman weak and woman mortal, through the spirit's open portal
I would read the Punic record of mine earthly being o'er—

I would feel that fire returning which within my soul was burning
When my star was quenched in darkness, set to rise on earth no more.
When I sank beneath Life's burdens in the streets of Baltimore.

Ah, these memories sore and saddening! Ah, that night of anguish
    maddening!
When my lone heart suffered shipwreck on a demon-haunted shore—
When the fiends grew wild with laughter, and the silence following
    after
Was more awful and appalling than the cannon's deadly roar—
Than the tramp of mighty armies thro' the streets of Baltimore,

Like a fiery serpent crawling, like a maelstrom madly-boiling,
Did this Phlegethon of fury sweep my shuddering spirit o'er,
Rushing onward, blindly reeling—tortured by intensest feeling
Like Prometheus when the vultures to his quivering vitals tore—
Swift I fled from death and darkness thro' the streets of Baltimore.

No one near to save or love me, no kind face to watch above me,
Though I heard the sound of footsteps like the waves upon the shore—
Beating—beating—beating—beating—now advancing—now retreating
With a dull and dreary rhythm, with a long, continuous roar—
Heard the sound of human footsteps in the streets of Baltimore.

There, at length, they found me lying, weak and 'wildered, sick and
    dying,
And my shattered wreck of being to a kindly refuge bore;
But my woe was past enduring, and my soul cast off its mooring,
Crying, as I floated onward, "I am of the earth no more!
I have forfeited Life's blessings in the streets of Baltimore."

Where was thou, O Power Eternal, when the fiery fiend infernal
Beat me with his burning fasces till I sank to rise no more!
Oh! was all my lifelong error crowded in that night of terror?
Did my sin find expiation which to judgment went before,
Summoned to a dread tribunal in the streets of Baltimore?

Nay, with deep, delirious pleasure I had drained my life's full measure
Till the fatal fiery serpent fed upon my being's core;
Then, with force and fire volcanic, summoning a strength Titanic,
Did I burst the bonds that bound me—battered down my being's door—
Fled, and left my shattered dwelling to the dust of Baltimore.

"Streets of Baltimore": This poem, similar in style and rhyme to Poe's "The Raven," appeared anonymously in a New York newspaper a decade after his death. The poem was purported to have been dictated to a spiritualistic medium by the dead poet himself. **Punic record:** perhaps used here to mean a pattern of initial successes followed by a final defeat (as in the case of Carthage during the Punic Wars against Rome in the third and second centuries B.C.). "Punic" may also mean "perfidious," anticipating the phrase "lifelong error" and the word "sin" in lines 28 and 29, respectively. **Phlegethon:** the river of fire in the ancient Greek underworld. **Prometheus:** the Titan in Greek myth who stole fire from Mount Olympus and gave it to humankind in defiance of Zeus. In retaliation Zeus decreed that Prometheus be bound to a rock and that an eagle feed upon the thief's liver, which daily regrew what had been earlier devoured. **they found me lying:** En route from Richmond, Virginia, to Philadelphia to accept $100 for completing an editing job, Poe stopped in Baltimore. There he broke his temperance pledge and was found senseless in the gutter near a polling place on Lombard Street on October 3, 1849. He died in a hospital four days later of "congestion of the brain." **fasces:** a bundle of rods containing an axe. **Titanic:** of great size and strength (from Titan, in Greek mythology a member of a race of gods who lost their supremacy over the world after a great battle with the Olympian deities).

34. Fitz-James O'Brien

Fitz-James O'Brien, a journalist, author, and playwright, was born in County Limerick, Ireland, about 1828. While attending the University of Dublin, he wrote two poems — "Loch Ine" and "Irish Castles" — both of which later appeared in *Ballads of Ireland*. After dissipating an £8,000 inheritance while working as a journalist in London, he moved to New York in 1852, apparently to escape an illicit love affair. Although he was able to earn a living by writing for major periodicals in America, including *Harper's Magazine*, *Vanity Fair*, and *Atlantic Monthly*, his works never attracted the attention he thought they deserved and the financial rewards he had expected. As a result, he volunteered for the Union army at the onset of the Civil War, going so far as to recruit a volunteer regiment called the McClellan Rifles. He was subsequently appointed to the staff of General Frederick Lander and went to the front in Virginia. While leading thirty-five Union cavalrymen on a cattle raid in 1862, he was hit in the shoulder by a Confederate bullet. He died six weeks later of complications caused by tetanus, a young man of only thirty-three.

Because his works often deal with psychology and pseudoscience, O'Brien is regarded as one of the forerunners of modern science fiction. His best known stories are "The Diamond Lens," about a man who falls in love with a being he sees through a microscope in a drop of water; "What

Was It?" in which a man is attacked by something he experiences in every way except through sight; and "The Wondersmith," about robots which turn upon their creators. Among his successful plays was "A Gentleman from Ireland."

Fitz James O'Brien

by A. E. Watrous (1859-1902)

This was our poet —one who strode
　　These streets in ante-bellum ages,
And smoked on street-car steps, and rode
　　Down Broadway on the tops of stages.

A Dublin gownsman, London rake,
　　For grim romance, pathetic ditty;
No color from 'cross the seas he'd take,
　　But loved, and learned, and wrote our city.

'Twas here he sowed each splendid crop
　　Of fecund wind—here did he reap
Fine whirlwinds. From the base or top
　　His path was lighter, being steep.

He swayed the sceptre, felt the lash,
　　Wrought starving nights—by sated days
Petted his trooper's brown moustache,
　　And sought and strolled life's sunny ways.

From here he sailed forth to crown
　　A flaring life with flaming death.
God rest him! There outside the town
　　He waits the Doomsday trumpet's breath.

Poor Fitz! they say—yet when I'm dead
　　I'll ask no pity, if a line
Of all I've writ in some one's head
　　Shall run as some of his in mine.

ante-bellum: a Latin phrase meaning "before the war," in this case the Civil War. **Broadway:** a fashionable thoroughfare in New York City. **Doomsday:** the day of the Last Judgment, at the end of world.

35. Patrick Breen

Patrick Breen emigrated from his native County Carlow, Ireland, in 1829 and settled near Toronto, where he married a woman he had known in the old country. Within a few years the couple moved to the United States, living successively in Illinois and Iowa Territory, where Patrick was deeded 320 acres of land near Keokuk. In April 1846 the nine members of the Breen family and their friend — Irish-born Patrick Dolan — set out for California. With children ranging in age from infancy to fourteen years, the Breens traveled in three wagons. After arriving at Fort Laramie, they were joined by several other families, including those of George Donner and James Reed. (Almost 35 percent of the emigrants had Irish surnames.) Reed, an Irish-born Protestant, soon found himself banished from the party for killing another man in an argument.

On July 20 Donner made the tragic mistake of leading the wagons onto the unfamiliar Hastings Cutoff around the south side of Great Salt Lake. Because of delays along the way, they arrived in the eastern Sierras at the end of October, dangerously late in the season to attempt a crossing. As they feared, snow prevented their passage, and they resigned themselves to spending the winter at the base of the mountains. The Breens built cabins at the lake, and in December they took the remaining members of the Reed family into their shelter. In her diary the Reeds' daughter Virginia recorded her experience in the Breens' cabin. "The Breens were the only Catholic family in the Donner party and prayers were said aloud regularly in that cabin night and morning. . . .," she wrote. "I was very fond of kneeling by the side of Mr. Breen and holding . . . [little torches] so that he might be able to read. . . ."

Faced with starvation, fifteen emigrants tried to cross the Sierras on snowshoes. On the sixth day out, they decided that they might have a chance to survive if one of their number was sacrificed. They agreed that whoever drew the longest slip would be their victim. Dolan, who drew the death card, said: "I am ready; take my life and save your own." When no one in the group would kill him, though, it was agreed that they would struggle on until death brought one of them down. On Christmas Day Dolan became delirious and deranged, pulling off his boots and most of his clothes and running out into the storm. He died that evening. The next day some of the group cut the flesh from Dolan's arms and legs, roasted it over the fire, and ate it, "averting their faces from each other, and weeping."

An account of the Donner party's ordeal in the Sierra Nevada was contained in a twenty-nine-page diary which Breen kept between November 20, 1846, and March 1, 1847. Of the eighty-one members who were stranded that winter, two-thirds of the men, one-third of the children, and one-quarter of the women perished. The survivors were ultimately rescued but not before additional instances of cannibalism, as this entry from Breen's diary indicates: ". . . Mrs. Murphy said here yesterday that [she] thought she would commence on Milt. & eat him. I dont [know] that she has done so yet, it is distressing[.] The Donn[ers] told the California folks that they [would] commence to eat the dead people . . . , if they did not succeed that day or next in finding their cattle then under ten or twelve feet of snow & did not know the spot or near it. . . ."

The following excerpt is from *The Donner Party*, a 254-page poem written by George Keithley, and is narrated in the voice of George Donner. This short selection probably relates an incident prior to the horrors experienced in the Sierra Nevada.

One Day near Dusk

From *The Donner Party* by George Keithley (b. 1935)

One day near dusk I left camp to look
for a place to piss in a clump of cottonwoods
whose paper leaves had gone from green to gold.
Not far from where I stood I thought I saw

something stirring in the grass— a dog
shook himself in the shade perhaps
pestered by a lively lizard, or the breeze

fluttered a few leaves. But when I took
another step closer I was able
to see someone sprawled beneath the trees.

He lay flat on his back. I saw the face
of our good friend Breen, and I was afraid
poor Patrick probably drove himself to death

searching for shelter where his wife would not
complain about the hot sun, and even
the blessed birds could communicate with heaven.

Perhaps he suffered terrible stomach trouble
from the fried potatoes that he ate. Or he might
have been brought down by a severe snakebite.

Then I noticed how his hands held his Bible
all but motionless and I finally perceived

that he was simply sleeping with the black book

propped on his chest as though a huge crow
crouched upon his shirt and lifted
its wide wings in rhythm with his breath.

The red sun achieved a brilliant glow
and small birds sang in the slants of light
while Breen slept as easy as the dead.

Since he was safe and I of course had other
business anyway, I hid in the shade
only a little longer and then returned
toward our camp feeling suddenly relieved.

36. James Buchanan

James Buchanan, the fifteenth president of the United States, was born in a Pennsylvania log cabin in 1791. His father and paternal grandparents were born in County Donegal, Ireland, while his maternal grandmother had emigrated from northern Ireland. The future president lived in Mercersburg, Pennsylvania, from 1796 to 1807, when he entered Dickinson College in Carlisle. Buchanan was expelled from the college, however, for "every sort of extravagance and mischief," although he later returned and was graduated *cum laude*. Buchanan later went into politics "as a distraction from a great grief," presumably the death of Anne Coleman, the twenty-three-year-old woman to whom he had been engaged. According to the story behind this unfortunate episode, when she heard her fiancé's name linked with another woman, Miss Coleman broke the engagement. The later discovery of Miss Coleman's dead body in a Philadelphia hotel led to rumors that she had committed suicide. Buchanan's private life was thereafter dogged by the suspicion that he had — in the words of Carl Sandburg — "hounded a young woman to her grave."

Prior to becoming the only Pennsylvanian to be elected president of the United States, Buchanan served in both the U.S. House and the Senate and was secretary of state and American minister to Russia and Britain. While living in retirement at "Wheatland," his home in Lancaster, Pennsylvania, the former president wrote *Mr. Buchanan's Administration on the Eve of the Rebellion* in defense of his policies toward the seceded Southern states.

James Buchanan
1791–1868

by Stephen Vincent Benét (1898–1943)

Poor James Buchanan!
He didn't know what to do,
For the South was getting its dander up
And the North was angry, too.

"You're villains and knaves for holding slaves!"
The Abolitionists groan,
But the Southerners swear it's their own affair
And the north must leave it alone.

Poor James Buchanan:
He fiddled and fussed and blew,
While the argument went from bad to worse
As arguments often do.
"We'd rather be done with the Union
Than let you Yankees boss us!"
"You Southerners crow you're the whole blame show,
But just you try to cross us!"

It was "Shan't!" and "Won't!" and "Can't!" and "Don't!"
And "Liar!" and "You're another!"
Till the whole wide land was split in two
And brother set against brother,
Till, at last, with a "There!" and a haughty stare,
In martial precipitation,
The Southern States left the Union's gates
To set up a separate nation.

Poor James Buchanan!
He twiddled his four years through,
And left the mess for somebody else
As weak men always do.
For when times are dark and the outlook stark,
The government needs a man on
Its chair of State, not an addlepate
Like weary old James Buchanan.

Abolitionists: political activists who sought an immediate end to slavery in the
United States.

James Buchanan
by Martha Keller (b. 1902)

Perhaps he leaned upon a gate,
Or lingered in a parlor's gloom.
But anyhow they changed his fate—
That face, that hour, and that room.

For gossip like the elements
Went roaring through the town at will,
Which citizens-with-better-sense
Repeated—as we do it still.

He should have known that such a pause
With such a girl would seem to his
Affianced Anne sufficient cause
For having words—so little is.

He didn't. Neither did he dream
The two-tongued tattle of the town
Could injure so her self-esteem,
Or shake her faith and break it down.

Perhaps it was because she blamed
Her own response, so eager, so
Romantic, the reaction shamed
And shook her like a vertigo.

She chose to break and not to bend.
Because she could no longer bear
Uncertainty, she made an end
And found contentment in despair.

Because, for her, perfection died—
Like all the final, the intense,
She fell in love with suicide.
Experience has better sense.

No love is ever what it seemed.
But it is lack, not life, that kills—
Not love, but love-as-it-is-dreamed.
Reality has lesser ills . . . .

She fled by stage. With every sway
Of slipping wheels, and jar and jolt
Of road and rut, she watched the spray
Of mud that ringed the axle bolt.

And in some inn, alone, afraid,
Alone again, alone by night,
She watched the flowered carpet, frayed
And florid in the candlelight.

Until at last, because she fled
A heart too heavy to be hid—
She put a pistol to her head.
At least, that's what they said she did . . . .

Though he—however ill-advised—
Kept silence for a lifetime, these:
One woman, once, one place, he prized,
Plain truth, all learning, and tall trees.

And yet, for nearly fifty Falls
I wonder what they made him feel—
His pillared porch and empty walls?
The creakings of a carriage wheel?

37. Thomas Jefferson Davis

Descended through his mother (Jane Cook) from Scotch-Irish ancestors, Thomas Jefferson Davis, the president of the Confederacy, was born in Kentucky in 1808. Following his graduation from the U.S. Military Academy, he did frontier duty in Wisconsin Territory and later served with distinction in the Mexican War. After six years as a U.S. senator from Mississippi, in 1853 he became secretary of state to President Franklin Pierce. Besides improving the nation's military academy and increasing the number of army personnel, he arranged for the purchase of southern New Mexico and Arizona and almost succeeded in acquiring slaveholding Cuba from Spain.

Again appointed to the Senate from Mississippi, Davis became a forceful voice for states' rights, strict interpretation of the Constitution, and support for the Union. When South Carolina became the first state to secede, Davis continued to hope that the other Southern states would not follow suit. Perhaps because he believed that the North would use force to restore the Union, he was willing to accept almost any compromise to prevent war as long as it guaranteed the constitutional rights of sovereign states. But when Mississippi seceded in early 1861, Davis resigned from Congress, intending to return home to defend his state but soon finding himself unanimously elected president of the fledgling Confederate States of America. Although Davis sent peace commissioners to Washington, D.C., to try to negotiate a peaceful settlement to the nation's sectional dispute, President Lincoln declined to receive them.

Despite Davis's eventual alignment with the Confederate cause, his views on slavery were atypical of his region and social position. He believed, for example, that the South's "peculiar institution" was a temporary one on the slaves' road to "perfectibility" and that Christianity and Anglo-Saxon culture would prepare the slaves for eventual emancipation and citizenship. Besides allowing his own slaves a high degree of self-government, he educated the most promising of them. In addition, scores of letters from his slaves attest to the genuine affection they had for him.

Later in his life, after the collapse of the Confederacy, the former president likened the system of settlement and confiscations carried out in Ireland by Cromwell to what he expected to happen to the people of the defeated South. "There was no excuse for it here; there had been some in Ireland," Davis wrote. "Between the conquering forces of Cromwell and the Irish there were essential differences of race, religion, habits, laws, and hopes. There had been war for centuries, and no promise of future tranquility on less rigorous terms." Davis saw "the further parallel that both countries suffered for loyalty to what each regarded as the rightful government; Ireland, for devotion to the Royal Family of the Stuarts; and the South, for its fidelity to the principles defined by the Constitution of 1787."

Jefferson Davis Inaugural

Capitol Portico: Montgomery, Alabama

by John Beecher (1904–1980)

A brazen star
marks where his haughty feet set
who later fled
in womanly disguise while near and far
the vengeful victor spoke in flame
and insult till the broken land was red
not with blood and embers only but with shame

A star inlaid
marks where he postured on the marble for a day
with his people ranged below
and seeking to stay history he bayed
the sun like Joshua
The sun impenitently set
and once more rose on irreversible woe

a brazen star: The approximate site of Davis's inauguration as president of the Confederacy in February 1861 is marked by a brass star in the pavement in front of the west portico of the Alabama state capitol. **in womanly disguise:** When Union troops approached Davis to arrest him in Georgia during the last days of the Civil War, the president of the Confederacy covered himself with his wife's raincoat, which he had donned in the dark, thinking it was his own. His wife than covered his head and shoulders with her shawl. **he bayed the sun like Joshua:** During the battle of Gibeon, Joshua, Moses' successor as leader of the Israelites, prayed that the sun stay its course in the sky so the Israelite cause would be aided by prolonged daylight (Joshua 10: 2–14).

Jefferson Davis

by Walker Meriwether Bell

"Our hearts, our hopes, our prayers, our tears,
Our faith triumphant o'er our fears,
Are all with thee, are all with thee."
                                        Longfellow

Calm martyr of a noble cause,
    Upon they form in vain
The Dungeon shuts its cankered jaws,

And clasps its cankered chain;
For thy free spirit walks abroad,
And every pulse is stirred
With the old deathless glory thrill
Whene'er thy name is heard.

The same that lit each Grecian eye,
Whene'er it rested on
The wild pass of Thermopylae—
The plain of Marathon;
And made the Roman's ancient blood
Bound fiercely as he told,
"How well Horatio kept the bridge,
In the brave days of old."

The same that makes the Switzer's heart
With silent rapture swell,
When in each Alpine height he sees
A monument to Tell:
The same that kindles Irish veins
When Emmet's name is told;
What Bruce to Caledonia is,
Kosciusko to the Pole—

Art thou to us!—thy deathless fame,
With Washington entwined,
Forever in each Southern heart
Is hallowed and enshrined;—
And though the tyrant give thy form
To shameful death—'t were vain;
It would but shed a splendor round
The gibbet and the chain.

Only less sacred in our eyes,
Thus blest and purified,
Than the dear cross on which our Lord
Was shamed and crucified,
Would the vile gallows tree become,
And through all ages shine,
Linked with the glory of thy name,
A relic and a shrine!

Dungeon: Jefferson Davis's prison cell at Fort Monroe, Virginia. **Thermopylae:**
the pass in eastern Greece where a force of 6,000–7,000 Greeks under King Leonidas

of Sparta initially held off a Persian invasion in 480 B.C. Most of the Greeks fled, however, when the Persians gained access to the pass. In the end, only 300 Spartans and 800 Thespians under Leonidas fought to the death to defend Thermopylae. **Marathon:** the plain in northeast Attica where an Athenian force of 10,000 defeated 25,000 Persians in 490 B.C. The Greeks lost only 192 men; the Persians, 6,400. **Horatio:** Horatius Cocles, the Roman hero of the sixth century B.C. who held off an Etruscan army at the Sublician Bridge across the Tiber into Rome long enough for his compatriots to demolish the span behind them. When the bridge gave way, Horatius fell into the water but swam to the other side, successfully avoiding a barrage of enemy missiles. **Switzer:** a citizen or inhabitant of Switzerland. **Tell:** William Tell, the legendary hero of the Swiss struggle for independence from Austrian domination during the fourteenth century. **Emmet:** Robert Emmet (1778–1803), an Irish patriot executed for his involvement in an uprising against British rule in 1803. In his speech to the jury he asked that no man write his epitaph until "my country takes her place among the nations of the earth." **Bruce:** Robert the Bruce (1274–1329), the king of Scotland who defeated the English at Bannockburn and eventually forced them to recognize Scottish independence. **Caledonia:** the ancient Roman name for the Scottish Highlands. **Kosciusko:** Tadeusz Kosciusko (1746–1817), a Polish soldier who fought in the American Revolution and later led an uprising for Poland's independence from Austrian, Prussian, and Russian rule.

Jefferson Davis

by Harry Thurston Peck (1856–1914)

No paltry promptings of unglutted hate
   The Nation feels for him who erst assailed
Her life, and strove against the will of fate
To found an Empire and destroy a State.
   She stands today magnificently mailed
In loyal love, too gloriously great
   For thought of vengeance that were all too late.

And he whose death her sons would once have hailed
   With joy, now slinks through dark Oblivion's gate,
With this his epitaph: When others quailed,
   He staked his all upon one cast of fate
   And lost—and lived to know that he had failed!

38. John Mitchell

A native of County Londonderry, Ireland, John Mitchell at age thirty abandoned a legal career for one as a revolutionary. Disenchanted with the nonviolent and constitutional approach taken by Daniel O'Connell to achieve an independent Irish parliament, Mitchel joined the Young Ireland movement. From the pages of the *United Irishman*, he openly preached armed resistance to Britain and repeal of the constitutional union of that country and Ireland. Within six months, however, he was arrested and convicted of treason and condemned to fourteen years' imprisonment in Tasmania.

Following his escape in 1853, after only five years of exile, Mitchel was treated to enthusiastic welcomes from the Irish in San Francisco and New York. Buoyed by this experience, he established the *Citizen*, which he dedicated to the cause of Irish independence and which quickly came to enjoy a circulation of 50,000. His newfound status in New York soon dimmed, though, when he attacked the temporal power of the papacy and became an outspoken defender of slavery, the latter an extremely odd position for a champion of Irish liberty.

After being rejected for military service in the Confederate army because of poor eyesight, Mitchell accepted a position as editor of the *Richmond Enquirer*. As in the past, he used his pen to justify the Southern cause and to argue the states' rights position. In addition, as a member of a Confederate ambulance committee, he helped evacuate the wounded from the battlefields of Spotsylvania and the Wilderness. Within two years two of his sons had made the supreme sacrifice — John a casualty of the Union shelling of Fort Sumter, and Willy killed in Pickett's Charge at Gettysburg. His third son lost an arm during an engagement near Richmond.

By the spring of 1864 Mitchel had turned against President Jefferson Davis, apparently because of the latter's failure to prosecute the war more aggressively. From his new editorial position at the *New York Daily News*, a notoriously pro-Southern publication, the Irishman continued that paper's violent opposition to President Andrew Johnson's reconstruction policies. For his fulminations in the press, Mitchel was arrested by the military authorities and was confined to Fortress Monroe in Virginia. He never recovered physically and mentally from the four-month imprisonment.

John Mitchel

by John Boyle O'Reilly (1844–1890)

Dead, with his harness on him:
Rigid and cold and white,
Marking the place of the vanguard

> Still in the ancient fight.
>
> The climber dead on the hill-side,
>   Before the height is won:
> The workman dead on the building,
>   Before the work is done!
>
> O, for a tongue to utter
>   The words that should be said—
> Of his worth that was silver, living,
>   That is gold and jasper, dead!
>
> Dead—but the death was fitting:
>   His life to the latest breath,
> Was poured like wax on the chart of right,
>   And is sealed by the stamp of Death!
>
> Dead—but the end was fitting:
>   First in the ranks he led;
> And he marks the height of his nation's gain,
>   As he lies in his harness—dead!

39. Michael Corcoran

Michael Corcoran was born in 1827 in Sligo, Ireland, into a family whose estates had been confiscated by the British in the seventeenth century. Although as a young man he entered the Irish constabulary, he resigned in 1849 in protest against British mistreatment of his native land. Once in America, he enlisted in the New York State Militia's Sixty-Ninth Regiment and rapidly rose up the ranks. When he refused to parade his regiment for the visiting Prince of Wales, he became not only the darling of the New York Irish but also the object of a court-martial. The charges were dropped, however, when he offered his services and those of his men to the newly forming Union army.

Corcoran's Sixty-Ninth Militia fought valiantly at the first battle of Manassas (Bull Run) in July 1861 but suffered heavy losses (192 men killed, wounded, and missing) during the Union defeat. (The following song — "Boys That Wore the Green" — recounts the Sixty-Ninth's exploits at Bull Run.) Corcoran himself was captured and remained a Confederate prisoner for thirteen months because he refused to agree never again to take up arms. He was one of fourteen Union officers sent to Libby Prison in

Richmond, Virginia, to be held in exchange for an equal number of Confederate sailors. After his release he made a triumphal return to New York and was promoted to the rank of brigadier general.

The Irishman subsequently organized the Corcoran Legion, composed mostly of Irish immigrants and eventually consisting of the 155th, 164th, 170th, and 184th New York regiments. In late 1862 the legion defended Suffolk, Virginia, against Confederate troops, and from July 1863 to May 1864 it helped defend Washington D.C. In December 1863, at the age of thirty-six, Corcoran was killed in an accidental fall from a horse.

Boys That Wore the Green

author unknown

On the twenty-first of July, beneath a burning sun,
McDowell met the Southern troops in battle, at Bull Run:
Above the Union vanguard, was proudly dancing seen,
Beside the starry banner, old Erin's flag of green.

Colonel Corcoran lead [*sic*] the Sixty-ninth on that eventful day,—
I wish the Prince of Wales were there to see him in the fray;—
His charge upon the batteries was a most glorious scene,
With gallant New York firemen, and the boys that wore the green.

In the hottest of the fire there rode along the line
A captain of a Zouave band, crying, "Now, boys, is your time;"
Ah! who is he so proudly rides, with bold and dauntless mien?
'Tis Thomas Francis Meagher, of Erin's isle of green!

The colors of the Sixty-ninth, I say it without shame,
Were taken in the struggle to swell the victor's fame;
But Farnham's dashing Zouaves, that run with the machine,
Retook them in a moment, with the boys that wore the green!

Being overpowered by numbers, our troops were forced to flee,
The Southern black horse cavalry on them charged furiously;
But in that hour of peril, the flying mass to screen,
Stood the gallant New York firemen, with the boys that wore the green.

Oh, the boys of the Sixty-ninth, they are a gallant band,
Bolder never drew a sword for their adopted land;
Amongst the fallen heroes, a braver had not been,
Than, you, lamented Haggerty, of Erin's isle of green.

Farewell, my gallant countrymen, who fell that fatal day,
Farewell, ye noble firemen, now mouldering in the clay;
Whilst blooms the leafy shamrock, whilst runs the old machine,
Your deeds will live, bold Red Shirts, and Boys that Wore the Green!

McDowell: General Irwin McDowell (1818–1885), the commander of the Union troops who converged at the important railroad junction at Bull Run on July 21, 1861. After ten hours of fighting, the federal troops fell back in retreat, bested by Confederate forces under generals Joseph Johnston and Pierre Beauregard. **Erin:** a literary name for Ireland. **New York firemen:** Colonel Noah Farnham's Eleventh New York "Fire Zouaves." **Thomas Francis Meagher:** a native of County Waterford, Ireland, and captain of Company K, Sixty-Ninth New York Regiment. He later organized and commanded the Irish Brigade. **Farnham's dashing Zouaves:** Colonel Noah Farnham's Eleventh New York "Fire Zouaves." **Haggerty:** James Haggerty, captain of Company A, Sixty-Ninth New York Regiment. He was killed at Bull Run, where the Sixty-Ninth lost thirty-eight killed, fifty-nine wounded, and ninety-five missing, about 16 percent of its strength.

40. Thomas Meagher and the Irish Brigade

Thomas Meagher was born in Waterford, Ireland, in 1823, the son of a prominent merchant who for a time was a member of the British parliament. The younger Meagher attended the Jesuit college at Clongowes-Wood in Kildare and the English college at Stonyhurst. At the age of twenty-three, a year after joining the Young Ireland party, he made his debut as an orator at the "monster rally" at Kilkenny attended by Daniel O'Connell. A year later, however, Meagher made his break with O'Connell's constitutionalist approach to political change and adopted a more militant nationalist position, thereby earning the nickname "Meagher of the Sword."

In 1848 Meagher traveled to Paris to seek French assistance for an Irish uprising and returned to Dublin with an Irish tricolor. Following a speech in which he made incendiary remarks, he was arrested for sedition and condemned to death for high treason. The sentence was soon commuted to banishment to Tasmania. (A poem he wrote en route, aboard H.M.S. *Swift* in July 1849, appears below.) He escaped from Tasmania two and a half years later.

Almost from the moment of his arrival in America, Meagher was lionized by the New York Irish. After a period of time on the lecture circuit, he undertook the study of law and was admitted to the bar in 1855, thereafter combining a legal career with the editorship of the *Irish News*. When the Civil War broke out, Meagher raised Company K, the "Irish Zouaves," for the Sixty-Ninth New York State Militia Regiment, serving as a captain of that unit under Colonel Michael Corcoran at the first battle of Bull Run.

At the end of the Sixty-Ninth's three-month active service, Meagher organized and commanded the Irish Brigade, whose banner boasted an Irish harp, a wreath of shamrocks, and the Gaelic motto "They shall never retreat from the charge of lances." Though its initial regiments were the Sixty-Third, Sixty-Ninth, and Eighty-Eighth New York State Volunteers, the brigade was later augmented by the Twenty-Eighth Massachusetts and the 116th Pennsylvania volunteer infantry regiments. The Irish Brigade fought in all of the major campaigns of the Army of the Potomac and lost more than 4,000 men during the war. Eleven of its members were awarded the Congressional Medal of Honor. Of the five officers who commanded the brigade, three were killed or mortally wounded: Colonel Richard Byrnes, Colonel Patrick Kelly, and Brigadier General Thomas A. Smyth.

After the war Meagher became secretary and acting governor of Montana Territory. On July 1, 1867, after boarding a steamboat at Fort Benton, Montana, he mysteriously disappeared, allegedly in the waters of the Missouri River.

Songs in Exile

by Thomas Francis Meagher (1823–1867)

Although it is our lot to range
    The earth's wide surface o'er,
Yet still our hearts can know no change,
    We're Paddies evermore.

Place us beneath yon burning sky,
    On Africa's arid shore,
Yet e'en within the torrid zone
    We're Paddies evermore.

Let beef be tough, and biscuit dry,
    And milkless tea outpour,
We'll shed no tear, we'll heave no sigh,
    We're Paddies evermore.

Though short our day, and quenched our light
    Before that day be o'er,
Yet still our hearts can know no night,
    We're Paddies evermore.

Let sharks and dolphins shun the hook,

> Baited from purser's store,
> We'll catch them yet by hook or crook,
> We're Paddies evermore.
>
> Though Neptune come with tar and soap
> Our bearded chins to score,
> Still with this shaver we will cope,
> We're Paddies evermore.
>
> Although the whitening surge beat high,
> And loud the tempest roar,
> Yet quail we not when death seems nigh,
> We're Paddies evermore.
>
> Although the Cape no hope may bring,
> Our tone we will not low'r,
> For still in Table Bay we'll sing,
> We're Paddies evermore.
>
> And when we tread Van Dieman's [sic] strand,
> Transported to that shore,
> In prayer we'll bless our native land,
> As Paddies evermore.

Paddies: a slang term (often disparaging) for Irishmen. **Neptune:** the Roman god of the sea. **Cape:** Cape of Good Hope, on the southwest tip of Africa. **Table Bay:** an inlet off the coast of South Africa. **Van Dieman [sic]:** Van Diemen, the former name of Tasmania, an island state of Australia.

The Ballad of the Sixty-Ninth

by Joseph I. C. Clarke (1846–1925)

> Clouds black with thunder o'er the Southern states;
> North, East and West a sickening fear;
> The Union on the dark laps of the Fates,
> And nowhere sign the skies would clear.
> Would hate haul down the flag we loved so well—
> The star-flag that at Yorktown flew?
> For answer came the hurtling of a shell,
> With the Union cleft in two!
>
> Never since out of chaos came the world

Sprang such resolve as took us then:—
　"Thro' blood and fire, with that brave flag unfurled,
　　The Union shall be whole again."
At Lincoln's call men swarmed from towns and farms;
　　An ecstasy shook all the land.
Tramp! tramp! the people's bravest rose in arms.
　　With them the Irish took their stand.

For here their slave rags had away been cast,
　　Freedom had met them at the door,
To share such empire lovelit, rich and vast
　　As never fronted man before.
Our great Republic! Shall the kings behold,
　　Neath slavery's thrust, its overthrow?
Loud, righteous, quick our regiment's answer rolled:—
　　"The Irish Sixty-Ninth says, No!"

Tramp! tramp! At Corcoran's command they've swung
　　Down Broadway's length a thousand strong,
Their flag of green by grand Old Glory flung,
　　Their steps like music to the cheering throng,
The great Archbishop, blessing rank and file,
　　Bends o'er them—soldier, gun and blade,
On every face the bold-heart Irish smile
　　That looks in Death's eyes unafraid.

Mother of Irish regiments, march in pride;
　　No idle presage in your tread!
The way is long; the battle ground is wide;
　　High will be the roster of your dead.
Ever you'll find the battle's crest and front,
　　Then march to seek new fighting ground;
Ever, when shattered in the battle brunt,
　　Men for the gaps will still be found.

You'll be baptized in fire in Blackburn's Ford,
　　Bull Run shall see two hundred fall—
You fancy south when north the rout has poured;
　　At Rappahannock like a wall;
You'll strike at Fair Oaks; clash at Gaine's Mill;
　　And ramp like tigers over Malvern Hill;
Stand and be hammered at Chancellorsville;
　　Antietam's corn shall redden at your name,

The while you deal the blow that stuns;
   At Marye's Heights your men shall feed on flame
      Up to the muzzles of the guns;

At Gettysburg fire-dwindled on you'll press,
      And then remanned again seek fight;
All through the tangle of the Wilderness,
      You'll battle day and night;
At Petersburg you'll spring to the assault;
      Only at Appomattox shall you halt!

Let Nugent, Meagher, Cavanagh be praised,
      MacMahon [*sic*], Kelly, Haggerty, Clark [*sic*],
But the thousands three that the regiment raised,
      As surely bore the hero-mark.
Fame's darling child, the Sixty-Ninth shall shine:—
      Never in Duty's honor to lag;
Forty-eight times in the battle line,
      Never, never to lose a flag.

Tramp! tramp! you saw the Union split in twain,
      Tramp! tramp! You saw the nation whole.
Your red blood flowed in torrents not in vain;
      It fed the great Republic's soul.
Your drums still roll; your serried ranks still form:
      From manhood's service no release.
Ready at call to ride the battle storm,
      But best the pledge, the guard of Peace.

Fates: the three goddesses of destiny in Greek and Roman mythology. **Yorktown:** the Revolutionary War battlefield in Virginia where the British surrendered on October 19, 1781. **hurtling of a shell:** an allusion to the Confederate bombardment of Fort Sumter in Charleston, South Carolina, on April 12, 1861. **Irish took their stand:** More than 160,000 Irish-born soldiers fought in the Union army during the Civil War. **Corcoran:** Michael Corcoran (1827–1863), a native of County Sligo, Ireland, and colonel of the Sixty-Ninth New York Regiment. He was captured at Bull Run. **Blackburn's Ford:** Of the thirty-six battles or engagements in which either the Sixty-Ninth Regiment or the Irish Brigade participated, the poem mentions eleven, in the following order: Blackburn's Ford (Bull Run) (July 18, 1861), Rappahannock (November 7, 1863), Fair Oaks (May 31–June 1, 1862), Gaine's Mill (June 27, 1862), Malvern Hill (July 1, 1862), Chancellorsville (May 1–5, 1863), Antietam (September 17, 1862), Marye's Heights (Fredericksburg) (December 12–15, 1862), Gettysburg (July 1–4, 1863), Wilderness (May 5–7, 1864), and Petersburg (June 16–18, 1864). **Archbishop:** John Hughes (1797–1864), a native of County Tyrone, Ireland, and the first archbishop of New York City. Hughes's vicar general actually blessed the brigade, since Hughes was in Europe on a mission in behalf of the Union cause. **Nugent:** Robert Nugent (?–1901), a native of County Down, Ireland, and lieutenant colonel of the Sixty-Ninth New York Regiment. He later served as general of the Sixty-Ninth New York Volunteers and commander of the Irish Brigade. **Meagher:** Thomas Meagher (1823–1867), a native of County Waterford, Ireland, and captain of Company K, Sixty-Ninth New York Regiment. He later organized and commanded the Irish Brigade. **Cavanagh:** James Cavanagh (1831–1901), a native of County Tipperary, Ireland, and captain of Company C, Sixty-Ninth New York Regiment. **MacMahon [*sic*]:** Henry McMahon, lieutenant of Company G, Sixty-Ninth New York Regiment. **Kelly:** either James Kelly, a native of County Monaghan, Ireland, and captain of Company H, Sixty-Ninth New York Regiment, or Patrick Kelly (?–1864), a native of County Galway, Ireland, and captain of Company E. After the Irish Brigade was formed, Patrick Kelly became lieutenant colonel of the Eighty-Eighth New York and succeeded Meagher as commander of the Irish Brigade. Kelly was killed at Petersburg. **Haggerty:** James Haggerty, captain of Company A, Sixty-Ninth New York Regiment. He was killed at Bull Run, where the Sixty-Ninth lost thirty-eight killed, fifty-nine wounded, and ninety-five missing, about 16 percent of its strength. **Clark [*sic*]:** Thomas Clarke, captain of Company D, Sixty-Ninth New York Regiment. He was wounded at Bull Run.

The Irish Sixty-Ninth

by John Galusha

Ye Erin sons of hill and plain,
Come listen to my feeble strain,
Perhaps you'll think it all a dream,
Though every line is true.
I'll sing to you of our long campaign
Through summer sun and winter's rain,
To Richmond's gates and back again,
I will relate to you.

It was in August, sixty-one,
When Colonel Owens [*sic*] took command,
And brought us into Maryland
Where let it rain or shine.
He drilled us—every day we rose
To learn us how to thrash our foes,
And more than once they felt the blows
Of the Irish Sixty-ninth.
In February, sixty-two,
While passing in a grand review,
We were told our foes we would pursue
And Richmond overthrow.

To Washington we went straight way,
And sailed in steamers down the bay
Until we were forced next day
To land at Fort Monroe.

At Hampton then we camped around,
Until brave Little Mac came down
And ordered us up to Yorktown
Our strength there to combine.
And there we worked both night and day,
And drove the rebel hordes away,
And marching through the town next day
Went the gallant Sixty-ninth.

From Yorktown then we sailed away,
And landed at West Point next day,
And gaily marched along the way,
And camped among the pines.
And there we stayed three weeks or more,
Until we heard the cannons roar
And musketry come like a shower
Along the Rebel lines.

Then double quick away we went,
Across the river we were sent
To drive the Rebels back we meant,
No man fell out of line.
Where Philadelphia's noble sons
Had nobly spotted Pickett's guns,
And when away the Rebels run,
Cheered the gallant Sixty-ninth.

Then on Antietam's field again
We boldly faced the iron rain.
Some of our boys upon the plain
They found a bloody grave,
Where our brave general, Little Mac,
Made boastingly to clear the track
And to send the ragged Rebels back
Across the Potomac's waves.
At Fairoaks then long weeks we lay,
Had picket fighting night and day,
I've seen our brave boys borne away
And some in death grow pale.

And in that seven day's fight, going back
Over bloody fields we left our track
Where other regiments they fell back,
We stood at Glendale.

Next day out on the battle field,
Old veterans they were forced to yield,
For the rebels had a stone wall shield
Protecting front and rear.
[They gave us constant] shot and shell.
It was like the gaping jaws of hell,
And many's the brave man round us fell.
We boldly did our share.

O'Keen [*sic*], our colonel, nobly stood
Where the grass was turning red with blood,
And growing to a crimson flood.
We still kept in our line,
And many got a bloody shroud,
Though Philadelphia's sons were proud
And sang of deeds in praises loud
Of the gallant Sixty-ninth.

Erin: a literary name for Ireland. **Colonel Owens [*sic*]:** Colonel Joshua T. Owen of the Sixty-Ninth Pennsylvania Regiment. **Fort Monroe:** a federal fortress in Hampton, Virginia. **Little Mac:** the Union general George McClellan. **Yorktown:** the siege of Yorktown, Virginia (April 16–May 4, 1862). **West Point:** a site in Virginia where the Mattaponi and Pamunkey rivers unite to form the York River. **Pickett's guns:** an allusion to the Confederate general George Pickett, perhaps at the battles of Fredericksburg (December 12–15, 1862) or Gettysburg (July 1–3, 1863). **Antietam's fields:** the battle of Antietam (September 17, 1862). **Fairoaks:** the site of the battle of Fair Oaks (or Seven Pines), May 31–June 1, 1862. **seven days' fight:** the battle of Seven Days (June 25–July 1, 1862). **Glendale:** an engagement fought on June 30, 1862. **O'Keen [*sic*]:** Colonel Dennis O'Kane of the Sixty-Ninth Pennsylvania Regiment. His men pushed back a Confederate attempt to break the Union line at Gettysburg, although he died of wounds sustained on July 3, 1863.

At Fredericksburg

by John Boyle O'Reilly (1844–1890)

God send us peace, and keep red strife away;
    But should it come, God send us men and steel!
The land is dead that dare not face the day
    When foreign danger threats the common weal.

Defenders strong are they that homes defend:
    From ready arms the spoiler keeps afar.
Well blest the country that has sons to lend
    From trades of peace to learn the trade of war.

Thrice blest the nation that has every son
    A soldier, ready for the warning sound;
Who marches homeward when the fight is done,
    To swing the hammer and to till the ground.

Call back that morning, with its lurid light,
    When through our land the awful war-bell tolled;
When lips were mute, and women's faces white
    As the pale cloud that out from Sumter rolled.

Call back that morn: an instant all were dumb,
    As if the shot had struck the Nation's life;
Then cleared the smoke, and rolled the calling drum,
    And men streamed in to meet the coming strife.

They closed the ledger and they stilled the loom,
    The plough left rusting in the prairie farm;
They saw but "Union" in the gathering gloom;
    The tearless women helped the men to arm;

Brigades from towns—each village sent its band;
    German and Irish—every race and faith;
There was no question then of native land,
    But — love the Flag and follow it to death.

No need to tell their tale: through every age
    The splendid story shall be sung and said;
But let me draw one picture from the page —
    For words of song embalm the hero dead.

The smooth hill is bare, and the cannons are planted,
    Like Gorgon fates shading its terrible brow;
The word has been passed that the stormers are wanted,
    And Burnside's battalions are mustering now.
The armies stand by to behold the dread meeting;
    The work must be done by a desperate few;
The black-mouthèd guns on the height give them greeting—
    From gun-mouth to plain every grass blade in view.
Strong earthworks are there, and the rifles behind them

Are Georgia militia—an Irish brigade—
Their caps have green badges, as if to remind them
    Of all the brave record their country has made.

The stormers go forward—the Federals cheer them;
    They breast the smooth hillside—the black mouths are dumb;
The riflemen lie in the works till they near them,
    And cover the stormers as upward they come.
Was ever a death-march so grand and so solemn?
    At last, the dark summit with flame is enlined;
The great guns belch doom on the sacrificed column,
    That reels from the height, leaving hundreds behind.
The armies are hushed—there is no cause for cheering;
    The fall of brave men to brave men is a pain.
Again come the stormers! and as they are nearing
    The flame-sheeted rifle-lines, reel back again.
And so till full noon come the Federal masses—
    Flung back from the height, as the cliff flings a wave;
Brigade on brigade to the death-struggle passes,
    No waving rank till it steps on the grave.

Then comes a brief lull, and the smoke-pall is lifted,
    The green of the hillside no longer is seen;
The dead soldiers lie as the sea-weed is drifted,
    The earthworks still held by the badges of green.
Have they quailed? is the word. No: again they are forming—
    Again comes a column to death and defeat!
What is it in these who shall now do the storming
    That makes every Georgian spring to his feet?

"O God! what a pity!" they cry in their cover,
    As rifles are readied and bayonets made tight;
"'Tis Meagher and his fellows! their caps have green clover;
    'Tis Greek to Greek now for the rest of the fight!"
Twelve hundred the column, their rent flag before them,
    With Meagher at their head, they dashed at the hill!
Their foemen are proud of the country that bore them;
    But, Irish in love, they are enemies still.
Out rings the fierce word, "Let them have it!" the rifles
    Are emptied point-blank in the hearts of the foe;
It is green against green, but a principle stifles
    The Irishman's love in the Georgian's blow.
The column has reeled, but it is not defeated;

In front of the guns they re-form and attack;
Six times they have done it, and six times retreated;
    Twelve hundred they came, and two hundred go back.
Two hundred go back with the chivalrous story;
    The wild day is closed in the night's solemn shroud;
A thousand lie dead, but their death was a glory
    That calls not for tears—the Green Badges are proud!

Bright honor be theirs who for honor were fearless,
    Who charged for their flag to the grim cannon's mouth;
And honor to them who were true, though not tearless,—
    Who bravely that day kept the cause of the South.
The quarrel is done—God avert such another;
    The lesson it brought we should evermore heed;
Who loveth the Flag is a man and a brother,
    No matter what birth or what race or what creed.

Fredericksburg: At Fredericksburg, Virginia, on December 12, 1862, Thomas Meagher led the Irish Brigade in six suicidal charges against Marye's Heights, in the futile attempt losing 545 men, half the brigade's strength. **Sumter:** Fort Sumter in Charleston, South Carolina, whose bombardment by the Confederates on April 12, 1861, began the Civil War. **Gorgon fates:** any of three sister monsters of Greek mythology. They had snakes for hair, and their eyes turned anyone who looked at them into stone. **Burnside:** Ambrose Burnside (1824–1881), the Union commander of the Army of the Potomac until he suffered 12,600 casualties at Fredericksburg.

Meagher's Brigade

by Hugh Farrar McDermott

Now the green plumes nod to the rising sun,
As it leads the way to each bristling gun;
And the soldier's soul is a harp of joy,
Tuned to the glory of Fontenoy.

Solid in mass as woods of oak,
Fierce for the fray as lions awok[e]
Column on column, with martial tread,
Defy the terror of shell and lead.

With shout and yell and stunning peal,
Their courage leaps upon their steel!
With shock and dash, and plunge and stroke,
'Mid roaring seas of fire and smoke,

Their desperate valor shakes the earth,
When the foe cries out: "Who gave them birth?"

With fearless breasts and rushing tread,
Again they charge the rain of lead,
And in the battle's clash and roar,
Anoint their brows with Freedom's gore.

When hand to hand they press attack,
The thund'ring cannon sweep them back;
As more they see red currents flow,
More fiercely on they charge the foe;
And as the dying gasp for life,
Their spirit still impels the strife,—
Like wounded eagles poising high,
They soar in triumph ere they die.

Now cheering with his bugle blast,
The gallant Meagher flies swiftly past;
Through teeming groans and clash and jar,
His trumpet voice thus sounds afar:
"Again to the charge, old Erin's sons!
Again to the charge! Press on your guns!
Behold the green! Think of its fame!
Think how your sires baptized its name!"

Again they charge; it is their last;
On battle mounds their die is cast,
They sink as 'neath the simoon's blast.

O God, how grand! in battle's rage,
    Despising life, defying death,
Victory alone could those assuage
    Whose names expired with parting breath;
Fame blushed for Fame as heroes fell;
    They died for glory more sublime;
While Freedom struck their funeral knell,
    Which rings for aye on the ear of time.

In lonely dell, on hill and plain,
    Where fade the slain and blooms the sod,
Memory shall dwell, with pride and pain,
    While Freedom lives the soul of God;
And poets strike a joyous lay,

A plaintive dirge for its refrain,
When power of wrong has passed away,
And nature's laws shall rule again.

Fontenoy: the battle of 1745 in which the six Irish regiments of the French army turned the tide for Louis XIV by helping defeat the Allied forces. During the battle the Irish regiments numbered about 4,000 of the 60,000 French troops and suffered 656 of the 3,870 casualties on the French side. While smashing through the Allied right flank, the Irish troops shouted, "Remember Limerick!" — a cry to avenge the surrender of that Irish city to the army of William III in 1691. **Meagher:** Thomas Meagher (1823–1867), the Irish native who formed the Irish Brigade in the Union army during the Civil War. **Erin:** a literary name for Ireland. **simoon's blast:** the hot, dry, suffocating sandwind that sweeps across the African and Asiatic deserts at intervals during spring and summer.

Thomas Francis Meagher
by James J. Bourke

As rolls Montana's tideless wave,
    Far westward out where sinks the sun,
It sweeps above a nameless grave
Where sleeps a Tribune bright and brave;
    A soldier whose campaigning's done—
A soldier on whose conquering sword
    Both gods and men might look with pride;
An orator whose lightning word
Could flash like meteor of the Lord—
    Who loving lived and loving died.

The regal sun, the watching stars,
    The moon when in its rounded crest,
Fling forth in rays of slanting bars
Deep through the rush of watery wars
    A cross of silver o'er his breast,
Down where his whitening bones are strewn
    Beneath the river's ceaseless roll;
And sobbing winds that night or noon,
His wailing mourners hymn their tune,
    And sigh soft dirges for his soul.

Full many a stately galley speeds
    In gleam of glory o'er the place,
Where, far below the throbbing reeds
And shrouded by the water weeds,

Lies stark his pale, uncoffined face;
And travellers list with bated breath
    While pilots tell the tale of doom—
How he who wore the victor's wreath
Sank battling here with night and death,
    And found an unannointed tomb.

But, ah, no trophy crowns the spot
    Where cold and pulseless wastes the heart
That dared of yore, when youth was hot,
The hangman's rope, the felon's lot,
    To act for Eire a true man's part;
The waters seethe with hurrying dread
    Above the dull and lampless brain,
The tongue of fire is mute and dead,
And sands are round the God-like head,
    And all but prayer for him is vain.

Yet had he, when his sands were run,
    Been laid to sleep in hallowed clay,
The land for whom his work was done,
Beneath whose flag he'd fought and won
    Would strew his grave with flowers to-day,
The marble pile they'd upward rear
    Till flame-like it would flaunt the skies,
And many a broken lance and spear
They'd place around the warrior's bier
    And shattered drum and banner-prize.

They mourn him in the land he loved,
    His priceless worth, his conquering arm,
They miss him where in grace he moved—
For camp and council both have proved
    His master mind to guide or charm.
And many a tale will yet be told,
    By camping fires in future wars,
Of him who with his clansmen bold
Shook out the old green banners fold
    To fight beneath the Stripes and Stars

And hosts will whisper listening guests
    The Southern foeman's wild refrain,
When glared he o'er the green-plumed crests,
And sprigs of green on Irish breasts—

"Here comes that damned Green Flag again!"
And hearts will fire and pulses bound
    At thoughts of Antietam's day;
When hemmed by fire and foeman round,
The Irish stormed the vantage ground—
    And claimed the glory of the fray.

And Fredericksburg's hard foughten field,
    Where men were mown like autumn grain,
Shall prove, though oft it broke and reeled—
That Irish valor could not yield,
    Though wheel-deep lay he mangled slain.
What time that Meagher with glance of pride,
    Points out the range of belching guns—
"Go take them now," he laughing cried;
And while the storm of death rung wide,
    They straight obeyed like duteous sons.

Oh, these are memories that evoke
    The noblest traits that stamp our race,
For though the rift of fire and smoke,
Where wild the Irish slogan broke,
    When foe met foeman face to face,
We know that each day's battle close
    Though fierce and bloody'd been the fight,
Saw wounded soldiers tend the foes,
Heard pitying words that heavenward rose,
    And prayers above the dead at night.

But we, with whom the chieftan [*sic*] grew
    Who proudly led this bold brigade,
Whose voice, whose form, whose face we knew,
Whose fiery soul, whose courage true,
    Are with us dreams that will not fade;
Who've heard his glorious burning words,
    Like Him the Roman chief of old,
Who bade the slaves gird on their swords,
And smite to doom their tyrant lords,
    And Heaven would aye them guiltless hold.

And we within the circling bound
    Of this proud city of the Gael,
The rebel Emmet's camping ground,
The scene of Edward's martyr wound,

The throbbing heart of Innisfall—
Shall we erect no storied urn,
    Or marble statue carven fair,
To him whose God-like words could burn,
Who never more may now return,
    Like wearied child her breast to share.

Oh, pile the stone and heap the cairn,
    And carve the likeness of his face,
And twine at foot the oak and fern,
That coming nations yet may learn
    He lived the Isaiah of our race.
But if you'd fill your glorious part,
    And glance upon your work with pride,
And image true of Meagher impart,
Oh, place a shamrock o'er his heart—
    For it he loved, for it he died!

Thomas Francis Meagher: a native of County Waterford, Ireland, and captain of Company K, Sixty-Ninth New York Militia. He later organized and commanded the Irish Brigade. **Montana's tideless wave:** the Missouri River. **nameless grave:** After the Civil War, Thomas Meagher became acting governor of Montana Territory. He drowned in the Missouri River near Fort Benton on July 1, 1867. His body was never recovered. **Tribune:** in ancient Rome one of ten officers elected to protect the interests of the plebeians. **Eire:** Ireland. **Green Flag:** the ensign of the Irish Brigade. The heavily fringed flag was a deep green and bore in the center an embroidered Irish harp, with a sunburst above it and a wreath of shamrocks beneath. A crimson scroll, in Irish letters, carried the motto "They shall never retreat from the charge of lances." **Antietam's day:** September 17, 1862, when Union forces stopped a Confederate advance into Maryland and Pennsylvania. The Irish Brigade suffered 113 dead and 422 wounded. **Fredericksburg's hard foughten field:** the battle of December 13, 1862, in which the Irish Brigade lost 545 men — half its number — in six suicidal charges against Marye's Heights at Fredericksburg, Virginia. **the Roman chief of old:** possibly Eunus, a Syrian who led a slave revolt in the Roman province of Sicily in 139 B.C. after announcing the gods' blessings for such an undertaking. **proud city of the Gael:** Dublin, Ireland. **Gael:** used here to refer to the Irish. **Emmet:** Robert Emmet (1778–1803), an Irish patriot arrested and executed in Dublin for his involvement in an uprising against British rule in 1803. In his speech to the jury he asked that no man write his epitaph until "my country takes her place among the nations of the earth." **Edward's martyr wound:** the mortal wound sustained by Lord Edward Fitzgerald (1763–1798) during his arrest for treason in 1798. Fitzgerald had joined the United Irishmen movement in its attempt to create an independent Irish republic and had engaged in negotiations for French military support. **Innisfall:** also *Inisfail*, a Gaelic word meaning "Isle of Destiny," one of many ancient names for Ireland. **Isaiah:** a Hebrew prophet of the eighth century B.C.

Poetical Address Before the Irish Brigade
by Dr. Lawrence Reynolds

Whether he's fated in far lands to roam,
Or pines beneath a stranger's sway at home,
There is, in every year, one sacred day,
When Ireland's son feels full of hope and gay.
Sees sorrow's sad shade from life's scenes depart,
And faded joys flash fresh upon his heart;
While fancy tells the blissful time will come
When fame and freedom yet shall bless his home.

Why should we not, on this our hallowed day,
On freedom's soil, feel full of hope and gay?
When every hill around, and every vale
Tells to all time a spirit-thrilling tale,
That here the conflict for the rights of man,
Man's natural rights and dignity began.
That hence were chased by freemen of all lands
The monarch's minions and his hireling bands.
That in this happy country, none shall bleed
For difference of thought, or race or creed;
But all shall dwell in holy unity,
The sons of order, love and liberty.

What has Columbia by just laws become?
Her children's Eden and the exile's home.
'Tis only on her shore, since time began,
Man walked in pride, and felt himself a man;
Looked up to God, and down on such vile things
As flattering courtiers and inflated kings.
Gave proud defiance to each threat'ning foe,
And cordial welcome to each child of woe.

Oh! shall we ever, ever be again
The peaceful, happy people we were then?
Each by the other's skill and friendship blest,
The enterprising East, the fertile West,
The South by love cemented to the North—
The modern envied Eden of the earth.

Alas! as in the world's young sinless hours,
The wily serpent lurked in Eden's bowers,

And blasted all the peace and rapture there;
So breathed the serpent words of misery here,
Burst every bond of holy brotherhood,
And bathed the country in fraternal blood.
The crafty politician's guilesome tongue
Poured cheating words the mislead crowd among,
And brought that plague, than famine direr far,
That heaviest curse of mankind, civil war.

The storm came on, the crouching coward bowed
His craven head beneath the murky cloud:
In his concealment trembled in his soul,
To see the flash and hear the thunder roll.
At once you gallant Irish, you came forth,
And proved your manhood, loyalty and worth;
And, unseduced, unwavering, undismayed,
You raised for battle your renowned Brigade,
And proved how pure the loyalty you vowed,
By deeds of daring, and by floods of blood.
Your chief you chose to lead you to the war,
Your native chieftain, the intrepid Meagher,
Who dared already in his early youth,
The patriot's doom for freedom and for truth;
And never since from foeman's fire he shrank—
Our first in danger, as our first in rank.

You fought, how gloriously you fought, how well,
The page of wondering history shall tell.
On Yorktown's walls, the rebel flag was seen
To droop its folds beneath the Irish green.
From Williamsburg, the traitor legion fled
From the fierce charge by Irish valor lead;
And Fair Oaks saw the victors of a day
Before your green flag fade like mists away.
Already Richmond lay before your view,
And owned her destined conquerors in you.
But politicians, to the nation's grief,
Marred the wise projects of your youthful chief.
Why was withheld the stipulated aid?
Why was McDowell's promised corps delayed?
While Southern thousands rushed to Richmond's aid
And closed the gaps that Irish valor made.

From that came on that trial most severe,

Which gallant heroes are compelled to bear;
To leave a conquest all but won, and fly
Before an oft-defeated enemy.

In countless thousands, on the rebels came,
With cries of vengeance and with hearts of flame—
They came to hurl destruction on our rear,
But you, Green Erin's bold Brigade[,] were there,
And glorying in the post given you by Mac,
The thundering tide of traitors you tossed back.

Bright on the warrior's memory flashes still,
Your bright advance at eve on Gaines's Mill.
From early dawn you heard the cannon's roar,
And every hour it deepened more and more—
Nearer and nearer comes the battle's sound—
Your General moves your ready ranks around,
That chafe at every moment of delay:
"Advance!" You cheer, and cheering, bound away.
The battle raged from morning until eve;
The field, the Union forces slowly leave.
On came the rebels, in a countless host,
They cleave the loyal ranks, and all is lost;
Horse, foot, artillery, one jumbled mass;
Over that narrow bridge: how shall they pass?
They gnash their teeth, and scowl in fierce despair.
The stream before—the foemen in their rear.
Who, who are they, who through the flying crowd
Pass, with firm tread and bearing sternly proud?
Who, who are they, whose green flags gaily fly?
They near the hill: they face the enemy;
With hurried pace they mount—from on the hill,
They wave their flags of green, and all is still.
The foe retires; pursuit and panic cease,
And all is silence, sweet repose and peace;
Save where brave Porter's rescued corps rend Heaven
With grateful shouts for Ireland's warriors given.

Still in the rear the loyal lines we close;
And slow retiring, keep at bay our foes.
At Savage Station next the Irish band,
Calm and resolved, before their vanguards stand.
They come; they cheer and rush, our ranks to pierce;
Our cannon greets them with a welcome fierce;

Our bullets whistle thick around their ears;
Our changing lines advance with heavy cheers.
High in our front ranks streams the banner green;
Our foes look on it, and desert the scene.

With each repulse, inflamed to greater wrath,
Like famished wolves they follow on our path.
O'er White Oak Swamp, we break the narrow bridge,
And wait their onset, on the rising ridge.
Along the line a dreadful fight soon rose:
Here our troops conquered, there prevailed the foes.
A weak point in our line their leader found,
And moved, to flank us, and our troops surround.
The veteran Sumner still kept fighting on,
But saw his forces yield, hope almost gone.

When on his eye a gladsome vision broke,
Our coming green flag, and the hero spoke:
"Irish brigade, while through the day I fought,
Your gallant band with anxious eye I sought,
But now I care not, since you are with me,
For all the hosts of Jackson and of Lee."
The veteran spoke, we cheered, the charge he led,
Our bayonets glittered, and the foeman fled,
And unattacked along our road we go,
And stand at Malvern Hill, to meet the foe.

When the sun rose on mountain, vale, and rill,
What scene so lovely as sweet Malvern Hill?
The noble mansion topp'd the gradual slope,
And gave the view variety and scope.
The fertile plain diversified and broke
By graceful fir-tree, and by lordly oak;
The plump sheep fed, and sheaves of heavy grain,
Were frequent piled throughout the broad domain,
While in the rear, the James's [*sic*] River flowed,
Whose winding tide with gorgeous grandeur glowed.

The noon stole on, the beauties of that hour
Ask Titian's coloring and Caracchi's [*sic*] power;
The painter and the poet here might gaze,
Paint scenes sublime and pen immortal lays.
What pity that war's tumults harsh and rude,
Should e'er on this sweet solitude intrude,

That the wild havoc, and sad waste of war,
Should nature's bounties and her beauties mar.

The cannon now resounds, the hurrying drum
Loud beats to arms and tells the foemen come,
Quick forms in line and marches our Brigade,
As gay as if they formed for their parade,
Upon their bayonets bright the sunbeams dance,
The skirmishers come out, spread wide, advance.
The leaders on each side exhaust their skill,
But hours wear on and they but skirmished still.
At length Magruder heads his tiger band,
And boldly seeks to meet us, hand to hand;
Like beasts of prey o'er th' intervening space,
His frantic followers loudly yelling, race.
Quick from our rear impetuous courtiers bound,
Their rapid gallop shakes the echoing ground;
Rushing along, "give way, give way," they cry,
Comes on their heels, the horse Artillery.
They sweep by, while a cloud of dust conceals
The panting horses and the whirling wheels;
Down the steep hill with headlong haste they go,
Wheel round their guns and point them at the foe.
Magruder comes, the word to fire is given,
And gaping earth and quivering man are riven;
A new host rushes o'er the gory plain—
Again the cannon roars, that host is slain.
Once more the desperate charge Magruder led,
Once more the cannon roared, and all lay dead.

The crimson sun was sinking from the sky,
Tinging the light clouds with a saffron dye;
The battle's smoke and the advancing night,
Concealed that sun—those clouds so fair and bright.

'Tis darkness, yet not silence, on the throbbing ear
Peals the war's tumult and the Irish cheer;
Now lurid lightnings through the darkness shine
As the last volley flies from all our line.
Our rifles rattle and our cannons roar,
But to our challenge foes reply no more.

That night we marched, and on the coming morn
In safety camped, held our foiled foes in scorn;

On the damp ground our wearied limbs we toss;
Our comrades welcome, or lament their loss.
From very peril saved, and every ill,
By our own courage, and McClellan's skill.

We leave Virginia's desolated soil,
A desert, where no thrifty peasant's [*sic*] toil,
Whence the green grass and golden grain have fled—
A country now, the country of the dead.
To fairer scenes we're called away by war.
That loyal State may warfare never mar—
Sweet Maryland, thou brave and peaceful State
'Mid tumult calm, 'mid turbulence sedate.
Were all they sister States true, firm like thee,
This nation from war's ravages were free.
When our lov'd country's madness shall be past
And peace and late repentance come at last,
All shall before thy useful virtues bow,
And own the noblest of her States are thou.
We marched, the land one blooming garden seemed,
With cattle and with grain, the rich land teemed.
A bluer sky, a milder atmosphere,
A halo shed by peace, was beaming there;
The gentlemen we met there frank and warm,
Saw woman's lovely face, and graceful form.

At home, in peace, too little do we prize,
The love-light beaming in fond woman's eyes,
The kind attentions and the gentle tone,
That tell the heart that beats for us alone.
But when in toil and danger far we roam,
From all the comforts and the love of home,
How cold we look upon the sunny sky,
The tree with branches broad, or towering high,
The fairy glen, the river fleet and bright,
And all that nature forms to glad the sight;
Oh! then we own this world a joyless place
Without dear woman's form and angel face.

The promises by the arch plotters made
To their deluded followers, quickly fade;
Where splendor and profusion reigned, that home
Has a sad scene of poverty become.
There's nothing now in all the beggared South,

To clothe the naked back, or feed the mouth,
And Lee and Jackson the sad desert leave,
Rich Maryland to plunder and deceive.
In gangs their hungry followers throng the road,
The baggage that they bear is no great load;
To all they meet, they're most polite and kind,
And scatter proclamations on the wind;
Yet take the people's goods and food away,
And in return give promises to pay;
But no recruits her sturdy patriots give,
And the foiled traitors are compelled to leave.
They leave in haste, they have no time to spare;
They hear McClellan close upon their rear;
They leave a guard his progress to delay,
While the main body flies in fear away.
South Mountain's pass the onward road commands,
And there their strong rear guard for battle stands,
Not long it stands—bold Burnside's rapid horse,
Leads to the charge, th' avenging Union force;
His soldiers following, mount the hill and shout,
Rush to the assault, and the scared rebels rout.

When next morn's sun upon the bright earth burst
We followed fast, our bold Brigade the first—
Ever the first to meet the foe in fight,
Ever the last to guard the rear in flight.
The gladdening peasants crowding to the road,
The path the foemen took, unquestioned showed;
A curious spectacle was witnessed then,
Six thousand following sixty thousand men.
O'ertaken, all their force they mass, and stand;
Without a fight they cannot leave this land:
And a position strong their leader chose,
McClellan's further progress to oppose.

Through rich deep soil the clear Antietam glides,
And tall hills grandly rise on both its sides;
That on the east, like a huge sentinel,
Looks down upon the plain, and western hill.
There, in a wide gap, cut through the tall wood,
Our chief McClellan, through that conflict stood;
Guiding with counsels, ever wise and right,
The varying fortunes of that desperate fight;
While on the west side, Jackson, Hill and Lee

Drew out the flower of Southern chivalry.

The gallant Hooker on our right, the first
Upon the foeman's flank, with fury burst;
Close by his side a lofty hill arose,
Defended by a triple line of foes.
And from that hill those foes to force, was made
The arduous duty of our brave Brigade.
You Irish lads, e'er full of mirth and fun,
How gay your hearts when rose that morning's sun;
With laughter loud you waded through the rill,
With manly bearing, breasted the steep hill;
Beyond that hill a well-protected road,
To aid our foes, a rifle-pit bestowed;
Above its banks they scarcely raise their head,
On our advance they rained a shower of lead;
Down falls the Green Flag, on the crimson plain,
Crowds rush to seize it, and it floats again;
The standard-bearer falls, a third, a score,
Still the unwavering line, it flutters o'er;
An anxious group around McClellan stand,
The spy-glass turned on us from every hand:
An Aide-de-camp cries out in agony—
"The day is lost to us, the Irish fly";
McClellan gazing on the battle scene,
Sees raised again, the glorious flag of green;
Sees, while his eyes with victory's radiance shine,
The volley flying from our closed-up line,
The foe retiring, and exclaims "Hurra,"
"The Irish win the hill, and win the day."
All looked; the Irish on the hill-top stood,
The foe were hid amid the neighboring wood;
What now can Lee, what now can Jackson do?
How 'scape the conquering foeman that pursue,
How back to their homes, can they ever get?
McClellan holds their whole host in a net.

High o'er the river, Harper's [*sic*] Ferry stands
And from its heights the neighboring roads commands;
A force placed there, the foeman to oppose,
Basely resign that fortress to our foes.
Then Jackson rushed through with his aid to Lee,
And now through it their beaten armies flee:
Oh! had some heroic chief held Bolivar,

The foe were seized, and ended this sad war.

Along the country with proud hopes we go,
With conquest flushed, and careless of the foe,
Already we see Richmond's battered wall
At last before McClellan's genius fall.
When, lo! a letter to our camp is brought,
A letter with terrific misery fraught;
And 'mid his conquests from us is removed—
The chief we trusted in, the man we loved.

Who can forget, while memory holds her power,
The bitter sorrows of that parting hour?
While the old cannon poured his last salute,
Each heart beat wildly, tho' the tongue was mute.
Tremble the standard-bearers, strong and brave,
While the green flags he loved, they sadly waved,
And many an eye that fired at threat'ning death,
Now droops the load of manly tears beneath,
And gratified, yet weighed down by our grief,
A woman's weakness, conquers our brave chief.

Yet we performed the loyal patriot's part,
And marched along with sad foreboding heart.
At Falmouth with the foe's outposts we fight,—
They fly and burn the bridge they crossed in flight;
Sumner at once would o'er the river dash,
But young men think the veteran too rash—
"We'll wait a day,—and cross with then pontoon,
They're ordered 'long, and must be with us soon."
We wait another and another day,
And still the pontoons linger on the way.
Ah! now at last, indeed the tale is true,
The lazy pontoons slowly creep to view,
Yet wait—to cross so early is not fit,
They have not finished quite their rifle-pit.
Wait some days longer till the Richmond train,
Shall bring down corps of chosen men again.
Wait, wait! that stone-wall upon Mary's Hill [sic]
Is not quite finished, Lee is at it still.
Those triple rows they're forming for defense,
Will not be ready for some few days hence.
Now all that Lee and Jackson planned is done,
Now throw the bridge across, and boys charge on.

We crossed the bridge, at our success amazed,
On Fred'ricksburgh [*sic*] our gallant soldiers seized,
Formed where the railroad thro' the city run,
In streets commanded by the foemen's guns.
Thence thro' the water, up the hill we go,
To fire through stone-walls, at our laughing foe.
Our cannons fire behind us, with great skill,
But fire[,] like water, won't run up the hill,
And Lee and Jackson think it a good joke,
To hear our cannon and to see our smoke.
What crowds of wounded combatants we meet
Hurrying along thro' every dangerous street;
And, oh, what numbers, miserably slain,
Die, unavenged, upon the battle plain;
Yet even there, the Irish won renown,
And with new glory left the riddle town.
The nearest slain, close by the stone-wall gap,
Wore the green box-wood in their Irish cap.

We miss full many of the light of heart,
Who in our perils and our sports took part;
They died, for every man is born to die:
For them we shed no tear, we heave no sight,
But tell with admiration and with pride,
How well they fought, how gallantly they died.
Is there who wearies Heaven with coward prayer,
His life to age's helplessness to spare?
Who begs this boon, on his sick bed to lie,
And of diseases inch by inch to die?
More glorious was our lost companions' lot,
To fall where raged the battle loud and hot,
And bound from their post on that crimson sod,
Where freedom triumphed, to the breast of God.
Their last gaze fixed upon their flag of green,
Which waved in glory—o'er the battle scene.
And the last sound that feel upon their ears
Their comrades volley and their comrades' cheers.
Like them we swear to fill a hero's grave,
Like them to perish, or the Union save.

No hatred, no desire of gold accursed,
Called us to mingle in this strife at first,
But human wisdom, human love ne'er planned,
Laws like our laws, a Government so grand;

We shared its glory, and its peril share,
And here before that God, who hears, we swear,
The stars may fall from yon blue vault of Heaven,
But not one Star shall from that flag be riven;
Which o'er his troops, when human rights were won,
Was waved by mankind's hero—Washington.
The earth may melt, the sun the ocean drain,
Those laws shall stand, that Government remain.

Welcome, brave comrades, to our sports to-night,
You whom we met, in many a desperate fight,
Your birth, your valor, and your flag the same,
You're our Brigade in everything but name.
Welcome, you Irish Ninth, come from that shore,
Against whose granite ocean's billows roar;
And ne'er tossed back those billows, that proud rock
As you e'er backward hurled the foeman's shock.
At Gaines' Mill, with what true aim you fired,
What numbers fell, as slowly you retired.
With stubborn strength, you fought thro' all the day,
And kept the numerous foe, in fear away.
And when at eve, our banners topped the hill,
The foeman thought the Ninth opposed them still:
They fled, the green flag which they gazed upon,
And we gained glory, that your prowess won.
At Malvern Hill we saw your heroes pass
From fight, with your lost Colonel—gallant Cass.
Glory and peace to him, who left behind
No bolder spirit, and no nobler mind,
And welcome here, brave Thirty-Seventh, no band
E'er gave more honor to green Erin's land.
Brave Kearney's [*sic*] pet, the favorites of him
Whose glory makes great heroes' glory dim.
At Williamsburg, how bold you charged the foe;
At Fair Oaks, hosts of foemen you laid low.
Fierce, fierce the fray, and bloody is the work
When charge the Irish Rifles of New York.
Welcome, brave Sixty-Ninth, you gallant band,
That give to fame, fair Pennsylvania's land,
We thank you for your presence here to-night,
We thanked you for your aid in many a fight.
Although you're robbed of glory's envied wreath,
At Savage Station our famed Eighty-Eighth,
They rushed to charge the foe, and end the fight;

They came too late, you put the foe to flight.
But when did brave men ever charge in vain,
When led by such a hero as O'Kane.

Welcome, brave Second, to a merrier scene,
That when at Glendale, waved your flag of green,
When flying foemen hurried from your cheer,
Your voice is much more pleasant to us here.
And welcome Houston [*sic*], to our sports to-night—
The gay, the gallant, generous and polite.
And last, not least, our bosom friends we see,
Our brave, kind-hearted friends of Tammany.
And welcome Hooker, with a soldier's cheer,
We greet our noblest soldier's presence here;
McClellan's right hand, Valor's favorite son,
The honors that you wear you nobly won.
Full many a gem left California's mine,
But none so precious as that heart of thine:
A heart no danger or no foe can bend,
That none can ever conquer but a friend.
Since by your sway our Army has been blest,
You proved the generous feelings of your breast;
A father's care for every man you showed,
Cared for his comfort, clothing, tent and food;
Shed o'er our gloomy souls a lambent light
And fired our bosoms for the coming fight.
There's not one man, our famed green flag beneath,
But follows thee, to victory or death.
Yet Richmond shall behold her 'leaguered wall
Before the might of Hooker's soldierly fall;
He shall command, the woes of war to cease,
And by his valor give our Country peace:
A hapless fate shall fall upon the foe,
That hears our battle-cry, Hurrah for Joe!

Lawrence Reynolds: a native of Waterford, Ireland, who served as a surgeon with the Sixty-Third New York Volunteers. He had fled from Ireland after the failed 1848 uprising. He wrote and delivered this "poetical address" as part of the Irish Brigade's celebration of St. Patrick's Day during the Peninsular Campaign in March 1862. **Columbia:** the United States of America, usually personified as a female figure. **Meagher:** Thomas Francis Meagher, a native of County Waterford, Ireland, and captain of Company K, Sixty-Ninth New York Militia. He later organized and commanded the Irish Brigade. **Yorktown's walls:** Confederate entrenchments at Yorktown, Virginia, the first obstacle in Major General George McClellan's attempt to seize the Peninsula en route to the capture of Richmond, the Confederate capital. McClellan laid siege to Yorktown from April 16 to May 4, 1862, by which time reports of additional Union troops led the Confederates to abandon their defensive position. **Williamsburg:** the site of an engagement north of Yorktown, Virginia, on May 5, 1862. **Fair Oaks:** the site of a battle in Virginia on May 31-June 1, 1862. On the second day of the engagement, McClellan ordered in the Irish Brigade to stop a Confederate attack. The men of the Brigade charged with a savage battle shout — half-English and half-Gaelic — which one observer described as "worth a division." **Richmond:** the capital of Virginia and the object of McClellan's failed Peninsular Campaign. **McDowell's promised corps:** Although General McClellan demanded that 40,000 men under General Irwin McDowell (1818–1885) be sent from northern Virginia to the peninsula, McDowell was prevented from doing so because he was busy trying to stop "Stonewall" Jackson's depredations in the Shenandoah Valley. **Erin:** a literary name for Ireland. **Mac:** probably the Union general Irwin McDowell. **Gaines's Mill:** a battle in Virginia on June 27, 1862, during which the Irish Brigade stalled a Confederate charge, saved the Ninth Massachusetts from being destroyed by "Stonewall" Jackson, and covered the retreat of a collapsing Union line. **Porter:** Fitz John Porter (1822-1910), the Union general who commanded the First Division, Third Corps, during the Peninsular Campaign. **Savage Station:** an engagement in Virginia on June 29, 1862, when the Irish Brigade was used as a rear guard. **White Oak Swamp:** an engagement in Virginia on June 30, 1862, when the Irish Brigade fiercely protected the withdrawal of McClellan's troops. **Sumner:** Edwin Vose Sumner (1797-1863), who led the First Division, Second Corps, during the Peninsular Campaign of 1862 and was breveted a major general after the battle of Fair Oaks on May 31-June 1, 1862. On the first day of the battle, he told the Irish Brigade that if they failed the battle was lost. "I'll go to my stars on you," he said, pointing to his epaulets. "I want to see how Irishmen fight, and when you run, I'll run too." **Jackson:** Thomas "Stonewall" Jackson (1824–1863), the famous Confederate officer who received his nickname when General Barnard Bee tried to rally his men at Manassas by pointing out Jackson: "Look! There stands Jackson like a stone wall! Rally behind the Virginians!" **Lee:** Robert E. Lee (1807–1870), the Confederate commander of the Army of Northern Virginia. **Malvern Hill:** the site of a battle in Virginia on July 1, 1862, when the Irish Brigade's Eighty-Eighth New York Regiment forced General Robert E. Lee's Louisiana Tigers to retreat. **James's [*sic*] River:** the James River in Virginia. **Titian:** an Italian painter (c. 1477–1576). **Caracchi [*sic*]:** Carracci, one of three painters (Annibale, Agostino, or Ludovico) from a sixteenth-century family in Bologna, Italy. **Magruder:** John Bankhead Magruder (1810–1871), the Confederate officer whose dilatoriness and failure to commit all his men at Malvern Hill (July 1, 1862) contributed to the Union victory. **McClellan:** the Union commander George McClellan (1826-1885). **Little Mac:** Major General George McClellan. **South Mountain:** a battle on September 14, 1862, during which Union troops, directed by Major General Ambrose Burnside, seized control of the passes through South Mountain, Maryland. The Confederates were forced to withdraw toward Antietam Creek. **Burnside:** Ambrose Burnside (1824–1881), the Union commander of the Army of the Potomac until he suffered 12,600 casualties at Fredericksburg, Virginia. **Antietam:** Antietam Creek, near Sharpsburg, Maryland, the site of the battle of Antietam (September 17, 1862). During this bloodiest of Civil War battles, the Irish Brigade played a conspicuous part in the Union victory by pushing the enemy back to its second line. One Irish regiment lost half its men while another lost a third. The brigade suffered more than 500 casualties (113 dead and 422 wounded) at the "Bloody Lane," a sunken road where today stands a handsome memorial to the brigade. **Hill:** Ambrose Powell Hill (1825–1865), the Confederate general whose troops late in the day drove back a Union advance at Antietam. **Hooker:** Joseph Hooker (1814–1879), the Union commander whose troops attacked the Confederates near the Dunker church at Antietam. When Reynolds published this "poetical address," he dedicated it to General Hooker, "who was ever dear to the Irish, from his valor, and under whom they expect that your advance will be a succession of victories, and that this glorious Union will be preserved now and forever." **Green Flag:** the ensign of the Irish Brigade. The heavily fringed flag was a deep green and bore in the center an embroidered Irish harp, with a sunburst above it and a wreath of shamrocks beneath. A crimson scroll, in Irish letters, carried the motto "They shall never retreat from the charge of lances." **o'er the river:** Harpers Ferry is located at the confluence of the Potomac and the Shenandoah rivers. **Harper's [*sic*] Ferry:** Harpers Ferry, a heavily defended Union position which Brigadier General Julius White surrendered on September 15, 1862, under threat from Confederate forces commanded by "Stonewall" Jackson. The surrender resulted in the capture of 12,000 federal troops. **Bolivar:** actually Bolivar Heights, a Union position west of Harpers Ferry. This Union position was threatened when Confederates placed batteries on School House Ridge opposite. **The chief we trusted in:** Major General George McClellan, whom the War Department ordered to Trenton, New Jersey, to await a new assignment. **Falmouth:** the site of the Irish Brigade's winter quarters in 1862, located across the Rappahannock River from Fredericksburg, Virginia. **Mary's Hill [*sic*]:** Marye's Heights, the scene of six suicidal charges by the Irish Brigade during the battle of Fredericksburg, Virginia, on December 13, 1862. The brigade lost 545 men (killed, wounded, or missing) out of 1,300 engaged. **Fred'ricksburgh [*sic*]:** Fredericksburg. (See the previous entry.) **Irish Ninth:** the Ninth Massachusetts Infantry Regiment, rescued by the Irish Brigade from being destroyed by "Stonewall" Jackson at Gaines's Mill (June 26, 1862). **Cass:** Colonel Thomas Cass (1821-1862), a native of Ireland who organized and was the first commander of the Ninth Massachusetts Infantry Regiment. He was killed at the battle of Malvern Hill, Virginia. **Thirty-Seventh:** the Thirty-Seventh New York Infantry, also known as the Irish Rifles. **Kearney [*sic*]:** Philip Kearny, the popular Union commander whose men played significant roles in the battles of Williamsburg, Fair Oaks, and Glendale during the Peninsular Campaign. **Irish Rifles:** the Thirty-Seventh New York Infantry. **Sixty-Ninth:** the Sixty-Ninth Pennsylvania Infantry. **Eighty-Eighth:** the Eighty-Eighth New York Infantry, one of the many Celtic units in the Irish Brigade. **O'Kane:** Colonel Dennis O'Kane of the Sixty-Ninth Pennsylvania Infantry. His men pushed back a Confederate attempt to break the Union line at Gettysburg, although he died of wounds to the chest and/or abdomen. **Second:** the Second Corps of the Union army's First Division. **Glendale:** an engagement fought on June 30, 1862. **Houston [*sic*]:** either First Lieutenant Charles E. Huston of the 142nd Pennsylvania Infantry or Lieutenant James Huston of the Eighty-Second New York Infantty. **Tammany:** the Democratic political machine organization in New York City. **Joe:** General Joseph Hooker (1814–1879).

On Raising a Monument to the Irish Legion

by Charles Graham Halpine ("Private Miles O'Reilly") (1829–1866)

To raise a column o'er the dead,
       To strew with flowers the graves of those
Who, long ago, in storms of lead,
And where the bolts of battle sped,
       Beside us faced our Southern foes;
To honor these—th' unshriv'n, unhearsed—
       To-day we sad survivors come,
With colors draped, and arms reversed,
And all our souls in gloom immersed,
       With silent fife and muffled drum.

In mournful guise our banners wave;
       Black clouds above the "sunburst" lower;
We mourn the true, the young, the brave
Who, for this land that shelter gave,
       Drew swords in peril's deadliest hour—
For Irish soldiers fighting here
       As when Lord Clare was bid advance,
And Cumberland beheld with fear
The old green banners swinging clear
       To shield the broken lines of France.

We mourn them; not because they died
       In battle, for our destined race,
In every field of warlike pride,
From Limerick's wall to India's tide,
       Have borne our flag to foremost place;
As if each sought the soldier's trade,
       While some dim hopes within him glows,
Before he dies, in line arrayed,
To see the old green flag displayed
       For final fight with Ireland's foes.

For such a race the soldier's death
       Seems not a cruel death to die,
Around their names a laurel wreath,
A wild cheer as the parting breath
       On which their spirits mount the sky;
Oh, had their hope been only won,
       On Irish soil their final fight,

And had they seen, ere sinking down,
Our em'rald torn from England's crown,
    Each dead face would have flashed with light.

But vain are words to check the tide
    Of widowed grief and orphaned woe;
Again we see them by our side,
As, full of youth and strength and pride,
    They first went forth to meet the foe!
Their kindling eyes, their steps elate,
    Their grief at parting hid in mirth;
Against our foes no spark of hate,
No wish but to preserve the State
    That welcomes all th' oppressed of earth.

Not a new Ireland to invoke,
    To guard the flag was all they sought;
Not to make others feel the yoke
Of Poland, feel the shot and stroke
    Of those who in the legion fought;
Upon our great flag's azure field
    To hold unharmed each starry gem—
This cause on many a bloody field,
Thinned out by death, they would not yield—
    It was the world's last hope to them.

Oh ye, the small surviving band,
    Oh, Irish race wherever spread,
With wailing voice and wringing hand,
And the wild *kaoine* of the dear old land,
    Think of her Legion's countless dead!
Struck out of life by ball or blade,
    Or torn in fragments by the shell,
With briefest prayer by brother made,
And rudely in their blankets laid,
    Now sleep the brave who fought so well.

Their widows—tell them not of pride,
    No laurel checks the orphan's tear;
They only feel the world is wide,
And dark, and hard—nor help nor guide—
    No husband's arm, no father near;
But at their nod our fields were won,

And pious pity for their loss
In streams of gen'rous aid should run
To help them say: "Thy will be done,"
        As bent in grief they kiss the Cross.

Then for the soldiers and their chief
        Let all combine a shaft to raise—
The double type of pride and grief,
With many a sculpture and relief
        To tell their tale to after days;
And here will shine—our proudest boast
        While one of Irish blood survives:
"Sacred to that unfalt'ring host
Of soldiers from a distant coast,
        Who for the Union gave their lives.

"Welcomed they were with generous hand,
        And to that welcome nobly true,
When war's dread tocsin filled the land,
With sinewy arm and swinging brand,
        These exiles to the rescue flew.
Their fealty to the flag they gave,
        And for the Union, daring death.
Foremost among the foremost brave,
They welcomed vict'ry and the grave,
        In the same sigh of parting breath."

Thus be their modest history penned,
        But not with this our love must cease;
Let prayers from pious hearts ascend,
And o'er their ashes let us blend
        All feuds and factions into peace.
Oh, men of Ireland! here unite
        Around the graves of those we love,
And from their homes of endless light
The Legion's dead will bless the sight,
        And rain down anthems from above!

Here to this shrine by reverence led,
        Let Love her sacred lessons teach;
Shoulder to shoulder rise the dead,
From many a trench with battle red
        And thus I hear their ghostly speech:

> "Oh, for the old earth, and our sake,
>   Renounce all feuds, engend'ring fear,
> And Ireland from her trance shall wake,
> Striving once more her chains to break
>   When all her sons are brothers here."
>
> I see our Meagher's plume of green,
>   Approving nod to hear the words,
> And Corcoran's wraith applauds the scene,
> And bold Mat Murphy smiles, I ween—
>   All three with hands on ghastly swords—
> Oh, for their sake, whose names of light
>   Flash out like beacons from dark shores—
> Men of the old race! in your might,
> All factions quelled, again unite—
>   With you the Green Flag sinks or soars!

"sunburst": a feature of the regimental flags of the Irish Brigade. The heavily fringed flags were a deep green and bore in the center an embroidered Irish harp, with a sunburst above it and a wreath of shamrocks beneath. A crimson scroll, in Irish letters, carried the motto "They shall never retreat from the charge of lances." **Lord Clare:** Charles O'Brien (1699–1761), Sixth Viscount Clare, the commander of the Irish troops in the army of Louis XIV. At the battle of Fontenoy in 1745, the Irish Brigade turned the tide for France by helping defeat the Allied forces under the Duke of Cumberland. **Cumberland:** the Duke of Cumberland, the son of George II and the commander of the British, Austrian, and Dutch forces against Louis XIV at Fontenoy in 1745. **Limerick's wall:** an allusion to the siege of Limerick by the army of William III in 1691. **yoke of Poland:** During the late eighteenth century part or all of Poland was annexed by Austria, Prussia, and Russia. *kaoine*: probably *caoin* (pronounced "cuin"), a Gaelic verb meaning "weep, lament, mourn." **Meagher's plume of green:** the sprigs of boxwood worn like ensigns. **Corcoran:** Michael Corcoran (1827–1863), a native of County Sligo, Ireland, and colonel of the Sixty-Ninth New York Militia Regiment. **Mat Murphy:** perhaps Mathew Murphy, first mustered into the Sixty-Ninth New York Regiment as a second lieutenant at the age of twenty-two.

When the Sixty-Ninth Comes Back
by Joyce Kilmer (1886–1918)

The Sixty-ninth is on its way—France heard it long ago,
And the Germans know we're coming, to give them blow for blow.
We've taken on the contract, and when the job is through
We'll let them hear a Yankee cheer and an Irish ballad too.

The Harp that once through Tara's Halls shall fill the air with song,
And the Shamrock be cheered as the port is neared by our trium-
    phant throng.
With the Potsdam Palace on a truck and the Kaiser in a sack,
New York will be seen one Irish green when the Sixty-ninth comes
    back.

We brought back from the Border our Flag —'twas never lost;
We left behind the land we love, the stormy sea we crossed.
We heard the cry of Belgium, and France the free and fair,
For where there's work for fighting-men, the Sixty-ninth is there.

    The Harp that once through Tara's Halls shall fill the air with song,
    And the Shamrock be cheered as the port is neared by our trium-
        phant throng.
    With the Potsdam Palace on a truck and the Kaiser in a sack,
    New York will be seen one Irish green when the Sixty-ninth comes
        back.

The men who fought at Marye's Heights will aid us from the sky,
They showed the world at Fredericksburg how Irish soldiers die;
At Blackburn Ford they think of us, Atlanta and Bull Run;
There are many silver rings on the old flagstaff but there's room for
    another one.

    The Harp that once through Tara's Halls shall fill the air with song,
    And the Shamrock be cheered as the port is neared by our trium-
        phant throng.
    With the Potsdam Palace on a truck and the Kaiser in a sack,
    New York will be seen one Irish green when the Sixty-ninth comes
        back.

God rest our valiant leaders dead, whom we cannot forget;
They'll see the Fighting Irish the Fighting Irish yet.
While Ryan, Roe, and Corcoran on History's pages shine,
A wreath of laurel and shamrock waits the head of Colonel Hine.

    The Harp that once through Tara's Halls shall fill the air with song,
    And the Shamrock be cheered as the port is neared by our trium-
        phant throng.
    With the Potsdam Palace on a truck and the Kaiser in a sack,
    New York will be seen one Irish green when the Sixty-ninth comes
        back.

France heard it long ago: During World War I, the "Fighting 69th" — redesignated the 165th Infantry — sent 3,500 men overseas to fight in France. The unit gained additional fame because of its commander, William ("Wild Bill") Donovan, and its chaplain, Fr. Francis Duffy. The regiment's historian, the poet Joyce Kilmer, became a battlefield sergeant and was killed while on an observation mission with Donovan. After the war, when the regiment marched up Fifth Avenue in New York on April 28, 1919, its members were greeted with Victor Herbert's musical setting for Kilmer's poem "When the Sixty-Ninth Comes Back." **The Harp that once through Tara's Halls:** an allusion to a song of the same name by the Irish poet Thomas Moore (1779–1852). **Potsdam Palace:** Sans-Souci Palace, in Potsdam, built by King Frederick the Great of Prussia (1740–1786). **Kaiser:** Wilhelm II (1859–1941), the German monarch during World War I. **Marye's Heights, Fredericksburg, Blackburn Ford, Bull Run:** Civil War engagements in which the Irish Brigade was involved. **Ryan:** one of twenty-nine men by that name who joined the Sixty-Ninth New York Militia Regiment between 1861 and 1864. **Roe:** probably Thomas Roe, who joined Company A, Sixty-Ninth New York Militia Regiment, in 1864. **Corcoran:** Michael Corcoran (1827–1863), a native of County Sligo, Ireland, and colonel of the Sixty-Ninth New York Regiment. He was captured at Bull Run. **Colonel Hine:** Charles De Lane Hine (1867–1927), major of U.S. Volunteers in the Spanish-American War and colonel of the Sixty-Ninth New York Infantry in World War I.

41. Philip Kearny

Philip Kearny's earliest paternal ancestor in America was an Irish emigrant who settled in Perth Amboy, New Jersey, sometime after 1704. The latter-day Kearny was trained at the French Cavalry School in Saumur, France, and later enlisted in the U.S. army for duty on the western frontier. In 1847, while leading an attack on Churubusco, Mexico, he sustained a hit that resulted in the amputation of his left arm. After the Mexican War he returned to France to fight for Napoleon III in the Franco-Italian conflict.

With the outbreak of the American Civil War, Kearny returned to his native land and was given command of the First New Jersey Brigade in the Union army. Seemingly unhindered by his earlier injury, he was often seen holding the reins of his horse in his teeth as he directed his men with his right arm. Just before the Second Battle of Bull Run, however, he was fired upon and killed after unwittingly crossing Confederate lines at Chantilly, Virginia, on September 1, 1862.

The fallen Kearny was eulogized in superlative terms. The Union general John Pope described his fellow officer with unusual eloquence: "Tall and lithe in figure, with a most expressive and mobile countenance, and a manner which inspired confidence and zeal in all under his command, no one could fail to admire his chivalric bearing and his supreme courage. He seemed to think that it was his mission to make up the shortcomings of others, and in proportion as these shortcomings were made plain, his exertions and exposure were multiplied." General Winfield Scott, meanwhile, praised Kearny as "the bravest man I ever knew, and a perfect soldier." In 1912 Kearny's body was exhumed from Trinity Churchyard in New York City and interred at Arlington National Cemetery in Virginia. Two years later his grave was adorned with a life-size equestrian statue of the "little general."

Kearny at Seven Pines

by Edmund Clarence Stedman (1833–1908)

So that soldierly legend is still on its journey,—
    That story of Kearny who knew not to yield!
'T was the day when with Jameson, fierce Berry, and Birney,
    Against twenty thousand he rallied the field.
Where the red volleys poured, where the clamor rose highest,
    Where the dead lay in clumps through the dwarf oak and pine,
Where the aim from the thicket was surest and nighest,—
    No charge like Phil Kearny's along the whole line.

When the battle went ill, and the bravest were solemn,
    Near the dark Seven Pines, where we still held our ground,
He rode down the length of the withering column,
    And his heart at our war-cry leapt up with a bound;
He snuffed, like his charge, the wind of the powder,—
    His sword waved us on and we answered the sign:
Loud our cheer as we rushed, but his laugh rang the louder,
    "There's the devil's own fun, boys, along the whole line!"

How he strode his brown steed! How we saw his blade brighten
    In the one hand still left,—and the reins in his teeth!
He laughed like a boy when the holidays heighten,
    But a soldier's glance shot from his visor beneath.
Up came the reserves to the mellay [*sic*] infernal,
    Asking where to go in,—through the clearing or pine?
"O, anywhere! Forward! 'T is all the same, Colonel:
    You'll find lovely fighting along the whole line!"

O, evil the black shroud of night at Chantilly,
    That hid him from sight of his brave men and tried.
Foul, foul sped the bullet that clipped the white lily,

The flower of our knighthood, the whole army's pride!
Yet we dream that he still—in that shadowy region
    Where the dead form their ranks at the war drummer's sign,—
Rides on, as of old, down the length of legion,
    And the word still is Forward! along the whole line.

Jameson, Berry, and Birney: Charles Jameson (1827–1862), Hiram Berry (1824–1863), and David Birney (1825–1864), Union brigadier generals in Kearny's division during the Peninsular campaign. **Seven Pines:** also known as the battle of Fair Oaks (May 31–June 1, 1862). **mellay [*sic*]:** melee. **Chantilly:** a Union victory in Virginia (August 31, 1862), after which Kearny was fired upon and killed after unwittingly crossing the Confederate lines. "Poor Kearny," lamented the Confederate general A. P. Hill. "He deserved a better death than that."

Dirge for a Soldier

by George Henry Boker (1823–1890)

Close his eyes; his work is done!
    What to him is friend or foeman,
Rise of moon, or set of sun,
    Hand of man, or kiss of woman?
                Lay him low, lay him low,
                In the clover or the snow?
                What cares he? he cannot know:
                Lay him low!

As man may, he fought his fight,
    Proved his truth by his endeavor;
Let him sleep in solemn night,
    Sleep forever and forever.
                Lay him low, lay him low,
                In the clover or the snow!
                What cares he? he cannot know:
                Lay him low!

Fold him in his country's stars,
    Roll the drum and fire the volley!
What to him are all our wars,
    What but death-bemocking folly?
                Lay him low, lay him low,
                In the clover or the snow!
                What cares he? he cannot know:
                Lay him low!

> Leave him to God's watching eye;
> Trust him to the hand that made him.
> Mortal love weeps idly by:
> God alone has power to aid him.
> Lay him low, lay him low,
> In the clover or the snow!
> What cares he? he cannot know:
> Lay him low!

42. Patrick Cleburne

Patrick Cleburne was born in County Cork, Ireland, on St. Patrick's Day 1828. Although he apprenticed himself to a druggist at the age of 18, he failed the apothecaries' exam administered at Trinity College, Dublin, primarily because of his deficiencies in the classical languages. To escape this humiliation, he sought anonymity in a British infantry regiment, although after three years he left the service for America in 1849. He eventually obtained a job as a druggist's clerk in Helena, Arkansas.

As national events rushed headlong toward civil war, Cleburne threw in his lot with the Confederacy. Elected captain of the First Arkansas Regiment, he was known as a strict disciplinarian, but he insisted that his men be treated with respect and he never condoned punishment that disgraced the individual. On one occasion when he learned that one of his drunken soldiers had been whipped with the buckle end of a belt, he took steps to ensure that the officer who had ordered the punishment lost his commission.

In 1863, during a battle at Richmond, Kentucky, the Irishman was wounded in the mouth. The bullet which entered his left jaw destroyed two lower teeth and lodged in his mouth, rendering him incapable of speech and thus useless as a commanding officer during that engagement. Although Cleburne later fought in Alabama and Tennessee, he showed the most daring at Chickamauga, where he and his men repulsed Sherman and covered the retreat of General Braxton Bragg from Lookout Mountain in Georgia. For his actions during these crucial engagements, he became known as the "Stonewall Jackson of the West."

As the fortunes of the Confederacy waned during the last year of the war, Cleburne risked military advancement with what some regarded as a dangerous suggestion. Seeing that the Southern ranks were becoming thinner, he proposed that slaves be enlisted in the Confederate army and that they be granted their freedom for serving. Though at first ignored, his suggestion was later embodied in a bill which the Confederate Congress passed on March 3, 1865.

A year after the battle at Richmond, Cleburne was shot and killed during an engagement at Franklin, Tennessee. Before the battle he had said to a companion, "Well, Govan, if we must die, let us die like men." The Irishman's last words were spoken to a fellow officer: "We will resume this conversation at the first convenient moment." His death on the battlefield occurred only fifteen minutes after an unusual act of charity toward one of his men. As Cleburne rode into battle he noticed that one of his soldiers was leaving tracts of blood on the ground while walking barefoot over the frozen cornfield. Cleburne took off his boots and gave them to the soldier, dying soon later in his own bare feet.

Death of Cleburne
by Virginia A. Frazer

I.

The gray war-horse, impatient, champs his bit,
    His spreading nostrils sniff the coming fight,
But still as stone his rider's eagle eye
    Looks on the serried lines that meet his sight.

Each feature tells a tale they may not know—
    A volume may be spoken in each breath;
But grave and stern, with silence on his lips,
    The gallant Cleburne waits the charge of death.

Behind their works loom up the lines of blue,
    Before, the timber felled by cautious hands
To break the ranks of gray; 'twixt these a floor,
    To thresh with leaden flail the Southern bands.

"Charge!" wildly, with the ringing rebel yell
    That flings its piercing echo on the breeze,
The men, like gray stars on a somber field,
    Crash through the crackling limbs of fallen trees.

"Charge!" and the horse no longer paws the earth,
    For in the front, with Cleburne at their head,
His men advance, to sternly do or die—
    Their death-march sounding in the rattling lead!

Again they move—above the deafening roar
    Of belching guns the weird yell rings again,
And in the flash it seems the gates of hell
    Had yawned wide as they gained the open plain!

There was no time for parleying or fear.
    What though the men were grain before the flail?
What though their works were only bloody dead?
    'T was *victory* or *death*—they *could not* quail!

The storm of shot, and bursting of the shell,
    And sweep of hurtling grape with burning breath,
Pour on the Southern host, undaunted, yet
    Still facing close the horrid hail of death!

And in the storm the stern form and his horse
    Gleam like an upraised statue through the cloud;
The flying bullets, whizzing, pass him by;
    Ay, even death seems loath to weave his shroud!

The outer works are carried! on and on!
    For victory smiles. On with the rebel yell!
Scale now the inner works, or let the guns
    Of foes shout out a glorious funeral-knell!

They knew not how it was—a rift revealed
    The horse and rider, then the scene was dim;
But on the inner works the death-hail rang
    In dying Cleburne's ears a battle-hymn!

II.

'T is midnight's hour, and through the lifting clouds
    The struggling moonbeams gaze on Franklin's field,
Upon the war-stained corse of friend and foe,
    And weirdly kiss the lips forever sealed.

The ghastly calm seems steeped in human gore,
    The ditch bears in its depth the bloody tide;
The cold December winds mourn round the spot
    Where Cleburne, with his charger, nobly died.

No more for him rings out the battle-cry,

No more the stern lips echo back its tone;
   And as in life he led the Irish bands,
     In death his life-blood mingled with *his own*.

III.

The hand of Time plows deep the battle-field,
   For at his voice the thundering cannons cease;
The sword is rusting—from its unused sheath
   The spider swings the gauzy flag of peace.

Throughout, the city wears a sable pall—
   Remembering in love her silent guest;
Just at the water's edge the steamer waits,
   To bear lamented Cleburne to his rest.

In reverence grouped around the hero's corse,
   The honored and the humble silent grieve,
When through the throng a brawny arm makes way,
   Its useless mate a ragged, empty sleeve.

No sound breaks rudely on the solemn hush:
   The crowd falls back, and at the coffin's head
The grim form kneels to make the sacred cross
   Above the cold heart of the hallowed dead.

The upraised eyes are hard with harder life,
   Unused to weep; but as the prayer was done,
One big tear splashed upon the coffin-lid—
   Loved Erin's tribute to her hero son!

corse: corpse.

Cleburne

author unknown

Another ray of light hath fled, another Southern brave
Hath fallen in his country's cause and found a laureled grave—
Hath fallen, but his deathless name shall live when stars shall set,
For, noble Cleburne, thou art one this world will ne'er forget.

'Tis true, thy warm heart beats no more, that on thy noble head
Azrael placed his icy hand, and thou art with the dead;

The glancing of thine eyes are [*sic*] dim; no more will they be bright
Until they ope in Paradise, with clearer, heavenlier light.

No battle news disturbs thy rest upon the sun-bright shore,
No clarion voice awakens thee on earth to wrestle more,
No tramping steed, no wary foe bids thee awake, arise,
For thou art in the angel world, beyond the starry skies.

Brave Cleburne, dream in thy low bed, with pulseless deadened heart;
Calm, calm and sweet, O warrior rest! thou well hast borne thy part,
And now a glory wreath for thee the angels singing twine,
A glory wreath, not of the earth, but made by hands divine.

A long farewell—we give thee up, with all thy bright renown,
A chieftain here on earth is lost, in heaven an angel found.
Above thy grave a wail is heard—a nation mourns her dead;
A nobler for the South ne'er died, a braver never bled.

A last farewell—how can we speak the bitter word farewell!
The anguish of our bleeding hearts vain words may never tell.
Sleep on, sleep on, to God we give our chieftain in his might;
And weeping, feel he lives on high, where comes no sorrow's night.

Azrael: in Jewish and Islamic theology the angel who separates the soul from the
body at the moment of death.

"Oh, No, He'll Not Need Them Again"
author unknown

Oh, no! he'll not need them again—
No more will he wake to behold
The splendor and fame of his men,
The tale of his victories told!
No more will he wake from that sleep
Which he sleeps in his glory and fame,
While his comrades are left here to weep
Over Cleburne, his grave and his name.

Oh, no! he'll not need them again;
No more will his banner be spread
O'er the field of his gallantry's fame—
The soldier's proud spirit is fled!
The soldier who rose 'mid applause,

From the humblemost place in the van—
I sing not in praise of the cause
    But rather in praise of the man.

Oh, no! he'll not need them again;
    He has fought his last battle without them.
For barefoot he, too, must go in,
    While barefoot stood comrades about him;
And barefoot they proudly marched in,
    With blood flowing fast from their feet;
They thought of the past victories won,
    And the foes that they now were to meet.

Oh, no! he'll not need them again;
    He is leading his men to the charge,
Unheeding the shells, or the slain,
    Or the showers of the bullets at large
On the right, on the left, on the flanks,
    He dashingly pushes his way,
While with cheers, double-quick and in ranks,
    His solders all followed that day.

Oh, no! he'll not need them again;
    He falls from his horse to the ground!
Oh anguish! oh, sorrow! oh, pain!
    In the brave hearts that gathered around.
He breathes not of grief, nor a sigh
    On the breast where he pillowed his head,
Ere he fix'd his last gaze upon high—
    "I'm killed, boys, but fight it out," said.

Oh, no! he'll not need them again;
    But treasure them up for his sake;
And oh! should you sing a refrain
    Of the memories they still must awake,
Sing it soft as the summer-eve breeze,
    Let it sound as refreshing and clear;
Tho' grief-born, there's that which can please
    In thoughts that are gemmed with a tear.

43. Father William Corby

William Corby was born in 1833 in Detroit, where his father, Daniel Corby of King's County, Ireland, had settled. When he was twenty years old, the young Corby entered the University of Notre Dame and within a year had joined the Congregation of the Holy Cross, the teaching religious order which administered the university. After his ordination he combined pastoral work with his duties as a professor and the director of the Manual Labor School at the university.

When the Civil War began, Corby was commissioned chaplain of the Eighty-Eighth New York Infantry, one of the many Celtic units in the Irish Brigade. In that capacity he participated in all the campaigns of the Army of the Potomac, seeing service most notably at the battles of Antietam, Fredericksburg, Chancellorsville, Gettysburg, Spotsylvania, and Petersburg. He is best remembered for granting general absolution to the members of the Irish Brigade at Gettysburg.

That scene was later described by St. Clair Mulholland, himself a native of Ireland and at the time a major in the brigade: "While this is customary in the armies of Catholic countries in Europe, it was perhaps the first time it was ever witnessed on this continent. . . . Father Corby stood on a large rock in front of the brigade. Addressing the men, he explained what he was about to do, saying that each one could receive the benefit of the absolution by a making a sincere act of contrition and firmly resolving to embrace the first opportunity to confess his sins, urging them to do their duty, and reminding them of the high and sacred nature of their trust as soldiers and the noble object for which they fought. . . . The brigade was standing at 'Order arms!' As he closed his address, every man, Catholic and non-Catholic, fell on his knees with his head bowed down. Then stretching his right hand toward the brigade, Father Corby pronounced the words of absolution . . . ."

After the war Corby returned to Notre Dame, first assuming administrative duties there and then serving as provincial general of the Holy Cross Congregation in the United States. During his tenure at the university, he oversaw an ambitious building program, the broadening of academic offerings, and the establishment of a law school.

Father Corby

by James J. Creswell

All day, up Round Top's crested crown,
Two armor'd hosts are led;
Two banners wave, as night goes down,
Each over its soldier dead.

For far away, o'er ridge and slope,
    The lone Palmetto tree
Still cheers those rebel lines to hope,
    Their leader, gallant Lee.

Old Gettysburg to-day must stand,
    Or with the flag go down!
Thus vow'd our boys of Northern land,
    To save that loyal town.
Our fathers' flag—to heroes given—
    To-day shall wave *their* deed;
Shall wave each fold in sight of heaven!
    Thus spoke our dauntless Mead [*sic*].

Fall in! the thundering guns sing loud,
    Thro' morning's peaceful air;
Fall in! a soldier needs no shroud.
    No time for soldier pray'r.
A moment Nugent's men may rest,
    To jest or laugh the while,
Each folds upon a loyal breast
    The Green of his loved Isle.

A moment—'neath yon shelving stone—
    Within that awful field —
Those heroes bend in deep atone,
    While Death's dark shadows yield;
A soldier-priest, with hands extend
    Absolves their sins! Forgiven—
Short shrift was theirs, Faith makes amend
    Beneath approving heaven.

Forward! Thro' bristling lines of steel
    Their gory work soon done,
The shattered columns backward reel
    Our field to-day is won;
To-night the moon's pale rays shall rest—
    Each in his narrow bed—
To-morrow flowers with perfume prest
    We garland round our dead!

Old Gettysburg yet lives to tell
    When night each star bends down,

> How rebel hail of shot and shell,
> Plow'ed thro that loyal town.
> And well hath Gettysburg relied
> On soldier boys' brave deed
> While little Round Top points with pride
> To Corby's loyal creed.

Round Top's crested crown: Little Round Top, a position on the Gettysburg battlefield which three Irish companies helped capture. **Palmetto tree:** the palm tree emblem on the flag of South Carolina, adopted when it seceded in 1861. **Mead [*sic*]:** George Gordon Meade (1815–1872), the great-grandson of an Irish emigrant and the commander of the Army of the Potomac. The Union troops under his command successfully repulsed the Confederate drive at Gettysburg. **Nugent:** Robert Nugent (?–1901), a native of County Down, Ireland, and lieutenant colonel of the Sixty-Ninth New York Regiment. He later served as general of the Sixty-Ninth New York Volunteers and commander of the Irish Brigade.

A Miracle of War

by Smith Johnson

> Two armies stood in stern array
> On Gettysburg's historic field—
> This side the blue, on that the gray—
> Each side resolved to win the day,
> Or life to home and country yield.
>
> "Take arms!" "Fall in!" rang o'er the line
> Of Hancock's ever-valiant corps—
> For to the left the cannons chime
> With music terribly sublime,
> With death's unceasing, solemn roar.
>
> With spirits ardent, undismayed,
> With flags uplifted toward the sky,
> There stands brave Meagher's old brigade
> Those noble laurels ne'er will fade
> Upon the page of history.
>
> "All forward, men!" No, pause a while—
> Dead silence follows like parade
> At "order arms," for 'long the file
> There moves a priest with holy smile—
> The priest of Meagher's old brigade.

All eyes were toward him reverent turned,
    For he was known and loved by all,
And every face with fervor burned,
And with a glance his mission learned—
    A mission of high Heaven's call.

Then spake the priest: "My comrades, friends,
    Ere long the battle fierce will surge,
Ere long the curse of war descends—
At such a moment God commends
    You from the soul all sin to purge.

"Kneel, soldiers; lift your hearts to God,
    In sweet contrition crush the pride
Of human minds; kneel on the sod
That soon will welter in your blood—
    Look up to Christ, who for you died."

And every man, whate'er his creed,
    Kneels down, and whispers pass along
The ranks, and murmuring voices plead
To be from sin's contagion freed
    And turned from path of mortal wrong.

Across the vale the gray lines view
    The priest and those who, kneeling now,
For absolution humbly sue,
And joining hearts, the gray and blue,
    Together make the holy vow.

* * * * * * * * * * *

The smoke of battle lifts apace,
    And o'er the field lie forms of men,
With glazen eyes and pallid face—
Dead—yet alive, for God's sweet grace.
    Has saved them, from the death of sin.

Hancock: Winfield Scott Hancock (1824–1886), the major general who rallied the Union troops on Cemetery Hill on the first day of Gettysburg. **Meagher's old brigade:** the Irish Brigade. **priest of Meagher's old brigade:** Fr. William Corby, the chaplain of the Eighty-Eighth New York Infantry.

44. Thomas Jonathan "Stonewall" Jackson

Born in 1824 in what is now West Virginia, Thomas "Stonewall" Jackson claimed Irish roots on both sides of his family tree. His paternal great-grandfather was born in either 1715 or 1719 near Coleraine, Ireland, and his mother was born in Virginia, a daughter of Irish settlers named Thomas and Margaret Neale.

Jackson's youth provides numerous examples of his enterprise and seriousmindedness. Eager to learn more than the short school sessions offered, for instance, he promised to teach a slave how to read and write if the latter supplied him with fire wood so he could peruse his books each night. The teenage Jackson was employed in the construction of the Parkersburg and Staunton Turnpike and each Sunday walked three miles to church. The local justice of the peace was so impressed by Jackson's sense of responsibility that he obtained for the seventeen-year-old boy an appointment as a constable. The following year Jackson enrolled in the U.S. Military Academy.

Beginning in 1858, Jackson lived in Lexington, Virginia, while he taught natural philosophy, optics, acoustics, astronomy, and analytical mechanics at Virginia Military Institute there. The future general followed a strict routine that reflected his military training. He rose at six in the morning, took a cold bath (no matter what the weather), led family prayers at seven, ate breakfast, and headed off to V.M.I. by eight. His wife recorded the remainder of his daily schedule: "Upon his return home at eleven o'clock, he devoted himself to study until one. The first book he took up daily was his Bible, which he read with a commentary, and the many pencil-marks upon it showed with what care he bent over its pages. From his Bible he turned to his text-books, which engaged him until dinner, at one o'clock."

The famous Confederate officer received his nickname during the battle of Manassas in 1861. As Jackson and his men awaited attack behind Henry House Hill, General Barnard Bee tried to rally his men by pointing out Jackson: "Look! There stands Jackson like a stone wall! Rally behind the Virginians!" Two years later at Chancellorsville, Jackson was accidentally shot by Confederate pickets after returning to his lines to announce his victory against the right wing of the Union line. Jackson was hit twice in the left arm and once in the right hand. After his shattered arm was amputated the next morning, General Robert E. Lee said: "He has lost his left arm, but I have lost my right." Fearing that Jackson might be captured, Lee ordered his removal to Fairfield plantation at Guinea Station. There Jackson died on May 10, 1863, soon after uttering his famous last words: "Let us cross over the river, and rest under the shade of the trees."

Stonewall Jackson's Way

by John Williamson Palmer (1825–1906)

Come, stack arms, men! Pile on the rails,
    Stir up the camp-fire bright;
No growling if the canteen fails,
    We'll make a roaring night.
Here Shenandoah brawls along,
There burly Blue Ridge echoes strong,
To swell the Brigade's rousing song
    Of "Stonewall Jackson's way."

We see him now — the queer slouched hat
    Cocked o'er his eye askew;
The shrewd, dry smile; the speech so pat,
    So calm, so blunt, so true.
The "Blue-Light Elder" knows 'em well;
Says he, "That's Banks—he's fond of shell;
Lord save his soul! we'll give him—" well!
    That's "Stonewall Jackson's way."

Silence! ground arms! kneel all! caps off!
    Old Massa's goin' to pray.
Strangle the fool that dares to scoff!
    Attention! it's his way.
Appealing from his native sod,
In forma pauperis to God:
"Lay bare Thine arm; stretch forth Thy rod!
    Amen!" That's Stonewall's way."

He's in the saddle now. Fall in!
    Steady! the whole brigade!
Hill's at the ford, cut off; we'll win
    His way out, ball and blade!
What matter if our shoes are worn?
What matter if our feet are torn?
"Quick step! we're with him before morn!"
    That's "Stonewall Jackson's way."

The sun's bright lances rout the mists
    Of morning, and, by George!
Here's Longstreet, struggling in the lists,
    Hemmed in an ugly gorge.

> Pope and his Dutchmen, whipped before;
> "Bay'nets and grape! hear Stonewall roar;
> "Charge, Stuart! Pay off Ashby's score!"
>   In "Stonewall Jackson's way."
>
> Ah! Maiden, wait and watch and yearn
>   For news of Stonewall's band!
> Ah, Widow, read, with eyes that burn,
>   That ring upon thy hand!
> Ah! Wife, sew on, pray on, hope on;
> Thy life shall not be all forlorn;
> The foe had better ne'er been born
>   That gets in "Stonewall's way."

Shenandoah: a valley in northwestern Virginia, used by the Confederates as an invasion route to threaten Washington, D.C., Baltimore, Harrisburg, and Philadelphia. **Blue Ridge:** a mountain range extending from southern Pennsylvania to northern Georgia. **Blue-Light Elder:** "Stonewall" Jackson, so called because of his strict Presbyterian personal behavior. **Banks:** Nathaniel Banks (1816–1894), a Union officer who conducted operations in the Shenandoah Valley. **Old Massa:** "Stonewall" Jackson, referred to here in Southern dialect for "Old Master." *In forma pauperis:* a Latin phrase meaning "in the appearance of a poor man." **Hill:** Ambrose Powell Hill (1825–1865), a Confederate general who was on Jackson's march around the Union right flank at Chancellorsville. When Jackson was wounded, Hill took command of the corps but was himself wounded carrying his chief to the rear. **Longstreet:** James Longstreet (1821–1904), the Confederate general who inflicted great losses on the Union army at Fredericksburg but arrived too late to play a part in the battle of Chancellorsville. **Pope:** John Pope (1822–1892), the Union general whose pursuit of Jackson at Second Bull Run was frustrated when James Longstreet sent five divisions into the Union flank. **Stuart:** J. E. B. Stuart (1833–1864), the Confederate cavalry officer who took command of Jackson's corps when the latter was wounded at Chancellorsville. **Ashby:** Turner Ashby (1828–1862), Jackson's cavalry commander during the Shenandoah Valley campaign.

"The Brigade Must Not Know, Sir!"

by John Williamson Palmer (1825–1906)

> "Who've ye got there?"—"Only a dying brother,
>   Hurt in the front just now."
> "Good boy! he'll do. Somebody tell his mother
>   Where he was killed, and how."
>
> "Whom have you there?"—"A crippled courier, Major,
>   Shot by mistake, we hear.

He was with Stonewall." "Cruel work they've made here;
    Quick with him to the rear!"

"Well, who comes next?"—"Doctor, speak low, speak low, sir;
    Don't let the men find out!
It's Stonewall!"—"God!"—"The brigade must not know, sir,
    While there's a foe about!"

Whom have we here—shrouded in martial manner,
    Crowned with a martyr's charm?
A grand dead hero, in a living banner,
    Born of his heart and arm:

The heart whereon his cause hung—see how clingeth
    That banner to his bier!
The arm wherewith his cause struck—hark! how ringeth
    His trumpet in their rear!

What have we left? His glorious inspiration,
    His prayers in council met.
Living, he laid the first stones of a nation;
    And dead, he builds it yet.

Stonewall Jackson

by Herman Melville (1819–1891)

The Man who fiercest charged in fight,
    Whose sword and prayer were long—
        Stonewall!
    Even him who stoutly stood for Wrong,
How can we praise? Yet coming days
    Shall not forget him with this son.

Dead is the Man whose Cause is dead,
    Vainly he died and set his seal—
        Stonewall!
    Earnest in error, as we feel;
True to the things he deemed was due
    True as John Brown or steel.

Relentlessly he routed us;
    But *we* relent, for he is low—
        Stonewall!

> Justly his frame we outlaw; so
> We drop a tear on the bold Virginian's bier,
> Because no wreath we owe.

John Brown: the abolitionist (1800–1859) who was executed for treason for his raid on Harpers Ferry in 1859.

The Dying Words of Stonewall Jackson
by Sidney Lanier (1842–1881)

> "Order A. P. Hill to prepare for battle."
> "Tell Major Hawks to advance the commissary train."
> "Let us cross the river and rest in the shade."
>
> The stars of Night contain the glittering Day
> And rain his glory down with sweeter grace
> Upon the dark World's grand, enchanted face—
> 　All loth to turn away.
>
> And so the Day, about to yield his breath,
> Utters the stars unto the listening Night,
> To stand for burning fare-thee-wells of light
> 　Said on the verge of death.
>
> O hero-life that lit us like the sun!
> O hero-words that glittered like the stars
> And stood and shone above the gloomy wars
> 　When the hero-life was done!
>
> The phantoms of a battle came to dwell
> I' the fitful vision of his dying eyes—
> Yet even in battle-dreams, he sends supplies
> 　To those he loved so well.
>
> His army stands in battle-line arrayed:
> His couriers fly; all's done: now God decide!
> —And not till then saw he the Other Side
> 　Or would accept the shade.
>
> Thou Lord whose sun is gone, they stars remain!
> Still shine the words that miniature his deeds.
> O thrice-beloved, whe'er thy great heart bleeds,
> 　Solace hast thou for pain!

A. P. Hill: Ambrose Powell Hill (1825–65), the Confederate general who was on Jackson's march around the Union right flank at Chancellorsville. When Jackson was wounded, Hill took command of the corps but was himself wounded carrying his chief to the rear. **Major Hawks:** Wells J. Hawks, Jackson's chief commissary officer. Prior to the war he had served a term as mayor of Charlestown, West Virginia, and three terms in the state legislature and was Charlestown's foremost businessman.

Death of Stonewall Jackson

by Henry Lynden Flash (b. 1835)

Not midst the lightning of the stormy fight,
　　Not in the rush upon the vandal foe,
Did kingly Death, with his resistless might,
　　Lay the great leader low.

His warrior soul its earthly shackles broke
　　In the full sunshine of a peaceful town;
When all the storm was hushed, the trusty oak
　　That propped our cause went down.

Though his alone the blood that flecks the ground,
　　Recording all his grand, heroic deeds,
Freedom herself is writhing with the wound,
　　And all the country bleeds.

He entered not the Nation's Promised Land
　　At the red belching of the cannon's mouth;
But broke the House of Bondage with his hand—
　　The Moses of the South!

O gracious God! not gainless is the loss;
　　A glorious sunbeam gilds thy sternest frown;
And while his country staggers 'neath the Cross,
　　He rises with the Crown.

Under the Shade of the Trees

by Margaret Junkin Preston (1820–1897)

What are the thoughts that are stirring his breast?
　　What is the mystical vision he sees?
—"Let us pass over the river and rest
　　Under the shade of the trees."

Has he grown sick of his toils and his tasks?
   Sighs the worn spirit for respite or ease?
Is it a moment's cool halt that he asks
   Under the shade of the trees?

Is it the gurgle of waters whose flow
   Ofttime has come to him, borne on the breeze,
Memory listens to, lapsing so low,
   Under the shade of the trees?

Nay—though the rasp of the flesh was so sore,
   Faith, that had yearnings far keener than these,
Saw the soft sheen of the Thitherward Shore
   Under the shade of the trees;—

Caught the high psalms of ecstatic delight—
   Heard the harps harping, like soundings of seas—
Watched earth's assoiléd ones walking in white
   Under the shade of the trees.

Oh, was it strange he should pine for release,
   Touched to the soul with such transports as these,—
He who so needed the balsam of peace,
   Under the shade of the trees?

Yes, it was noblest for him—it was best
   (Questioning naught of our Father's decrees),
There to pass over the river and rest
   Under the shade of the trees!

General Jackson Crosses Jordan

by Martha Keller (b. 1902)

The air of heaven was black with smoke,
Black with battle, loud with lead,
When Thomas Jonathan Jackson spoke,
And these were the words that Jackson said,

   As the blood of his arm ran over his breast
   And he lay and bled with his hand in Lee's:
   "Let us pass over the river and rest—
   Rest in the shade of the trees."

By the roads and ridges, creeks and crags,
    Where men would follow, he led them on,
Led the rebels in bloody rag
    From dawn to dark and dark to dawn.
With bandages for their battle flags —
    They followed Jackson to hell and gone.

The arm he lost was a mortal loss.
(He lost his left, but Lee his right.)
The one more river he had to cross
Was wicked water and black as night.

But over Jordan, deep and wide,
As wide a water as kingdom come,
A flock of angels on either side—
Waited for to carry him home.

He was a deacon, good and grim.
    He, alone, was a mighty host,
A rebel yell and a battle hymn.
    His were the men that marched the most.
Stonewall wasn't the word for him—
He was a phantom, he was a ghost.

The angels waiting on either bank
Blew for him till their trumpets burst.
But he slipped so fast around the flank
That he got to heaven first.
In clouds as white as a cloud of tents,
There in a sunshine bright as braid,
He called the roll of his regiments—
And rested in the shade.

His were the men no men could beat.
    (He won his battle by breaking rules.)
With empty bellies and bloody feet,
    (Regulations were made for fools,)
He led them up to the judgment seat—
    (Fast as horses, tough as mules.)

Jordan: a river between modern Israel and Jordan which the biblical Hebrews crossed from the east on their way into the Promised Land.

45. Richard Dowling

Richard Dowling was born in Tuam, Ireland, in 1838 and at the age of ten came to New Orleans with his sister. On the eve of the Civil War, he was part-owner of a liquor-importing business in Galveston, Texas, and the owner of "The Bank of Bacchus," a saloon and billiard parlor whose specialty was a drink called "Kiss Me Quick and Go."

During the War Between the States, Dowling volunteered for the Confederate army. He quickly advanced to the rank of lieutenant and helped recapture Galveston on January 1, 1863. Three weeks later he and his Davis Guards — an all-Irish unit of Company F, Texas Heavy Artillery — received orders to abandon Fort Sabine, a defensive position guarding a six-mile-long pass on the boundary of Texas and Louisiana, in anticipation of a planned Union attack involving 5,000 troops. When Dowling's more immediate commanding officer, however, advised him to use his own discretion, the Davis Guards choose to defend the pass.

By the beginning of September, the Guards had constructed Fort Griffin, an earthwork for their six guns, and were awaiting the Union advance. Before the three federal gunboats off the coast opened fire to cover the landing of their 1,200 troops, however, the Davis Guards fired off 137 rounds. A shot fired by gunner Michael McKernan tore a hole through the boiler of the gunboat *Sachem*, causing the vessel's crew to jump overboard to escape the steam and boiling water. The Irish gunners then turned their fire on the *Clifton*, making its way up the channel with a complement of seventy-seven sharpshooters. When a shot from Fort Griffin broke the gunboat's wheel rope, the vessel went out of control and crashed into the banks of the channel. Although the Irish unit killed fifty Union soldiers and captured 350 others as well as two gunboats, it suffered no losses during the forty-five-minute battle.

For this victory — the most spectacular engagement in Texas during the war — Dowling and his men were accorded heroes' welcomes. President Jefferson Davis, for whom the Guards were named, described the battle as "the Thermopylae of the Civil War" — although this time the defenders were victorious. In his volume *The Rise and Fall of the Confederacy*, Davis later wrote: "There is no parallel in ancient or modern warfare to the victory of Dowling and his men at Sabine Pass, considering the great odds against which they had to contend." Two weeks after the battle, the *Houston Telegraph* editorialized: "Let no one hereafter cast any imputations on the honest Irish soldier. . . . The noble men belonging to the Davis Guards, who are all natives of the green Emerald Isle, deserve well of the nation. . . . Inured to hard labor, nobly did they stand by the guns and fight to the last." Dowling himself reported that "All my men behaved like heroes. Not a man flinched from his post. Our motto was 'Victory or Death.'"

Ballad of Dick Dowling
by A. M. Sullivan (1896–1980)

Before the oil-stained eddies glistened
Along the steaming Sabine meadows,
Before the wildcat drillers listened
For the belch from the earth's deep shadows,

The sleepy silences had heard
Below the shell road to The Pass
The sound of many an angry word
From lips of steel and from tongues of brass.

The year was eighteen and sixty-three,
The first week of a hot September.
A copper mist burned on the sea
And the sky was stained three shades of umber

When sentinels on Fort Griffin's wall
Saw lights flash through the murk and haze,
Red and green and blue, then all
The spectrum set the sky ablaze.

The guards who saw the colors flame
Cried alarum to the drowsy men,
And one, Dick Dowling was his name,
Studied each flash with a soldier's ken.

"The lights are talking and what they tell
Have an ugly meaning for the Davis Guards,"
Dick Dowling whispered, "and I can spell
Trouble ahead in the rainbow words."

Dick propped the rampart for his fighting brood
With iron rails and with broken logs,
And the bastion built of rubble and wood
Leered with defiance across the bogs.

Fort Griffin hunched at the Sabine Pass,
Blocking the Yankee road to the west;
The water darkened like leaden glass,
And that night no man took his rest.

The Union gunboats came on in force
To clear the river and take the land
With fifteen hundred men and horse
And General Franklin in command.

Confederate Chieftain was J. B. Magruder,
With Lieutenant Odlum at the Sabine post,
And young Dick Dowling at the fort and leader
Who measured the need against the cost.

General Magruder was in Houston town
When he heard the news. The time was short.
Should they fight or run? With a sudden frown
He scribbled a message to the fort:

"The foe are many and we are few,
Lieutenant Dowling, yours the voice
To spike or fire the guns, and you
Alone can make a soldier's choice."

The Davis Guards, they were Irishmen
Who spoke with a soft and singing tongue,
From Dublin quay and the Kerry fen,
Peasant and scholar, and all were young.

They left their land in the days of famine,
Away from hunger the men took flight.
They left forbidden pools of the salmon,
They left their fields in the hour of blight.

Dick, red-thatched and twenty-two,
Spoke to his merry and quiet men,
"They are many and we are few.
Now is our chance—and never again.

"Who stands with me? And leave who will
Leaves now before the foeman speaks."
And no man moved from the sodden hill.
The color rose in Dowling's cheeks

And the fire sparked in Dowling's eyes,
"Here we stand when the gunboats come,
Here we fight till the last man dies
Or the Yanks march in to a captive drum."

At dawn Dick Dowling sat by the kettle
Munching dark bread, sipping dark tea
When a cannon boomed and red hot metal
Splashed the cinders on Dowling's knee.

The ball from the *Clifton* came sudden and rude
And no man asked for his second sup.
Dick Dowling murmured, "His aim is good.
Man your stations. Up, men, up!"

Balls hit the bastions and disappeared
Like marbles hurled at a giant sponge.
The *Clifton*'s gunners cursed and jeered,
Heard the silence and thought it strange.

Back drew the *Clifton* from the Oyster Reef,
Back to the waters where the transports tossed,
And Dowling's gunners aired their grief
At Dick for the fighting moments lost.

At three the boats crept back for duty,
The *Clifton* first and the *Sachem* second,
The *Arizona* and the *Granite City*
Pushed their bows where the Lone Star beckoned.

The gunboats belched and the sky rained iron,
Hot and cold, but the range grew dim
As dust clouds swarmed on the fort's environ
And Dowling's gunners looked at him.

"When shall we answer?" "Not now," he said,
"Our range is only a mile and a half.
I'll tell you when," and he risked his head
For a look at the foe and a gentle laugh.

"The Yankee guns spill more in a minute
Than we can answer with all our powder.
This is our game and we can win it;
They talk loud, but we'll talk louder

"With a range point blank and no gun misses.
Closer they come. Now watch my fuse.
Look for the moment when my powder hisses
And the rich man fall for the poor man's ruse."

Rumor was rife on the Union craft
That dummy cannon were guarding the fort,
And gunboats drinking a shallow draft
Bellowed their challenge without retort.

Close to the shore the *Sachem* drifted
Five hundred yards from McKernan's gun,
Clear as a picture as the warm wind shifted
And the bright brass glistened in the turning sun.

Dick Dowling, who came from Tuam town
In Galway, signalled above the noise.
He lit his taper, waved up and down.
"Now is the moment. Blast 'em boys."

The *Sachem* strummed a poisonous lyre
Of grape and canister, like a siren daft;
Michael McKernan was the first to fire
And he centered his sights twixt fore and aft.

"Make this count, Mike," Dowling shouted
Over the whine of the *Sachem*'s shell.
His eye was keen and no man doubted
His gun would sound the *Sachem*'s knell.

Mike hit the mark as the fort spoke thunder,
And the *Sachem* reeled with a massive shock,
Her boilers blew, and her bow went under,
And her bridge deck scattered like a broken crock.

The white flag climbed the *Sachem*'s mast,
Asking pity for a mortal wound
And the *Clifton* met the second blast,
Withered in anguish and ran aground.

The gunners in the fort took careful aim
At the *Arizona*'s cushioned hide,
And her cotton bales leaped high in flame
When the red hot metal burst inside.

The gunboat ran with a crippled gait,
Tossing her stores in the muddy water,
And none of the troopships dared to wait
As the *Clifton* and *Sachem* asked for quarter.

The gunboats counted their fatal toll —
One hundred killed, three hundred taken,
With cannon lost and the easy goal
To clear the Sabine Pass forsaken.

The fight was over in half an hour
When the *Granite City* ran for the sea,
But not in glory as Fort Griffin's tower
Lifted the banner of victory.

Twenty-two transports with mud-churning wheels
Scurried from the battle like a harried pack
As six iron terriers barked at their heels
And barked so loud they never came back.

Dick Dowling's loss was a single man
Nicked by a splinter in the hand and knee;
None other hurt since the fight began
And nothing spoiled but porridge and tea.

Crocker, captain of the *Clifton*, asked,
"Who leads the gunners of the deadly aim?"
A young voice spoke, his visage masked,
"Lieutenant Dowling, sir's my name."

"You, lad? And where are all of your men?"
"Here they are, all forty-seven,"
Dick laughed, "We were sitting at breakfast when
You tried to send us to Hell—or Heaven,

"And all hands quit to answer back
And since Fate picks our side the winner,
Captain, t'would be a social lack
Unless we asked your boys to dinner."

Dick and his Jefferson Davis Guards
Will live forever at the Sabine Pass
Inviting the ghosts of the Irish bards
Who sing by the sandless hourglass.

He stands in bronze and he stands in granite,
Facing the river where the fleet turned tail;
The stone lists the Davis Guards upon it,
Names that rhyme in the songs of the Gael:

Daugherty, Delany, Donovan, Degan,
Hennessey, Hasset, Drummond and Flood,
Higgins and Huggins, Fleming and Egan,
And Hurley who boasted his royal blood.

Monahan, Plunkett, Gleason and Powers,
And Sullivan three from the town of Kenmare,
McDonnell and Wilson from Antrim's wet bowers,
Malone from Wexford, O'Hara from Clare.

McKeever from Louth and Wilson from Derry,
Walsh out of Wicklow, McNealis, McGrath
From the mountains of Cork, and Fitzgerald from Kerry
And Michael McKernan, the lad from Armagh.

In bronze and granite men sing of their glory
From Beaumont south to the wide Rio Grande.
If you pause at The Pass you can read the proud story
Of young Dick Dowling and his stalwart band.

General Franklin: William Franklin (1823–1903), a Union major general who took part in an expedition to Sabine Pass, Texas, in September 1863. **J. B. Magruder:** John Bankhead Magruder (1810–1871), the Confederate major general who supervised the retaking of Galveston, Texas, in January 1863 and drove off the blockading Union fleet. **Lieutenant Odlum:** Frederick Odlum, Dowling's wife's uncle. **Crocker:** Frederick Crocker, captain of the *Clifton*, an 892-ton, 210-feet-long sidewheel steamer used in the Union attempt to seize Sabine Pass. **He stands in bronze:** A nine-feet-tall bronze statue of Dowling stands in Sabine Pass Battleground State Historic Park, fifteen miles south of Port Arthur, Texas. **Names that rhyme in the songs of the Gael:** The forty-seven members of the Davis Guards were Patrick Abbott, Michael Carr, Abner Carter, Pat Clair, James Corcoran, Thomas Daugherty, Hugh Deagan, Michael Delaney, Dan Donovan, Jonathan Drummond, Michael Egan, Pat Fitzgerald, James Fleming, John Flood, William Gleason, Tom Hagerty, William Hardy, John Hassett, John Hennessey, James Higgins, Tim Huggins, Tim Hurley, William Jett, Pat Malone, Alex McCabe, Pat McDonnell, Tim McDonough, John McGrath, John McKeever, Michael McKernan, Dan McMurray, Jonathan McNealis, Michael Monoghan, Peter O'Hara, Lawrence Plunkett, Maurice Powers, Edward Pritchard, Charles Rheins, Michael Sullivan, Pat Sullivan, Thomas Sullivan, Mathew Walsh, John Westley, John White, Joseph Wilson, Dr. George Bailey, and Lieutenant N. H. Smith. **Gael:** used here to refer to the Irish. **Beaumont:** a town in southeastern Texas along the Nueces River, about twenty-five miles from the Gulf of Mexico. **Rio Grande:** an 1,800-mile-long river forming the border between Texas and Mexico and flowing into the Gulf of Mexico.

46. Philip Sheridan

Although Sheridan's memoirs claim that he was a native of Albany, New York, he actually may have been born aboard the ship which carried his parents from Ireland to America. According to one theory, he may have invented an American birth in order to be eligible for the presidency of the United States.

Sheridan found that his Catholicism and Famine-Irish background were distinct handicaps at the U.S. Military Academy, but it was his temper that almost ended his military career. An unfortunate incident occurred at the beginning of his senior year, when a cadet sergeant began to berate Sheridan during a parade march. Provoked by the verbal harassment, Sheridan cursed the sergeant and lunged at him with his bayonet. Perhaps because he missed his intended target, Sheridan was suspended from the academy for only a year.

Sheridan's subsequent career during the Civil War belied his earlier disgrace. He practically saved the army of General William Rosecrans by holding off a Confederate advance, and he contributed to General Grant's victory at Chattanooga while in command of the Twentieth Corps of the Army of the Cumberland. As a result, Grant placed him in charge of the 10,000-man cavalry corps of the Army of the Potomac.

On the morning of October 19, 1864, Sheridan's troops were encamped at Cedar Creek, Virginia, although Sheridan himself was in Winchester to the north, returning from a military conference in Washington. Sheridan's absence provided the Confederate general Jubal Early with the perfect opportunity for a lightning attack. Within minutes the Confederates had captured more than 1,000 prisoners, and fleeing Union soldiers clogged the road north from Middletown.

Sheridan, meanwhile, alarmed by the gunfire he could hear in the distance, hastened from Winchester to rally his men. Although standing only 5'5" and weighing but 130 pounds, "Little Phil" struck awe into his troops when they saw him mounted on his horse, Rienzi, ordering them to regroup and counterattack. When his men began to chant his name, he cried, "Don't cheer me. Fight, damn you, fight!" Sheridan and his men turned disaster into victory by killing or capturing a large portion of Early's command. He renamed his horse "Winchester" in honor of his victory.

Sheridan's success at Cedar Creek was the final major victory in his campaign to clear Confederate troops from the Shenandoah Valley. The statistics which he soon dispatched to Grant showed that he had more than fulfilled his order to "eat out Virginia clear and clean, so that crows flying over it for the balance of the season will have to carry their own provender with them." His report portrayed an appalling litany: the seizure or destruction of 425,000 bushels of wheat, 77,000 bushels of corn, 20,000 tons of hay, 15,000 swine, 12,000 sheep, 11,000 cattle, and 4,500 horses and mules.

In the last year of the conflict, "Little Phil" carried out a series of raids that prepared the way for major Union victories. In an attempt to break the Confederate communications line around Richmond, his men destroyed ten miles of railroad track, cut off telegraph communication to the city, and captured many supply trains. In one final raid he left General Robert E. Lee with only one railroad line of communication with the South, thereby forcing Lee's evacuation of Petersburg and his retreat to Appomattox. After Grant and Sherman, Sheridan is generally regarded as the third most important Union general of the Civil War.

Sheridan's Ride

by Thomas Buchanan Read (1822–1872)

Up from the South, at break of day,
Bringing to Winchester fresh dismay,
The affrighted air with a shudder bore,
Like a herald in haste to the chieftain's door,
The terrible grumble, and rumble, and roar,
Telling the battle was on once more,
And Sheridan twenty miles away.

And wider still those billows of war
Thundered along the horizon's bar;
And louder yet into Winchester rolled
The roar of that red sea uncontrolled,
Making the blood of the listener cold,
As he thought of the stake in that fiery fray,
And Sheridan twenty miles away.

But there is a road from Winchester town,
A good, broad highway leading down;
And there, through the flush of the morning light,
A steed as black as the steeds of night
Was seen to pass, as with eagle flight,
As if he knew the terrible need;
He stretched away with his utmost speed;
Hills rose and fell; but his heart was gay,
With Sheridan fifteen miles away.

Still sprang from those swift hoofs, thundering South,
The dust, like smoke from the cannon's mouth;
Or the trail of a comet, sweeping faster and faster,

Foreboding to traitors the doom of disaster.
The heart of the steed, and the heart of the master,
Were beating like prisoners assaulting their walls,
Impatient to be where the battle-field calls;
Every nerve of the charger was strained to full play,
With Sheridan only ten miles away.

Under his spurning feet the road
Like an arrowy Alpine river flowed,
And the landscape sped away behind
Like an ocean flying before the wind,
And the steed, like a barque fed with furnace ire,
Swept on, with his wild eye full of fire.
But, lo! he is nearing his heart's desire;
He is snuffing the smoke of the roaring fray,
With Sheridan only five miles away.

The first that the general saw were the groups
Of stragglers, and then the retreating troops.
What was done! what to do? a glance told him both;
Then, striking his spur with a terrible oath,
He dashed down the line, 'mid a storm of huzzas,
And the wave of retreat checked its course there, because
The sight of the master compelled it to pause.
With foam and with dust, the black charger was gray;
 By the flash of his eye, and the red nostril's play,
He seemed to the whole great army to say,
"I have brought you Sheridan all the way
From Winchester, down to save the day!"

Hurrah! hurrah for Sheridan!
Hurrah! hurrah for horse and man!
And when their statues are placed on high
Under the dome of the Union sky,
The American soldiers' Temple of Fame;
There with the glorious general's name,
Be it said, in letters both bold and bright,
"Here is the steed that saved the day,
By carrying Sheridan into the fight,
From Winchester — twenty miles away!"

A steed as black as the steeds of night: Rienzi, a horse about three years old
when Sheridan acquired it in 1862, while he was stationed near Rienzi, Mississippi.

Sheridan at Cedar Creek
by Herman Melville (1819–1891)

Shoe the steed with silver
        That bore him to the fray,
When he heard the guns at dawning—
        Miles away;
When he heard them calling, calling—
        Mount! nor stay:
                Quick, or all is lost;
                They've surprised and stormed the post,
                They push your routed host—
        Gallop! retrieve the day.

House the horse in ermine—
        For the foam-flake blew
White through the red October;
        He thundered into view;
They cheered him in the looming,
        Horseman and horse they knew.
                The turn of the tide began,
                The rally of bugles ran,
                He swung his hat in the van;
        The electric hoof-spark flew.

Wreathe the steed and lead him—
        For the charge he led
Touched and turned the cypress
        Into amaranths for the head
Of Philip, king of riders,
        Who raised them from the dead.
                The camp (at dawning lost)
                By eve, recovered—forced,
                Rang with laughter of the host
        As belated Early fled.

Shroud the horse in sable—
        For the mounds they heap!
There is firing in the Valley,
        And yet no strife they keep;
It is the parting volley,
        It is the pathos deep.
                There is glory for the brave

Who lead, and nobly save,
But no knowledge in the grave
Where the nameless followers sleep.

amaranths: plants of the genus *Amaranthus*, grown for their showy blossoms or foliage. **Early:** Jubal Early (1816–1894), the Confederate general whose outnumbered troops were defeated by Sheridan at Cedar Creek on October 19, 1864. **Lee:** Robert E. Lee (1807–1870), the Confederate commander of the Army of Northern Virginia.

To Sheridan
(from one who loves him very dearly)
by Charles Graham Halpine ("Private Miles O'Reilly") (1829–1866)

Phil Sherry was of knightly build,
    A soldier of renown,
His sabre flashed on many a field,
    His flag o'er many a town;
And when the limbs to weakness grow
    Now filled with youthful flame,
Our children's children yet shall glow
    To bold Phil Sherry's name.

With stormy oath and bugle-blast,
    And eyes of kindling fire,
When the skies of war were overcast,
    And hope might well expire,
Our Phil with gleaming hand and heel
    Led on his fiery flock,
And the victor foe would turn and reel
    Beneath his desperate shock.

Who has not heard, with tears and smiles,
    Of the hot and headlong ride,
When, after twenty galloping miles,
    He checked the rebel tide?
And how, when Lee was brought at length
    To final bay or flight,
'Twas Phil that hurled our final strength,
    And won our final fight?

Oh, gallant leader of the brave,
    Whose fame for aye endures,

Soil not the crest that victory gave
    By work that is not yours.
Leap in the saddle once again,
    Let your wild plumes outflow,
Nor help to crush the beaten men
    Who sank beneath your blow.

To baser hands, to meaner souls,
    Resign the odious task —
'Tis love this passionate cry controls,
    'Tis for your fame I ask.
I want you still an image high,
    Niched in my heart—its king;
Oh, once more let your pennons fly,
    Let "boots and saddles" ring!

You were not framed—the soul God placed
    Within your fiery clay—
That rarest gift of heaven to waste
    In the wranglings of to-day;
The base intrigues, the ready lies,
    The cold and coward hates—
The bark that in the darkness flies,
    The pitfall at the gates.

Those form the politician's trade—
    Too base for you to know;
To fight deceit you were not made—
    You need a manlier foe;
And I tell you, Phil, I'd rather seek
    For friends in the foes we fought,
Than trust any "loyal" Southern sneak
    Whom success to our side has brought.

Sheridan

by Richard Watson Gilder (1844–1909)

Quietly, like a child
  That sinks in slumber mild,
No pain or troubled thought his well-earned peace to mar,
Sank into endless rest our thunderbolt of war.

Though his power to smite

Quick as the lightning's light,—
His single arm an army, and his name a host,—
Not his the love of blood, the warrior's cruel boast.

But in the battle's flame
How glorious he came!—
Even like a white-combed wave that breaks and tears the shore,
While wreck lies strewn behind, and terror flies before.

'Twas he,—his voice, his might,—
Could stay the panic-flight,
Alone shame back the headlong many-leagued retreat,
And turn to evening triumph morning's foul defeat.

He was our modern Mars;
Yet firm his faith that wars
Ere long would cease to vex the sad, ensanguined earth,
And peace forever reign, as at Christ's holy birth.

Blest land, in whose dark hour
Arise to loftier power
No dazzles of the sword to play the tyrant's part,
But patriot-soldiers, true and pure and high of heart!

Of such our chief of all;
And he who broke the wall
Of civil strife in twain, no more to build or mend;
And he who hath this day made Death his faithful friend.

And now above his tomb
From out the eternal gloom
"Welcome!" his chieftain's voice sounds o'er the cannon's knell;
And of the three one only stays to say "Farewell!"

Mars: the Roman god of war.

Interpolation Sounds

from *Leaves of Grass* by Walt Whitman (1819–1892)

(General Philip Sheridan was buried at the Cathedral, Washington, D.C., August, 1888, with all the pomp, music, and ceremonies of the Roman Catholic service.)

Over and through the burial chant,
Organ and solemn service, sermon, bending priests,
To me come interpolation sounds not in the show—plainly to me,
    crowding up the aisle and from the window,
Of sudden battle's hurry and harsh noises—war's grim game to sight
    and ear in earnest;
The scout call'd up and forward—the general mounted and his aids
    around him—the new-brought word—the instantaneous order
    issued;
The rifle crack—the cannon thud—the rushing of men from their tents;
The clank of cavalry—the strange celerity of forming ranks—the slender
    bugle note;
The sound of horses' hoofs departing—saddled, arms, accoutrements.

47. Mathew Brady

A native of upstate New York who described himself as the son of an
Irishman, Mathew Brady opened his first studio in New York City in 1842,
while he was only nineteen. For four consecutive years he won a silver
medal for his daguerreotype entries at the annual American Institute exhibit, and in 1849 he was awarded the first gold medal ever presented for
that genre. He subsequently earned recognition at the New York and London world fairs. About 1855, however, he abandoned the daguerreotype
for the wet-plate process known as photography.

At the commencement of the Civil War, Brady persuaded President
Lincoln and the head of the Secret Service to let him and his assistants
accompany Union troops into battle. Invariably seen wearing a linen duster
and a broad-brimmed flat hat, Brady frequently risked his life to remain
close to his "What-is-it" Wagon, which he used as a dark room. In the
general panic at the first battle of Bull Run, the wagon was overturned,
although Brady was able to retrieve some of his wet plates. A writer for
Humphrey's Journal acknowledged Brady's ability to capture and convey
the horrors of the battlefield: "His are the only reliable records at Bull's
Run. . . . His pictures, though perhaps not as lasting as the battle pieces on
the pyramids, will nonetheless immortalize those introduced in them.
Brady has shown more pluck than many of the officers and soldiers who
were in the fight. He went — not exactly like the [Irish] 'Sixty-Ninth,'
stripped to the pants — but with his sleeves tucked up and his big camera
directed upon every point of interest on the field. . . . [I]t is certain that
[those who took flight] did not get away from Brady as easily as they did
from the enemy. He has fixed the cowards beyond the possibility of a

doubt."

Impoverished by the panic of 1873, Brady found temporary financial relief when the U.S. Government purchased 2,000 of his photographs for $25,000. He continued as a photographer in Washington until he was struck by a vehicle and died the next year.

A Photo by Brady

by George Keithley (b. 1935)

His large faith looks like ours and he believes
like us that his camera's report
records nature. The silent lives
of men are filmed where they were flung out
in the sunny grass and the scene achieves
simplicity . . . A flat calm distorts
the field of vision as though the men's
mouths made no more noise below his lens.

On the grey grass or the sky nothing flies
from fear. There's some withdrawal
of smoke, a haze beneath the trees
where the surprised troops fall along the hill.
Each figure rests in an insane ease—
all conscious grace, all that is natural
halted as sunlight floods the aperture.
Heavy flank fire floats in the air.

Wedged against the trees a white
church bleaches the hilltop. With pure
release men sprawl in the grass, prostrate,
their shirts blown open on the pasture.
The long sense of balance is accurate
and quiet . . . A thoughtless leisure
on their legs and groin and arms as the church-ground
takes the sun and their pale breasts burn unbound.

48. Father Abram Ryan

Abram Ryan was born in Hagerstown, Maryland, in 1838, to emigrants from County Tipperary, Ireland. While attending the Christian Brothers' School in St. Louis, Missouri, he fell in love with a young girl named Ethel, who, like him, however, had decided to enter religious life. About their brief romance the budding poet wrote: "They met to part from themselves and the world.... / And in the heart of that last parting hour, Eternity was beating." He later described her as "A fair, sweet girl, with great brown eyes / That seemed to listen just as if they held / The gift of hearing with the power of sight."

At the outbreak of the Civil War, the newly ordained Ryan was an ardent supporter of the South. Although he failed to secure an official military chaplaincy, he seems to have served in an unofficial capacity. According to one authority, Ryan was at the battle of Marye's Heights at Fredericksburg, Virginia, at the end of 1862. (It may have been here that he reputedly seized a musket and fought side by side with the Confederate troops.) Four months later he was mourning the death of his brother on the battlefield, a personal tragedy that prompted him to write the poems "In Memory of My Brother" and "In Memoriam—David J. Ryan C.S.A." Toward the end of the war, when no other clergyman would do so, he ministered to smallpox victims at a prison in New Orleans. While still in the Crescent City, he was accused of refusing to bury a dead soldier because he was a Yankee. When the priest was ordered to appear before Benjamin Butler, the Union general in charge of the occupied city, Ryan defended himself. "Why, I was never asked to bury him and never refused," he said, adding gratuitously, "The fact is, General, it would give me great pleasure to bury the whole lot of you."

Ryan achieved more lasting fame because of his verse. Though he wrote poems of a religious nature, he is better known for his Civil War poetry, the most familiar works being "The Conquered Banner," "The Sword of Robert Lee," "The Lost Cause," and "March of the Deadless Dead." Despite the popularity of his verse, he viewed his work as of little importance. He described his efforts as "written at random — off and on, here, there, anywhere — just when the mood came, with little of study and less of art, and always in a hurry."

After what he regarded as the War of Southern Independence, the priest-poet toured the country on the lecture circuit, sometimes to raise funds for the relief of plague victims and Southern orphans and widows. It was not until the late 1870s that he seems to have reconciled himself with the victorious North. He did so after the South's former enemies sent money, nurses, and doctors to help fight the yellow fever epidemic that devastated parts of the South in 1878. His final rapprochement was expressed in "Reunited" and "Requiem for the Federal Dead."

Father Ryan's Death
by William D. Kelly (1814–1890)

Your saddest tears, O April skies, drop down,
    And let the voices of your sobbing breeze,
      Sigh the most plaintive of their threnodies
For him, who, girt with sacerdotal gown,
When war's wild tumult stirred each Southern town,
    And filled the land with its discordancies,
      Sang high above them all such melodies
Their very sweetness won the South renown;
Poet! God rest thee, now thy songs are sung;
    Father! heaven gain thee, now thy toil is o'er;
Whoever listened to thy tuneful tongue
    Telling the mystic secrets of its lore,
Trusts that thy voice, celestial choirs among,
    Hymns the new song of love forevermore.

49. Ulysses S. Grant

Born in Point Pleasant, Ohio, in 1822, Ulysses S. Grant was the great-grandson of John Simpson, who entered this world in Dungannon, County Tyrone, Ireland, in 1738. After settling in Pennsylvania, Simpson married and had a son, who in turn headed west and took up residence in Ohio. Hannah, the daughter of this latter Simpson, married Jesse Grant and gave birth to their son — Hiram Ulysses Grant. (He became known as "Ulysses Simpson Grant" when his name was incorrectly entered on army documents.) Another Irish strain may have entered the famous general's pedigree through Rachel Kelley, his paternal grandmother.

After a succession of failures as a farmer, a real estate salesman, and a clerk, Grant found favor with Mars during the War Between the States. His victory at Fort Henry and Fort Donelson, Tennessee, earned him the confidence of President Lincoln, whose faith was rewarded when Grant captured Vicksburg in July 1863. As the newly appointed commander of all Union troops between the Alleghenies and the Mississippi River, Grant achieved a major victory at Chattanooga, where his 80,000 troops defeated General Braxton Bragg's 64,000 Confederates at the end of 1863. The next year, in command of all the Union armies, Grant moved east, setting off a campaign that dogged Robert E. Lee through Virginia until the Confederate general surrendered at Appomattox in April 1865.

In January 1879, after two terms as president, Grant arrived in Dublin, Ireland, during a journey around the world. After visiting such landmarks as Trinity College, the Bank of Ireland, and the Royal Irish Academy, the former U.S. president was presented with the Freedom of the City by the Lord Mayor. In a speech outside City Hall, Grant acknowledged the honorary citizenship accorded him but boasted of America's Irishmen: "I am by birth a citizen of a country where there are more Irishmen, either native born or descendants of Irishmen, than you have in all Ireland. I have had the honor and pleasure, therefore, of representing more Irishmen and their descendants when in office than the Queen of England does."

From Dublin Grant traveled to Dundalk, Omagh, and Strabane before arriving in Londonderry. While there he gave an address in which he referred to his own Ulster roots and praised his host city, "whose history is so well known throughout America." He also expressed his hope that more Irish would immigrate to the United States when "you become more crowded and want more room," although he humorously warned his listeners that they would not be able to obtain American citizenship "as rapidly as you have made me a citizen here today."

By 1885 Grant was impoverished because of bad business investments and was suffering from throat cancer. After retiring to Wilton, New York, he worked feverishly on his memoirs so his family would have an income after his death. He completed the volume just four days before dying on July 23, 1885. The publication of the former president's memoirs later earned almost $500,000 for his family.

Grant's funeral procession through New York City in 1885 was seven miles long and attracted a million people. His body was originally placed in a temporary vault in Riverside Park until the General Grant National Memorial ("Grant's Tomb") in New York City was completed twelve years later. The circular Greek Revival tomb, the largest mausoleum in the United States, is adorned with heroic bronze busts of five other Civil War generals. Along the south façade are engraved Grant's words — "Let us have peace."

Can't

by Harriet Prescott Spofford (1835–1921)

How history repeats itself
    You'll say when you remember Grant,
Who, in his boyhood days, once sought
    Throughout the lexicon for "can't."

He could not find the word that day,
    The earnest boy whose name was Grant;
He never found it through long years,

With all their power to disenchant.

No hostile host could give him pause;
    Rivers and mountains could not daunt;
He never found that hindering word—
    The steadfast man whose name was Grant.

The Battle of Lookout Mountain

by Kinahan Cornwallis (1839–1917)

Then came a bloody battle in the clouds—
Clouds that—alas!—to many proved their shrouds.
A thousand feet above the Vale it raged—
On Lookout Mountain desperately waged—
And from the Valley those who viewed the fight,
Ne'er saw a grander—more terrific—sight
Till smoke and mist concealed it from the view—
A fight from dawn to dusk that hotter grew
Till all the Rebel hosts were put to flight—
Confused, disordered, and in awful plight;
For Bragg to check the Union army failed,
And Lookout Mountain's rugged top was scaled,—
Its fortress captured, and the vict'ry hailed,—
And Missionary Ridge, from west to east.
"On vict'ries now—behold—!" said Grant, "we feast!"
'Twas not till night the long day's battle ceased,
And then triumphant were the Boys in Blue,
Who Chattanoogan Valley captured, too,
And with the stars and stripes adorned the view.
"Well done!" said Grant, "you climbed that Mountain well,
Of harder fighting hist'ry ne'er will tell!"
Grant led his forces grandly, and the foe
Surrendered, died, or fled to plains below,
Pursued by Sherman's and by Hooker's fire.
Bragg and Rebellion met disaster dire.

Kentucky now—with Tennessee—was freed
From Rebel raids, while Burnside, much in need—
At Knoxville—gained not glory but relief.
"I hail," said Grant, "one consequence as chief;
It opens Georgia to the Union arms,
And fills the groaning South with fresh alarms,

> For fifteen thousand men its battle cost—
> The captured, wounded and the dead it lost."
> November, 'Sixty-three, grew dark indeed
> To Rebel eyes. Reverses gathered speed.

Lookout Mountain: a mountain ridge near Chattanooga, Tennessee, which Union troops under Major General Joseph Hooker scaled and seized from its Confederate defenders on November 24, 1863. This engagement was part of the battle of Chattanooga, which pitted 80,000 Union troops under General Grant against General Braxton Bragg's 64,000 Confederates. **Bragg:** Braxton Bragg (1817–1876), the commander of the Confederate army in Tennessee. **Boys in Blue:** Union soldiers, so called from their blue uniforms. **stars and stripes:** the Union flag. **Sherman:** William T. Sherman (1820–1891), one of the most formidable Union generals in the Civil War. **Hooker:** Joseph Hooker (1814–1879), the Union commander whose troops captured Lookout Mountain on November 24, 1863. **Burnside:** Ambrose Burnside (1824–1881), the Union commander of the Army of the Potomac until he suffered 12,600 casualties at Fredericksburg.

Grant at Appomattox

by Gertrude Claytor (1890?–1973)

Now it was Spring,
Buds were thick on the shattered bough,
Now you could hear the high bird-trill,
The rustle of wind, the rain—
For guns were still.
Fields that were choked with blood
Thawed in the rain, drew breath,
Conquering spears of green rose from the load of death.

Though a hundred years go by
Rhythm is still the same,
Shadow and shock of steel,
Smoke and the fruit of flame,
Blue of the sky, the Gray—
Caught and forever bound,
The old that is folded away,
The new that peoples the ground.
The fallow dust must yield,
The soldier turn from the field.

Grant looked on the sodden land
With the plume of life just showing,
On the tree with the battered bough,

On the bough where the buds were growing;
He looked on the field of death,
On wheat that prodded the loam
And he said to the vanquished men,
"Take the horses and mules, go home,
Go home for the Springtime plowing."
The weary men went home,
And remembered the words of Grant,
The seed of the word was sown
In the fields they were soon to plant.

As a tide will rise from the sea,
The heart will rise in flood
Breaking its barriers—free—
Cool with the cooling blood—
This was his day, his theme,
His flood in the sea of time,
Warrior, dreamer and dream.
Here at the end was Lee,
Strong in vast defeat,
So had the cycle turned—
So was the dream complete.
Lee and the proffered sword—
After the Wilderness—Peace,
Out of the wilderness, Lord.

Lee: Robert E. Lee (1807–1870), the Confederate commander of the Army of Northern Virginia, who surrendered to Grant at Appomattox, Virginia, in April 1865.

General Grant — the Hero of the War

by George Moses Horton (1797?–1883?)

Brave Grant, thou hero of the war,
Thou art the emblem of the morning star,
Transpiring from the East to banish fear,
Revolving o'er a servile Hemisphere,
At large thou hast sustained the chief command
And at whose order all must rise and stand,
To hold position in the field is thine,
To sink in darkness or to rise and shine.

Thou art the leader of the Fed'ral band,
To send them at thy pleasure through the land,

Whose martial soldiers never did recoil
Nor fail in any place to take the spoil,
Thus organized was all the army firm,
And led unwavering to their lawful term,
Never repulsed or made to shrink with fear,
Advancing in their cause so truly dear.

The love of Union burned in every heart,
Which led them true and faithful from the start,
Whether upon water or on land,
They obeyed their marshal's strict command,
By him the regiments were all surveyed,
His trumpet voice was by the whole obeyed,
His order right was every line to form,
And all be well prepared to front the storm.

Ye Southern gentlemen must grant him praise,
Nor on the flag of Union fail to gaze;
Ye ladies of the South forego the prize,
Our chief commander here to recognize,
From him the stream of general orders flow,
And every chief on him some praise bestow,
The well-known victor if the mighty cause
Demands from every voice a loud applause.

What more has great Napoleon ever done,
Though many battles in his course he won?
What more has Alexander e'er achieved,
Who left depopulated cities grieved?
To him we dedicate the whole in song,
The verses from our pen to him belong,
To him the Union banners are unfurled,
The star of peace the standard of the world

Napoleon: Napoleon Bonaparte (1769–1821), the French military commander and emperor who controlled western Europe from 1809 to 1812. **Alexander:** Alexander the Great (356–323 B.C.), the Macedonian conqueror whose empire extended from Greece to India.

Great Grant, Glorious in Our Wars

by Thomas Bailey Aldrich (1836–1907)

Great Captain, glorious in our wars—

No meed of praise we hold from him;
About his brow we wreathe the stars
The coming ages shall not dim.

The cloud-sent man! Was it not he
That from the hand of adverse fate
Snatched the white flower of victory?
He spoke no word, but saved the State.

Yet History, as she brooding bends
Above the tablet on her knee,
The impartial stylus half suspends,
And fain would blot the cold decree:

"The torn hand and sleepless care
That stayed disaster scare availed
To serve him when he came to wear
The civic laurel; there he failed."

Who runs may read; but nothing mars
The nobler record unforgot.
Great Captain, glorious in our wars—

All else the heart remembers not.

A Bumper to Grant

by Charles Graham Halpine ("Private Miles O'Reilly") (1829–1866)

Come, fill your glasses, fellows,
    And stand up in a row,
On a presidential drinking
    We are going far to go;
Let us have no more sobriety—
    At least no more to-night—
While for President Ulysses Grant
    We take our foremost flight.
                Oh, for President Ulysses
                Let every glass be bright—
                May he rule the country he has saved,
                And God defend the right.

His hand is soft to meet a friend,
    And mailed to meet a foe—
He's the Mississippi River horse,

Resistless as its flow;
He's the conqueror of leaguered towns,
    And victor in the field—
No foe has ever grappled Grant
    That was not forced to yield.
            So to President Ulysses
            Brim every glass to-night—
            May he rule the country he has saved,
            And God defend the right.

In the world to-day no prouder name
    Is borne on any breeze,
And with Grant to steer the ship of state,
    Our flag shall rule the seas;
No "dominion" shall be north of us,
    And south of us no foe—
Our stars and stripes in the Canadas,
    And likewise Mexico.
            For with President Ulysses
            There'll be few who care to fight—
            May he rule the country he has saved,
            And God defend the right.

No more shall Irish officers
    In English dungeons pine,
No more shall Seward's endless notes
    In endless terror whine;
We'll assert our place of nationhood,
    And take our proper rank,
With iron-clads to guard our shores,
    And rebellion in the bank:
            All this when Grant is President
            To whom our faith we plight—
            May he rule the country he has saved,
            And God defend the right.

Oh, the Queen of the Antilles
    Must be wooed and must be won,
With her groves of palm and orange
    Flashing brightly in the sun;
And our brethren of the beaten states,
    Who suffer wrong to-day,
Will find a generous hand held out
    When Grant has come to sway;

> For generous is Ulysses
> To the men who felt his might—
> May he rule the country he has saved,
> And God defend the right.

We are sick of old Thad Stevens,
    We are sick of Butler too;
Sick of Kelly, Ashley, Sumner,
    And that God forsaken crew.
Let the men who faced the music
    When the storm ran high and hard,
All join to make Ulysses Grant
    Our captain of the guard.
                For with candidate Ulysses
                We can make the bulliest fight
                To rule the country he has saved
                And God defend the right.

Then old John Bull at Liverpool
    Will some day wake and groan,
Finding Farragut at anchor
    And his ports wide open thrown:
"Settle up your Anglo-rebel bills,
    And quickly, if you please,
For General Grant is our President,
    And I command the seas."
                To this we pledge Ulysses,
                And to him we drink to-night—
                May he rule the country he has saved,
                And God defend the right.

So, boys, a final bumper,
    While we all in chorus chant—
"For next President we nominate
    Our own Ulysses Grant."
And if asked what state he hails from,
    This our sole reply shall be,
"From near Appomattox Court-house,
    With its famous apple tree."
                For 'twas there, to our Ulysses,
                That Lee gave up the fight—
                Now boys, "To Grant for President,
                And God defend the right."

stars and stripes: the American flag. **Seward:** William Seward (1801–1872), the U.S. secretary of state who conducted lengthy negotiations with England over the *Trent* affair. **Queen of the Antilles:** Cuba, in rebellion against Spain since 1868. **beaten states:** the defeated states of the Confederacy. **Stevens and Butler:** Thaddeus Stevens (1792–1868) and Benjamin Butler (1818–1893), Massachusetts congressmen who advocated a punitive policy toward the Southern states after the Civil War. **Kelly:** William Darrah Kelly (1814–1890), a Pennsylvania congressman who supported military occupation of the defeated South and the extension of suffrage to the freed slaves. **Ashley:** James Ashley (1824–1896), an Ohio congressman who initiated the move to impeach President Andrew Johnson. **Sumner:** Charles Sumner (1811–1874), a Massachusetts senator who insisted that Southern states grant suffrage to freed black slaves as a condition of readmission to the Union. **John Bull:** England. **Farragut:** David Glasgow Farragut (1801–1870), the Union naval officer whose fleet captured New Orleans and Mobile Bay and helped Grant gain control of the Mississippi River (July 1863). **Anglo-rebel bills:** U.S. claims against Britain for damage inflicted on Union shipping during the Civil War by the *Alabama*, a Confederate ship built in England. **Lee:** Robert E. Lee (1807–1870), the Confederate commander who surrendered to Grant in April 1865.

Grant

by James Whitcomb Riley (1843–1916)

Sir Lancelot rode overthwart and endlong in a wide forest, and held no path but as wild adventure led him. . . . And he returned and came again to his horse, and took off his saddle and his bridle, and let him pasture; and unlaced his helm and ungirdled his sword, and laid him down to sleep upon his shield before the cross. — Age of Chivalry.

What shall we say of the soldier, Grant,
   His sword put by and his great soul free
How shall we cheer him now or chant
   His requiem befittingly?
The fields of his conquest now are seen
   Ranged no more with his armèd men—
But the rank and file of the gold and green
   Of the waving grain is there again.

Though his valiant life is a nation's pride,
   And his death heroic and half divine,
And our grief as great as the world is wide,
   There breaks in speech but a single line:—
We loved him living, revere him dead!—
   A silence then on our lips is laid:
We can say no thing that has not been said,
   Nor pray one prayer that has not been prayed.

But a spirit within us speaks: and lo,
    We lean and listen to wondrous words
That have a sound as of winds that blow,
    And the voice of waters and low of herds;
And we hear, as the song flows on serene,
    The neigh of horses, and then the beat
Of hooves that scurry o'er pastures green,
    And the patter and pad of a boy's bare feet.

A brave lad, wearing a manly brow,
    Knit as with problems of grave dispute,
And a face, like the bloom of the orchard bough,
    Pink and pallid, but resolute;
And flushed it grows as the cloverbloom.
    And fresh it gleams as the morning dew,
As he reins his steed where the quick quails boom
    Up from the grasses he races through.

And ho! as he rides what dreams are his?
    And what have the breezes to suggest?—
Do they whisper to him of shells that whiz
    O'er fields made ruddy with wrongs redressed?
Does the hawk above him an Eagle float?
    Does he thrill and his boyish heart beat high,
Hearing the ribbon about his throat
    Flap as a Flag as the winds go by?

And does he dream of the Warrior's fame—
    This western boy in his rustic dress?
For, in miniature, this is the man that came
    Riding out of the Wilderness!—
The selfsame figure—the knitted brow—
    The eyes full steady— the lips full mute—
And the face, like the bloom of the orchard bough,
    Pink and pallid, but resolute.

Ay, this is the man, with features grim
    And stoical as the Sphinx's own,
That heard the harsh guns calling him,
    As musical as the bugle blown,
When the sweet spring heavens were clouded o'er
    With a tempest, glowering and wild,
And our country's flag bowed down before
    Its bursting wrath as a stricken child.

Thus, ready mounted and booted and spurred,
    He loosed his bridle and dashed away!—
Like a roll of drums were his hoofbeats heard,
    Like the shriek of the fife his charger's neigh!
And over his shoulder and backward blown,
    We heard his voice, and we saw the sod
Reel, as our wild steeds chased his own
    As though hurled on by the hand of God!

And still, in fancy, we see him ride
    In the blood-red front of a hundred frays,
His face set stolid, but glorified
    As a knight's of the old Arthurian days:
And victor ever as courtly, too,
    Gently lifting the vanquished foe,
And staying him with a hand as true
    As dealt the deadly avenging blow.

So, brighter than all of the cluster of stars
    Of the flag enshrouding his form today,
His face shines forth from the grime of wars
    With a glory that shall not pass away:
He rests at last: he has borne his part
    Of salutes and salvos and cheers on cheers—
But O the sobs of his country's heart
    And the driving rain of a nation's tears!

Lancelot: the greatest of King Arthur's knights. **overthwart and endlong:** across and lengthwise. **Sphinx:** the colossal recumbent figure of an imaginary creature having the body of a lion and the head of a human located near the pyramids of Giza. **Arthurian days:** the reign of King Arthur, a legendary ruler of Britain, whose life was based on the exploits of one or more historical figures of the sixth century A.D.

In Memory of General Grant

by Henry Abbey (1842–1911)

White wings of commerce sailing far,
    Hot steam that drives the weltering wheel,
Tamed lightning speeding on the wire,
    Iron postman on the way of steel,—
These, circling all the world, have told
    The loss that makes us desolate;

For we give back to dust this day
      The God-sent man who saved the state.

When black the sky and dire with war,
      When every heart was wrung with fear,
He rose serene, and took his place,
      The great occasion's mighty peer.
He smote armed opposition down,
      He bade the storm and darkness cease,
And o'er the long-distracted land
      Shone out the smiling sun of peace.

The famous captains of the past
      March in review before the mind:
Some fought for glory, some for gold,
      But most to yoke and rule mankind.
Not so the captain dead to-day,
      For whom our half-mast banners wave:
He fought to keep the Union whole,
      And break the shackles of the slave.

A silent man, in friendship true,
      He made point-blank his certain aim,
And, born a stranger to defeat,
      To steadfast purpose linked his name:
For while the angry flood of war
      Surged down between its gloomy banks,
He followed duty, with the mien
      Of but a soldier in the ranks.

How well he wore white honor's flower,
      The gratitude and praise of men,
As General, as President,
      And then as simple citizen!
He was a hero to the end:
      The dark rebellion raised by Death
Against the Powers of Life and Light,
      He battled hard, with failing breath.

O hero of Fort Donelson,
      And wooded Shiloh's frightful strife!
Sleep on! for honor loves the tomb
      More than the garish ways of life.
Sleep on! sleep on! Thy wondrous life

Is freedom's most illustrious page;
And fame shall loudly sound thy praise
In every clime, to every age.

Fort Donelson: a Tennessee battle (February 1862) that was the Union's first major success. Grant's victory forced the Confederates to withdraw from Kentucky and most of Tennessee. **Shiloh:** a Union victory in Tennessee (April 1862), in which each side lost a quarter of its troops.

Vanquished

by Francis Fisher Browne (1843–1913)

Not by the ball or brand
Sped by a mortal hand,
Not by the lightning stroke
When fiery tempests broke,—
Not mid the ranks of War
Fell the great Conqueror.

Unmoved, undismayed,
In the crash and carnage of the cannonade,—
Eye that dimmed not, hand that failed not,
Brain that swerved not, heart that quailed not.
Steel nerve, iron form,—
The dauntless spirit that o'erruled the storm.

While the Hero peaceful slept
A foeman to his chamber crept,
Lightly to the slumberer came,
Touched his brow and breathed his name.
O'er the stricken form there passed
Suddenly an icy blast.

The Hero woke, rose undismayed,
Saluted Death, and sheathed his blade.
The Conqueror of a hundred fields
To a mightier Conqueror yields;
No mortal foeman's blow
Laid the great Soldier low:

Victor in his latest breath—
Vanquished but by Death.

What Best I See in Thee

To U.S.G. return'd from his World's Tour
from *Leaves of Grass* by Walt Whitman (1819–1892)

What best I see in thee,
Is not that where thou mov'st down history's great highways,
Ever undimm'd by time shoots warlike victory's dazzle,
Or that thou sat'st where Washington sat, ruling the land in peace,
Or thou the man whom feudal Europe feted, venerable Asia
        swarm'd upon,
Who walk'd with kings with even pace round the world's prome-
        nade:
But that in foreign lands, in all thy walks with kings,
Those prairie sovereigns of the West, Kansas, Missouri, Illinois,
Ohio's, Indiana's millions, comrades, farmers, soldiers, all to the
        front,
Invisibly with thee walking with kings with even pace the round
        world's promenade
Were all so justified.

Death of General Grant

from *Leaves of Grass* by Walt Whitman (1819–1892)

As one by one withdraw the lofty actors,
From that great play on history's stage eterne,
That lurid, partial act of war and peace—of old and new con-
        tending,
Fought out through wrath, fears, dark dismays, and many a long
        suspense;
All past—and since, in countless graves receding, mellowing,
Victor's and vanquish'd—Lincoln's and Lee's—now thou with
        them,
Man of the mighty days—and equal to the days!
Thou from the prairies!—tangled and many-vein'd and hard has
        been thy part,
To admiration has it been enacted!

The Death of Grant

by Ambrose Bierce (1842–1914?)

Father! whose hard and cruel law

Is part of thy compassion's plan,
　Thy works we presumptuously scan
　For what the prophets say they saw.

Unbidden still the awful slope
　Walling us in we climb to gain
　Assurance of the shining plain
That faith has certified to hope.

In vain!—beyond the circling hill
　The shadow and the cloud abide.
　Subdue the doubt, our spirits guide
To trust the record and be still.

To trust it loyally as he
　Who, heedful of his high design,
　Ne'er raised a seeking eye to thine,
But wrought thy will unconsciously,

Disputing not of chance or fate,
　Nor questioning of cause or creed;
　For anything but duty's deed
Too simply wise, too humbly great.

The cannon syllabled his name;
　His shadow shifted o'er the land,
　Portentous, as at his demand
Successive bastions sprang to flame!

He flared the continent with fire,
　The rivers ran in lines of light!
　Thy will be done on earth—if right
Or wrong he cared not to inquire.

His was the heavy hand, and his
　The service of the despot blade;
　His the soft answer that allayed
War's giant animosities.

Let us have peace: our clouded eyes,
　Fill, Father, with another light,
　That we may see with clearer sight
Thy servant's soul in Paradise.

The Dead Comrade

by Richard Watson Gilder (1844–1909)

Come, soldiers, arouse ye!
Another has gone;
Let us bury our comrade,
His battles are done.
    His sun it is set;
He was true, he was brave,
He feared not the grave,
There is naught to regret.

Bring music and banners
And wreaths for his bier—
No fault of the fighter
That Death conquered here.

Bring him home ne'er to rove,
Bring him home to his rest,
And over his breast
Fold the flag of his love.

Great Captain of battles,
We leave him with thee!
What was wrong, oh forgive it;
His spirit make free.
    Sound taps, and away!
Out lights, and to bed!
Farewell, soldier dead!
Farewell—for a day.

Grant — 1885

by John Boyle O'Reilly (1844–1890)

Blessed are Pain, the smiter,
And Sorrow, the uniter!
For one afflicted lies—
A symboled sacrifice—
And all our rancor dies!

No North, no South! O stern-faced Chief,
One weeping ours, one cowlèd Grief—
Thy Country—bowed in prayer and tear—
For North and South—above thy bier!

For North and South! O Soldier grim,
The broken ones to weep for him
Who broke them! He whose terrors blazed
In smoking harvests, cities razed;
Whose Fate-like glance sent fear and chill;
Whose wordless lips spake deathless will—
Till all was shattered, all was lost—
All hands dropped down—all War's red cost
Laid there in ashes—Hope and Hate
And Shame and Glory!

Death and Fate

Fall back! Another touch is thine;
He drank not of thy poisoned wine,
Nor blindly met they blind-thrown lance,
Nor died for sightless time or chance—
But waited, suffered, bowed and tried,
Till all the dross was purified;
Till every well of hate was dried;
And North and South in sorrow vied,
And then—at God's own calling—died!

On a Bust of General Grant

by James Russell Lowell (1819–1891)

Strong, simple, silent are the [steadfast] laws
That sway this universe, of none withstood,
Unconscious of man's outcries or applause,
Or what man deems his evil or his good;
And when the Fates ally them with a cause
That wallows in the sea-trough and seems lost,
Drifting in danger of the reefs and sands
Of shallow counsels, this way, that way, tossed,
Strength, silence, simpleness, of these three strands
They twist the cable shall the world hold fast
To where its anchors clutch the bed-rock of the Past.

String, simple, silent therefore such was he
Who helped us in our need; the eternal law
That who can saddle Opportunity
Is God's elect, though many a mortal flaw
May minish him in eyes that closely see,
Was verified in him; what need we say
Of one who made success where others failed,
Who, with no light save that of common day,
Struck hard, and still struck on till Fortune quailed,
But that (so sift the Norns) a desperate van
Ne'er fell at last to one who was not wholly man. . . .

Nothing ideal, a plain people's man
At the first glance, a more deliberate ken
Finds type primeval, theirs in whose veins ran
Such blood as quelled the dragon in his den,

Made harmless fields, and better worlds began;
He came grim-silent, saw and did the deed
That was to do; in his master-grip
Our sword flashed joy; no skill of words could breed
Such sure conviction as that close-clamped lip;
He slew our dragon, nor, so seemed it, knew
He had done more than any simplest man could do.

Yet did this man, war-tempered, stern as steel
Where steel opposed, prove soft in civil sway;
The hand hilt-hardened had lost tact to feel
The world's base coin, and glozing knaves made prey
Of him and of the entrusted Commonweal;
So Truth insists and will not be denied.
We turn our eyes away, and so will Fame,
As if in his last battle he had died
Victor for us and spotless of all blame,
Doer of hopeless tasks which praters shirk,
One of those still plain men that do the world's rough work.

minish: an archaic form of "diminish." **Norns:** the three Norse goddesses of fate.
glozing: flattering. **praters:** people who utter foolish talk.

Grant at Rest

by James J. Meehan

Not like the tombs where sleep Egyptian kings,
    Raised up by bondmen driven from afar,
Is thy last home; a song of glory rings
    Above the cannon of forgotten war.

Gone are the steeds of strife and battle now;
    Furled are the flags that billowed over them;
Folded the hands and quiescent the brow
    That faced their call and knew their requiem.

O Rover, flowing onward by the shore,
    Keep green the grass that rises from the sod
Where men that are shall falter nevermore,
    And slaves that were uplift free hands to God!

Grant's Tomb Revisited
by Karl Shapiro (b. 1913)

Something unkempt about it
As if the tomb itself were moribund,
Sepulchre of our own Napoleon,
Litter fluttering under the battleflags
And few white faces.
We've all seen better days,
Hiram Ulysses.
They say the neighborhood is in transition
And only the Hudson keeps an even keel.

The stocky tower rises dirtily,
Imperial, republican,
With sculptures all wrong for today.
I'm puzzled why you like this place.
Pose me under the big stone eagle
Amidst the sociological decay.

Who collared this mausoleum with bright tiles,
Flashing, swooping childwork of the age,
Leaping around like a Luna Park?
Take my picture under the Mirò arch,
A neighborhood Mirò, not so bad at that.

Let's go upstairs, that's what it's all about
Where only a single guard remains inside
And seems almost surprised to see
Only two visitors, not in a group.

"One million people turned out for the event
"Buildings all over the city draped in black
"Sixty thousand marchers up Broadway
"Stretched seven miles, the President
"Cabinet, Supreme Court, almost the entire Congress
"Ship on the Hudson fired a salute

And there below
The two monogamous crypts
Eight and a half tons each
From the days when there was no doubt
About a reciprocity of might,
The General on the left and Julia on the right.

Napoleon: Napoleon Bonaparte (1769–1821), the French military commander and emperor who controlled western Europe from 1809 to 1812. **Hiram Ulysses:** Grant's first and middle names. He became known as "Ulysses Simpson Grant" when his name was incorrectly entered on the papers needed for an appointment to the U.S. Military Academy. His mother was Hannah Simpson Grant. **Hudson:** the Hudson River. Grant's Tomb is located near the Hudson River, at Riverside Drive and 122nd Street in New York City. **Luna Park:** one of the amusement parks on Coney Island, New York. **Miró:** Joan Miró (1893–1983), a Spanish painter, sculptor, and printmaker known for his use of exuberant colors and playful, surrealist images. **Julia:** Grant's wife, Julia Dent, whom he married in 1848.

50. Horace Greeley

Horace Greeley, who coined the phrase "Go west, young man," was descended on his mother's side from Scotch-Irish emigrants who settled in what in now Londonderry, New Hampshire, in 1718. As founder and editor of the *New York Tribune*, he set a new standard in American journalism by replacing the usual interest in the lurid with an emphasis on social and political reform. Through his editorials he attacked slavery and economic monopolies, opposed capital punishment, supported the rights of labor, and advocated the free distribution of government lands to western settlers. The focus of his efforts was summarized in his remark that newspapers should be "as sensitive to oppression and degradation in the next street as if they were practised in Brazil or Japan."

As the slavery issue intensified during the 1850s, Greeley favored disunion rather than complicity in the extension of the "peculiar institution" into the western territories. When civil war finally came, he insisted that Congress and President Lincoln emancipate the slaves, partially in the belief that the Union could not "afford to repel the sympathies and reject the aid of Four Millions of Southern people." As war dragged on, however, he urged Lincoln to negotiate a peace with the South, arguing that "our bleeding, bankrupt, almost dying country . . . shudders at the prospect of fresh conscriptions, of further wholesale devastations, and of new rivers of human blood."

In 1848, at a mass meeting of the Friends of Ireland in New York City, Greeley claimed that the immigration of thousands of Irish into America each year gave the United States the right to comment on Britain's policy toward its island colony. He particularly refuted the British charge that defects in the Irish character were responsible for the appalling state of the island by stressing the hard work which the Irish immigrants had contributed to America. He even questioned the very basis of Britain's claim upon Ireland: "In confessing that they know not how to make the Irish people contented, peaceful, prosperous and happy, [English] statesmen admit that they have not the ability to govern Ireland, and therefore have no moral right to persist in this attempt."

Fifteen years later an editorial in the *Tribune* commented on the upcoming gubernatorial race: "The nomination of Fernando Wood and [John] Hoffman, neither of whom has a drop of Irish blood in his veins, for Mayor of a city, three-fourths of whose Democratic voters are Irish, is an insult to the honor of the Old Sod . . . . The Irish vote in New York is enough to elect two Mayors. . . . Nominate an Irishman, elect an Irishman, and then, when you call upon him in City Hall, you've got an Irish Mayor as sure as there's never a snake nor a toad in Ireland."

Horace Greeley

by Edmund Clarence Stedman (1833–1908)

Earth, let thy softest mantle rest
    On this worn child to thee returning,
Whose youth was nurtured at thy breast,
    Who loved thee with such tender yearning!
He knew thy fields and woodland ways,
    And deemed thy humblest son his brother:—
Asleep, beyond our blame, or praise,
    We yield him back, O gentle Mother!

Of praise, of blame, he drank his fill;
    Who has not read the life-long story?
And dear we hold his fame, but still
    The man was dearer than his glory.
And now to us are left alone
    The closet where his shadow lingers,
The vacant chair,—that was a throne,—
    The pen, just fallen from his fingers.

Wrath changed to kindness on that pen;
    Though dipped in gall, it flowed with honey;
One flash from out the cloud, and then
    The skies with smile and jest were sunny.
Of hate he surely lacked the art,
    Who made his enemy his lover:
O reverend head and Christian heart!
    Where now their like the round world over?

He saw the goodness, not the taint,

> In many a poor, do-nothing creature,
> And gave to sinner and to saint,
> But kept his faith in human nature;
> Perchance he was not worldly-wise,
> Yet we who noted, standing nearer,
> The shrewd, kind twinkle in his eyes,
> For every weakness held him dearer . . . .

51. Andrew Johnson

Andrew Johnson, the seventeenth president of the United States, entered this world in 1808 in Raleigh, North Carolina, the great-grandson of William McDonough and Catherine Shaucnosee, both born in Dublin, Ireland, in 1712 and 1716, respectively. (His paternal grandfather immigrated to America from Ballyeaston, County Antrim, about 1750.)

In 1843 Johnson began a career in Congress that spanned a decade in the House and one term in the Senate, in each case as a representative of Tennessee. In both chambers he consistently combined Jacksonian populism with Jeffersonian agrarianism. Besides introducing constitutional amendments for the popular election of the president and for limits to the terms of Supreme Court justices, he opposed federal expenditures, sponsored a homestead act, supported slavery, and proclaimed the superiority of the white race. As the nation careened toward civil war, though, he remained a staunch Union Democrat, calling secession treason and insisting that the government uphold the Constitution and enforce federal laws (but without coercing the states). He eventually became the only senator from a seceding state to remain in Congress. Shortly after federal troops regained portions of Tennessee, he was appointed military governor of the state. In 1864 he was elected vice president on a "Union ticket" with the Republican Abraham Lincoln.

After succeeding to the presidency upon Lincoln's assassination, Johnson followed a generally conciliatory policy toward the defeated South. In the belief that the seceded states had never legally left the Union, he insisted that the federal government had no right to dictate to the former states of the Confederacy. As a result, he did not demand that they grant suffrage to the freed slaves and only suggested that the states ratify the Thirteenth Amendment (abolishing slavery). In addition, he vetoed a bill to grant citizenship and legal equality to freedmen. His later broad amnesty for former Confederates only angered his Radical Republican opponents even more.

Johnson's political enemies in Congress struck back with a series of punitive laws against the South. In addition to setting up military rule in the former Confederacy, the Radical Republicans denied "readmission" to the Union until the southern states granted black suffrage and ratified the Fourteenth Amendment (defining citizenship and guaranteeing equal protection of the laws). In the meantime, the House brought impeachment charges against the president when he dismissed his secretary of war in violation of the Tenure of Office Act, which required senatorial approval for a president's dismissal of any of his appointees. In the face of eleven impeachment charges, Johnson negotiated with several fence-sitting senators, promising patronage to one, appointing another to his cabinet, and reassuring a third that he would no longer obstruct the congressional Reconstruction program. The embattled president was acquitted by the Senate on May 26, 1868.

The President to Congress

by Charles Graham Halpine ("Private Miles O'Reilly") (1829–1866)

Andy Johnson is my name,
    Tennessee my nation,
"Swinging round" it is my game,
    And President my station.
Yankee Doodle may squirm and screech,
    Yankee Doodle Dandy,
But Yankee Doodle won't impeach
    His "great plebeian," Andy.

Uncle Thad is drunk or mad
    When he the scheme proposes,
For heaven's own plan made me the man
    To be your "second Moses!"
Let Ashley and Phillips preach,
    Yankee Doodle Dandy,
But Wall Street can not yet impeach
    The "second Moses," Andy.

It seems that I'm the "anvil" now,
    And Congress is "the hammer;"
The sparks of fight fly far and bright,
    And deafening is the clamor;
But no "dead duck" by hunter struck,
    Yankee Doodle Dandy,
So far can reach as to impeach
    The "circle-swinging Andy."

I had better, p'r'aps, have shut my mouth
    Than Congress so have pelted;
Perhaps too quickly for the South
    My bowels may have melted;
But 'twas a generous fault, you'll own,
    Yankee Doodle Dandy,
And not enough to cost his throne
    To your repentant Andy.

You've stripped me of my dearest power—
    To use it none were braver;
Even Mrs. Cobb can't get a job
    Of pardoning now to save her;
I'm only President in name,
    Yankee Doodle Dandy,
Then why impeach, and blast the fame
    Of the once "most pop'lar Andy"?

I can't appoint the man I want
    To aid my re-election;
My spoils are lost, and, tempest-tossed,
    My friends are in dejection.
I nominated men of fame,
    Yankee Doodle Dandy,
But the Senate won't confirm a name
    That so much as smells of Andy.

And once—'twas the Cleveland scrape,
    When the boys required a preacher —
My private Miles, wid his "winnin smiles,"
    Seduced even Father Beecher!
But worse to keep than to seduce,
    Yankee Doodle Dandy,
For Beecher, as never did my "goose,"
    Took wings and fled from Andy.

Along the railroads, near and far,
    With patriot resolution,
I left "the flag with every star."
    Likewise "the Constitution"
I did the level best I could,
    Yankee Doodle Dandy,
But "by fantastics misunderstood"
    Is the epitaph of Andy.

> Impeach me if you think 'twill pay—
> But it won't pay, I'll be bound, sirs;
> For, driving things this reckless way,
> You'll drive 'em in the ground, sirs.
> The people may have thought me wrong,
> Yankee Doodle Dandy,
> But a punishment too long and strong
> Will win them back to Andy.

Uncle Thad: Thaddeus Stevens (1792–1868), a Massachusetts congressman who advocated a punitive policy toward the Southern states after the Civil War. **Ashley:** James Ashley (1824–1896), an Ohio congressman who initiated the move to impeach President Andrew Johnson. **"second Moses!":** During the election campaign of 1864, Johnson promised blacks that he would be their "Moses," leading them out of slavery. **Phillips:** Wendell Phillips (1811–1884), who called for confiscating the estates of the former "slave oligarchy" in the South and distributing them to the freed slaves. **I had better, p'r'aps, have shut my mouth / Than Congress so have pelted:** One of the impeachment charges against Johnson was that he had brought Congress into disrepute through some of his speeches. **Mrs. Cobb:** a woman accused of using her influence to broker pardons. **Cleveland scrape:** a movement for a new political party, to which Henry Ward Beecher, the famous orator and abolitionist, at first lent his support. **private Miles:** Private Miles O'Reilly, a pseudonym of Charles Graham Halpine.

52. Ancient Order of Hibernians

The Ancient Order of Hibernians was founded in 1836 to protect the Irish and their churches from anti-immigrant violence in New York City. The order also successfully fought the stereotype of the Irishman found in the American theater at the time. The Hibernians later agitated for Irish independence, supported literary and religious activities, and encouraged the study of Irish history and culture. The organization also served as an insurance agency, paying sick benefits and burial expenses for its members. Although the order was originally open only to native-born Irishmen, since 1884 all Roman Catholics of Irish descent have been eligible for membership.

An Irish Night in Chicago
by Patrick Coughlan

We tender kindly greeting to the boys and girls meeting,
    While the pleasant hours are fleeting at Apollo Hall tonight;
And the memory we'll treasure of this night of joyous pleasure,
    As each couple treads the measure of the dance with keen delight.
For what sight is more entrancing than an Irish girl dancing,
    With the love-light ever glancing from her bright and roguish eye,
And her partner, bold and loving, through the figures proudly moving,
    As he catches looks approving from his comrades standing nigh.

Yes, a welcome we're extending, and every effort bending
    To make joy for those attending our festival and ball—
The maidens true and tender, in all their lovely splendor,
    Sure our hearts make quick surrender to each charming beauty's
        thrall.
We welcome young or old men, the timid or the bold men,
    The fiery or the cold men; yes, men from any place;
And we'll toast in brimming glasses those joyous lads and lasses,
    Who represent the masses of our gallant Irish race.

And our greeting won't be colder when welcoming the soldier,
    Where could you find men bolder than the gallant Clan-na-Gael?
Those boys, so rough and ready, whose hearts are true and steady,
    And to fight they're ever ready, for their native Innisfail.
They'll prove the good condition of their soldier erudition,
    By a splendid exhibition of their military skill,
And they'll show how they're preparing for that day, when they'll be
        steering

To their distant native Erin, her tyrants blood to spill,.

And, as with bumpers flowing, we indulge in speeches glowing,
    Of the time when we'll be going to either victory or death;
We show, with much emotion, our hearts' and souls' devotion
    To the land beyond the ocean, where we first drew living breath.
For the boys of this Division have come to the decision,
    To make real that glorious vision, that grand entrancing sight,
When with rifles brightly gleaming and the green flag proudly stream-
      ing,
    For their native land redeeming the Clan-na-Gael will fight.

Now accept our invitation without any hesitation,
    But fill out an application and to join our ranks contrive;
Sure long enough you've slumbered by disunion still encumbered,
    So now come and be numbered in our grand "Division Five."
We preach fraternal feeling to our countrymen appealing,
    While at altars lowly kneeling, to preserve St. Patrick's faith;
And recite the olden story of our saints and sages hoary,
    And emulate their glory in our matchless A. O. H.

Clan-na-Gael: a secret society formed in 1867 by Irish refugees to use violence to end British rule in Ireland. **Innisfail:** also *Inisfail*, a Gaelic word meaning "Isle of Destiny," one of many ancient names for Ireland. **Erin:** a literary name for Ireland. **this Division:** Division Five of the Ancient Order of Hibernians. **A. O. H.:** abbreviation for the Ancient Order of Hibernians.

53. The Fenian Raids

In May 1866, Buffalo, New York, was one of three staging areas for a planned invasion of Canada by the Fenians, an American offshoot of the Irish Revolutionary Brotherhood pledged to the use of force to free Ireland from British rule.

The initial Fenian invasion force was led by John O'Neill, a native of County Monaghan, Ireland, and a veteran of the Civil War. Early on June 1, 1866, two Fenian detachments of 600 men crossed the Niagara River from a point north of Buffalo. Within thirty minutes they had raised the green Fenian standards on Canadian soil. The next morning 840 Canadians under Lieutenant Colonel Alfred Booker arrived at Ridgeway, Ontario. As Booker began to lead his poorly provisioned men north to Stephensville for a planned rendezvous with additional Canadian forces, they were surprised by O'Neill and his men but succeeded in forcing them to retreat.

The Canadian advantage that morning slipped away when the appearance of several mounted Fenians along Ridge Road caused the Canadian vanguard to fear a cavalry attack. When the defenders formed a square in order to repel the expected Fenian charge, they came under a barrage of enemy bullets from O'Neill's troops. The Canadians retreated a mile and a half south, pursued to Ridgeway by Fenians. The Canadians lost ten killed and thirty-seven wounded, compared to the Fenians' eight dead and sixteen wounded.

The Fenians encamped in the ruins of Old Fort Erie that night and waited for promised reinforcements from Buffalo. When it appeared that they would not be rescued, the Fenians abandoned their camp early on June 3 and recrossed the Niagara River. An armed U.S. tug overtook the returning raiders and forced them to surrender. The glorious adventure came to an inglorious end when 700 Fenians were taken into custody by American authorities.

In 1870 O'Neill led a force of 200 men across the border again, only to see them retreat in the face of stiff Canadian resistance near the village of Eccles Hill in Quebec. While riding to the rear for reinforcements, O'Neill was arrested by a U.S. marshal sent to enforce the neutrality laws. Although sentenced to two years' imprisonment, O'Neill was released in three months after obtaining a pardon from President Ulysses S. Grant.

Despite the folly of the Fenians' efforts, O'Neill attempted even a third invasion of Canada. In September 1871, without the support of the Fenian council, he and a few followers seized the Hudson's Bay post in what is now Manitoba before being arrested by American troops. He later became an agent for a group of land speculators who attempted to attract Irish settlers to Nebraska. The town of O'Neill in Holt County, Nebraska, is named for him.

Ridgeway

by Scian Dubh

There's a flush on the cheek of the gallant O'Neill!—
　　There is blood on his lips and strange light in his eye;
And there's death in the gleam of his chivalrous steel,
　　As it sweeps round his head like a flash round the sky,
While his horse, white with foam, plunges deep, mid the foe,
Through the red land he opens at every blow!

In that hurricane swoop of the sons of the Gael,
　　And their merciless shout that rings out on the air,
See the face of the tyrant grows haggard and pale,
　　For he knows the wild longing for vengeance that's there;
See him crushed with the terrible cry that he hears,
Bursting forth from the lips of seven hundred long years.

Breast to breast! crash on crash! hand to hand! hip and thigh!
　　And the field is a desert!—the foemen are fled!
And again the bright "Sun-burst" waves proudly on high,
　　While low down in the dust lies the banner of red,
And the clarion of triumph sends forth a long peal,
For the sons of the Gael and their gallant O'Neill!

O'Neill: John O'Neill, an Irish native and Civil War veteran who led three disastrous Fenian invasions of Canada between 1866 and 1871. **sons of the Gael:** here used to refer to the Fenian invaders. **"Sunburst":** a feature of the regimental flags of the Irish Brigade. The heavily fringed flags were a deep green and bore in the center an embroidered Irish harp, with a sunburst above it and a wreath of shamrocks beneath. A crimson scroll, in Irish letters, carried the motto "They shall never retreat from the charge of lances."

54. Myles Keogh

Myles Keogh was born in County Carlow, Ireland, in 1840 or 1842, one of thirteen children. Attracted by the prospect of a military career, the young Keogh traveled to Italy to enlist in the papal army, which in 1860 was waging war against the Italian nationalists who hoped to incorporate the Papal States into a unified Italy. The Irishman served with distinction and rose through the ranks to become second lieutenant in the Battalion of St. Patrick and then lieutenant in the Papal Guards. Before leaving Rome in 1862, he was awarded the *Pro Petri Sede* ("For the See of Peter") medal and the Cross of the Order of St. Gregory the Great.

After immigrating to New York City in 1862, Keogh continued his military career, but now with the U.S. army. He joined the Union forces as a cavalry captain and went on to see action in more than a hundred battles. For his bravery and good conduct during the war, he was breveted lieutenant colonel in the volunteers, while his services at Gettysburg earned him the rank of major. Within weeks after Lee's surrender, Keogh transferred to the Seventh Cavalry and was quickly commissioned captain.

In May 1876 Keogh was at Fort Abraham Lincoln in Dakota Territory, preparing to lead Company I of the Seventh Cavalry in George Custer's disastrous expedition against the Sioux. As the cavalry marched off to its fate the following month, it did so to the strains of "Garry Owen," the famous Irish air that Keogh may have introduced to the Seventh's regimental band. If, as Dr. John Langellier maintains, Custer was among the first killed at the Little Bighorn, Keogh was the ranking officer during the battle. Whatever the case, his body and Custer's were among the few which escaped mutilation.

After the battle Keogh's horse, Comanche, was found seven miles from the scene of the American defeat, its saddle twisted under its belly. One Indian was apparently tempted to take the saddle blanket but changed his mind when he saw that it was heavily stained with blood. When another Indian yelled at the horse and threw a clod of dirt at it, the horse refused to move. By order of the secretary of war, a soldier was detailed to look after him as long as he lived, and no one was ever afterwards permitted to ride him.

Keogh had bought his famous mount at Ellis Station, Kansas, in 1868. The $90 horse stood fifteen hands in height and weighed 925 pounds. When Comanche died in 1891 at the age of twenty-nine, it was rendered almost immortal by the skillful hands of a taxidermist. Today the horse is on display at the University of Kansas in Lawrence.

Miles Keogh's Horse
by John Hay (1838–1905)

On the bluff of the Little Big-Horn,
    At the close of a woeful day,
Custer and his Three Hundred
    In death and silence lay.

Three Hundred to Three Thousand!
    They had bravely fought and bled;
For such is the will of Congress
    When the White man meets the Red.

The White men are ten millions,
    The thriftiest under the sun;
The Reds are fifty thousand,
    And warriors every one.

So Custer and all his fighting men
    Lay under the evening skies,
Staring up at the tranquil heaven
    With wide, accusing eyes.

And of all that stood at noonday
    In that fiery scorpion ring,
Miles Keogh's horse at evening
    Was the only living thing.

Alone from that field of slaughter,
    Where lay the three thousand slain,
The horse Comanche wandered,
    With Keogh's blood on his mane.

And Sturgis issued this order,
    Which future times shall read,
While the love and honor of comrades
    Are the soul of the soldier's creed.

He said—
        Let the horse Comanche
    Henceforth till he shall die,
Be kindly cherished and cared for
    By the Seventh Cavalry.

He shall do no labor; he never shall know
    The touch of spur or rein;
Nor shall his back be ever crossed

By living rider again.

And at regimental formation
   Of the Seventh Cavalry,
Comanche draped in mourning and led
   By a trooper of Company I,

Shall parade with the Regiment!

                              Thus it was
Commanded and thus done,
   By order of General Sturgis, signed
By Adjutant Garlington.

Even as the sword of Custer,
   In his disastrous fall,
Flashed out a blaze that charmed the world
   And glorified his pall,

This order, issued amid the gloom,
   That shrouds our army's name,
When all foul beasts are free to rend
   And tear its honest fame,

Shall prove to a callous people
   That the sense of a soldier's worth,
That the love of comrades, the honor of arms,
   Have not yet perished from earth.

Sturgis: Samuel Davis Sturgis (1822–1889), an officer in the Seventh Cavalry who saw service in the Indian campaigns.

55. Henry McCarty (Billy the Kid)

Born in New York City in 1859, the notorious outlaw was the son of Patrick McCarty and his Irish-born wife, Catherine Devine. The young McCarty followed his family to Kansas and then to New Mexico, where his recently widowed mother married William Antrim. Antrim's name provided Henry with a variety of pseudonyms ("Henry Antrim," "Kid Antrim," and "William Antrim").

In 1877, after having spent two years working as a cowboy, a teamster, and a general laborer, McCarty killed an Irish blacksmith named Frank Cahill during a fistfight that began when Cahill called the Kid a "pimp" and when the teenager, in turn, called the smith a "sonofabitch." Although indicted for murder, McCarty (now using the alias William Bonney) escaped and headed for New Mexico, where he later worked as a ranchhand for John Tunstall, a man who seems to have been a substitute father for McCarty. In addition to his ranch, Tunstall operated a bank and general store in Lincoln. Unfortunately for Tunstall, though, this new enterprise competed with a similar store owned by James Dolan and Laurence Murphy, both natives of Ireland. The commercial rivalry reached a climax when Tunstall was killed by members of the Murphy-Dolan gang. Enraged by the murder, McCarty swore vengeance on "every son of a bitch who helped kill John."

During the spring of 1878, the young McCarty and his confederates tracked down Tunstall's killers. Among the five members of the Dolan-Murphy gang who fell victim to the avengers was Sheriff William Brady, who had led the posse that killed Tunstall. During the better part of 1880, McCarty was on the run for killing a would-be assassin at Fort Sumner, New Mexico. Returning to the fort later that year, the Kid and his followers ran into a posse led by Sheriff Pat Garrett. In the gunfire that ensued, McCarty escaped but surrendered a week later when cornered in Stinking Springs.

The following spring, while awaiting execution in the Lincoln County Courthouse for the murder of Brady, McCarty again escaped. This time the young outlaw slipped out of his handcuffs (while on a visit to the privy), grabbed a six-gun, and killed his two guards. As he calmly rode out of town, he shouted, "You won't follow me any more with that gun." In July 1881 McCarty returned to Old Fort Sumner to visit a ladyfriend. There he was confronted by Sheriff Garrett, who had been waiting for him in the dark. A bullet from the lawman's gun struck McCarty in the heart and instantly killed him.

The Ballad of Billy the Kid
by Henry Herbert Knibbs (1874–1945)

No man in the West ever won such renown
As young Billy Bonney of Santa Fe town,
And of the wild outlaws that met a bad end,
None so quick with a pistol or true to a friend.

It was in Silver City his first trouble came,
A man called Billy's mother a very foul name;
Billy swore to get even, his chance it came soon,
When he stabbed that young man in Joe Dyer's saloon.

He kissed his poor mother and fled from the scene,
A bold desperado and not yet fifteen;
He hid in a sheep-camp but short was his stay,
For he stole an old pony and rode far away.

At monte and faro he next took a hand,
And lived in Tucson on the fat of the land;
But the game was too easy, the life was too slow,
So he drifted alone into Old Mexico.

It was not very long before Billy came back,
With a notch in his gun and some gold in a sack;
He struck for the Pecos his comrades to see,
And they all rode to Lincoln and went on a spree.

There he met his friend Tunstall and hired as a hand
To fight with the braves of the Jingle-Bob brand;
Then Tunstall was murdered and left in his gore;
To avenge that foul murder Young Billy he swore.

First Morton and Baker he swiftly did kill,
Then he slaughtered Bill Roberts at Blazer's sawmill;
Sheriff Brady and Hindman in Lincoln he slew,
Then he rode to John Chisum's along with his crew.

There he stood off a posse and drove them away,
In McSween's House in Lincoln he made his next play;
Surrounded he fought till the house was burned down,
But he dashed through the flames and escaped from the town.

Young Billy rode north and Young Billy rode south,
He plundered and killed with a smile on his mouth;
But he always came back to Fort Sumner again
For his Mexican sweetheart was living there then.

His trackers were many, they followed him fast,
At Arroyo Tiván he was captured at last;
He was taken to Lincoln and put under guard,
And sentenced to hang in the old court-house yard.

J. Bell and Bob Ollinger [*sic*] watched day and night,
And Bob told Young Billy he'd made his last fight.
Young Billy gave Ollinger scarcely a glance,
But sat very still and awaited his chance.

One day he played cards with J. Bell in the room,
Who had no idea how close was his doom;
Billy slipped off a handcuff, hit Bell on the head,
Then he snatched for the pistol and shot him down dead.

Bob Ollinger heard and he ran to the spot
To see what had happened and who had been shot;
Young Billy looked down from a window and fired,
Bob Ollinger sank to the ground and expired.

The Young Billy escaped on a horse that was near,
As he rode forth from Lincoln he let out a cheer;
Though his foes they were many he feared not a one,
So long as a cartridge remained in his gun.

But his comrades were dead or had fled from the land,
It was up to Young Billy to play a lone hand;
And Sheriff Pat Garrett he searched far and wide,
Never thinking the Kid in Fort Sumner would hide.

But when Garrett heard Billy was hiding in town,
He went to Pete Maxwell's when the sun had gone down;
The door was wide open, the night it was hot.
So Pat Garrett walked in and sat down by Pete's cot.

Young Billy had gone for to cut him some meat,
No hat on his head and no boots on his feet;
When he saw two strange men on the porch in the gloom,
He pulled his gun quick and backed into the room.

Billy said, Who is that? and he spoke Maxwell's name,
Then from Pat Garrett's pistol the answer it came —
The swift, cruel bullet went true to its mark,
And Young Billy fell dead on the floor in the dark.

So Young Billy Bonney he came to his end,
Shot down by Pat Garrett who once was his friend;
Though for coolness and courage both gunmen ranked high,
It was Fate that decided Young Billy should die.

Each year of his life was a notch in his gun,
For in twenty-one years he had slain twenty-one.
His grave is unmarked and by desert sands hid,
And so ends the true story of Billy the Kid.

Billy Bonney: one of Henry McCarty's many pseudonyms. **Silver City:** Silver City, New Mexico. **he stabbed that young man in Joe Dyer's saloon:** This episode is generally regarded as apocryphal. **monte and faro:** gambling card games. **Pecos:** the principal tributary of the Rio Grande, rising in the Sangre de Cristo Mountains northeast of Santa Fe, New Mexico, and flowing south and southeast into Texas. **Jingle-Bob brand:** a mark used by the rancher John Chisum to identify his more than 60,000 cattle. The brand was made by slashing the animal's dewlap (the fold of skin under the throat), thereby leaving a hanging chunk of hide and flesh. **Morton:** William Morton, whose corpse was found with ten bullet wounds (nine in the body and one in the head). **Baker:** Frank Baker, found with five bullets in his body. **he swiftly did kill, . . . Then he slaughtered:** It is more accurate to say that Billy the Kid was among the group that murdered the men mentioned in this stanza. **Bill Roberts:** actually Andrew Roberts (aka "Buckshot" and "Bill Williams"). **Sheriff Brady:** William Brady (1829–1878), a native of County Cavan, Ireland. **Hindman:** Deputy Sheriff George Hindman. **John Chisum:** a powerful rancher (1824–1884), who owned more than 60,000 longhorn cattle in Lincoln County, New Mexico. **McSween's House:** the home of Alexander McSween (1843–1878), John Tunstall's partner and a prominent lawyer in Lincoln County, New Mexico. **his Mexican sweetheart:** possibly Celas Gutiérres or Paulita Maxwell. According to gossip at the time, Paulita was pregnant with Billy's child. **J. Bell:** Deputy U.S. Marshal James W. Bell. **Bob Ollinger [*sic*]:** Deputy U.S. Marshall Robert Olinger (1850–1881). His part in the death of the Kid's friend John Jones may have been the reason for the brutal way in which Billy killed him. **Pete Maxwell:** the manager of his family's ranch, sheep herds, and employees in and around Fort Sumner, New Mexico, whose abandoned buildings Maxwell's father had bought from the government in 1871. **his grave is unmarked:** Billy is buried in the military cemetery at Fort Sumner, New Mexico. The inscription on his tombstone reads: "The Boy Bandit King — He Died as He Had Lived."

Billy the Kid (or William H. Bonney)

by N. Howard Thorp (1867–1940)

Bustin' down the canyon,
Horses on the run,
Posse just behind them,
'T was June first, seventy-one.

Saddle guns in scabbards,
Pistols on saddle bow,
The boys were ridin' for their lives—
The Kid en Alias Joe.

Thirty miles west of the Gila
They bade the posse good-bye,
For they couldn't keep up with the lightweight Kids,
No matter how hard they'd try.

From the land of the Montezuma,
Past the hills of the Mogollons,
By night en day they made their way
Till they landed in Tombstone.

Those were frontier towns, old pardner;
'T was a game of take en give,
And the one who could draw the fastest
Was the only one who'd live.

Whiskey en women en poker,
Monte en Faro en Stud,
Just a short wild race, who'd keep the pace
Would land in a river of blood.

Fightin' en drinkin' en gamblin',
Nigger en Mex en White;
'T was a riot of sin, let the best man win;
'T was drink, when called, or fight.

En every one claimed a woman,
Though none of their claims would stand
'Gainst the kid, who was quicker'n lightning
With a gun in either hand.

Believing that John H. Tunstall
Was the man who was in the right,
He offered him his services
In the Lincoln County fight.

The Kid rode with Brewer's posse
Who avenged John Tunstall's loss,
Killing William Morton, en Baker
Roberts en Joe Ross.

Locked in the Dolan house in Lincoln,
Then used as a county jail,
Handcuffed en with a double guard,
Trailing a ball en chain,

He killed his guards, Bell en Olinger,
In the jail yard in daylight,
Stole the horse of the probate clerk
En on him made his flight.

Caught a-napping at last in Sumner,
In Pete Maxwell's room one night,
Not knowing he was waylaid,
Not knowing with whom to fight;

A chance shot fired by Garrett,
A chance shot that found its mark;
'T was lucky for Pat the Kid showed plain,
While Garrett was hid in the dark.

If Garrett was game, I don't know it;
He never appeared so to me;
If any of you fellows think so,
I'll refer you to Oliver Lee.

Gila: a river rising in southwestern New Mexico and flowing west across Arizona into the Colorado River near Yuma, Arizona. **land of Montezuma:** Mexico. Montezuma was the Aztec ruler whose empire was conquered by Spanish troops led by Hernando Cortez. **Mogollons:** a range of mountains in western New Mexico. **Monte, Faro, and Stud:** gambling card games. **Brewer's posse:** led by Dick Brewer (John Tunstall's foreman) and composed of Charlie Bowdre, William McCloskey, John Middleton, Frank McNab, Henry Brown, J. G. Scurlock, Wayt Smith, and Jim French. **William Morton:** whose corpse was found with ten bullet wounds (nine in the body and one in the head). **Baker:** Frank Baker, found with five bullets in his body. **Roberts:** Andrew Roberts (aka "Buckshot" and "Bill Williams"). **Bell:** Deputy U.S. Marshal James W. Bell. **Olinger:** Deputy U.S. Marshall Robert Olinger (1850–1881). His part in the death of the Kid's friend John Jones may have been the reason for the brutal way in which Billy killed him. **Pete Maxwell:** the manager of his family's ranch, sheep herds, and employees in and around Fort Sumner, New Mexico. **game:** lame. **Oliver Lee:** one of two men sought by Pat Garrett in connection with the mysterious death of Albert J. Fountain in 1896. The two suspects were tried and acquitted.

Billy the Kid, *Version 1*
author unknown

Billy was a bad man
And carried a big gun,
He was always after Greasers
And kept 'em on the run.

He shot one every morning,
For to make his morning meal.
And let a white man sass him,
He was shore to feel his steel.

He kept folks in hot water,
And he stole from many a stage;
And when he was full of liquor
He was always in a rage.

He kept things boilin' over,
He stayed out in the brush,
And when he was full of dead eye,
Other folkses better hush.

But one day he met a man
Who was a whole lot badder.
And now he's dead,
And we ain't none the sadder.

Greasers: a slang term for swaggering young toughs.

Billy the Kid, *Version 2*
author unknown

I'll sing you a true song of Billy the Kid,
I'll sing of the desperate deeds that he did,
Way out in New Mexico long, long ago,
When a man's only chance was his own forty four.

When Billy the Kid was a very young lad,
In the old Silver City he went to the bad;
Way out in the West with a gun in his hand
At the age of twelve years he first killed his man.

Fair Mexican maidens play guitars and sing
A song about Billy, their boy bandit king,
How ere his young manhood had reached its sad end
He'd a notch on his pistol for twenty-one men.

'Twas on the same night when poor Billy died
He said to his friends: "I am not satisfied;
There are twenty-one men I have put bullets through,
And Sheriff Pat Garrett must make twenty-two."

Now this is how Billy the Kid met his fate:
The bright moon was shining, the hour was late,
Shot down by Pat Garrett, who once was his friend,
The young outlaw's life had now come to its end.

There's many a man with a face fine and fair
Who starts out in life with a chance to be square,
But just like poor Billy he wanders astray
And loses his life in the very same way.

Silver City: Silver City, New Mexico.

56. Jesse James

The notorious outlaw Jesse James was born in 1847 in Kearney, Missouri, where he and his older brother Frank lived with their mother, Zerelda Cole James, a Catholic who traced her roots to Ireland. In 1863 Union troops attacked the James home, beating Jesse and hanging his stepfather (who survived). Almost immediately Jesse and his brother joined the Confederate guerrilla force of the infamous William Quantrill. The following year the brothers were part of a band of approximately 200 guerrillas who looted Centralia, Missouri, held up a train, and killed twenty-five Union troops on board. That same day these raiders defeated an equal number of cavalrymen.

After the war the James brothers employed their guerrilla tactics in peacetime robbery. During the next fifteen years they ranged through eleven states and territories, carrying off an estimated twenty-five raids. After joining forces with the three Younger brothers, they terrorized the Midwest with their robberies. In retaliation, Pinkerton railroad detectives attacked the James house with a bomb, hoping to kill the outlaw brothers, who, it turned out, were not at home. Instead, the bomb tore off Zerelda's right arm and killed her eight-year-old son.

Jesse James later lived as a fugitive in St. Joseph, Missouri, with his wife and children under the alias "Tom Howard." In April 1882 the family's house was the scene of James's death at the hands of Robert and Charles Ford, former confederates of the outlaw's who hoped to share a $10,000 reward from several railroad companies. Although Robert Ford had originally intended only to turn James over to authorities, he shot James in the back of the head when the latter began to suspect Ford's treachery. According to Ford's account of the episode, he killed James while the famous outlaw straightened a picture on the wall. (Ford was henceforth known as "that dirty little coward who shot Mister Howard.") Although the Fords were convicted of murder and were sentenced to be hanged, they were pardoned by the governor.

Jesse James

by Rosemary Carr Benét (1900–1962)

Among our country's outlaws
There are some lusty names,
But many a voice would make a choice
Of Jesse Woodson James.

No wishy-washy man was he
Of milk and *aqua pura.*
He shook the ground for miles around
His native soil, Mizzoura.

"Allow me!" said his brother,
His helpful partner, Frank.
Then out they'd sail to rob the mail
Or polish off a bank.

The sheriffs found, unlike the hound,
His bite worse than his bark.
He shot as well as William Tell
Though apples weren't his mark.

And those who came to spoil his game
Found people sometimes coy.
For lots would say, "It's Jesse's way,
He's just a home-town boy."

"They done him wrong when he was young.
Perhaps he should have borne it.
But we have found it is not sound
To step upon a hornet."

He robbed and looted banks and trains.
He took what wasn't his'n.
He thumbed his nose at all of those
Who sadly muttered, "Prison!"

A price was out upon his head.
His luck began to crack.
Two of his men turned traitor then
And shot him in the back.

Jesse died at thirty-five,
Frank lived to threescore-ten.
Of their kind you will not find
Two more daring men.

Some call Jess Missouri's pride,
Some say he's her shame,
All we can say is, anyway
He earned his outlaw fame.

aqua pura: a Latin phrase meaning "pure water." **William Tell:** the legendary hero of the Swiss struggle for independence from Austrian domination during the fourteenth century.

Jesse James

author unknown

Jesse James was a lad that killed a-many a man;
He robbed the Danville train.
But that dirty little coward that shot Mr. Howard
Has laid poor Jesse in his grave.

Poor Jesse had a wife to mourn for his life,
Three children, they were brave.
But that dirty little coward that shot Mr. Howard
Has laid poor Jesse in his grave.

It was Robert Ford, that dirty little coward,

I wonder how he does feel,
For he ate of Jesse's bread and he slept in Jesse's bed,
Then laid poor Jesse in his grave.

Jesse was a man, a friend to the poor,
He never would see a man suffer pain;
And with his brother Frank he robbed the Chicago bank,
And stopped the Glendale train.

It was his brother Frank that robbed the Gallatin bank.
And carried the money from the town;
It was in this very place that they had a little race,
For they shot Captain Sheets to the ground.

They went to the crossing not very far from there,
And there they did the same;
With the agent on his knees, he delivered up the keys
To the outlaws, Frank and Jesse James.

It was on Wednesday night, the moon was shining bright,
They robbed the Glendale train;
The people they did say, for many miles away,
It was robbed by Frank and Jesse James.

It was on Saturday night, Jesse was at home
Talking with his family brave,
Robert Ford came along like a thief in the night
And laid poor Jesse in his grave.

The people held their breath when they heard of Jesse's death,
And wondered how he ever came to die.
It was one of the gang called little Robert Ford,
He shot poor Jesse on the sly.

Jesse went to his rest with his hand on his breast;
The devil will be upon his knee.
He was born one day in the county of Clay
And came from a solitary race.

This song was made by Billy Gashade,
As soon as the news did arrive;
He said there was no man with the law in his hand
Who could take Jesse James when alive.

Gallatin bank: On December 7, 1869, the James brothers robbed the Davies County Savings Bank in Gallatin, Missouri. One of the men killed the cashier and wounded another bank employee. **Captain Sheets:** Captain John W. Sheets, the cashier killed in the Gallatin bank robbery. **Glendale train:** On October 8, 1879, the James brothers stole $6,000 from a train on the Chicago and Alton line near Glendale Station in Jackson County, Missouri.

Jesse James

author unknown

Jesse James was a man, and he had a robber band;
And he flagged down the eastern bound train.
Robert Ford watched his eye,
And he shot him on the sly,
And they laid Jesse James in his grave.

    Poor old Jesse, poor old Jesse James,
    And they laid Jesse James in his grave.
    Robert Ford's pistol ball,
    Brought him tumbling from the wall,
    And they laid Jesse James in his grave.

Jesse James' little wife
Was a moaner all her life,
When they laid Jesse James in his grave.
She earned her daily bread
By her needle and her thread,
When they laid Jesse James in his grave.

Jesse James

(A Design in Red and Yellow for a Nickel Library)
by William Rose Benét (1886–1950)

Jesse James was a two-gun man,
    (*Roll on, Missouri!*)
Strong-arm chief of an outlaw clan.
    (*From Kansas to Illinois!*)
He twirled an old Colt forty-five;
    (*Roll on, Missouri!*)
They never took Jesse James alive.
    (*Roll, Missouri, roll!*)

Jesse James was King of the Wes';
    (*Cataracks in the Missouri!*)
He'd a di'mon' heart in his lef' breas';
    (*Brown Missouri rolls!*)
He'd a fire in his heart no hurt could stifle;
    (*Thunder, Missouri!*)
Lion eyes an' a Winchester rifle.
    (*Missouri, roll down!*)

Jesse James rode a pinto hawse;
Come at night to a water-cawse;
Tetched with the rowel that pinto's flank;
She sprung the torrent from bank to bank.

Jesse rode through a sleepin' town;
Looked the moonlit street both up an' down;
Crack-crack-crack, the street ran flames
An' a great voice cried, "I'm Jesse James!"

Hawse an' afoot they're after Jess!
    (*Roll on, Missouri!*)
Spurrin' an' spurrin'—but he's gone Wes'.
    (*Brown Missouri rolls!*)
He was ten foot tall when he stood in his boots;
    (*Lightnin' light the Missouri!*)
More'n a match fer sich galoots.
    (*Roll, Missouri, roll!*)

Jesse James rode outa the sage;
Roun' the rocks come the swayin' stage;
Straddlin' the road a giant stan's
An' a great voice bellers, "Throw up your han's!"

Jesse raked in the di'mon' rings,
The big gold watches an' the yuther things;
Jesse divvied 'em then an' thar
With a cryin' child had lost her mar.

The U.S. troopers is after Jess;
    (*Roll on, Missouri!*)
Their hawses sweat foam, but he's gone Wes';
    (*Hear Missouri roar!*)
He was broad as a b'ar, he'd a ches' like a drum,
    (*Wind an' rain through Missouri!*)

An' his red hair flamed like Kingdom Come.
    (*Missouri down to the sea!*)

Jesse James all alone in the rain
Stopped an' stuck up the East'-bound train;
Swayed through the coaches with horns an' a tail,
Lit out with the bullion an' the registered mail.

Jess made 'em all turn green with fright
Quakin' in the aisles in the pitch-black night;
An' he give all the bullion to a pore ole tramp
Campin' nigh the cuttin' in the dirt an' damp.

The whole U.S. is after Jess;
    (*Roll on, Missouri!*)
The son-of-a-gun, if he ain't gone Wes';
    (*Missouri to the sea!*)
He could chaw cold iron an' spit blue flame;
    (*Cataracks down the Missouri!*)
He rode on a catamount he'd larned to tame.
    (*Hear that Missouri roll!*)

Jesse James rode into a bank;
Give his pinto a tetch on the flank;
Jumped the teller's window with an awful crash;
Heaved up the safe an' twirled his mustache;

He said, "So long, boys!" He yelped, "So long!
Feelin' porely today—I ain't feelin' strong!"
Rode right through the wall a-goin' crack-crack-crack—
Took the safe home to mother in a gunny-sac.

They're creepin', they're crawlin', they're stalkin' Jess;
    (*Roll on, Missouri!*)
They's a rumor he's gone much further Wes';
    (*Roll, Missouri, roll!*)
They's word of a cayuse hitched to the bars
    (*Ruddy clouds on Missouri!*)
Of a golden sunset that busts into stars.
    (*Missouri, roll down!*)

Jesse James rode hell fer leather;
He was a hawse an' a man together;
In a cave in a mountain high up in air

He lived with a rattlesnake, a wolf, an' a bear.

Jesse's heart was as sof' as a woman;
Fer guts an' stren'th he was sooper-human;
He could put six shots through a woodpecker's eye
And take in one swaller a gallon o' rye.

They sought him here an' they sought him there,
     (*Roll on, Missouri!*)
But he strides by night through the ways of the air;
     (*Brown Missouri rolls!*)
They say he was took an' they say he is dead,
     (*Thunder, Missouri!*)
But he ain't—he's a sunset overhead!
     (*Missouri down to the sea!*)

Jesse James was a Hercules.
When he went through the woods he tore up the trees.
When he went on the plains he smoked the groun'
An' the hull lan' shuddered fer miles aroun'.

Jesse James wore a red bandanner
That waived on the breeze like the Star-Spangled Banner;
In seven states he cut up dadoes.
He's gone with the buffler an' the desperadoes.

Yes, Jesse James was a two-gun man
     (*Roll on, Missouri!*)
The same as when this song began;
     (*From Kansas to Illinois!*)
An' when you see a sunset burst into flames
     (*Lightnin' light the Missouri!*)
Or a thunderstorm blaze—that's Jesse James!
     (*Hear that Missouri roll!*)

cayuse: a horse, especially an American Indian pony. **Hercules:** a hero of classical myth who possessed great strength and was renowned for his exceptional feats. **dadoes:** the plural of "dado," that part of a pedestal between the base and the cornice; probably a reference to Jesse James's habit of shooting up the columns of the banks he robbed.

57. William "Buffalo Bill" Cody

The famous scout, buffalo hunter, and showman was born in Le Claire, Iowa, in 1846. Although the claim by Cody's grandmother Lydia Martin that her ancestors were of Irish nobility was most likely an exaggerated one, Cody was probably of Irish ancestry. A biography which was produced during his life asserted that Cody's Irish ancestors had immigrated to America in 1747. In addition, genealogists doing research on another Cody family derived the surname from the Irish Odo, a name which the passing of time, they say, transformed into MacOdo, then Codo, and finally Cody.

After serving as a civilian scout and guide for the U.S. cavalry in Kansas following the Civil War, Cody was hired to supply twelve head of buffalo per day to feed 100 workers constructing the Kansas Pacific Railroad. His technique was ingenious: while hunting from his mount, he closed in on the lead buffalo, killed it with his .50-calibre Springfield rifle, turned the rest of the herd in a milling circle, and picked off the rest of his quota. He claimed to have killed 4,280 buffalo in less than eighteen months.

Beginning in 1868, Cody was employed as chief scout for the Fifth Cavalry. In one year he guided seven expeditions and took part in nine military engagements. Although he was awarded the Congressional Medal of Honor for his services in the Indian wars, he was considered a friend by many Native American tribes. In 1878 he wrote: "Every Indian outbreak that I have ever seen has resulted from broken promises and broken treaties by the government." That same year a former commander of the Fifth Cavalry commented that Cody's eyesight was better than a field-glass, his knowledge of terrain was perfect, and his stamina was legendary. Cody was regarded as such an expert rider that the *New York World* wrote that he could ride with a cup of water on his head and not spill a drop. He assumed such epic proportions that his story was told in 700 dime novels and a best-selling autobiography.

In 1883 Cody opened his famous Wild West "Exhibition" in Omaha, Nebraska. For the next thirty years the Wild West train transported 600 Indians, broncobusters, cowboys, and sharpshooters as well as 500 cattle, bison, and elk to thousands of towns and cities in the U.S. and Europe. When the show arrived in England, the *Birmingham Gazette* noted that "Additional interest is attached to the buffaloes by the fact that they are almost the only survivors of what is nearly an extinct species. According to Colonel Cody there are not so many buffaloes on the whole American continent as there are in the exhibition."

Buffalo Bill

by Carl Sandburg (1878–1967)

Boy heart of Johnny Jones—aching today?
Aching, and Buffalo Bill in town?
Buffalo Bill and ponies, cowboys, Indians?

Some of us know
All about it, Johnny Jones.
Buffalo Bill is a slanting look of the eyes,
    A slanting look under a hat on a horse.
He sits on a horse and a passing look is fixed
    On Johnny Jones, you and me, barelegged,
A slanting, passing, careless look under a hat on a horse.

Go clickety-clack, O pony hoofs along the street.
Come on and slant your eyes again, O Buffalo Bill.
Give us again the ache of our boy hearts.
Fill us again with the red love of prairies, dark nights,
    lonely wagons, and the crack-crack of rifles sputtering
    flashes into an ambush.

58. Molly Maguires

The poems in this section chronicle the events surrounding two of as many as fifty murders allegedly committed by the Molly Maguires, a secret organization that used intimidation and violence in its struggle against the mine operators in northeastern Pennsylvania during the late 1870s.

On September 3, 1875, Jimmy Kerrigan and two accomplices—Michael Doyle and Edward Kelly — carried out their plan to kill a mine boss by the name of John Jones. On the testimony of a young lawyer who had witnessed the murder, a posse captured the three suspects and imprisoned them. When a mob threatened to lynch the trio, however, the suspects were transferred to the Carbon County prison at Mauch Chunk. During the subsequent legal proceedings, Kerrigan and Doyle confessed to their part in the murder. In fact, intent upon assuring himself a place in the annals of labor history, Kerrigan recast his confession into the form of a ballad ("Jimmy Kerrigan's Confession" below), a versification which later appeared in the Mauch Chunk newspaper. Doyle, meanwhile, was even more prolific. "Doyle's Pastime on St. Patrick's Day" was the first of three ballads which he composed while awaiting execution. In another ballad, entitled "Michael J. Doyle," the condemned man lamented his inability to visit his beloved home at Mount Laffee one more time. Kelly, the third murderer, was also convicted and sentenced to be hanged.

Some of the testimony offered during the trial was subsequently used to indict Alexander Campbell, a saloon keeper, on the charge that he had hired Doyle and Kelly to murder Jones. Not surprisingly, Campbell, an emigrant from Donegal, Ireland, and an influential if low-key member of the Mollies, was found guilty and sentenced to the gallows. The only surprise at the trial was the appearance for the prosecution of James McKenna, an Irish Catholic formerly known among the Mollie Maguires as one of their own but revealed at the trial as James McParlan, an undercover agent for the mine owners.

Until the day of his execution, Campbell continued to proclaim his innocence. "It's hard to die innocent, but I shall not be the first to die thus," he declared. "God knows that I am innocent of any crime, and the people know it, and the Commonwealth [of Pennsylvania] knows it." To make his point in a dramatic way, Campbell ground his right hand in the dust on the floor of his cell and, striking the wall with it, left there the imprint of his dirtied palm. "There is the proof of my words," he shouted. "That mark of mine will never be wiped out. There it will remain forever to shame the county that is hangin' an innocent man." (After Campbell's execution his jailers were unable to remove the hand print, despite repeated painting and plastering. It is said that even today the hand print remains visible on the wall.)

Though many people in the region rejoiced that the power of the Molly Maguires seemed finally broken, others became sympathetic to the cause out of disgust with Kerrigan's testimony, McParlan's treachery, and the hysteria which had accompanied the trials. This sympathetic point of view found expression in "The Doom of Campbell, Kelly and Doyle," written after the trials by Michael Reddy of Yorktown, Schuylkill County. Two final ballads — "Hugh McGeehan" and "Thomas Duffy" — tell the tales of two men sentenced to die for the murder of a policeman named Benjamin Yost. (McGeehan was convicted of the actual murder, while Duffy was found guilty of complicity.)

Jimmy Kerrigan's Confession
by Jimmy Kerrigan (c. 1845–1898)

You know I am that squealer they talk so much about,
And sure you know the reason, of which I have no doubt.
If not, I will tell you as nearly as I can,
So please in kindness listen to Jimmy Kerrigan.

I fought for my country as you will plainly see,
And I always did my duty when we met with General Lee.

Indeed, on many a battlefield we saw the rebels flee,
I and my comrades marching 'longside me.

And when the war was over and I at home again
Had married and settled down in a comfortable way,
Carroll, Donahue and Campbell did lead me astray.
And it's them that I may thank for where I am today.

On the first day of September in eighteen seventy-five,
Returning from my work, at Carroll's I did arrive
To take my beer, as usual, but did not get a fill,
When Carroll said, "Kerrigan, here are men for Summit Hill."

Says I, "Why, Carroll, I have got to work, with them I cannot go."
"Kerrigan, you know better, and what you say is not so."
So lastly I consented and fixed myself in style
To lead, as he requested, young Kelly and Michael Doyle.

We arrived at Alex Campbell's at half-past nine or ten.
When Campbell did accomp'ny us from there to Summit Hill
Saying, "Hugh, these are chaps we've talked about, and who have
    left their homes
To satisfy the rest of us—to kill the hated Jones."

Hugh got the pistols ready to see if they were free.
Then handed one to Doyle, young Kelly and to me
Saying, "Take these, boys, we'll arrange the rest all right,
If you'll but try to have it done against tomorrow night."

On Thursday we had a glance at Jones but failed the deed to do.
The command "Thou shalt not kill" once more appeared in view.
But Campbell he insisted and the following day we went
And did the bloody deed over which we now repent.

And when we were arrested that day about noon,
All of us were in life's full bloom.
Kelly, I think, a little past nineteen
Led astray, as it was thought, by a chap named Jerry Kane.

When Doyle was tried and I saw it was no use
For me to hold my tongue, I resolved to let it loose;
I told the whole story from beginning to end
And think that since I have told it the country's on the mend.

I had one to assist me who was both good and true
To religion and to country, nor less to me and you:
His name was James McParlan; he's a credit to his race.
A clever chap, young in years, and honesty's in his face.

That this society was a shame to Irishmen you know,
Though outside the coal region I learn it is not so.
For there they do their duty and churches they supply
To teach the way of holiness and fit all men to die.

But not so in the coal fields where by church they are accursed,
And excommunicated, which still made matters worse;
They craved to be admitted into her fold, you know,
Through those notorious criminals—Tom Fisher and Kehoe.

Tom Fisher and Kehoe were county delegates
For Schuylkill and for Carbon; but now they have pale pates,
For crimes which they encouraged and sent vile men to do,
And though they now would squeal on them, their squealing will not do.

Moral

And before I do lay down my pen, I'll address these words to ye,
Abstain from drinking liquor, and from all bad company;
For if you don't, you will it rue unto the day you die,
And with this I shall leave you, and bid you all good-bye.

Jimmy Kerrigan: a chief witness in the prosecution of such Molly Maguires as James Carroll, Alexander Campbell, Jack Kehoe, and John Donahue. **Carroll, Donahue and Campbell:** James Carroll, John Donahue, and Alexander Campbell (hanged, respectively, for the murders of policeman Benjamin Yost; mine superintendent Morgan Powell; and Morgan Powell and mine superintendent John P. Jones. **young Kelly and Michael Doyle:** hanged for the murder of mine superintendent John P. Jones. **Hugh:** Hugh McGeehan (hanged for the murder of policeman Benjamin Yost). **James McParlan:** James McKenna, an Irish Catholic who infiltrated the Molly Maguires while acting as an undercover agent for the mine owners. **this society:** the Ancient Order of Hibernians. The Molly Maguires in the Pennsylvania coal region obtained from the state legislature a charter recognizing them as a chapter of the Ancient Order of Hibernians. The enemies of the Molly Maguires, including the local clergy, regarded this charter as an attempt to hide the secret society's true nature. **Tom Fisher:** hanged for the murder of mine superintendent Morgan Powell. **Kehoe:** Jack Kehoe, the "King of the Molly Maguires" (hanged for the murder of mine foreman Frank W. Langdon). **Schuylkill and Carbon:** counties in the Pennsylvania coal region; their respective seats are Pottsville and Jim Thorpe.

Doyle's Pastime on St. Patrick's Day
by Michael J. Doyle (?–1877)

It was early on this morning,
    As on my bunk I did sleep;
I was awakened by the brass bands
    A-playing on the street.

So I did rise and rub my eyes,
    No more this day to sleep;
And when I thought the day it was
    I jumped up to my feet.

First Chorus

Saying, can I walk or can I talk,
    Or can I anyone see? No!
But closed up in a dismal cell
    In hopes of liberty.

And when I came to myself,
    And in my cell did hear
The music that the band did play,
    It gave me good cheer.

And when the tune was finished,
    And the band it ceased to play,
I passed remark upon myself,
    And on them these words did say:

But shortly after that,
    Before a half hour passed,
The turnkey he came in,
    And gave me my breakfast.

Second Chorus

Can I walk or can I talk,
    Or can I anyone see? No!
But this one thing I can do—
    Is to eat my grub pretty free.

When he was about to go,

> After I got my coffee and bread;
> I spoke some words to him,
>   And these are the words I said:
>
> So then I sat down,
>   My breakfast for to eat,
> For, when a man is in good health,
>   I tell you it goes sweet.
>
> Now to conclude and finish,
>   With one more thing to say,
> This is a nice way to be
>   On St. Patrick's Day!

Michael J. Doyle: hanged for the murder of mine superintendent John P. Jones.

Michael J. Doyle
by Michael J. Doyle (?–1877)

Mount Laffee, oh my happy home! Of thee I love to sing,
No spot on earth's more dear to me than to which my heart doth cling.
For to cross the old school house hill 'twere my joy to roam,
And call to mind the happy hours I spent at father's home.

When Mike Keely and I would go home at night, our day's work bein'
     done,
We would have a talk and take a walk to where we would find some fun.
At nine or ten we would return again to the parents at our homes,
And there we would find them and with them enjoy a poem.

Let others speak of where they will, perhaps their own glorious home.
But give me sweet Mount Laffee still, my birth, I claim my own.
Where all the people, both great and small, kindness have in store,
And with the help of kind Providence, we will see them all once more.

Of all the scenes that's passed there is one before my sight,
When we was leaving home the sun was shining bright,
Each heart was then free and light and gentle in every tone,
And pleasant were the words we spoke, when we was leaving home.

We made the train in hit of time, to look for work was our design,
It's little we thought that day our troubles to meet at noon,
When a crowd of men did arrest us with p'inted guns in their hands

and a revolver with every man,
But we not knowing what was wrong to them ourselves we did resign

A hearing for to undergo they marched us over through the town,
Unto the station house there for everyone that wished to look on,
Some would say, "Those are the men," whilst others would nod their
     head;
One woman she came in, which my quick ear had overheard:

"I can swear those ain't the men," but in a very short time she left again.
Next comes in Mauch Chunk police and in this manner they did begin:
"First bring out the biggest man until we get the handcuffs on."
And when they had our three hands bound they marched us o'er the
     town.

Around the town like all pell mell until we reached this dismal cell,
Which by experience I can tell is not much short of an earthly hell;
This cell is like a graveyard vault to which I do declare,
It's better for to live in hopes than die in dark despair.

Can I walk or can I talk or can I anyone see?
No! but locked up in a dismal cell in hopes of liberty.
So now to conclude and finish my verses, I hope to the company I've
     said nothing wrong;
My name is Michael J. Doyle, I was born in Mount Laffee, and I am the
     poet of this little song.

Michael J. Doyle: hanged for the murder of mine superintendent John P. Jones.
Mount Laffee: a village on the south side of Pottsville, Pennsylvania. **Mauch
Chunk:** a town in Carbon County, Pennsylvania.

The Doom of Campbell, Kelly and Doyle
by Mike Reddy

Kind-hearted Christians, I pray you give attention,
     It's of a young man, down in jail he doth lie,
For the shooting of the boss, John P. Jones,
     A murderer's death he is doomed for to die.

They say Doyle and Kelly committed the murder,
     And that it was plotted by some cruel gang;
And likewise Jimmy Kerrigan that weak-hearted creature
     That told all about it, 'fraid he would hang.

In years after this when he will be at his freedom,
    When people will see him their blood it will boil.
They will say, "There goes that weak-hearted creature
    That swore away the lives of Campbell, Kelly and Doyle."

The Commonwealth lawyers have done hard time against them;
    The ones that have done it are Hughes and Albright.
They say that the Hibernians are a great band of criminals
    That go about robbing and murdering at night.

Now Hughes and Albright, stop throwing your slander
    When the whip is in your hand; don't crack her free
Lest early some morning or late in the evening
    You may trip on a brick and come down on your knee.

Now bad luck to Mrs. Murphy that speaks of her buttermilk,
    She's the woman can swear without toil,
As brave as a lion she stood quite defiant
    To swear away the lives of Campbell, Kelly and Doyle.

Here's success to brave Kalbfus, that noble defender,
    He done his endeavor their lives for to save,
But the opposite party had plead hard against him,
    Which leaves Doyle to fill up a murderer's grave.

So now to conclude and finish my verses,
    I hope to the company I have said nothing wrong;
My name is Mike Reddy, I still live in Yorktown
    And I am the poet of this little song.

Doyle and Kelly: Michael Doyle and Edward Kelly (hanged for the murder of mine superintendent John P. Jones). **Hughes and Albright:** Judge F. W. Hughes and General Charles Albright of Schuylkill County, the prosecution lawyers. **Hibernians:** the Ancient Order of Hibernians, which, at least in the Pennsylvania coal region, supported the tactics of the Molly Maguires. **Mrs. Murphy:** She testified that Doyle had obtained buttermilk at her home, thus establishing his presence in the vicinity of Jones's murder and thus negating his alibi. **Kalbfus:** Daniel Kalbfus of Carbon County, the defense counsel.

Hugh McGeehan

by Hugh McGeehan (c. 1852–1877)

Come all ye true-born Irishmen wherever you may be,

I hope you pay attention and listen unto me.
For if ever you do get in jail, you'll surely rue the day,
And curse the hour when you first set sail all for Americ-a.

Just think on poor Tom Munley, all in his mannerly prime,
He is sentenced to be hung for an atrocious crime.
The jury found him guilty and the Governor says he must die,
So now poor Tom is sentenced to be hung which seals his destiny.

It would break your heart to listen as he sits in the jail,
To hear his wife and children at his cell door weep and wail.
He kisses little children and through the iron door
Sayin', "Adieu, my little ones, farewell to ye evermore."

Just think, James McKenna, the detective, has gained himself a name,
And in the detective agency has risen to great fame.
He said he came amongst our people in November 'seventy-three
Which leaves many's the wife and babe to mourn and curse his memory.

He came amongst our people in a very quiet time,
He was the foremost plotter of that atrocious crime.
He should be tried for murder, condemned he ought to be,
And along with his poor victims, die on the gallows tree.

That's not half of what he done as unto you I'll tell,
He plotted other murders and that you know full well.
Himself and Jimmy Kerrigan says they done it up in style,
While in Mauch Chunk they swore away the lives of Campbell, Kelly
    and Doyle.

One day up in Tamaqua he met four or five men,
James Carroll and James Roarity with Boyle, Duffy and Hugh McGeehan.
He spent his money freely and great joy he did maintain,
And with his good behavior their confidence did gain.

By this villain, like Judas of old, they were sold for cursed gold, their
    lives he did betray.
It's for Franklin B. Gowen of high renown he drove us to the range;
He broke down our glorious union, upon us did hardship bring,
And in every paper now you read he is styled our Railroad King.

My name is Hugh McGeehan, I am scarcely twenty-four,
In was born in the County Donegal, on Erin's pleasant shore.
I left my foster parents there, like many of my race,

But now I'm held in durance vile, bowed down with sore disgrace.

The first place that I worked a shaft was in the Jeddo mine,
And there the men can testify how well I served my time.
The day I left my native land I took a solemn oath,
That liquor vile of any kind should ne'er go down my throat.

So now I still am keeping it until the day I die,
Let it be on a bed of roses or on the gallows high.
So now I am accused of murder and the same I do deny,
And when my trial will come on, the traitors I will defy.

By the Holy Virgin Mary, I'll tell to you what's true,
I never knew Jimmy Kerrigan, or any of his crew.
I never kept his company and that he knows full well,
But to save his guilty neck he would swear a saint to hell.

Hugh McGeehan: hanged for the murder of policeman Benjamin Yost. **Tom Munley:** hanged for the murder of mine foremen Thomas Sanger and William Uren. **James McKenna:** an Irish Catholic who infiltrated the Molly Maguires while acting as an undercover agent for the mine owners. **Jimmy Kerrigan:** a chief witness in the prosecution of such Molly Maguires as James Carroll, Alexander Campbell, Jack Kehoe, and John Donahue. **Mauch Chunk:** a town in Carbon County, Pennsylvania. **Campbell, Kelly and Doyle:** Alexander Campbell, Edward Kelly, and Michael Doyle (hanged, respectively, for the murders of mine superintendents Morgan Powell and John P. Jones; John P. Jones; and policeman Benjamin Yost). **James Carroll and James Roarity:** hanged for the murder of policeman Benjamin Yost. **Boyle, Duffy:** James Boyle and Thomas Duffy (hanged for the murder of policeman Benjamin Yost). **Tamaqua:** a town in Schuylkill County, Pennsylvania. **Judas:** the Apostle who betrayed Jesus. **Franklin B. Gowen:** a lawyer, railroad executive, mine operator, and bitter foe of labor organizations. This son of Irish immigrant parents ultimately broke the miners' union in Pennsylvania. **Jeddo Mine:** one of several mines by that name in Schuylkill and Luzerne counties in Pennsylvania.

Thomas Duffy
author unknown

Come all ye true-born Irishmen,
I hope you will pay attention and listen unto me,
Concerning ten brave Irishmen all in their youthful bloom,
Who died in Pennsylvania on the twenty-first of June.

Thomas Duffy and James Carroll as you can plainly see,

They were murdered by false perjurers all on the gallows tree.
Thomas Duffy on the brink of death did neither shake or fear,
But he smiled upon his murderers although his end was near.

He took his brother by the hand and kissed him o'er and o'er
Saying, "Farewell, my faithful brother, I shall never see you more,
Till your spirit from this world has fled to that celestial shore
Where perjurers can't enter to shake loving hearts any more.

"Take my advice, dear Patrick, and follow in my wake.
Let perjurers do all they can, my heart they will never shake."
He scorned his prosecutors although he stood alone,
As did many a gallant Irishman before England's king and throne.

He said, "We are not defeated; up or with our banner high,
Although our parents were [mis]treated we will show them how to die."
He mounted on the scaffold with a firm and steady tread,
Resembling a young nobleman a-going up to bed.

He looked upon the circle that stood around him there,
And smiled upon his brother whose heart was in despair.
"Give me your hand, dear Patrick, fret not for my sad fate,
But before I will bid this world adieu, the truth to you I'll state.

"I never saw James Kerrigan, the truth to you I'll tell,
Save once at Carroll residence where I treated him right well.
I never asked James Carroll to shoot a man for me,
Nor offered him ten dollars, as my God I hope to see.

"I bear no living creature the slightest hate or spite,
But as I am going to face my God my conscience it is light.
But why should I tarry longer in this dark world of owe?
My faith was never stronger and I am longing for to go."

The rope was dropped around his neck and the warrant to him read,
And in twenty minutes after, brave Duffy he was dead.
God rest his soul; he perished there to friends and country true,
And he kept his secrets to the last as Irishmen should do.

Bright angels thronged the jail yard until they saw him dead,
And taking a last look at him his spirit with them fled.
Tom Duffy was as true a man as ever blessed our sod,
And now we hope his soul's at rest with Mary and with God.

Thomas Duffy and James Carroll: hanged for the murder of policeman Benjamin Yost. **James Kerrigan:** a chief witness in the prosecution of such Molly Maguires as James Carroll, Alexander Campbell, Jack Kehoe, and John Donahue. **Mary:** the mother of Jesus.

Thomas Duffy
by Manus Coll

My name is Tommy Duffy, I am scarcely twenty-four;
I was born in County Donegal, on Ireland's Emerald shore.
I left my aging parents, like many of my race,—
And now I'm held in durance vile, besmirched in black disgrace.

I was just about eighteen years old when to this land I came,
No sin lay on my conscience, and on my head no shame;
The first place that I earned me pay was in the Jeddo Mine,
And there, the men can testify how well I served me time!

The day I left my native land, I swore a solemn oath,
No liquor, grog of any kind would e'er go down my throat.
And now I'm still a-keeping it, and will until I die,
Be it on a bed of roses, or on a gallows high.

I stand accused of murder foul, the same I do deny.
And now my trial will soon come off—the traitors I defy!
But perjury has got its way throughout our happy land,
And like O'Connell, I'll have them swear on every upraised hand.

May God have mercy on these men, their deeds they can't secrete,
When called to face an angry God, before the Judgment Seat.
But such is life for Irishmen, and ever more 'twill be,
For it always was since that bad day, when Paddy's land was free.

By all that's holy Up Above, now what I say is true!
I never knew "Powder" Kerrigan, nor any of his crew.
I never kept his company, which he must know right well,
But to save his guilty neck, Alas; he'd swear a Saint to Hell.

So here's to all my kindly friends; my enemies also,
And to my foster parents, whom I have brought so low,
As for my loved and pretty wife, to me she is most dear,
I know that she will grieve for me, whilst I am lying here.

But wait, me lads, a little while, and soon you'll see me free,
To face the Bosses, one and all, that tried to bury me,
I'll walk among my fellow men, with head erect and strong,
To show my vile accusers that they are in the wrong!

Tommy Duffy: hanged for the murder of policeman Benjamin Yost. **Jeddo Mine:** one of several mines by that name in Schuylkill and Luzerne counties in Pennsylvania. **O'Connell:** Daniel O'Connell (1775–1847), a leader in the effort to repeal the political union between Ireland and England in the nineteenth century. The allusion in the poem is to the following episode. While defending in court twenty-five Irishmen accused of killing about twenty armed men, O'Connell was frustrated at every turn by the prosecution's leading witness, a policeman who convincingly testified that he had seen the crimes committed. After being tipped off that the witness's father was a notorious sheep stealer, O'Connell asked the policeman whether he knew anyone who stole sheep. When the witness repeatedly swore that he knew no such person, the wily defense attorney exposed the man's family secret, whereupon the discredited policeman revealed himself as a perjurer. **Paddy's land:** Ireland. Paddy is a slang term (often disparaging) for an Irishman. **"Powder" Kerrigan:** James Kerrigan, a Dublin-born leader of the Molly Maguires. He received his nickname from an episode that occurred in a mine shaft 300 feet below ground. When Kerrigan noticed there was no room for him to sit among the miners warming themselves around a coal fire, he decided to make a place for himself. He deftly removed the keg of powder he was carrying on his shoulder, leaned over his comrades around the flames, and placed the keg on the hot coals. An article in *McClure's Magazine* described the denouement: "Men scattered in terror, right and left, whereupon Kerrigan calmly lifted the keg of powder off the coals, lit his pipe and began smoking."

59. James McNeill Whistler

Descended from an Irish branch of an old British family, Whistler denied that he was a native of Lowell, Massachusetts, where he was born in 1834 ("I shall be born when and where I want, and I do not choose to be born at Lowell . . . ."). Instead, he claimed to have been born in St. Petersburg, Russia, where his American-born father superintended the building of the St. Petersburg–Moscow Railroad and where the youngster first took drawing lessons. After returning to the United States for his education, he spent three years at the U.S. Military Academy before heading for Paris in 1855, never to return to America.

During his subsequent career Whistler was noted for his portraits, marine scenes, and landscapes. His most famous work — *Portrait of My Mother* (originally called *An Arrangement in Grey and Black*) — is now in the Louvre. While in London, he become known for his acerbic wit and eccentric dress. His artistic creed is summed up in his notion that a painting has "no mission to fulfill" but is a "joy to the artist, a delusion to the philanthropist, and a puzzle to the botanist." Although he disdained critics, he conceded their usefulness because "they keep one always busy . . . either fighting or proving them idiots." When the art critic John Ruskin mocked him for asking 200 guineas for one particular painting — "for flinging a pot of paint in the public's face" — Whistler successfully sued him for slander, although the artist was awarded only a farthing.

To Whistler, American

On the loan exhibit of his paintings at the Tate Gallery.

by Ezra Pound (1885–1972)

You also, our first great,
Had tried all ways;
Tested and pried and worked in many fashions,
And this much gives me heart to play the game.

Here is a part that's slight, and part gone wrong,
And much of little moment, and some few
Perfect as Dürer!
"In the Studio" and these two portraits, if I had my choice!
And then these sketches in the mood of Greece?

You had your searches, your uncertainties,
And this is good to know—for us, I mean,
Who bear the brunt of our America

And try to wrench her impulse into art.

You were not always sure, not always set
To hiding night or tuning "symphonies";
Had not one style from birth, but tries and pries
And stretched and tampered with the media.

You and Abe Lincoln from that mass of dolts
Show us there's chance at least of winning through.

Tate Gallery: the London art gallery where Ezra Pound viewed Whistler's work in 1911. **Dürer:** Albrecht Dürer (1471–1528), the first northern European artist to combine Italian Renaissance influences with the late Gothic art of the North.

60. Elisha Kent Kane

Elisha Kent Kane, one of America's most famous Arctic explorers, was descended from John O'Kane, his emigrant great-grandfather, who left Ireland for New York soon after 1750. After graduating from the University of Pennsylvania's medical school, Elisha Kane served as physician on various maritime expeditions. Among them was the unsuccessful search in 1850 for survivors of Sir John Franklin's disastrous attempt to find the Northwest Passage five years before. Kane told his story in a stirring narrative, which, in abridged form, was republished as *Adrift in the Arctic Ice Pack.*

In 1853 Kane accompanied a second expedition to the Arctic in search of an open polar sea that many scientists believed existed. After passing into unknown waters now known as Kane Basin, the members of the crew were stricken with scurvy but continued in their search, discovering an ice-free channel which they named for John Pendleton Kennedy, the secretary of the navy. (Fifty-four years later Kennedy Channel was used by Robert E. Peary on his trek to the Arctic Circle.) After spending a disastrous second winter in the Arctic, Kane and his crew managed to escape, reaching Upernivik, Greenland, after eighty-three days, in August 1855. The expedition's astronomical, meteorological, geological, and anthropological investigations provided the foundation for future study of the Arctic.

Kane
by Fitz-James O'Brien (1828–1862)

Aloft upon an old basaltic crag,
   Which, scalpt'd by keen winds that defend the Pole,
   Gazes with dead face on the seas that roll
Around the secret of the mystic zone,
A mighty nation's star-bespangled flag
          Flutters alone,
And underneath, upon the lifeless front
   Of that drear cliff, a simple name is traced;
Fit type of him who, famishing and gaunt,
   But with a rocky purpose in his soul,
          Breasted the gathering snows,
          Clung to the drifting floes,
By want beleaguer'd, and by winter chased,
Seeking the brother lost amid that frozen waste.

Not many months ago we greeted him,
   Crown'ed with the icy honors of the North,
   Across the land his hard-won fame went forth,
And Maine's deep woods were shaken limb by limb;
His own mild Keystone State, sedate and prim,
   Burst from decorous quiet as he came;
   Hot Southern lips with eloquence aflame
Sounded his triumph. Texas, wild and grim,
Proffer'd its horny hand. The large-lung'd West
          From out its giant breast,
Yell'd its frank welcome. And from main to main,
          Jubilant to the sky,
          Thunder'd the mighty cry,
          HONOR TO KANE!

In vain, in vain beneath his feet we flung
   The reddening roses! All in vain we pour'd
   The golden wine, and round the shining board
Sent the toast circling, till the rafters rung
   With the thrice-tripled honors of the feast!
   Scarce the buds wilted and the voices ceased
Ere the pure light that sparkled in his eyes,
Bright as auroral fires in Southern skies,
   Faded and faded! And the brave young heart
That the relentless Arctic winds had robb'd
Of all its vital heat, in that long quest
For the lost captain, now within his breast
   More and more faintly throbb'd.

His was the victory; but as his grasp
Closed on the laurel crown with eager clasp,
        Death launch'd a whistling dart;
And ere the thunders of applause were done
His bright eyes closed forever on the sun!
Too late, too late the splendid prize he won
In the Olympic race of Science and of Art!
Like to some shatter'd berg that, pale and lone,
Drifts from the white North to a tropic zone,
        And in the burning day
        Wastes peak by peak away,
        Till on some rosy even
It dies with sunlight blessing it; so he
Tranquilly floated to a Southern sea,
        And melted into heaven.

He needs no tears, who lived a noble life;
    We will not weep for him who died so well,
    But we will gather round the hearth, and tell
The story of his strife;
    Such homage suits him well,
    Better than funeral pomp or passing bell.
What tale of peril and self-sacrifice!
Prison'd amid the fastnesses of ice,
    With hunger howling o'er the wastes of snow!
    Night lengthening into months, the ravenous floe
Crunching the massive ships, as the white bear
Crunches his prey. The insufficient share
        Of loathsome food,
The lethargy of famine, the despair
    Urging to labor, nervously pursued,
    Toil done with skinny arms, and faces hued
Like pallid masks, while dolefully behind
Glimmer'd the fading embers of a mind!
That awful hour, when through the prostrate band,
Delirium stalk'd, laying his burning hand
    Upon the ghastly foreheads of the crew.
    The whispers of rebellion, faint and few
    At first, but deepening ever till they grew
Into black thoughts of murder; such the throng
Of horrors bound the hero. High the song
Should be that hymns the noble part he play'd!
Sinking himself, yet ministering aid

To all around him. By a mighty will
Living defiant of the wants that kill,
Because his death would seal his comrades' fate;
    Cheering with ceaseless and inventive skill
Those Polar waters, dark and desolate.
Equal to every trial, every fate,
    He stands, until Spring, tardy with relief,
            Unlocks the icy gate,
And the pale prisoners thread the world once more,
To the steep cliffs of Greenland's pastoral shore
            Bearing their dying chief.

Time was when he should gain his spurs of gold
    From royal hands, who woo'd the knightly state;
The knell of old formalities is toll'd,
    And the world's knights are now self-consecrate.
No grander episode doth chivalry hold
    In all its annals, back to Charlemagne,
    Than that lone vigil of unceasing pain,
Faithfully kept through hunger and through cold,
    By the good Christian knight, ELISHA KANE!

brother lost: Sir John Franklin. **Keystone State:** Pennsylvania. **lost captain:** Kane himself, after the 1853–1855 expedition, which one biographer called the archetypical victory in defeat. **Tranquilly floated to a Southern sea / And melted into heaven:** Kane died in Cuba. **whispers of rebellion:** In 1854 nine men under Kane's command protested his decision to spend a second winter in the Arctic and decided to find their way to South Greenland. When the mutineers returned in December, Kane nursed them back to health as best he could. **Charlemagne:** the eighth- and ninth-century Frankish king and Emperor of the Romans.

Dr. Kane in Cuba

by Elizabeth H. Whittier (1815–1864)

A Noble life is in thy care,
    A scared trust to thee is given;
Bright Island! let thy healing air
    Be to him as the breath of Heaven.

The marvel of his daring life—
    The self-forgetting leader bold—
Stirs, like the trumpet's call to strife,
    A million hearts of meaner mould.

Eyes that shall never meet his own
    Look dim with tears across the sea,
Where from the dark and icy zone,
    Sweet Isle of Flowers! he comes to thee.

Fold him in rest, O pitying clime!
    Give back his wasted strength again;
Soothe, with thy endless summer time,
    His winter-wearied heart and brain.

Sing soft and low, thou tropic bird,
    From out the fragrant, flowery tree,—
The ear that hears thee now has heard
    The ice-break of the winter sea.

Through his long watch of awful night,
    He saw the Bear in the Northern skies,
Now, to the Southern Cross of light
    He lifts in hope his weary eyes.

Prayers from the hearts that watched in fear
    When the dark North no answer gave,
Rise, trembling, to the Father's ear,
    That still His love may help and save.

Bright Island: Cuba, where Kane died in 1857. **Sweet Isle of Flowers:** Cuba. **Bear:** either the Great Bear (the most prominent northern constellation) or the Little Bear (the northernmost constellation). **Southern Cross:** a southern constellation near Centaurus, having the form of a cross.

Elisha Kent Kane

by George Henry Boker (1823–1890)

O Mother Earth, thy task is done
    With him who slumbers here below;
From thy cold Arctic brow he won
    A glory purer than thy snow.

Thy warmer bosom gently nursed
    The dying hero; for his eye
The tropic Spring's splendors burst,—
    "In vain!" a thousand voices cry.

"In vain, in vain!" The poet's art
    Forsook me when the people cried;
Naught but the grief that fills my heart,
    And memories of my friend, abide.

We parted in the midnight street,
    Beneath a cold autumnal rain;
He wrung my hand, he stayed my feet
    With "Friend, we shall not meet again."

I laughed; I would not then believe;
    He smiled; he left me; all was o'er.
How much for my poor laugh I'd give!—
    How much to see him smile once more!

I know my lay demeans the dead
    That sorrow is an humble thing,
That I should sing his praise instead,
    And strike it on a higher string.

Let stronger minstrels raise their lay,
    And follow where his fame has flown;
To the whole world belongs his praise,
    His friendship was to me alone.

So close against my heart he lay,
    That I should make his glory dim,
And hear a bashful whisper say,
    "I praise myself in praising him."

O, gentle mother, following night
    His long, long funeral; march, resign
To me the right to lift this cry,
    And part the sorrow that is thine.

O, father, mourning by his bier,
    Forgive this song of little worth!
My eloquence is but a tear,
    I cannot, would not rise from earth.

O, stricken brothers, broken band,—
    The link that held the jewel lost,—
I pray you give me leave to stand
    Amid you, from the sorrowing host.

> We'll give his honours to the world,
> We'll hark the echoes from afar;
> Whene'er our country's flag's unfurled
> His name shall shine in every star.
>
> We feel no fear that time shall keep
> Our hero's memory. Let us move
> A little from the world to weep,
> And for our portion take his love.

61. Carry Moore Nation

Carry Moore, America's fiery temperance advocate, was born in Bryantsville, Kentucky, in 1846. Her father, George Moore, was descended from a pioneer Irish settler in the area, while her mother was a manic-depressive who fancied that she was Queen Victoria. Carry Moore later used her own mystic experiences to justify her temperance mission as divinely inspired.

Shortly after moving with her parents to Belton, Missouri, in 1867, Moore married Charles Gloyd, a man whose alcoholism destroyed the marriage. Once she had left him, she supported herself by teaching school — until she was fired, reputedly after a dispute over the correct pronunciation of the letter "a." Before long, however, she married David Nation, a minister, lawyer, and newspaper editor. Although this second marriage lasted twenty-four years, it was generally unhappy for both spouses. When Mrs. Nation moved to Kansas to become the pastor of a church, her husband divorced her on the grounds of desertion.

In the late 1890s Carry Nation began having the visions which prompted her to start a crusade against the evils of drink. As a member of the Woman's Christian Temperance Union, she was known throughout the world for her hatchet, which she used without mercy in her saloon-smashing sprees. These were all the more threatening because of her 175-pound, almost six-foot physical presence. In Wichita, for example, she trashed the Hotel Carey and other distinguished saloons, destroying quantities of liquor worth thousands of dollars. She justified her role as a hellion on the theory that, wherever saloons were illegal, any citizen had the right to destroy not only their demon rum but also their furniture. She, in turn, was the victim of violence, often being shot at, clubbed, or cut. Although she was arrested about thirty times, she was able to pay her fines from the proceeds of her lectures and the sale of souvenir hatchets.

After making a public speech in 1911, Nation suffered a mental breakdown. As a result, she spent the last five months of her life in a hospital in Leavenworth, Kansas. In reviewing her life, she once mused: "I can see where I have made mistakes — many of them — but they were mistakes of the head and not of the heart."

That Little Hatchet

by C. Butler-Andrews

A century was fading fast,
When o'er its closing decade passed
A matron's figure, chaste, yet bold,
Who held within her girdle's fold
      A bran' new hatchet.

The jointists smiled within their bars,
'Mid bottles, mirrors and cigars—
The woman passed behind each screen,
And soon occurred a "literal" scene—
      Rum, ruin, racket!

At first she "moral Suasion" tried,
But lawless men mere "talk" deride:—
'Twas then she seized her household ax
And for enforcing law by acts,
      Found nought to match it.

The work thus wrought with zeal discreet,
Has saved that town from rum complete;
Proving that woman's moral force
Like man's, is held, as last resource,
      By sword or hatchet.

And following up that dauntless raid,
The nation welcomes her crusade;
All o'er the land, pure women charmed,
Are eager forming, each one armed
      With glittering hatchets.

Talk of "defenders of the nation!"
Woman's slight arm sends consternation
'Mong its worst foes, on social fields,
Worse than the "Mauser," when she wields

The "smashing" hatchet.

Mohammed sought by arts refined,
To raise his standard o'er mankind;
But found success for aye denied,
Until at length he boldly tried
             The battle-hatchet.

When soon his power imperial, shone
O'er countless tribes, in widening zone;
And wine was banished from the board
Of Moslem millions, by the sword
             And victor's hatchet.

And men, once slaves, their freedom gained
By force, and power at length attained;
So, cultured brains and force combined,
Shall mark the sphere of womankind
             And surely reach it.

In valor, more Joan d'Arc's are needed,
Woman's high social power's conceded,
But she herself, must blaze the path
To public morals, by her own worth
             And "Little Hatchet."

jointists: habitués of disreputable places of entertainment. **"Mauser":** a Mauser rifle, named for its inventor and adopted by the German military in 1871 and perfected in 1884. **Mohammed:** an Arab prophet (A.D. 570–632) and the founder of Islam. **Joan d'Arc:** the French peasant girl (c. 1412–1431) who raised the English siege of Orleans and drove the English army out of France.

62. John Morrissey

Born in County Tipperary, Ireland, in 1831, John Morrissey emigrated with his parents to Troy, New York, at the age of three. He spent many of his early years as a "runner" hired to allure newly arrived immigrants to his employer's boarding house in New York City. Before he was eighteen he had compiled a rap sheet for burglary, assault, and battery. His pugilistic talents were soon enlisted by the local Tammany Hall politicians, who made him the head of the Dead Rabbits, their dependable gang of toughs.

Morrissey eventually parlayed his talent into a professional boxing career. In his first professional fight, his opponent, George Thompson, deliberately lost on a foul in the eleventh round, apparently because he feared being killed by Morrissey's armed backers. In his next fight, in 1853, the Irishman was being bested by Yankee Sullivan — an Irishman whose real name was James Ambrose — when Morrissey's supporters began to riot and threaten his opponent. Sullivan left the ring to fight some of the brawlers and was disqualified for not returning to the ring when the next round began. Five years later Morrissey won the American bareknuckle heavyweight championship in a bout with John Heenan, who broke his hand on a ring post early in the bout and conceded in the eleventh round. Morrissey retired undefeated at the age of forty.

The former boxer — who was illiterate until his twenty-first birthday — subsequently made a name for himself as a gambling impresario and a politician. He eventually owned fifteen gambling parlors, and in 1864 he built the first thoroughbred racetrack at Saratoga, New York. Two years later he was elected to the first of two terms in Congress. For helping uncover the corruption of Boss Tweed, the leader of Tammany Hall, Morrissey came under attack from the political machine that had once used him. He twice won election to the New York senate by defeating the Tammany candidates.

The following song — "Morrissey and the Russian Sailor" — relates an imaginary incident, while "John Morrissey My Jo, John" is an earnest prayer by its author that Morrissey "not be corrupted by his associations in Congress." (The latter work is narrated with an Irish accent.)

Morrissey and the Russian Sailor

author unknown

Come all you sons of Erin, attention now I crave,
While I relate the praises of an Irish hero brave,
Concerning a great fight, me boys, all on the other day,
Between a Russian sailor and bold Jack Morrissey.

It was in Terra del Fuego [*sic*], in South America,
The Russian challenged Morrissey and unto him did say,
"I hear you are a fighting man, and wear a belt I see.
What do you say, will you consent to have a round with me?"

Then up spoke bold Jack Morrissey, with a heart so stout and true,
Saying, "I am a gallant Irishman that never was subdued.
Oh, I can whale a Yankee, a Saxon bull or bear,
And in honor of old Paddy's land I'll still those laurels wear."

These words enraged the Russian upon that foreign land,
To think that he would be put down by an Irishman.
He says, "You are too light for me. On that make no mistake.
I would have you to resign the belt, or else your life I'll take."

To fight upon the tenth of June these heroes did agree,
And thousands came from every part the battle for to see.
The English and the Russians, their hearts were filled with glee;
They swore the Russian sailor boy would kill bold Morrissey.

They both stripped off, stepped in the ring, most glorious to be seen,
And Morrissey put on the belt bound round with shamrocks green.
Full twenty thousand dollars, as you may plainly see,
That was to be the champion's prize that gained the victory.

They both shook hands, walked round the ring, commencing then to
      fight.
It filled each Irish heart with joy for to behold the sight.
The Russian he floored Morrissey up to the eleventh round,
With English, Russian, and Saxon cheers the valley did resound.

A minute and a half our hero lay before he could rise.
The word went all around the field: "He's dead," were all their cries.
But Mossissey raised manfully, and raising from the ground,
From that until the twentieth the Russian he put down.

Up to the thirty-seventh round 'twas fall and fall about,
Which made the burly sailor to keep a sharp lookout.
The Russian called his second and asked for a glass of wine.
Our Irish hero smiled and said, "The battle will be mine."

The thirty-eighth decided all. The Russian felt the smart
When Morrissey, with a fearful blow, he struck him o'er the heart.
A doctor he was called on to open up a vein.

He said it was quite useless, he would never fight again.

Our hero conquered Thompson, the Yankee Clipper too;
The Benicia boy and Shepherd he nobly did subdue.
So let us fill a flowing bowl and drink a health galore
To brave Jack Morrissey and Paddies evermore.

Erin: a literary name for Ireland. **Terra del Fuego** [*sic*]: Tierra del Fuego, a group of islands at the southern tip of South America. **Paddy's land:** Ireland. Paddy is a slang term (often disparaging) for an Irishman. **Thompson:** George Thompson, whom Morrissey fought for the championship of California. **Yankee Clipper:** probably Yankee Sullivan. **Benicia boy:** John Heenan (1835–1873), so named because he had done construction work for the Pacific Mail Steamship Company in Benicia, California, where he threw a thirty-two-pound sledge for twelve hours a day.

John Morrissey My Jo, John

an earnest cry and prayer that he may not be corrupted
by his associations in Congress

by Charles Graham Halpine (1829–1866)

John Morrissey my jo, John,
    When first I kenned ye weel,
Your airms were like twa iron flails,
    Your hands like slugs o' steel;
But now ye've gaithered self, John,
    An' to Congress ye maun go,
Where they fight less fairly than yourself,
    John Morrissey my jo.

John Morrissey my jo, John,
    Wi' braid and monly breast,
Ye have faced fu' mony a mon, John,
    To try which more was best;
There were tough knocks fairly dealt, John,
    But to Congress now ye go,
Where they gouge an' strike below the belt,
    John Morrissey my jo.

John Morrissey my jo, John,
    We have played an' drunk thegither,
An' fu' mony a "tiger" fight, John,
    We have had wi' one anither;

Oh, at cheatin' still ye mocked, John,
    But to Congress now ye go,
Where the dice are cogged and the cards are stocked,
    John Morrissey my jo.

John Morrissey my jo, John,
    Wi' grief our hearts are stirred,
For still to friend an' foe, John,
    Your bond was aye your word;
But I fear ye'll learn to lie, John,
    When to Congress now ye go,
For twad tak a saint to resist the taint,
    John Morrissey my jo.

John Morrissey my jo, John,
    On your good pluck ye relied,
An' against no pitted foe, John,
    The "hocussing game" ye tried;
But ye'll find it "hocus" all, John,
    When to Congress now ye go,
A' we fear frae your high stand ye'll fall,
    John Morrissey my jo.

John Morrissey my jo, John,
    These politicians deal
From a far-box false-bottomed
    Wi' springs o' patent "steal."
Will your scruples never melt, John
    When to Congress now ye go?
Can ye deal the same square game ye dealt,
    John Morrissey my jo.

John Morrissey my jo, John,
    It never was kenned your plan
To kick a fallen foe, John,
    Or spurn a helpless man;
But you'll find a different rule, John,
    When to Congress now ye go,
For they kick the South, having gagged its mouth,
    John Morrissey my jo.

John Morrissey my jo, John,
    My heart in terror beats,

> For you've got into unco' company—
> A gang o' patent cheats.
> Ye have fought an' gambled fair, John,
> But to Congress now ye go,
> An' I fear they may corrupt you there,
> John Morrissey my jo.

63. John L. Sullivan

The Boston-born Sullivan, the champion pugilist of the world, inherited his size from his 190-pound mother and his pugnacity from his father, a short-tempered immigrant from Tralee, Ireland. The young Sullivan became a plumber's apprentice but was dismissed when he broke his employer's nose during an argument. The youngster went on to knock out his first opponent in the ring at age nineteen, boasting afterwards that "I can lick any sonofabitch alive!"

By the mid 1880s Sullivan was approaching the zenith of his popularity. In 1882 he was matched with Paddy Ryan in the world champion bareknuckle contest in Gulfport, Mississippi. The bout ended in the ninth round when Sullivan knocked out Ryan, the previous champion. "When Sullivan struck me," said Paddy, "I thought that a telegraph pole had been shoved against me endways." Nursing a particular animus for "foreign fighters," Sullivan gave the Englishman Charlie Mitchell such a trouncing the next year that the police stopped the fight to save the limey's life.

On the eve of Sullivan's departure for Europe four years later, his fans gave him a $10,000 gold belt adorned with his name in diamonds. After a three-hour grudge match with Mitchell in France, the two pugilists were arrested, but Sullivan fled the country. While in Great Britain, the "Knocker-out" met the Prince of Wales and broke all rules of protocol with his informality. "I'm proud to meet you," he said to the royal. "If you ever come to Boston he sure to look me up; I'll see that you're treated right." In Dublin, meanwhile, Sullivan was greeted by two brass bands playing "See, the Conquering Hero Comes" and after a week left with four jugs of whiskey and seventeen shillelaghs.

In 1889 Sullivan went seventy-five rounds with Jake Kilrain in the last bareknuckle championship bout in America. The battle, which lasted just over two hours in heat that topped 100 degrees, pitted an overweight Sullivan against the challenger Kilrain. Although the latter boxer hoped simply to wear down his opponent by delaying tactics, "Trip-Hammer Jack" Sullivan took the offensive and began laying into Kilrain with staggering blows. Kilrain's seconds finally threw in the towel. Years later the poet Vachel Lindsay remembered witnessing the event, referring to it in his poem "John L. Sullivan, the Strong Boy of Boston."

By 1892 "His Fistic Highness" had earned just over $1 million and had knocked down an estimated 200 opponents. His drinking and riotous lifestyle, however, had brought him to the verge of bankruptcy. To pay off his debts, he was forced to sell his diamond belt and to accept a challenge from "Gentleman Jim" Corbett, eight years his junior. Knocked out in the twenty-first round of the only bout he ever lost, "the Boston Hercules" rose to his feet to deliver his valedictory address. "I fought once too often," he said through a broken nose. "But I am glad that it was an American who licked me and that the championship stays in this country."

From **John L. Sullivan, The Strong Boy of Boston**
by Vachel Lindsay

> When I was nine years old, in 1889,
> I sent my love a lacy Valentine.
> Suffering boys were dressed like Fauntleroys,
> While Judge and Puck in giant humor vied.
> The Gibson Girl came shining like a bride
> To spoil the cult of Tennyson's Elaine.
> Louisa Alcott was my gentle guide. . . .
> Then . . .
> I heard a battle trumpet sound
> Nigh New Orleans
> Upon an emerald plain
> John L. Sullivan
> The strong boy
> Of Boston
> Fought seventy-five red rounds with Jake Kilrain.

. . . .

Fauntleroys: boys dressed in black velvet and a lace collar, a style in imitation of Cedric Errol, the seven-year-old child in "Little Lord Fauntleroy," a story by Francis Burnett (1894–1927). *Judge:* a humorous weekly founded in 1881 by a group of writers and artists who had resigned from *Puck*. **Puck:** a humorous weekly founded as a German-language publication in 1869 but published in an English edition beginning in 1877. **Gibson Girl:** between about 1890 and 1910 the prototype of the ideal woman (from a sketch by illustrator Charles Gibson). **Tennyson's Elaine:** a lady in Tennyson's *Idylls of the King* whose love of Lancelot is so great that she dies of it. **Louisa Alcott:** a nineteenth-century New England author, best known for her semi-autobiographical *Little Women* and *Little Men*.

John L. Sullivan

author unknown

Oh, J. Sullivan! Oh, J. Sullivan!
Oh, John Lycurgus Sullivan, all hail!!
Thou Bottomless infinitude! Thou god! Thou you!
Thou Zeus with all-compelling hand!
Thou glory of the mighty Occident! Thou Heaven-born!
Thou Athens-bred! Thou light of the Acropolis!
    Thou son of a gambolier!
59 inches art thou around thy ribs; twice twain knuckles
    hast thou; and again twice twain.
Thou scatterest men's teeth like antelopes at play.
Thou straightenest thine arm, and systems rocks, and eye-balls
    change their hue.
Oh, thou grim granulator! Thou soul-remover! Thou
    lightsome, coy excoriator!
Thou cooing dove! Thou droll, droll John!
Thou buster!
Oh, you! Oh, me too! Oh, me some more!
Oh, thunder!

Lycurgus: Sullivan's middle name was actually Lawrence. Lycurgus was a Spartan lawgiver of the ninth century B.C. **Zeus:** the supreme deity of the ancient Greeks. **Acropolis:** the citadel of Athens, Greece, and the site of the Parthenon, the temple to the goddess Athena. **gambolier:** one who frolics or skips about, as in dancing or playing.

The Famous Knocker-out

author unknown

You valiant Sons of Erin's Isle,
    And sweet Columbia too,
Come, gather 'round, and listen while
    I chant a stave for you.
Oh! Fill your glass up, every man,
    With Irish whiskey, stout;
And drink to John L. Sullivan,
    The famous "Knocker-out."

Chorus
Oh! The chorus swell for bold John L.,
    We'll fling it to the breeze,

> Yes, shout it loud, so England's crowd
> > Shall hear it o'er the seas:
> The great and small, he's drowned them all
> > In many a clever bout;
> Hurrah for John L. Sullivan,
> > The famous "Knocker-out."
>
> They sent men here from England's shore,
> > The best they could produce,
> The great John L. to try and floor,
> > But 'twasn't any use.
> Try how they would, they never could
> > Give Sullivan the rout,
> For like a giant tree he stood,
> > This famous "Knocker-out" . . . .

Erin: a literary name for Ireland. **Columbia:** the United States of America, usually personified as a female figure.

John L. Sullivan Enters Heaven

(after Vachel Lindsay's "Gen. William Booth Enters into Heaven")
by Robert Frost (1874–1963)

Sullivan arrived at the very lowest Heaven
Which is sometimes mistaken for the very highest Hell,
Where barkeeps, pugilists, jockeys, and gamblers
And the women corresponding (if there are any) dwell.
> They done queer things, but they done 'em on the level,
> And thus they escape the jurisdiction of the Devil.

Sullivan felt, and he couldn't find his ticket.
He though for a moment he would have to go to Hell.
But the gatekeeper told him, "You don't need a ticket:
Everybody needs you: Your name's John L.
> There's a lot of fighting characters been setting up waiting
> To see if you were up to your mundane rating."

Sullivan asked, "They've been setting up to see me?"
And the gatekeeper answered, "They have like Hell!
They've been setting up to try you, and see if they can lick you,
And settle who's who in the Fields of Asphodel.
> So you may as well be ready to take them all on —

Hercules and Pollux and the whole doggone

"Fraternity of sluggers, I mean the first-raters
(We send the second-raters to entertain Hell).
I seen Herc's hands all wound with lead and leather
Till they looked like the balls on a great dumb-bell.
    He's mad because the deeds you matched his with
    Were sound printed facts, while his were just myth."

Sullivan said "I guess I'm in for trouble."
He cracked the gate a little and then said "Hell!
I hope I ain't expected to take all them together.
If I take them in succession I'll be doing damn well.
    I wish I'd staid in Boston or Chelsea, and would of
    If I'd had the least encouragement to think I could of."

The gatekeeper said "You don't need to worry;
The way to do's to rush them and give them sudden Hell.
They've been so purged of earthliness they don't weight nothing
While you weigh something, and will for a spell.
    They's nothing to sustain them but their jealousy of you,
    While you still feel the good of Boston beans, you do."

Sullivan burst into heaven roaring.
The devils beyond the board fences of Hell
Put the whites of their eyes to crannies and knotholes
To see who was driving the angels pell-mell.
    They said 'twas the greatest punch of all times.
    Ring the bells of Heaven! Sound the gladsome chimes!

Asphodels: Mediterranean lilies which the Greeks associated with Hades and the Elysian Fields (the abodes of the dead in the afterlife). **Hercules:** a hero of classical myth who possessed great strength and was renowned for his exceptional feats. **Pollux:** in Greek mythology a champion boxer and the brother of Castor.

64. Henry W. Grady

Of Irish ancestry through his father (a Confederate soldier killed at Petersburg in 1864), Henry Grady experienced mixed results during his first forays into journalism. While attending the University of Virginia after the war, he penned gossipy news items for the *Atlanta Constitution* under a nom de plume. Later, when, as editor of a newspaper in Rome, Georgia, he was forbidden by his publisher to attack local political corruption, he purchased the two other newspapers in town and combined them into a bully pulpit. Although this venture was a financial failure, he and two associates tried again with a publication of their own, the equally short-lived *Atlanta Herald*. After a stint with the *New York Herald* and with the help of a $20,000 personal loan, Grady bought a 25-percent interest in the *Atlanta Constitution*.

As managing editor, Grady helped make the *Constitution* the most popular newspaper in the region and the vehicle for promoting his vision of the postbellum South. He urged Southerners to develop local resources, diversify their crops, and promote manufacturing. He realized, however, that the economic resurgence of the former Confederacy would be impossible without the help of Northern investors. In turn, financial backing would not be forthcoming until the South had achieved social stability by resolving the race issue. In this regard Grady believed that white Southerners would acquiesce to the political rights granted African Americans after the war in return for an acknowledgment of white supremacy and the maintenance of segregation.

Grady preached his gospel not only on the editorial page but also in a series of speeches throughout the country. Before addressing the New England Society of New York in 1886, he betrayed his trepidation at speaking where no Southerner had ever appeared before: "I have thought of a thousand things to say, five hundred of which if I say they will murder me when I get back home, and the other five hundred of which will get me murdered at the banquet." In his actual address he lauded Lincoln as "the typical American" and jokingly pointed out that his fellow speaker, William T. Sherman, was "considered an able man in our parts, though some people think he is a kind of careless man about fire." The central message of the address, however, was that Southerners had accepted the results of the Civil War, bore no animosity toward the North, and were interested in economic development and racial and national harmony.

Henry W. Grady

by James Whitcomb Riley (1849–1916)

True-hearted friend of all true friendliness!—

Brother of all true brotherhoods!—Thy hand
     And its late pressure now we understand
Most fully, as it falls thus gestureless
And Silence lulls thee into sweet excess
     Of sleep. Sleep thou content!—Thy loved Southland
     Is swept with tears, as rain in sunshine; and
Through all the frozen North our eyes confess
     Like sorrow—seeing still the princely sign
Set on they lifted brow, and the rapt light
     Of the dark, tender, melancholy eyes—
     Thrilled with the music of those lips of thine,
And yet the fire thereof that lights the night
     With the white splendor of thy prophecies.

65. John Boyle O'Reilly

Born near Drogheda, Ireland, in 1844, John Boyle O'Reilly became active in the Fenian movement to overthrow British rule in Ireland even while he was a member of a British regiment. When his efforts to recruit other Irish soldiers to the cause were uncovered, he was court-martialed and found guilty of conspiracy and failure to inform the authorities of "an intended mutiny." Although he was sentenced to death, that penalty was commuted to life imprisonment and finally to twenty years of penal servitude. In 1869, however, O'Reilly escaped from imprisonment in Western Australia. He first took passage on an American whaling ship and at the Cape of Good Hope boarded another American ship bound for Liverpool. There he shipped aboard the *Bombay* as "third mate" and headed for Philadelphia.

After moving to Boston, O'Reilly began a literary career that made him one of the most popular writers and commentators on the Irish-American scene. As editor of the *Pilot*, the most influential "Irish paper" in America, he became a spokesman for racial and religious tolerance, American patriotism, Irish nationalism, and the Jeffersonian ideals of the Democratic Party. Despite his support for the rights of Irish-American citizens, O'Reilly condemned sectarianism. After the 1871 Orange Riots between Catholic and Protestant Irish in New York City, for instance, he thundered on the editorial page of the *Pilot*: One way to end this discord is "when America, tired out and indignant with her squabbling populations, puts her foot down with a will and tells them all — Germans, French, Irish, Orange — 'You have had enough now. There is only ONE flag to be raised in this country and that flag is the Stars and Stripes.'" Even in the face of a growing xenophobic nativist movement, he attacked efforts to establish an "Irish" political party to counter anti-immigrant measures.

The esteem in which this naturalized American was held by his contemporaries is evident in the frequency with which he was called upon to provide the appropriate patriotic sentiment on various civic occasions. Before a gathering of the Grand Army of the Republic in 1886, for example, he delivered a Memorial Day oration entitled "The Common Citizen Soldier," usually regarded as his best speech. Two years later he read his poem "Crispus Attucks" at the dedication of the Boston Massacre Monument on the Boston Common, and in 1889 he read a poem at the dedication of the Pilgrim Monument at Plymouth, Massachusetts. He also wrote "Liberty Lighting the World" for the unveiling of the Statue of Liberty.

Following his death in 1890, O'Reilly was universally praised for his ability to foster cultural understanding. One eulogist emphasized his ability to abolish the old distinction between English American and Irish American: "[T]his Roman Catholic, on New England soil, in daily association with the sons of Puritans, — the sons of men who hated the Papacy as the instrument of Satan, and whose descendants have not entirely got beyond the narrowness of their forefathers, — could yet describe in fitting terms, and show the appreciation of his mind and soul for, the achievements of the founders of New England."

The Dead That Never Die

John Boyle O'Reilly
Born June 28, 1844. Died August 10, 1890.

by Joseph Smith (1853–1929)

Why should a soul aflame with song
    Linger among the shadowed silences of Time
And creep with palsied age along
    The dull, dumb trails of earth, when ways sublime
And star-lit paths beyond the sun,
    Call it to come to wear the robe and crown
That song and suffering have won
    When the brave singer his burden had laid down.

To die, to lay our burdens down
    At the full measure of reputation's tide,
When the mind's harvest is full grown,
    E'er yet the founts of love and labor shall have dried,

Is but to pass from mortal toil
     Into immortal rest and youth eternal,
Where sin and stain no more assoil,
     To dwell mid endless spring in fields supernal.

When in the zenith of our day,
     When earth's acclaim is sweetest in our ears,
Each added hour is but delay
     That leads to waning powers and sterile year.
Wisely the ancient sage hath said
     Those whom the Gods on high love all die young
And to Elysian fields are led
     By nymphs rejoicing when their song is sung.

Why grieve when Heav'n reclaims its own
     And bids the singer, touched with celestial fire,
To stand beside the glitt'ring throng
     Among his songful peers of th' immortal choir.
While yet his song was in the heart
     And stirring the souls of all his mortal ken
Death whispered it is time to part
     From kin and kind and all the things of men.

And so he died down by the sea
     Whose murm'rous music chanted in his soul
Like echoes from antiquity,
     Like songs of bards that down dead cent'ries roll.
Death came gently as the breeze
     That whispers softly on a summer eve
Out of the placid summer seas, —
     As tender as the sighing wood-guests grieve.

We may not cavil with the ordered plan
     Of Him, who even marks the sparrow's fall;
We only know the singer and the man
     Who, by the sea, responding to Death's call,
Went forth to life and love that never end,
     To us was brother and to all men friend.

* * * * * * * * *

To-day we come as pilgrims to a shrine
     To call a kindly spirit back from space,
To fill the cask of death with Life's red wine,

And look once more into a vanished face.
To say to death and dust and swift decay
    We have in memory an alchemy
That is more potent than your allies gray,
    That tells all earth O'Reilly will not die.

In that green field of memory he lives,
    That field that no defection ever mars,
Where Death's dread distance but enchantment gives
    To those we love who've journeyed to the stars.
We see him still with his brave head erect,
    With friendly smile, with keen and kindly eye,
With the great heart and soul of the elect—
    And seeing say O'Reilly will not die.

But yesterday he sang his songs for us;
    We saw him standing in the crowded ways,
His splendid face lit up with kindliness,
    Urging the worker onward with his praise.
The fires of hell through which his soul once flamed
    Destroyed the dross but left the metal pure—
A soul recast, heroically framed—
    A man whose work and worth shall long endure.

In youth he felt the alien tyrant's scourge,
    His ripening manhood bore the convict's chain;
And yet, with soul unspoiled he sought to purge
    The world of wrong and hate and greed and gain.
To him the beaten and oppressed were kin;
    A brother in the sweating slave he saw,
A soul immortal found he 'neath each skin;
    He went to Christ not custom for the law.

The fabled land he charted with his pen
    To make a home for brotherhood and youth.
He cradled in a heart that loved all men,
    And fashioned in a brain that loved all truth.
He gave Bohemia, sunlit, to his age,—
    A vale of faerie built on Fancy's strand,—
Where praise and honor were the worker's wage
    And weary hearts preferred to any land.

What though he sleep 'neath Holyhood's green sod

In that cool bed where pain forever ends,
What though he wait the trumpet call of God,
He lives immortal in the hearts of friends,
The friends that prize the winged words he penned,
The friends that praise the beauty of his thought;
Yea! He will live to all that world a friend
Which loves the gospel of good will he taught.

Not by their hoardings do we measure men
When death has closed the chapter of their lives;
Not for their place and power we treasure them,
But for the garnered good for which each strives—
The kindly act that gives the crushed relief,
The helpful arm that saves stumbling friend,
The silent pressure of the hand in grief,
The loyal faith, unwav'ring to the end.

Time marches on, the metered cent'ries pass,
The seasons wax and wane, the day's career
Is but a brief, swift shadow in the glass,
All things material die and disappear.
Yet may great minds write on the page of Time
Some word and thought to baffle death and fate,
To light the paths that lead to ways sublime,
For souls that in the womb of Time still wait.

The kingdoms flourish for a day and fade;
The conq'ror's laurels shrivel and decay,
The spoils of commerce in the balance weighed
Seem rust and dross beside the poet's bay.
Immortal only are the things ignored
By pride and place and monarchy and mart.
His fame's secure who writes the kindly word
That's graved upon some fellow mortal's heart.

Elysian fields: in Greek mythology a land of bliss and contentment on the banks of the river Oceanus (in the west), where the good and the heroic lived after death. **he died down by the sea:** O'Reilly died at his home in Hull, Massachusetts, at the tip of the Nantasket Beach peninsula across the bay from Boston. **pilgrims to a shrine:** This poem was read at the dedication of a memorial to O'Reilly on the grounds of his home in Hull, Massachusetts, in 1917; his former home is now the town library. **Bohemia:** a state of mind that glories in freedom and artistic expression. **faerie:** the imaginary land of the fairies. **Holyhood's green sod:** O'Reilly is buried in Holyhood Cemetery in Brookline, Massachusetts.

At the Poet's Shrine

by Joseph I. C. Clarke (1846–1925)

Out of the luminous ether where your soul
Abides alway,
God send it that your shining eyes look down
On us to-day—
Brave-hearted poet, buoyant prince of song,
Whose numbers the long years across
Still sound as true, as clear and strong
As when they leaped forth in a flood
To glorify the deeds and men long gone.
Your flaming phrase lives on.
You held the live thrill of our Irish blood,
The pulse that beats in rhythm with a world
Of joy or pain;
That stirs to high resolve and deep disdain
Of small conformities and barren gain,
But ever throbs with sure intent
To prop the right and scarify the wrong.
O, noble soul, whose ways were ever bent
Along the heights to range, and flaunt
A flag of freedom never to be furled!

How flashed your eyes with rapture as you saw
Draw near the reign of universal law,
With shoulder-touch, with brother glance, and smile
To make the millions one the earth round.
Yet in what breast rose faster righteous wrath
When knave or autocrat was found
In arms athwart the people's path?
You would be with us in our war to-day—
Soldier as well as singer crowned with flowers—
With sword and word a freeman's part to play
In headlong charge or foot to foot advance
For all men's liberty as well as ours.

You rose to right the wrongs of Inisfail,
Nor stayed to count the cost.
You gloried in her broken blades and spears
Clutched by the faithful in the battles lost,
To be rehammered for a new assault
In that fierce strife that knows no halt,

Which Erin wages for her land and life.
You felt the biting of the prison chain,
The pangs that noble minds assail
In far off dungeons with a deadly sting;
Yet never once took counsel of your fears.
Who else could sing your Exile of the Gael,
Whose clamorous stanzas ring and ring
With echoes of a thousand fighting years?

Now, in this mighty land where first you knew
How freemen lived and ruled, where order grew,
And where for you life's dreams came true,
We meet about the modest shrine that held
Your living hopes, and where you shaped new dreams,
Holding the hand of that one woman dear,
Your little girls all gathered at your knee,
With teeming Boston city crooning near,
And Ireland calling softly oversea.

Here oft beneath the glimmer of the moon,
In whose pale gold and silver on the wave,
Hard fact and fine imaginings would blend,
You traveled back o'er many a vivid page,
Now writ in genius mood, now traced
In tears and blood upon the age.
The boy who frolicked by the storied Boyne
Looked wondering at the care-browed man
Who smiled upon him, both hearts still attune.
Thro' Austral forest wilds again you fled
To freedom, stumbling thro' the brake,
And sprang to slay th' uncoiling Dukite snake.

With straining eyes you watched o'er waters for
The coming of the ship that bore your fate,
And doubted was it ship's light or a star
That rose at midnight o'er the ocean verge,
Till morning burning into fiery noon
Had placed in yours a horny hand—
The sun-browned skipper's from the Yankee land.
Ecstatic hour, relived here o'er and o'er,
The prison gloom far back, the ocean deeps before
On Australasian seas you spread your sail
And sighted first the spouting Amber Whale,

Wherein you buried your harpoon.
Thro' Java's straits your good ship bore
Tossing the sunlit spray.
Once more you boated full of joy and youth
With Golu [*sic*] off the land of the Malay.

Here oft you felt the fairy breezes blow
From dim Romance lands of the long ago,
Or penned defiant in a manful strain
A gospel of the land of artist brain,
Bohemia.
But ever broader grew your vision's sweep,
The singer rising to the seer,
And ever in the world-heart warm and deep
You sounded with the plummet of the mind,
Voicing America's great civic will,
Her guarded freedom in the State,
And, fervent yearning, dreamed mankind
Uplifted, marching back thro' Eden's gate.

So wrought our poet here, but in the town
Made daily commerce in the hives of men,
A brave, sweet spirit in the human coil,
Preaching in prose with voice and pen,
And putting in his lightest word the pure
Convictions of his life:
Homing at eve, glad-hearted, fain,
As would the humblest son of toil.

Then in full tide and splendor of his verse,
In all vigor of his deed and thought,
His form lay cold one summer morning here—
The blighted August of a mournful year.
All that was life and manhood was as naught.
The lips were silent and the forehead wan,
America and Ireland sorrowed at his bier;
Vainly did lovers, scholars, bards rehearse
The story of his brilliant lays, his human love:
The bolt had fallen, and the light had gone.

Piteous the picture of the souls bereaved,
But here his glory lingers on,
And we who then in dusking twilight grieved,

Turn to the radiance that ever shone
Around him, and still lives for all in song
That will outlast the cycles of decay.
The high ideals are eternal guides
To immortality beyond the reach
Of rising and of falling tides;
And they were yours, O'Reilly, man and boy,
To suffer and to bear a heart of cheer;
To sing brave songs that mirrored truth and joy,
With love and love of beauty at their core,
These marked the glory of his day.
For him forever let but joy bells fling
To each and air their chimes,
As in celestial rhymes.
The people's poet is the future's king.

Inisfail: a Gaelic word meaning "Isle of Destiny," one of many ancient names for Ireland. **Erin:** a literary name for Ireland. **Exile of the Gael:** the title of a poem by O'Reilly. **We meet about the modest shrine:** This poem was read at the dedication of a memorial to O'Reilly on the grounds of his home in Hull, Massachusetts, in 1917; his former home is now the town library. **one woman dear:** Mary Murphy, whom O'Reilly married on August 15, 1872. She was the daughter of John and Jane (Smiley) Murphy, residents of Charlestown, Massachusetts, and natives, respectively, of counties Fermanagh and Donegal, Ireland. **your little girls:** the O'Reillys' four daughters (Molly, Eliza, Agnes, and Blanid, born between 1873 and 1880). **Boyne:** a river in eastern Ireland, on whose northern bank is located the town of Drogheda, O'Reilly's birthplace. **Austral forest wilds:** the forbidding terrain of western Australia, where O'Reilly was imprisoned in a British penal colony. **Dukite snake:** a red snake found in the wilds of Australia and the subject of O'Reilly's poem "The Dukite Snake." **sun-browned skipper:** David Gifford, the captain of the American whaling ship that rescued O'Reilly from Australia in 1869. Four years later O'Reilly dedicated his first book — *Songs of the Southern Seas* — to Gifford, but news of the dedication arrived two hours after the captain's death. **Amber Whale:** a reference to an incident that occurred while O'Reilly was still aboard Gifford's ship, when the Irishman almost drowned during the pursuit of a whale. O'Reilly later wrote the poem "The Amber Whale" about the episode. **Java:** the main island of Indonesia. **Golu [*sic*]:** Golo, one of the Lubang Islands off the coast of the Philippines on the South China Sea. **Malay:** an extensive group of islands in the Indian and Pacific oceans. **Bohemia:** a state of mind that glories in freedom and artistic expression. **His form lay cold one summer morning here:** O'Reilly died on August 10, 1890, at his home in Hull, Massachusetts.

John Boyle O'Reilly
by Denis A. McCarthy (1870–1931)

"Great men grow greater by the lapse of time,"—
So sang O'Reilly once in deathless rhyme;
And so, to-day, with eyes and hearts that brim,
May we most truly sing the same of him.

Great men grow greater. Men of minor mold,
Assessed by time, high place must fail to hold;
But ever stronger, ever still more sure,
The claim of real greatness rests secure.

Great men grow greater. Lesser men may tower
Above their generation for an hour,
But whatsoe'er their merit in its prime,
It fails to stand the austere test of time.

Great men grow greater. Lesser men decline,
More feebly still their little lanterns shine;
While all the brighter glows the lambent flame
That shows, down times' defiles, the great one's name.

To-day we gather, honor due to give
To one whose name seems destined still to live
When long forgot shall be the names and worth
Of those who walked with him the ways of earth.

To-day we pause a little in the round
Of common things, with sympathy profound,
To pay a tribute to the matchless mind
Which oped its treasures to enrich mankind.

But little need has he of carven stone.
Or bronze memorial—he has found a throne,
A veritable shrine in every heart
That loves the beauty of the poet's art.

And he is numbered with the happy dead
Whose deeds to immortality are wed,
Whose fate himself expressed in deathless rhyme,
Whose fame "grows greater by the lapse of time."

"Great men grow greater by the lapse of time": a line from O'Reilly's poem "The Test of a Nation." **To-day we gather:** This poem was read at the dedication of a memorial to O'Reilly on the grounds of his home in Hull, Massachusetts, in 1917; his former home is now the town library.

The Poet

To John Boyle O'Reilly

by Joseph I. C. Clarke (1846–1925)

Strong voice for Freedom, love-illumined soul;
   Sharp sword of Truth, held firm in hand and bare;
Great hope-thrilled singer, who beyond earth's dole
   Heard songs of joy which will for us endure,
     Eternal joy be thine!
Pow'r was about thee; light was in thy face,
   And in thine eyes far, mystic visions shone,
Where kin and alien clasped in world-embrace,
   And Right's battalions marched in thunder on,
     Making thy song divine.

First sang to thee o'er Ireland's uplands green,
   The skylark's melody as morn grew bright,
Filling thy soul with love and rapture keen.
   In sunrise glory and of lofty flight
     Thy song to thee was born.
But ever round thee rose deep tones of pain
   From Ireland's heart wrung, and thy dark eyes filled
As wailed the women o'er their famine-slain,
   As men were driven from the fields they tilled,
     As children wept forlorn.

Then fierce and passionate thy song began—
   A cry for vengeance on the tyrant's horde.
The stripling chanted, but the full-grown man
   Laid singing by and lifted up the sword,
     To smite if so to save.
Soldier and poet, God so shaped thy ways,
   That though death faced thee amid prison chains
And hate and torment dogged thee weary days,
   Fair Freedom found thee, and thy song remains
     A clarion to the brave.

Thy darkest dungeon thou hast made to shine;
   Thy sufferings are coined in songs of gold;
The whole world's longing is transformed to thine,
   Lamp of the true and Leader of the bold,
     Singer of days to be.
Uplifted prophet, lightnings of the air

About thee played and storm clouds at thy feet,
Rolled chasing amid moans of man's despair,
While thy brave harp did songs of hope repeat,
And dawning days of glee.

For 'mid the voiceful volume of thy song—
The loud, high chords that rang from land to land—
Sweet undertones of Love were swept along,
As to the wave replies the singing sand
In silver-whispered sound.
Yea, these our hearts heard as when angels sing.
Thine eagle flight we watched and heard the dove,
And ev'ry height scaled by thy daring wing
Still brought us closer to thy human love.
Beloved outleaps renowned.

Out of thy far green island comes a sigh,
Out of our Free America a moan,
For we are human, and to die's to die.
And Fame doth not for Death's dull blow atone,
Deathless albeit thy rhyme;
But not for us the shadow or the tear;
Thy living spirit like a breath of flame,
Radiant and beautiful doth still appear,
A light to glory in, a joy to name,
While Death is slain by Time.

Sing to us, bard and brother, from the skies,
Hurl against Wrong the terror of thy lance,
So we may hearken when the million cries,
And what thou carried'st forward we'll advance,
To fight while there be need
The rusted tyrannies that die so hard,
The lawless might that rules by dint of fear,
The Greed that measures travail by the yard,
The cynic who meets virtue with a sneer,
The thought that mocks high deed.

And here where Liberty enthroned doth keep
Thy name and fame a firstling of her heart,
Our eyes thy spirit follow in its sweep
To fair, sad Ireland, where she stands apart
Praying a brighter day.
O Mother Nature take thy perfect son,

Whose life a psalm was, and whose lips thine pressed,
And learned thy secrets; now the day is done
Lay him in peace upon they mighty breast,
His white brow twined with bay.

To John Boyle O'Reilly

by James Berry Bensell (1856–1886)

As when a man along piano keys
Trails a slow hand, and then with tough grown bold
Strikes pealing chords, by some great master old
Woven into a gem of melodies,
All full of summer and the shout of seas,—
So do thy rhythmic songs my soul enfold.

First some sweet love-note, full as it can hold
Of daintiness, comes like the hum of bees;
Then, rising grandly, thou dost sound a chord
That rings and clamors in the heart of hearts,
And dying as receding waves, departs
Leaving us richer by a lusty hoard
Of noble thoughts.

O poet! would that we
Might strike one note like thine,—but just for thee!

John Boyle O'Reilly

by Paul Laurence Dunbar (1872–1906)

Of noble minds and noble hearts
Old Ireland has goodly store;
But thou wert still the noblest son
That e'er the Isle of Erin bore.
A generous race, and strong to dare,
With hearts as true as purest gold,
With hands to soothe as well as strike,
As generous as they are bold,—
This is the race thou lovedst so;
And knowing them, I can but know
The glory thy whole being felt
To think, to act, to be, the Celt!

Not Celt alone, America
    Her arms about thee hath entwined;
The noblest traits of each grand race
    In thee were happily combined.
As sweet of song as strong of speech,
    Thy great heart beat in every line.
No narrow partisan wert thou;
    The cause of all oppressed was thine!
The world is cruel still and cold,
But who can doubt thy life has told?
Though wrong and sorrow still are rife
Old Earth is better for thy life!

Erin: a literary name for Ireland.

John Boyle O'Reilly

by James Whitcomb Riley (1849–1916)

Dead? this peerless man of men—
    Patriot, Poet, Citizen!—
Dead? and ye weep where he lies
    Mute, with folded eyes!

Courage! All his tears are done;
Mark him, dauntless, face the sun!
    He hath led you.—Still, as true,
    He is leading you.

Folded eyes and folded hands
Typify divine commands
    He is hearkening to, intent
    Beyond wonderment.

'Tis promotion that has come
Thus upon him. Stricken dumb
    Be your moanings dolorous!
    God knows what He does.

Rather, as your chief, *aspire*!—
Rose and seize his toppling lyre,
    And sing Freedom, Home and Love,
    And the rights thereof!

Ere in selfish grief ye sink,
Come! catch rapturous breath and think—
Think what sweep of wing hath he
Loosed in endless liberty.

66. Henry James Jr.

Henry James Jr., one of America's most influential novelists and critics, traced his Irish ancestry through his grandfather, William James, a Protestant emigrant from County Cavan, Ireland, who settled in Albany, New York, in 1789. As a youngster, the American James became habituated to life in Europe and in later life spent most of his time there. Although in 1862 he entered Harvard law school, he spent most of that year reading fiction and preparing himself for a career as a writer. Perhaps as a result of his own experiences as an American in Europe, many of his works reflect a tension between the ideals of the New World and those of the Old. As David Galloway, the author of *Henry James: The Portrait of a Lady*, has pointed out, James was concerned with "the moral and psychological changes effected in an ingenuous character, usually an American, who suddenly finds himself exposed to the cultural richness of Europe." The subtext to James's realism and the struggle between innocence and evil is the strong possibility that new experiences may corrupt the protagonist, leaving him or her disillusioned and cynical.

Unlike his sister Alice, James refused to identify with Ireland's political aspirations. Although he correctly foresaw the failure of the home rule bill being debated in Parliament in 1886, he expected that the British colony would eventually win "an Irish parliament for Irish affairs" when England realized that Ireland would injure her "less with [home rule] than she does without it." Despite — or perhaps because of — his own Irish Presbyterian roots, James ironically complained that Ireland was in some ways more emancipated than many so-called civilized countries, since the Irish reveled in "odious forms of irresponsibility & license." "[T]hey seem to me," he continued, "an inferior & 3rd rate race, whose virtues are of the cheapest & shallowest kind, while their vices are peculiarly cowardly & ferocious. They have been abominably treated in the past — but their wrongs appear, to me, in our time, to have occupied the conscience of England only too much to the exclusion of other things."

Henry James
by Robert Louis Stevenson (1850–1894)

Who comes to-night? We open the doors in vain.
Who comes? My bursting walls, can you contain
The presences that now together throng
Your narrow entry, as with flowers and song,
As with the air of life, the breath of talk?
Lo, how these fair immaculate women walk
Behind their jocund maker; and we see
Slighted *De Mauves*, and that far different she,
Gressie, the trivial sphynx; and to our feast
Daisy and *Barb* and *Chancellor* (she not least!)
With all their silken, all their airy kin,
Do like unbidden angels enter in.
But he, attended by these shining names,
Comes (best of all) himself—our welcome James.

jocund maker: Henry James Jr., at the head of several female characters from his works of fiction. **DeMauves:** Countess Euphemia Cleve, a character in "Madame de Mauves." She is the American wife of the philandering Count Richard de Mauves. **Gressie:** Georgina Gressie Benyon Roy, a character in "Georgina's Reasons." While still married to Raymond Benyon, she abandons their infant son in Italy and nonchalantly marries William Roy. **Daisy:** Annie P. (Daisy) Miller, an unsophisticated but naturally flirtatious American girl abroad in *Daisy Miller*. **Barb:** Lady Barbara, a relative of Lord Deepmere in *The Americans*. **Chancellor:** Olive Chancellor, a morose, well-to-do, unmarried feminist in *The Bostonians*.

67. Michael "King" Kelly

Michael "King" Kelly — the son of an Irish immigrant papermaker in Troy, New York — was playing with the Cincinnati Reds when "Pop" Anson brought him to Chicago in 1879. Kelly was a versatile player for the White Stockings, doing duty as catcher, shortstop, and outfielder and earning a reputation as an umpire-baiter. His sale to Boston in 1887 for $10,000 caused an uproar and earned him the nickname the "Ten Thousand Dollar Beauty." As the number-one baseball idol of his day, he achieved immortality with his base-stealing record (84) and his base-running slide, the subject of the popular song "Slide, Kelly, Slide." He was known for his disregard of the rules both on and off the field. (When asked if he drank while playing, he replied, "It depends on the length of the game.") Toward the end of his life, he slid from a stretcher during his final illness, reputedly observing that "This is my last slide." At the time of his death, he was playing the lead role in *Casey at the Bat*.

Slide, Kelly, Slide
by John W. Kelly (1875–?)

I played a game of baseball. I belong to Casey's nine!
The crowd was feeling jolly and the weather it was fine;
A nobler lot of players I think were never found,
When the omnibusses landed that day upon the ground.
The game was quickly started, they sent me to the bat;
I made two strikes. Says Casey, "What are you striking at?"
I made the third, the catcher muffed, and to the ground it fell;
I run like a divil to first base, where the gang began to yell:

Chorus:
Slide, Kelly, slide! Your running's a disgrace!
Slide, Kelly, slide! Stay there, hold your base!
If someone doesn't steal you, and your batting doesn't fail you,
They'll take you to Australia! Slide, Kelly, slide!

'Twas in the second inning they called on me, I think,
To take the catcher's place while he went to get a drink;
But something was the matter, sure I couldn't see the ball;
And the second one came in, broke my muzzle, nose and all.
The crowd up in the grandstand they yelled with all their might.
I ran toward the club house, I thought there was a fight.
'Twas the most unpleasant feeling I ever felt before;
I knew they had me rattled, when the gang began to roar:

Chorus:
Slide, Kelly, slide! Your running's a disgrace!
Slide, Kelly, slide! Stay there, hold your base!
If someone doesn't steal you, and your batting doesn't fail you,
They'll take you to Australia! Slide, Kelly, slide!

They sent me out to centre field, I didn't want to go.
The way my nose was swelling up, I must have been a show;
They said on me depended victory or defeat;
If a blind man was to look at us he'd know that we were beat.
Sixty-four to nothing! was the score when he got done,
And everybody there but me said they had lots of fun.
The news got home ahead of me, they heard I was knocked out.
The neighbors carried me in the house, and then began to shout:

Chorus:

Slide, Kelly, slide! Your running's a disgrace!
Slide, Kelly, slide! Stay there, hold your base!
If someone doesn't steal you, and your batting doesn't fail you,
They'll take you to Australia! Slide, Kelly, slide!

Casey's nine: the baseball team in the poem "Casey at the Bat," written by Ernest L. Thayer and first recited publicly in 1888. According to Thayer, the poem's famous slugger was named for Daniel Henry Casey, a high school classmate in Worcester, Massachusetts. When Thayer needed a name for his mythical ballplayer, he thought of the 200-pound, six-foot-two-inch teenager, who had almost beaten him up for remarks he made in a newspaper article. Thayer described his choice of Casey's name as "a taunt thrown to the wind. God grant he never catches me."

68. Chester A. Arthur

Chester A. Arthur, the twenty-first president of the United States, claimed Irish descent from his father, William, who was born in County Antrim, Ireland, in 1796, and who was a graduate of Belfast College. After emigrating in 1816 to Durham, Quebec, the elder man became a Baptist preacher, ministering to eleven parishes in New York and Vermont. The future president was born in the latter state in 1829.

Chester Arthur's political career was marked by the contrast between his idealism and his pragmatism. Although he headed the corrupt New York Customs House and was a member of one of the state's notorious political machines, he continued his father's commitment to securing civil rights for African Americans. In the "Lemmon Slave Case," for instance, the younger Arthur successfully argued that slaves brought into New York while in transit to a slave state were legally free. In another case he obtained a judgment that recognized equal rights for blacks and whites on public transportation within the state.

In 1880, when the Republican national convention was deadlocked on a presidential candidate, the delegates finally nominated James A. Garfield for the number-one slot. Arthur was selected as the vice-presidential candidate primarily to satisfy the New York faction known as the "Stalwarts." During the fall campaign, in an effort to disqualify Arthur for the vice presidency, a Democratic operative claimed that Arthur was not a native-born citizen, having been born in Ireland and brought to the United States at the age of fourteen by his father. Although Arthur went out of his way to admit that he was of Irish descent — in order to attract Irish-American voters — he denied the charge about the place of his birth. The opposition operative responded with another tale, this time that Arthur had been born in Canada.

Arthur succeeded to the presidency after Garfield was assassinated by a dismissed government clerk who shouted "I am a Stalwart!" as he pulled the trigger. The new president surprised the politicians of his era by breaking with the Republican machine that had supported him and by taking stances that won him the respect of political reformers. Besides supporting civil service reform and signing the 1883 Pendleton Act (which established a commission to administer civil service exams), he vetoed an $18 million pork-barrel rivers and harbors bill and prosecuted those charged with fraud in the awarding of government mail contracts. When Arthur left office in 1885, reformers in both parties agreed that the "reformed crook" "had done well . . . by not doing anything bad."

Chester A. Arthur

by Richard Armour (1906–1989)

The shot that killed Garfield shot Arthur from Vice
Up to President, which (for Prince Arthur) was nice.
His friends never dreamt that he ever would get
To such a high place, no (good gracious, no) Chet!

For Chester A. Arthur, side whiskers and all,
Was a dude and a dandy, good looking and tall.
His cellar was stacked with the finest of wines
Or, his tongue slightly twisted, "the winest of fines."

And his wardrobe? This elegant man of affairs
Is famed for his trousers—he had eighty pairs!
And the crease upon each was as sharp, people say,
As a blade, and a blade (gay) was Chester A. A.

But the greatest surprise to his friends, the sensation,
Wasn't Chester's becoming the head of the nation.
What came as a shock was that Chester the Charmer,
The slightly spoiled spoilsman, became a reformer!

And to friends who'd expected their share of the loot
When Garfield was shot in the rear of his suit,
To friends who'd been patiently waiting and trusting,
This change in old Chet was, well, downright disgusting.

69. James G. Blaine

James G. Blaine — speaker of the House of Representatives, U.S. senator, and secretary of state — was born in 1830 to an Irish mother and a Scotch-Irish Presbyterian father. Blaine's first American ancestor was James Blaine, who had emigrated from Londonderry, northern Ireland, in 1745 and settled near Lancaster, Pennsylvania.

James G. Blaine's nomination for president in 1884 by the Republican Party caused the Democrats to fear the loss of their traditional Irish allies. The Republicans first played up their candidate's roots — his Irish Catholic mother and his Irish-American cousin (Sister Angela Gillespie, a famous Civil War nurse). Blaine himself did his part, paying tribute to "the ancient faith in which my mother lived and died" and referring to Sister Angela as literally his sister. The Grand Old Party also reminded Irish voters about Blaine's generally aggressive stance toward Great Britain while serving as secretary of state. In Boston, meanwhile, the Irish Land League claimed that if Blaine was elected "Ireland would be free in thirty days." And in New York a huge rally for Blaine opened with an acknowledgment of the event's historic nature: "To think of thousands of Irish Democrats assembled together to endorse the nomination of the Republican Party."

Blaine's chances of winning the Irish vote en bloc disappeared, however, because of a famous slur and the withering attacks of the Irish-American press. The *Irish American* labeled the Republican "the tattooed candidate, who is charged with being a renegade to the faith of his mother, and whose whole political record is a foul blot on the reputation of the Irish race for honor and probity." The paper also reminded the voters of the Republican Party's "unvarying anti-Irish proclivities." Meanwhile, while making a pro-Blaine statement , the Reverend Samuel Burchard let slip an unfortunate allusion to the Democratic Party's historical connection with saloonkeepers, Catholic immigrants, and secessionists: "We are Republicans, and don't propose to leave our party, and identify ourselves with the party whose antecedents have been RUM, ROMANISM, AND REBELLION."

Blaine of Maine

by "Ironquill" (Eugene Ware) (1841–1911)

> Lashed to his flagship's mast,
> Old Farragut, through iron-guarded bays,
> Through fleets of fire, through batteries ablaze,
> By shot and shell harassed,
> While wreck and ruin seemed to block his way,

And splintered spars spread sprinkling on the spray,
Guiding his fleet throughout the frightful fray,
　　Into the harbor passed;
　　　　And sullen forts grew calm and still
　　　　Beneath the victor's iron will,
　　Subdued and crushed at last.

　　　　O Blaine! amid the glare
Of party ruin, take the ship of state;
We bind thee to its mast, thou statesman great;
　　And thine must be the care
To guide it on through rocks and reefs that vex
The changing channel with a thousand wrecks.
And though the surge shall sweep its sacred decks,
　　We know thou wilt not spare
Thy efforts to conduct it by
The rocks and reefs that seem to lie
　　Around it everywhere.

Old Farragut: David Glasgow Farragut (1801–1870), the Union naval officer whose fleet captured New Orleans (April 1862) and Mobile Bay (August 1864) and helped Ulysses S. Grant gain control of the Mississippi (July 1863).

70. Grover Cleveland

Grover Cleveland, the only U.S. president to serve two nonconsecutive terms, was born in Caldwell, New Jersey, in 1837. His maternal grandfather was Abner Neal, a Protestant of Anglo-Irish extraction who had emigrated from Ireland in the late 1700s, apparently driven from his native country because of his political activities. One of the president's great-great-great-grandfathers was Richard Lamb of Dublin, who died in either 1736 or 1737 on his way to New England.

Perhaps because of his Irish roots, Cleveland twice offered what help he could in defense of Fenian prisoners captured during ill-fated attempts to invade Canada. After the first unsuccessful attempt — led by John O'Neill in May 1866 — Cleveland and some other Democratic lawyers handled the prisoners' case for free. When a similar invasion failed four years later, the Fenian prisoners were taken to Canada for trial. Because the future president was occupied with another legal case in Buffalo, he made arrangements for a friend of his to defend the Fenians without charge.

After the invaders were convicted, Cleveland was among those who petitioned President Ulysses S. Grant to commute the prison sentence.

During the presidential campaign of 1876, Cleveland became the object of attacks against his character. A Buffalo newspaper first published the insinuation that Cleveland was the father of an illegitimate son, the issue of a relationship with a widow named Mrs. Halpin. Although Cleveland never knew for sure that he was the father of the child, he agreed to take responsibility for him when Halpin claimed that Cleveland was the boy's father. When the mother began drinking while nursing the child, Cleveland indirectly took steps to have the boy committed to the care of an orphan asylum, the expenses of which Cleveland agreed to pay. After Halpin kidnapped the child, the authorities intervened and recommitted him to the orphanage, although he was later adopted by a distinguished New York family. During the campaign Cleveland's detractors titillated the voters with the jeer: "Ma, Ma, where's my Pa? Gone to the White House, Ha, Ha, Ha!"

Cleveland

by William Goldsmith Brown (1812–1911)

Yes, quietly; drumbeat nor trumpet's peal,
    Nor martial tramping, should the end proclaim
Of this great civic life; the grief we feel
    No blazon asks; nor asketh aught his fame.

For his was that best courage peace tries best,—
    Sedate defiance of all clamors shrill;
Scorn of mere shows; stern putting to the test
    Of men and causes; and unconquered will.

His, therefore, is this solemn pause of all,
    This deep remembrance of old ardors true—
Dear as our youth—in us who, at his call,
    Bared stripling arms plain patriot work to do.

Silence, keep silence, o'er this wasted frame,—
    Wreck of that burly strength which once he gave.
Better than drums, or outcry of his name,
    Is silence—and the woman by his grave.

Grover Cleveland
by Joel Benton (1832–1911)

Bring cypress, rosemary and rue
For him who kept his rudder true;
Who held to right the people's will,
And for whose foes we love him still.

A man of Plutarch's marble mold,
Of virtues strong and manifold,
Who spurned the incense of the hour,
And made the nation's weal his dower.

His sturdy, rugged sense of right
Put selfish purpose out of sight;
Slowly he thought, but long and well,
With temper imperturbable.

Bring cypress, rosemary and rue
For him who kept his rudder true;
Who went at dawn to that high star
Where Washington and Lincoln are.

Plutarch: the Greek philosopher and author (A.D. c. 46–c. 120) whose biographies of ancient Greeks and Romans were intended to teach moral lessons.

71. William Jennings Bryan

Bryan, whose first Scotch-Irish ancestor settled in Virginia in 1650, came to Lincoln, Nebraska, in 1887, eager to practice law but quickly attracted by the lure of politics. After two terms in the House of Representatives, he accepted a position as editor-in-chief of the *Omaha World Herald* and began a career as a public lecturer on the Chautauqua circuit. At the Democratic national convention in 1896, Bryan's dramatic denunciation of the gold standard in his "Cross of Gold Speech" led to his selection as the party's presidential candidate. Although he crisscrossed the country on an 18,000-mile campaign swing, he was defeated by William McKinley, the Republican candidate. Bryan again lost to McKinley four years later.

Following this second electoral defeat, Bryan began to publish the *Commoner*, a weekly newspaper which he used to attack the influence of money in the political process. After another failed presidential bid — against William Howard Taft — in 1908, the "Great Commoner" was instrumental in securing the nomination of Woodrow Wilson for the presidency in 1912. He served for two years as Wilson's secretary of state until he resigned in disagreement with the president's policy toward Germany prior to World War I. As an early advocate of the idea that a declaration of war should be ratified in a national referendum, Bryan declared: "I so believe in the right of the people to have what they want that I admit the right of the people to go to war if they really want it. There should be a referendum vote about it, however, and those who voted for war should enlist first, together with the jingo newspaper editors."

At a dinner hosted in honor of Bryan by the mayor of Dublin in 1913, someone asked the famous American when he had dropped the "O" from his name. Bryan replied by asking the members of the audience whether they had ever heard of an O'Brian prior to the eleventh-century Irish king Brian Boru. When no one offered an answer, Bryan explained that "Bryan" had been the original name and that the "O" had been added by others, not eliminated by his ancestors.

Twelve years later in Dayton, Tennessee, Bryan successfully prosecuted John Scopes, a high school teacher accused of violating a state statute forbidding the teaching of biological evolution. During the trial Bryan proclaimed his belief in the literal interpretation of the Bible against the ridicule of the defense attorney, Clarence Darrow. The famous "monkey trial" daily attracted 10,000 spectators and 200 reporters.

From **Bryan, Bryan, Bryan, Bryan**
by Vachel Lindsay (1879–1931)

I

In a nation of one hundred fine, mob-hearted, lynching,
      relenting repenting millions,
There are plenty of sweeping, swinging, stinging, gorgeous
      things to shout about,
And knock your old blue devils out.

I brag and chant of Bryan, Bryan, Bryan,
Candidate for president who sketched a silver Zion,
The one American Poet who could sing outdoors,
He brought in tides of wonder, of unprecedented splendor,
Wild roses from the plains, that made hearts tender,
All the funny circus silks
Of politics unfurled,
Bartlett pears of romance that were honey at the cores,
And torchlights down the street, to the end of the world.

There were truths eternal in the gab and tittle-tattle.
There were real heads broken in the fustian and the rattle.
There were real lines drawn:
Not the silver and the gold,
But Nebraska's cry went eastward against the dour and old,
The mean and cold.

It was eighteen ninety-six, and I was just sixteen
And Altgeld ruled in Springfield, Illinois,
When there came from the sunset Nebraska's shout of joy:
In a coat like a deacon, in a black Stetson hat
He scourged the elephant plutocrats
With barbed wire from the Platte.
The scales dropped from their mighty eyes.
They saw that summer's noon
A tribe of wonders coming
To a marching tune.

. . . .

And all these in their helpless days
By the dour East oppressed,
Mean paternalism
Making their mistakes for them,
Crucifying half the West,
Till the whole Atlantic coast
Seemed a giant spider's nest.

And these children and their sons

At last rode through the cactus,
A cliff of mighty cowboys
On the lope.
With gun and rope.
And all the way to frightened Maine the old East heard them call,
And saw our Bryan by a mile lead the wall
Of men and whirling flowers and beasts,
The bard and the prophet of them all.
Prairie avenger, mountain lion,
Bryan, Bryan, Bryan, Bryan,
Gigantic troubadour, speaking like a siege gun,
Smashing Plymouth Rock with his boulders from the West,
And just a hundred miles behind, tornadoes piled across the sky,
Blotting out sun and moon,
A sign on high.

. . . .

III

Then we stood where we could see
Every band,
And the speaker's stand.
And Bryan took the platform.
And he was introduced.
And he lifted his hand
And cast a new spell.
Progressive silence fell
In Springfield,
In Illinois,
Around the world.
Then we heard these glacial boulders across the prairie rolled:
"The people have a right to make their own mistakes. . . .
You shall not crucify mankind
Upon a cross of gold."

. . . .

IV

July, August, suspense.
Wall Street lost to sense.
August, September, October,
More suspense,
And the whole East down like a wind-smashed fence.

Then Hanna to the rescue,

Hanna of Ohio,
Rallying the roller tops,
Rallying the bucket-shops,
Threatening drouth and death,
Promising manna,
Rallying the trusts against the bawling flannelmouth;
Invading miners' cellars,
Tin-cans, socks,
Melting down the rocks,
Pouring out the long green to a million workers,
Spondulix by the mountain-load, to stop each new tornado,
And beat the cheapskate blatherskite,
Populistic, anarchistic,
Deacon-desperado.

V

Election night at midnight:
Boy Bryan's defeat.
Defeat of western silver,
Defeat of the wheat.
Victory of letterfiles
And plutocrats in miles
With dollar signs upon their coats,
Diamond watchchains on their vests
And spats on their feet.
Victory of custodians,
Plymouth Rock,
And all that inbred landlord stock.
Victory of the neat.
Defeat of the aspen groves of Colorado valleys,
The blue bells of the Rockies,
And blue bonnets of old Texas,
By the Pittsburg [*sic*] alleys.
Defeat of alfalfa and the Mariposa lily.
Defeat of the Pacific and the long Mississippi.
Defeat of the young by the old and silly.
Defeat of tornadoes by the poison vats supreme.
Defeat of my boyhood, defeat of my dreams.

VI

Where is McKinley, that respectable McKinley,
The man without an angle or a tangle,

Who soothed down the city man and soothed down the farmer,
The German, the Irish, the Southerner, the Northerner,
Who climbed every greasy pole, and slipped through every crack;
Who soothed down the gambling hall, the bar-room, the church;
The devil vote, the angel vote, the neutral vote,
The desperately wicked, and their victims on the rack,
The gold vote, the silver vote, the brass vote, the lead vote,
Every vote? . . .

Where is McKinley, Mark Hanna's McKinley,
His slave, his echo, his suit of clothes?
Gone to join the shadows, with the prompts of that time,
And the flame of that summer's prairie rose.

Where is Cleveland whom the Democratic platform
Read from the party in a glorious hour,
Gone to join the shadows with pitchfork Tillman,
And sledge-hammer Altgeld who wrecked his power.

Where is Hanna, bulldog Hanna,
Low-browed Hanna, who said: "Stand pat"?
Gone to his place with old Pierpont Morgan.
Gone somewhere . . . with lean rat Platt.

Where is Roosevelt, the young dude cowboy,
Who hated Bryan, then aped his way?
Gone to join the shadows with mighty Cromwell
And tall King Saul, till Judgment day.

Where is Altgeld, brave as the truth,
Whose name the few still say with tears?
Gone to join the ironies with Old John Brown,
Whose fame rings loud for a thousand years.

Where is that boy, that Heaven-born Bryan,
That Homer Bryan, who sang from the West?
Gone to join the shadows with Altgeld the Eagle,
Where kings and the slaves and the troubadours rest.

Zion: a synonym for Jerusalem, especially after David captured it (c. 1000 B.C.).
Altgeld: John Peter Altgeld (1847–1902), the governor of Illinois who protested
the use of federal troops in the Pullman strike of 1894 and who supported Bryan
for president in 1896 and 1900. **elephant plutocrats:** Republicans and their special interest groups and policies (e.g., eastern bankers, railroad owners, protec-

tive tariffs, and the gold standard). Bryan blamed these for the plight of the farmer. **Platte:** a river flowing east through central Nebraska to the Missouri River. **Plymouth Rock:** the site in Plymouth, Massachusetts, where the Pilgrims landed in 1620; used here to represent the nation's eastern elite. **You shall not crucify mankind / Upon a cross of gold:** a line from Bryan's "Cross of Gold Speech," in which he denounced the gold standard. **Wall Street:** Eastern financial interests. **Hanna:** Marcus Hanna (1837–1904), the American industrialist and politico who was responsible for William McKinley's successful presidential campaign against Bryan in 1896. **drouth:** an archaic form of the word "drought." **trusts:** monopolistic corporations. **flannelmouth:** deceptive speech. **Spondulix:** money or cash; a coin. **blatherskite:** a person who talks nonsense; used here to mean Bryan. **McKinley:** William McKinley (1843–1901), the successful Republican presidential candidate against Bryan in 1896 and 1900. **Cleveland:** Grover Cleveland (U.S. president 1885–1889 and 1893–1897). **Tillman:** Benjamin Tillman (1847–1918), a South Carolina governor and senator and spokesman for the agrarian interests in the country. He was known as "pitchfork Ben" for promising to "stick my pitchfork" through President Cleveland's ribs. **Pierpont Morgan:** an American entrepreneur (1837–1913), whose vast financial and industrial empire made him the symbol of plutocracy. **Platt:** Thomas Platt (1833–1910), the New York senator who dominated that state's politics until Theodore Roosevelt was elected governor. **Roosevelt:** Theodore Roosevelt (1858–1919), who condemned many of Bryan's reform ideas but later became a leader of the reform movement. **Cromwell:** Oliver Cromwell (1599–1658), the military leader of the parliamentary forces against Charles I during the English civil war. **King Saul:** the first king of Israel (c. 1020—c. 1000 B.C.). **Old John Brown:** the well-known abolitionist (1800–1859), who was executed for treason for his raid on Harpers Ferry, Virginia (now West Virginia).

From **The Chautauqua**
by John Beecher (1904–1980)

I

Great Commoner

> Their iron-tired wagon wheels grating
> on the raw bricks awakened her at daybreak.
> All morning they rolled in from the tall corn,
> the prairie folk, red-faced and sober-sided,
> for this was Bryan's day in Egypt. Around
> the big top wagons filled the field but still
> their streams debouched down every black mud track
> from Karnack, Olive Branch, Lickcreek and Buncombe.
> The July sun climbed up the implacable sky
> of Illinois, turning the circus tent
> into a huge and sweltering oven where

the sweating multitudes on folding chairs
waved palm-leaf fans, awaiting the silver tongue
to peal its mystic message to their ears:
"You shall not press on labor's brow this crown
of thorns; you shall not crucify mankind
upon a cross of gold!" The managers
in panic sought my mother, though her turn
to declaim a Shakespearean play entire
was not scheduled until that night. "For God's
sake help us out! Please come and entertain them!
The tent's already full and he's not due
till noon!" The five thousand upturned faces
stirred her to tears, transfigured as they were
by expectation of the Messiah. What might
she substitute to slake their needs of him?
"Tomorrow and tomorrow and tomorrow
Creeps in this petty pace from day to day
To the last syllable of recorded time
And all our yesterdays have lighted fools
The way to dusty death"? That wouldn't do!
"The barge she sat in, like a burnished throne,
Glowed on the water"? Wrong Egypt. Jaques
the melancholy? "All the world's a stage
And all the men and women merely players;
They have their exits and their entrances;
And one man in his time plays many parts"?
Hardly the proper text to preface Bryan
the incorruptible, sworn enemy
of Wall Street and the wicked Eastern trusts.
She chose what seemed most fit, the Hoosier bard's
"Little Orphant Annie" and "The Raggedy Man,"
conjuring cooling visions with "When the Frost
is on the Punkin," making them weep with Field
for Little Boy Blue's untimely end and all
his battered toys still to be put away.
Then a murmur rose like wind in the ripe corn
and grew to a roar as the rotund prophet
stalked up to the platform. "Bryan, it's Bryan!"

. . . .

Bryan's day in Egypt: a metaphor for Bryan's role as a new Moses. **Karnack, Olive Branch, Lickcreek and Buncombe:** towns in Illinois. **"You shall not press on labor's brow . . .":** a line from Bryan's "Cross of Gold Speech," in which he denounced the gold standard. **Messiah:** a metaphor for Bryan's role as a political savior. **"Tomorrow and tomorrow and tomorrow . . ."**: lines from Shakespeare's *Macbeth* (V. v. 17ff). **"The barge she sat in, . . ."**: lines from Shakespeare's *Antony and Cleopatra* (II. ii. 196ff). **Jaques the melancholy:** a moody and changeable character in Shakespeare's *As You Like It*. **"All the world's a stage . . .":** lines from Shakespeare's *As You Like It* (II. vii. 139ff). **Wall Street:** Eastern financial interests. **Eastern trusts:** monopolistic corporations. **Hoosier bard:** James Whitcomb Riley (1849–1916), an American poet whose work idealized childhood, small town life, and ordinary people. **"Little Orphant Annie," "The Raggedy Man," "When the Frost is on the Punkin":** poems by James Whitcomb Riley. **Field:** Eugene Field (1850–1895), an author and editorialist. **Little Boy Blue:** the main character in a story of the same name by Eugene Field about the death of a child.

Bryan's Last Battle
(*The Scopes Trial*)
author unknown

Of all the tales of human struggle, hear this one from Tennessee,
The Holy Bible there on trial, its mighty truths must stricter be.
Its stubborn foe was evolution, the learned could not understand
How in its pages, white and holy, we surely read the fate of man.
Oh, who will go and end this struggle? Oh, who will go and be the man?
And face the foe so learned and mighty, and for the Holy Bible stand?

I see a man, though old in years, a strong and mighty man is he;
Amid the nation's sighs and tears, he starts for sunny Tennessee.
And when he reached the town of Dayton, he faced the foe, to them he
        said,
"I will not here deny my Maker, the Bible's good enough for me."
Yes, Bryan went to end the struggle, there was no greater man than he
To face the foe so learned and mighty, and give the Bible victory.

Evolution tries to take us back to live in monkeyland,
Bryan took the Holy Bible and stood for God-created man.
"I love this book my mother taught me, with pages pure and white as
        snow,
I'll place my faith in the Holy Bible, till all the world its riches know.
Oh, who will grieve those saints in glory, who struggle here for a brighter
        day,
And walk with faith and truth and virtue, and points us to a starlit way?"

Oh, Lord, keep the little town of Dayton; 'twas Bryan's last great cause to
        win.
He won with truth and love and virtue, when he struggled there with a
        world of sin.

Then let us cling to the Holy Bible, our rule of life, and faith our guide,
He proved its truth in every heartthrob, and upon its glorious faith he
　　died.
The Bible shows me the Rose of Sharon, it points me to a perfect day,
And leads me to the Rock of Ages, my Savior's love is a starlit way.

upon its glorious faith he died: Bryan died five days after the Scopes trial. **Sharon:** a fertile pasture land in biblical Palestine, extending from the Mediterranean Sea to the mountains of Samaria. Its roses and lilies were remarkable for their beauty, and for the prophet Isaiah the fruitfulness of the plain prefigured the peace and tranquility of the Messianic Kingdom.

72. John Frederick Finerty

John Finerty, the Chicago journalist and congressman, was born in Galway, Ireland, in 1846. At the age of eighteen he came to the United States and almost immediately volunteered for the Union army. During a career as a newspaper reporter, he worked for three Chicago journals — the *Republican*, the *Tribune*, and the *Times*. While on the staff of the last publication, he reported the Indian wars, including Custer's campaign against Sitting Bull in 1876. Finerty later served one term in the House of Representatives and was among the Irish who uncharacteristically supported James G. Blaine, the Republican presidential nominee in 1884. Long active in Irish and Irish-American affairs, he served numerous times as president of the United Irish League of America and the United Irish Societies of Chicago. He was the editor of the *Chicago Citizen* and the author of *Warpath and Bivouac* and *People's History of Ireland*.

In Memoriam, John F. Finerty
by Joe Fogarty

Erin, call your children from the four ends of the earth,
Tell them softly, gently, to cease their joy and mirth,
To don the sad black crape, the sable badge of grief,
For death has called and taken Ireland's greatest chief.
John Finerty, the honest man, the noblest of them all,
Is numbered with the honored dead, he's now beyond recall;
That voice is stilled for ever, that thousands loved to hear,
That manly form is vanished that thrilled with hope and cheer.

With fear our foes oft trembled at the mention of his name,
Whilst Irish cheers a million fold attestified his fame;
A hero on the firing line, an orator in the hall,
A true man always ready to answer freedom's call,
Fluent and keen his mighty pen, in voicing Erin's cause,
Untiring in his constant fight against oppressive laws.
No braver son had Ireland to wield both sword and pen,
And in defense of Erin's rights he'd face ten thousand men.

The landlord class he did assail, with Charles Stewart Parnell,
With vigor and with vehemence he tolled their funeral knell;
He lived to see them vanish like snow before hot rain,
Usurping breed of shoneens, spawn of a vicious reign;
For Ireland, all for Ireland, was his slogan night and day,
With hands upraised and ready he always sought the fray.
With Redmond for Home Rule he kept fighting manfully,
He told the Saxon hypocrites that Ireland must be free.

Death, cruel death, assailed him in sight of freedom's goal,
And a nation's tears bewail him, with grief beyond control;
Ireland will ne'er forget the noble work he's done,
Whilst Galway with heartrending keen laments her favorite son;
Our church has lost a pillar, too, bold, stern, stout and strong—
He stood beside her priests and nuns 'gainst prejudice and wrong.
"By force," he said, "we're not subdued, but by another means—
Disunion is the weapon that keeps intact our chains.

"Then let us all be soldiers in this fight for liberty;
With shouts of joy we'll rend the skies when motherland is free."
Such was the watchword of the chief that we lament today,
A soldier's place his sole desire, in the midst of all the fray.
He fought uphill for native land, with courage all his own,
And long with love he strove to place dead Banba on her throne.
He shed light on Saxon ways, with his trusty, strong X-ray,
He unmasked them before the world in the clear, bright light of day.

Poor Ireland has a champion lost, her swordsman is no more,
A wave of grief a mountain high has swept the Shamrock shore.
He's parted with this world of woe, has bowed to death's decree,
But in spirit he'll be with us in our fight for liberty.
His life works should a model be for every Irish heart,
And Erin's chains will crumble when each man does his part.
'Twixt tears and sobs my feeble pen indites his elegy—
May the joys of heaven be thine, John, forever in eternity.

Erin: a literary name for Ireland. **Charles Stewart Parnell:** the Irish patriot (1846–1891) and leader of the Home Rule Movement in the 1880s. **shoneens:** persons who prefer English rather than Irish cultural standards and attitudes. **Redman:** John Redman (1856–1918), the parliamentary leader of the Irish Nationalist Party. **Home Rule:** limited self-government for Ireland. **Saxon hypocrites:** the English. **Banba:** in Irish mythology the queen of the Tuatha Dé Danann (pre-Celtic deities of Ireland). Her name became synonymous with Ireland itself.

73. Finley Peter Dunne

One of America's most famous ethnic humorists, Dunne was born to Irish immigrants in the predominantly Irish neighborhood of Bridgeport, near Chicago. In 1884 the sixteen-year-old Dunne began a newspaper career that saw him work for six Chicago newspapers, first as a police and sports reporter, then as a features and editorial writer, and finally as managing editor of the *Post*. In 1890 he created the first of three Irish characters whom he used as vehicles for satire or political commentary in his columns: Colonel Thomas Jefferson Dolan; Colonel Malachi McNeery, based on the pensive real-life saloon keeper James McGarry; and Martin Dooley, the more famous derivative of the previous character.

In more than 300 weekly columns, Dunne used Mr. Dooley to recreate what Charles Fanning called "the first fully realized Irish ethnic neighborhood in American literature." Although on many occasions Dooley waxes nostalgic about the Great Famine and the hardships of immigration and assimilation, he also dispenses insight into the Irish character and the human condition. After opining, for example, that "f'r an impetchoos an' darin' people th' Irish is th' mos' cowardly whin it comes to mathrimony that iver I heerd tell iv," Dooley cites "Dacey th' plumber, who'd niver 'v married if he hadn't got into th' wrong buildin' whin he wint to take out a license f'r his dog, an' got a marriage license instid." Other Dooley pieces illustrate the gap between the immigrants and their more Americanized children: After scandalizing the neighborhood by wearing bloomers while riding a bicycle, Molly Donahue is sent off to confession, where she receives "a pinance th' like iv which ain't been knowed in Bridgeport since Cassidy said Charles Stewart Parnell was a bigger man thin th' pope."

Dunne received national attention with the publication of *Mr. Dooley in Peace and War* and *Mr. Dooley in the Hearts of His Countrymen*, which were followed by five other volumes of "observations." One of Dooley's famous remarks was about Thanksgiving: "'Twas founded be th' Puritans

to give thanks f'r bein' presarved fr'm th' Indians, and . . . we [Irish] keep
it to give thanks we are presarved fr'm th' Puritans."

The following poem owes its origin to a comment by Dunne that the
ancestors of John F. Finerty, a fellow newspaperman, were born in Ireland. Finerty, then the editor of the *Chicago Citizen*, replied with "Dooley's
Lamentation."

Dooley's Lamentation

by John F. Finerty (1846–1908)

My name is Pether Dooley,
    My age is thirty-two
I'm a native of sweet Archy Road,
    Not far from Healy's Slough!
My parents were thrue Irish,
    Though "Scotch" is now in vogue,
And they blarneyed all creation
    With their "pure Roscommon brogue!"

Whin first I met McGarry,
    In the year of '92,
He filled me with philosophy
    On the banks of Healy's Slough!
But soon he grew unruly—
    I made of him some fun—
So I changed his name to Dooley
    An' mine to Finley Dunne!

How many an hour I rambled
    'Mid hills of sand and junk!
How many a time I gamboled
    'Mid fields of cabbage-skunk,
'Twas sweet to watch the sunset,
    And hear the bull-frogs mew,
In those days of happy innocence
    On the banks of Healy's Slough!

Bad luck to you, McGarry,
    An' your pure Roscommon brogue!
You led me into throuble,
    You blarneying owld rogue!
Your tongue ran on so clever,
    Your words seemed ever new,

An' you soaked me with philosophy
  On the banks of Healy's Slough!

But now I have grown famous—
  My works are much in vogue—
An' the English rave in chorus
  Of my "pure Roscommon brogue!"
They've "pirated" my labors—
  The ruthless Saxon crew—
I'll abuse them to my neighbors
  On the banks of Healy's Slough!

Then fare you well, McGarry!
  An' farewell Pether Dunne!
I'm swallowed up in "Dooley"
  An' vanished is my fun!
Oh for the owld time evenings
  When I heard the bull-frogs mew,
And watched the purple sunset
  On the banks of Healy's Slough!

Archy Road: actually Archer Avenue, at the heart of Bridgeport, located below the south branch of the Chicago River. **Healy's Slough:** (pronounced "slew"), a creek that ran out of the Chicago River diagonally southeast across Archer Avenue. **My parents:** Dunne's parents were Peter and Ellen (Finerty) Dunne. **Roscommon:** a county in north central Ireland. **McGarry:** James McGarry, the real-life saloon keeper on whom Dunne's fictional character Colonel Malachi McNeery was based.

74. John Goff

Born in County Wexford, Ireland, in 1848, John Goff was orphaned at the age of nine and briefly supported himself as a telegrapher for the British government. After coming to the United States when he was fifteen, he obtained a position as a telegraph operator in New York City and later as a clerk in two dry goods establishments. He attended night classes at Cooper Union and, after serving as a clerk for a U.S. district attorney, studied law and in 1876 was admitted to the New York bar.

Two years earlier Goff had taken a leading role in what was known as "Goff's Irish Rescue Party." Composed of John Boyle O'Reilly (the editor of the *Boston Pilot*), John Devoy, and others, the party successfully carried out the rescue of six Fenian prisoners from a British penal colony in Australia. Replicating the scheme that had effected O'Reilly's escape from Australia seven years earlier, the rescuers hired a New Bedford whaler, the *Catalpa*, under the command of Captain George Anthony. With the groundwork laid by two Fenian leaders who had preceded the ship to Australia, the prisoners deserted their work detail and made their way to the shore, where they were eventually picked up by the *Catalpa*. The six Fenians arrived safely in New York City in 1876.

In 1888 Goff became assistant district attorney for New York City. His effectiveness in prosecuting local politicians for election fraud led to his appointment five years later as chief counsel to a committee investigating corruption in the city's police department. For his success in exposing such criminality, the voters elected him city recorder and later a district justice of the New York supreme court. While on the bench he presided over some of the most celebrated criminal trials of the era, including those of Lefty Louie and Dago Frank.

The Boy from Wexford
(John W. Goff 1848–1924)

by A. M. Sullivan (1896–1980)

He was the "boy from Wexford who fought with heart and hand.
Aye, fought with mind and soul at Honor's sharp command,
"Drove out the beast whose paws have tracked in public places,"
And he fought until he saw defeat on evil faces.

O, sing the praise of Wexford, and praise for Gorey town
And the warrior of words who cut marauders down;
O, ring the champion's shield that fended off the stain
Of compliment and laurel for a moment's golden gain.

Inquisitor of traitors, procurers, knaves and thieves,
He seized the ugly truth, and pinned it on their sleeves
For all the land to see, for all the world to scorn,
For all a city's people to count their shame and mourn.

Aye, mourn the broken vigil, that a beast with laden craw
Should feed in the city's trough, and trample the sovereign law.
John Goff had words to brand the drowsy citizen
Who nodded while his sacred halls became a harlot's den.

Noble son of Banba, the Fianna's fighting son,
He bade the world to listen till Eire's cause is won
Remembering ninety-eight—and father and son who stood
Against the ancient despot, and risked the hangman's hood.

Goff, Devoy, O'Reilly—they made the anvils chime
With song and broke the chains, and cancelled England's crime
Against six exile Fenians on Australia's barren floor
And snatched them out of bondage behind the penal door.

Sing now the "Boys of Wexford" for one who met the foe
And gave no coward's inch, but matched him blow for blow
Until the weight of truth broke tyrant's arm and blade,—
Tough was the Wexford steel from which John Goff was made.

"boy from Wexford who . . .": a slightly altered line from the refrain in the poem "The Boys of Wexford." The original line begins "We are the Boys of Wexford who . . . ." **Gorey town:** Goff's birthplace in County Wexford. **Noble son of Banba:** Goff is apostrophized as a son of Banba, who in Irish mythology was the queen of the Tuatha Dé Danann (pre-Celtic deities of Ireland). Her name became synonymous with Ireland itself. **Fianna:** in Irish legend a band of professional soldiers of superhuman strength, size, and courage. **Eire:** the Irish name for Ireland. **ninety-eight:** an allusion to an unsuccessful uprising against the British in Wexford, Ireland, in 1798. **Devoy and O'Reilly:** John Devoy (1842–1928) and John Boyle O'Reilly (1844–1890), Irish natives who with Goff planned the rescue of six Fenian prisoners from an Australian penal colony. Devoy and O'Reilly had earlier been arrested for recruiting followers to the Fenian cause from within the ranks of the British army. Devoy was released on condition that he go into exile; O'Reilly was transported to Australia but escaped in 1869. **six exile Fenians:** Richard Cranston, Thomas Darragh, Michael Harrington, Thomas Hassett, Martin Hogan, and James Wilson.

75. William Randolph Hearst

William Randolph Hearst was born in San Francisco in 1863 into a politically influential family that traced its descent to Scottish ancestors who had immigrated to America in 1680. Hearst's paternal grandmother (Elizabeth Collins), however, was of Irish ancestry, her family having emigrated from Galway. According to a family story, Hearst's Irish Catholic governess, Eliza Pike, was concerned that his mother had not had the infant baptized. One day when the mother was out of the city, Eliza spirited young Willie to a Catholic church, where he was baptized by a priest. When the boy's mother returned and learned what the governess had done, Mrs. Hearst reminded her employee that the family was Episcopalian. Eliza replied: "It doesn't matter so long as the baby is Christian."

In 1876 Willie and his mother, Phoebe, traveled to Europe. While touring Ireland, the pair saw unbelievable poverty, which Phoebe tried to describe to her husband, George, in a letter from Belfast. "Many of them are highly educated, warm hearted and hospitable," she wrote about the Irish people, "but the poor classes are <u>terribly</u> poor. Willie wanted to give away all his money and clothes, too, and really, I felt the same way. If we could have relieved half of them. . . . Willie says he does not like this country very much because the men are so bad to the women and horses. He saw the women working out[side] barefooted and thinly clad. The horses in the south of Ireland are so poor and overworked. The whole country is beautifully cultivated."

After assuming ownership of the *San Francisco Examiner* from his father, a U.S. senator and mining entrepreneur, the younger Hearst made it a financial success. In 1895 he bought the *New York Journal* and proceeded to wage a circulation battle with the *New York World*, using such devices as sensationalism, editorial crusades, banner headlines, and color comics. His sensationalistic coverage of Spanish atrocities in Cuba in the mid 1890s helped provoke an American declaration of war against Spain. By 1937 he owned twenty-five large dailies throughout the United States and through their pages wielded a powerful influence. In the poem "Doxology" below, Bert Leston Taylor uses irony to satirize the God-like Hearst, while John Beecher's excerpt is unambiguously critical.

In the 1970s Hearst's son, William Randolph Hearst Jr., wrote in his autobiography that he had interviewed the famous Irish nationalist Eamon De Valera on numerous occasions. After mentioning that De Valera had led Ireland for thirty-five years, the journalist mentioned the statesman's claim that Hearst's father had "helped us to be a nation."

Doxology

by Bert Leston Taylor ("B.L.T.") (1866–1921)

Praise Hearst, from whom all blessings flow!
Praise Hearst, who runs things here below.
Praise them who make him manifest—
Praise Andy L. and all the rest.

Praise Hearst because the world is round,
Because the seas with salt abound,
Because the water's always wet,
And constellations rise and set.

Praise Hearst because the grass is green,
And pleasant flow'rs in spring are seen;
Praise him for morning, night and noon.
Praise him for stars and sun and moon.

Praise Hearst, our nation's aim and end,
Humanity's unselfish friend;
And who remains, for all our debt,
A modest sweet white violet.

Doxology: a hymn of praise to God; the metrical formula beginning "Praise God from whom all blessings flow."

From Part II of **And I Will Be Heard**
by John Beecher (1904–1980)

. . . .

William Randolph Hearst
you are another public character
I feel like saying something to.
Long ago
I stopped reading your lousy papers
and if I did happen to pick one up
the last thing I would turn to
would be your editorials.
I don't know what you are saying at the moment
but you must be getting careful
because otherwise I would be hearing about it from somewhere.
All I want to talk to you about
is an estate you have in California
called San Simeon.
I saw it for the first time last Christmas Eve

driving by on the highway just as dark was coming down
and I didn't know there was such a place in this country
or such brass
as you must have had
to dare build it just for yourself.
Do you know
how the Oakies have to live in California
or haven't you bothered to look around?
And those folks whose farms blew away
or were tractored off the land
back in Oklahoma, Texas and Arkansas
have you seen their faces?
I had just come from seeing them
when I drove by your place
San Simeon
on Christmas Eve.
The gall of you
to dare call that place after a disciple of Christ
and to pretend in your newspapers
that you
William Randolph Hearst
are a defender of the Christian faith

against infidels.

. . . .

San Simeon: Hearst's lavish estate on the California coast, completed at a cost of $30 million. The main building, a Spanish-Moorish castle, contains about 150 rooms. **Oakies:** a derogatory term for Oklahomans, specifically those who fled Oklahoma in the 1930s because of economic depression, dust storms, and foreclosures on their farms. **disciple of Christ:** St. Simeon. Sources differ about the name of the saint for whom the bay below Hearst's mansion was originally named: Simon the Zealot (one of Christ's apostles, the name "Simon" being the Hellenized form of the Hebrew "Simeon") or Simeon Stylites (a fifth-century Syrian anchorite).

76. The Sinking of the *Maine*

As the revolution against Spanish rule in Cuba dragged on at the end of the 1890s, American sympathy for the Cubans grew. American investments in the island's economy were increasingly threatened, and the Spanish atrocities inflamed the American public. In January 1898 the United States sent the battleship *Maine* to Cuba to protect American lives and property and to evacuate U.S. citizens if the situation there collapsed into chaos. On February 15, while the *Maine* lay in Havana harbor, the ship was sunk in an explosion. Of the crew's 350 men and officers, 252 were killed in the explosion and eight others died subsequently. Among those casualties — dead, missing or injured — sixty-four men bore distinctively Irish surnames or were natives of Ireland. Two of the uninjured also bore Irish surnames. This large percentage of casualties among those of Irish birth or descent made such a profound impression on the poet Joseph Clarke that he penned "The Fighting Race." This poem — his most famous — appeared in the *New York Sun* on St. Patrick's Day 1898.

The list of the Irish and Irish-American dead contained the following: James Boyle (New York City), Anthony Conroy (Galway), William Cosgrove (no place listed), Charles Curran (County Donegal), William Donoughty (Londonderry, Ireland), Patrick Flynn (County Waterford), Patrick Gaffney (County Roscommon), Thomas Harty (New York City), Patrick Hughes (King's County, Ireland), John McManus (Davenport, Iowa), Joseph Scully (Baltimore, Md.), Joseph Seery (County Kildare), and Owen Sheridan (County Cavan).

The missing men of Irish birth or ancestry, meanwhile, were Lewis Barry (Halifax, N.S.), George Brosnan (Brooklyn, N.Y.), Thomas Caine (Portsmouth, Va.), Michael Cochrane (Fall River, Mass.), Michael Flaherty (Portsmouth, Va.), Patrick Grady (County Kildare), Michael Griffin (Dublin), William Hanrahan (Cohoes, N.Y.), William Hough (New York City), Michael Kane (County Galway), Edward Kean (Chicago, Ill.), Frank Kelly (South Boston, Mass.), Hugh Kelly (Brooklyn, N.Y.), John Kelly (Brooklyn, N.Y.), Thomas Kinsella (Washington, D.C.), Edward Lawler (Liverpool, England), John Lydon (New York City), Bernard Lynch (Portland, Me.), Matthew Lynch (Providence, R.I.), Hugh McGonigle (County Donegal), John McDermott (New York City), Michael Malone (New York City), Joseph Monahan (Roxbury, Mass.), Edward Moore (Charles City, Va.), Cornelius Murphy (County Cork), Charles Nolan (Boston, Mass.), James O'Connor (Bayonne, N.J.), Thomas O'Hagan (New York City), Patrick O'Neill (County Louth), Henry O'Regan (East Boston, Mass.), John Powers (County Cork), Thomas Quigley (New York City), Charles Quinn (Boston, Mass.), Joseph Reilly (New York City), John Shea (New York City), Patrick Shea (Willimantic, Conn.), Thomas Shea (New York City), Martin Tuohey (Brooklyn, N.Y.), and Joseph Walsh (Brockton, Mass.).

Another dozen Irish and Irish Americans were injured in the explosion, while two who escaped unscathed bore Irish surnames. The injured were Franics Cahill (Salem, Mass.), John Coffey (Somerville, Mass.), Daniel Cronin (New York City), Michael Flynn (Philadelphia, Pa.), Patrick Foley (Orange, N.J.), Joseph Kane (Worcester, Mass.), Michael Lanahan (Louisville, Ky.), Harry McCann (Vallejo, Calif.), John McDevitt (Listowel, Ireland), William McGuiness (County Tyrone), and Jeremiah Shea (Haverhill, Mass.). John Dolan (Brookline, Mass.) and Michael Meehan (County Sligo) escaped harm.

The Fighting Race
by Joseph I. C. Clarke (1846–1925)

"Read out the names!" and Burke sat back,
    And Kelly drooped his head.
While Shea—they called him Scholar Jack—
    Went down the list of the dead.
Officers, seamen, gunners, mariners,
    The crews of the gig and yawl,
The bearded man and the lad in his teens,
    Carpenters, coal passers—all.
Then, knocking the ashes from out his pipe,
    Said Burke in an offhand way:
"We're all in that dead man's list, by Cripe!
    Kelly and Burke and Shea."
"Well, here's to the *Maine*, and I'm sorry for Spain,"
    Said Kelly and Burke and Shea.

"Wherever there's Kellys there's trouble," said Burke,
    "Wherever fighting's the game,
Or a spice of danger in grown man's work,"
    Said Kelly, "you'll find my name."
"And do we fall short," said Burke, getting mad,
    "When it's touch and go for life?"
Said Shea, "It's thirty-odd years, bedad,
    Since I charged to drum and fife
Up Marye's Heights, and my old canteen
    Stopped a rebel ball on its way.
There were blossoms of blood on our sprigs of green—
    Kelly and Burke and Shea—
And the dead didn't brag." "Well, here's to the flag!"
    Said Kelly and Burke and Shea.

"I wish 'twas in Ireland, for there's the place,"
     Said Burke, "that we'd die by right,
In the cradle of our soldier race,
     After one good stand-up fight.
My grandfather fell on Vinegar Hill,
     And fighting was not his trade;
But his rusty pike's in the cabin still,
     With Hessian blood on the blade."
"Aye, Aye," said Kelly, "the pikes were great
     When the word was 'clear the way!'
We were thick on the roll in ninety-eight—
     Kelly and Burke and Shea."
"Well, here's to the pike and the sword and the like!"
     Said Kelly and Burke and Shea.

And Shea, the scholar, with rising joy,
     Said, "We were at Ramillies,
We left our bones at Fontenoy
     And up in the Pyrenees,
Before Dunkirk, on Landen's plain,
     Cremona, Lille and Ghent,
We're all over Austria, France and Spain,
     Wherever they pitched a tent.
We've died for England from Waterloo
     To Egypt and Dargai;
And still there's enough for a corps or crew,
     Kelly and Burke and Shea."
"Well, here is to good honest fighting blood!"
     Said Kelly and Burke and Shea.

"Oh, the fighting races don't die out,
     If they seldom die in bed,
For love is first in their hearts, no doubt,"
     Said Burke; then Kelly said:
"When Michael, the Irish Archangel, stands,
     The angel with the sword,
And the battle-dead from a hundred lands
     Are ranged in one big horde,
Our line, that for Gabriel's trumpet waits,
     Will stretch three deep that day,
From Jehoshaphat to the Golden Gates—
     Kelly and Burke and Shea,"
"Well, here's thank God for the race and the sod!"
     Said Kelly and Burke and Shea.

by Cripe: a euphemistic expression for a particular profanity. **bedad:** an Irish interjection meaning "by God." **Marye's Heights:** the Confederate position at the battle of Fredericksburg in 1862. The Irish Brigade assaulted this position in six suicidal charges, losing 545 men — half its strength — in the futile attempt. **Vinegar Hill:** the site of a skirmish against the British garrison in Wexford, Ireland, in 1798. **Hessian:** pertaining to German mercenaries hired by the British during the American Revolution. These mercenaries came not only from the state of Hesse but also from other small German principalities (Ansbach, Anhalt-Zerbst, Brunswick, and Waldeck). **Ramillies:** a battle of 1706, in which the French were defeated by an Allied force under the Duke of Marlborough. Three Irish regiments under Colonel Charles O'Brien fought with the French. **Fontenoy:** a battle of 1745, in which the six Irish regiments of the French army turned the tide for Louis XIV by helping defeat the Allied forces. During the battle the Irish regiments numbered about 4,000 of the 60,000 French troops and suffered 656 of the 3,870 casualties on the French side. While smashing through the Allied right flank, the Irish troops shouted "Remember Limerick!", a cry to avenge the surrender of that Irish city to the army of William III in 1691. **Pyrenees:** a mountain chain between France and Spain. **Landen's plain:** a battlefield in Flanders, where the French defeated William III of England in 1693. The Irish exile Patrick Sarsfield was killed during the engagement and was buried on the battlefield. **Cremona:** the Italian city in which the French garrison (including 600 Irish soldiers) recovered from a surprise attack by Imperialist troops. In turning the tide, the two Irish battalions of colonels Arthur Dillon and Walter Bourke lost 350 men killed, wounded, or captured. **Lille:** the French town whose commander repulsed several assaults by Imperialist troops in August and September 1708. **Ghent:** the Belgian city near which the French repulsed pursuing British and Austrian troops on July 12, 1708. **Waterloo:** the Belgian village near which Napoleon was defeated on June 18, 1815. **Dargai:** possibly Dargal, a town in Pakistan. **Gabriel's trumpet:** an allusion to the time when the archangel Gabriel will announce the Day of Judgment. **Jehoshaphat:** the Valley of Jehoshaphat ("The Lord has judged"), a most likely hypothetical place mentioned in the apocryphal Book of Joel (3:2) as the site of the Last Judgment. **Golden Gates:** the gates of heaven.

77. The Spanish-American War

Throughout the military history of the United States, the Irish and their descendants have played an extremely important and often illustrious role. An estimated 30 to 50 percent of the Americans who fought in the Revolutionary War were of Irish birth or ancestry, some of the most famous being John Barry, Richard Montgomery, John Sullivan, and Timothy Murphy. The War of 1812 boasted such famous Irish Americans as Andrew Jackson, Thomas Macdonough, and Steven Decatur, while a quarter of General Zachary Taylor's troops during the Mexican War were Irish born. With the experience they acquired in the Mexican War, James Shields, Philip Kearny, and Philip Sheridan went on to greater glory in the Civil War, during which between 144,000 and 170,000 Irish-born fought for the Union.

The following poem — whose title is a Gaelic slogan meaning "Clear the Way" — sings the praise of those men of Irish birth or ancestry who gave their lives in the nation's wars. Its main focus, however, is on the presence of those soldiers and sailors in the war with Spain in 1898. It is particularly interesting for its allusions to the daring men of the *Merrimac*, to the men killed in the explosion of the *Maine*, and to William O'Neill (one of Teddy Roosevelt's companions in the Rough Riders). The story of the *Merrimac* is told in the last three poems of this section; O'Neill is the subject of two poems in the next section.

Fag a Ballagh

author unknown

. . . .

At Bloody Lane, at San Juan hill;
At Las Guasimas, Siboney,
Porto Rico, and El Caney;
The earth is pillowed with the graves
Of old Ireland's sons, Erin's braves.
Were with Schley at Santiago,
With young Bagley on the *Winslow*;
Were marines at Guantanamo,
Were with Dewey and fighting Jack,
Kelly, Murphy, Mike, and Mac,
And shared with Hobson the *Merrimac*.

Against old Spain their strength they hurled—
Stars and Stripes and the Green unfurled,

Irish blood to avenge the *Maine*,
Till Irish brows, besprent like rain,
Were mixed all in the bloody brew,
Where swords and guns in flinters flew,
Where cannister hot, grape and shot,
Hissed o'er that awful bloody spot
Where floated grand Old Glory.

Hear you not their old slogan roar,
Loud sounding o'er Potomac's shore,
As onward these brave heroes bore
The Stars and Stripes, their own galore,
Sweeping about in bloody rout,
With dash and crash and deafening shout,
The Spaniard, old in story.

See their charge on hill and valley,
In wood and dale, Old Glory's rally;
Hear their war cry, "Fag a Ballagh!"
O'Boyle, O'Neill, McCoy, McCalla,
The stubborn Spaniard backward bearing,
Those fighting, daring sons of Erin,
Those dashing, smashing sons of Erin.

The sun rose red o'er Siboney plain,
Rough Riders rode o'er heaps of slain,
And Spanish blood poured out like rain
On Siboney so gory.
To halt Roosevelt, Dons now tried,
So they marched forth in Spanish pride.

Then Roosevelt, Rough Rider, cried,
O'Neill, Rough Rider, by his side,
"Forward! Charge!"To the front we ride
Where the brave O'Neill serenely died,
His sprigs of green in crimson dyed.

They left their bones on Bunker Hills [*sic*],
At Stoney Point [*sic*], and the Antilles;
They fought and bled at New Orleans,
Mexico, and the Philippines.
'Neath Pekin's walls they rest unseen,
Blossoms of blood their sprigs of green.

Fag a Ballagh: also spelled *Faugh a Ballaugh*, Gaelic for "Clear the Way." **Bloody Lane:** perhaps the sunken road on the battlefield at Antietam, where the Irish Brigade suffered more than 500 casualties during the Civil War. In the context of this poem the phrase more likely refers to Bloody Ford, the nickname for a ford across the Aguadores River near San Juan Hill. The ford received its nickname from the dead and wounded Americans who were the victims of Spanish snipers at the crest of the hill. **San Juan hill:** a Spanish outpost in Cuba stormed by American troops on July 1, 1898. **Las Guasimas:** the site of a skirmish in which 1,000 American troops forced a Spanish rear guard of 1,500 to abandon its position between Siboney and Santiago, Cuba, on June 24, 1898. **Siboney:** a site eleven miles east of Santiago, Cuba, that was captured by 6,000 American troops on June 23, 1898. **Porto Rico:** probably a reference to Admiral William Sampson's bombardment of San Juan, Puerto Rico, on May 12, 1898, in an attempt to find out whether the Spanish fleet lay inside. Sampson learned that the enemy fleet had slipped into the harbor of Santiago, Cuba. **El Caney:** a battle in which a 521-man Spanish garrison six miles northeast of Santiago, Cuba, was overrun by Americans on July 1, 1898. **Erin:** a literary name for Ireland. **Schley:** Commodore Winfield Scott Schley (1839–1911), whose cruiser squadron defeated the Spanish fleet when it tried to slip past the American blockade of the harbor of Santiago, Cuba, on July 3, 1898. **Bagley:** Ensign Worth Bagley, an American killed when his ship, the torpedo boat *Winslow*, was crippled by Spanish fire at Cárdenas, Cuba, on May 11, 1898. **Guantanamo:** a harbor about forty miles east of Santiago, Cuba, where 650 U.S. Marines landed on July 10, 1898. The Marines intended to establish a coaling station there for use by American ships blockading Santiago. **Dewey:** Admiral George Dewey (1837–1917), whose victory at the battle of Manila on May 1, 1898, ended Spanish power in the Philippines. **fighting Jack:** John J. Pershing (1860–1948), the First Lieutenant of the African-American Tenth Cavalry. **Kelly:** John Kelly, a water-tender on the *Merrimac*. **Murphy:** J. C. Murphy, a coxswain on the *Iowa*. **Hobson:** Richmond Pearson Hobson (1870–1937), a Spanish-American War hero, who, with a crew of seven other men, tried to blockade the harbor of Santiago, Cuba, with the *Merrimac*, an old naval collier. **Stars and Stripes:** the American flag. **the Green unfurled:** an Irish banner ("the Green"). *Maine*: the U.S. battleship sunk in the harbor of Havana, Cuba, on February 15, 1898. Of the 260 crew members who were casualties, sixty-four men bore distinctively Irish surnames or were natives of Ireland. Two of the uninjured men also bore Irish surnames. **besprent:** sprinkled over. **flinters:** also "flinders," small fragments, splinters. **Old Glory:** the American flag. **their old slogan:** perhaps the cry "Remember the *Maine*!", a call for war against Spain directed at Congress ("Loud sounding o'er Potomac's shore"). **O'Neill:** William O'Neill (1860–1898), a native of Ireland who helped organize the Arizona Volunteers, a group which later became part of the First U.S. Volunteer Cavalry Regiment (the "Rough Riders"). Not long after he and his men landed in Cuba, the popular officer was cut down by enemy fire on San Juan Hill. **McCoy:** Frank McCoy, who served with the Tenth Cavalry in Cuba, where he saw service at Las Guasimas and was wounded in the San Juan Hill engagement. His first paternal American ancestor came from Ireland sometime before 1750. **McCalla:** Bowman McCalla, who led a party that successfully cut two telegraphic cables between Cienfuegos, Cuba, and Spain on May 11, 1898. He later served in the Philippines and led a detachment of 112 sailors and marines to the rescue of the foreign legations in Peking, China, during the Boxer uprising. His great-grand-mother was from County Antrim, Ireland. **Rough Riders:** the First U.S. Volunteer Cavalry Regiment, recruited from the cattle ranges and the mining camps of the West and led by Theodore Roosevelt. **Dons:** Spanish lords or gentlemen; used here to refer to Spanish military officers. **wily Don:** Pascual Cervera y Topete, the admiral of the Spanish fleet in Santiago harbor. **Bunker Hills [*sic*]:** Bunker Hill: actually Breed's Hill, the scene of a battle between the British and American colonials in Charlestown, Massachusetts, on June 17, 1775. Seven of the American officers in that engagement were natives of Ireland, five had Irish immigrant parents, and another five were of Irish descent. Fifty-four of the American casualties had Irish surnames, and twenty were natives of Ireland. **Stoney Point [*sic*]:** Stony Point, the last major northern battle of the American Revolution, when General Anthony Wayne's troops captured a 600-man British garrison on the Hudson River in June 1779. **Antilles:** probably a reference to Saint Eustatius and Tobago, two islands in the Antilles (West Indies), which were captured in 1780 by the Dillon Regiment of the Irish Brigade in the service of France. The regiment was under the command of Count Arthur Dillon, a member of an originally Irish family which had settled in France at the end of the seventeenth century. (*See* the poem "Dillon's Brigade" in Section 12.) **New Orleans:** the scene of an American victory by Andrew Jackson and his 5,500 men against a British force of 9,000 troops in January 1815. Jackson's parents were natives of Ireland. **Mexico:** an allusion to the Mexican War (1836–1838) between the United States and Mexico. **the Philippines:** an allusion to the Americans' capture of the islands during the Spanish-American War and to the subsequent efforts of Filipino nationalists to oust the U.S. military. **Pekin's walls:** an allusion to a fifty-five-day siege of the legation district of Peking, China, by a fanatical Chinese group known as the Boxers in 1898. One of the Americans killed on this mission was Captain Henry J. Reilly, a native of Ireland and the commander of Battery F of the Fifth U.S. Artillery. (See the poem "Reilly of F" in Section 80.)

78. The Men of the *Merrimac*

Despite the American blockade around Cuba at the beginning of the Spanish-American War, six Spanish warships under Admiral Cervera slipped past the blockading ships and into Santiago harbor. The American admiral William Sampson responded to this development with a plan to seal up the enemy fleet by sinking a ship at the narrowest part of the harbor channel. Lieutenant Richmond Hobson was selected to carry out this undertaking with the *Merrimac* (an old naval collier) and a crew of volunteers. Two of the seven volunteers who were selected for this gamble were Irish Americans — Francis Kelly of Boston, a twenty-eight-year-old water tender aboard the *Merrimac*, and J. C. Murphy, a coxswain from the U.S.S. *Iowa*. The other volunteers were Randolph Clausen, a coxswain on the *New York*; Osborn Deignan, a coxswain on the *Merrimac*; George F. Phillips, a machinist on the *Merrimac*; Daniel Montagu, a seaman on the *Brooklyn*; and George Charette, a gunner's mate on the *New York*.

According to the American plan, the *Merrimac* would be sunk when its torpedoes were fired in succession, beginning forward, so as to throw her down by the bow. During a training session Murphy was told that he would be given a signal to cut the *Merrimac*'s anchor rope and the lashings on the starboard side. He was then to cross over to the port side of the vessel and prepare to fire torpedo #1. After being told about the dangers he could expect from the rushing chain and the breaking hawsers, he examined the anchor lashing, noticed the ax that he would use to cut the anchor rope, found the end of the signal-cord, and inspected the wire ends for making contact with the torpedo. "It shall be done, sir," Murphy said, showing that he understood his duties. Charette, meanwhile, was to fire torpedoes #2 and #3. Deignan, after putting the helm hard aport, was to "lay down" to torpedo #4 and be ready to fire by the time #3 went off. An additional man was to be selected from the relief crew to attend to torpedo #5. After stopping the *Merrimac*'s engine, Kelly and Phillips were to open the sea connections — thereby flooding the vessel — and come up on deck. Phillips was to stand by to fire torpedo #6, and Kelly torpedo #8.

As often happens, however, even the best laid plans can go awry. The *Merrimac* had not gone very far up the channel when it came under heavy attack from the Spanish shore batteries and suffered damage to its steering mechanism. When the collier began to drift out of control, Kelly and two other men remained below deck trying to fix one of the boilers. After Hobson decided to sink the vessel by exploding its torpedoes, Kelly emerged on deck and proceeded to put on a life preserver. Almost immediately he was thrown to the deck by the explosion of a large projectile, as a result of which his right upper lip was cut away. After regaining consciousness, Kelly rushed down into the engine room but stopped when he saw that the water had risen around the cylinders. He then returned to the deck and took his place at torpedo #8, only to find that the projectile's cells and connections had been destroyed. In the end, only torpedoes #1 and #5 fired properly, the others having been disabled by shrapnel. (When Murphy fired torpedo #1, he suffered a wound to his right hip, a gash about twelve inches in length and perhaps a half inch in depth.) The *Merrimac* continued to drift until it sank, unfortunately in a position that left the channel open. Hobson and his men had abandoned the collier before it finally went down, escaping on a catamaran. They were picked up by Cervera himself and for thirty-three days were imprisoned in Morro Castle.

The Men of the *Merrimac*
by Clinton Scollard (1860–1932)

Hail to Hobson! Hail to Hobson! hail to all the valiant set!
Clausen, Kelly, Deignan, Phillips, Murphy, Montagu, Charette!
Howsoe'er we laud and laurel we shall be their debtors yet!
Shame upon us, shame upon us, should the nation e'er forget!

Though the tale be worn with the telling, let the daring deed be sung!
Surely never brighter valor, since this wheeling world was young,
Thrilled men's souls to more than wonder, till praise leaped from every
    tongue!

Trapped at last the Spanish sea-fox in the hill-locked harbor lay;
Spake the Admiral from his flagship, rocking off the hidden bay,
"We must close yon open portal lest he slip by night away!"

"Volunteers!" the signal lifted; rippling through the fleet it ran;
Was there ever deadlier venture? was there ever bolder plan?
Yet the gallant sailors answered, answered well-nigh to a man!

Ere the dawn's first rose-flush kindled, swiftly sped the chosen eight
Toward the batteries grimly frowning o'er the harbor's narrow gate;
Sooth, he holds his life but lightly who thus gives the dare to Fate.

They had passed the other portal where the guns grinned, tier o'er tier,
When portentous Morro thundered, and Socapa echoed clear,
And Estrella joined the chorus pandemoniac to hear.

Heroes without hands to waver, heroes without hearts to quail,
There they sank the bulky collier 'mid the hurtling Spanish hail;
Long shall float our starry banner if such lads beneath it sail!

Hail to Hobson! Hail to Hobson! hail to all the valiant set!
Clausen, Kelly, Deignan, Phillips, Murphy, Montagu, Charette!
Howsoe'er we laud and laurel we shall be their debtors yet!
Shame upon us, shame upon us, should the nation e'er forget!

Hobson: Lieutenant Richmond Pearson Hobson (1870–1937). **Clausen:** Randolph Clausen, a coxswain on the *New York*. **Kelly:** John Kelly, a water-tender on the *Merrimac*. **Deignan:** Osborn Deignan, a coxswain on the *Merrimac*. **Phillips:** George F. Phillips, a machinist on the *Merrimac*. **Murphy:** J. C. Murphy, a coxswain on the *Iowa*. **Montagu:** Daniel Montagu, a seaman on the *Brooklyn*. **Charette**: George Charette, a gunner's mate on the *New York*. **Spanish sea-fox:** Pascual Cervera y Topete, the admiral of the Spanish fleet in the harbor of Santiago, Cuba. **Admiral:** William Sampson (1840–1902), whose fleet blockaded six Spanish warships in Santiago harbor. **Morro:** the Spanish fortification on the eastern side of the entrance into Santiago harbor. **Socapa and Estrella:** the Spanish batteries on the western and eastern sides, respectively, of the neck leading into Santiago harbor.

Hobson of Santiago

by John Jerome Rooney (1866–1934)

Richmond Hobson—that is his name!
	Gallant South, be proud of him,
For he is made of old hero stuff—
	Heart and soul and body and limb!

Dauntless soul of the ancient mold,
	Fashioned of metal tried and true,
Here's the cup of a Nation's heart
	Brimming with love for you!

Admiral Sampson, bold and grim,
	Close by Santiago lay,
Holding the Spanish Admiral's fleet
	Trapped in the narrow bay—

Trapped, yet not secure enough
	To quiet the Yankee sailor's fear—
For the channel out to the Carib sea
	Was all unblocked and clear!

What if Cervera—desperate now—
	Should slip, some night, when the tempest blew,
Out of the bay to the friendly deep
	The Yankee squadron through?

Give him a chance—a running chance—
    In his Windward Strait, with his greyhound keels,
And, Sampson, you'll see, thro' your two-inch glass,
    A pair of Spanish heels!

"What's to be done?" the Admiral thought—
    "What's to be done to keep him there
Till we starve him out or shell him out—
    Or capture him in his lair?

"Here is the plan!" said Hobson then—
    "We'll block him in till the blue-coats come—
We'll put the cork in his little jug
    And fasten it like a drum!"

"But who will do the trick for me?—
    Who will go to his certain fate
In some sturdy hulk, we well may spare,
    And sink her in the strait?"

"I!" said Lieutenant Hobson, "I!"
    And twice two thousand men said "I!"
Not a man or boy in the Yankee fleet
    Was afraid that day to die!

"Seven we need," the Admiral said—
    "Seven to settle the Spaniard's debt—
Phillips, Montague [*sic*], Deignan, Kelly,
    Murphy and George Charette!

"And, Lieutenant, you shall take the ship—
    The good, stout collier *Merrimac*—
Into the channel's narrowest neck
    And sink her in her track!"

And there was another hero there—
    Whom the Admiral quite forgot to name,
Coxswain Clausen, who'd slipp'd aboard—
    Pledged fast to death or fame!

'Twas three-o'-the-clock—the moon was hid—
    The lightning flashed in a fitful glare,
The great fleet lay, in a watchful sleep,
    Like an eagle poised in air:

The word was said—the *Merrimac*,
   Lifting her anchor, drifted away
From the flagship's side—the stanch *New York*—
   Down to the slumbering bay:

Into the narrow mouth she went—
   Under her ten-knot steam she dashed—
While high above, on the frowning crew,
   The lights of Morro flashed!

Then came a shot from the signal gun—
   A warning call to the ships and shore—
And the darkness flamed with the tongues of fire
   And shook with the thunder roar!

Crash on crash—and a storm of shell
   Roared from the landward batteries
Till the air was rent with the surging sound
   Like the boom of many seas!

Yet, straight plunged the gallant *Merrimac*
   Over the mines of the wily Don—
The muskets cracked, the hoarse shells shrieked—
   But still the ship went on!

Estrella battery, just ahead,
   Belched out her sheets of steel and flame—
With never a pause, thro' the narrowing neck,
   The eight grim heroes came!

"Helm hard aport!"—the ship hove to—
   The anchor fell, the engines stopped—
And across the channel, from side to side,
   The fated vessel dropped!

The touch of a button—a muffled roar—
   And, forward, to port, a quick, fierce shock —
The plates were rent and the bulkheads crushed
   Like a lightning-riven rock!

She shuddered and shook with an ague spell—
   She moaned and tossed like a god in pain—
Then down she went—and carried below
   The last mad hope of Spain!

Over the side went the valiant crew,
    Hobson and all his gallant men—
And the heart of the Spanish Admiral
    Was touched and softened then!

"Fire not a shot at yon catamaran—
    For a braver foe ne'er sailed the sea—
And, I vow, these fearless Yankee lads
    Shall honor my ship and me!"

Nobly done and nobly said,
    Seaman from chivalrous Arragon [sic] —
The Yankee heart, wherever it be,
    Salutes and thanks the Don!

But Richmond Hobson—that is his name!
    Gallant South, be proud of him—
Builded of stanch old hero-stuff,
    Heart and soul and body and limb!

Dauntless soul, of the ancient mold,
    Fashioned of metal tried and true,
Here's the cup of a Nation's heart
    Brimming with love for you!

Richmond Hobson: Lieutenant Richmond Pearson Hobson (1870–1937). **Gallant South:** Hobson was born in Greensboro, Alabama. **Admiral Sampson:** William Sampson (1840–1902), whose fleet blockaded six Spanish warships in the harbor of Santiago, Cuba. **Spanish Admiral:** Pascual Cervera y Topete, the admiral of the Spanish fleet in Santiago harbor. **Cervera:** (See the previous note.) **Windward Strait:** the Windward Passage, a strait in the West Indies between Cuba and Hispaniola. **keels:** flat-bottomed barges. **blue-coats:** probably American army troops. **Phillips:** George F. Phillips, a machinist on the *Merrimac*. **Montague [sic]:** Daniel Montagu, a seaman on the *Brooklyn*. **Deignan:** Osborn Deignan, a coxswain on the *Merrimac*. **Kelly:** John Kelly, a water-tender on the *Merrimac*. **Murphy:** J. C. Murphy, a coxswain on the *Iowa*. **George Charette:** a gunner's mate on the *New York*. **Clausen:** Randolph Clausen, a coxswain on the *New York*. **Morro:** the Spanish fortification on the eastern side of the entrance into Santiago harbor. **wily Don:** Pascual Cervera y Topete, the admiral of the Spanish fleet in Santiago harbor. In Spanish-speaking countries a don is a lord or a gentleman. **Estrella battery:** the Spanish battery on the eastern side of the neck leading into Santiago Harbor. **Arragon [sic]:** Aragon, a region in northeastern Spain.

Eight Volunteers

by Lansing C. Bailey (1870-1913)

Eight volunteers! on an errand of death!
    Eight men! Who speaks?
Eight men to go where the cannon's hot breath
    Burns black the cheeks.

Eight men to man the old *Merrimac*'s hulk;
Eight men to sink the old steamer's black bulk,
Blockade the channel where Spanish ships skulk,—
    Eight men! Who speaks?
"Eight volunteers!" said the Admiral's flags!

    Eight men! Who speaks?
Who will sail under El Morro's black crags?—
    Sure death he seeks.
Who is there willing to offer his life?
Willing to march to this music of strife,—
Cannon for drum and torpedo for life?
    Eight men! Who speaks?

Eight volunteers! on an errand of death!
    Eight men! Who speaks?
Was there a man who in fear held his breath?
    With fear-paled cheeks?
From ev'ry war-ship ascended a cheer!
From ev'ry sailor's lips burst the word "Here!"
Four thousand heroes their lives volunteer!
    Eight men! Who speaks?

El Morro: the Spanish castle or fortification on the eastern side of the entrance into Santiago harbor.

79. William "Buckey" O'Neill

Born in Ireland in 1860, William O'Neill was that uniquely western type of Renaissance man: editor, gambler, newspaper owner, lawyer, sheriff, miner, explorer, politician, soldier, and hero. While working as a typesetter for the *Phoenix Herald*, he displayed such skill in "bucking the tiger" — making a particular move in the card game faro — that he was given the nickname "Buckey." He later became the editor of the *Arizona Gazette*, a reporter for the *Tombstone Epitaph*, the editor of the *Prescott Miner*, and the owner-editor of *Hoof and Horn*, a cattleman's journal. In 1889, while sheriff of Yavapai County, O'Neill led a posse that nabbed four cowboys who had stolen $1,300 from an Atlantic & Pacific train east of Flagstaff. The 600-mile, three-week pursuit ended with a shootout before the outlaws were taken to Kanab, Utah, for trial.

With the outbreak of hostilities between the United States and Spain, O'Neill helped organize the Arizona Volunteers, a group which later became part of the First U.S. Volunteer Cavalry Regiment, also known as the "Rough Riders." His enthusiasm for supporting the war effort against Spain may have been the result of his belief that Arizona would secure statehood and "stardom" if her young men rallied to the flag. In a letter written to a friend some time in May 1898, O'Neill asked the rhetorical question, "Who would not gamble for a new star in the flag?"

Whatever O'Neill's aspirations for Arizona, the Fates had decreed otherwise for the Irish aspirant. Not long after he and his men landed in Cuba, the popular officer was cut down by enemy fire on San Juan Hill. Theodore Roosevelt, the colonel of the First U.S. Volunteer Cavalry, recorded the tragic episode of July 1, 1898: "The most serious loss that I and the regiment could have suffered befell just before we charged. Buckey O'Neill was strolling up and down in front of his men, smoking his cigarette, for he was inveterately addicted to the habit. He had a theory that an officer ought never to take cover — a theory which was, of course, wrong, though in a volunteer organization the officers should certainly expose themselves very fully, simply for the effect on the men; our regiment toast on the transport running, 'The officers; may the war last until each is killed, wounded, or promoted.' As O'Neill moved to and from, his men begged him to lie down, and one of the sergeants said, 'Captain, a bullet is sure to hit you.' O'Neill took his cigarette out of his mouth, and blowing out a cloud of smoke laughed and said, 'Sergeant, the Spanish bullet isn't made that will kill me.' A little later he discussed for a moment with one of the regular officers the direction from which the Spanish fire was coming. As he turned on his heel a bullet struck him in the mouth and came out at the back of his head; so that even before he fell his wild and gallant soul had gone out into the darkness."

O'Neill's death was all the more ironic because of another tragic episode which had occurred when American troops first landed at Daiquiri, Cuba. During the landing, two African-American cavalrymen were pulled under the water by the surf. Although O'Neill tried to rescue the two men, he was ultimately unsuccessful. After his death his widow received condolences from Prescott's African-American citizens, who described their former mayor as a true and tried friend.

Rough Rider O'Neill
by Joseph I. C. Clarke (1846–1925)

When the cresset of war blazed over the land
    And a call rang fierce thro' the West,
Saying, "Rough Riders, come to the roll of the drum,"
    They came with their bravest and best,
With a clatter of hoofs and a stormy hail—
    Sinewy, lean, tall and brown;
Hunters and fighters and men of the trail,
    From hills and plains, from college and town;
With the cowboys' yell and the redman's whoop,
    Sons of thunder and swingers of steel;
And, leading his own Arizona troop,
    Rode glad and fearless "Bucky" O'Neill.

In the ranks there was Irish blood galore,
    As it ever is sure to be
When the Union flag is flung to the fore,
    And the fight is to make men free.
There were Kellys and Murphys and Burkes and Boyles—
    The colonel owned an O'Brien strain—
And the lift of the race made a glow on each face
    When they met on the Texan plain;
But the man of them all, with the iron will—
    Man and soldier from crown to heel;
A leader and master in games that kill—
    Was soft-spoken Captain "Bucky" O'Neill.

On the watch in the valley or charging the height,
    In a plunge 'cross the steep ravine,
San Juan or Las Guasimas, battle or fight,
    Or a rush thro' the jungle screen,
Where the wave of the war took the battling host
    The Rough Riders fronted the storm,
And their dead on the rocks of red glory tossed

Amid spray with their life-blood warm.
What wonder, then, holding his chivalrous vow
        To stoop not, nor crouch not, nor kneel,
That Death in hot anger struck full on the brow
        Of the dauntless "Bucky" O'Neill.

O, battle that tries out the hearts of the strong,
        To your test he had answered true,
Who bent not his head and balked but at wrong,
        Nor murmured what billet he drew!
In the cast of the terrible dice of doom
        It came fair to his hand as well
To mount the high crest where the great laurels bloom
        Or to die at the foot where he fell.
And of such are the victors, and these alone
        Shall be stamped with the hero seal,
And stirrup to stirrup they'll ride to the Throne,
        From the colonel to "Bucky" O'Neill!

The colonel owned an O'Brien strain: an allusion to Roosevelt's distant Irish ancestry, although the O'Brien reference is unclear. Roosevelt's ancestors included John Barnwell (who came to America from County Meath, Ireland, in 1701) and John Barnhill (who was born in northern Ireland about 1729). **San Juan:** a Spanish outpost in Cuba stormed by American troops on July 1, 1898. **Las Guasimas:** a skirmish in which 1,000 American troops forced a Spanish rear guard of 1,500 to abandon its position on June 24, 1898.

The Rough Riders

by John Steven McGroarty (1862–1944)

Souls of the rough riding men, the first-born and the last,
Come and gather 'round us from out the storied past,
Come from the field of Monmouth, the red-dyed Rapidan,
Come with Putnam and Marion, Stonewall and Sheridan;
Far from silent bivouacs that sleep in ancient dust,
Leap again to saddle, unsheath you[r?] swords of rust,
List to the bugle ringing clear on the desert sky,
Calling the war-worn troopers that now go riding by.

Come and gather 'round us, souls of hard riding men,
Who fought with swinging sabers, of old, o'er hill and glen,
Souls of the strong adventurers who blazed the bloody trail
Down from the guns of Lexington to Shenandoah's vale;

Halt your ghostly riders, your squadrons side by side,
While they ride by who rode, as you, upon a battle tide,
Wanderers of the savage hills and desert's blinding plain,
Who spilled their eager hearts against the chivalry of Spain.

We'll dream again they're gathered from near and far away,
That host that to the Alamo rode down one sun-kissed day.
The bronco busters of the plain, the hunters from the hill,
The keepers of the rainless wastes that love and lure them still;
Brood of the trackless wilderness, swart with desert's breath,
Spawn of the brown Southwest whose trails are dim with death.
We'll dream once more they're mustered, here 'neath skies aglow,
A thousand strong in the rendezvous as then at the Alamo.

And as the dust-brown columns sweep on with thunder tread,
Full will we fling a cheer for him, the chieftain at the head,
A cheer for him the chieftain, who led them on the way,
At whose clear call to glory they galloped to the fray,
Him they trailed to victory where flamed the flag unfurled,
The one great heart of all best loved of all the world.
We'll lift our hearts to greet him as breaks the vision, then,
Of Roosevelt still riding with his rough riding men.

Sing from your throat, O bugle, as they ride forth at dawn,
From Caney and Guaysimas [*sic*] and the hill at San Juan;
Turn again, O Memory, with heart that holds them dear,
Again their steeds are champing, the hoof-beats sounding near;
Home from crimson fights they won, home they come at last,
To ride in full review before the spirits of the past,
Here, where one silent trooper waits upon the way
The last rung trumpet call that wakes the Judgment Day.

Onward they come in full view, the living and the dead,
Troop and the plunging squadron, their leader at the head;
And he will halt his charger as all the columns wheel,
Where face to face they stand again—Roosevelt and O'Neill.
Up to the Colonel's lips will leap his saber in salute
To him, the well-loved Captain, who sits the stirrups mute,
Smiling as when he answered to freedom's crowding roll,
And death flung to the darkness his wild and gallant soul.

So shall they come with Memory from near and far away,
The host that from the Alamo rode out one sunlit day.
Back they come to mountain and desert's shining plain,

The living and the gloried dead, the wounded and the slain;
Every saddle set once more as when they rode to war,
To strike for a new republic, to die for a new born star;
Not a gap in the ranks of dream that sailed the tropic sea—
Colonel, Captains and troopers all, home from *Cuba free*.

So shall they come and pass away as evening's shadow falls,
And good-night songs and reveille the singing bugle calls,
Leaving this one lone sentry upon the grim plateau
Over the purpled buttes aflame and shifting dunes below,
Here in his silent stirrups with desert stars agleam,
Soul of the wild adventure, heart of the deathless dream,
One faithful, sun-browned trooper that waits upon the way
The last rung trumpet call that wakes the Judgment Day.

Monmouth: a Revolutionary War battle fought at Monmouth Courthouse, New Jersey, in June 1778. **Rapidan:** a tributary of the Rappahannock River in Virginia. The battle of Fredericksburg was fought nearby in December 1862. **Putnam:** Israel Putnam (1718–1790), a Revolutionary War general who distinguished himself at the battle of Bunker Hill in June 1775. **Marion:** Francis Marion (1732?–1795), a Revolutionary War general who organized paramilitary bands of patriots to harass loyalists and British forces. **Stonewall:** Thomas "Stonewall" Jackson (1824–1863), the Confederate general who died of wounds sustained when he was accidentally killed by fire from his own men. **Sheridan:** Philip Sheridan (1831–1888), the commander of the 10,000-man cavalry corps of the Army of the Potomac. **Lexington:** a Revolutionary War battle fought at Lexington, Massachusetts, on April 19, 1775; also a Civil War engagement in which Union cavalry were routed by Confederate mounted troops at Lexington, Tennessee, on December 8, 1862. **Shenandoah's vale:** a valley in northwestern Virginia that saw heavy fighting during the Civil War. **Alamo:** the former mission in San Antonio, Texas, where a force of Americans and Texans was massacred by an army under Mexican dictator Santa Anna in March 1836. Of the 187 defenders of the Alamo, thirty-four were either Irish natives or men of Irish ancestry or with traditional Irish surnames. **Caney:** a battle in which a 521-man Spanish garrison in Cuba was overrun by Americans on July 1, 1898. **Guaysimas [*sic*]:** Guasimas, a skirmish in which 1,000 American troops forced a Spanish rear guard of 1,500 to retreat on June 24, 1898. **San Juan:** a battle in which the Rough Riders and four African-American regiments captured a Spanish outpost on July 1, 1898. **one lone sentry:** the statue of a Rough Rider, presumably O'Neill, located in front of the county courthouse in Prescott, Arizona. The statue was dedicated in 1907 and is inscribed with these words: "Erected by Arizona in honor of the first U.S. Volunteer Cavalry, known to history as Roosevelt's Rough Riders, and to the memory of Captain William O. O'Neill and his comrades who died while serving their country in the war with Spain."

80. Henry J. Reilly

In 1898 a fanatical Chinese group known as the Boxers led a violent uprising against Westerners in China. After a number of missionaries and members of the foreign legations were killed in Peking, the Boxers began a fifty-five-day siege of the legation district of the capital. In response, American troops were sent to China to help Austrian, British, French, German, Italian, Russian, and Japanese troops rescue the legations.

One of the Americans on this mission was Captain Henry J. Reilly, a native of Ireland and the commander of Battery F of the Fifth U.S. Artillery. On August 15, 1900, his men distinguished themselves by blasting open the first gate into the Chinese capital. Reilly's thirty-eight-year military career was cut short, however, when he was killed by a Chinese bullet as he stood atop the Chien Gate observing his men fire their guns. He was buried the next day on the grounds of the American legation. Just before the flag-draped coffin was lowered into the ground, the American minister moved forward to retrieve the Stars and Stripes. "Don't touch that flag," General Chaffee, the U.S. military commander, cried. "If it's the last American flag in China it will be buried with Reilly." The following April Reilly's remains were moved to Arlington National Cemetery in Virginia. He was survived by a wife and two sons and two daughters.

Reilly of F

by John Jerome Rooney (1866–1934)

I

Know you the story, friends, know you the story?
    No hero is mine of the plume and the lance—
Yet worthy to claim the green bay of glory
    In the lay of the singer of oldest romance.
Then, when the song of the minstrel is gone,
Forget not how Reilly—brave Reilly went on!

II

Out from the East, like a bolt from the sky,
    Thrilled the wild rumor of danger and dread—
Out from the East flamed a prayer and a cry—
    A cry of the living, a cry of the dead—
Straight to the heart of the nations it came,
And the nations were shaken, as wind shakes a flame!

III

There 'mid the millions of Mongols, they stood—
    One grain in the desert, a drop in the sea—
Mothers and children—brave men of our blood—
    What is their fate? Say, what shall it be?
How can we name the thing that we fear?
The heart, at the thought, is palsied and seer!

IV

Onward! the cry of the East and the West—
    Onward! spoke Chaffe, Columbia's son:
The nations were calling for their bravest and best
    For the work of a giant before them undone.
No time now to palter with quavering breath—
'Twas action and rescue — 'twas rescue or death!

V

And the word came to Reilly—it spoke not again—
    Brave Reilly with all his bold lads of the guns—
(Ah, if any came out from El Caney's red rain,
    'Twas by the grace of the Lord—not Hispania's sons!)
Oh, a stancher band never turned face to the foe
As onward with Reilly, straight onward they go!

VI

They battered the walls of the forts of Taku,
    They lifted the door-knock and pounded it well—
And the door?—the door was a breach looking thro'
    An entrance well dusted by shrapnel and shell.
The fort, like a mist of the morning, was gone,
And Reilly went on—bold Reilly went on!

VII

On by the railroad—still onward they press'd—
    Thro' rampart—thro' swamp, like a sword of the Lord—
True sons of the East, true sons of the West,
    A knight of King Arthur confronting a horde!
And Battery F, unafraid of the brunt,
Kept its pace, and its guns, right up to the front!

VIII

See! See! the walls of the Capital rise
    Away to the right, a vision of power—
They are flashing a signal—our loved one's replies—
    They are lost had the guns been delayed but an hour.
Like a cyclone they open and thunder their doom
And the flame from their mouths is the light in our gloom!

IX

Battery F opened up like a hell,
    With a roar like a lion—a serpent's fierce hiss—
Solid shot under! above with the shell!
    Gates were not made to be pounded like this.
Trembles the portal—with a shot it is gone—
And Reilly went on—bold Reilly went on!

X

From the compound a cheer, like a voice from the grave,
    Rolls upward and out and upward again;
The Lord—He is gracious and mighty to save,
    And he works by the hands of His valiant of men!
Still, was work to be done—stern work to be done—
Ere the wall'd town within was level'd and won.

XI

Then "Forward," called Reilly—and forward they swept
    To the walls where the foe had rallied his horde.
Like a boy, to a ladder the Captain has leapt,
    You can see, far in front, the gleam of his sword.
Then up thro' the smoke, like a wraith, he has gone—
And Reilly went on—bold Reilly went on!

XII

O sweet harp of Erin, sound gently thy lay!
    O star of Columbia, be swift with thy light!
He fell—and the summit of Glory that day
    Was the rampart he scaled alone in the fight.
In a beam of the splendor a moment he shone—
And Reilly went on—brave Reilly went on!

Mongols: conquerors who invaded northern China in the thirteenth century; used here to mean Chinese. **Chaffee:** Adna Romanza Chaffee (1842–1914), the U.S. brigadier general whose troops were victorious at the battle of Caney in Cuba during the Spanish-American War. He later commanded the American troops in China who helped rescue foreigners besieged in Peking during the Boxer Rebellion. **Columbia:** the United States of America, usually personified as a female figure. **El Caney:** a battle fought in Cuba on July 1, 1898, during the Spanish-American War. **Hispania:** Spain. **Taku:** a city on the east coast of China, about 100 miles east of Peking. Two of Taku's three forts were located on the north side of the entrance to the Pei Ho River; the third was on the south side of the entrance. **King Arthur:** a sixth-century warrior and leader of the Britons against the Germanic invaders. **Capital:** Peking, China. **Erin:** a literary name for Ireland.

81. William McKinley

William McKinley, the twenty-fifth president of the United States, was descended from James MacKinlay, who had accompanied William III to Ireland and fought with the Presbyterian king at the battle of the Boyne in 1690. James's son David — the president's great-great-great-grandfather — was born in northern Ireland (probably County Antrim) about 1705 and sailed for Pennsylvania about forty years later.

William McKinley was born in Niles, Ohio, in 1843 and during the Civil War served with the Twenty-Third Ohio Regiment. At the battle of Antietam, the young McKinley was attached to the Union commissary. Realizing that the men in his brigade had eaten only a scant breakfast before the engagement, he drove a mule team loaded with food rations and hot coffee right into the thick of the fighting. For this unusual attention to duty, he was promoted to second lieutenant. Rutherford B. Hayes, a major at the time, described McKinley's action as "a thing that had never occurred under similar circumstances in any other army in the world."

After the war McKinley practiced law and then entered politics, serving as a U.S. congressman for fourteen years and as governor of Ohio for four. In 1896 he was elected president on a Republican platform that supported the gold standard and protective tariffs, policies which "radicals" like William Jennings Bryan blamed for the plight of the American farmer. Although McKinley initially opposed war with Spain over that country's repressive and often brutal policies in Cuba, he was gradually pushed by public opinion to ask Congress to declare war.

After acquiring the Philippines as a prize of victory in that conflict, the United States proceeded to impose its rule on a people who were thought to be unfit for self-government and resisted American efforts to "civilize" them. In the process, the Americans killed about 8,000 Filipinos, having adopted the very policies which they had condemned the Spanish for using in Cuba.

McKinley was in the first year of his second term when he became a victim of this new American imperialism. On September 6, 1901, while shaking hands with visitors to the Temple of Music at the Pan-American Exposition in Buffalo, New York, the president was shot and died eight days later. The assassin — Leon Czolgosz, an anarchist who opposed the American campaign against the Philippine insurrectionists — had approached the chief executive with a handkerchief covering the revolver in his hand. McKinley's last words were, "Goodbye all. It is God's will. His will, not ours, be done."

McKinley

author unknown

'T is not the President alone
    Who, stricken by that bullet, felt
The assassin's shot that laid him prone
    Pierced a great nation's heart as well;
And when the baleful tidings sped
    From lip to lip throughout the crowd,
Then, as they deemed their ruler dead,
    'T was Liberty that cried aloud.

Ay, Liberty! for where the foam
    Of oceans twain marks the coast
'T is there, in Freedom's very home,
    That anarchy has maimed its host;
There 't is that it has turned to bite
    The hand that fed it; there repaid
A country's welcome with black spite;
    There, Judas-like, that land betrayed.
For 't is no despot that's laid low,
    But a free nation's chosen chief;
A free man, stricken by a blow
    Base, dastardly, past all belief.
And Tyranny exulting hears
    The tidings flashed across the sea;
While stern Repression hugs her fears,
    And mouths them in a harsh decree.

Meanwhile the cloud, though black as death,

Is lined with hopes, hopes light as life,
And Liberty that, scant of breath,
      Had watched the issue of the strife,
Fills the glad air with grateful cries
      To find the sun no more obscured,
And with new yearnings in her eyes
      Climbs to her watch-tower—reassured.

Faithful Unto Death

by Richard Handfield Titherington (1861–1935)

His work is done, his toil is o'er;
      A martyr for our land he fell—
      The land he loved, that loved him well;
Honor his name for evermore!

Let all the world its tribute pay,
      For glorious shall be his renown;
      Though duty's was his only crown,
Yet duty's path is glory's way.

For he was great without pretence;
      A man of whom none whispered shame,
      A man who knew nor guile nor blame;
Good in his every influence.

On battle-field, in council-hall,
      Long years with sterling service rife
      He gave us, and at last his life—
Still unafraid at duty's call.

Let the last solemn pageant move,
      The nation's grief to consecrate
      To him struck down by maniac hate
Amid a mighty nation's love;

And though the thought it solace gives,
      Beside the martyr's grave to-day
      We feel 't is almost hard to say:
"God reigns and the Republic lives!"

Outward Bound

by Edward Sydney Tylee

Farewell! for now a stormy morn and dark
  The hour of greeting and of parting brings;
Already on the rising wind yon bark
    Spreads her impatient.

Too hasty keel, a little while delay!
  A moment tarry, O thou hurrying dawn!
For long and sad will be the mourners' day
    When their beloved is gone.

But vain the hands that beckon from the shore:
  Alike our passion and our grief are vain.
Behind him lies our little world: before
    The illimitable main.

Yet, none the less, about his moving bed
  Immortal eyes a tireless vigil keep—
An angel at the feet and at the head
    Guard his untroubled sleep.

Two nations bowed above a common bier,
  Made one forever by a martyred son—
One in their agony of hope and fear,
    And in their sorrow one.

And thou, lone traveler, of a waste so wide,
  The uncharted seas that all must pass in turn,
May the same star that was so long thy guide
    O'er thy last voyage burn.

No eye can reach where through yon sombre veil
  That bark to its eternal fares;
No earthly breezes swell its shadowy sail;
    Only our love and prayers.

Two nations: possibly a reference to the class and sectional warfare that had characterized the campaigns of 1896 and 1900.

McKinley
by James Whitcomb Riley (1849–1916)

He said: "It is God's way;
    His will, not ours, be done."
And o'er our land a shadow lay
    That darkened all the sun;
The voice of jubilee
    That gladdened all the air
Fell sudden to a quavering key
    Of suppliance and prayer.

He was our chief—our guide—
    Sprung of our common earth.
From youth's long struggle proved and tried
    To manhood's highest worth;
Through toil, he knew all needs
    Of all his toiling kind,
The favored striver who succeeds,
    The one who falls behind.

The boy's young faith he still
    Retained through years mature—
The faith to labor, hand and will,
    Nor doubt the harvest sure—
The harvest of Man's love—
    A Nation's joy that swells
To heights of song, or deep whereof
    But sacred silence tells.

To him his Country seemed
    Even as a mother, where
He rested—slept; and once he dreamed—
    As on her bosom there—
And thrilled to hear, within
    That dream of her, the call
Of bugles and the clang and din
    Of war—And o'er it all

His rapt eyes caught the bright
    Old Banner, winging wild
And beck'ning him, as to the fight
    When—even as a child—

He awakened—And the dream
Was real! And he leapt
As led the proud flag through a gleam
Of tears the Mother wept.

His was a tender hand—
Even as a woman's is—
And yet as fixed, in Right's command,
As this bronze hand of his;
This was the soldier brave—
This was the Victor fair—
This is the Hero Heaven gave
To glory here—and There.

Old Banner: the Union flag, perhaps as opposed to the "new" Confederate ensign.

82. Theodore Roosevelt

Although the Dutch ancestry of Theodore Roosevelt, the twenty-sixth president of the United States, is well known, his Irish roots are often overlooked. Among his ancestors were John Barnwell (who came to America from County Meath, Ireland, in 1701) and John Barnhill (who was born in northern Ireland about 1729). Barnhill's granddaughter Margaret Barnhill of Philadelphia married Cornelius Van Schaack Roosevelt, the president's paternal grandfather.

During 1881 the twenty-two-year-old Roosevelt visited Europe with his new bride, Alice. In a letter to his mother from Killarney, Ireland, the future president described his impressions of the Emerald Isle: "After breakfast today, Alice and I started off on a jaunting car together with a very nice old Irishman for guide, and drove through beautiful lanes, bounded by white hawthorne hedges, and passing by more than one stately manor house . . .; then we got into the Kerry mountains, and the country became wild, rugged and barren, the yellow gorse surrounding the peat bogs, and in some of the glens or perched right on the mountain side, could be seen the small cabins, built of turf or stone, often without windows or chimney: adjoining each was a small potato field, a larger one of oats, and two or three lean cows, or else a few goats feeding on the mountain side. . . . A beautiful country; but with a terrible understratum of wretchedness with an example of which I was today brought face to face.

I passed a man lying on the road, insensible from sheer hunger! He was trying to get to Cork; I, or rather some peasants under my directions, revived him after a while: and I had him fed and sent to Cork and gave him ten shillings."

Though Roosevelt boasted of his Irish blood, he left an unflattering picture of some of the Irish members of the New York Assembly. "The [committee] Chairman," he wrote, "is an Irishman named Murphy, . . . a Fenian; he is a tall, stout man with a swollen, red face, a black moustache . . . and has had a long experience in politics — so that to undoubted pluck and a certain knowledge of parliamentary forms he adds a great deal of stupidity and a decided looseness of ideas as regards the 8th Commandment. Next comes John Shanley of Brooklyn, an Irishman, but born in America; much shrewder than Murphy and easier to get along with, being more Americanized, but fully as dishonest; . . . a Tammany Hall gentleman named McManus, a huge, fleshy, unutterably course and low brute who was formerly a prize fighter, at present keeps a low, drinking and dancing saloon, and is more than suspected of having begun life as a pickpocket."

Following his election to the presidency in 1904, however, Roosevelt was much more flattering in his estimation of the Irish electorate. "One of the things I am most pleased with in the recent election," he boasted, "is that while I got, I think, a greater proportion of the Americans of Irish birth or parentage and of the Catholic religion than any previous Republican candidate, I got this proportion purely because they knew I felt in sympathy with them and in touch with them, and they and I had the same ideals and principles, and not by any demagogic appeals about creed or race, or by any demagogic attack upon England."

The poems in this section are but a few of the scores which have been written about one of the nation's most colorful chief executives. The most complete collection of such works is the 1923 volume *Roosevelt as the Poets Saw Him*, edited by Charles Hanson Towne. The first poem below is a humorous account of Roosevelt's role in promoting a negotiated settlement to the Russo-Japanese War (1904-1905).

The Ballad of Sagamore Hill

by Wallace Irwin (1876-1959)

'Tis morning, and King Theodore
   Upon his throne sits he
As blithely as a King can sit
   Within a free countree,
And now he thinks of submarines,
   And now of peace and war.

His royal robe he handeth Loeb,
    Then wireth to the Czar:

"Come off, come off, thou Great White Czar,
    Come off thy horse so high!
Send envoys straight, and arbitrate
    Thy diplomatic pie."
Then straightway to the Mik-a-doo
    This letter he doth limn,
"Come off thy perch, thou Morning Sun,
    And do the same as him!"

Then straightway from the Rising Sun
    Come envoys three times three,
Komura neat and Sato sweet,
    (An Irish Japanee).
Small men are they with domey brains,
    And in their fingers gaunt
A list of seven hundred things
    They positively want.

Then straightway from St. Petersburg
    Come envoys six times two,
De Witty grand and Rosen bland
    And Nebotoffkatoo—
Volkyrieoffskygrandovitch—
    (Here see the author's note,
"The balance of that noble's name
    Came in another boat.")

'Twas on the royal yacht *Mayflower*
    They met, that noble crew.
"De Witty grand, shake Sato's hand—
    Komura, how-dee-do!"
While forty thousand gun-salutes
    Concuss on Oyster Bay,
A proud man is King Theodore
    Upon that trysting day!

To Portsmouth town, to Portsmouth town,
    The sweating envoys puff,
To speak of tin and Saghalien
    And eke to bluff and bluff—
But Theodore at Oyster Bay

Doth while the times between
By taking trips and dives and dips
    Within his submarine.

For many a day the Japanese
    Uphold their fingers gaunt,
And mention seven hundred things
    They positively want—
For many a day the Muscovites
    Down-plant their Russian shoes,
And mention seven hundred things
    They positively refuse.

Till happy from his submarine
    King Theodore doth peep,
And stops a wireless telegram
    That buzzeth o'er the deep:
"O Theodore, O goodly King,
    The envoys call our bluff—
Despite the fuss the stubborn Russ
    Disgorgeth not the stuff."

"Come hither, Mr. Serge de Witt!
    King Theodore doth say,
"Now tell me quick by the Big Stick
    Why dost refuse to pay?"
"Come hither, Baron Kom-u-ra,
    And sit upon my lap—
Why dost thou cuss and make a fuss,
    Thou naughty, naughty Jap?"

To Portsmouth back, to Portsmouth back,
    The envoys then do flee,
And each is sad and mild and meek
    As an envoy ought to be,
And as they speak of Terms of Peace
    Politeness doth ensue—
Like Prince Alphonse and Duke Gaston,
    'Tis ever "After you!"

So soon the terms of Peace are signed
    And put upon a shelf,
And Theodore doth straightway take
    Great credit to himself.

> The bugles call and roses fall
>> On good King Theodore,
> As round the Stick the kodaks click
>> Full twelve times thirty-four.
>
> And now when ancient grandsires sit
>> Within the evening gray,
> And oysters frolic noisilee
>> All over Oyster Bay,
> The graybeard tells his little niece
>> How Theodore did trek
> To drag the gentle Bird of Peace
>> To Portsmouth—by the neck.

Sagamore Hill: Roosevelt's home on Oyster Bay, Long Island, New York. **Loeb:** William Loeb, Roosevelt's private secretary. **Czar:** Nicholas II of Russia. **Mik-a-doo:** Mikado, a title of the Japanese emperor (meaning "exalted gate," or door of the imperial palace). **Morning Sun:** a title of the Japanese emperor. **Rising Sun:** Japan, often called the Land of the Rising Sun. **Komura:** Jutaro Komura (1855–1911), the Japanese diplomat who concluded the Treaty of Portsmouth (1905) ending the Russo-Japanese War. **Sato:** Sato Aimaro, one of three secretaries who accompanied the Japanese peace delegation. He performed his additional duty of dealing with the press with such humor that he was dubbed "the genial Sato" by the journalists. **St. Petersburg:** the capital of Russia from 1712 to 1918. **De Witty:** Serge Witte (1849–1915), the chief Russian envoy in peace negotiations with Japan at the end of the Russo-Japanese War (1904-1905). **Rosen:** Baron Roman Romanovitch Rosen, the Russian minister in Tokyo. **Nebotoffkatoo:** possibly a humorous liberty with the name of Constantine Nabakoff, a secretary to the Russian delegation. **Volkyrieoffskygrandovitch:** probably a humorous neologism created by joining common Russian syllables to a variant spelling of the Norse word *Valkyrie* (in Norse mythology any of the female spirits who bring the souls of slain warriors to Valhalla). **Oyster Bay:** the Long Island, New York, site of Roosevelt's home "Sagamore Hill." **Portsmouth:** The negotiations between the Russian and the Japanese envoys began on August 8, 1905, at the Portsmouth Naval Shipyard in Kittery, Maine, just across the Piscatagua River from Portsmouth, New Hampshire. **Saghalien:** also Sakhalin, an island off the extreme east coast of Siberia. **Muscovites:** inhabitants of Moscow or Russians generally. **Big Stick:** an allusion to the West African proverb which Roosevelt admired: "Speak softly and carry a big stick; you will go far." **Alphonse . . . Gaston:** a pair of Frenchmen created by Fred Opper for the comic pages of the Hearst Sunday editions in the early 1900s. The two men were characterized by their excessive good manners ("You first, my dear Alphonse!" "No, no — you first, my dear Gaston!"). **terms of Peace:** By the Treaty of Portsmouth (1905), Japan acquired Port Arthur, the southern half of Sakhalin Island, and Russia's sphere of influence in southern Manchuria. (For helping negotiate the treaty, Roosevelt received the Nobel Peace Prize the next year.) **Stick:** See "Big Stick" above. **kodaks:** from Kodak, the trademark name for a portable, roll-film camera introduced by George Eastman in 1888.

Roosevelt
by Vachel Lindsay (1879–1931)

When the stuffed prophets quarrel, when the sawdust
    comes out, I think of Roosevelt's genuine sins.
Once more my rash love for that cinnamon bear,
    Begins!

His sins were better than their sweetest goodness.
His blows were cleaner than their plainest kindness.
He saw more than they all, in his hours of black blindness.
The hour of his pitiful spiritual fall
He was more of an angel than all of this host,
When with Lucifer's pride his soul was burnt out,
When, still in the game, he gave up the ghost.

His yarns were nearer the sky than their truth.
His wildest tales, in his fish-story hour,
Nearer true than their truth.
When with art and with laughter he held supreme power,
He was white as the moon, and as honest as youth.

And now their sworn word is but barnyard mud.
And their highest pride is to hide in a hole.
They talk of "dollars" and "dollars" and "dollars"
And "dollars" and "dollars," and hate his clean soul.

(Oh money, money—that *never* can think,
Money, money, that *never* can rule,
Always an anarchist, always an idiot,
Always King Log—never King Stork,
Always rotting, reeking:—always a fool.)

Roosevelt was proud like a singer.
Roosevelt's pride was that of a scribe,
Or the pride of a father, the pride of a ruler,
The pride of the thoroughbred chief of a tribe,
The pride of Confucius, the pride of a student!
He hated a coward, he hated a fool,
He knew that money is always a fool.

When they tear each others' newspaper-hearts
I think of Roosevelt's genuine code.

He hated the paste-board, the smeary, the fake.
He hated the snake, the frog and the toad.

Oh a moose with sharp antler!
Oh a panther of panthers—Oh a fox of foxes
Often caught in tight boxes!
Yet we know he would always bark out the truth.
He loved the curious political game:—
But we know he loved better:—truth, God, and *youth*.

A peacock of peacocks! An eagle of eagles!
Defeating, within himself, the quick fox.
A buffalo roaring—a world-lion roaring!
Defeating within himself the bright fox,—
Then ranging out through the wilderness trail,
Killing the jackal—felling the ox.

Megalomaniac, envious, glorious,
Envying only the splendors of worth.

Emulating the cleanest on earth,
(Those who were, therefore, the strongest on earth).
Emulating thoroughbreds—always.
Peacock! Lion! Cinnamon bear!
Skyscrapers—steeples and plains for abode!
He was mostly the world's fine cinnamon bear,
He was mostly our glittering cinnamon bear,
Sitting there in an old rocking chair,
In the White House yard, taking the air.

He told us Aesop's new fables, each day—
President seven big glorious years!
Seven years of wonder. Must they all fade away,
In the quarrels of the rat with the loud-voiced cootie
Told by the zinc-throated, varnished "loud-speaker,"
Told by wireless, while the world sits breathless,
Or by megaphone,
By line-o'-type, or by letter ripe:—
The quarrels of the angle-worm with the toad?

Who elected these pole-cats rulers of men?

Let us start a gay nation over again!

Let us start a circus as honest as Barnum's,
With three clean rings, and plenty to see,
Athletes, not snakes, on the trapeze tree.

Let us start our nation over again,
In the names of legitimate rulers of men,
In the names of the great, and the famous dead:—
Yes, the name of the glittering cinnamon bear,
Never so wicked or sore in the head,
But he fed the children honey and bread.
He taught them the names of the great and the dead,
From the Irish Sagas, to Carson and Boone.

He loved the villages, Deadwood, Medora,
Tuskeegee and Tuscarora,
Mexicali and Farmington,
Calexico and Bennington,
Arlington and Lexington,
Oyster Bay, Mount Vernon.

He loved the cities Denver, Manhattan,
And the wide great spaces
From the Amazon to Saskatoon—
He loved the heroes, Columbus, Whitman, Lincoln,
He loved the heroes! He loved George Washington!—
Who was honest as youth and white as the moon.

"Great-heart!" Roosevelt! Father of Men!
He fed the children honey and bread.
He taught them the Ten Commandments and prayer,
Rocking there in his old rocking chair,
Or riding the storms of dream that he rode.

Join hands, poets, friends, companions!
Let us start a new world on the Roosevelt Code!

Let us start our nation over again
In the name of the honest, proud cinnamon bear,
Rocking there in his old rocking chair
Or riding the terrible storms that he rode!

Lucifer: a proud, rebellious archangel who was expelled from heaven. **King Log ... King Stork:** characters in Aesop's fable "Frogs Asking for a King." In reply to the frogs' request, Jupiter first sent them a log. When the new ruler permitted his subjects such familiarities as jumping on his back, the frogs learned to despise their king and asked Jupiter for a more active and imperious ruler. To the frogs' chagrin, the successor King Stork proved a tyrant who ruled through intimidation. **Confucius:** a Chinese philosopher and teacher (551?–478? B.C.). **Aesop:** a sixth-century B.C. Greek writer of fables. **Carson:** Christopher ("Kit") Carson (1800–1868), an American scout and frontiersman. **Boone:** Daniel Boone (1734–1820), an American pioneer. **Deadwood:** a town in South Dakota, in an area of the Black Hills that was the subject of some of Roosevelt's best prose. **Medora:** a town in North Dakota, the site of a log cabin in which Roosevelt lived between 1883 and 1885 while working on the Maltese Cross Ranch. **Tuskeegee:** a city in Georgia, the seat of Tuskeegee Institute, established in 1881 by Booker T. Washington, the African-American leader whose invitation to the White House by Roosevelt caused howls of disapproval from many Southerners. **Tuscarora:** a town in the Pennsylvania anthracite coal region; a Nevada village in a gold and silver district of the state. **Mexicali:** a city in northwest Mexico, on the Mexican-U.S. border. **Farmington:** one of several towns or villages by that name in the United States. **Calexico:** a city in southern California, on the Mexican-U.S. border. **Bennington:** probably Bennington, Vermont, the site of a victory over a British force by American militiamen led by General John Stark. **Arlington:** probably Arlington National Cemetery (in Arlington County, Virginia), the final resting place of many of the nation's military heroes. **Lexington:** probably Lexington, Massachusetts, where the first major battle of the American Revolution was fought on April 19, 1775. **Oyster Bay:** the Long Island, New York, site of Roosevelt's home "Sagamore Hill." **Mount Vernon:** George Washington's home along the Potomac River in Virginia. **Amazon:** a river in South America. **Saskatoon:** a city in Saskatchewan, Canada. **Whitman:** Walt Whitman (1819–1892), an American poet.

Our Colonel

by Arthur Guiterman (1871–1943)

Deep loving, well knowing
    His world and its blindness,
A heart overflowing
    With measureless kindness,

Undaunted in labor,
    (And Death was a trifle),
Steel-true as a sabre,
    Direct as a rifle,

All Man in his doing,
    All Boy in his laughter,
He fronted, unruing,
    The Now and Hereafter,

A storm-battling cedar,
    A comrade, brother—
Oh, such was our Leader,
    Beloved as no other!

When weaker souls faltered
    His courage remade us
Whose tongue never paltered,
    Who never betrayed us.

His hand on your shoulder
    All honors exceeding,
What breast but was bolder
    Because he was leading!

And still in our trouble,
    In peace or in war-time,
His word shall redouble
    Our strength as aforetime.

When wrongs cry for righting,
    No odds shall appal us;
To clean, honest fighting
    Again he will call us.

And, cowboys or dough-boys,
    We'll follow his drum, boys,
Who never said, "Go, boys!"
    But always said "Come, boys!"

Roosevelt

by Robert H. Davis (1869–1942)

He came from out the void
Buoyed upon the surging tides.
He braved the West,
Defied the wide frontiers;
He trekked the continents
And enthroned his name
Among the white, the black, the brown, the yellow men.
He trod the frond,
Fording the darkened streams
That glide through jungles

To the tropic sea.
He spanned the globe,
He swept the skies,
And moved beneath the eaters of the deep.
He entered all the portals of the world.
A vibrant, thrilled, exhaustless, restless soul;
Riding at last the very stars—
Asleep.

Theodore Roosevelt (or Half-Mast the Flag)

by Samuel Valentine Cole (1851–1925)

Half-mast the flag, and let the bell be tolled:
    A tower of strength he was, whose presence drew
The people around him, and to-day is rolled
    A wave of unaccustomed sorrow through
The land he loved; whatever now be said,
The latest great American is dead.

How quick he slipped from us—this man of might,
    Heroic courage, life-abounding ways!
When God's great angel in the silent night
    Brought, though invisible to others' gaze,
Some whispered message, he obediently heard,
Left all, and followed him without a word.

We loved this man who loved not fame, or wealth,
    But service, first; not perfect, or divine,
But humanlike, and full of moral health,
    And prompt to look beyond the outward sign
Of race, or creed, or party, find the plan
Of God himself, and recognize the man.

How true his vision was! And how his voice
    Seemed as a breeze does on a sultry day!
Long years ago he made life's master-choice,
    Like a brave knight of conscience, and alway
Dared wield the club of language clear and strong
To shield the right and batter down the wrong.

He stood for honest purposes: unroll
    The record of his years, you seek in vain
For life's disfigurements—there lies the scroll,

No blots upon it, nothing to explain;
But what is worthy and to all men's sight
As open as a landscape to the light.

Farewell, great Soul! Thou surely wilt fare well
    On that mysterious and adventurous way
Which thou hast gone; in those realms also dwell
    Truth, right, and honor, and God's love bears sway
To these, as in our bounds of time and place,
Thou art no stranger; they will know thy face.

There Washington and Lincoln stretch to thee
    The hand of welcome; they are working still
For some high end as once for liberty;
    Thou art at one with them in aim and will,
The peer of them in doing well thy part,
And their companion in the Nation's heart.

So lived this man, and died, and lives again—
    A white dynamic memory in the land.
Oh, what a heritage, my countrymen!
    He'll plead forever now, with voice and hand,
Our righteous causes, and his power will grow.
Cease tolling, bell, and let the bugles blow!

Roosevelt

by T. E. Thomas

'Twas not in him to deal with cringing touch
Or remonstrate with fawning plaint—
His honest, virile heart was never faint.
Nor had he faith in those whose acts were such
That led to doubt their aim in any fight.
To him all things were either wrong or right;
No compromise was his, with purpose whole,
He favored or opposed with all his soul.

No foeman's steel brought terror to his eyes;
No sycophancy could he endure,
Nor aught that was not plain and pure.
His friendship was no traitors' paradise;
He measured men and deeds with common sense,

And gave to each in turn fair recompense
As they deserved, of either blame or praise,
For his were always, not devious ways.

A master mind was his, both brilliant and profound,
Gifted with a reasoning rare;
Boldly 'twas his to do and dare,
With precept manly and with judgment sound.
No sophist's plea nor sham could bar his way;
Each act with him must bear the open light of day;
No half-way measure sought, could satisfy
Or meet his questioning of How or Why.

He served his time, his people, and his land,
And as he sowed, so did he reap.
The silent summons found him in his sleep.
Peaceful in death, in resignation grand,
His glorious soul has through the portal flown
To meet the only master it had ever known.
From earth's great trials triumphantly it passed,
Fighting at Armageddon to the last.

Armageddon: the place where the final battle between good and evil will be fought.

Roosevelt

by Peter Fandel

Columbia,
If aught but loss of honor
Or decay of principle
May set the well springs of thy tears aflow,
The occasion now is thine.
For he, thy champion supreme,
Who took his heartbeats from thine own,
Was snatched from thee all unforewarned
And left thee desolate and bereft.
Yes, he thy son, who ever stood by thee
And all his soul in loving beyance [*sic*] held
Unto thy intimate counsel and demand,
In the very hour of thy sorest need
Has fallen a prey to the grim reaper—Death.
How proud he was! how faithful, and how strong!

He, with the indomitable courage of a lion,
Stood constant guard beside thee and
With jealous eye scanned every act
That dared assail thy honor or besmirch.
Strong sinewed, both of mind and limb,
He feared no ill-designing foe,
Nor the enmity of those who tried
To shield corruptive will or suffered wrong
Behind the barriers of they glorious aegis,
He was a man of men—
One who summed our divergent strength
And roused our conscience from submissive sloth
Against the infesting evils of the day.
He rested not nor slumbered,
But breathed his fiery spirit in the land
Till it became therewith aflame
And scourged the felonious sin thereof.
And it from labors in the vicious pit
He came not forth entirely unscathed,
Or, in devotion to the cause,
Perchance sometimes o'erreached himself,
The blame should not be counted his;
For noble souls to virtues may transmute
Oft traits of human frailty
And thus be more deserving still.
But, when, by the receding past,
He in perspective true shall once be brought
And loom forth free from personal animosities
And the contrarieties of feeling
And strange antagonisms of mind
That dis-esteem in shallow mortals breed,
He shall appear in true proportions—
Proportions that shall measure well
With those of our heroic dead
Who live on still in our institutions
And are their glory and enduring worth.

Columbia: the United States of America, usually personified as a female figure.
beyance [*sic*]: abeyance.

83. Edward MacDowell

Edward MacDowell, a distinguished nineteenth-century American composer, was of Scotch-Irish ancestry, his grandfather having been born in Belfast, Ireland, of Scottish parents. Although MacDowell's initial musical training in the United States was from South American instructors, his subsequent musical preparation was decidedly European. In 1876 he was admitted to the Paris Conservatoire, but, after developing a dislike for French music, he decided to pursue his education in Germany. He was soon appointed head piano instructor at the Darmstadt Conservatory. On a later visit to Franz Liszt to play his (MacDowell's) First Piano Concerto, the American musician was so nervous that he could not ring the bell to the famous European's house. For the next two years MacDowell concentrated on composing orchestral pieces and symphonic poems.

Following his return to Boston with his new wife, MacDowell realized that he must devote his time to performance and instruction rather than composition. He was soon lionized as the foremost American composer and pianist and, as a result, developed a growing clientele of piano and composition students. This increasing fame may have been influential in his appointment in 1896 to the first professorship of music at Columbia University. Although he established a male chorus and a university orchestra, he was distressed by the realization that his music classes carried no academic credit and that few of his students were prepared for the calibre of musical instruction he hoped to give them. He vainly requested that the academic world place greater emphasis on the fine arts.

MacDowell's widow carried out his wish that his summer estate at Peterborough, New Hampshire, be turned into an artists' colony. Leonard Bernstein, Aaron Copland, and Virgil Thomson were among the composers who subsequently spent time in residence at the 500-acre property. Since 1960 the MacDowell Medal has been awarded annually to a distinguished composer, artist, or writer.

The Absent Guest
by Robert Underwood Johnson (1853–1937)

Go, wreathe his chair with laurel,
And brim his glass with wine,
And let one silent place proclaim
The presence we divine.

To sorrow for so pure a soul,
So warm a heart as he,
Makes never discord at a feast

Given to Harmony.

The dream he dreamed by starlight
   Is not less fair by sun:
That Beauty may to Beauty join
   Till all the arts be one;

That each who serves the Muses,
   And weaves the magic thrall
With words, or sounds, or speechless earth,
   May brother be to all.

On this wide hearth he lighted
   A new-inspiring flame,
Whose torch to kindling torch for aye
   Shall whisper of his fame.

Join hands for that Ideal
   He loved and worshiped most. . . .
Our absent guest, I said? . . . Ah, no!
   He is our absent host.

Muses: the nine Greek goddesses who presided over the arts.

84. Augustus Saint-Gaudens

Saint-Gaudens was born in Dublin to a French father and an Irish mother (Mary McGuiness), but within six months of his birth his family sailed for America, eventually settling in New York City. There the youngster first showed his artistic bent by sketching the shoemakers in his father's shop. He later studied drawing at Cooper Union and the National Academy of Design.

By 1867 Saint-Gaudens was working as a cameo cutter in Paris and attending a small art school, where, as he reported, "I modeled my first figures from the nude." Within a year he was studying sculpture at the Ecole des Beaux-Arts and startling his comrades by singing the "Marseillaise." Although he suffered from illness and financial worries after proceeding to Rome, he designed *Hiawatha* there and received various commissions, among them requests for copies of busts of Demosthenes and Cicero. The hold which the Eternal City had on him is evident when

— once again living in New York — he would "turn on the water at the little wash-basin, let it run continuously with a gentle tinkle, and thus recall the sound of the fountain in the garden at Rome."

After returning to the United States, Saint-Gaudens received a variety of commissions. His most famous were *Admiral Farragut* (New York City), *The Puritan* (Philadelphia), *Lincoln* (Chicago), *General John Logan* (Chicago), the *Shaw Memorial* (Boston), *General William Sherman* (New York City), the *Adams Monument* (District of Columbia), and *Diana* (for the tower of the original Madison Square Garden). He was also commissioned to design statues of Robert Louis Stevenson (Edinburgh, Scotland) and Charles Stewart Parnell (Dublin, Ireland). In 1905 he created designs for several U.S. coins, including a rendering of "Liberty" for the $20-gold piece. (His model for the figure "Liberty" was Mary Cunningham, an Irish immigrant girl.)

Saint-Gaudens was a founder of the Society of American Artists, received honorary degrees from Harvard, Princeton, and Yale, and was elected to the Royal Academy. As a teacher at the Art Students' League, he advised his pupils "to develop technique and then to hide it." On one occasion, as he wended his way through a studio full of the accoutrements of his "trade" — scaffolds, plaster casts, and clay models — he remarked that "People think a sculptor has an easy life in a studio. It's hard labor, in a factory."

Saint-Gaudens

Born in Dublin, Ireland, March 1, 1848
Died in Cornish, New Hampshire, August 3, 1907

by Robert Underwood Johnson (1853–1937)

I

Uplands of Cornish! Ye, that yesterday
Were only beauteous, now are consecrate.
Exalted are your humble slopes, to mate
Proud Settignano and Fiesole,
For her new-born is Italy's new birth of Art.
In your belovèd precincts of repose
Now is the laurel lovelier than the rose.
  Henceforth there shall be seen
An unaccustomed glory in the sheen
Of yonder lingering river, overleant with green,
Whose fountains hither happily shall start,

Like eager Umbrian rills, that kiss and part,
  For that their course will run
  One to the Tiber, to the Arno one.
O hills of Cornish! chalice of our soiled wine,
        Ye shall become a shrine,
For now our Donatello is no more!
        He who could pour
His spirit into clay, has lost the clay we wore,
        And Death, again, at last,
  Has robbed the Future to enrich the Past.
        He, who so often stood
At joyous worship in your Sacred Wood,
        He shall be missed
  As autumn meadows miss the lark,
Where Summer and Song were wont to keep melodious tryst.
  His fellows of the triple guild shall hark
  For his least whisper in the starry dark.
  Her, in his memory, Youth shall dedicate
Laborious years to that unfolding which is Fate.
        By Beauty's faintest gleams
  She shall be followed over glades and streams.
        And all that is shall be forgot
        For what is not;
  And every common path shall lead to dreams.

II

Poet of Cornish; comrade of his days:
  When late we met,
With his remembrance how thine eyes were wet!
  Thy faltering voice his praise
        More eloquently did rehearse
Than on his festal day thy liquid verse
Since once to love is never to forget,
Let us defer our plaint of private sorrow
Till some less-unethereal to-morrow.
        To-day is not the poet's shame
        But the dull world's; not yet
Shall it be kindled at the living flame
        Whose treasured embers
        Ever the world remembers.
Not so the sculptor—his immediate bays
No hostile climate whithers or delays.

Let us forego the debt of friendly duty;
A nation newly is bereft of beauty.
Sing with me now his undeferrèd fame,—
    For Time impatient is to set
This jewel in his country's coronet.
When all men with new accent speak his name,
And all are blended in a vast regret,
There is no place for grief of thee or me:
One reckons not the rivers in the sea.
Sing not to-day the hearth despoiled of fire:
    Ours be the trumpet, not the lyre.
            Death makes the great
The treasure and the sorrow of the State.
            Nor is it less bereaved
            By what is unachieved.
Oh, what a miracle is Fame!
We carve some lately unfamiliar name

Upon an outer wall, as challenge to the sun;
            And half its claim
            Is deathless work undone.
Although the story of our art is brief,
Thrice in the record, at a fadeless lead,
Falls an unfinished chapter; thrice the flower
Closed ere the noonday glory drank its dew;
Thrice have we lost of promise and of power—
The torch extinguished at its brightest hour—
His comrades all, for whom he twined the rue.
        But though they stand authentic and apart
This is in our new land the first great grief of Art.

III

Yet, sound for him the trumpet, not the lyre—
Him of the ardent, not the smouldering, fire:
Whose boyhood knew full streets of martial song
    When the slow purpose of the throng
Flamed to a new religion, and a soul.
He knew the lure of flags; caught first the far drums' roll;
        Thrilled with the flash that runs
        Along the slanted guns;
Kept time to the determined feet
        That ominously beat

Upon the city's floor
The firm, mad rhythm of war.
With envious enterprise
He saw the serried eyes
That, level to the hour's demand,
Looked straight toward Duty's promised land.
That to be boy was to be promised fast
With the great world of battle sweeping past,
While every hill and hollow
Heard the heart-melting music, calling "Follow!"
The day o'er-brimmed with longing and the night
As though doomed heroes summoned us to see
Thermopylaes and Marathons.
—Ah, had he known who was to be
Their laureate in bronze!

But who can read To-morrow in To-day?
Fame makes no bargain with us, will not say
Do thus, and thou shalt gain, or thus and lose;
Nay, will not let us for another choose
The trodden and the lighted way.
She burns the accepted pattern, breaks the mould,
Prefers the novel to the old,
Revels in secrets and surprise;
And while the wise
Seek knowledge at the sages' gate
The schoolboy by a truant path keeps rendezvous with Fate.

IV

This is the honey in the lion's jaws:
That from the reverberant roar
And wrack of savage war
Art saves a sweet repose, by mystic laws
Not by long labor learned
But by keen love discerned;
For this it bears the palm:
To show the storms of life in terms of calm.
Not what he knew but what he felt,
Gave secret power to this Celt.
Master of harmony, his sense could find
A bond of likeness among things diverse,
And could their forms in beauty so immerse

That to the enchanted mind
Ideal and real seems a single kind.

Behold our gaunt Crusader, grimly brave,
        The swooping eagle in his face,
        The very genius of command,
And her not less, with her imperious hand,—
The herald Victory holding equal pace.
        Not trulier in the blast
        Moves prow with mast;
Line mates with flowing line, as wave with following wave—
        Rider and homely horse
        Intent upon their course
As though she went not with them. Near or far,
One is their import: she the dream, the star—
And he the prose, the iron thrust—of War.

V

    So, on the traveled verge
Of storied Boston's green acropolis
That sculptured music, that immortal dirge
    That better than towering shaft
        Has fitly epitaphed
The hated ranks men did not dare to hiss!
When Duty makes her clarion call to Ease
    Let her repair and point to this:
        Why seek another clime?
        Why seek another place?
We have no Parthenon, but a nobler frieze,—
Since sacrifice than worship nobler is.
It sings—the anthem of a rescued race;
It moves—the epic of a patriot time,
And each heroic figure makes a martial rhyme.
    How like ten thousand treads that little band,
    Fit for the van of armies! What command
    Sits in that saddle! What renouncing will!
    What portent grave of firm-confronted ill!
    And as a cloud doth hover over sea,
    Born from its waters and returning there,
    Fame, sprung from thoughts of mortals, swims the air
    And gives them back her memories, deathlessly.

VI

I wept by Lincoln's pall when children's tears
    That saddest of the nation's years,
Were reckoned in the census of her grief;
        And flooding every eye,
        Of low estate or high,
The crystal sign of sorrow made men peers.
    The raindrop on the April leaf
Was not more unashamed. Hand spoke to hand
A universal language; and whene'er
The hopeful met 't was but to mingle their despair.
    Our yesterday's war-widowed land
To-day was orphaned. Its victorious voice
Lost memory of the power to rejoice.
For he whom all had learned to love was prone.
The weak had slain the mighty; by a whim
The ordered edifice was overthrown
And lay in futile ruin, mute and dim.
O Death, thou sculptor without art,
What didst thou to the Lincoln of our heart?
            Where was the manly eye
            That conquered enmity?
            Where was the gentle smile
            So innocent of guile—
            The message of good-will
            To all men, whether good or ill?
            Where shall we trace
Those treasured lines, half humor and half pain,
That made him doubly brother to the race?
For these, O Death, we search thy mask in vain!

Yet shall the Future be not all bereft:
Not without witness shall its eyes be left.
The soul, again, is visible through Art,
Servant of God and Man. The immortal part
Lives in the miracle of a kindred mind,
That found itself in seeking for its kind.
The humble by the humble is discerned;
And he whose melancholy broke in sunny wit
Could be no stranger unto him who turned
From sad to gay, as though in jest he learned
Some mystery of sorrow. It was writ:
The hand that shapes us Lincoln's must be strong

As his that righted our bequeathèd wrong;
The heart that shows us Lincoln must be brave,
An equal comrade unto king or slave;
The mind that gives us Lincoln must be clear
　　　As that of seer
To fathom deeps of faith abiding under tides of fear.
What wonder Fame, impatient, will not wait
　　　To call her sculptor great
Who keeps for us in bronze the soul that saved the State!

VII

Most fair his dreams and visions when he dwelt
His spirit's comrade. Meager was his speech
Of things celestial, save in line and mould;
But sudden cloud-rift may reveal a star
As surely as the unimpeded sky.
The deer has its deep forest of retreat:
Shall the shy spirit have none? Be, then,
The covert unprofaned wherein withdrew
The soul that 'neath his pensive ardor lay?
Find the last frontier — Man is still unknown ground.

Things true and beautiful made a heaven for him.
Childhood, the sunrise of the spirit world,
Yielded its limpid secrets to his eye.
He was in Friendship what he was in Art—
Wax to receive and metal to endure.
Looking upon his warriors facing death,
Heroes seem human, such as all might be
Yet not without the consecrating will!
Age is serener by his honoring;
And when he sought the temple's inmost fane
The angels of his Adoration lent
Old hopes new glory, and his reverent hand
Wrought like Beato at the face of Christ.

But what is this that, neither Hope nor Doom,
Waits with eternal patience at a tomb?
A brooding spirit without name or date,
　　　Or race, or nation, or belief;
　　　Beyond the reach of joy or grief,
　　　Above the plane of wrong or right;

A riddle only to the sorrowless; the mate
Of all the elements in calm—still winter night,
Sea after tempest, time-scarred mountain height;
Passive as Buddha, single as the Sphinx,—
Yet neither that sweet god that seems to smile
On mortal good and guile,
Nor wide-eyed monster that into Egypt sinks
And Beats and Nature links;
But something human, with an inward sense
Profound, but nevermore intense;
And though it doth not stop to teach,
It will with each
Attuned to beauty hold a muted speech;
In its Madonna-lidded meditation
Not more a mystery than a revelation;
Listen! It doth to Man the Universe relate.
O Sentinel before the Future's Gate!
If thou be Fate, art thou not still *our* Fate?

For those who fain would live, but must breathe on
Prisoners of this prosaic age—
Ah, who for them shall read that page
Since wingéd Shelley and wise Emerson are gone?

VIII

How shall we honor him and in his place
His comrades of the Old and Happy Race
Whose Art is refuge Sorrow comes not nigh,
Though Art be twin to Sorrow? They reply
From all the centuries they outsoar,
From every shore
Of that three-continent sea
To which the streams of our antiquity
Fell swift and joyously:
"How, but to live with Beauty?"

Across our Western world without surcease
How many a column sounds the name of Greece!
The sun, loth-lingering on the crest of Rome,
Finds here how many an imitative dome!
O classic quarries of our modern thought,
What blasphemies in stone from you are wrought!

For though to Law, Religion, or the State,
These stones to Beauty first are dedicate,
Yet to what purpose, if we but revere
The temple, not the goddess?—if whene'er
The magic of her deep obsession seem
To master any soul, we call it dream?
    Come let us live with Beauty!
Her name is ever on our lips; but who
Holds Beauty as the fairest bride to woo?
The gods oft wedded mortals; now alone
May man the Chief Immortal make his own.
To Time each day adds increment of age
But Beauty ne'er grows old. There is no gauge
To count the glories of the counted hours.
Flowers die, but not the ecstasy of flowers.
    Come, let us live with Beauty!
What infinite treasure hers! and what small need
Of our cramped natures, whose misguided greed,
Hound-like, pursues trails of Luxury
Or sodden Comfort! Who shall call us free—
Content if but some casual wafture come
From fields Elysian, where the valleys bloom
With life delectable? Such happy air
Should be the light we live in; unaware
It should be breathed, till man retrieves the joy
Philosophy has wrested from the boy.
    Come, let us live with Beauty!

Who shall put limit to her sovereignty?
   Who shall her loveliness define?
Think you the Graces only three? —
   The Muses only nine?
Beyond our star-sown deep of space
Where, as for solace, huddles world with world
(A human instinct in the primal wrack),
Mayhap there is a dark and desert place
      Of deeper awe
With but one outer star, there hurled
By cataclysm and there held in leach by law:
If lonely be that star, 't is not for Beauty's lack.
She was ere there was any need of Truth,
She was ere there was any stir of Love;
And when Man came, and made her world uncouth

With sin, and cities, and the gash of hills,
And forests, and a thousand brutish ills, —
        Moved by eternal ruth
She hid her wounds and gave him, from above,
The magic all his happiness is fashioned of.

IX

Knights of the five arts that our sculptor prized:
How shall ye honor him and, in his place,
Those others of the Old and Happy Race
Who lived for beauty, and the golden lure despised?

Painter of music, Architect of song,
Sculptor in color, Poet in clay and bronze,
And thou whose unsubstantial fancy builds
Abiding symphonies from stone and space!
Mount ye to large horizons: ever be
As avid of other beauty as your own.
As nations greater are than all their states,
More than the sum of all the arts is Art.
High are their clear commands, but Art herself
Makes holier summons. Ever open stand
The doors of her free temple. At her shrine
In service of the world, whose hurt she heals,
Ye, too, physicians of the mind and heart—
Shall ye not take the Hippocratic oath?
Have ye not heard the voices of the night
Call you from kindred, comfort, sloth and praise,
To lead into the light the willing feet
That grope for order, harmony and joy?—
To reach full hands of bounty unto those
Who starve for beauty in our glut of gold?

How shall we honor him whom we revere—
Lover of all arts and of his land?
How, but to cherish Beauty's every flower?—
How, but to live with Beauty, and so be
Apostles of Rejoicing to mankind?

Cornish: a town in New Hampshire, near which Saint-Gaudens had his summer home and studio. **Settignano:** Desiderio da Settignano (1428?–1464), an Italian sculptor and one of the leading Florentine artists of the Renaissance. **Fiesole:** a small Italian hill town, located near Florence and known for its Renaissance villas. **precincts of repose:** probably "Aspet," Saint-Gaudens' summer home and studio near Cornish, New Hampshire. The sculptor is buried on the property. **yonder lingering river:** the Connecticut River near Cornish, New Hampshire. **Umbrian hills:** a region in central Italy. **Tiber . . . Arno:** the rivers on which Rome and Florence are respectively located. **our Donatello:** Saint-Gaudens; a reference to the famous Florentine sculptor (1386?–1466). **Poet of Cornish:** Percy Wallace MacKaye (1875–1956), poet, playwright, and essayist. In 1905 he wrote and staged a masque honoring Saint-Gaudens in which the Boston Symphony and more than seventy members of the Cornish summer colony participated. **Thermopylaes and Marathons:** two battles of the Persian War (500–479 B.C.), the former a Greek defeat and the latter an Athenian victory. **gaunt Crusader:** Saint-Gaudens' equestrian statue of William T. Sherman, located at Fifty-Ninth Street and Fifth Avenue in New York City. The work includes a statue of Victory carrying an olive branch before the mounted Union general. **Boston's green acropolis:** Boston Common. **sculptured music:** the Shaw Memorial, Saint-Gaudens' bas-relief sculpture in honor of Colonel Robert Gould Shaw and the other officers and men of the Fifty-Fourth Massachusetts Regiment, one of the state's Civil War units. Located opposite the State House, on the edge ("verge") of Boston Common, the memorial depicts Shaw and his men as they passed the State House on May 28, 1863, after receiving their regimental colors from Governor John Andrew. Although Shaw and his officers were white, the enlisted men in this regiment were all free African Americans who had volunteered to fight during the Civil War. **hated ranks:** a reference to the racial prejudice against the African Americans in the Fifty-Fourth Massachusetts Regiment. **Parthenon:** the temple of the Greek goddess Athena, built in the fifth century B.C. on the acropolis in Athens. "Parthenon" is derived from the Greek word for virgin, an appellation commonly given to Athena. **Who keeps for us in bronze the soul that saved the State:** a reference to Saint-Gaudens' two statues of Abraham Lincoln in Chicago. **fane:** temple. **angels of his Adoration:** Saint-Gaudens' large relief *Adoration of the Cross by Angels*, sculpted for St. Thomas Church in New York City. **Beato:** perhaps Pietro Beato, a little-known seventeenth-century Neapolitan painter. **A brooding spirit without name or date:** the Adams Monument in Rock Creek Cemetery in Washington, D.C., commissioned by Henry Adams for his wife's grave. Saint-Gaudens referred to it as the "Mystery of the Hereafter." **Buddha:** an Indian religious leader of the sixth-century B.C. **Sphinx:** the colossal recumbent figure of an imaginary creature having the body of a lion and the head of a human located near the pyramids of Giza. **Shelley:** Percy Bysshe Shelley (1792–1822), an English lyric and dramatic poet. **Emerson:** Ralph Waldo Emerson (1803–1882), an American poet, lecturer, and essayist. **comrades of the Old and Happy Race:** from the context probably Saint-Gaudens' fellow artists. **fields Elysian:** in Greek mythology a land of bliss and contentment on the banks of the river Oceanus (in the West), where the good and the heroic lived after death. **Graces:** the ancient Greek and Roman goddesses of beauty and kindness, usually represented as three in number. **Muses:** the nine Greek goddesses who presided over the arts. **ruth:** pity; sorrow. **Knights of the five arts:** subsequently identified in the poem as "Painter of music, Architect of song, / Sculptor in color, Poet in clay and bronze, / And thou whose unsubstantial fancy builds / Abiding symphonies from stone and space!" **Hippocratic oath:** an oath embodying the ethical obligations of physicians, usually attributed to the Greek physician Hippocrates (c. 460–c. 377 B.C.).

85. Henry Ford

Among the Irish ancestors of Henry Ford, the famous automobile manufacturer, was his paternal grandfather, John Ford, a Protestant tenant farmer near Clonakilty in County Cork, Ireland. In 1847 the older Ford left his homeland for America, bringing with him his wife and their seven children. One of the sons, William, subsequently met and married the daughter of Patrick O'Hern, also a native of County Cork. Their son Henry was born on his parents' forty-acre farm in Dearborn, Michigan, in 1863.

Despite the occasional critical remarks about Ford in the following poetic excerpt, the automaker was an exponent of an idealistic business theory and enlightened industrial policies. Believing that the business of business was not only to make a profit but also to make the world "a better place in which to live," the auto executive was convinced that the Ford Motor Company had succeeded at doing both. Part of this service role, he believed, was to build a vehicle "so low in price that no man making a good salary will be unable to buy one — and enjoy with his family the blessings of hours of pleasure in God's great open spaces." Though his management style was paternalistic, Ford's policies — the eight-hour day, profit-sharing, a high daily wage — seemed to herald an end to the war between capital and labor (and thus any need for unions). By realizing that "a worker" was also "a consumer," he saw that "good wages to labor, good earnings to farmers, prosperity in the masses, make a good market for cars."

In the early 1920s Ford visited Ireland to open his company's first factory outside the United States. During the visit he pledged £5,000 for the Hospital Building Fund in Cork. The next day, however, the local press reported that he had promised to donate £10,000. When officials from the hospital fund offered to correct the error with a new headline ("Henry Ford Did Not Give £10,000 to Hospital"), the American manufacturer realized that he had been "taken in" and promised to make the larger donation. His only condition was that he be allowed to choose the biblical quotation that would adorn the hospital: "I came among mine own — and they took me in."

From Part II of **And I Will Be Heard**
by John Beecher (1904–1980)

. . . .

I think everybody knows
that Henry Ford
has done a lot for this country.

He had an idea
a great idea
and when he was laughed at
he believed in it all the harder
and put it over
and the American people
backed him
and gave him a lot of their money
in the form of profits
to use
because his was the kind of an idea
that took a lot of money
to be worked out.

But then Henry Ford appeared to get
a funny idea
a wrong idea
that this was his money
that he had "made" it himself
and he got another idea
that he knew all the answers
and that "history is bunk."
Now American history is not bunk.
The kind Henry Ford would like to have written is
but not the kind I am writing in this piece.
If the kind of American history I am writing
was bunk
there wouldn't have been any Henry Ford
and he ought to know it.
He used to know it
but lately
he is acting
as if he had forgotten.

Henry Ford says
to the people who work for him
I will treat you better than anybody else will
and pay you more
but you have got to be thankful
and do exactly what I say do
and let me tell you
exactly what to think
whether to take a drink or not

not to join a union
et cetera.
Recently the United States Senate
through one of its committees
heard what was going on
what Henry Ford was up to
having guys' teeth knocked out
for coming around his plants
telling "his" people
they ought to join something
the American law
gives them a right to join
if they want to
but Henry Ford thinks
they oughtn't to
which is all right if he wants to think it
but is not all right
is all wrong
when he tries to stop them
with blackjacks
and if Henry Ford had the sense God gave a june bug
he would know that it wouldn't even work
for very long.

By God Henry Ford
you have got to stop it
you have got to lay off that stuff
and lay off quick
or the American people
who don't belong to you at all
but to whom you yourself belong
are going to teach you a lesson.
They gave you their money
our money
everybody's money
to do something for all of us
that needed doing
and nobody else but you could do.
That money you have got
is a trust
and don't you forget it.

Listen, Henry Ford.

We are hearing a lot these days
about the "Fifth Column"
about "Trojan Horses"
and parachute troops in disguise
who go around with dynamite
and flame-throwers
disrupting communications behind the lines
setting destructive fires
holding strategic bridgeheads
and spreading stories of disaster, which is the worst
    thing they do.

Pretty soon
I expect you to begin hollering
like you usually do in a crisis
I expect you to begin popping off
and pointing with alarm
and trying to scare everybody half to death
but be careful this time
be mighty careful
or the American people
will get on to you.
We will begin to think
that it is you
that came out of the Trojan Horse
yes you
that came dropping down out of the enemy bomber
in a parachute
disguised as an old woman.

. . . .

Fifth column: sympathizers and saboteurs and/or spies of an enemy behind home lines of defense. **Trojan Horse:** a device to undermine an enemy from within.

86. Ireland at the Fair

Ireland at the Fair

An Ode for St. Patrick's Day, March 17, 1915
by Joseph I. C. Clarke (1846–1925)

From far-off Holy Island by the right
Of those who love this golden land;
Who've shared the burden of the fight
From snowy peak to ocean strand,
That won for thee the crests of high estate,
Here gathered, and with souls elate
And harps of gladness, at thy feast we stand.
Unto the winds we fling our banners gay,
Amid the beauties of thy home of light,
For all the world upbuilded and outspread
In jeweled splendor by the matchless bay,
Where thou does grandly celebrate
The making of the wondrous waterway
Linking Pacific and Atlantic seas,
And in clear tones that no discordance mars,
Forever to attest
The peace-crowned wedding of the East and West
Beneath our flag of stars.

We bring the joy, the genial grace,
The worth, the valor of our ancient race
That here in root and blossom thrives:
The clear glance of the Irish eye
That gleams with life, and winces not to die,
The warm tones of the Irish voice,
In all that makes for glory to rejoice,
The strong clasp of the Irish hand,
Willing in service, weighty in command,
Yea, lift we up, exalting thee, to-day
The hands that toil, the hands that grip the sword
The holy hands that raise to praise the Lord,
The smooth white hands of woman fair and pure,
Pledging to thee our Irish hearts, our lives,
Long as the mountains and the sea endure,
O golden California!

Hail to thee, free-limbed queen,

Thy white feet on the mountains hoar,
Thy gaze o'er valleys deep between
That glow in harvest gold or silver green.
Around thee pinnacle and peak and dome
Where the swift wind and eagle make their home,
And the sheer rock falls in mile-deep sweep,
Fall, too, glad waters in their shining leap,
As 'neath the sun's enamored rays they flow
From out the white breasts of the snow.

Oh, the glory of thy wind-blown hair,
The frolic brilliance of thy fearless eyes,
The sun tan on thy forehead rounded fair,
With one star-diamond shining there,
Filleted, my queen, with virgin gold.
Of pearl mist is thy flowing robe, I wist,
That in thy stride, thro' fold on fold,
Chaste beauties, fled as glimpsed, we may behold.
Sierra queen, thus dost thou move at dawn
On main breeze wings swiftly drawn
From crag to crag in aerial flights,
Commanding the rock ramparts upward hurled,
Foreordained as thy fortress heights
When broke the mad young mornings of the world.

Then, as the sun springs up the east,
And ev'ry peak from out the mist defines,
While the land breeze stirs
To music all the silver firs,
The tall sequoia and the sugar pines
And forest harmonies thine anthem sing,
Fair on a snowy shimmer of a cloud,
Thou sweepest to our noonday feast
Adown thy broad rich valley where thy sons,
Of thee, their queen in joyance proud,
Hail thee from the cities of the plain,
Salute thee from the plough or growing grain,
Or hardby [sic] streams whose water foaming runs,
Or where the hardy miner digs for gold,
Until in swelter of the deserts bare
The heat-haze shimmering is uprolled,
Save where the sage brush and the cactus share
The blue-green patches in the stony glare.

Swift now thy flight across the coastal chain.
Lo, from their crests the glory of the main!
The long waves breaking in a front of foam,
Onrushing ever in an endless host,
The deep blue dotted with the distant sails,
Or smoke-plumes out upon the ocean trails.
Now northward over fields and flow'rs
Seamed silver-bright with shining rails.
Behold fair cities by the sea arise,
Whose spires and gardens in the morning gleam.
And on the broad-sloped land the blessing lies
Of toil-worn beauty under the sun and show'rs:
The scented shadows of the orange groves,
With glimmer of fair faces thro' the leaves,
The palm trees waving their wide silken plumes,
The trembling grasses that the hillsides drape,
The crimson roses, the white apple blooms
And sunshine dropping golden to the grape
And vales whose green they'll gild with wheaten sheaves,
And mottled herds of cattle in long droves.

Hark, on thine ear four sweet bells ring
The Angelus from Mission shrines of old,
That still among their groves show tiles of red,
Where long the good Franciscan padres led
The red man's choirs the praise of Christ to sing.
So bendest thou in pray'r thy perfect head,
For thou rememberest their far first call
That lured thee from thy summits ice-enthroned,
While canticles that pious lips intoned
In laud of Mary and the Lord of all
Gave strange new comfort to thy soul.

But on thy flight
To find thy goal
And thy delight to-day
By San Francisco bay.
Fast by the ocean with the ocean's thrill
Deep-pulsing and wide throbbing in her breast,
Warm with the kindlings of her high desire,
Firm in the posture of unshaken will,
Triumphant risen over quake and fire,
Thy golden daughter, virgin of the West.
Miraculous, immaculate,

In supple strength with outstretched arms she stands
In welcome to the peoples of all lands
Who've flocked in worship to her Golden Gate.
As thine, our hearts are with her in her pride,
Our Irish hearts, our Celtic joy
That nothing human can destroy.
Mark you, my queen,
Our flag of gold and green
Its magic sheen outflaunting on the bay.
The very breezes as its fold they toss
Have blown from Ireland's shores,
Thrilling an Irish rondelay [*sic*]
From where the wild Atlantic roars,
And gambolling the Continent across,
Came o'er the mountains jauntily at play
To kiss our harp-strung flag of green,
Yea, this is Ireland's day.

We come to thee,
The grand, the free,
Remembering, remembering,
Old Ireland far away,
Her hills and vales,
Her olden tales,
Her glories and her fate,
And still the day of her arising wait,
And for its lordly coming pray.

Mother Ireland! Mother Ireland!
From thy sainted isle,
Smile on us, dear mother, smile,
Incline thine ear
This fair St. Patrick's morn
To hear
The wonder story, to thy glory born,
Of sons who crossed the sea,
And here by good St. Francis' bay,
Two thousand stormy leagues away,
Still love thee, and still long to see thee free.

What of thy sons, Mother Erin, in thousands
Who came with their sinews, their thews and their brains?
A tale worth the telling in numbers heroic!
The Argonauts, dust covered, crossing the plains,

Seeking new empire far out to the sunset.
Creaking of wagons and straining of reins,
Fighting off red men and thirsting for water,
Camping and singing by night 'round the fires.
Sons of old Ireland, rough-bearded among them,
From cold Donegal to the mouth of the Suir,
Scholars and doctors and toilers from Dublin,
Antrim and Kerry, Tyrone, Tipperary,
Carlow and Wexford and Galway — galore,
Chorusing songs of their land in the firelight
Or chants of their rhymers new born on the trail:
E'en now we may hear the wild melody rising,
Yet haunting as harps sounding far on the wind:
The prairie, lads, the Rockies, boys
    The deserts and the plains,
And rude and rough as runs the road,
    There's many a mile remains.
It's only, lads, in moonlit dreams,
    We'll roam in Irish lanes.
So up and top your saddles, boys,
    As soon as break of day.
It's far we are from Ireland,
    But it's far to Monterey[.]
Hurrah, hurrah for Ireland!
    And slainthe, Monterey!

The mad queen sure has hold of us,
    And bids us to behold
New lands without a landlord,
    And streams on beds of gold,
A princess each to welcome us,
    And a plough to break the mold.

Says one, "I want no Indian queen:
    A Spanish dame for me."
But cries my heart for my colleen,
    My life, my wife to be.
Oh, what's the land, the gold without
    My maid of Killalee [*sic*] ?
So spring to your cayuses, boys,
    As soon as chirps the day.

The golden land's ahead of us,
    The call's from Monterey:

Hurrah, hurrah the Golden land!
  And slainthe, Monterey!

They came with the rest in the glamor of gold,
Over the high mountain passes they struggled,
With pick and with shovel and rocker they toiled,
And plucked the gold nuggets and sifted the dust.
Hardly they won it, and wildly they spent it;
Then on by the streams till they yielded no more.
Some from the Isthmus came, rocked on the ocean,
Farmers for plough lands and priests for devotion,
A pioneer Ireland that swarmed down the valleys,
Breathing in freedom the air of the free.
Some 'neath the starry flag over the mountains
Marched with our Kearny for seizing and holding
The land in the lap of the Union forever,
Its outpost majestic, confronting the sea,
Hardy the race for its battle with nature,
Charming with laughter its heaviest toil,
Sturdy to build up the towns and the cities,
Brainy to plan them and wisely to rule,
Learnèd to lead in the forum and school.
Names that shine still on the peaks of endeavor,
Rise from our hundreds of thousands in clusters
Winning, deserving live honors and trust;
Broderick, Tobin, Donahue, Doyle.
Phelans that, father and son, win our tribute,
Mackay, Flood, Fair of the silver bonanzas;
Soldiers who rose on the red field to glory
Pouring their lives that the Union might live,
Treading the ways that the patriots trod;
Prelates whose ministries flamed 'fore our altars,
Lighting man's road to the feet of our God.
And rough-clad or silk-clad, the Celt, man and woman,
Warm-hearted, loyal, enjoying and loving,
Humble or boldly upreaching for fame,
Stands for the Commonwealth's safety and honor,
To live and to strive or to die in her name.

Holy Island: Ireland. **hardby** [*sic*]: hard by. **Angelus:** a Catholic prayer recited three times a day to commemorate the angel Gabriel's message to Mary that she had been selected to be the mother of Jesus. **Thy golden daughter, virgin of the West:** the city of San Francisco. **Golden Gate:** a strait between San Francisco and the Pacific Ocean. **Erin:** a literary name for Ireland. **Argonauts:** persons who moved to California during the gold rush of 1849; from the name of the men in Greek mythology who accompanied Jason aboard the ship *Argo* in search of the Golden Fleece. **Donegal:** a county in northwestern Ireland. **Suir:** a river in southern Ireland. **Antrim, Kerry, Tyrone, Tipperary, Carlow, Wexford, Galway:** counties in Ireland. **slainthe:** actually *sláinte* (pronounced "slaun-cha"), an Irish toast meaning "good health." **Killalee** [*sic*]**:** Killaloe, a town in southeastern Ireland. **cayuses:** horses, especially Indian ponies. **rocker:** a cradle used to wash sand or gravel to separate gold or other heavy metal. **Isthmus:** the Isthmus of Panama. **starry flag:** the American flag. **Kearny:** Stephen Kearny (1794–1848), the military commander whose Army of the West helped conquer California during the Mexican War. **Broderick:** David Broderick (1820–1859), a U.S. senator from California, killed in a duel with a political opponent. **Tobin:** Richard Montgomery Tobin (1866–1952), a San Francisco banker and civic leader and assistant naval attaché at the American Embassy in Paris at the end of World War I. **Donahue:** Peter Donahue (1822–1885), whose San Francisco foundry was the first in the western United States. **Doyle:** John T. Doyle (1819–1906), a lawyer who succeeded in obtaining for the Catholic Church in California a $904,000 judgment against Mexico. The payment represented twenty-one years of interest accrued to a fund originally established to support missionary work in California. **Phelans:** James Phelan (1824–1892), an Irish native and a San Francisco merchant-capitalist, and his son, James Duval Phelan (1861–1930), a San Francisco mayor and a U.S. senator from California (1915–1921). **Mackay, Flood, Fair:** John Mackay, James Flood, and James Fair, the "Silver Kings," whose "Big Bonanza" strike in Nevada in 1873 resulted in more than $1 million in gold and silver.

87. Woodrow Wilson

President Woodrow Wilson's paternal grandfather, James Wilson, was a native of Strabane, County Tyrone, northern Ireland, and had immigrated to Philadelphia in 1807. Aboard the ship which brought him to America was his future wife, Amy Adams, an Irish native who liked to say that she lived so close to Scotland that she could see the linen flying on the clotheslines across the Northern Channel. In Philadelphia Wilson found employment with the *Aurora*, a newspaper which was edited by William Duane and which generally supported the views of Thomas Jefferson. Wilson's youngest son — Joseph Ruggles Wilson — attended Jefferson College in Canonsburg, Pennsylvania, and later followed a call to the Presbyterian ministry. He was ordained in 1849, shortly after his marriage to Janet Woodrow, a member of a 600-year-old Scottish family.

The couple's son — the future American president — served as president of Princeton University and governor of New Jersey before being elected the nation's chief executive in 1912. While president, Wilson saw his foreign policy toward Great Britain complicated by the failure of the Easter Rising in Dublin in 1916 and by the policy of national self-determination which he proclaimed in his Fourteen Points. Although Irish-American politicians condemned Britain for crushing the rebellion and executing its leaders, Wilson refrained from doing anything that would jeopardize the Anglo-American war effort. (Wilson's Presbyterian Scotch-Irish roots often placed him at odds with the Catholic Celtic Irish.) He did, however, suggest to the British that American public opinion would never be satisfied short of some degree of Irish independence.

While on the surface Wilson's call for self-determination seemed to encompass Irish independence, the president believed that the Irish Question was an internal matter to be resolved by the British. Once, when a delegation of Irish Americans requested to see the president in order to press the case of Irish home rule, Wilson ordered his Secret Service man to eject the delegation's leader from the building. Wilson was further embarrassed when more than 5,000 supporters of Irish freedom sent a delegation to France to state their case at the Paris Peace Conference. Although Wilson received the delegation, he admitted that his "first impulse was to tell the Irish to go to hell." Despite a resolution by the U.S. Senate requesting that the Irish-American delegates get a hearing at the Versailles conference, Wilson refused to accommodate them further, thereby causing American Hibernophiles to join forces with Wilson's enemies.

Woodrow Wilson
by Katherine Lee Bates (1859–1929)

Spirit long shaping for sublime endeavor,
A Sword of God, the gleaming metal came
From stern Scotch ancestry, where whatsoever
Was true, was pure, was noble, won acclaim;
From scholar sires of holy consecration
Whose saints were Knox and Calvin. In the flame
And on the anvil, in that strong creation
Of blade from ore, did not Geneva call
Unto Geneva? For the world's salvation
Was wrought that brand, a splendor over all,
Deep-scored by many a skilled artificer
With runes, cross-hilted, jeweled for the hall,
Keen-edged for combat, burning through base slur
And cruel calumny, Excalibur.

Upflung upon an agony exceeding
All agonies this haggard earth has borne,
On his one heart beat all the frantic pleading
Of all the starved, plague-ridden, battle torn,
Perishing peoples, while those furtive foemen,
Old Selfishness, Derision, Faith Forsworn,
Let fly their venomed arrows, practised bowmen,
From ambush. So the wrestling, glorious dream
That winged his heart was brought to dust, an omen
Ill for humanity, prompt to blaspheme
A brightness dimmed, a roseate vision paled.
Yet from that trampled heart the immortal gleam
Ascends a living League of Nations hailed
By Christmas chimes. Its champion has not failed.

Knox and Calvin: John Knox and John Calvin, the founders of Presbyterianism in the sixteenth century. Wilson was a life-long member of the Presbyterian Church. **Geneva:** In the sixteenth century Geneva was John Calvin's home and religious headquarters; in 1920 the Swiss city became the seat of the League of Nations. **Excalibur:** King Arthur's famous sword. **League of Nations:** the international organization proposed by Wilson and created after World War I to promote world peace through collective security.

The Leader

by Robert Underwood Johnson (1853–1937)

This is the man they deemed of languid blood
    A schoolman versed in books, who, Hamlet-like,

Showed but heat-flashes powerless to strike—
His resolution blighted in the bud.

They knew him not—nor we, who trusted him.
See! how his brooding purpose, taking form,
Falls like swift lightning from long-gathered storms,
While fateful thunder shakes the round world's rim.

His country, stirred by him to lofty strife,
Sharing his vision, with high passion thrills;
It climbs, renouncing minor goods and ills,
And stands beside him at the crown of life.

To a new knighthood he ordains the brave,
To be soul-worthy of a freeman's birth—
Not for our wrongs alone, but that on earth
None shall be master, none shall be slave.

But yesterday a secret of his heart,
His welcome message floods the globe like light;
It cheers the farthest darkness by its might;
Its boldness makes the undissceptered start.

Where it has spread, by sea or mountain side
Or by the bivouac of the caravan,
The lowliest feels a part of Heaven's plan
And stands erect with newly wakened pride.

Beleaguered Liberty takes heart again,
Hearing afar the rescuing bugles below;
And even in the strongholds of the foe
His name becomes the whispered hope of men.

Hamlet-like: indecisive, like Shakespeare's character Hamlet. **welcome message:** probably Wilson's Fourteen Points, his blueprint for the postwar era, based on such principles as open diplomacy, collective security through a general association of nations, freedom of the seas, and national self-determination.

Woodrow Wilson

by Donald Gillies

Strange justice walks abroad tonight.
The pale, forsaken figure, whose

Exalted quest was peace, has found
    The peace none may refuse.

Teacher, Statesman, Leader freed
    From living strife and mortal pain—
Exhausted with the weight of dreams
    And hopes too great to gain.

Beside the Thames, they share tonight
    Potomac's sorrow and good-bye
For him who rose, when aid was life,
    A comrade and ally.

On Paris streets, young soldiers pause
    To talk of him who sought to bring
On sown, green fields of home, an end
    To war's red harvesting.

Beyond the Rhine, the vanquished know
    No greed of empire touched his brain,
But faith more sovereign than power
    And greater than domain.

The tongue that wakened half a world
    Is silent now; at rest the mind
That knew the ultimate of praise
    And venom of mankind.

Slow to the tomb the body goes—
    Times to no dim drum;
Let those who scorned his faith stand forth
    And scoff his martyrdom!

Thames . . . Potomac: the rivers on which London and Washington, D.C., are respectively located. **Rhine:** the river between Germany and France.

The Warrior Passes

by Hubert Kelley

In S Street trod the phantom guard—
    The men of Argonne, men of Aisne—
Who battled well and battled hard

And, sorely wounded, died in vain.
Forgotten dead were on parade—
    A mangled crew, if men would know—
But still with faces undismayed,
    They marched with majesty, and, lo,

On S Street to the rendezvous—
    The darkest house—they came at last:
The sergeant silently withdrew,
    The lipless bugler shrilled a blast;
The President! The gallant call
    Startled the shadows with its flame,
And from the doorway, gaunt and tall,
    The President, the Chieftain, came!

Martyred and old, the Chieftain came
    To meet the warrior guard of death.
His brow was hurt, his body lame,
    His heart was still, and still his breath.
His greatness, like a shining cloak,
    Obscured his broken form and bend:
The ghastly sergeant wheeled and spoke,
    The rifles mounted to "Present!"

In S Street, in the street of grief,
    The deathly guard of honor trod,
Bearing the spirit of their Chief
    Into the cabinet of God.
How different another day!
    The thundering cheers that would not cease!
When glittering Paris thronged the way
    Into the rendezvous of peace!

They marched away, the guard of death,
    Silent and grim behind the Great;
And phantom youth without a breath
    Whispered unto his mangled mate,
"What is the thing about his face
    That makes me dream of something dim—
A crucifix at some torn place
    And the shell-scarred face of Him?"

S Street: the street in Washington, D.C., where Wilson's home at the time of his
death was located. **Argonne . . . Aisne:** two famous battlefields of World War I.

Woodrow Wilson

by Robinson Jeffers (1887–1862)

It said "Come home, here is an end, a goal,
Not the one raced for, is it not better indeed? Victory you know requires
Force to sustain victory, the burden is never lightened, but final defeat
Buys peace: you have praised peace, peace without victory."

He said "It seems I am traveling no new way,
But leaving my great work unfinished how can I rest? I enjoyed a vision,
Endured betrayal, you must not ask me to endure final defeat,
Visionless men, blind hearts, blind mouths, live still."

It said "Yet perhaps your vision was less great
Than some you scorned, it has not proved even so practicable; Lenin
Enters this pass with less reluctance. As to betrayals: there are so many
Betrayals, the Russians and the Germans know."

He said "I knew I have have enemies, I had not thought
To meet one at this brink: shall not the mocking voices die in the grave?"
It said "They shall. Soon there is silence." "I dreamed this end," he said,
      "when the prow
Of the long ship leaned against dawn, my people

Applauded me, and the world watched me. Again
I dreamed it at Versailles, the time I sent for the ship, and the obstinate
      foreheads
That shared with me the settlement of the world flinched at my threat
      and yielded.
That is all gone. . . . Do I remember the darkness?"

It said "No man forgets it but a moment.
The darkness before the mother, the depth of the return." "I thought,"
      he answered,
"That I was drawn out of this depth to establish the earth on peace. My
      labor
Dies with me, why was I drawn out of this depth?"

It said "Loyal to your highest, sensitive, brave,
Sanguine, some few ways wise, you and all men are drawn out of this
      depth
Only to be these things you are, as flowers for color, falcons for swift-
      ness,

Mountains for mass and quiet. Each for its quality

Is drawn out of this depth. Your tragic quality
Required the huge delusion of some major purpose to produce it.
What, that the God of the stars needed your help?" He said "This is my last
Worst pain, the bitter enlightenment that buys peace."

Lenin: Vladimir Ilyich Lenin (1870–1924), the famous Russian revolutionary leader.

Woodrow Wilson

by Roselle Mercier Montgomery (?–1933)

The eagle has passed on! . . . into the blue . . .
And all the chattering of the sparrow dies.
They could not bear to see the eagle rise
Beyond the reaches that their small wings knew,
Above the housetops they could compass too—
But though they strove to blind the eagle's eyes
With fluttering wings . . . to stay him with their cries,
He rose and passed . . . above, beyond their view.
An eagle always is a lonely one—
The far heights call to him and he must go;
But little birds cannot look on the sun,
And what an eagle knows they cannot know . . .
When he is gone, the small ones know, at last,
That there, above their heads, an eagle passed!

Woodrow Wilson

by S. Omar Barker (b. 1894)

There will be those to-day who weep their own
    Who fell in battle or upon the sea;
And those who, when they mourn, will think of all
    America's brave dead. Well, as for me,
I too have tears and sad remembering
    For every man of them, named or unknown.
Yet from the throng one gray, gaunt face appears
    Of him who battled, at the last, alone.

Condemn him if you will: his is the place
    Of honor in our land due every man
Whose soul has glimpsed ideals and whose heart
    Has fought to prove them true. Lone veteran
Of visions was his role unto the last.
    Repudiated, still he dared to face
The world, head up, and loyal unto death
    To his great plan of peace for all the race.

He was lone out-post for that world-old hope
    Humanity can never quite release:
He gave his heart, his life, his soul, to hold
    Our eyes upon the gleam of lasting peace.
If he was right (God knows he may have been!)
    Come, bring heart-laurel for his sleeping head!
If he was wrong, still true his heart and brave
    His fight: His place is with our soldier-dead.

Woodrow Wilson

by Robert Underwood Johnson

Could he return to us, how would we greet him?
    Streets paved with flowers and vocal with song,
Children with forests of laurel to greet him,
    Some from the candid, who once thought him wrong;
Honor and praise from the foes of his fighting.
    Friend of the many, misled by the few,
The young would remember the wrongs of his righting;
    The old would forget not the world he made new.

Fame shall recount his dark night of decision
    When the fate of all peoples was trembling in doubt;
Poets shall sing of the might of his vision
    And History weep while the multitudes shout.
Land of his love, long remembrance keep fair for him—
    Him who fell forward in Liberty's war.
Mother of martyrs, Columbia, wear for him,
    Proud on thy grateful breast, Valor's gold star.

Columbia: the United States of America, usually personified as a female figure.

88. Eugene O'Neill

Much has been made of the autobiographical nature of works by the playwright Eugene O'Neill, the winner of four Pulitzer prizes for literature. In *Bound East for Cardiff*, a short drama staged in 1916, he incorporated some of the "life experiences" he had enjoyed since leaving Princeton University during his freshman year: steamship voyages as a seaman; life as a derelict in Argentina, Liverpool, and New York; an attempted suicide; and newspaper work on the *New London Telegraph*. In his more famous *Long Day's Journey into Night*, his creation of a family named Tyrone is an allusion to County Tyrone, Ireland, the ancestral home of the O'Neills. The character James Tyrone is unmistakably the author's famous actor-father (a native of Kilkenny), while Edmund, one of the grown sons in the play, is the playwright himself. Mary Tyrone, the mother in the drama, is clearly intended to be the author's own mother, Mary (Quinlan) O'Neill.

In real life O'Neill's attitude toward Ireland was famously ambivalent. Although he was proud of his Irish ancestry, in real life he spoke critically of the "Old Sod" in front of his father. The playwright frequently alluded to his O'Neill roots and relished the story of "Red" O'Neill. According to the legend, during a boat race "Red" cut off his hand and threw it onto the shore in order to be the first to "touch" land and thereby win the large tract of property that was the object of the contest. On one occasion O'Neill the playwright confided that "One thing that explains more than anything about me is the fact that I'm Irish."

In 1936 O'Neill became the first American playwright to be awarded the Nobel Prize for literature. The famous Anglo-Irish playwright Bernard Shaw said that he was "very pleased" about the choice of O'Neill, while two other Irish authors weighed in with praise: Lennox Robinson ("O'Neill's contribution to the drama is very valuable indeed") and William Butler Yeats ("I have the greatest admiration for his work"). But in O'Neill's eyes the greatest recognition came from the Irish ambassador in Washington, who praised him on behalf of the Irish Free State for adding, along with Shaw and Yeats, to the credit of old Ireland. Yeats had earlier flattered O'Neill by requesting his permission to stage his *Days Without End* at the Abbey Theater in Dublin.

When O'Neill's pet Dalmatian died while the playwright and his third wife were living in California, the author helped himself through the grieving process by writing a panegyric in which he adopted the persona of his faithful Fido. Although the 250-word testament describes the dog's weariness with a life plagued by blindness and deafness, it may actually express the dramatist's battle with Parkinson's disease. The first few lines suggest the vanity of vanities: "Dogs are wiser than men. They do not set great store upon things. They do not waste their days hoarding property . . . [and] worrying about how to keep the objects they have, and to obtain the objects they have not. There is nothing of value I have to bequeath except my love and my faith . . . ."

Mourning Becomes Eugene O'Neill
by Arthur Guiterman (1871–1943)

> Eugene G. O'Neill
>> Moans a great, great deal.
>
> Eugene G. O'Neill
>> Disrupts the evening meal.
>
> Eugene G. O'Neill,
>> Tart as lemon peel,
>> Sad as cold boiled veal,
>> Weighing woe and weal,
>> What anguish must he feel!
>
> Eugene G. O'Neill,
>> Slightly off his keel
>> With sombre, Freudian zeal,
>> Makes the blood congeal,
>> The senses reel.
>
> Eugene G. O'Neill
>> Probes with bitter steel
>> Wounds that none may heal.
>
> Three ouches and a squeal
>> For Eugene G. O'Neill!

Eugene G. O'Neill: O'Neill's middle name was Gladstone, after the British prime minister who proposed legislation granting Irish Home Rule.

89. F. Scott Fitzgerald

F. Scott Fitzgerald, the novelist whose love-hate relationship with the wealthy formed the basis of much of his work, including *The Great Gatsby*, was born in St. Paul, Minnesota, in 1896. His dual American and Irish ancestry seems to have been the cause of the identity crisis that plagued him for most of his life. Through his paternal forebears, Fitzgerald was descended from prominent figures in the history of colonial Maryland. (He was named, in fact, for Francis Scott Key, the author of the "Star Spangled Banner" and a cousin of his paternal grandmother.) His maternal grandfather, Philip McQuillan, had emigrated from County Fermanagh, Ireland, in 1843, settling eventually in St. Paul, where he operated a wholesale grocery business and left a fortune worth more than $125,000. Yet despite this grandfather's financial success, Fitzgerald regarded his maternal ancestry as "straight 1850 potato-famine Irish." The author's cultural schizophrenia is evident in his remark that "I am half black Irish and half old American stock. . . . The black Irish half of the family had the money and looked down upon the Maryland side of the family who . . . had 'breeding.' So . . . spent my youth alternately crawling in front of the kitchen maids and insulting the great."

Fitzgerald's most autobiographical work is *This Side of Paradise*, published in 1920 and generally regarded as the first realistic American college novel. Besides containing references to the sixty-four books and ninety-eight writers that influence Amory Blaine — the Fitzgerald-like protagonist — the work chronicles the influence of Monsignor Darcy, a character based on Monsignor Cyril Fay, who had become for Fitzgerald something of a surrogate father in St. Paul. In 1917, when it appeared that Fitzgerald might be sent overseas with his infantry unit, Fay had written the second lieutenant a poem entitled "A Lament for a Foster Son, and He going to the War Against the King of Foreign." Part of the poem, which Fitzgerald later incorporated into *This Side of Paradise*, includes these lines: "May Patrick of the Gael and Columb of the Churches and the / five thousand Saints of Erin be better than a shield to him / And he go into the fight."

Before his death in 1940, the famous Irish-American author requested to be buried with his Maryland ancestors in St. Mary's Catholic Cemetery in Rockville, Maryland. The local bishop denied permission, however, probably because of Fitzgerald's defection from the Catholic Church. Instead, he was buried in Rockville Union Cemetery. Thirty-five years later, after St. Mary's Cemetery had been declared a historic monument, Fitzgerald's daughter obtained permission to transfer his remains to the site. In a gesture of reconciliation, the archbishop of Baltimore said: "F. Scott Fitzgerald came out of the Maryland Catholic tradition. He was a man touched by the faith of the Catholic Church. There can be perceived in his work a Catholic consciousness of reality. He found in his faith an understanding of the human heart caught in the struggle between grace and death. His characters are involved in this great drama, seeking God and seeking love. As an artist he was able with lucidity and poetic imagination to portray this struggle. He also experienced in his own life the mystery of suffering and, we hope, the power of God's grace."

On Editing Scott Fitzgerald's Papers
by Edmund Wilson (1895–1972)

Scott, your last fragments I arrange tonight,
Assigning commas, setting accents right,
As once I punctuated, spelled, and trimmed
When, passing in a Princeton spring, now dimmed—
A quarter-century ago and more—
You left your "Shadow Laurels" at my door.
That was the tale of one who sang and shone,
Lived for applause but had his life alone,
In some beglamoured, shimmering, bluish-green,
Imagined Paris wineshop of nineteen;
Who fed on drink for weeks, forgot to eat,
"Worked feverishly," nourished on defeat
A lyric pride, and lent a lyric voice
To all the tongueless, knavish tavern boys,
The liquor-ridden, the illiterate;
Got stabbed one midnight by a tavern mate—
Betrayed, but self-betrayed by stealthy sins—
And faded to the sound of violins.

Tonight, in this dark, long Atlantic gale,
I set in order such another tale,
While tons of wind that take the world for scope
Rock blackened fathoms where marauders grope
Our blue and bathed-in Massachusetts ocean;
The Cape shakes to the depth bomb's dumbed concussion;
And guns can interrupt me in these rooms,
Where now I seek to breathe again the fumes
Of iridescent drinking dens, retrace
The bright hotels, regain the eager pace
You tell of. . . . Scott, the bright hotels turn pale;
The pace limps or stamps; the fumes are stale;
The horns and violins blow faint tonight.
A rim of darkness that devours light
Runs like the wall of flame that eats the land;

Blood, brain, and labor pour into the sand;
And here among our comrades of the trade
Some buzz like husks, some stammer, much afraid,
Some mellowly give tongue and join the drag
Like hounds that bay the bounding anise bag,
Some swallow darkness and sit hunched and dull,
The stunned beast's stupor in the monkey skull.

I climbed, a quarter-century ago and more
Played out, the college steps, unlatched my door,
And, creature strange to college, found you there—
The pale skin, hard green eyes, and yellow hair—
Intently cleaning up before a glass
Some ravage wrought by evenings at the Nass;
Nor did you stop abashed, thus pocked and blotched,
But kept on peering while I stopped and watched.
Tonight, from days more distant now, we find,
Than holidays in France were, left behind,
Than spring of graduation from the fall
That found us grubbing below City Hall,
Through storm and darkness, time's contrary stream,
There gleams surprisingly your mirror's beam
To bring before me still, in graver guise,
The glitter of the hard and emerald eyes;
The cornea tough, the aqueous chamber cold,
Those glassy optic bulbs that globe and hold,
They pass their image on to what they mint,
Suffuse your tales of summer with their tint,
And leave us to turn over, iris-fired,
Not the great, Ritz-sized diamond you desired
But jewels in a handful, lying loose:
The opal's green chartreuses, shifting blues,
Its shadowy-vivid vein of red that flickers,
Tight phials of the spirit's light mixed liquors;
Some zircons livid, tinsel rhinestones; but
Two emeralds, green and lucid, one half cut,
One cut consummately—and both take place
In Letters' most expensive Cartier case.

And there I have set them out for final show,
And come to the task's dead end, and dread to know
The eyes struck dark, dissolving in the wrecked
And darkened world, the light of intellect
That spilled into the spectrum of tune, taste,

> Scent, color, living speech is gone, is lost;
> And we must dwell among the jagged stumps,
> With owls digesting mice to gruesome lumps
> Of skin and gristle, monkeys scared by thunder,
> Great buzzards that descend to grab the plunder.
> And I, your scraps and sketches sorting yet,
> Can never thus relight one sapphire jet,
> However close I look, however late,
> But only spell and point and punctuate.

"Shadow Laurels": Fitzgerald's one-act play about an American who goes to Paris to learn more about his dead father. **The Cape:** Cape Cod, Massachusetts. **the Nass:** possibly Nassau Hall, Princeton University's original 1756 building, still a prominent feature of the campus. **Letters':** an obscure allusion. **Cartier:** the famous family jewelry business founded in France in 1847 by Louis-François Cartier.

90. Charles A. Lindbergh

Although the famous aviator's Swedish roots are well known, his Irish ancestry through his maternal great-grandmother, Emma Kissane, is rarely recognized. Lindbergh's place in the annals of aviation history was won when he made the first nonstop flight across the Atlantic in May 1927 in the *Spirit of St. Louis*. Built by the Ryan Aircraft Company in San Diego, California, the plane made its 3,500-mile flight from New York to Paris in thirty-three and a half hours.

Twenty-seven hours after leaving Long Island, New York, Lindbergh approached the coast of Ireland, although at the time he was uncertain of his exact position. After sighting a tiny boat and than a man's head thrust through one of its portholes, the pilot closed the throttle of the plane and glided to within fifty feet of the fishing vessel. "Which way is Ireland?" Lindbergh cried out. Disappointed that he heard no response, he banked his plane and pointed it in what he hoped was the direction of Europe. Within an hour he sighted a coastline which his charts identified as Valencia and Dingle Bay off the southwestern tip of Ireland. To his amazement he had arrived at this point two and a half hours ahead of his calculated time. He later recorded his impression of the Emerald Isle: "I've never seen such beauty before — fields so green."

During the 1930s, as clouds of war threatened Europe, Lindbergh became the spokesman for American noninterventionism on the Continent. Although he urged Britain, France, and the United States to increase the preparedness of their military aviation, he counseled against entering a war against Nazi Germany. He feared not only that France and Britain could not defeat Hitler but also that war would see the loss of more than a million American soldiers and the destruction of western civilization. Painted by his critics as pro-Nazi and anti-Semitic, Lindbergh never regained his former reputation, even though he abandoned his noninterventionist position when the U.S. entered the war.

From Part II of **And I Will Be Heard**
by John Beecher (1904–1980)

. . . .

And Charles Augustus Lindbergh
I remember the day
when you
were the American people
brave
invincible
what we all deep down knew we all of us were
and I remember another day
when we all grieved with you
and your child was our child
and we forgave you
when you moved to England
and we understood
why you wanted to be private.
But now
you want to be public again
and you are handing us
some pretty funny stuff.
It is all right to tell us Hitler's bombers won't be here next
week
because you are an expert on bombers
and you may know
even though you experts have been wrong all along about
Hitler
still you have a right to say what you really think.
But just don't go on from that
to making politics out of it.
Be sure you aren't trying to put ahead some party or other.
Watch it.
We still remember
Hermann Goering pinning a medal on you

and we have a picture in our heads of Hitler looking on
and that day
you could have been the American people again
if you had just quietly told that Hermann Goering
where to shove his medal.

your child was our child: In 1932 Lindbergh's infant son was kidnapped from the family home in New Jersey and was later found murdered. This tragedy and the trial of the kidnapper (Richard Bruno Hauptmann) received sensational world-wide publicity. **Hermann Goering:** the Nazi air force chief (1893–1946), from whom Lindbergh unwittingly accepted a German medal but later refused to return it.

Wings
by Blanche W. Schoonmaker

How did he know, the young sky-rover,
The windy way it was safe to go?
Beating a path through sun and darkness,
How does the golden plover know?

Skill and science were riding with him,
Knowledge and poise at his shoulder stayed,
Yet in that whirl of straining hours,
How was he sure and unafraid?

Soul attuned to a magic summons,
Pulse attuned to the motor's song,
Cutting a path through sun and darkness,
Mile after conquering mile along—

So he followed a luring splendor,
Fanned to flame by Disaster's breath,
Face to face with eternal secrets,
Gallantly holding the hand of Death!

Flight like the flight of the golden plover,
Fast and far with the storm-clods blown:
How was it done, O wings of daring?
Even the birds fly not alone!

plover: a shorebird.

Lindbergh

by Aline Michaelis

Alone, yet never lonely,
    In all that blue expanse;
The skies were his, his only,
    When Lindbergh flew to France.
Like hero made immortal
    Who storms at Asgard's door,
Beyond the cloud's bright portal
    Men saw his swift plane soar.

Bifrost, the bridge he crossed on—
    Its rainbow spanned the sea—
And while his plane was tossed on
    The air's infinity.
Great Odin, in Valhalla,
    Peered down to see him fly,
When, swifter than the swallow,
    He swept across the sky.

Thor watched and Bragi, singing,
    Told all that matchless flight,
And sent a new name ringing
    Down halls forever bright.
Who knows what promise fed him
    Through hours lone and long?
Who knows what vision led him
    Unto the waiting throng?

Alone, yet never lonely,
    Serene, beyond mischance,
The world was his, his only,
    When Lindbergh flew to France!

Asgard's door: In Scandinavian mythology Asgard was the dwelling-place of the gods. **Bifrost:** in Scandinavian mythology the bridge (rainbow) between heaven and earth. **Odin:** in Scandinavian mythology the god of war, who presided over Valhalla, the great hall in the celestial regions to which the Valkyries carried the souls of heroes slain in battle. **Thor ... Bragi:** in Scandinavian mythology the sons of Odin, respectively regarded as the god of thunder and the god of poetry. **waiting throng:** the 150,000 people who greeted Lindbergh's arrival at Le Bourget Airfield in Paris.

Flying Charlie

by Louise Ayres Garnett (?–1937)

(Who said: *And I looked down and saw the most beautiful country
my eyes ever beheld . . . and it was Ireland.* And whose mother
said: *Charlie gets a lot of Irish from my mother's side.*)

You must have heard it calling you, Ireland, your Ireland,
You must have heard it calling you from over across the sea.
You saw its banners fly to you,
Far and wide and high for you,
Making a singing sky for you, for you, its flying Charlie.

Ourself that's racing through your veins, your Ireland, your
    Ireland,
Called, Charlie, clap your wings on, be stepping along the
    sky.
We'll wear our greenest green for you,
It's proud we'll be to be seen by you,
And she'll watch, the dark Rosaleen, for you, for you, her
    flying Charlie . . . .

We can't be claiming the all of you for Ireland, your Ireland,
America's mixed the Viking with the blood that is our own;
But the Irish heart in the breast of you
Has put the zip and the zest in you—
A drift of dreams go west with you . . .
So we're willing to call the rest of you the whole world's
    flying Charlie!

    O it's Flying Charlie for you and me,
    It's him that's the king of air and sea,
    For Charlie go bragh *from the Land of the Free,*
        The whole world's flying Charlie.

Rosaleen: a poetic name for Ireland. **Viking:** one of the Scandinavians who raided,
traded, and settled throughout Europe during the eighth to the eleventh centuries. ***Charlie* go bragh:** "Charlie forever!" (a parallel to the Irish cry *Erin go bragh!*
— "Ireland forever!").

A Signature
by Robert H. Davis (1869–1942)

What was that glinting
Silver thing
That flashed like something wild a-wing,
And fled on the crest of the morning,
Leaping the coast of Newfoundland
Like a jewel the zenith adorning?

What is that glittering over the sea,
Remote in the heavens,
Higher and higher,
Plunging for Ireland,
Swift as an arrow tipped with desire?

What is that shimmering
High above England
Weaving the mists,
Invading the Channel?
What does it bring,
This shadowy thing?

Avant! Over France
Like an eagle it hovers
Aloft in the blue;
Spiraling, gliding,
Coming to rest,
A pant in its breast
Weary of riding.

Mon Dieu! It is mortal
Out of the void
Hurrying by
Signing the name of
LINDBERGH
On the land
And the sea
And the sky.

Newfoundland: the most easterly of Canada's ten provinces. **Channel:** the English Channel (between England and France). **Avant!:** Forward! **Mon Dieu!:** a French phrase meaning "My God!"

Skoal! Charles Lindbergh, Skoal!

author unknown

"Speak! speak! thou fearless boy!
Who, to our breathless joy,
Hast with thy wingèd toy
    Tamed the Atlantic!
Wrapt not in eagle-down,
But with your harness on,
You flew where none had flown,
    And we are frantic."

Then from those Northern eyes
Laughter began to rise,
Thinking of sleety skies
    Passed now forever,
And of the water's flow
Under the ice and snow,
As he resolved to go
    Back to land never.

"I am no Viking old!
My deeds are young and bold;
We came through all that cold—
    I and my engine.
Before you had toasted me,
Hailing my victory,
Let those nine pistons be
    Honored with mention.

"Over Long Island Sound,
By the Grand Bank around,
We left the solid ground
    Darkened behind us.
Then fell the evening—
Frozen and evil thing—
With only the compass ring
    There to remind us.

"Sleep there was none now;
I and my swift prow
Sped as we wondered how
    Broad was the ocean.

Rising ten thousand feet—
Still came the angry sleet!
Ah! then the early, sweet
    Morning in motion.

"All day I felt the pull
Of the steel miracle. . . .
Ireland was beautiful,
    Then France was near us."
Now from the flowing bowl
Spoke forth a nation's soul:
"Skoal! Charles Lindbergh, skoal!
    New York to Paris!"

Skoal!: a Norse exclamation of good wishes. **Viking:** one of the Scandinavians who raided, traded, and settled throughout Europe during the eighth to the eleventh centuries. **Long Island Sound:** the body of water between Connecticut and Long Island, New York. **Grand Bank:** a plateau under the Atlantic Ocean southeast of Newfoundland, Canada.

Our Boy

by Oliver Herford (1863–1935)

Wings and the Boy I sing, who, braving Fate,
And the tempestuous Sea-God's ancient hate,
Three thousand miles on wings unswerving sped
Through ice-barbed winds, o'er moving mountains dread,
And to the stricken watchers on the shore
Of sorrowing France, Columbia's message bore.

Wings and the Boy! Companions linked as one.
Prince of the Air, Columbia's bravest son,
Modest as brave—the glory of the deed
Joyously sharing with his wingèd steed,
Named for a gallant Knight—by happy chance,
The Spirit of Saint Louis, King France.

Wings and the Boy I sing: a witty parallel to the first line of Vergil's *Aeneid*: "Arms and the man I sing!" **Sea God:** the Greek god Poseidon. **Columbia:** the United States of America, usually personified as a female figure. **Saint Louis:** a thirteenth-century king of France, often regarded as the ideal of chivalric kingship.

Lindbergh
by Wendell Phillips Stafford (1861–?)

Lone eagle of the wild Atlantic plain,
Tall, laughing boy, with sun-glints in your eyes,
Playfellow of the lightning and the rain,
Co-sentry with old watchers in the skies,
Light-hearted prologue to the epic muse,
Glad reuniter of long-riven parts,
Bright Hermes of the nations, bringing news
Of love still flaming in all human hearts!
"Do I deserve all this?" Oh, more, far more,
More than the grateful world can ever pay.
A fouler fog than hides Newfoundland's shore
Your little bark's propellor [*sic*] whirled away.
Fly on, above the mist of sordid things:
Rise, like the sun, with healing in your wings!

Hermes: a Greek god and the messenger of the other gods. **Newfoundland:** the most easterly of Canada's ten provinces.

91. Will Rogers

Despite his later "poorboy persona," the famous cowboy humorist Will Rogers was the son of a successful rancher and banker. His father was of mixed Irish and Cherokee ancestry and held a prominent position in the Cherokee Nation. Proud of his Indian blood, Will Rogers once boasted to a Boston audience: "My ancestors didn't come over on the Mayflower — they met the boat." About his Irish ancestry he quipped: "These Irish, you got to watch 'em. There was a few of 'em sneaked into Oklahoma and got mixed up with the Rogerses and the Cherokees, and I am a sort of an offshoot — an Irish Indian." After the famous Florenz Ziegfeld said that he thought Rogers had a touch of Jewish blood, the humorist described a possible family crest: "a shillelagh with a tomahawk on one end, and a percent sign on the other."

As a youngster Rogers enjoyed roping calves, a skill which he perfected on his classmates, cajoling them to "stoop over, run down the hall, and beller like a calf." After leaving high school, he became known as "The Cherokee Kid," a rope artist and rough rider with Texas Jack's Wild West Circus. (His most famous rope trick was lassoing a horse and its rider simultaneously with two ropes.) While touring the country with this troupe and others, he began to exploit the amusement which his drawl elicited by engaging in self-deprecating banter with the audiences. After making the switch to vaudeville, he quickly became a Broadway star with his intermittent appearance in the Ziegfeld Follies between 1916 and 1925.

In the meantime Rogers had begun what developed into a promising journalistic career. Beginning with a series of weekly articles for the *New York Times*, he gradually went on to attract an audience of 40 million readers with his "daily telegram," a short paragraph that became syndicated in 350 newspapers. After touring Europe as President Coolidge's "ambassador of good will" and as a correspondent for the *Saturday Evening Post*, Rogers wrote *Letters of a Self-Made Diplomat to His President*, the first of several longer volumes in a humorous style.

Because of his later popularity as a lecturer and radio speaker, it was probably only natural that Rogers should make the transition to motion pictures. By 1919 he and his family had moved to California, where he reached the pinnacle of his acting career between 1929 and 1935. (He made a total of seventy films.) In the midst of the Depression, he was earning $200,000 per motion picture. His annual income as an actor, writer, lecturer, and radio personality was estimated at $600,000, a figure that made him the highest paid entertainer of his era. He was generous in his charity, however, especially to the Red Cross during World War I and the Depression.

Oklahoma's Will

In memory of Will Rogers, Aug. 15, 1935
by Ruth Olive Angel

We mourn him not for repartee alone
    (Thousands there are with gift of witty tongue)
But more for something in the sharp, clean tone
    He put upon a thought, and how he swung
His philosophic lasso till its noose
    Tripped us with genial laughter, kin to youth,
And when we paused and tried to struggle loose
    We found ourselves held fast by homely truth.

But greater still, we love the simple way
    He wore the cloak of culture unadorned
With just enough of gayness to be gay
    And just enough of kindness to be mourned.
So proudly now we stand grief-bowed and still
    While all the world pays tribute to "Our Will."

92. The Five Sullivan Brothers

When the five Sullivan brothers — ranging in age from twenty to twenty-nine — were killed during the battle of Guadalcanal in November 1942, a spokesman for the Navy said that the loss of the brothers was the heaviest blow suffered by any American naval family.

The five — Albert, Madison, Joseph, Francis, and George — had enlisted together the previous January on condition that they not be separated during the war. After the local recruiter had refused to guarantee their request — reminding them that the Navy placed members of the same family in different assignments — the brothers wrote a letter of protest to the Navy Department in Washington. In its official reply the Navy agreed to waive its rule and allow the four unmarried brothers to serve together. (Albert, the married brother and the father of a child, was also eventually allowed to serve with his siblings.)

The boys' mother knew that she would be unable to dissuade them, especially now that they were also intent on joining in order to avenge the death of their best friend aboard the U.S.S. *Arizona*. She therefore consoled herself with the belief that George and Francis — who had already served in the Navy — would be able to assure not only their own safety but that of their brothers. In her heart, though, she realized that the boys were fatalists. "They felt that when your number was up, there was nothing you could do about it but die fighting," she later said. "They would take their chances together." George had even presciently observed: "If the worse comes to worst, why we'll all have gone down together."

The brothers perished after their ship, the U.S.S. *Juneau*, was sunk by Japanese fire in the Solomon Islands. Four of the brothers died immediately from the explosion, while George was among the 140 of the ship's 700 men who initially survived. For days George lay adrift on a raft, crying out for his missing brothers and becoming increasingly deranged from drinking salt water and from exposure to the burning sun. In his madness he jumped overboard — only to be ripped apart by three sharks as he screamed "Help me! Help me!"

Subsequent events catapulted the martyred brothers into the national spotlight. In February 1944 they were honored by a mass at St. Patrick's Cathedral in New York City and by the announcement that a newly built destroyer would be named for them. That same month the Sullivans' forty-three-year-old uncle, Patrick Henry Sullivan, joined the crew of the new destroyer, while their sister, Genevieve, took her brothers' place in the war effort by joining the WAVES. The brothers gained further recognition with the 1944 Hollywood film *The Sullivans* (retitled *The Fighting Sullivans*).

In August 1995, Albert Sullivan's granddaughter, Kelly Sullivan Loughren, participated in ceremonies marking the launching of a new destroyer. As she smashed a bottle of champagne against the ship's prow, she said: "In honor of my grandfather and his brothers, I christen thee *The Sullivans*. May the luck of the Irish always be with you and your crew." *The Sullivans* and its crew of twenty-six officers and 315 sailors were invited to visit Ireland the following summer during the gathering of the O'Sullivan clan and in honor of the fiftieth anniversary of the Irish navy.

In Memoriam

by A. M. Sullivan (1896–1980)

I

Five Irish lads stood tiptoe on the prairie
Stared over the plumed high corn of Iowa
And saw the blue Pacific lap the dusk
And where the sky sloped down on the winter wheat
They watched the wind sweep through the green shoal water
And their hearts beat faster with the distant rumble
In the dark flotillas of the thunder heads.

II

Six centuries long the Sullivans of Kerry
Have looked to the west from bastions of Bearehaven
Looked through the mists of Dingle toward the Blaskets
Hugging the horizon like great men-of-war,
Looked through the Gulf Stream's breath beyond the pennons
Of Spanish ships with wine and spice for Galway,
Looked for the land of youth and the land of promise
And they sailed west with the faith and songs of Kerry
Landing them where whim of wind and commerce brought them,
Boston, New York, Penn's city on the Bay,
Savannah, Charleston, the diked-up Creole city.
Hewers of wood and breakers of land, they gouged
The waterways across New York, New Jersey,
Built plank roads through the swamps, and bridged the rivers,
Drove spikes with rhythm of the panting engine
And caught the dreams of empire in their hands.
Somewhere along the road their hearts made anchor
On prairie land, and sons and daughters came
With the blueness of deep water in their eyes.

III

If oil will soothe the ferment of the ocean
A drop of blood will bring the sea to boil
And spread the rancor till all shores are stained
By the wrack that purges from hearts of men.
December Seven. The little men of Nippon
Feathered like falcons with unhooded eyes
Fall on Pearl Harbor drugged in Sunday slumber,
And make the stain that honor must erase.
The sons of Kerrymen rush to the quarrel
Out of the midlands and their pulse is tuned
To tides of tempest though they've seen no ship
Save the argosies that drift across the moon.

IV

Five Sullivans from Iowa go forth to battle
Linked arm in arm, and make the willing bargain,
Win all, lose all, they take the cruiser *Juneau*
Which burrows southward through the dangerous isles
And plumbless depths and distance of the blue water,
The old mirage of the winter wheat come true.
The Jap and Yank played many a game of tag
Through mist and rain, and coral reef and atoll,
But the Jap was *it* when the hide and seek was ended
And eight and twenty keels of the mute Mikado
Plummeted down three miles with seams wide open.
Nine Yankee craft went under, one the *Juneau*
Her skin of steel ripped open but the mouths
Of her long guns spat flame across the water
Till water chilled their gullets with a hiss
Of fury, and they spoke no more in anger.

V

Sing out the paean for the Yankee valor
With foemen vanquished and with shame avenged
But brothers five who came from Iowa
Will look no more on wind in the winter wheat
Nor hear the dry husks rustle in the Autumn;
They sleep with friend and enemy below
The curved blue arches of the Coral Sea.
Though sons of Kerry sail on every ocean
The Sea's the sea the blessed wide world over,
And the Gael who steers by shadow of the gull,

With O'Bruidar the Rogue, and Brendan the saintly rover
Knows he shall hear through grottos of dark water
The heavenly horn that summons sailors home.

prairie: The Sullivan brothers grew up in Waterloo, Iowa. Their paternal grandparents were emigrants from County Cork, Ireland. **Kerry:** a county in southwestern Ireland. **Bearehaven:** or Bere Haven, a body of water between Bere Island and the Beara Peninsula, at the northwestern end of Bantry Bay on the west coast of Ireland. **Dingle:** a peninsula at the western end of County Kerry. **Blaskets:** a group of islands off Dingle Peninsula. **Gulf Stream:** the strong ocean current that flows in the northwest Atlantic Ocean. **Galway:** a town on the west coast of Ireland. **Penn's city on the bay:** Philadelphia. **diked-up Creole city:** New Orleans. **December Seven:** December 7, 1941, the day of the Japanese attack on Pearl Harbor, Hawaii. **Nippon:** the Japanese name for Japan. **Pearl Harbor:** the Hawaiian operating base of the U.S. Pacific fleet, attacked by Japan in 1941. **eight and twenty keels:** During the six separate naval actions fought between August 7 and November 30, 1942, and known as the battle of Guadalcanal, the Japanese actually lost twenty-four warships (two battle ships, four cruisers, one light carrier, eleven destroyers, six submarines). **Mikado:** an archaic title of the Japanese emperor. **Nine Yankee craft:** During the battle of Guadalcanal (August 7–November 30, 1942), the Americans lost at least ten warships (six cruisers, one carrier, three destroyers). **Coral Sea:** an area of the Pacific Ocean between the northeast coast of Australia and the Solomon Islands. **Gael:** an Irishman. **O'Bruider the Rogue:** possibly a Gaelicized version of "Brodir," the name of an eleventh-century Viking king of the Isle of Man. **Brendan:** a sixth-century Irish monk who sailed to the Orkneys, Iceland, and, some say, the North American coast.

93. William "Wild Bill" Donovan

The son of Irish immigrants, William Donovan was born in 1883 in Buffalo, New York, where initially he practiced law. In 1911 he joined the New York National Guard and later served under General John Pershing, first on the Mexican border in 1916 and then in France in the last months of World War I. During his service in Europe, he was colonel of the 165th Regiment (formerly the "Fighting Irish" 69th) in the Forty-Second Division. According to one account, he received his nickname while training new recruits in France. "I have fifty pounds on my back, the same as you," he said challengingly, "and I'm twenty years older than any of you boys." Anonymously from within the ranks came the response, "Yeah, but we ain't no wild man like you, Bill." Wounded three times in combat and hailed as a national hero for his leadership, he was awarded the Distinguished Service Cross, the Distinguished Service Medal, and the Medal of Honor.

After the war Donovan resumed his legal career and tried his luck in the political arena. His tenure as a federal attorney and as head of the Justice Department's criminal division was broken by unsuccessful runs as the Republican candidate for lieutenant governor of New York in 1922 and for the governorship a decade later. Sometime during this period a former law partner said that Donovan would not be satisfied until he was the first Catholic president of the United States.

With the outbreak of World War II in Europe, Donovan pressed the U.S. government to create an intelligence network for the nation. In 1942, when the Office of Strategic Service was established as a result of his efforts, he was named its director. In that capacity he oversaw the agency's efforts at intelligence gathering, counterintelligence, underground activities, psychological warfare, propaganda, and sabotage. In 1957, when Donovan was awarded the National Security Medal, he became the first American to have received the nation's four highest decorations.

On Learning of the Death of "Wild Bill" Donovan

by Carleton S. Coon (1904–1981)

Wild, people called him, who had heard of his fame
And wild he was in heart and in feyness.
But more than wild was the man with the wile of Odysseus.
Like the King of the Assassins he welded together
An army of desperate, invisible soldiers,
Each as bold as himself in single deeds
But none as keen as himself, the leader of all, commander of men

Who could ask, "Jim, will you limpet that ship?"
Knowing the answer, for none would refuse him, or
"Carl, a free ride to Albania? Yes? Then you're off,
Ten minutes to Zero," and we would all die for him.
Die for him some of us did, but he died for us all.
Some who are left would burn him whole, like a Viking jarl in his
    ship.
Others would cover his bones with a colossal marble cross.
Each to his taste, say I, Yankee, Irishman, Italian.
As many tombs will he have in our hearts as the scattered
    remains of Osiris.
How lucky we were that he came when he did in the long tide of
    history.
Hail to Wild Bill, a hero of men and a name to hang myths on.
As American as chowder, Crockett, and Putnam.
A free fighter's hero, may God give him peace.

feyness: the state of being under a spell or in an excited state of mind. **Odysseus:** one of the heroes of the *Iliad* and the protagonist of the *Odyssey*, known for his cunning stratagems (e.g., the Trojan Horse and his killing of the Cyclops Polyphemus). **King of the Assassins:** probably Hasan ibn al-Sabbah, the founder of a secret fraternity of Muslim fanatics, active in Persia and Syria c. 1090–1272, whose chief object was to assassinate Crusaders. **Viking jarl:** a Scandinavian noble or chieftain who raided, traded, and settled throughout Europe during the eighth to the eleventh centuries. **Osiris:** the Egyptian god of the dead. He was killed and dismembered into fourteen pieces by his brother, Set. **Crockett:** David Crockett (1786–1836), the colorful frontiersman who served three terms in Congress before moving to Texas, where he was killed while defending the Alamo from a Mexican army. **Putnam:** Israel Putnam (1718–1790), an American Revolutionary general, who distinguished himself at the battle of Bunker Hill in 1775.

94. John F. Kennedy

In 1963, just months before his assassination, John Kennedy visited Ireland for what he described as one of the most moving experiences of his life. The president was proud that he and his siblings were 100 percent Irish, their grandfathers having borne the names Kennedy, Fitzgerald, Hickey, and Hannon. During his visit to New Ross, County Wexford, where his great-grandfather Patrick Kennedy was born in 1820, the mood was one of exaltation. "The pubs were open at five o'clock in the morning," one local said, "and most of the town was drunk by eight, for days on end. They were dancing there on the quay. If the town wasn't burned down that night, it never will be." Kennedy displayed his usual charm and said that "There is an impression in Washington that there are no more Kennedys in Ireland, that they are all in Washington." When he asked the Kennedys in the audience to raise their hands, he added, "Well, I am glad to see a few cousins who didn't catch the boat." To one of those cousins, Mary Kennedy Ryan, the president extended his thanks for the salmon and the hot tea which she had served him that day.

Kennedy continued his triumph to Ireland's two largest cities. In Cork he joked about his family's privileged status while introducing one of the members of his American entourage. "And now I would like to introduce to you the pastor at the church I go to," he said playfully. "He comes from right here in Cork — Monsignor O'Mahoney. He is the pastor of a poor, humble flock in Palm Beach, Florida."In Dublin, meanwhile, the president laid a wreath on the graves of the leaders of the 1916 Easter Rising. He also was awarded two honorary degrees, one from Trinity College and the other from rival National University. Ever the politician, Kennedy said he felt part of both institutions and that "if they ever have a game of Gaelic football or hurling, I shall cheer for Trinity and pray for National."

As he prepared to depart from Shannon Airport, Kennedy quoted a poem that the wife of Ireland's president, Eamon De Valera, had taught him, promising, like the poet, "to come back and see old Shannon's face again." One of the gifts which the president was given was a specially designed O'Kennedy coat of arms, an escutcheon with an added strong arm grasping an olive branch and arrows. After his wife had the coat of arms made into a seal ring for him, Kennedy one day delighted in telling her: "I used my Irish seal on a letter today — to the Queen of England!"

The "Inauguration Poem" below was written just before John Kennedy took the presidential oath of office in January 1961. When the author — A. M. Sullivan — learned that Robert Frost would read a poetic tribute to the new president at the event, Sullivan withdrew his own poem from distribution and deferred publication. Unknown to Sullivan, however, a copy of the poem was sent to Kennedy's personal secretary, who expressed the president's wish to keep it for the archives.

Inauguration Poem

by A. M. Sullivan (1896–1980)

I salute you, John F. Kennedy
With neither paean [n]or threnody
But with a rhyme, half-prayer, half-praise
For courage on this day of days.
Kennedy of the ancient Gaels
Derives from head, the leading man;
Hail! scion of a stalwart clan
Who placed his heart upon the scales
When there was duty to be weighed
And valor was the coin you paid.
The ballot box has built a throne
Higher than any ermined chair
Where you must sit, exposed, alone
And guarded by our faith and prayer.
No king or knave has held the power
We place into your hand this hour.
The trust we offer has more strength
Than secret weapons to be hurled
With eyes of anger 'round the world
Measured in time or folly's length,
Such as the atom's flowering tuber
Spreading its malice in a game
More deadly than when Satan came
As Genghis Khan or Schickelgruber [sic] .
The earth is but a shriveled grape
And meaningless in time and space
Except for people on its face,
A world from which none can escape
Unless he choose the vacuum
Between the stars and Kingdom Come
And here is where we make our stand
With half the world at your command.
There was a time in mortal pride
We boasted God stood at our side.
Maybe He did but took offense
At crass presumption of a child
By grandeur and by wealth beguiled
And these are years of penitence
And we must ravel out the skies
Of destiny till we regain

The golden thread and learn the price
Minted of willing sacrifice.
Lead us on, but friend and foe
Choose with a candid yes and no
And when a new path must be taken
And the easy trail forsaken
The only error to be made
Is faith's decision long delayed.
Aye, listen with two patient ears
But speak in candor with one tongue
Clearly as if a bell were rung
To let truth echo down the years
Without the sly, subjunctive blur
Of a hydra-headed sophister
Who tangles meaning in a knot
Frustrating sage or polyglot.
Young men who come to share your burden
Have a lordly purse of intellect
But you're the sovereign architect
To shape the plan for blame or guerdon.
Look to the past, if not for long—
John Harvard and Lord Baltimore
Can counsel you in the bloodless war
With a word of thunder to the wrong
That's conjured in the human mind
With reason numb and justice blind.
Be right with words, but seldom clever;
The world's too full of clever men
If Congress seats them now and then
The White House beds them hardly ever.
Eyes shift from small to the immense
From mediocre to the superb
But you must watch the active verb
And speak it in the present tense
Lest in our godly pantomime
Our ego runs ahead of time.
God light the vow upon your lip
With wings of flame across the land
And may your strong uplifted hand
Hold firm the helm of statesmanship,
With the full blessing of the crew
And one who didn't vote for you.

paean: a song of praise, triumph, or thanksgiving. **threnody:** a poem, speech, or song of lamentation, especially for the dead. **Gaels:** inhabitants of Ireland or Scotland speaking Irish or Scottish Gaelic. **Genghis Khan:** the Mongol conqueror (c. 1162–1227) and ruler of an empire stretching from the Caspian Sea to the Sea of Japan. **Schickelgruber [*sic*]:** Schicklgruber, an indirect reference to Adolf Hitler. Hitler's father, Alois, was the illegitimate son of Maria Anna Schicklgruber and Johann Nepomuk Hüttler (of which the name "Hitler" is a corruption). **hydra-headed:** having many facets or aspects. **sophister:** a sophist, one who reasons skillfully but speciously rather than honestly. **guerdon:** a reward or recompense. **John Harvard:** the seventeenth-century benefactor for whom Harvard College was named in 1639. **Lord Baltimore:** George Calvert (c. 1580–1632), who hoped to create in Maryland a haven for persecuted English Catholics.

Footnote to Tragedy
for JFK November 22, 1963
by A. M. Sullivan (1896–1980)

Whether we agreed on grain or taxes,
The price of steel, the Bay of Pigs Fiasco,
The Harvard dons, is immaterial now.
I didn't vote for you[,] John Kennedy,
And what is done is done beyond recall,
Past judgment or debate of right or wrong.
What matters most of all is that I write
Bold yea or nay in wisdom or in folly
Because a young man wagered golden years
Against the black wind with a flaming word
And won the cup of bloody sacrifice.
You took the risk for us who catch the coins
Of valor's mint and time's brief charities.
You found men's hidden worth beneath the skin,
And color blind, you looked around the earth
And felt one pulse throb in the living heart
And touched the braille of beauty in the soul
Of poet, peasant and social heretic.
No sceptre held such power as your fist,
Free gift of free-born citizens; no needle
Stitched so bright a garment for the truth
As the instant logic of your index finger.
Time abdicates at forty-six for you
Whose spectre lifts from nadir of the grave
To zenith as you wear the crown of peace
Mid praise and prayer of one who salts the ink

And shapes the alphabet upon the page
Of grief's old testament this blemished hour.

Bay of Pigs: the Cuban bay that was the scene of a failed invasion by 1,300 Cuban refugees in April 1962. Kennedy took full responsibility for the failure.

Thanksgiving, 1963

by Molly Kazan (1907–1963)

(Written shortly after President Kennedy was assassinated)

I think that what he gave us most was pride.
It felt good to have a President like that:
bright, brave and funny and goodlooking.

I saw him once drive down East Seventy-
          second Street
in an open car, in the autumn sun
(as he drove yesterday in Dallas).
His thatch of brown hair looked as though
          it had grown extra thick
the way our wood animals in Connecticut
grow extra fur for winter.
And he looked as though it was fun to be alive,
to be a politician,
to be President,
to be a Kennedy,
to be a man.

He revived our pride.
It felt good to have a President
who read his mail,
who read the papers,
who read books and played tough football.
It was a pleasure and a cause for pride
to watch him take the quizzing of the press
with cameras grinding—
take it in his stride,
with zest.

He'd parry, thrust, answer or duck
and fire a verbal shot on target,
hitting with the same answer, the segregation-

ists in a Louisiana hamlet and a govern-
		ment in South East Asia.
He made you feel that he knew what was
		going on
in both parties.
He would come out of the quiz with an "A"
in Economics, Military Science, Constitutional
		Law, Farm Problems and the moonshot
		program
and still take time to appreciate Miss May
		Craig.

We were privileged to see him on the worst day
(till yesterday),
the Bay of Pigs day,
and we marveled at his coolth and style
and were amazed at an air (that plainly was
		habitual)
of modesty
and even diffidence.
It felt good to have a President
who said, It was my fault.
And went on from there.

It felt good to have a President
who looked well in Vienna, Paris, Rome, Berlin
and at the podium of the United Nations
—and who would go to Dublin,
put a wreath where it did the most good
and leave unspoken
the satisfaction of an Irishman
en route to 10 Downing Street
as head of the U.S. government.

What was spoken
was spoken well.
What was unspoken
needed to be unspoken.
It was none of our business if his back hurt.

He revived our pride.
He gave grist to our pride.
He was respectful of our intellect;
he was respectful of excellence;

he was respectful of accomplishment and skill;
he was respectful of the clear and subtle uses of
        our language;
he was respectful of courage.
And all these things he cultivated in himself.

He was respectful of our heritage.
He is now part of it.

He affirmed our future.
Our future is more hopeful
because of his work
but our future is not safe nor sure.
He kept telling us that.
This is a very dangerous and uncertain world.
I quote. He said that yesterday.

He respected facts.
And we must now live with the fact of his
        murder.

Our children cried when the news came. They
        phoned and we phoned
and we cried and we were not ashamed of
        crying but we were ashamed of what
        had happened.
The youngest could not remember any other
        President, not clearly.
She felt as if the world had stopped.

We said, It is a shame, a very deep shame.
But this country will go on
more proudly
and with a clearer sense of who we are
and what we have in us to become
because we had a President like that.
He revived our pride.
We are lucky that we had him for three years.

Miss May Craig: a female correspondent. In his book *Kennedy*, Theodore C. Sorensen wrote that President Kennedy "knew that May Craig's questions were more likely to be puzzling than weighty, but he always shared the television viewers' curiosity about what her question would be and he always called on her."
Bay of Pigs day: an allusion to the failed invasion of Cuba by 1,300 Cuban refu-

gees in April 1962. **put a wreath:** on the graves of the leaders of the 1916 Easter Rising. **10 Downing Street:** the London residence of the British prime minister.

J. F. K.

by Loyd Haberly (1896–1981)

A bullet laid tall Lincoln low
But that was tragedies ago.

Now our own martyr, brave and good,
The President of Brotherhood,
Is gone, as moles go, into dirt
Where cold strifes thaw and no spites hurt.

Between the known and the unknown
He paced the strange streets of alone,
His mind being duty-bound to show
A blind tomorrow where to go.

Shot in Frontierland, he still talks to time
Of men released by Earth to float and climb
Out there beyond all praise and all abuse
Where silence keeps what silence cannot use.

Let us pray here.
That flag his child touched as she bowed
Beside his bier made us too proud
Of what we thought we were.

his child: Kennedy's daughter, Caroline.

Kennedy *Ucciso*

by Richard Hugo (1923–1982)

Don't scream at me you God damn' wops,
nine at night. I know what the headline says.
Blasted by some creep in Dallas.
Don't ask me who Johnson is.
Don't ask *racismo* [*sic*], *comunismo*?
I don't know. That fountain lit
and flowing over naked ladies, fish,
animals and birds, is blurred. You and words

in giant print keep banging at my head.

I voted for him, not my kind of man.
My kind could not be president,
just a target for the cold. You slip in
noisy knives of why. *Un gran uomo*?
Certamente. I know, here this very year.
Yes, a Catholic, Yes. Yes. Very rich.
A man who put some sixty million lives
on some vague line and won.
I'd vote for him again. But here
in the *piazza* where the fountain
makes wet love to ladies and stone swans
I want your questions and my hate to end.

The fountain runs in thighs of lovely stone.
Ladies do quite well, subduing swans
and lizards, giving in to fish. You Romans,
quite *simpatici*. Someday we'll be you.
I weep in the *piazza*, perfect wop.
Take your questions to a sainted star.
My Italian fails. *Come si dice*:
He was not afraid of what we are.

wops: a slang and disparaging word for Italians or people of Italian descent.
Johnson: Lyndon Baines Johnson, Kennedy's vice president and successor. *racismo*
[*sic*]: actually *razzismo*, Italian for "racism." *comunismo*: Italian for "Communism."
un gran uomo: Italian for "a great man." *Certamente*: Italian for "certainly." *pi-azza*: Italian for "plaza." *simpatici*: Italian for "nice, likeable, pleasant." *Come si
dice*: Italian for "It is said that . . ."

From **After His Assassination a Place of Peace**
by George Keithley (b. 1935)

I

After his assassination a place of peace,
a church
impatient with piety,
pleas for Kennedy—
"Receive, receive, your servant Jack."
Long lines of mourners murmur and turn back.
St. John's belfry wheel winds, and unreels its chimes.

The amber lamps upon the roof
of the radio tower pulse on and off.
Throughout the hour
wire reports grow like fine steel vines.

Thru this electric speech a siren climbs
above the trees and screams
for the body borne away,
given to the grass.

> Poor death, beggaring death
> seeking a gift of us
> that has our breath.

In our restless peace
what can my hand touch
that will bloom? Or our arms reach
that will bear?

. . . .

St. John's: probably St. John's Church, the "Church of the Presidents," opposite
Lafayette Square in Washington, D.C.

Escort for a President

by John Beecher (1904–1980)

I

Rapt to our screens we watch him borne inert
and casketed into the plane he stepped
from a few hours ago invulnerable,
serene and radiant. Young Zeus he seemed
at breakfast, brandishing his thunderbolts
and vaunting of the billions he'd dispensed
to Texans slavering for contracts. Votes
he angled for with grisly bait but was
first casualty of his dread TFX
although the instrument which took his life
was obsolete as bow and arrow. Lord,
Thine irony is more cruel than Thy wrath.

II

The land's sad face averts itself, now bleak
and sere that's starred with blue bonnets in spring

and Dallas underwing diminishes,
the azure shafts that oil and cattle built,
the marts where Santa holds his blazing court.
Small Jesús flattens nose upon plate glass
but José's out of work and so is María.

    III
Assumed into a myth more speedily
than Lincoln was or Roosevelt he floats
across the fabled river so far down
it seems the life-line on some ancient palm.
Mortality is sloughed in upper air
above the Mississippi. Brooding here
another myth circles on eagle wings
biding its time. Crossed hairs upon a back
as on a head brought to a baleful term
two young men's lives. Medgar, here's company.

    IV
Now swarming up the air with cries like doves
or angels come black girls from Birmingham
with blood upon their Sunday finery
and faces blown away. Here also wheel
two black boys slain in cleanlier wise by bullets
upon that Sabbath day. May they escort
a president upon his journey home?

Zeus: the chief god of the Greek pantheon. **TFX:** Tactical Fighter Experimental, a new aircraft developed for use by both the Navy and the Air Force. **Jesús . . . José . . . María:** names probably intended to represent the Hispanic Americans who watched the televised coverage of events after Kennedy's death, in this case through the windows of a TV appliance store. **Medgar:** Medgar Evers, an American civil rights leader who was killed by a sniper in 1963. **black girls from Birmingham:** four African-American girls who were killed when the Sixteenth Street Baptist Church in Birmingham, Alabama, was hit by a bomb on September 15, 1963.

Kennedy

by Michael Heffernan (b. 1942)

One late afternoon I hitched from Galway down to Kinvara on
the edge of the Burren, one of those long midsummer days when
the sun labors at last out of all-day rain and sets very late in the

evening. In dark pubs all up and down the street the townsmen
hunched to their pints silent and tentative as monks at supper.
Thinking to take my daily Guinness, I stopped, and Kennedy was
there, his picture on the mantel behind the bar.

A black-headed citizen, half in his cups, sidled over and smiled.
Ah Kennedy Kennedy, a lovely man, he said, and bought me a
Guiness. Ah yes, a lovely man, I said, and thank you very much.
Yes Kennedy, and they slaughtered him in his youth the filthy
communists, he said, and will you want another. Yes, slaughtered
him in his youth, I said, and thanked him very much.

All night, till closing time, we drank to Kennedy and cursed the
communists—all night, pint after pint of sour black lovely stout—
and when it came Time, I and my skin and the soul inside my
skin, all sour and lovely, strode where the sun still washed
the evening, and the fields lay roundabout, and Kinvara slept in
the sunlight, and Holy Ireland, all all asleep, while the grand brave
light of day held darkness back like the whole Atlantic.

Galway: a city on the west coast of Ireland. **Kinvara:** a village and bay at the head
of Galway Bay. **Burren:** a barren and crevassed region in County Clare. **Guinness:**
a brand of Irish beer produced by the family of the same name.

In Arlington Cemetery

by Stanley Koehler (b. 1915)

In the city of memorials,
among tombstones and small
headstones, I look through the cold
not for a monument
but for a grave with ferns
and evergreens lent
from the season past. A flame burns
in the air, not a leaf
to shelter it, blown like our grief,
variable and new, endless and old.

Uphill, over open ground,
on the wind's edge are coming
echoes of drummers drumming
on tight-stretched skin,

tattooing the stillness
to the funeral sound
of hoofs at the hobble,
unharnessed, held in
to the ritual pace;
and of wheels on the cobble.

The carriage circles a green park
with its temple, the dark
porch where the Form in his chair
sheds a marble tear
for what is fated like him:
statues for whom
there are robes of stone.
Love waves in her car
while Hate takes aim
through a lens from far—
off, and History bleeds, an old charade,
and Madmen fly
the line of parade
down empty walks, and from the shocked
stage the Actor's shout
is driven out.
Still, in those marble eyes
deepgrained as memory,
the barns are burning, the streets are blocked,
while motorcade and obsequies

through iron gates
to somber guns and the horn's last notes
continually come.
For this to end, for the drum
to be stilled at last,
more than this green bough
will be cut and cast.

The flame leaps up. Fresh as our vow,
it makes a gentle monument at night
with the simplicity of light.

Arlington Cemetery: Arlington National Cemetery, in Virginia, where John Kennedy was buried on November 25, 1963. **city of memorials:** Arlington Cemetery. **flame:** the eternal flame at the grave of John Kennedy. **temple . . . Form:** The interior of the Lincoln Memorial ("temple") is dominated by a gigantic seated statue ("Form") of Abraham Lincoln. **Actor's shout:** *Sic Semper Tyrannis* ("Thus always to tyrants"), shouted by the actor John Wilkes Booth after his assassination of Lincoln.

Two Women at JFK Gravesite

by Margaret Gibson

Sun begins on the harp of trees, on snow
that the storm shoved down in the dark.
A troop of boys runs by.

Somebody near us, muffled, says,
in Arlington National Cemetery
we used to sled down these roads
when we were young and the stones
here were stones merely where the dead
were, frozen together.

The buds on the tulip trees prick
as we splinter through the wind.
The flame is nearly level to the stone.
We do not let ourselves feel what others
report to feel
because somehow

the Greek house, the hill, the sky
of monuments dismay our love until
awe dies and with it cheap propriety.
The dead, we know, rot as immaculate
children run down the hills
holding their cold ears

and the storm is shouting miles up the river
dropping ice like bullets on the unsuspect.
The ironic flame chatters in the weather,
our innocence spreads like a city at his feet.
We have killed no man with hate
or with love.

Before the stone circle of a hero's words
a man plainly cries, thinking
how the sweet cheat of his fate
goes bankrupt here, how no body

not of any woman consoles the discrepancies
in his dreams.

The sun is face down in the distant river.
We pick our way back softly, shunning
heroes like ice, ignoring the hurt
ordinary men, numbers 31-623, 25
who alive might have wanted us
and a simple cupboard life

before the abstract truckled and cajoled
and they went down, stunned
like fallen children from their toys.

Arlington National Cemetery: the site in Virginia — across Memorial Bridge from
the nation's capital — where John Kennedy was buried on November 25, 1963.
flame: the eternal flame at the grave of John Kennedy. **Greek house:** Arlington
House, the Greek-Revival former residence overlooking Arlington National Cemetery. **stone circle of a hero's words:** a series of concrete and granite blocks located near Kennedy's grave and inscribed with quotes from his inaugural address. **hurt / ordinary men:** the thousands of men whose military service earned
them a place in Arlington Cemetery and whose tombstones are inscribed with
identification numbers.

For John Kennedy of Harvard
by Edward Pols (b. 1919)

A tumult of images insist,
Repeat, repeat, traverse, and re-traverse,
Until the dreadful Sunday's counterpoint—
She with your children pacing to the drum,
While here the prisoner comes, and dies
Under the blind resurge of violent Dallas—
Is on the night screen one more time rehearsed
And we believe at last
What on the Friday we so feared to know.

That Friday night St. Patrick's bells
Came to me in an old Maine house
The while against them spoke—spoke
The banal words each of us finds when moved
And when a public voice exacts reply—
Spoke the various accents of the city.

Some nuance unmanned me yet again
(Or was it the passing of my youth that struck?)
So, lest the children see my tears,
I walked awhile between the arbor and the barn
And thought of you passing once in 'thirty-seven
In the spring of freshman year and of your life
On the Yard walk past Widener's steps and
Up the slope towards Palmer House that was:
There stood a Norway maple on that hill
Which every spring spread out a cope
Of greeny gold upon the ground, and there we passed,
Treading the bright minuscule blossom down,
In the slant light of morning and of our lives.

Your smile held then—how shall I say?—a thought
Too much assurance, and your walk a pride
To daunt a green and envious boy who'd wrought
A manner but no ease for all he tried
To be at home: you seemed to own the place
I loved but did not yet possess. But stay,
There comes to mind the man of forty-five:
A man who wore that humor in his face
Did not let youth or wealth or rank betray
Him to forget this truth: when we arrive
Who come here late, the place we meant to find
And win and love is altered out of mind.

So, much of worth in what we take is lost—
That Harvard gone of Eliot and of James,
That land of Arcady before the host
Of yours and mine sailed here to stake their claims.
Provincial places though (your smile confides)
And not perhaps as open to the world
As we with myriad ties of blood and faith
Have made them in your time; and this abides,
For all the poise that's vanished with your wraith,
For all that Camelot's banners need be furled:
They changed to take us in, but we
Transformed them out of all they could foresee.

The tree is gone that once bestrewed the ground
Each springtime with a green-gold grace:
Now buildings flank that place,
While, moved and turned around,

Cropped Palmer House looks strange—
So all things shift and change—
But though your life is gone and my youth
I see you now in truth
Transfigured, resplendent in our ruth.
They say you were still half symbol,
Being given so little time;
Come, let us take you so, but in this sense:
In that region of possibility you fill
There, still, your bright incontinent essence
Inclines to its own completion, still
Shapes almost its own actuality, still contrives
Some reason, measure, humor in our lives.

Sunday's counterpoint: November 24, 1963, the third day after Kennedy's assassination in Dallas, Texas. **She with your children:** Jacqueline Kennedy and the two Kennedy children (John and Caroline). **prisoner:** Lee Harvey Oswald, Kennedy's assassin, who was killed by Jack Ruby while in police custody in Dallas on Sunday, November 24, 1963. **Friday:** November 22, 1963, the day on which Kennedy was assassinated. **St. Patrick's:** probably St. Patrick's Cathedral in New York City (whose bells the author heard via radio or TV). **'thirty-seven:** Kennedy began his freshman year at Harvard in September 1936. **Yard:** Harvard Yard, an area of the Harvard campus northeast of Harvard Square in Cambridge. The Yard is dominated by Massachusetts Hall, University Hall, Sever Hall, and the Widener Memorial Library. **Widener:** the Widener Memorial Library on the Harvard campus. **Palmer House:** perhaps the Dana-Palmer House, a private residence built in 1820 in the southeast corner of Harvard Yard. **man of forty-five:** Kennedy celebrated his forty-fifth birthday in May 1962. **Eliot:** Charles Eliot, the president of Harvard from 1869 to 1909. **James:** William James, who began his pioneering research in human psychology at Harvard. **Arcady:** any real or imaginary place offering peace and simplicity. **host / Of yours and mine:** probably the influx of immigrants into Boston and the rest of the nation. **Camelot:** in Arthurian legend the place where King Arthur held his court and where the Round Table was located; a name given to the Kennedy administration. **ruth:** pity, sorrow, remorse.

Hero

by William Stafford (1914–?)

What if he came back, astounded
to find his name so honored, schools
named after him, a flame at his tomb,
his careless words cherished? How could
he ever face the people again, knowing
all he would know in that great clarity
of the other side? (His eyes flare into

the eyes of his wife. He searches his brother's
drawn face turned toward him suddenly still.)

No. Better abandoned in the ground
recklessly cast back into the trash of
our atoms, all once loved let languish:
a lost civilization loses by particulars,
faith eroded by faithlessly treating
its servants. (Remember the slippering
progress the hearse made?—dwindling importantly
where faces could never really turn round?)

Our words apologize for such chill,
engulfing perspectives. We look deep into
the branded time helplessly and then come
chattering back for assurance, to shore up
our relics: *Arma virumque cano*. Such effort
it takes to build the high walls of Rome.

his wife: Jacqueline Bouvier Kennedy. **his brother's / drawn face:** probably a reference to Kennedy's brother Robert. ***Arma virumque cano:*** "Arms and the man I sing!" — the first line of *The Aeneid*, Vergil's epic Latin poem about the founding of Rome by Aeneas.

John Fitzgerald Kennedy

by John Masefield (1878–1967)

All generous hearts lament
    the leader killed,
The young chief with the
    smile, the radiant face,
The winning way that turned
    a wondrous race
Into sublimer pathways,
    leading on.
Grant to us life that though
    the man is gone
The promise of his spirit be
    fulfilled.

Farewell to a President

by Joseph A. Casper (b. 1941)

This trip he made, was it to no avail,
Driving down that Texan trail.
The crowds all cheered, as he smiled back,
Then came the sound of a rifle crack.
His car sped forward to the hospital near,
But life for the President ended here.
The suspected killer was caught nearby,
But not before a policeman died.
They held him in their county jail,
When being moved his face turned pale.
A shot rang out, he fell down,
Killed by a man who was in town.
Meanwhile the President was flown away,
To the Capitol where he did stay.
His casket there, it lie [*sic*] in State,
So that all the world could see his fate.
The T-V viewers, the people there,
All could see and the sorrows share.
The 25th day of November, that was the day,
Our dear President won on his way.
The people stood by and all looked grim,
When out stepped his son and saluted him.
His wife, his daughter, his family dear,
All looked down and standing near.
The men of the Armed Forces did their share,
To show for the President they did care.
Six white horses, and one on the side,
Took our President on his last ride.
First to the Church where you heard the mass,
Then over the bridge, through the gates they did pass.
Arlington National Cemetery, that's where they went,
To bury our 35th President.
The casket was set atop of the grave,
Our flag was held by servicemen brave.
A 21 gun salute, for a hero so true,
Who has given his life, for his country and you.
The bugler blew the taps aloud,
Not a stir or a sound was heard from the crowd.
The family left, then the dignitaries too,
And down went the casket for a life anew.
So hoping his life was not given in vain,
And by his quotation there's a lot we can gain.
"It's not what your country can do for you, but what
    you can do for your country."

suspected killer: Lee Harvey Oswald. **policeman:** Police Officer J. D. Tippit, shot to death two miles from the scene of Kennedy's assassination. **Killed by a man who was in town:** Lee Harvey Oswald was killed by Jack Ruby while in police custody in Dallas on Sunday, November 24, 1963. **his son . . . . / His wife, his daughter:** John Jr., Jacqueline, and Caroline Kennedy, respectively. **Church:** St. Matthew Catholic Church in Washington, D.C., where Kennedy's funeral was held on November 25, 1963. **Arlington National Cemetery:** the site in Virginia — across Memorial Bridge from the nation's capital — where Kennedy was buried on November 25, 1963. **"It's not what your country can do for you . . . :** Kennedy's quotation actually began, "Ask not what your country can do for you . . . ."

To J.F.K. 14 Years After
by Roger Weaver

Your sculptured lips are sealed
beneath the rushing scene
where Winter lies congealed
over everything.

The empty sky leers
about a silent hive.
Not all your peers
wish you alive,

wish you in deeper peace
than we know here
where children of Cochise
still love every year.

Your coins please crowds
who hoard half dollars,
and gossips stitch shrouds
for your dead and living brothers.

What can lips say true
when truth goes unreported
and news becomes the hue
of privacies unguarded?

Regardless of the fashion
to lower you this year,
I still wish with passion
that you were here.

Cochise: c. 1815–1874, a chief of the Apaches. **Your coins:** various types of fifty-cent pieces minted since 1964 bearing the profile of John F. Kennedy.

95. Jacqueline Bouvier Kennedy Onassis

Despite the French blood which Jacqueline Bouvier inherited from her father, her mother was 100 percent Irish, the family's first American ancestor having come from Ireland to New York City in the 1840s. Jacqueline's grandfather — James Thomas Lee — was vice president of Chase Manhattan Bank and president and chairman of the board of New York Central Savings Bank. At his death he left a $12 million estate.

When John and Jackie Kennedy celebrated their tenth wedding anniversary in 1963 at Hammersmith Farm in Newport, Rhode Island, the president gave his wife the inventory of a New York art dealer with permission to buy anything on the list. The first lady, in turn, presented her husband with a leather scrapbook containing photographs of the newly landscaped White House Rose Garden. She also gave him a St. Christopher medal to replace the one which he had buried with their prematurely born son, Patrick Bouvier Kennedy, who had died the month before.

Following her husband's assassination in November 1963, Mrs. Kennedy's dignity and stoic bearing helped the nation and the world cope with their grief. Images of her cradling her husband's head in her lap as the presidential limousine sped to a hospital in Dallas were engraved in the nation's consciousness, as was the image of her bloodied clothing. A few days later, in an interview with Theodore H. White, the former first lady alluded to a line from the musical *Camelot*: "Don't let it be forgot, that once there was a spot, for one brief shining moment that was known as Camelot." White's subsequent article drew heavily on the Camelot imagery, and from then on the Kennedy administration was associated with the presumed magic of King Arthur's court.

After the assassination of her brother-in-law, Robert Kennedy, in 1968, Jacqueline Kennedy and her children went into a kind of self-imposed exile. "I hate this country," she reportedly said. "I despise America and I don't want my children to live here anymore. If they're killing Kennedys, my kids are number one targets. . . . I want to get out of this country." That same year she married the Greek shipping magnate and billionaire Aristotle Onassis. With a $26-million settlement obtained after her new husband died, Mrs. Onassis returned to New York, where she worked as an editor for $10,000 a year. In July 1999, only three years after her own death, her son, John Fitzgerald Kennedy Jr., died in an airplane accident at the age of thirty-eight.

Jacqueline

by Will Inman (b. 1923)

And when she strides
soul uplifted
with unbrazen eyes,
his coffin cannot contain him,
her footsteps deliver him
in rhythms of dignity
down the avenues of our pulsedrums
that, mourning, we receive,
and, accepting his death, we
take unto us the living
flesh of his meanings.

96. Robert Kennedy

The seventh of the nine children born to Joseph and Rose Kennedy, Robert Kennedy was a graduate of Harvard University and the University of Virginia Law School. His first work as an attorney was with the Justice Department, prosecuting graft and income-tax cases. He later served as counsel on a Senate committee investigating labor racketeering. As attorney general for his brother, Kennedy prosecuted school desegregation cases and threw his support behind the 1964 Civil Rights Act.

For months after his brother's assassination in 1963, Kennedy was deeply depressed and unable to speak in public. While preparing to keep a long-scheduled commitment to address a St. Patrick's Day dinner in Scranton, Pennsylvania, he decided to include in his remarks a poem by Thomas Osborn Davis about the death of the Irish patriot Owen Roe O'Neill. The final lines of the poem seemed apropos of his brother: "Oh! why did you leave us, Owen? why did you die? / Your troubles are all over, you're at rest with God on high; / But we're slaves, and we're orphans, Owen! — why did you die?" An assistant urged him not to use the poem, however, saying that he would never be able to read it without breaking down. Kennedy replied that he had been practicing in front of a mirror, mastering the lines so that he could repeat them without faltering. "I can't yet, but I will by the time I speak," he accurately predicted.

When it became clear that he would not be Lyndon Johnson's vice presidential running mate, Kennedy successfully ran for the U.S. Senate from New York. In Congress he supported the expansion of the federal welfare system and denounced the Vietnam War. After declaring his candidacy for the presidency, he rolled to five victories in the six primaries that he entered, until he was assassinated in Los Angeles in June 1968 by Sirhan Sirhan, a Jordanian immigrant.

A Flower from Robert Kennedy's Grave
by Edward Sanders (b. 1939)

> *During demonstrations at Nixon's second inau-*
> *guration, we watched his limo pass, on the way*
> *to the White House; then I drove over to Ar-*
> *lington Cemetery.*

January 20, 1973

After
a winding walk
up past the white stones
of snuff,

past the guardhouse
circling circling
around the Catholic henge
to John Kennedy's bright taper
burning on the ground
in windy cold winter after-speech
afternoon

    then walk down
    to the left-hand

        edge of the hill-
ock—there in speechless serenity,
           built onto the steepness
           a small
           elegant
           perfectly proportioned
           white cross 'bove
           white flat marble marker

    Robert Francis Kennedy

    nearby a fount jets horizontal

over a slab o' stone

water curving down abruptly on the
rock front lip

                    R.F.K.'s words of race heal
                    writ upon the rock above
                    the flat-fount.

Across the walkway
by the grave
a long red rose
with a vial of water
slipped upon the stem end
& wrapped with shiny tape
lay singly
& to the left of it a
basket of yellow chrysanthemums

        and this: that
        only a whining hour past,
        Richard Nixon
        oozed down Pennsylvania Avenue
        flashing V's from a limousine
        behind a stutter-footed wary pack of Marines
                                    their
            bayonets stabbing the January
        in a thickery of different directions
            like small lance hairs
                    pricked up on the forehead of a
                    hallucinated drool fiend
                        during a bummer

but big enough to stab the
            throats of hippie rioters

                    buddy.

    I picked a yellow petal

    from thy grave
            Mr. Robert Kennedy

    & brought it home

from Arlington, where many young mourners
stood crying quietly this inauguration day

Picked a dream
            Mr. Robert Kennedy
brought it home in our hearts
burning like a brand in a fennel stalk

Picked a thought-ray
Robert Kennedy

        brought it back from this
        henge of park-side
        eternity

buses of protesters parked
in the lots beneath your hill

        Tears splash
        in the vessels
        of the sun

        Picked yellow
        molecules bunched
        in beauty
        from the beauty fount
        Mr. Robert Kennedy

The peace-ark
glides in the vastness,
though weirdness clings to your death.

But nothing can touch the ark
sails through the trellis of evil
brazen American wrought of light hate

Nothing can touch it
not even pyramidal battlements of gore-spore
nor tricky's pitiless flood
of dungeonoid luciphobian losers.

Arlington Cemetery: the site in Virginia — across Memorial Bridge from the
nation's capital — where John Kennedy was buried on November 25, 1963. **Richard Nixon:** the winner of the presidential election of November 1968. Robert

Kennedy had campaigned for the Democratic presidential nomination during that election cycle. **Pennsylvania Avenue:** the thoroughfare in Washington, D.C., on which the White House is located. **luciphobian:** fearing light.

R.F.K.

Stanza #1 of "Robert Kennedy: 1925–1968"

by Robert Lowell (1917-1977)

Here in my workroom, in its listlessness
of Vacancy, some old Victorian house,
airtight and sheeted for old summers,
far from the hornet yatter of the bond—
is loneliness, a thin smoke thread of vital
air. What can I catch from you now?
Doom was woven in your nerves, your shirt,
woven in the great clan; they too were loyal,
and you too more than loyal to them, to death.
For them like a prince, you daily left your tower
to walk through dirt in your best cloth. Untouched,
alone in my Plutarchan bubble, I miss
you, you out of Plutarch, made by hand—
forever approaching our maturity.

Plutarch: a Greek philosopher and author (A.D. c. 46–c. 120), whose biographies of ancient Greeks and Romans were intended to teach moral lessons.

Our Bobby Is Now Gone

by Larston D. Farrar (1915–1970)

When a dedicated man,
With a noble goal in mind
Meets a Near East Fancy Dan,
With a hatred for his kind,
You can view the unexpected,
On the TV 'fore your eyes,
For no matter how respected,
Our hero falls and dies.
Our Bobby—dear Bobby—really was the one,
And now, without warning, he suddenly is gone.
The road that looms ahead,
Seems terrible and sad,
Because it's like he said,

The country has it bad.
He ran a famous race,
And, against the odds, he won,
You can see his smiling face,
Before he saw the killer's gun.
Our Bobby—dear Bobby—really was the one,
And now, without warning, he suddenly is gone.
'Twas a sad and tragic day,
That morning in LA,
When a fanatic off the lobby,
Took aim and killed our Bobby.
The sun was bright
His eyes were blue,
He strove to share his light,
With you, and you, and you.
Now Bobby was the one,
And yet our Bobby's gone.
"How bad is it?" he cried,
And Ethel could not tell.
He lapsed and then he died,
And we heard the last death knell.
"Don't pick me up," he called,
As she nestled by his side.
The people were appalled,
When they heard that he had died.
In the Capitol dome at night,
When you look at it just right,
You can see his friendly grin,
And you feel he yet may win.
Remember now this truth,
And know I kid you not.
He worked for the poor and youth,
And he lived to kill the rot.
There were giants in those days—
The two killed in fair weather.
They were victims of a craze,
And now they sleep together.
We will not see his like so soon,
The shock of hair and voice so smooth.
But fate may still give us a boon,
And teach us, too, to know the truth.
Our Bobby—dear Bobby—really was the one,
And now, without warning, he suddenly is gone.

Near East Fancy Dan: Sirhan Sirhan, the Jordanian immigrant who killed Kennedy. **famous race:** the California Democratic primary, which Kennedy won on June 6, 1968. He was killed soon after acknowledging his victory that night. **killer:** Sirhan Sirhan, a Jordanian immigrant. **fanatic:** Sirhan killed Kennedy ostensibly because of the senator's support of Israel. **Ethel:** Ethel Kennedy, the senator's wife. **two killed in fair weather:** Martin Luther King Jr. and Robert Kennedy, killed, respectively, in April and June 1968.

Farewell to a Senator

by Joseph A. Casper (b. 1941)

A fighting man, a man was he.
He fought for people's liberty.
President he may have been,
If only the world was free from sin.
In California, he'll be remembered the most,
And all through the U.S.A., coast to coast.
It was in Los Angeles, this story began,
At the California primary, in which he ran.
The Senator won, votes went his way.
Then came the shots, that made it a gloomy day.
Six persons were injured, the Senator was one,
And they caught the assassin with the gun.
The Senator lie [*sic*] in an unconscious state,
But the doctors could not change his fate.
He died on the 6th day of June, 1968,
In the same manner of John his brother of late.
From Los Angeles to New York, his body was flown,
To Saint Patrick's Cathedral, where it was known,
His body there would lie in state, until the mass,
And thousands of people, by his casket would pass.
His body was then brought by rail,
To journey, on his last long trail.
The mourners waited, as the trains rolled by,
All were somber, many with tears in their eyes.
The casket was in the twenty-first car,
As the funeral trains traveled afar.
Through New York, New Jersey, Pennsylvania, to Delaware,
Maryland and Washington, D.C., as people waited there.
The trains arrived, darkness had set in,
They carried the casket, the Navy Band played a Hymn.
The funeral procession then left Union Station,
Seen on T.V., all over the Nation.

Down Constitution Avenue the cortege moved along,
At the Lincoln Memorial, there was sung a song.
The Battle Hymn of the Republic, for which we all stand,
As did Lincoln, the Kennedys all three so grand.
They will all be together in Heaven above,
To talk of the things, they all did love.
Then over the Memorial Bridge he was taken,
To be sent to Heaven, where he shall awaken.
To National Arlington Cemetery, for his last ride,
To be buried by his brother John, side by side.
So, Robert F. Kennedy, a man was he,
Who died, fighting, for American's [*sic*] freedom and equality.

California primary: June 6, 1968. **assassin:** Sirhan Sirhan, a Jordanian immigrant. **Union Station:** the railroad terminal in Washington, D.C., located near the Capitol and built in 1903–1907 in the neoclassical style (after the Roman Baths of Caracalla and the Baths of Diocletian). **Constitution Avenue:** a thoroughfare in Washington, D.C., generally linking the Ellipsis and the U.S. Capitol Building at either end. **Battle Hymn of the Republic:** a musical composition written in 1861 by Julia Ward Howe to the tune of "John Brown's Body." It became the unofficial anthem of the Union cause during the Civil War. **Kennedys all three:** Robert Kennedy; John Kennedy; and Joseph Kennedy Jr., the oldest of the Kennedy brothers, who was killed in 1944 while flying a top secret mission across the English Channel. **Memorial Bridge:** one of several bridges across the Potomac River connecting the District of Columbia with the opposite Virginia shore. **National Arlington Cemetery:** actually Arlington National Cemetery in Virginia. **buried by his brother:** Robert Kennedy's grave is located near his brother's, not next to it as this line implies.

97. Eugene McCarthy

This U.S. senator and four-time candidate for the presidential nomination was born in Minnesota in 1916, the son of a cattleman of Irish descent. After receiving an M.A. from the University of Wisconsin, McCarthy joined the faculty of St. John's University in Collegeville, Minnesota, where he had earned his undergraduate degree. During World War II he served in military intelligence, and after the war he taught at the College of Saint Thomas in St. Paul, Minnesota.

McCarthy was first elected to the U.S. House of Representatives in 1949 on the Democratic-Farmer-Labor ticket. After a decade in the House he was elected to the first of two terms in the Senate. There he enjoyed a reputation as an independent and gave expression to his scholarly bent through such articles as "The State and Human Freedom," "Morality in Government," and Freedom and Political Authority." In a speech given in 1951, for instance, the senator warned against a trend that by the end of the century would become a dangerous reality: the growing intrusiveness of government "into areas of culture and the social and private lives of its citizens." Later in that decade he wrote that the Christian statesman should be alert "to protect and defend the rights of individuals, or religious institutions and other institutions from violation by the state or by other institutions, or by persons."

By 1968 McCarthy had become an outspoken opponent of Lyndon Johnson, particularly of the president's prosecution of the Vietnam War. In his challenge to Johnson for the Democratic presidential nomination, McCarthy made an impressive showing in the New Hampshire primary that year. Though he rolled to three primary victories, he lost four of five matchups with Senator Robert Kennedy, who was also campaigning on an antiwar theme. After Kennedy's assassination, the Democratic Party nominated Vice President Hubert Humphrey. McCarthy ran for the presidency three more times: in 1972 as a Democrat against George McGovern, in 1976 as an independent, and twelve years later on the Consumer Party ticket.

For Eugene McCarthy

Stanza #7 of "To Summer" by Robert Lowell (1917–1977)

I love you so. . . . Gone? Who will swear you wouldn't
have done good to the country, that fulfillment wouldn't
have done good to you—the father, as Freud says:
you? We've so little faith that anyone
ever makes anything better—the same and less—

or that ambition ever makes the ambitious;
the state lifts us, we cannot change the state—all
was yours though, lining down the balls for hours,
freedom in the hollow bowling-alley:
crack of the globe, the boys. . . . Picking a quarrel
with you is like picking the petals of the daisies—
the game, the passing crowds, the rapid young
still brand your hand with sunflecks . . . coldly willing
to smash the ball past those who bought the park.

July 6, 1968

July 6, 1968: a date during McCarthy's campaign for the Democratic presidential nomination (November 1967–August 1968).

98. Georgia O'Keeffe

Georgia O'Keeffe, one of the world's most recognizable artists, was the daughter of Francis Calyxtus O'Keeffe, a native of Ireland whose parents had fled oppressive taxation of their prosperous woolen business in County Cork. Although her father abandoned Catholicism and allowed his children to be raised as Protestants, Georgia was permitted to attend Sacred Heart School in Sun Prairie, Wisconsin. In contrast to the starkness of the Congregational church which she usually attended with her family, the art and ritual which she found when she occasionally attended Catholic services with her uncle hit a responsive chord in her artistic nature. In addition, her desire to be like her paternal grandmother — Mary Catherine O'Keeffe — may have made the older woman's Catholicism all the more attractive to the young girl. At the very least Georgia wished that she had been given her grandmother's name and later said, "I love the Irish [in me]." Although the artist never converted to the religion of her father's family, she remained influenced by its imagery and even dressed like a nun, a habit which caused her to be mistaken for a Catholic sister one time during a visit to Vienna.

After studying at the Chicago Art Institute and Columbia University in New York, O'Keeffe intermittently tried her hand at painting and drawing. Through these media she found that she could "say things that I couldn't say in any other way — things that I had no words for." The artist first drew serious critical attention when Alfred Stieglitz, a pioneer in photography and her future husband, included some of her charcoal drawings in a show at his New York studio. Through these and other works she soon became known for her experimentation in subject matter and technique. (Some of her most famous paintings depict gigantic flower blossoms or bleached animal bones and skulls.) Despite the acclaim which her work received, she was distressed that some critics saw symbols of feminine sexuality in her designs, although she once said that her paintings were her children. By 1939 she was being hailed by the New York World's Fair Tomorrow Committee as one of the twelve most outstanding women of the previous fifty years.

Long before settling permanently in Abiquiu, New Mexico, O'Keeffe had spent many winters there. She was equally familiar with her summer house and studio at nearby Ghost Ranch. The almost hypnotic effect which the ranch had on her can be glimpsed in a letter to her husband in 1937: "At 5:30 I went out and walked — just over the queer colored land — such ups and downs — so much variety in such a small space . . . I've been up on the roof watching the moon come up — the sky very dark — the moon large and lopsided — and very soft . . . ." She remained at Abiquiu until her death in 1986, just two years shy of her one hundredth birthday.

O'Keeffe Retrospective

by May Swenson (1913–1989)

Into the sacral cavity can fit the skull of a deer,
the vertical pleat in the snout, place of the yoni.
Within the embrasure of antlers that flare, sensitive
tips like fingers defining thighs and hips, inner horns
hold ovary curls of space.

Where a white bead rolls at the fulcrum of widening knees,
black dawn evolves, a circular saw of polished speed;
its bud, like Mercury, mad in its whiz, shines, although
stone jaws of the same delta, opposite, lock agape—
blunt monolithic hinge, stranded, grand, tide gone out.

A common boundary has hip and hill, sky and pelvic basin.
From the upright cleft, shadow-entwirled, early veils
of spectral color—a tender maypole, girlish, shy, unbraids
to rainbow streams slowly separated.

A narrow eye on end, the lily's riper crack of bloom:
stamen stiff, it lengthens, swells, at its ball (walled pupil)
a sticky tear of sap. Shuttlecock (divided muzzle of the dried

deer's face, eyeholes outline the ischium) is, in the flap of
the jack-in-the-pulpit, silken flesh. As windfolds of
the mesa (regal, opulent odalisque) are, saturate orange, sunset.

Cerulean is solid. Clouds are tiles, or floats of ice
a cobalt spa melts. Evaporating, they yet grip their shapes;
if walked on, prove not fluff and steam. These clouds
are hard. Then rock may be pillow, stones vacant spaces.
Look into the hole: it will bulk. Hold the rock: it will empty.

Opposite, the thousand labia of a gray rose puff apart,
like smoke, yet they have a fixed, or nearly fixed, union,
skeletal, innominate, but potent to implode, flush red,
tighten to a first bud-knot, single, sacral.
Not quite closed, the cruciform fissure in the deer's
nose bone, symphysis of the pubis.

Where inbetweens turn visible blues, white objects vanish,
except — see, high at horizon on a vast canvas sky —
one undisciplined tuft, little live cloud, blowing:
fleece, breath of illusion.

yoni: in Hinduism a representation of the external female genitals. **Mercury:** a Roman deity and the messenger of the other gods. **Shuttlecock:** The reference here is unclear. **ischium:** the backward-facing lower bone of each half of the vertebrate pelvis. **jack-in-the-pulpit:** any North American plant of the genus *Arisaema*, having an upright spadix (spike of minute flowers) arched over by a spathe (a leaflike plant part). **Cerulean:** deep blue. **labia:** the lower petals of a flower having parts shaped like lips. **innominate:** having no name. **symphysis:** a joining of two complementary bones along the midline of the body, as at the halves of the lower jaw. **pubis:** one of the paired anterior bones of the vertebrate pelvic girdle.

99. Eamon De Valera

The first president of the Irish provisional government was born in New York City in 1882, the son of Catherine Coll of County Limerick and a Spaniard named Vivion De Valera. The younger De Valera was educated in Ireland and was a mathematics teacher when in 1913 he joined the Irish Volunteers, an organization formed to resist the opponents of Home Rule in Ireland. During the Easter uprising against the British in 1916, De Valera played a prominent role and escaped execution by the British only because of his American birth. While still imprisoned he was subsequently elected president of the revolutionary Sinn Fein ("We Ourselves") Party, whose candidates won three-quarters of the Irish seats in the British parliament in 1918 but refused to take their seats at Westminster. At the beginning of the next year Sinn Fein proceeded to set up its own parliament (Assembly of Ireland), appointed ministers to run the country, and confirmed De Valera as president of the nascent republic.

Though the new Irish republican government tried to survive by ignoring the British authorities, the latter had no intention of letting Ireland escape the imperial orbit. The resulting conflict over who would govern Ireland took the form of a guerrilla war, chiefly between the Royal Irish Constabulary and the Irish Republican Army. De Valera spent a portion of this war for independence on a fund-raising mission to the United States. When the truce of 1921 led to a treaty in which the British recognized the Irish Free State, the agreement's exclusion of Northern Ireland and its oath of allegiance to the Crown caused De Valera to reject the new constitutional arrangement. In the civil war that followed he supported the republican resistance to the Free State government and for a time was imprisoned.

Following his release in 1924, De Valera formed a republican opposition party (Fianna Fáil — "Warriors of Ireland"), which by 1932 had won control of the government. As head of the new ministry, De Valera proceeded to sever political and constitutional ties with Britain — abolishing the oath to the Crown, taking the island nation out of the British Commonwealth, and declaring Irish sovereignty. His policy of neutrality during World War II brought the country temporary prosperity and De Valera repeated electoral success. During the 1950s, however, Fianna Fáil's fortunes slipped until 1957, when the party obtained a majority in the Irish parliament. Two years later De Valera resigned as head of government to run successfully for the presidency, a post he won again in 1966.

De Valera at Ninety-Two
by Brendan Kennelly (b. 1936)

To sit here, past my ninetieth year,
Is a joy you might find hard to understand.
My wife is dead. For sixty years
She stood by me, although I know
She always kept a secret place in her heart
For herself. This I understood. There must always be
A secret place where one can go
And brood on what cannot be thought about
Where there is noise and men and women

Some say I started a civil war.
There are those who say I split the people.
I did not.
The people split themselves,
They could not split me.
I think now I was happiest when I taught
Mathematics to teachers in their training.
From nineteen hundred and six to nineteen sixteen
I taught the teachers.
Then the trouble started.
In jail, I often sat for hours
Especially at evening
Thinking of those mathematical problems
I loved to solve.
Here was a search for harmony,
The thrill of difficulty,
The possibility of solution.
Released from jail, I set about
Making a nation,
A vicious business,
More fools among my friends than in my enemies,
Devoted to what they hardly understood.

Did I understand? You must understand
I am not a talker, but a listener.
Men like to talk, I like to listen.
I store things up inside.
I remember what many seem to forget.
I remember my grandfather
Telling of his brother's burial in Clare.
The dead man was too tall
To fit in an ordinary grave
So they had to cut into a neighbor's plot,
Break the railings round a neighbor's grave

To bury a tall man.
This led to war between the families,
Trouble among the living,
Over a patch o' land for the dead.
The trouble's still there. Such things, as you know,
Being a countryman yourself,
Are impossible to settle.
When my grandfather scattered things on the kitchen floor
He used strange words from the Gaelic.
I wonder still about the roots of words.
They don't teach Latin in the schools now.
That's bad, that's very bad.
It is as important to know
Where the words in your mouth come from
As where you came from yourself.
Not to know such origins
Is not to know who you are
Or what you think you're saying.
I had a small red book at school,
'Twas full of roots,
I still remember it.

Roots . . . and crops. Origins . . . and ends.

The woman who looks after me now
Tells me to sip my brandy.
Sometimes I forget I have a glass in my hand
And so I do what I'm told.
I have been blind for years.
I live in a world of voices
And of silence.
I think of my own people, the tall men,
Their strange words, the land
Unmoved by all our passions about it,
This land I know from shore to shore,
The Claremen roaring their support
And all the odds and ends
(What was that word he had for them?)
Scattered on my grandfather's kitchen floor.

wife: Sinéad Flanagan. **Clare:** a county on the west coast of Ireland. **you:** Brendan Kennelly, who wrote this poem in the form of answers by De Valera to a series of questions put to him by the poet.

Works Consulted

Adams, Franklin P., ed. *Innocent Merriment: An Anthology of Light Verse.* New York: McGraw-Hill Book Company, Inc., 1942.

Armour, Richard. *Our Presidents.* New York: W. W. Norton & Company, 1964.

Armstrong, William Clinton, ed. *Patriotic Poems of New Jersey.* Newark: New Jersey Society of the Sons of the American Revolution, 1906.

Azoy, A. C. M. *Charge! The Story of the Battle of San Juan Hill.* New York: Longmans, Green and Company, 1961.

Barnes, Ruth A., ed. *I Hear America Singing.* New York: The John C. Winston Company, 1937.

Barnhill, A. Virgil, Jr. *Some Descendants of Robert Barnhill, I.* Knoxville: Arviba Publishers, 1994.

Barton, George. *Angels of the Battlefield: A History of the Labors of the Catholic Sisterhoods in the Late Civil War.* 2nd rev. ed. Philadelphia: The Catholic Art Publishing Company, 1898.

Bates, Samuel P. *History of Pennsylvania Volunteers, 1861-65.* Vol. 7. Harrisburg: n.p., 1869; Wilmington, N.C.: Broadfoot Publishing Company, 1993.

Beecher, John. *Collected Poems 1924–1974.* New York: Macmillan Publishing Company, Inc., 1974.

Benét, Rosemary, and Stephen Benét. *A Book of Americans.* New York: Farrar and Rinehart Inc., 1933.

Berton, Pierre. *Flames Across the Border: The Canadian-American Tragedy, 1813–1814.* Boston: Little, Brown and Company, 1981.

Blair, Walter. *Davy Crockett: Legendary Frontier Hero.* Springfield, Ill.: Lincoln-Herndon Press, 1986.

Boatner, Mark Mayo. *The Civil War Dictionary.* New York: David McKay Company, Inc., 1959.

Braxton, Joanne M., ed. *The Collected Poetry of Paul Laurence Dunbar.* Charlottesville: University of Virginia Press, 1993.

Breen, Walter. *Walter Breen's Complete Encyclopedia of U.S. and Colonial Coins.* New York: FCI Press, Inc., 1988.

Brewer, E. Cobham, ed. *The Reader's Handbook.* Philadelphia: J. B. Lippincott Company, 1899.

Brewton, Sara and John, eds. *America Forever New: A Book of Poems.* New York: Thomas Y. Crowell Company, 1968.

Browne, Francis F., ed. *Bugle-Echoes: A Collection of Poems of the Civil War.* Chicago: A. C. McClurg & Company, 1916.

Burns, Roger A. *The Bandit Kings: From Jesse James to Pretty Boy Floyd*. New York: Crown Publishers, Inc., 1995.

Busey, John W. *These Honored Dead: the Union Casualties at Gettysburg*. Hightstown, N.J.: Longstreet Press, 1988.

Bushong, Millard Kessler. *Historic Jefferson County*. Boyce, Va.: Carr Publishing Company, Inc., 1972.

The Cambridge Biographical Dictionary. Cambridge: Cambridge University Press, 1994.

Camp, James, et al., eds. *Pegasus Descending: A Treasury of the Best Bad Poems in English*. New York: The Macmillan Company, 1971.

Campbell, John H. *History of the Friendly Sons of St. Patrick and of the Hibernian Society for the Relief of Emigrants from Ireland*. Philadelphia: Hibernian Society, 1892.

Cane, Melville, et al., eds. *The Golden Year*. Freeport, N.Y.: Books for Libraries Press, 1966.

Capps, Claudius Meade, ed. *The Blue and the Gray: The Best Poems of the Civil War*. Boston: Bruce Humphries, Inc., 1943.

Carter, Samuel, III. *Blaze of Glory: The Fight for New Orleans, 1814–1815*. New York: St. Martin's Press, 1971.

Cassidy, Lewis. "Edward Douglass White." *The Journal of the American Irish Historical Society* 26 (1927).

Cavanagh, Michael. *Memoirs of Gen. Thomas Francis Meagher*. Worcester, Mass.: The Messenger Press, 1892.

Clark, Parks, and Edd Winfield, eds. *Southern Poets*. New York: American Book Company, 1936.

Clarke, Joseph I. C. "At the Poet's Shrine." *Journal of the American Irish Historical Society* 6 (1917): 244–247.

———. *The Fighting Race and Other Poems and Ballads*. 3rd ed. New York: The American News Company, 1911.

———. "Ireland at the Fair." *Journal of the American Irish Historical Society* 14 (1914–15): 292–297.

———. "John Barry—A Poem." *Journal of the American Irish Historical Society* 13 (1913–14): 305–309.

———. "Saratoga." *Journal of the American Irish Historical Society* 13 (1913–14): 288–289.

———. "Sullivan." *Journal of the American Irish Historical Society* 12 (1912–13): 225–232.

Cleary, James Mansfield, ed. *Proud Are We Irish: Irish Culture and History As Dramatized in Verse and Song*. Chicago: Quadrangle Books, 1966.

Codrescu, Andrei, ed. *American Poetry Since 1970: Up Late*. New York: Four Walls Eight Windows, 1987.

Colum, Padraic, ed. *An Anthology of Irish Verse*. New York: Liveright Publishing Corporation, 1948.

The Complete Poetical Works of James Whitcomb Riley. New York: Grosset &

Dunlap, 1932.

Condon, William H. *Life of Major-General James Shields*. Chicago: Press of the Blakely Printing Company, 1900.

Connolly, S. J. *The Oxford Companion to Irish History*. Oxford: Oxford University Press, 1998.

Conyngham, David P. *The Irish Brigade and Its Campaigns*. Boston: William McSorley & Company, 1867.

Coogan, Tim Pat. *Eamon de Valera: The Man Who Was Ireland*. New York: Harper Collins, 1993.

Corby, William. *Memoirs of Chaplain Life: Three Years with the Irish Brigade in the Army of the Potomac*. Edited by Lawrence Frederick Kohl. New York: Fordham University Press, 1992.

Cowles, Anna Roosevelt, ed. *Letters from Theodore Roosevelt to Anna Roosevelt Cowles 1870–1918*. New York: Charles Scribner's Sons, 1924.

Crane, Brinton. *A Decade of Revolution 1789–1799*. New York: Harper & Row, 1963.

Crockett, David. *Davy Crockett's Own Story*. New York: Citadel Press, 1955.

Crowley, Denis Oliver, ed. *Irish Poets and Novelists*. 3rd ed. San Francisco: n.p., 1893.

Croy, Homer. *Jesse James Was My Neighbor*. New York: Duell, Sloan and Pearce, 1949.

Crystal, David, ed. *The Cambridge Encyclopedia*. Cambridge: Cambridge University Press, 1990.

Curtis, Edmund. *A History of Ireland*. 4th ed. rev. London: Methuen & Company, Ltd., 1942.

Day Lewis, C., ed. *English Lyric Poems 1500–1900*. New York: Appleton-Century-Crofts, Inc., 1961.

de Breffny, Brian. *Irish Family Names: Arms, Origins and Locations*. New York: W. W. Norton & Company, Inc., 1982.

de Grummond, Jane Lucas. *The Baratarians and the Battle of New Orleans*. Baton Rouge: Louisiana State University Press, 1961.

Demeter, Richard. *Irish America: The Historical Travel Guide*. Vol. 1. 2nd ed. rev. and enl. Pasadena, Calif.: Cranford Press, 1998.

______. *Irish America: The Historical Travel Guide*. Vol. 2. Pasadena, Calif.: Cranford Press, 1996.

Deming, Norma H., and Katherine I. Bemis, eds. *Pieces for Every Day the Schools Celebrate*. New York: Noble and Noble, 1924.

Derr, Mark. *The Frontiersman: The Real Life and the Many Legends of Davy Crockett*. New York: William Morrow and Company, Inc., 1993.

Dinneen, Patrick. *An Irish-English Dictionary*. Dublin: The Educational Company of Ireland, 1927.

Dougherty, Daniel J. *History of the Society of the Friendly Sons of St. Patrick*. Philadelphia: Friendly Sons of St. Patrick, 1952.

Dunlop, Richard. *Donovan: America's Master Spy*. Chicago: Rand McNally

& Company, 1982.

Durant, John. *The Heavyweight Champions*. New rev. ed. New York: Hastings House, 1964.

Eckley, Grace. *Finley Peter Dunne*. Boston: G. K. Hall, 1981.

Editors of *The New Yorker*. *The New Yorker Book of Poems*. New York: The Viking Press, 1969.

Eggenberger, David, ed. *A Dictionary of Battles*. New York: Thomas Y. Crowell Company, 1967.

Emrich, Duncan, ed. *American Folk Poetry: An Anthology*. Boston: Little, Brown and Company, 1974.

Esthus, Raymond A. *Double Eagle and Rising Sun: The Russians and Japanese at Portsmouth in 1905*. Durham, N.C.: Duke University Press, 1988.

Fanning, Charles. *Finley Peter Dunne and Mr. Dooley: The Chicago Years*. Lexington: The University Press of Kentucky, 1978.

Faust, Patricia L. *Historical Times Illustrated Encyclopedia of the Civil War*. New York: Harper & Row, 1986.

Federal Writers Project of the Work Projects Administration. *New York City Guide*. New York: Random House, 1939.

Felleman, Hazel, ed. *The Best Loved Poems of the American People*. New York: Doubleday & Company, Inc., 1936.

Feuer, A. B. *The Spanish-American War at Sea: Naval Action in the Atlantic*. Westport, Conn.: Praeger Publishers, 1995.

Fleischer, Nat. *The Heavyweight Championship: An Informal History of Heavyweight Boxing from 1719 to the Present Day*. Rev. ed. New York: G. P. Putnam's Sons, 1961.

Foote, Shelby. *The Civil War: A Narrative*. Vol. 1 (Fort Sumter to Perryville). New York: Random House, Inc., 1986.

Ford, James L and Mary K., eds. *Every Day in the Year: A Poetical Epitome of the World's History*. New York: Dodd, Mead & Company, 1902.

Gale, Robert L. *A Henry James Encyclopedia*. New York: Greenwood Press, 1989.

Garraty, John A., and Mark C. Carnes, eds. *American National Biography*. 24 vols. New York: Oxford University Press, 1999.

Germain, Edward B., ed. *Surrealist Poetry in English*. New York: Penguin Books, 1978.

Gilbert, Felix, ed. *The Norton History of Modern Europe*. New York: W. W. Norton & Company, Inc., 1971.

Ginsberg, Allen. *Mind Breaths: Poems 1972–1977*. San Francisco: City Lights Books, 1978.

Glikes, Erwin A., and Paul Schwaber, eds. *Of Poetry and Power: Poems Occasioned by the Presidency and by the Death of John F. Kennedy*. New York: Basic Books, Inc., 1964.

Goring, Rosemary, ed. *Larousse Dictionary of Literary Characters*. New York: Larousse Kingfisher Chambers, Inc., 1994.

Grand Dictionnaire Encyclopédique Larousse. Paris: Librairie Larousse, 1985.

Gregg, John J. and Barbara T., eds. *Best Loved Poems of the American West*. Garden City, N.Y.: Doubleday & Company, Inc., 1980.

Guiterman, Arthur. *A Ballad-Maker's Pack*. New York: Harper & Brothers Publishers, 1921.

______. *Ballads of Old New York*. New York: Harper & Brothers Publishers, 1920.

______. *Brave Laughter*. New York: E. P. Dutton & Company, Inc., 1943.

______. *Gaily the Troubadour*. New York: E. P. Dutton & Company, Inc. 1936.

______. *I Sing the Pioneer*. New York: E. P. Dutton & Company, 1926.

Hafen, LeRoy, ed. *The Mountain Men and the Fur Trade of the Far West*. Vol. 7. Glendale, Calif.: The Arthur H. Clarke Company, 1969.

Halpine, Charles Graham. *Poetical Works of Charles G. Halpine*. New York: Harper & Brothers, 1869.

Haltigan, Patrick J. *The Irish in the American Revolution and Their Early Influence in the Colonies*. Washington, D.C.: Patrick J. Haltigan, 1908.

Harder, Kelsie B., ed. *Illustrated Dictionary of Place Names (United States and Canada)*. New York: Facts on File Publications, 1976.

Harmon, William, ed. *The Oxford Book of American Light Verse*. New York: Oxford University Press, 1979.

Harris, Mark, ed. *Selected Poems of Vachel Lindsay*. New York: The Macmillan Company, 1963.

Hass, Robert, ed. *Rock and Hawk: A Selection of Shorter Poems by Robinson Jeffers*. New York: Random House, 1987.

Hayward, John, ed. *The Oxford Book of Nineteenth-Century English Verse*. London: Oxford University Press, 1964.

Hennessy, Maurice. *The Wild Geese: The Irish Soldier in Exile*. Old Greenwich: The Devin-Adair Company, 1973.

Hewett, Janet B., ed. *The Roster of Union Soldiers, 1861–1865*. Wilmington, N.C.: Broadfoot Publishing Company, 1998.

Hinkel, John Vincent. *Arlington: Monument to Heroes*. Englewood Cliffs, N.J.: Prentice-Hall, Inc., 1965.

Hobson, Richmond Pearson. *The Sinking of the "Merrimac."* Annapolis: Naval Institute Press, 1987. Originally published by The Century Company, New York, 1899.

Horn, Maurice, ed. *The World Encyclopedia of Comics*. New York: Chelsea House Publishers, 1976.

Horstman, Dorothy, ed. *Sing Your Heart Out, Country Boy*. New York: E. P. Dutton & Company, Inc., 1975.

Hugo, Richard. *Selected Poems*. New York: W. W. Norton & Company, 1979.

Hunt, Frazier. *The Tragic Days of Billy the Kid*. New York: Hastings House Publishers, 1956.

Isenberg, Michael T. *John L. Sullivan and His America*. Urbana: University of Illinois Press, 1988.

Jobes, Gertrude. *Dictionary of Mythology, Folklore and Symbols.* New York: The Scarecrow Press, Inc., 1962.

Johnson, Allen, et al., eds. *Dictionary of American Biography.* 28 vols. New York: C. Scribner's Sons, 1928–88.

Johnson, Robert Underwood. *Collected Poems 1881–1919.* New Haven: Yale University Press, 1920.

Jones, Paul. *The Irish Brigade.* Washington, D.C.: Robert B. Luce, Inc., 1969.

Kaplan, Fred. *Henry James: The Imagination of Genius.* New York: William Morrow and Company, Inc., 1992.

Kauffman, Donald T., ed. *America in Verse: A Treasury of Patriotic Poetry.* New York: Pyramid Books, 1968.

Kazan, Molly. *Kennedy.* New York: Stein and Day, 1964.

Keithley, George. *The Donner Party.* New York: George Braziller, 1972.

———. *Song in a Strange Land.* New York: George Braziller, 1974.

Keller, Allan. *The Spanish-American War: A Compact History.* New York: Hawthorn Books, Inc., 1969.

Kennedy, Charles O'Brien, ed. *A Treasury of American Ballads: Gay, Naughty and Classic.* New York: The McBride Company, 1954.

Keystone Coal Industry Manual. Chicago: Maclean Hunter Publishing Company, 1991.

Kilmer, Joyce. *Poems, Essays and Letters.* Vol. 1. New York: George H. Doran Company, [1918].

Kodansha Encyclopedia of Japan. New York: International/USA Ltd., 1983.

Korson, George. *Minstrels of the Mine Patch Songs and Stories of the Anthracite Industry.* Philadelphia: University of Pennsylvania Press, 1938.

Laffin, John. *Brassey's Battles: 3500 Years of Conflict, Campaigns and Wars from A-Z.* London: Brassey's Defence Publishers, 1986.

Lasky, Victor. *J.F.K.: The Man and the Myth.* New York: The Macmillan Company, 1963.

Leckie, Robert. *The Wars of America.* 2 vols. New York: Harper & Row, 1968.

Leitch, Mary Sinton. "Dillon's Brigade." *The Recorder: The Bulletin of the American Irish Historical Society* 15 (April 1953): 13–14.

Lewis, Arthur H. *Lament for the Molly Maguires.* New York: Harcourt, Brace & World, Inc., 1964.

Lind, Michael. *The Alamo: An Epic.* Boston: Houghton Mifflin Company, 1997.

Lindsay, Vachel. *Collected Poems.* New York: Macmillan Publishing Company, 1973.

———. *Going-to-the-Stars.* London: D. Appleton and Company, 1926.

Lindsley, John Berrien. *The Military Annals of Tennessee.* Nashville: J. M. Lindsley & Company, 1886.

Long, Jeff. *Duel of Eagles: The Mexican and U.S. Fight for the Alamo.* New York: William Morrow and Company, Inc., 1990.

Lord, Walter. *A Time To Stand.* New York: Harper & Brothers, 1961.

Lowell, James Russell. *The Complete Poetical Works of James Russell Lowell*. Cambridge Edition. Boston: Houghton Mifflin Company, 1896.

Lowell, Robert. *Notebook 1967–68*. New York: Farrar, Straus and Giroux, 1969.

MacCloskey, Monro. *Reilly's Battery: A Story of the Boxer Rebellion*. New York: Richard Rosen Press, Inc., 1969.

Maclennan, Malcolm. *A Pronouncing and Etymological Dictionary of the Gaelic Language*. Edinburgh: John Grant, 1925.

MacManus, Seumas. *The Story of the Irish Race*. Rev. ed. New York: The Devin-Adair Company, 1968.

Major, Mabel, and T. M. Pearce, eds. *Signature of the Sun: Southwest Verse, 1900–1950*. Albuquerque: The University of New Mexico Press, 1950.

Marius, Richard, ed. *The Columbia Book of Civil War Poetry*. New York: Columbia University Press, 1994.

Martin, Ralph G. *Seeds of Destruction: Joe Kennedy and His Sons*. New York: G. P. Putnam's Sons, 1995.

McCarthy, Denis A. "John Boyle O'Reilly." *Journal of the American Irish Historical Society* 16 (1917): 255–256.

McGroarty, John Steven. *"Just California" and Other Poems*. Los Angeles: The Times-Mirror Press, 1933.

Memorial Services in the Congress of the United States and Tributes in Eulogy of Robert Francis Kennedy, Late Senator from the State of New York. Washington D.C.: U.S. Government Printing Office, 1968.

Merriam-Webster's Encyclopedia of Literature. Springfield, Mass.: Merriam-Webster, Inc., 1995.

Miller, James E., ed. *Complete Poetry and Selected Prose of Walt Whitman*. Boston: Houghton Mifflin Company, 1959.

Muller, Charles G. *The Darkest Day: 1814*. Philadelphia: J. B. Lippincott Company, 1963.

Mulholland, St. Clair A. *The Story of the 116th Regiment, Pennsylvania Volunteers in the War of the Rebellion*. Edited by Lawrence Frederick Kohl. New York: Fordham University Press, 1996.

Murphy, Bruce, ed. *Benét's Reader's Encyclopedia*. 4th ed. New York: Harper Collins Publishers, 1996.

Murphy, T. L. *Kelly's Heroes: The Irish Brigade at Gettysburg*. Gettysburg: Farnsworth House Military Impressions, 1997.

Neeser, Robert W., ed. *American Naval Songs & Ballads*. New Haven: Yale University Press, 1938.

Negri, Paul, ed. *Civil War Poetry: An Anthology*. Minneola, N.Y.: Dover Publications, Inc., 1997.

Newman, Peter. *A Companion to Irish History from the Submission of Tyrone to Partition 1603–1921*. Oxford: Facts on File, 1991.

Nolan, Frederick. *The West of Billy the Kid*. Norman: University of Oklahoma Press, 1998.

O'Brien, Michael J. "Chapter of Irish History in Thanksgiving History." *Journal of the American Irish Historical Society* 18 (1919): 163–168.

O'Callaghan, John Cornelius. *History of the Irish Brigades in the Service of France.* New York: P. O'Shea, 1887.

O'Connell, J. C. *The Irish in the Revolution and the Civil War, Spanish-American and Philippine Wars and Every Walk of Life.* Washington, D.C.: Trades Unionist Press, 1903.

O'Connor, Richard. *The Spirit Soldiers: A Historical Narrative of the Boxer Rebellion.* New York: G. P. Putnam's Sons, 1973.

Olcott, Charles S. *The Life of William McKinley.* Vol. 2. Boston: Houghton Mifflin Company, 1916.

O'Neal, Bill. *Encyclopedia of Western Gun-Fighters.* Norman, Okla.: University of Oklahoma Press, 1980.

O'Reilly, John Boyle, ed. *The Poetry and Song of Ireland.* New York: Gay Brothers & Company, 1887.

O'Rourke, Kevin. *Currier and Ives: The Irish and America.* New York: Harry A. Abrams, Inc., 1995.

O'Sheel, Shaemus. "Breakfast with Hercules Mulligan." In *Hercules Mulligan: Confidential Correspondent of General Washington* by Michael J. O'Brien. New York: P. J. Kenedy & Sons, 1937.

O'Toole, G. J. A. *The Spanish War.* New York: W. W. Norton & Company, 1984.

Pater, Alan F., ed. *Anthology of Magazine Verse and Yearbook of American Poetry.* 1980 ed. Beverly Hills: Monitor Book Company, Inc., 1980.

The Patriotic Anthology. Introduction by Carl Van Doren. New York: The Literary Guild of America, Inc., 1941.

Paulin, Tom, ed. *The Faber Book of Political Verse.* London: Faber and Faber, 1986.

Perkins, George, et al., eds. *Benét's Reader's Encyclopedia of American Literature.* New York: HarperCollins Publishers, 1991.

Phillips, J. J., et al., eds. *The Before Columbus Foundation Poetry Anthology: Selections from the American Book Awards, 1980–1990.* New York: W. W. Norton & Company, 1992.

Phisterer, Frederick. *New York in the War of the Rebellion 1861–1865.* 5 vols. 3rd ed. Albany: J. B. Ryan Company, 1912.

Piercy, Marge, ed. *Early Ripening: American Women's Poetry Now.* New York: Pandora Press, 1987.

Purcell, L. Edward. *Who Was Who in the American Revolution.* New York: Facts on File, 1993.

Read, Thomas Buchanan. *The Poetical Works of T. Buchanan Read.* New rev. ed. Philadelphia: J. B. Lippincott & Company, 1883.

Reeves, Thomas. *Gentleman Boss: The Life of Chester Alan Arthur.* New York: Alfred A. Knopf, 1975.

Reynolds, Lawrence. *Poetical Address Before the Irish Brigade.* Albany, N.Y.:

Michael O'Sullivan, 1863.

Rhyme with Reason: A Garland of Irish Shamrocks, Many of Them Grown in America. Chicago: P. G. Smyth, 1911.

Roberts, Frank C., ed. *Obituaries from The (London) Times 1961–1970.* Reading, Eng.: Newspaper Archive Developments Ltd., 1975.

Robinson, James I., Jr. *Stonewall Jackson: The Man, the Soldier, the Legend.* New York: Simon & Schuster Macmillan, 1997.

Roche, James Jeffrey. *Life of John Boyle O'Reilly.* Philadelphia: John J. McVey, 1891.

Rooney, John Jerome. "Ballad of Saucy Jack Barry." *Journal of the American Irish Historical Society* 9 (1910): 102–104.

______. "Hobson at Santiago," *New York Times,* 13 June 1898: 6

______. "The Irish Name." *Journal of the American Irish Historical Society* 2 (1899): 91–92.

______. "Reilly of F." *Journal of the American Irish Historical Society* 8 (1908–09): 243–245.

Rosenberger, Francis Coleman, ed. *Washington and the Poet.* Charlottesville: University Press of Virginia, 1977.

Sandburg, Carl, ed. *The American Songbag.* New York: Harcourt, Brace & World, Inc., [1927].

Scharf, Thomas. *History of Delaware 1609-1888.* Vol. 1. Philadelphia: L. J. Richards & Company, 1888.

Scharf, Thomas, and Thompson Westcott. *History of Philadelphia 1609–1884.* Philadelphia: L. H. Everts & Company, 1884.

Schoelwer, Susan Prendergast, and Tom W. Gläser. *Alamo Images: Changing Perceptions of a Texas Experience.* Dallas: DeGolyer Library and Southern Methodist University Press, 1985.

Schofield, William G. *Seek For a Hero: The Story of John Boyle O'Reilly.* New York: P. J. Kenedy & Sons, 1956.

Scudder, Horace Elisha, ed. *The Complete Poetical Works of John Greenleaf Whittier.* Cambridge Edition. Boston: Houghton Mifflin Company, 1894.

Seagrave, Pia Seija. *The History of the Irish Brigade.* Fredericksburg, Va.: Sergeant Kirkland's Museum and Historical Society, Inc., 1997.

Seltzer, Leon E., ed. *The Columbia Lippincott Gazetteer of the World.* Morningside Heights, N.Y.: Columbia University Press, 1952.

Shapiro, Karl. *New & Selected Poems, 1940–1986.* Chicago: The University of Chicago Press, 1987.

Shenk, Hiram, ed. *Encyclopedia of Pennsylvania.* Harrisburg: National Historical Association, Inc., 1932.

Sherman, Andew. *Life of Captain Jeremiah O'Brien.* Morristown, N.J.: George W. Sherman, 1902.

Sherman, Joan R., ed. *African-American Poetry of the Nineteenth Century.* Urbana: University of Illinois Press, 1992.

Sifakis, Stewart. *Who Was Who in the Civil War.* New York: Facts on File

Publications, 1988.

Silber, Irwin, ed. *Songs of Independence*. Harrisburg, Pa.: Stackpole Books, 1973.

Simpson, J. A., and E. S. C. Weiner, eds. *The Oxford English Dictionary*. 2nd ed. New York: Oxford University Press, 1989.

Smith, Dave, and David Bottoms, eds. *The Morrow Anthology of Younger American Poets*. New York: William Morrow and Company, Inc., 1985.

Smith, Joseph. "'The Dead That Never Die': John Boyle O'Reilly." *Journal of the American Irish Historical Society* 16 (1917): 231–234.

Smith, Page. *A New Age Begins: A People's History of the American Revolution*. 2 vols. New York: McGraw-Hill Book Company, 1976.

______. *The Shaping of America: A People's History of the Young Republic*. New York: McGraw-Hill Book Company, 1980.

______. *Trial by Fire: A People's History of the Civil War and Reconstruction*. New York: McGraw-Hill Book Company, 1982.

Sobel, Robert, and John Raimo, eds. *Biographical Dictionary of the Governors of the United States 1789–1978*. 4 vols. Westport, Conn.: Meckler Books, 1978.

Sorensen, Theodore C. *Kennedy*. New York: Harper & Row, 1965.

Stedman, Edmund Clarence, ed. *An American Anthology 1787–1900*. Boston: Houghton Mifflin Company, 1928.

______. *The Poems of Edmund Clarence Stedman*. Boston: Houghton Mifflin Company, 1908.

Stephen, Leslie, and Sidney Lee, eds. *Dictionary of National Biography*. 66 vols. London: Smith, Elden, & Company, 1885–1901.

Stevenson, Burton E., ed. *Great Americans As Seen by the Poets*. Philadelphia: J. B. Lippincott Company, 1933.

______, ed. *Poems of American History*. Rev. ed. Boston: Houghton Mifflin Company, [1922].

Stevenson, Burton E. and Elizabeth B., eds. *Days and Deeds: A Book of Verse for Children's Reading and Speaking*. Garden City, N.Y.: Doubleday, Page & Company, 1920.

Sullivan, A. M. "Ballad of Dick Dowling." In *Dick Dowling at Sabine Pass* by Frank X. Tolbert. New York: McGraw Hill Book Company, Inc., 1962.

______. "The Ballad of John O'Neil of Havre de Grace." *The Recorder: The Bulletin of the American Irish Historical Society* 15 (April 1953): 17.

______. "The Boy from Wexford." *The Recorder: The Bulletin of the American Irish Historical Society* 27 (February 1965): 11–12

______. "Fitz-James O'Brien: A Playboy of the Western World." *The Recorder: The Bulletin of the American Irish Historical Society* 18 (December 1955): 13–20.

______. "Footnote to Tragedy" and "Inauguration Poem." *The Recorder: The Bulletin of the American Irish Historical Society* 26 (February 1964): 14–15.

______. "In Memoriam." *The Recorder: The Bulletin of the American Irish His-*

torical Society 20 (December 1957): 29–30.

______. "The Man of Machias." *The Recorder: The Bulletin of the American Irish Historical Society* 24 (December 1960): 22–24.

______. *Tim Murphy: Morgan Rifleman and Other Ballads.* New York: The Declan X. McMullen Company, Inc., 1947.

Sullivan, Charles, ed. *America In Poetry.* New York: Harry N. Abrams, Inc., 1988.

Sweeny, William M. "General Hugh Brady, U.S. Army." *The Journal of the American Irish Historical Society* 24 (1925): 191–204.

Time-Life Books. *Vikings: Raiders from the North.* Alexandria, Va.: Time-Life Books, 1993.

Tinkle, Lon. *13 Days to Glory: The Siege of the Alamo.* New York: McGraw-Hill Book Company, Inc., 1958.

Towne, Charles Hanson, ed. *Roosevelt as the Poets Saw Him.* New York: Charles Scribner's Sons, 1923.

Trask, David F. *The War with Spain in 1898.* New York: Macmillan Publishing Company, Inc., 1981.

Troy, Robert. "The American Irish." *Journal of the American Irish Historical Society* 12 (1912–13): 96–97.

Tucker, Glenn. *Poltroons and Patriots.* Vol. 2. Indianapolis: The Bobbs-Merrill Company, Inc., 1954.

Urdang, Laurence, and Frederick G. Ruffner Jr., eds. *Allusions—Cultural, Literary, Biblical, and Historical: A Thematic Dictionary.* Detroit: Gale Research Company, 1982.

Vanden Heuvel, William, and Milton Gwirtzman. *On His Own: Robert Kennedy 1964–1968.* Garden City, N.Y.: Doubleday & Company, 1970.

Wakelyn, Jon L. *Biographical Dictionary of the Civil War.* Westport, Conn.: Greenwood Press, 1977.

Wallington, Nellie Urner, ed. *American History by American Poets.* 2 vols. New York: Duffield & Company, 1911.

Ward, Geoffrey C., et al. *The Civil War: An Illustrated History.* New York: Alfred A. Knopf, Inc., 1990.

Warner, Anne, ed. *Traditional American Folk Songs.* Syracuse: Syracuse University Press, 1984.

Warner, Denis and Peggy. *The Tide at Sunrise: A History of the Russo-Japanese War, 1904–1905.* New York: Charterhouse, 1974.

Warren, Robert Penn, ed. *Fifty Years of American Poetry.* New York: Harry N. Abrams, Inc., 1984.

Weems, John Edward. *The Fate of the Maine.* New York: Henry Holt and Company, 1958.

Weinberger, Eliot, ed. *American Poetry Since 1950.* New York: Marsilio Publishers, 1993.

Wetterau, Bruce. *World History: A Dictionary of Important People, Places, and Events, from Ancient Times to the Present.* New York: Henry Holt and

Company, 1994.

Whitman, Walt. *Leaves of Grass, 1891–1892*. Reprint, with a preface by Harold W. Blodgett and Sculley Bradley. New York: W. W. Norton & Company, Inc., 1973.

Whittelsey, Charles Barney. *The Roosevelt Genealogy 1649–1902*. Hartford: Charles Barney Whittelsey, 1902.

Who Was Who in America. Vol. 1 (1897–1942). Chicago: Marquis–Who's Who, 1968.

Who Was Who in America. Vol 3 (1951–1960). Chicago: The A. N. Marquis Company, 1960.

Woods, Ralph L., ed. *A Third Treasury of the Familiar*. New York: The Macmillan Company, 1970.

Woulfe, Patrick. *Irish Names and Surnames*. Rev. ed. Kansas City: Irish Genealogical Foundation, 1992.

Zaranka, William, ed. *The Brand-X Anthology of Poetry: A Parody Anthology*. Burnt Norton Edition. Cambridge: Apple-Wood Books, Inc., 1981.

Zentner, Christian, and Friedemann Bedürftig, eds. *The Encyclopedia of the Third Reich*. 2 vols. New York: Macmillan Publishing Company, 1991.